AMERICAN ENVIRONMENTAL STUDIES

The American Geography

JEDIDIAH MORSE

ARNO &
THE NEW YORK TIMES

WHITTEMORE LIBRARY
Framingham State College
Framingham, Massachusetts

Collection Created and Selected
by CHARLES GREGG of Gregg Press

Reprint Edition 1970 by Arno Press Inc.

Reprinted from a copy in
The State Historical Society of Wisconsin Library

LC# 70-125754
ISBN 0-405-02680-3

American Environmental Studies
ISBN for complete set: 0-405-02650-1

Manufactured in the United States of America

THE
AMERICAN
GEOGRAPHY;
OR,
A VIEW OF THE PRESENT SITUATION
OF THE
UNITED STATES OF AMERICA.

CONTAINING

Aftronomical Geography. Geographical Definitions. Difcovery, and General Defcription of America. Summary account of the Difcoveries and Settlements of North America; General View of the United States; Of their Boundaries; Lakes; Bays and Rivers; Mountains; Productions; Population; Government; Agriculture, Commerce; Manufactures; Hiftory; Concife Account of the War, and of the important Events which have fucceeded. Biographical Sketches of feveral illuftrio Heroes. General account of New England; Of its Boundaries; Extent; Divifions; Mountains; Rivers; Natural Hiftory; Productions; Population; Character; Trade; Hiftory. Particular Defcriptions of the Thirteen United States, and of Kentucky, The Weftern Territory and Vermont.—Of their Extent; Civil Divifions; Chief Towns; Climates: Rivers; Mountains; Soils; Productions; Trade; Manufactures; Agriculture; Population; Character; Conftitutions; Courts of Juftice; Colleges; Academies and Schools; Religion; Iflands; Indians; Literary and Humane Societies; Springs; Curiofities; Hiftories.

Illuftrated with two Sheet Maps—One of the Southern, the other of the Northern States, neatly and elegantly engraved, and more correct than any that have hitherto been publifhed.

To which is added, a concife Abridgment of the Geography of the Britifh, Spanifh, French and Dutch Dominions in America, and the Weft Indies—Of Europe, Afia and Africa.

By JEDIDIAH MORSE.

ELIZABETH TOWN:
PRINTED BY SHEPARD KOLLOCK, FOR THE AUTHOR.
M,DCC,LXXXIX.

To His EXCELLENCY

WILLIAM LIVINGSTON, Esq. *L.L.D.*

Governor of the State of NEW JERSEY,

This BOOK

Is most respectfully inscribed,

By his Excellency's

Most obliged, and

Most obedient Servant,

The AUTHOR.

MARCH 12, 1789.

PREFACE.

SO imperfect are all the accounts of America hitherto published, even by those who once exclusively possessed the best means of information, that from them very little knowledge of this country can be acquired. Europeans have been the sole writers of American Geography, and have too often suffered fancy to supply the place of facts, and thus have led their readers into errors, while they professed to aim at removing their ignorance. But since the United State have become an independent nation, and have risen into Empire, it would be reproachful for them to suffer this ignorance to continue; and the rest of the world have a right now to expect authentic information. To furnish this has been the design of the author of the following work; but he does not pretend that this design is compleated, nor will the judicious and candid expect it, when they consider that he has trodden, comparatively, an unbeaten path---that he has had to collect a vast variety of materials---that these have been widely scattered---and that he could derive but little assistance from books already published. Four years have been employed in this work, during which period, the Author has visited the several states in the Union, and maintained an extensive correspondence with men of Science; and in every instance has endeavored to derive his information from the most authentic sources; he has also submitted his manuscripts to the inspection of Gentlemen in the states which they particularly described, for their correction. It is possible, notwithstanding, and indeed very probable, that inaccuracies may have crept in; but he hopes there are none of any great importance, and that such as may be observed, will not be made the subject of severe censure, but ascribed to some pardonable cause. He flatters himself, however, that the work now offered to the public, will be found to be

PREFACE.

as accurate, compleat and impartial as the prefent ftate of American Geography and Hiftory could furnifh. After all, like the Nation of which it treats, it is but an infant, and as fuch folicits the foftering care of the country it defcribes; it will grow and improve as the nation advances towards maturity, and the Author will gratefully acknowledge ever friendly communication which will tend to make it perfect.

In the profecution of the work, he has aimed at utility rather than originality, and of courfe, when he has met with publications fuited to his purpofe, he has made a free ufe of them; and he thinks it proper here to obferve, that, to avoid unneceffary trouble, he has frequently ufed the words as well as the ideas of the writers, although the reader has not been particularly apprized of it.

For the Author diftinctly to acknowledge the obligations he is under to many citizens of thefe ftates, as well as to fome foreigners of diftinction, refidents among us, would fwell this preface to an improper length; he cannot forbear, however, to exprefs his peculiar obligation to EBENEZER HAZARD, ESQ. Poft Mafter General of the United States, for permiffion of free accefs to his very large and valuable *Collection* of papers, from which he has derived much of his hiftorical information. This collection has been made with unwearied care and minute exactnefs; and the papers, which are of unqueftionable authenticity, are the beft, and moft complete *depofitum* of facts relating to the hiftory of America from its firft fettlement, that is to be found in the United States. The Author's acknowledgments are likewife efpecially due to Captain THOMAS HUTCHINS, Geographer General of the United States, for his particular friendfhip and affiftance.

It is to be regretted, that fo few Maps could be introduced into the work; but the Author hopes to be enabled to increafe the number in future Editions. The Map of the fouthern ftates, was compiled from original and authentic documents, by Mr. Jofeph Purcell, of Charlefton, South Carolina, a Gentleman fully equal to the undertaking,

PREFACE.

dertaking, and is the most accurate yet published respecting that country, on so small a scale. The Map of the northern states was compiled principally by the Engraver, from the best Maps that could be procured; it was chiefly designed to give the reader an idea of the relative situation, and comparative extent of the several states and countries comprehended within its limits.

Indian names of rivers, &c. are spelled as they are pronounced, for the sake of expunging superfluous letters, and preventing persons unacquainted with the names from mistaking their true pronunciation.

The meridian which passes through Philadelphia is fixed, in this work, as the first, because of the size, the beauty, the improvements, and the central situation of that city.

The *Abridgment*, which is made principally from Zimmermann's Political Survey of the present state of Europe, and from Guthrie's Grammar, is added with a view to accommodate Schools and Private Families. Every citizen of the United States ought to be thoroughly acquainted with the Geography of his own country, and to have some idea, at least, of the other parts of the world; but as many of them cannot afford the time and expence, necessary to acquire a compleat knowledge of the several parts of the Globe, this book offers them such information as their situation in life may require; and while it is calculated early to impress the minds of American Youth with an idea of the superior importance of their own country, as well as to attach them to its interests, it furnishes a simplified account of other countries, calculated for their juvenile capacities, and to serve as an introduction to their future improvement in Geography.

CHARLESTOWN, *(Massachusetts)* March 12, 1789.

CONTENTS.

INTRODUCTION.

	Page
Of Astronomical Geography	1
The Planets	ibid
The Comets—The Solar System	ibid
The fixed Stars—The Earth	2
The Artificial Globe and its Circles	3
The Atmosphere, Winds, Tides, Clouds and Eclipses	5
	10

GEOGRAPHY 11

Definition, and explanation of Geographical terms	ibid.
Discovery of America	12
General Descripiton of America	16
Chronological account of the Discoveries and Settlements of N. America	21
North America, its Divisions	33

UNITED STATES 34

Boundaries and Contents	ibid
Lakes and Rivers	36
Bays	47
Face of the Country	48
Mountains	50
Soil—Vegetable and Animal Productions	52
Population, Character, &c.	63
Government	68
New Constitution	69
Cincinnati	79
Agriculture, Commerce and Manufactures	81
Military and Marine Strength	92
History	94
Stamp Act	97
Destruction of Tea, and Boston Port Bill	99
First Congress	101
Lexington Battle	103
General Washington's Appointment	104
Capture of Burgoyne	107
Capture of Cornwallis—Peace	112
Paper Money, and its consequences	117
Defects of the Old Confederation—Convention	123
Sketch of the Life of General Washington	127
——————————— General Montgomery	132
——————————— General Greene	134
——————————— Marquis de la Fayette	136

NEW ENGLAND 140

Divisions, Boundaries, Face of the Country, Mountains, &c.	ibid
Rivers—Natural Growth	142, 143
Productions, Population, Character &c.	144
Trade—History	149
————Indians	159

NEW

CONTENTS

	Page
NEW HAMPSHIRE	161
Boundaries, Divisions, Chief Towns, Rivers, Mountains, &c.	161, 162
Productions, Manufactures, Trade, Population, &c. &c.	164
Constitution, Colleges and Academies	165
History	166
MASSACHUSETTS	168
Boundaries, Rivers, capes, Islands	169
Light Houses, Religion, Civil Divisions	170, 171
Literary and Humane, Societies, Colleges, Academies, &c.	174, 175
Chief Towns	177
Constitution	179
Bridges—Trade, Manufactures, Agriculture	180, 181
Revenue—Mines—History	182, 183
Witchcraft Infatuation	186
Quaker Persecution	187
PROVINCE OF MAIN	193
Boundaries, Divisions, Rivers	194
Bays, Mountains, chief Towns, &c.	196
Climate, Soil, Produce, Timber, Trade, &c.	197
Mines, Animals, character, Religion, History	198
RHODE ISLAND	200
Civil Divisions—Population	201
Bays, Islands, Rivers, Climate, Productions, &c.	202
Trade, Light House, Chief Towns, &c.	203, 204
Religion, College	205, 206
Curiosities, Constitution, History, &c.	208, 209
CONNECTICUT	212
Boundaries, Rivers, Harbours	ibid
Climate, Soil, Productions, Trade, Manufactures	214, 215
Divisions, Population, Character, Religion	217, 219
Damages by the War, chief Towns	220, 221
Curiosities—Story of General Putnam and the Wolf	223
Colleges, Academies, &c.	225
Mines, Taxes, Constitution	227, 228
Practice of Law—New Inventions, History	230, 231
War between Mohegans and Narraganfetts	235
Law against Quakers	237
NEW YORK	243
Rivers, Bays and Lakes	ibid 246
Soil and Productions, Divisions, Population and Character	247
Chief Towns	253
Agriculture, Manufactures and Trade	261
Medicinal Springs	263
Minerals, Societies, Literature	265
Religion	267
Constitution, and Courts of Justice	270
Taxes, Indians	273

CONTENTS

	Page
Long and Staten Islands	275
History	276

NEW JERSEY — 282

Bays, Rivers, &c.	ibid
Divisions and Population	284
Mountains, Soil and Productions	286
Trade, Manufactures and Agriculture	287
Mines, Springs	289
Character, caves, Monument	291
Religion, Colleges, &c.	292
Chief Towns	295
Constitution, Law, Physic	297
History, &c.	298

PENNSYLVANIA — 302

Situation, Mines, Divisions	ibid 303
Rivers, Mountains, Productions, &c.	304, 306
Population, character, &c.	311
Religion	319
Moravian Settlements	320
Literary, and Humane Societies	325
Colleges, Academies, chief Towns	328
Trade, Manufactures and Agriculture	333
Springs, caves, Antiquities	338
Constitution	339
New Inventions—History	341

DELAWARE — 345

Climate, Divisions, Productions	ibid
Chief Towns, Religion, Population, constitution	346, 347
History	348

MARYLAND — 350

Divisions, Rivers, Soil, Productions	ibid 351
Population, character, chief Towns	352, 353
Trade, Religion, Colleges	354, 355
Constitution, History	356, 357

VIRGINIA — 360

Rivers	361
Mountains	363
Cascades and caverns	366
Mines and Minerals	369
Springs	371
Population, Militia	374, 379
Civil Division, Towns	380
Colleges and Literature	383
Religion, character, customs, &c.	386
Constitution and Laws	391
Manufactures and commerce	393
Revenue and Expences	396
History	398

INDIANA.

CONTENTS.

	Page
INDIANA	401
KENTUCKY, its Rivers, Springs, Soil, Population, &c.	402
NORTH CAROLINA	409
Rivers, Sounds, capes, Swamps, &c.	410
Divisions, Principal Towns, Productions, &c.	412
Trade, Diseases, Natural History, Religion	
Colleges, Population, character, customs, &c.	414, 415
Constitution, New Settlements and Roads	417
History	418, 419
SOUTH CAROLINA	421
Climate	423
Rivers, Mountains, Harbours, Divisions, &c.	ibid
Chief Towns	424, 425
Face of the country, Soil and Productions	427
Constitution, Laws, Literature, &c.	428, 429
Religion Population and character	430
Militia, Revenue, Taxes, Damages by the War, &c.	432
Commerce, State Debt, &c.	434
Courts of Law, History	435
	440
GEORGIA	443
Divisions, etc.	ibid
Chief Towns, Rivers, climate, etc.	444
Face of the country, Soil, Produce	446
Springs, curiosities, commerce, etc.	448
Population, character, Religion, Literature, etc.	450
Indians, Islands, History	452, 453
WESTERN TERRITORY, Extent, &c.	457
Rivers, Population, Soil and Produce	458, 460
Animals, Antiquities, Forts	463
Government and Divisions, etc.	464
VERMONT, Divisions.	499
Rivers, Mountains, Soil, climate, etc.	470
Militia, Population, character, curiosities, constitution	471
BRITISH AMERICAN DOMINIONS.	
New Britain	473
Canada	474
Nova Scotia	475
SPANISH DOMINIONS in North America.	
East and West Florida	476
Louisiana	477
New Mexico and California	478
Old Mexico or New Spain	479
SOUTH AMERICA.	
Terra Firma or Castile del Oro	482
Peru	

CONTENTS.

	Page
Peru	484
Chili	485
Paragua or la Plata	486
Brazil	487
Guiana	488
Amazonia	ibid
Patagonia	489
West India Islands	490

EUROPE. 490

Portugal	493
Spain	494
France	496
Italy	497
Switzerland	499
Turkey	501
Hungary	502
Germany	503
The Netherlands	505
Holland	506
Poland	508
Prussia	509
Russia	511
Sweden	513
Denmark	514
Great Britain and Ireland	515
European Islands, &c.	518

ASIA 519

Tartary	520
China	ibid
India	522
Persia	ibid

AFRICA ibid

Turkey in Asia	524
Asiatic Isles	525
Africa	ibid
Egypt	526
Barbary	ibid
Zaara, and Negroland	527
Ethiopia, African Isles	528
General Remarks	529
Appendix	532

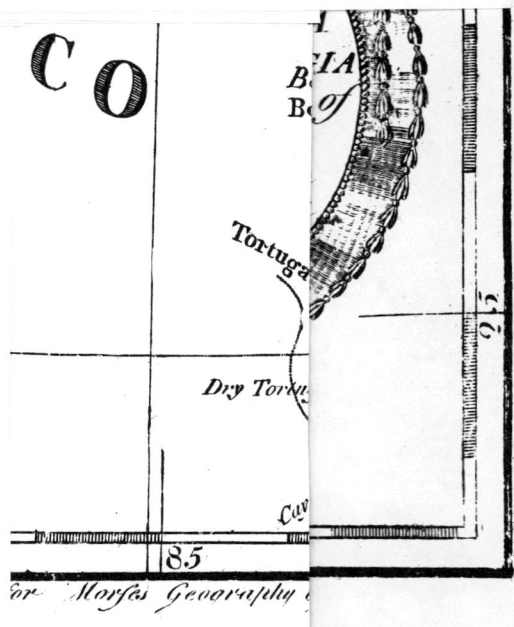

INTRODUCTION.

Of ASTRONOMICAL GEOGRAPHY.

A COMPLETE knowledge of *Geography*, cannot be obtained without some acquaintance with Astronomy. This Compendium, therefore, will be introduced with a short account of that Science. Astronomy* treats of the heavenly bodies, and explains their motions, times, distances and magnitudes. The regularity and beauty of these, and the harmonious order in which they move, shew that their Creator and Preserver possesses infinite wisdom and power.

Astronomy was first attended to by the Shepherds, on the beautiful plains of Egypt and Babylon. Their employment led them to contemplate the stars. While their flocks, in the silence of the evening, were enjoying sweet repose, the spangled sky would naturally invite the attention of the Shepherds. The observation of the heavenly bodies afforded them amusement, and at the same time assisted them in travelling in the night. A star guided the Shepherds to the manger where our blessed Saviour was born. By the aid of a lively imagination, they distributed the stars into a number of constellations or companies, to which they gave the names of the animals which they represented.

Of the Planets.] The sun is surrounded with seven spherical, opaque bodies, called *Planets* or wandering stars, which revolve about him as their centre at different distances, and in different periods as exhibited in the following

TABLE.

Sun and Planets.	Diameters in En. mil.	Distance from the Sun.	Annual periods round the Sun.			Square miles in surface.†
			y.	d.	h.	
Sun ☉	890,000					1,828,911,000,000
Mercury ☿	3,000	36,841,468	0	87	23	21,236,800
Venus ♀	9,330	68,891,486	0	224	17	691,361,300
Earth ⊕	7,970	95,173,000	1	0	0	199,859,860
Mars ♂	5,400	145,014,148	1	321	17	62,038,240
Jupiter ♃	94,000	494,990,976	11	314	18	20,603,970,000
Saturn ♄	78,000	907,956,130	29	174	0	14,102,562,000
Herschel	36,000	1800,000,000	82	34	0	7,577,406,000

* *From* astron a *star, and* nomos *the law or rule.*
† *These square miles are as computed by ancient astronomers.*

ASTRONOMICAL GEOGRAPHY.

The *seven* planets mentioned in the table are called *primary planets*; for befides thefe there are ten other bodies called *fecondary planets, moons,* or *fatellites,* which all revolve round their primaries from weft to eaft, and at the fame time are carried along with them round the fun, as follows :

The earth has one fatellite, viz. the moon ☽, which performs her revolution in 29d. 12h. 44m. at the diftance of about 60 femidiameters of the earth, or 209,100 miles, and is carried with the earth round the fun once in a year.

Jupiter has four moons; Saturn has five, and is alfo encompaffed with a broad ring. The diameter of the ring is, to the diameter of Saturn, as 9 to 4, and the fpace between the body of Saturn and the ring, is equal to the breadth of the ring.

The motion of the primary planets round the fun, and alfo the motion of the fatellites round their primaries, is called their *annual motion*. Befides this annual motion, they revolve round their own axes from weft to eaft, and this is called their *diurnal motion*.

The lately difcovered planet *Herfchel,* was firft obferved in 1782, by that celebrated aftronomer William Herfchel, L. L. D. F. R. S. In Great-Britain, it is called *Georgium Sidus*; but in France and America it has obtained the name of *Herfchel,* in honour to its learned difcoverer.

Comets.] The comets are large opaque bodies, which move in very eliptical orbits and in all poffible directions. Some revolve from weft to eaft; fome from eaft to weft; others from fouth to north, or from north to fouth. Their orbits have very different inclinations to the ecliptic. Some have conjectured, that the comets were intended by the All-wife Creator, to connect fyftems, and that each of their feveral orbits includes the fun, and one of the fixed ftars. The figures of the comets are very different. Some of them emit beams on all fides like hair, and are called hairy comets. Others have a long, fiery, tranfparent tail projecting from the part which is oppofite to the fun. Their magnitudes alfo are different. Some appear no bigger than ftars of the firft magnitude; others larger than the moon. They are fuppofed to be folid bodies, and very denfe; for fome of them in their neareft approach to the fun, were heated, according to Sir Ifaac Newton's calculation, 2000 times hotter than red hot iron; a degree of heat which would vitrify, or diffipate any matter known to us.

The number of comets belonging to our fyftem is not certainly known. Twenty-one have been feen. Of thefe, the periods of three only have been afcertained with accuracy. One appeared in the years 1531, 1607, 1682 and 1758; Its period is 75 years. Another was feen in 1532 and 1661, and is again expected in 1790; its period being 129 years. The third appeared laft in 1680, whofe period being 575 years cannot be expected to return until the year 2255.

Of the Solar-Syftem.] The feven planets, with their ten fatellites and the comets, conftitute the Solar, or as it is fome times called, the Copernican Syftem, in honour of Copernicus a native of Poland, who adopted the Pythagorean opinion of the heavenly bodies, and publifhed it to the world in 1530. This is now univerfally approved as the true fyftem. It has received great improvements from Gallileo, Sir Ifaac Newton, Dr. Halley, and other philofophers in almoft every age.

Of

Of the EARTH.

Of the fixed Stars.] The solar system is surrounded with the fixed stars; So called, because they at all times preserve the same situation in regard to each other. These stars, when viewed with the best telescopes, appear no larger than points, which proves that they are at an immense distance from us. Although their distance is not certainly known, yet it is the general opinion of astronomers, that they are at least 100,000 times farther from us, than we are from the sun; and that our sun viewed from a fixed star, would appear no bigger than a star does to us. A sound would not reach us from *Sirius*, or the dog-star, which is nearer to this earth than any of the fixed stars, in 50,000 years. A cannon ball flying at the rate of 480 miles an hour, would not reach us in 700,000 years. Light, which is transmitted from one body to another almost instantaneously, takes up more time in passing from the fixed stars to this earth, than we do in making a voyage to Europe; so that if all the fixed stars were now struck out of existence, they would appear to us to keep their stations for several months yet to come. It is impossible, therefore, that they should borrow their light from the sun, as do the planets.

The number of stars, visible to the naked eye at any one time, in the upper hemisphere, is not more than a thousand. A thousand more are supposed to be visible in the lower hemisphere; and by the help of a telescope, a thousand more have been discovered; so that the whole number of stars are reckoned at 3000. They are distinguished from the planets by their twinkling.

To consider these stars as designed merely to decorate the sky, and form a rich and beautiful canopy for this earth, would be derogatory to the wisdom of the Creator. Astronomers therefore, with much reason, have considered the fixed stars as so many suns, attended with a number of revolving planets, which they illuminate, warm and cherish. If this be true, there are as many systems as there are fixed stars. These may also revolve round one common centre, forming one immense system of systems. All these systems, we may conceive, are filled with inhabitants suited to their respective climes; and are so many theatres, on which the Great Creator and Governor of the Universe, displays his infinite power, wisdom and goodness. Such a view of the starry heavens, must fill the mind of every beholder, with sublime, magnificent and glorious ideas of the Creator.

Of the EARTH.

HAVING taken a cursory view of the heavenly bodies, we proceed to give a more particular account of the planet which we inhabit.

The Earth, though called a globe, is not perfectly round, but is widened at the equator, and flattered at the poles; so that its diameter from east to west, is about thirty miles longer, than from north to south. Its figure is an oblate-spheroid. It moves round the sun once in a year. This is called the earth's annual motion, to which we are indebted for the difference in the length of the days and nights, and for the variety in the seasons. The diameter of the earth's orbit, is 190,346,000 miles. And since the circumference of a circle, is to its diameter, as 335 is to 113, the circumference of the earth's orbit, is 597,987,646 miles. And as the earth describes

Of the EARTH.

scribes this orbit in 365 days and 6 hours, (or in 8766 hours,) it is plain that it travels at the rate of 68,217 miles every hour; so that its velocity in its orbit, is at least 142 times as great as the velocity of a cannon-ball, supposing the ball to move through eight miles in a minute, which it is found to do, nearly. At this rate it would take 22 years, and 228 days for a cannon-ball to go from this earth to the sun.

The earth is 25,038 miles in circumference; and by turning on its axis once in twenty-four hours from west to east, causes a continual succession of day and night, according as either side is turned to or from the sun; and occasions an apparent motion of the sun and heavenly bodies from east to west. This is called the earth's *diurnal*, or daily motion, by which the inhabitants on the equator are carried 1040 miles every hour.

That the earth is round like a globe is evident: *First*, From its having been circumnavigated, or sailed round by Magellan, Sir Francis Drake, Lord Anson, Captain Cook and others.* *Secondly*, From its shadow in eclipses of the moon, which shadow is bounded by a circular line.

As the earth is round and habitable on all sides, it will doubtless appear strange, that persons can stand directly opposite to us on the under side. But

---

* Magellan *sailed from Seville in Spain, under the auspices of Charles V. 10th of August,* 1519; *and having discovered the Magellanic Streights in South America, he crossed the Pacific Ocean, and arrived at the Philippine Islands where he was poisoned. His ship returned by way of the Cape of Good Hope, 8th September* 1522.

Sir Francis Drake *sailed from Plymouth,* 13th December 1577—*entered the Pacific Ocean, and steering round America, returned November 3d,* 1580. *He was a man of great generosity. The booty which he took, and even the wedges of gold given him in return for his presents to Indian chiefs, he divided in just proportional shares with the common sailors.*

Thomas Cavendish *sailed from Plymouth with two small ships the 1st of August,* 1586—*passed through the Streights of Magellan—took many rich prizes along the coasts of Chili and Peru; and near California possessed himself of the St. Annan Acapulco ship, with a cargo of immense value. He completed the circumnavigation of the globe the 9th of September,* 1588.

Between the years 1598, *and* 1626, Oliver de Nort, *of Utrecht,* James Mahu, George Spillenberger, *a Fleming,* William Schouten, *a Hollander, and* James the Hermit, *successively sailed round the globe.*

Lord Anson *sailed in September* 1740—*doubled Cape Horn in a dangerous season—lost most of his men by the scurvy, and with only one remaining ship, the Centurion, crossed the Great Pacific Ocean, which is* 10,000 *miles over—took a Spanish galleon, on her passage from Acapulco to Manilla, and returned home in June* 1744.

Byron—Bouganville, *a Frenchman*—Wallis *and* Carteret, *successively circumnavigated the globe, between the years* 1764 *and* 1769.

Captain Cook *in the ship Endeavour, sailed from Plymouth the 26th of August,* 1768, *and after a most satisfactory voyage, returned the 12th of June* 1771. *He set out on a second voyage the 14th of February,* 1776—*made many important discoveries, and was killed on the island of Owhyhee by the natives, the 14th of February,* 1779. *His ships under the command of Captain Clerk, returned the 16th of October,* 1780.

ARTIFICIAL GLOBE.

But this will eafily be conceived, when it is confidered that the earth attracts all bodies, on or near it's furface, towards its centre equally on all fides. If fo, the people who are oppofite to us ftand juft as firm as we do.

It is now ten o'clock in the morning, and we now think we are ftanding upright on the upper part of the earth. We fhall think the fame at ten o'clock this evening, when the earth fhall have turned half round, becaufe we fhall then perceive no difference of pofture. We fhall then be exactly in the pofition of thofe perfons who now ftand on the oppofite fide of the earth. Since they are as ftrongly attracted towards the centre of the earth as we are, they can be in no more danger of falling downward, than we are at prefent of falling upward.

ARTIFICIAL GLOBE.

AN artificial globe is a round body, whofe furface is every where equally remote from the centre; and on which the external form of our habitable world is reprefented, and all the parts of the earth and water are defcribed in their natural order, form, diftance and fituation.

In order to determine the fituation of places on the globe, it is fuppofed to be circumfcribed by feveral imaginary circles. Each circle is divided into 360 equal parts, called degrees; each degree is divided into 60 minutes, and each minute into 60 feconds.

Axis of the Earth.] The axis of the earth is an imaginary line paffing through its centre from north to fouth. The extreme points of the axis are called the poles.

Circles.] A circle paffing through the centre of a globe, and thereby dividing it into two equal parts or hemifpheres, is called a *great circle*. Of thefe there are fix.—The equator, the meridian, the ecliptic, the horizon, and two colures.

Circles dividing the fphere into unequal parts, are called *fmall or leffer circles*, of which there are four, the two tropics, and the two polar circles.

Equator.] The Equator is that line or circle which encompaffes the middle of the earth, dividing the northern half from the fouthern. This line is often called the *equinoctial*, becaufe, when the fun appears therein, the days and nights are equal in all parts of the world. From this line latitude is reckoned.

Meridian.] This circle is reprefented on the artificial globe by a brafs ring, and is divided into 360 degrees. It paffes through the poles of the earth, and the *zenith* and the *nadir*, croffing the equator at right angles, and dividing the globe into eaftern and weftern hemifpheres. It is called *meridian* from the latin *meridies, mid-day*; becaufe when the fun comes to the fouth part of this circle it is called noon, and the day is half fpent. There are an infinite number of meridians, which vary as you travel eaft or weft. Geographers affume one of the meridians for the firft; commonly that which paffes through the metropolis of their own country. The meridian of Philadelphia is the firft for Americans; that of London for the Englifh; and that of Paris for the French.

Ecliptic.]

ARTIFICIAL GLOBE.

Ecliptic.] The Ecliptic is a great circle, in whose plane the earth performs her annual revolution round the sun, or in which the sun seems to move round the earth, once in a year. This circle is called the *Ecliptic*, from the word *Eclipse*, because no eclipse of the sun or moon happens, but when the moon is in or near the plane of this circle. It makes an angle with the equator of 23° 30′, and intersects it in two opposite parts called the *equinoctial points*, because when the sun is in either of these points, he has no declination, and shines equally to both poles, and the day is then equal to the night all over the world. The times when the sun passes through these points, are the 21st of March, and the 21st of September: The former is called the *vernal*, the latter the *autumnal* equinox.

The ecliptic is divided into twelve equal parts of thirty degrees each, called signs. These begin at the vernal intersection of the ecliptic with the equator, and are numbered from west to east. The names and characters of the signs, with the months in which the sun enters them, are as follows:

Latin names of the signs.	English names.	Charac- ters.	Months in which the sun enters them.
1 Aries	The Ram	♈	March
2 Taurus	The Bull	♉	April
3 Gemini	The Twins	♊	May
4 Cancer	The Crab	♋	June
5 Leo	The Lion	♌	July
6 Virgo	The Virgin	♍	August
7 Libra	The Scales	♎	September
8 Scorpio	The Scorpion	♏	October
9 Sagittarius	The Archer	♐	November
10 Capricornus	The Goat	♑	December
11 Aquarius	The Water-Bearer	♒	January
12 Pisces	The Fishes	♓	February

Zodiac.] If two circles were drawn parallel to the ecliptic, at the distance of eight degrees on each side of it, the space, or girdle included between these two parallels, sixteen degrees broad, and divided in the middle by the ecliptic, will comprehend within it the orbits of all the planets, and is called the *Zodiac*.

Horizon.] The Horizon is represented on the artificial globe by a broad wooden circle, dividing it into upper and lower hemispheres. There are, geographically speaking, two horizons, the *sensible* and the *rational*. The sensible horizon is that circle which limits our prospect; where the sky and the land or water appear to meet. The rational or real horizon, is a circle whose plane passes through the centre of the earth, dividing it into upper and lower hemispheres.

The horizon is divided into four quarters, and each quarter into 90 degrees. The four quartering points, (viz.) east, west, north and south, are called the *Cardinal points*. The poles of the horizon are the zenith and the nadir. The former is the point directly over our heads; the latter the point directly under our feet.

Colures.] The colures are two meridian lines which divide the globe into four quarters. They are called *colures*, to distinguish them from other

ARTIFICIAL GLOBE.

other meridians. They both pass through the poles of the world, and one of them through the equinoctial points Aries and Libra; the other through the solstitial points Capricorn and Cancer: The former is called the equinoctial, the latter the solstitial colure.

Tropics.] The tropics are two circles drawn parallel to the equator, at the distance of 23°, 30′ on each side of it. These circles form the limits of the ecliptic, or the sun's declination from the equator. That which is in the northern hemisphere, is called the tropic of Cancer, because it touches the ecliptic in the sign Cancer; and that in the southern hemisphere, is called the tropic of Capricorn, because it touches the ecliptic in the sign Capricorn. On the 21st of June the sun is in Cancer, and we have the longest day. On the 21st of December the sun is in Capricorn, and we have the shortest day. They are called *tropics*, from the greek word τρεπω, *to turn*, because when the sun arrives at them, he returns again to the equator.

Polar Circles.] The two polar circles are described round the poles of the earth at the distance of 23° 30′. The *northern* is called the *Arctic circle*, from *Arctos*, or the bear, a constellation situated near that place in the heavens; the *southern*, being opposite to the former, is called the *Antarctic circle*.—The polar circles bound the places where the sun sets daily. Beyond them the sun revolves without setting.

Zones.] The tropics and polar circles, divide the globe into five parts, called *Zones*, or *Belts*; viz. One torrid, two temperate, and two frigid zones. The *Torrid Zone*, 47 degrees broad, is bounded by the tropics, and divided in the middle by the equator. It is called the torrid or burning zone, because the sun, being always over some part of it, makes it extremely hot.

Each of the *Temperate Zones* is 43 degrees in breadth. The one which lies between the tropic of cancer and the arctic circle, is called the north temperate zone; and the other, lying between the tropic of capricorn and the antarctic circle, is called the south temperate zone. The mildness of the weather in these spaces, which are between the extremes of heat and cold, has acquired to them the name of *temperate zones*.

The two *Frigid Zones*, so called on account of the extreme cold of those regions, are included between the polar circles and the poles. Each of them is 23° 30′ broad.

Climates.] By a number of other circles, drawn parallel to the equator, the earth is divided into climates.

A *Climate* is a tract of the earth's surface, included between the equator and a parallel of latitude, or between two parallels of such a breadth, as that the length of the day in the one, be half an hour longer than in the other. Within the polar circles, however, the breadth of a circle is such, that the length of a day, or the time of the sun's continuance above the horizon without setting, is a month longer in one parallel, as you proceed northerly, than in the other.

Under the equator, the day is always twelve hours long. The days gradually increase in length as you advance either north or south from the equator. The space between the equator, and a parallel line drawn at the distance of 8° 25′ where the days are twelve hours and a half long, is called the first climate; and by conceiving parallels drawn in this manner, at the increase of every half hour, it will be found that there

are

ARTIFICIAL GLOBE.

are twenty-four climates between the equator and each of the polar circles. Forty-eight in the whole.

Under the polar circles, the longest day is twenty-four hours. The sun, when at the tropics, skims the horizon without setting. As you advance from the polar circles to the poles, the sun continues above the horizon for days, weeks and months, in a constant increase until you arrive at the poles, where the sun is six months above the horizon; and the whole year may be said to consist of but one day and one night.

There are thirty climates between the equator and either pole. In the first twenty-four, between the equator and each polar circle, the period of increase for every climate is half an hour. In the other six, between the polar circles and either pole, the period of increase for each climate is a month. These climates continually decrease in breadth as you proceed from the equator, as may be seen by attending to the following table.

TABLE.

Names of countries and remarkable places, situated in the respective climates, north of the equator.

Within the first climate lie,

Climates.	Longest day.	Latitudes in which the respective climates begin and end.	Names of countries
		d. m.	
1	12½	8 25	1 The Gold coast in Africa, Cayenne and Surinam in S. Amer.
2	13	16 25	2 Abyssinia, Siam, Madras, Darien, Barbadoes.
3	13½	23 50	3 Mecca, Bengal, Canton, Mexico, Jamaica, Gaudelupe.
4	14	30 25	4 Egypt, Delhi, Canary Isles, E. Florida, Havanna.
5	14½	36 28	5 Gibraltar, Jerusalem, Nanking, Georgia and Carolinas.
6	15	41 22	6 Lisbon, Madrid, Asia-Minor, Virginia, Maryland, Philadel.
7	15½	45 29	7 Rome, Constantinople, Caspian Sea, New-England.
8	16	49 01	8 Paris, Vienna, Nova-Scotia, Newfoundland, Canada.
9	16½	52 00	9 London, Flanders, Prague, Dresden, Cracow.
10	17	54 27	10 Dublin, Warsaw, Holland, Hanover, Labrador.
11	17½	56 37	11 Edinburgh, Copenhagen, Moscow.
12	18	58 29	12 South Part of Sweden, Siberia.
13	18½	59 58	13 Orkney Isles, Stockholm.
14	19	61 18	14 Bergen in Norway, Petersburgh in Russia.
15	19½	62 25	15 Hudson's Straits.
16	20	63 22	16 South Part of West Greenland.
17	20½	64 06	17 Drontheim in Norway.
18	21	64 49	18 Part of Finland in Russia.
19	21½	65 21	19 Archangel on the White-Sea, Russia.
20	22	65 47	20 Hecla in Iceland.
21	22½	66 06	21 Northern Parts of Russia and Siberia.
22	23	66 20	22 New-North Wales in N. America.
23	23½	66 28	23 Davis's Straits in ditto.
24	24	66 31	24 Samoieda.
25	1 month	67 21	25 South Part of Lapland.
26	2 do.	69 48	26 West Greenland.
27	3 do.	73 37	27 Zemble Australis.
28	4 do	78 30	28 Zemble Borealis.
29	5 do.	84 05	29 Spitsbergen, or E. Greenland.
30	6 do.	90 0	30 Unknown.

Latitude.] The latitude of a place is its distance from the equator, north or south. The greatest latitude is that of the poles, which are ninety degrees distant from the equator.

ARTIFICIAL GLOBE.

The elevation of the pole above the horizon, is always equal to the latitude of the place; for to a person situated on the equator, both poles will rest in the horizon. If you travel one, two or more degrees north, the north pole will rise one, two or more degrees, and will keep pace with your distance from the equator.

Longitude.] Every place on the surface of the earth has its meridian. The *Longitude* of a place, is the distance of its meridian from some other fixed meridian, measured on the equator. Longitude is either east or west. All places east of the fixed or first meridian, are in east longitude; all west, in west longitude. On the equator, a degree of longitude is equal to sixty geographical miles; and of course, a minute on the equator is equal to a mile. But as all the meridians cut the equator at right angles, and approach nearer and nearer to each other, until at last they cross at the poles, it is obvious that the degrees of longitude will lessen as you go from the equator to either pole; so that in the sixtieth degree of latitude, a degree of longitude is but thirty miles, or half as long as a degree on the equator; as is evident from the following table.

A TABLE,

Shewing the number of miles contained in a degree of longitude in each parallel of latitude from the equator.

Degrees of latitude	Miles	60th parts of a mile	Degrees of latitude	Miles	60th parts of a mile	Degrees of latitude	Miles	60th parts of a mile	Degrees of latitude	Miles	60th parts of a mile
1	59	56	24	54	48	47	41	00	70	20	32
2	59	54	25	54	24	48	40	8	71	19	32
3	59	52	26	54	00	49	39	20	72	18	32
4	59	50	27	53	28	50	38	22	73	17	32
5	59	46	28	53	00	51	37	44	74	16	32
6	59	40	29	52	28	52	37	00	75	15	32
7	59	37	30	51	56	53	36	08	76	14	32
8	59	24	31	51	24	54	35	26	77	13	32
9	59	10	32	50	52	55	34	24	78	12	32
10	59	00	33	50	20	56	33	32	79	11	28
11	58	52	34	49	44	57	32	40	80	10	24
12	58	40	35	49	8	58	31	48	81	09	20
13	58	28	36	48	32	59	31	00	82	08	20
14	58	12	37	47	56	60	30	00	83	07	20
15	58	00	38	47	16	61	29	04	84	06	12
16	57	40	39	46	36	62	28	08	85	05	12
17	57	20	40	46	00	63	27	12	86	04	12
18	57	4	41	45	16	64	26	16	87	03	12
19	56	44	42	44	36	65	25	20	88	02	04
20	56	24	43	43	52	66	24	24	89	01	04
21	56	00	44	43	8	67	23	28	90	00	00
22	55	36	45	42	24	68	22	32			
23	55	12	46	41	40	69	21	32			

ARTIFICIAL GLOBE.

The Atmosphere.] The earth is surrounded by a thin, invisible fluid, composed of a mixture of saline, sulphurious, watery, earthy, and spirituous particles, rising to the distance of between forty-five and fifty miles from the earth's surface. This fluid is called the *atmosphere.* Experiment has shewn, that this atmosphere is essential to animal and vegetable life. It is a necessary vehicle of sound; and without it few things would be visible, excepting those upon which the rays of the sun fall in a direct line between the sun and the eye: But the rays of light, falling on the particles which compose the atmosphere, are thence reflected in every direction; in this way day-light is produced, even when the whole hemisphere is covered with clouds.

Winds.] Wind is air put in motion; the swifter this motion, and the more dense the air, the greater will be the force of the wind. If it be soft and gentle, it is called a breeze; if fresh and violent, a gale; if the gale be attended with rain and hail, it is called a storm. As the air is a fluid, its natural state is rest, which it always endeavours to keep, or recover by an universal equilibrium of all its parts. Whenever, therefore, this equilibrium is destroyed by the rarefaction of the air in particular parts, which renders it lighter in those parts than in others, there necessarily follows a motion of all the surrounding air towards these rarified parts, to restore the equilibrium; this motion is called *wind.* The velocity of the wind in a storm has been ascertained by Philosophers, and found to be about sixty miles an hour.

Tides.] By *tide* is meant the regular ebbing and flowing of the sea twice in twenty-four hours. The cause of the tides, is the attraction of the sun and moon, but chiefly of the latter. The waters of the immense ocean, as it were, forgetful of their natural rest, rise and roll in tides, obsequious to the strong attractive power of the moon, and the weaker influence of the sun. The moon in one revolution round the earth in twenty-four hours, produces two tides; of course there are as many ebbs. These tides, necessarily following the moon's motion, flow from east to west. This constant agitation of the waters of the ocean, together with their saltness, are wisely ordained by the Creator to preserve them from putrefaction.

Clouds.] Clouds are nothing but a collection of vapours, exhaled from the earth by the attractive influence of the sun, suspended aloft in the air, and soaring on the wings of the wind. They are elevated from a quarter of a mile to a mile from the earth, according to their density, and that of the air.

Eclipses.] An eclipse is a total or partial privation of the light of the sun or moon. When the moon passes between the earth and the sun, the rays of the sun are in part intercepted, and the sun is said to be in eclipse. When the earth intervenes between the sun and moon, the moon, having no light of her own, appears dark or dusky; and, as we say, she is eclipsed. An eclipse of the sun never happens but at a new moon; nor one of the moon but when she is full.

GEOGRAPHY.

GEOGRAPHY.

GEOGRAPHY is a science describing the surface of the earth as divided into land and water.

Geography is either *universal*, as it relates to the earth in general; or *particular*, as it relates to any single part.

The globe of the earth is made up of land and water, and is therefore called *terraqueous*. About one fourth of the surface of the globe is land; the other three fourths are water.

The common divisions of the land and water are as follows:

The divisions of land are,

I. *Into Continents.*] A continent is a large tract of land, comprehending several countries and kingdoms. These countries, &c. are contiguous to each other, and are not entirely separated by water. There are but two continents, the *eastern* and *western*. The eastern continent is divided into Europe, Asia and Africa; the western into North and South America.

II. *Islands.*] An island is a tract of land entirely surrounded by water; as Rhode Island, Hispaniola, Great-Britain, Ireland, New-Zealand, Borneo, Japan, &c.

III. *Peninsulas.*] A peninsula is almost an island, or a tract of land surrounded by water, excepting at one narrow neck; as Boston, the Morea, Crim Tartary and Arabia.

IV.

The divisions of water are,

I. *Into Oceans.*] An ocean is a vast collection of water, not entirely separated by land, and divides one continent from the other. There are three great oceans. The *Atlantic*, lying between America and Europe, three thousand miles wide. The *Pacific*, lying between Asia and America, ten thousand miles over. The *Indian-Ocean*, lying between Africa and the East Indies, three thousand miles wide.

II. *Lakes.*] A lake is a large collection of water in the heart of a country surrounded by land. Most of them, however, have a river issuing from them, which falls into the ocean; as Lake Ontario, Lake Erie, &c. A small collection of water, surrounded as above, is called a pond.

III. *Seas.*] A sea or gulf is a part of the ocean, surrounded by land excepting a narrow pass, called a strait, by which it communicates with the ocean; as the Mediterranean, Baltic and Red Seas; and the gulfs of Mexico, St. Lawrence and Venice.

IV.

GEOGRAPHY.

IV. *Isthmusses.*] An isthmus is a narrow neck of land joining a peninsula to the main land; as the isthmus of Darien, which joins North and South America; and the isthmus of Seuz, which unites Asia and Africa.

V. *Promontories.*] A promontory is a mountain or hill extending into the sea, the extremity of which is called a cape. A point of flat land projecting far into the sea is likewise called a cape; as Cape Ann, Cape Cod, Cape Hatteras.

VI. *Mountains, Hills,* &c. need no description.

IV. *Straits.*] A strait is a narrow passage out of one sea into another; as the straits of Gibraltar, joining the Mediterranean to the Atlantic; the Straits of Babelmandel, which unite the Red Sea with the Indian Ocean.

V. *Bays.*] A bay is a part of the sea running up into the main land, commonly between two capes; as Massachusetts Bay, between Cape Ann and Cape Cod; Delaware Bay, between Cape May and Cape Henlopen; Chesapeek Bay, between Cape Charles and Cape Henry.

VI. *Rivers.*] A River is a considerable stream of water, issuing from one or more springs, and gliding into the sea. A small stream is called a rivulet or brook.

Maps.] A map is a plain figure representing the surface of the earth, or a part of it, according to the laws of perspective. On the map of any tract of country, are delineated its mountains, rivers, lakes, towns, &c. in their proper magnitudes and situations. The top of a map is always north, the bottom south, the right side east, and the left side west. From the top to the bottom are drawn meridians, or lines of longitude; and from side to side the parallels of latitude.

DISCOVERY of AMERICA.

IT is believed by many, and not without some reason, that America was known to the ancients. Of this, however, history affords no certain evidence. Whatever discoveries may have been made in this western world, by Madoc Gwinneth, the Carthaginians and others, are lost to mankind. The eastern continent was the only theatre of history from the creation of the world to the year of our Lord 1492.

Christopher Columbus, a native of Genoa, has deservedly the honor of having first discovered America. From a long and close application to the study of geography and navigation, for which his genius was naturally inclined, Columbus had obtained a knowledge of the true figure of the earth, much superior to the general notions of the age in which he lived. In order that the terraqueous globe might be properly balanced, and the lands and seas proportioned to each other, he was led to conceive that another continent was necessary. Other reasons induced him to believe that this continent was connected with the East Indies.

As early as the year 1474, he communicated his ingenious theory to Paul, a physician of Florence, eminent for his knowledge of cosmography.

He

DISCOVERY of AMERICA.

He warmly approved it, suggested several facts in confirmation of it, and encouraged Columbus in an undertaking so laudable, and which promised so much benefit to the world.

Having fully satisfied himself with respect to the truth of his system, he became impatient to reduce it to practice. The first step towards this, was to secure the patronage of some of the European powers. Accordingly he laid his scheme before the senate of Genoa, making his native country the first tender of his services. They rejected his proposal, as the dream of a chimerical projector. He next applied to John II. king of Portugal, a monarch of an enterprising genius, and no incompetent judge of naval affairs. The king listened to him in the most gracious manner, and referred the consideration of his plan to a number of eminent cosmographers, whom he was accustomed to consult in matters of this kind. These men, from mean and interested views, started innumerable objections, and asked many captious questions, on purpose to betray Columbus into a full explanation of his system. Having done this, they advised the king to dispatch a vessel, secretly, in order to attempt the proposed discovery, by following exactly the course which Columbus had pointed out. John, forgetting on this occasion the sentiments becoming a monarch, meanly adopted their perfidious counsel.

Upon discovering this dishonourable transaction, Columbus, with an indignation natural to a noble and ingenious mind, quitted the kingdom, and landed in Spain in 1484.

Here he presented his scheme, in person, to Ferdinand and Isabella, who at that time governed the united kingdoms of Castile and Arragon. They injudiciously submitted it to the examination of unskilful judges, who, ignorant of the principles on which Columbus founded his theory, rejected it as absurd, upon the credit of a maxim under which the unenterprising, in every age, shelter themselves, " That it is presumptuous in any person, " to suppose that he alone possesses knowledge, superior to all the rest of " mankind united." They maintained, likewise, that if there were really any such countries as Columbus pretended, they would not have remained so long concealed; nor would the wisdom and sagacity of former ages have left the glory of this discovery to an obscure Genoese pilot.

Meanwhile, Columbus, who had experienced the uncertain issue of applications to kings, had taken the precaution of sending into England his brother Bartholomew, to whom he had fully communicated his ideas, to negociate the matter with Henry VII. On his voyage to England, he fell into the hands of pirates, who stripped him of every thing, and detained him a prisoner several years. At length he made his escape, and arrived at London in extreme indigence, where he employed himself some time in selling maps. With his gains he purchased a decent dress; and in person presented to the king the proposals which his brother had entrusted to his management. Notwithstanding Henry's excessive caution and parsimony, he received the proposals of Columbus with more approbation than any monarch to whom they had been presented.

After several unsuccessful applications to other European powers of less note, he was induced, by the intreaty and interposition of Perzez, a man of considerable learning, and of some credit with queen Isabella, to apply again

again to the court of Spain. This application, after much warm debate and several mortifying repulses, proved successful; not, however, without the most vigorous and persevering exertions of Quintanilla and Santangel, two vigilant and discerning patrons of Columbus, whose meritorious zeal in promoting this grand design, entitles their names to an honorable place in history. It was, however, to queen Isabella, the munificent Patroness of his noble and generous designs, that Columbus ultimately owed his success.

Having thus obtained the assistance of the court, a squadron of three small vessels was fitted out, victualled for twelve months, and furnished with ninety men. The whole expence did not exceed £4000. Of this squadron Columbus was appointed admiral.

On the 3d of August, 1492, he left Spain in the presence of a crowd of spectators, who united their supplications to Heaven for his success. He steered directly for the Canary Islands, where he arrived and refitted, as well as he could, his crazy and ill appointed fleet. Hence he sailed, September 6th, a due western course into an unknown ocean.

Columbus now found a thousand unforeseen hardships to encounter, which demanded all his judgment, fortitude and address to surmount. Besides the difficulties, unavoidable from the nature of his undertaking, he had to struggle with those which arose from the ignorance and timidity of the people under his command. On the 14th of September he was astonished to find that the magnetic needle in their compass, did not point exactly to the polar star, but varied toward the west; and as they proceeded, this variation increased. This new phenomenon filled the companions of Columbus with terror. Nature itself seemed to have sustained a change; and the only guide they had left, to point them to a safe retreat from an unbounded and trackless ocean, was about to fail them. Columbus, with no less quickness than ingenuity, assigned a reason for this appearance, which, though it did not satisfy himself, seemed so plausible to them, that it dispelled their fears, or silenced their murmurs.

The sailors, always discontented, and alarmed at their distance from land, several times mutinied, threatned once to throw their admiral overboard, and repeatedly insisted on his returning. Columbus, on these trying occasions, displayed all that cool deliberation, prudence, soothing address and firmness, which were necessary for a person engaged in a discovery, the most interesting to the world of any ever undertaken by man.

It was on the 11th of October, 1492, at ten o'clock in the evening, that Columbus, from the fore-castle, descried a light. At two o'clock next morning, Roderic Triana discovered land. The joyful tidings were quickly communicated to the other ships. The morning light confirmed the report; and the several crews immediately began *Te Deum*, as a hymn of thanksgiving to God, and mingled their praises with tears of joy, and transports of congratulation. Columbus, richly dressed, with a drawn sword in his hand, was the first European who set foot in the *New World* which he had discovered. The Island on which he thus first landed, he called St. Salvador. It is one of that large cluster of Islands known by the name of the Lucaya or Bahama Isles. He afterwards touched at several of the islands in the same cluster, enquiring every where for gold, which he
thought

thought was the only object of commerce worth his attention. In steering southward he discovered the islands of Cuba and Hispaniola, abounding in all the necessaries of life, and inhabited by a humane and hospitable people.

On his return he was overtaken with a storm, which had nearly proved fatal to his ships and their crews. At a crisis when all was given up for lost, Columbus had presence of mind enough to retire into his cabin, and to write upon parchment a short account of his voyage. This he wrapped in an oiled cloth, which he inclosed in a cake of wax, put it into a tight cask, and threw it into the sea, in hopes that some fortunate accident might preserve a deposit of so much importance to the world. He arrived at Palos in Spain, whence he had sailed the year before, on the 15th of March, 1493. He was welcomed with all the acclamations which the populace are ever ready to bestow on great and glorious characters; and the court received him with marks of the greatest respect.

In September of this year, (1493) Columbus sailed upon his second voyage to America; during the performance of which, he discovered the islands of Dominica, Marigalante, Gaudelupe, Montserrat, Antigua, Porto Rico and Jamaica; and returned to Spain 1496.

In 1498 he sailed a third time for America; and on the 1st of August discovered the CONTINENT. He then coasted along westward, making other discoveries for 200 leagues, to Cape Vela, from which he crossed over to Hispaniola, where he was seized by a new Spanish Governor, and sent home in chains.

In 1502 Columbus made his fourth voyage to Hispaniola; thence he went over to the Continent—discovered the bay of Honduras; thence sailed along the main shore easterly 200 leagues, to Cape Gracias a Dios, Veragua, Porto Bello and the Gulf of Darien.

The jealous and avaricious Spaniards, not immediately receiving those golden advantages which they had promised, and lost to the feelings of humanity and gratitude, suffered their esteem and admiration of Columbus to degenerate into ignoble envy.

The latter part of his life was made wretched by the cruel persecutions of his enemies. Queen Isabella, his friend and patroness, was no longer alive to afford him relief. He sought redress from Ferdinand, but in vain. Disgusted with the ingratitude of a monarch, whom he had served with so much fidelity and success, exhausted with hardships, and broken with the infirmities which these brought upon him, Columbus ended his active and useful life at Valladolid, on the 20th of May, 1506, in the 59th year of his age. He died with a composure of mind suited to the magnanimity which distinguished his character, and with sentiments of piety becoming that supreme respect for religion which he manifested in every occurrence of his life. He was grave though courteous in his deportment, circumspect in his words and actions, irreproachable in his morals, and exemplary in all the duties of his religion. The court of Spain were so just to his memory, notwithstanding their ingratitude towards him during his life, that they buried him magnificently in the Cathedral of Seville, and erected a tomb over him with this inscription,

COLUMBUS has given a NEW WORLD
To the KINGDOMS of CASTILE and LEON.

Among

Among other adventurers to the New World in purfuit of Gold, was Americus Vefpucius, a Florentine gentleman, whom Ferdinand had appointed to draw fea charts, and to whom he had given the title of chief pilot. This man accompanied Ojeda, an enterprizing Spanifh adventurer, to America; and having with much art, and fome degree of elegance, drawn up an amufing hiftory of his voyage, he publifhed it to the world. It circulated rapidly, and was read with admiration. In his narrative he had infinuated that the glory of having firft difcovered the continent in the New World, belonged to him. This was in part believed, and the country began to be called after the name of its fuppofed firft difcoverer. The unaccountable caprice of mankind has perpetuated the error; fo that now, by the univerfal confent of all nations, this new quarter of the globe is called AMERICA. The name of Americus has fupplanted that of Columbus, and mankind are left to regret an act of injuftice, which, having been fanctioned by time, they can never redrefs.

GENERAL DESCRIPTION of AMERICA.

BOUNDARIES and EXTENT.

THE Continent of America, of the difcovery of which a fuccinct account has juft been given, extends from Cape Horn, the fouthern extremity of the Continent in latitude 56° fouth, to the north pole; and fpreads between the 40th degree eaft, and the 100th degree weft longitude from Philadelphia. It is nearly ten thoufand miles in length from north to fouth; its mean breadth has never been afcertained. This extenfive continent lies between the Pacific Ocean on the weft, and the Atlantic on the eaft. It is faid to contain upwards of 14,000,000 fquare miles.

Climate, Soil and Productions.] In regard to each of thefe, America has all the varieties which the earth affords. It ftretches through the whole width of the five zones, and feels the heat and cold of two fummers and two winters in every year. Moft of the animal and vegetable productions which the eaftern continent affords, are found here; and many that are peculiar to America.

Rivers.] This continent is watered by fome of the largeft rivers in the world. The principal of thefe, are Rio de la Plata, the Amazon and Oronoke in South America—The Miffiffippi and St. Lawrence in North-America.

Gulfs.] The Gulf or Bay of *Mexico*, lying in the form of a bafon between North and South America, and opening to the eaft, is conjectured by fome, to have been formerly land; and that the conftant attrition of the waters of the Gulf Stream, has worn it to its prefent form. The water in the Gulf of Mexico, is faid to be many yards higher, than on the weftern fide of the continent in the Pacific Ocean.

Gulf Stream.] The *Gulf Stream* is a remarkable current in the Ocean, of a circular form, beginning on the coaft of Africa, in the climates where

DESCRIPTION of AMERICA.

the trade winds blow westerly, thence running across the Atlantic, and between the Islands of Cuba and South-America into the Bay of Mexico, from which it finds a passage between Cape Florida and the Bahama Islands, and runs north-easterly along the American coast to Newfoundland; thence to the European coast and along the coast southerly 'till it meets the trade winds. It is about 75 miles from the shores of the southern states. The distance increases as you proceed northward. The width of the stream is about 40 or 50 miles, widening toward the north, and its common rapidity three miles an hour.—A northeast wind narrows the stream, renders it more rapid, and drives it nearer the coast; northwest and west winds have a contrary effect.

Mountains.] The *Andes* in South America, stretch along the Pacific Ocean from the Isthmus of Darien, to the Straits of Magellan, 4300 miles. The height of Chimborazo, the most elevated point in this vast chain of mountains, is 20,280 feet; above 5000 feet higher than any other mountain in the known world.

North America, though an uneven country, has no remarkably high mountains. The most considerable, are those known under the general name of the *Allegany Mountains*: These stretch along in many broken ridges under different names, from Hudson's River to Georgia. The *Andes* and the *Allegany Mountains* are probably the same range, interrupted by the Gulf of Mexico. It has been conjectured that the West India islands were formerly united with each other, and formed a part of the continent, connecting North and South America. Their present disjointed situation is supposed to have been occasioned by the trade winds. It is well known that they produce a strong and continual current from east to west, which by beating against the continent for a long course of years, must produce surprizing alterations, and may have produced such an effect as has been supposed.

Number of Inhabitants.] It has been supposed that there are 160 millions of inhabitants in America. It is believed, however, that this account is exaggerated at least one half. This number is composed of Indians, Negroes, Mulattoes, and some of almost every nation in Europe.

Aborigines.] The characteristical features of the Indians of America, are, a very small forehead covered with hair from the extremities to the middle of the eyebrows. They have little black eyes, a thin nose, small and bending towards the upper lip. The countenance broad; the features coarse, the ears large and far from the face; their hair very black, lank and coarse. Their limbs small but well turned; the body tall, strait, of a copper color, and well proportioned; strong and active, but not fitted for much labour. Their faces smooth and free from beard, owing to a custom among them of pulling it out by the roots. Their countenances, at first view appear mild and innocent, but upon a critical inspection, they discover something wild, distrustful and sullen. They are dextrous with their bows and arrows; fond of adorning themselves with strings of beads and shells about their necks, and plates in their ears and noses. In summer they go almost naked; but in winter they cover themselves with the skins of beasts taken in hunting, which is their principal employment. They many times torture their prisoners in the

most

most shocking and cruel manner; generally scalp them, and sometimes broil and eat them. A great part of the Aborigines of America are gross idolaters, and worship the sun, moon, and stars. It is the opinion of many learned men, supported by several well established facts, that the Indians of America are remains of the ten tribes of Israel, and that they came to this continent in the manner hereafter mentioned.

Society among savages is extremely rude. The improvement of the talents which nature has given them, is of course, proportionably small. It is the genius of a savage to act from the impulse of present passion. They have neither foresight nor disposition to form complicated arrangments with respect to their future conduct. This, however, is not to be ascribed to any defect in their natural genius, but to their state of society, which affords few objects for the display either of their literary or political abilities. In all their warlike enterprizes they are led by persuasion. Their society allows of no compulsion. What civilized nations enforce upon their subjects by compulsory measures, they effect by their eloquence; hence the foundation of those masterly strokes of oratory, which have been exhibited at their treaties; some of which equal the most finished pieces that have been produced by the most eminent ancient or modern orators.

As a specimen, take the following from Mr. Jefferson's notes on Virginia. ' I may challenge the whole orations of Demosthenes and Cicero, and of any more eminent orator, if Europe has furnished more eminent, to produce a single passage, superior to the speech of Logan, a Mingo chief, to Lord Dunmore, when governor of this state. And, as a testimony of their talents in this line, I beg leave to introduce it, first stating the incidents necessary for understanding it. In the spring of the year 1774, a robbery and murder were committed on an inhabitant of the frontiers of Virginia, by two Indians of the Shawanee tribe. The neighbouring whites, according to their custom, undertook to punish this outrage in a summary way. Col. Cresap, a man infamous for the many murders he had committed on those much-injured people, collected a party, and proceeded down the Kanhaway in quest of vengeance. Unfortunately a canoe of women and children, with one man only, was seen coming from the opposite shore, unarmed, and unsuspecting an hostile attack from the whites. Cresap and his party concealed themselves on the bank of the river, and the moment the canoe reached the shore, singled out their objects, and, at one fire, killed every person in it. This happened to be the family of Logan, who had long been distinguished as a friend of the whites. This unworthy return provoked his vengeance. He accordingly signalized himself in the war which ensued. In the autumn of the same year, a decisive battle was fought at the mouth of the Great Kanhaway, between the collected forces of the Shawanees, Mingoes, and Delawares, and a detachment of the Virginia militia. The Indians were defeated, and sued for peace. Logan however disdained to be seen among the suppliants. But, lest the sincerity of a treaty should be distrusted, from which so distinguished a chief absented himself, he sent by a messenger the following speech to be delivered to Lord Dunmore.

" I appeal to any white man to say, if ever he entered Logan's cabin hungry, and he gave him not meat; if ever he came cold and naked, and

he

he clothed him not. During the courfe of the laft long and bloody war, Logan remained idle in his cabin, an advocate for peace. Such was my love for the whites, that my countrymen pointed as they paffed, and faid, " Logan is the friend of white men." I had even thought to have lived with you, but for the injuries of one man. Col. Crefap, the laft fpring, in cold blood, and unprovoked, murdered all the relations of Logan, not fparing even my women and children. There runs not a drop of my blood in the veins of any living creature. This called on me for revenge. I have fought it : I have killed many : I have fully glutted my vengeance. For my country, I rejoice at the beams of peace. But do not harbour a thought that mine is the joy of fear. Logan never felt fear. He will not turn on his heel to fave his life. Who is there to mourn for Logan?—Not one."

Of their bravery and addrefs in war they have given us multiplied proofs. No people in the world have higher notions of military honour than the Indians. The fortitude, the calmnefs, and even exultation which they manifeft while under the extremeft torture, is in part owing to thei favage infenfibility, but more to their exalted ideas of military glory, and their rude notions of future happinefs, which they believe they fhall forfeit by the leaft manifeftation of fear, or uneafinefs, under their fufferings. They are fincere in their friendfhips, but bitter and determined in their refentments, and often purfue their enemies feveral hundred miles through the woods, furmounting every difficulty, in order to be revenged. In their public councils they obferve the greateft decorum. In the foremoft rank fit the old men, who are the counfellors, then the warriors, and next the women and children. As they keep no records, it is the bufinefs of the women to notice every thing that paffes, to imprint it on their memories, and tell it to their children. They are, in fhort, the records of the council ; and with furprizing exactnefs, preferve the ftipulations of treaties entered into a hundred years back. Their kindnefs and hofpitality is fcarcely equalled by any civilized nation. Their politenefs in converfation is even carried to excefs, fince it does not allow them to contradict any thing that is afferted in their prefence. In fhort there appears to be much truth in Dr. Franklin's obfervation, " We call them favages, becaufe their manners differ from ours, which we think the perfection of civility ; they think the fame of theirs."

The firft peopling of America.] It has long been a queftion among the curious, how America was firft peopled. Various have been the theories and fpeculations of ingenious men upon this fubject. Dr. Robertfon* has recapitulated and canvaffed the moft probable of thefe theories, and the refult is,

I. That America was not peopled by any nation from the ancient continent, which had made any confiderable progrefs in civilization ; becaufe when America was firft difcovered, its inhabitants were unacquainted with the neceffary arts of life, which are the firft effays of the human mind toward improvement ; and if they had ever been acquainted with them, for inftance with the plow, the loom, and the forge, their utility would have been fo great and obvious, that it is impoffible they fhould have been

* Hift. America. Vol. I. Page 22.

been loſt. Therefore the anceſtors of the firſt ſettlers in America were uncivilized and unacquainted with the neceſſary arts of life.

II. America could not have been peopled by any colony from the more ſouthern nations of the ancient continent; becauſe none of the rude tribes of theſe parts poſſeſſed enterprize, ingenuity, or power ſufficient to undertake ſuch a diſtant voyage: but more eſpecially, becauſe, that in all America there is not an animal, tame or wild, which properly belongs to the warm, or temperate countries of the eaſtern continent. The firſt care of the Spaniards, when they ſettled in America, was to ſtock it with all the domeſtic animals of Europe. The firſt ſettlers of Virginia and New-England, brought over with them, horſes, cattle, ſheep, &c. Hence it is obvious that the people who firſt ſettled in America, did not originate from thoſe countries where theſe animals abound, otherwiſe, having been accuſtomed to their aid, they would have ſuppoſed them neceſſary to the improvement, and even ſupport of civil ſociety.

III. Since the animals in the northern regions of America correſpond with thoſe found in Europe in the ſame latitudes, while thoſe in the tropical regions, are indigenous, and widely different from thoſe which inhabit the correſponding regions on the eaſtern continent, it is more than probable that all the original American animals were of thoſe kinds which inhabit northern regions only, and that the two continents, towards the northern extremity, are ſo nearly united as that theſe animals might paſs from one to the other.

IV. It having been eſtabliſhed beyond a doubt, by the diſcoveries of Capt. Cook in his laſt voyage, that at *Kamſkatka*, in about latitude 66° north, the continents of Aſia and America are ſeparated by a ſtrait *only* 18 miles wide, and that the inhabitants on each continent are ſimilar, and frequently paſs and repaſs in canoes from one continent to the other; from theſe and other circumſtances it is rendered highly probable that America was firſt peopled from the northeaſt parts of Aſia. But ſince the Eſquimaux Indians are manifeſtly a ſeparate ſpecies of men, diſtinct from all the nations of the American Continent, in language, in diſpoſition, and in habits of life; and in all theſe reſpects bear a near reſemblance to the northern Europeans, it is believed that the Eſquimaux Indians emigrated from the north weſt parts of Europe. Several circumſtances confirm this belief. As early as the ninth century the Norwegians diſcovered Greenland, and planted colonies there. The communication with that country, after long interruption, was renewed in the laſt century. Some Lutheran and Moravian miſſionaries, prompted by zeal for propagating the Chriſtian faith, have ventured to ſettle in this frozen region. From them we learn, that the north weſt coaſt of Greenland is ſeparated from America, but by a very narrow ſtrait, if ſeparated at all; and that the Eſquimaux of America perfectly reſemble the Greenlanders in their aſpect, dreſs, mode of living, and probably language. By theſe deciſive facts, not only the conſanguinity of the Eſquimaux and Greenlanders is eſtabliſhed, but the poſſibility of peopling America from the north weſt parts of Europe. On the whole it appears rational to conclude, that the progenitors of all the American nations, from Cape Horn to the ſouthern limits of Labrador, from the ſimilarity of their aſpect, color, &c. migrated from the north eaſt parts of Aſia; and that the nations that inhabit Labrador.

Labrador, Esquimaux, and the parts adjacent, from their unlikeness to the rest of the American nations, and their resemblance to the northern Europeans, came over from the north west parts of Europe.

Having given a summary account of America in general; of its first discovery by Columbus, its extent, rivers, mountains, &c. of the Aborigines, and of the first peopling this continent, we shall next turn our attention to the discovery and settlement of North America.

A SUMMARY *account of the first* DISCOVERIES *and* SETTLEMENTS *of* NORTH AMERICA, *arranged in chronological order.*

NORTH AMERICA was discovered in the reign of Henry VII. a period when the Arts and Sciences had made very considerable progress in Europe. Many of the first adventurers were men of genius and learning, and were careful to preserve authentic records of such of their proceedings as would be interesting to posterity. These records afford ample documents for American historians. Perhaps no people on the globe, can trace the history of their origin and progress with so much precision, as the inhabitants of North America; particularly that part of them who inhabit the territory of the United States.

The fame which Columbus had acquired by his first discoveries on this western continent, spread through Europe, and inspired many with
1496 the spirit of enterprize. As early as 1496, four years only after the first discovery of America, John Cabot, a Venetian, obtained a commission from Henry VII. to discover unknown lands and annex them to the crown.

In the Spring he sailed from England with two ships, carrying with him his three sons. In this voyage, which was intended for China, he fell in with the north side of Terra Labrador, and coasted northerly as far as the 67th degree of latitude.

1497.] The next year he made a second voyage to America with his son Sebastian, who afterwards proceeded in the discoveries which his father had begun. On the 24th of June he discovered Bonavista, on the north east side of Newfoundland. Before his return he traversed the coast from Davis's straits to Cape Florida.

1502.] Sebastian Cabot was this year at Newfoundland; and on his return, carried three of the natives of that island to Henry VII.

1513.] In the spring of 1513, John Ponce sailed from Porto Rico northerly, and discovered the continent in 30° 8′ north latitude. He landed in April, a season when the country around was covered with verdure, and in full bloom. This circumstance induced him to call the country FLORIDA, which, for many years was the common name for North and South America.

1516.] In 1516, Sir Sebastian Cabot and Sir Thomas Pert, explored the coast as far as Brazil in South America.

This vast extent of country, the coast whereof was thus explored, remained unclaimed and unsettled by any European power, (except by the Spaniards in South America) for almost a century from the time of its discovery.

1524.]

1524.] It was not till the year 1524 that France attempted difcoveries on the American coaſt. Stimulated by his enterprizing neighbours, Francis I. who poſſeſſed a great and active mind, fent John Verrazano, a Florentine, to America, for the purpoſe of making difcoveries. He traverfed the coaſt from latitude 28° to 50° north. In a fecond voyage, fometime after, he was loſt.

1525.] The next year Stephen Gomez, the firſt Spaniard who came upon the American coaſt for difcovery, failed from Groyn in Spain, to Cuba and Florida, thence northward to Cape Razo, in latitude 46° north, in fearch of a northweſt paſſage to the Eaſt Indies.

1534.] In the fpring of 1534, by the direction of Francis I. a fleet was fitted out at St. Malo's in France, with defign to make difcoveries in America. The command of this fleet was given to James Cartier. He arrived at Newfoundland in May of this year. Thence he failed northerly ; and on the day of the feſtival of St. Lawrence, he found himfelf in about latitude 48° 30' north, in the midſt of a broad gulf, which he named St. Lawrence. He gave the fame name to the river which empties into it. In this voyage, he failed as far north as latitude 51°. expecting in vain to find a paſſage to China.

1535.] The next year he failed up the river St. Lawrence 300 leagues to the great and fwift *Fall.* He called the country New France ; built a fort in which he fpent the winter, and returned in the following fpring to France.

1542.] In 1542, Francis la Roche, Lord of Robewell, was fent to Canada, by the French king, with three ſhips and 200 men, women and children. They wintered here in a fort which they had built, and returned in the fpring. About the year 1550, a large number of adventurers failed for Canada, but were never after heard of. In 1598, the king of France commiſſioned the Marquis De la Roche to conquer Canada, and other countries not poſſeſſed by any Chriſtian prince. We do not learn, however, that la Roche ever attempted to execute his commiſſion, or that any further attempts were made to fettle Canada during this century.

1539.] On the 12th of May, 1539, Ferdinand de Soto, with 900 men, befides feamen, failed from Cuba, having for his object the conqueſt of Florida. On the 30th of May he arrived at Spirito Santo, from whence he travelled northward 450 leagues from the Sea. Here he difcovered a river a quarter of a mile wide and 19 fathoms deep, on the bank
1542 of which he died and was buried, May, 1542, aged 42 years.
1543 Aiverdo his fucceſſor, built feven brigantines, and the year following embarked upon the river. In 17 days he proceeded down the river 400 leagues, where he judged it to be 15 leagues wide. From the largeneſs of the river at the place of his embarkation, he concluded its fource muſt have been at leaſt 400 leagues above, fo that the whole length of the river in his opinion muſt have been more than 800 leagues. As he paſſed down the river, he found it opened by two mouths into the gulf of Mexico. Thefe circumſtances leave us to conclude, that this river, fo early difcovered, was the one which we now call the *Miſ-ſiſſippi.*

Jan.

DISCOVERY and SETTLEMENT of NORTH AMERICA. 23

Jan. 6, 1549.] This year king Henry VII. granted a pension for life to Sebastian Cabot, in consideration of the important services he had rendered to the kingdom by his discoveries in America.

1562.] The admiral of France, Chatillon, early in this year, sent out a fleet under the command of John Ribalt. He arrived at Cape Francis on the coast of Florida, near which, on the first of May, he discovered and entered a river which he called May river. It is more than probable that this river is the same which we now call St. Mary's, which forms a part of the southern boundary of the United States. As he coasted northward he discovered eight other rivers, one of which he called Port Royal, and sailed up it several leagues. On one of the rivers he built a fort and called it *Charles*, in which he left a colony under the direction of Captain Albert. The severity of Albert's measures excited a mutiny in which, to the ruin of the colony, he was slain. Two years after, Chatillon sent Rene Laudonier with three ships to Florida. In June he arrived at the river *May*, on which he built a fort, and, in honor to his king, Charles IX. he called CAROLINA.

1564

In August, this year, Capt. Ribalt arrived at Florida the second time, with a fleet of seven vessels to recruit the colony, which, two years before, he had left under the direction of the unfortunate Capt. Albert.

The September following, Pedro Melandes, with six Spanish ships, pursued Ribalt up the river on which he had settled, and overpowering him in numbers, cruelly massacred him and his whole company. Melendes, having in this way taken possession of the country, built three forts, and left them garrisoned with 1200 soldiers. Laudonier and his colony on May River, receiving information of the fate of Ribalt, took the alarm and escaped to France.

1567.] A fleet of three ships was this year sent from France to Florida, under the command of Dominique de Gourges. The object of this expedition, was to dispossess the Spaniards of that part of Florida which they had cruelly and unjustifiably seized three years before. He arrived on the coast of Florida, April 1568, and soon after made a successful attack upon the forts. The recent cruelty of Melendes and his company excited revenge in the breast of Gourges, and roused the unjustifiable principle of retaliation. He took the forts; put most of the Spaniards to the sword; and having burned and demolished all their fortresses, returned to France. During the 50 years next after this event, the French enterprized no settlements in America.

1568

1576.] Capt. Frobisher was sent this year, to find out a north west passage to the East-Indies. The first land which he made on the coast was a Cape, which, in honor to the queen, he called *Queen Elizabeth's Foreland*. In coasting northerly he discovered the straits which bear his name. He prosecuted his search for a passage into the western ocean till he was prevented by the ice, and then returned to England.

1579.] In 1579, Sir Humphry Gilbert obtained a patent from queen Elizabeth, for lands not yet possessed by any Christian prince, provided he would take possession within six years. With this encouragement he sailed for America, and on the 1st of August 1583, anchored in Conception Bay. Afterward he discovered and took possession of St. John's Harbour, and the country south. In pursuing his discoveries

1583

discoveries he lost one of his ships on the shoals of Sablon, and on his return home, a storm overtook him, in which he was unfortunately lost, and the intended settlement was prevented.

1584.] This year two patents were granted by queen Elizabeth, one to Adrian Gilbert, (Feb. 6.) the other to Sir Walter Raleigh, for lands not possessed by any Christian prince. By the direction of Sir Walter, two ships were fitted and sent out, under the command of Philip Amidas, and Arthur Barlow. In July they arrived on the coast, and anchored in a harbour seven leagues west of the Roanoke. On the 13th of July, they, in a formal manner, took possession of the country, and, in honor of their virgin queen Elizabeth, they called it *Virginia*. Till this time the country was known by the general name of *Florida*. After this VIRGINIA became the common name for all North America.

1585.] The next year, Sir Walter Raleigh sent Sir Richard Greenville to America, with seven ships. He arrived at Wococon Harbour in June. Having stationed a colony of more than a hundred people at Roanoke, under the direction of Capt. Ralph Lane, he coasted northeasterly as far as Chesapeek Bay, and returned to England.

The colony under Capt. Lane, endured extreme hardships, and must have perished, had not Sir Francis Drake fortunately returned to Virginia, and carried them to England, after having made several conquests for the queen in the West Indies and other places.

A fortnight after, Sir Richard Greenville arrived with new recruits ; and, although he did not find the colony which he had before left and knew not but they had perished, he had the rashness to leave 50 men at the same place.

1587.] The year following, Sir Walter sent another company to Virginia under Governor White, with a charter and twelve assistants. In July he arrived at Roanoke. Not one of the second company remained. He determined, however, to risque a third colony. Accordingly he left 115 people at the old settlement, and returned to England.

This year (Aug. 13) *Manteo* was baptized in Virginia. He was the first native Indian who received that ordinance in that part of America. On the 18th of August, Mrs. Dare was delivered of a daughter, whom she called VIRGINIA. She was the first English child that was born in North America.

1590.] In the year 1590, Governor White came over to Virginia with supplies and recruits for his colony ; but, to his great grief, not a man was to be found. They had all miserably famished with hunger, or were massacred by the Indians.

1602.] In the spring of this year, Bartholomew Gosnold, with 32 persons, made a voyage to North Virginia, and discovered and gave names to Cape Cod, Martha's Vineyard, and Elisabeth Islands, and to Dover Cliff. Elisabeth Island was the place which they fixed for their first settlement. But the courage of those who were to have tarried, failing, they all went on board and returned to England. All the attempts to settle this continent which were made by the Dutch, French, and English from its discovery to the present time, a period of 110 years, proved ineffectual. The Spaniards only, of all the European nations, had been successful. There is no account of there having been one European family,

family, at this time, in all the vaſt extent of coaſt from Florida to Greenland.

1603.] Martin Pring and William Brown, were this year ſent by Sir Walter Raleigh, with two ſmall veſſels, to make diſcoveries in North Virginia. They came upon the coaſt which was broken with a multitude of iſlands, in latitude 43° 30′ north. They coaſted ſouthward to Cape Cod Bay; thence round the Cape into a commodious harbour in latitude 41° 25′, where they went aſhore and tarried ſeven weeks, during which time they loaded one of their veſſels with ſaſſafras, and returned to England.

Bartholomew Gilbert, in a voyage to South Virginia, in ſearch of the third colony which had been left there by Governor White in 1587, having touched at ſeveral of the Weſt-India Iſlands, landed near Cheſapeek Bay, where, in a ſkirmiſh with the Indians, he and four of his men were unfortunately ſlain. The reſt, without any further ſearch for the colony, returned to England.

France, being at this time in a ſtate of tranquility in conſequence of the edict of Nantz in favor of the Proteſtants, paſſed by Henry IV. (April 1598) and of the peace with Philip king of Spain and Portugal, was induced to purſue her diſcoveries in America. Accordingly the king ſigned a patent in favor of De Mons, (1603) of all the country from the 40th to the 46th degrees of north latitude under the name 1604 of *Acadia*. The next year De Mons ranged the coaſt from St. Lawrence to Cape Sable, and ſo round to Cape Cod.

1605.] In May 1605, George's Iſland and Pentecoſt Harbor were diſcovered by Capt. George Weymouth. In May he entered a large river in latitude 43° 20′, (variation 11° 15′ weſt,) which Mr. Prince, in his Chronology, ſuppoſes muſt have been Sagadahok; but from the latitude, it was more probably the Piſcataqua. Capt. Weymouth carried with him to England five of the natives.

1606.] In the Spring of this year, James I. by patent, divided Virginia into two colonies. The *ſouthern* included all lands between the 34th and 41ſt degrees of north latitude. This was ſtyled the *firſt colony*, under the name of South Virginia, and was granted to the London Company. The *northern*, called the ſecond colony, and known by the general name of North Virginia, included all lands between the 38th and 45th degrees north latitude, and was granted to the Plymouth Company. Each of theſe colonies had a council of thirteen men to govern them. To prevent diſputes about territory, the colonies were prohibited to plant within an hundred miles of each other. There appears to be an inconſiſtency in theſe grants, as the lands lying between the 38th and 41ſt degrees, are covered by both patents.

Both the London and Plymouth companies enterprized ſettlements within the limits of their reſpective grants. With what ſucceſs will now be mentioned.

Mr. Piercy, brother of the Earl of Northumberland in the ſervice of the London Company, went over with a colony to Virginia, and diſcovered Powhatan, now James River. In the mean time the Plymouth company ſent Capt. Henry Challons in a veſſel of fifty-five tons to plant a colony in North Virginia; but in his voyage he was taken by a Spaniſh fleet and carried to Spain.

1607.] The London company this spring, sent Capt. Christopher New-
April 26.) port with three vessels to South Virginia. On the 26th of April
he entered Chesapeek Bay, and landed, and soon after gave to the most
southern point, the name of *Cape Henry*, which it still retains.
May 13.] Having elected Mr. Edward Wingfield president for the year,
they next day landed all their men, and began a settlement on
James river at a place which they called James-Town. This is
June 22.] the first town that was settled by the English in North America. The June following Capt. Newport sailed for England,
leaving with the president one hundred and four persons.
August 22.] In August died Capt. Bartholomew Gosnold, the first
projector of this settlement, and one of the council. The following winter James-Town was burnt.

During this time the Plymouth company fitted out two ships under the
command of Admiral Rawley Gilbert. They sailed for North Virginia
on the 31st of May, with one hundred planters, and Capt. George Popham
for their president. They arrived in August and settled about nine or ten
leagues to the southward of the mouth of Sagadahok river. A great
part of the colony, however disheartened by the severity of the winter, returned to England in December, leaving their president Capt. Popham,
with only forty-five men.

It was in the fall of this year that the famous Mr. Robinson with part
of his congregation, who afterwards settled at Plymouth in New-England, removed from the North of England to Holland, to avoid the cruelties of persecution, and for the sake of enjoying " purity of worship and
liberty of conscience."

This year a small company of merchants at Dieppe and St. Malo's,
founded Quebec, or rather the colony which they sent, built a few huts
there which did not take the form of a town until the reign of Lewis
XIV.

1608.] The Sagadahok colony suffered incredible hardships after the
departure of their friends in December. In the depth of winter, which
was extremely cold, their store-house caught fire and was consumed with
most of their provisions and lodgings. Their misfortunes were increased,
soon after, by the death of their president. Rawley Gilbert was appointed
to succeed him.

Lord chief Justice Popham made every exertion to keep this colony
alive by repeatedly sending them supplies. But the circumstance of his
death, which happened this year, together with that of president Gilbert's
being called to England to settle his affairs, broke up the colony, and
they all returned with him to England.

The unfavorable reports which these first unfortunate adventurers propagated respecting the country, prevented any further attempts to settle
North Virginia for several years after.

1609.] The London company, last year, sent Capt. Nelson with two ships
and one hundred and twenty persons, to James-Town; and this year Capt.
John Smith, afterwards president, arrived on the coast of South Virginia,
and by sailing up a number of the rivers, discovered the interior country.
In September Capt. Newport arrived with seventy persons, which increased the colony to two hundred souls.

Mr.

Mr. Robinfon and his congregation, who had fettled at Amfterdam, removed this year to Leyden, where they remained more than eleven years, till a part of them came over to New England.

The council for South Virginia, having refigned their old commiffion, requefted and obtained a new one; in confequence of which they appointed Sir Thomas Weft, Lord De la War, general of the colony; Sir Thomas Gates, his lieutenant; Sir Gerge Somers Admiral; Sir Thomas Dale high marfhal; Sir Ferdinand Wainman general of the horfe, and Capt. Newport vice admiral.

June 8.] In June Sir T. Gates, admiral Newport, and Sir George Somers, with feven fhips and a ketch and pinnace, having five hundred fouls on board, men women and children, failed from Falmouth for *July* 24,] South Virginia. In croffing the Bahama Gulf, on the 24th July, the fleet was overtaken by a violent ftorm and feparated. Four days after, Sir George Somers ran his veffel afhore on one of the Bermudas Iflands, which, from this circumftance, have been called the Somer Iflands. The people on board, one hundred and fifty in number, all got fafe on fhore, and there remained until the following May. The remainder of the fleet arrived at Virginia in Auguft. The colony was now increafed to five hundred men. Capt. Smith, then prefident, a little before the arrival of the fleet, had been very badly burnt by means of fome powder which had accidentally caught fire. This unfortunate circumftance, together with the oppofition he met with from thofe who had lately arrived, induced him to leave the colony and return to England, which he accordingly did the laft of September. Francis Weft, his fucceffor in office, foon followed him, and George Piercy was elected prefident.

1610.] The year following, the South Virginia or London company, fealed a patent to Lord De la War, conftituting him Governor and Captain General of South Virginia. He foon after embarked for America with Capt. Argal and one hundred and fifty men, in three fhips.

The unfortunate people, who, the year before, had been fhipwrecked on the Bermudas Iflands, had employed themfelves during the winter and fpring, under the direction of Sir Thomas Gates, Sir George Somers, and admiral Newport, in building a floop to tranfport themfelves to the continent. They embarked for Virginia on the 10th of May, with about one hundred and fifty perfons on board, leaving two of their men behind, who chofe to ftay, and landed at James-Town on the 23d of the fame month. Finding the colony, which at the time of Capt. Smith's departure, confifted of five hundred fouls, now reduced to fixty, and thofe few in a diftreffed and wretched fituation, they with one voice refolved to return to England; and for this purpofe, on the 7th of June, the whole colony repaired on board their veffels, broke up the fettlement, and failed down the river on their way to their native country.

Fortunately, Lord De la War, who had embarked for James-Town the March before, met them the day after they failed and perfuaded them to return with him to James-Town, where they arrived and landed the 10th of June. The government of the colony of right, devolved upon Lord De la War. From this time we may date the effectual fettlement of Virginia. Its hiftory from this period, will be given in its proper place.

As

As early as the year 1608, or 1609, Henry Hudson, an Englishman, under a commission from the king his master, discovered Long Island, New York, and the river which still bears his name, and afterwards sold the country or rather his right, to the Dutch. Their writers, however, contend that Hudson was sent out by the East-India company in 1609, to discover a northwest passage to China; and that having first discovered Delaware Bay, he came and penetrated Hudson's river as far as latitude 43°. It is said however that there was a sale, and that the English objected to it, though for some time they neglected to oppose the Dutch settlement of the country.

1610.] In 1610, Hudson sailed again to this country, then called by the Dutch *New Netherlands*, and four years after, the States General granted a patent to sundry merchants for an exclusive trade on the
1614 North river, who the same year, (1614) built a fort on the west side near Albany. From this time we may date the settlement of New-York, the history of which will be annexed to a description of the State.

Conception Bay, on the Island of Newfoundland, was settled in the year 1610, by about forty planters under governor John Guy, to whom king James had given a patent of incorporation.

Champlain, a Frenchman, had begun a settlement at Quebec 1608. St. Croix, Mount Mansel, and Port Royal were settled about the same time. These settlements remained undisturbed till 1613, when the Virginians, hearing that the French had settled within their limits, sent Capt. Argal to dislodge them. For this purpose he sailed to Sagadahok, took their forts at Mount Mansel, St. Croix and Port Royal, with their vessels, ordnance, cattle and provisions, and carried them to James-Town in Virginia. Quebec was left in possession of the French.

1614.] This year Capt. John Smith with two ships and forty-five men and boys, made a voyage to North Virginia, to make experiments upon a gold and copper mine. His orders were, to fish and trade with the natives if he should fail in his expectations with regard to the mine. To facilitate this business, he took with him *Tantum* an Indian, perhaps one that Capt. Weymouth carried to England in 1605. In April he reached the Island Monahigan in latitude 43° 30′. Here Capt. Smith was directed to stay and keep possession with ten men for the purpose of making a trial of the whaling business, but being disappointed in this, he built seven boats, in which thirty-seven men made a very successful fishing voyage. In the mean time the Capt. himself with eight men only, in a small boat, coasted from Penobscot to Sagadahok, Acocisco, Passataquack, Tragabizanda, now called Cape Ann, thence to Acomak where he skirmished with some Indians; thence to Cape Cod where he set his Indian Tantum ashore and left him, and returned to Monahigan. In this voyage he found two French ships in the Bay of Massachusetts, who had come there six weeks before, and during that time, had been trading very advantageously with the Indians. It was conjectured that there were, at this time, three thousand Indians upon the Massachusetts Islands.

In July, Capt. Smith embarked for England in one of the vessels, leaving the other under the command of Capt. Thomas Hunt to equip for a voyage to Spain. After Capt. Smith's departure, Hunt perfidiously allured twenty Indians (one of whom was *Squanto*, afterwards so serviceable to
the

Discovery and Settlement of North America. 29

the English) to come on board his ship at Patuxit, and seven more at Naufit, and carried them to the Island of Malaga, where he sold them for twenty pounds each, to be slaves for life. This conduct, which fixes an indelible stigma upon the character of Hunt, excited in the breasts of the Indians such an inveterate hatred of the English, as that, for many years after, all commercial intercourse with them was rendered exceedingly dangerous.

Capt. Smith arrived at London the last of August, where he drew a map of the country, and called it New-England. From this time North Virginia assumed the name of *New-England*, and the name *Virginia* was confined to the southern colony.

Between the years 1614 and 1620, several attempts were made by the Plymouth company to settle New-England, but by various means they were all rendered ineffectual. During this time, however, an advantageous trade was carried on with the natives.

1617.] In the year 1617, Mr. Robinson and his congregation, influenced by several weighty reasons, meditated a removal to America. Various difficulties intervened to prevent the success of their designs
1620 until the year 1620, when a part of Mr. Robinson's congregation came over and settled at Plymouth. At this time commenced the settlement of New-England.

The particulars relating to the first emigrations to this northern part of America; the progress of its settlement, &c. will be given in the history of New-England, to which the reader is referred.

In order to preserve the chronological order in which the several colonies, now grown into independent states, were first settled, it will be
1621 necessary that I should just mention, that the next year after the settlement of Plymouth, captain John Mason obtained of the Plymouth council a grant of a part of the present state of New-Hamp-
1623 shire. Two years after, under the authority of this grant, a small colony fixed down near the mouth of Piscataqua river. From this period we may date the settlement of New-Hampshire.

1627.] In 1627, a colony of Swedes and Fins came over and landed at Cape Henlopen; and afterwards purchased of the Indians the land from Cape Henlopen to the Falls of Delaware on both sides the river, which they called *New Swedeland Stream*. On this river they built several forts, and made settlements.

1628.] On the 19th of March 1628, the council for New-England sold to Sir Henry Roswell, and five others, a large tract of land, lying round Massachusetts Bay. The June following, Capt. John Endicot, with his wife and company, came over and settled at Naumkeag, now called Salem. This was the first English settlement which was made in Massachusetts Bay. Plymouth indeed which is now included in the Commonwealth of Massachusetts, was settled eight years before, but at this time it was a separate colony, under a distinct government, and continued so until the second charter of Massachusetts was granted by William and Mary in 1691; by which Plymouth, the Province of Main and Sagadahok were annexed to Massachusetts.

June 13, 1633.] In the reign of Charles the first, Lord Baltimore, a Roman Catholic, applied for and obtained a grant of a tract of land

upon

upon Chefapeek Bay, about one hundred and forty miles long and one hundred and thirty broad. Soon after this, in confequence of the rigor of the laws of England againft the Roman Catholics, Lord Baltimore, with a number of his perfecuted brethren, came over and fettled it, and in honor of queen Henrietta Maria, they called it MARYLAND.

The firft grant of Connecticut was made by Robert, Earl of Warwick, prefident of the council of Plymouth, to Lord Say and Seal, to
1631 Lord Brook and others, in the year 1631. In confequence of feveral fmaller grants made afterwards by the patentees to particular perfons, Mr. Fenwick made a fettlement at the mouth of Con-
1635 necticut river, and called it *Saybrook*. Four years after a number of people from Maffachufetts Bay came and began fettlements at Hartford, Wethersfield and Windfor on Connecticut river. Thus commenced the Englifh fettlement of CONNECTICUT.

Rhode Ifland was firft fettled in confequence of religious perfecution. Mr. Roger Williams, who was among thofe who early came over to Maffachufetts, not agreeing with fome of his brethren in fentiment, was very unjuftifiably banifhed the colony, and went with twelve others,
1635 his adherents, and fettled at Providence in 1635. From this beginning arofe the colony, now ftate of RHODE-ISLAND.

1664.] On the 20th of March, 1664, Charles the fecond granted to the Duke of York, what is now called NEW-JERSEY, then a part of a large tract of country by the name of New-Netherland. Some parts of New-Jerfey were fettled by the Dutch as early as about 1615.

1662.] In the year 1662, Charles the fecond granted to Edward, Earl of Clarendon and feven others, almoft the whole territory of the three Southern States, North and South Carolinas and Georgia. Two years
1664 after he granted a fecond charter enlarging their boundaries. The proprietors, by virtue of authority, vefted in them by their charter, engaged Mr. Locke to frame a fyftem of laws for the government of their intended colony. Notwithftanding thefe preparations, no
1669 effectual fettlement was made untill the year 1669, (though one was attempted in 1667) when Governor Sayle came over with a colony and fixed on a neck of land between Afhley and Cooper Rivers. Thus commenced the fetttlement of CAROLINA, which then included the whole territory between the 29th and 36th 30′ degrees north latitude, together with the Bahama Iflands, lying betweem latitude 22° and 27° north.

1681.] The Royal charter for Pennfylvania was granted to William Penn on the 4th March 1681. The firft colony came over the
1682 next year and fettled under the proprietor, William Penn, who acted as Governor from October 1682, to Auguft 1684. The firft affembly in the province of Pennfylvania was held at Chefter, on the 4th of December 1682. Thus William Penn, a Quaker, juftly celebrated as a great and good man, has the honor of laying the foundation of the prefent populous and very flourifhing STATE of PENNSYLVANIA.

The proprietory government in Carolina, was attended with fo many inconveniencies, and occafioned fuch violent diffentions among the fettlers, that the Parliament of Great-Britain was induced to take the province under their immediate care. The proprietors (except Lord Granville) accepted

accepted of £.22,500 sterling, from the crown for the property and jurisdiction. This agreement was ratified by act of Parliament in 1729. A clause in this act reserved to Lord Granville his eighth share of the property and arrears of quit-rents, which continued legally vested in his family 'till the revolution in 1776. Lord Granville's share, made a part of the present state of North-Carolina. About the year 1729, the extensive territory belonging to the proprietors, was divided into North and South Carolinas. They remained separate royal governments untill they became independent States.

1729

For the relief of poor indigent people of Great-Britain and Ireland, and for the security of Carolina, a project was formed for planting a colony between the rivers Savannah and Alatamaha. Accordingly application being made to King George the second, he issued letters patent, bearing date June 9th, 1732, for legally carrying into execution the benevolent plan. In honor of the king, who greatly encouraged the plan, they called the new province GEORGIA. Twenty-one trustees were appointed to conduct the affairs relating to the settlement of the province. The November following one hundred and fifteen persons, one of whom was General Oglethorpe, embarked for Georgia, where they arrived, and landed at Yamacraw. In exploring the country, they found an elevated pleasant spot of ground on the bank of a navigable river, upon which they marked out a town, and from the Indian name of the river which passed by it, called it Savannah. From this period we may date the settlement of GEORGIA.

1732

1654.] Kentucky was first discovered by James Macbride, and some others who were in company with him, in the year 1754. Col. Daniel Boon explored it in 1769.

1769

1773.] Four years after Col. Boon and his family, with five other families who were joined by forty men from Powle's valley, began the settlement of KENTUCKY, which is now one of the most growing colonies, perhaps, in the world, and will doubtless be erected into an independent state, as soon as the new government shall have been properly organized.

The tract of country called VERMONT, before the late war, was claimed both by New-York and New-Hampshire. When hostilities commenced between Great-Britain and her Colonies, the inhabitants considering themselves as in a state of nature, and not within any legal jurisdiction, associated and formed for themselves a constitution of civil government. Under this constitution, they have ever since continued to exercise all the powers of an independent State. Although Vermont has not been admitted into union with the other states, nor her jurisdiction acknowledged to be legal by the state of New-York, yet we may venture to date her political existence as a separate government, from the year 1777, because, since that time, Vermont has to all intents and purposes been a sovereign and independent State.

1777

The extensive tract of country lying northwest of the Ohio River within the limits of the United States, was erected into a separate *temporary* government by an Ordinance of Congress passed the 13th of July, 1787.

1787

Thus I have given a summary view of the first discoveries and progressive

32   DISCOVERY *and* SETTLEMENT *of* NORTH AMERICA.

five settlement of North America in their cronological order.—The following recapitulation will comprehend the whole in one view.

Names of places.	When settled.		By whom.
Quebec,		1608	By the French.
Virginia,	June 10,	1609	By Lord De la War.
New-foundland,	June,	1610	By Governor John Guy.
New-York,) New-Jersey,)	about	1614	By the Dutch.
Plymouth,		1620	By part of Mr. Robinson's congregation.
New-Hampshire,		1623	By a small English colony near the mouth of Piscataqua river.
Delaware,) Pennsylvania,)		1627	By the Swedes and Fins.
Massachusetts Bay,		1628	By Capt. John Endicot and company.
Maryland,		1633	By Lord Baltimore, with a colony of Roman Catholics.
Connecticut,		1635	By Mr. Fenwick, at Saybrook, near the mouth of Connecticut river.
Rhode-Island,		1635	By Mr. Roger Williams and his persecuted brethren.
New-Jersey,		1664	Granted to the Duke of York by Charles II. and made a distinct government, and settled some time before this by the English.
South-Carolina,		1669	By Governor Sayle.
Pennsylvania,		1682	By William Penn, with a colony of Quakers.
North-Carolina,	about	1728	Erected into a separate government, settled before by the English.
Georgia,		1732	By General Oglethorpe.
Kentucky,		1773	By Col. Daniel Boon.
Vermont,		1777	By emigrants from Connecticut and other parts of New-England.
Territory N. W. of Ohio river,		1787	By the Ohio and other companies.

The above dates are from the periods, when the first permanent settlements were made.

NORTH-AMERICA comprehends all that part of the western continent which lies north of the Isthmus of Darien. This vast extent of country, is divided between Spain, Great-Britain, and the Thirteen United States. Spain claims all the land west of the Mississippi, and east and west Florida. According to the treaty of 1783, all the country north of the northern boundary of the United States, and east of the river St. Croix, belongs to Great-Britain. The remaining part is the territory of the *Thirteen United and Independent States.*

DIVI-

{ 33 }

DIVISIONS OF NORTH AMERICA.

Names of States and Colonies.	length	breadth	lat. capt. towns.	lon. from Philadel.	chief towns.	distance and bearing from Philadelphia.	belonging to	No. of census inhabts.	t'k'n.
New-Hampshire,	80	60	43,5	3,54 E.	Portsmouth.	408 miles N. E.	} Thirteen United States, lying along the sea coast from north east to south west. Total 3,083,522	102,000*	1787
Massachusetts,	450	154	42,25	3,39 E.	Boston.	343 N. E.		360,000*	1787
Rhode-Island,	68	40	41,30	3,24 E.	Newport.	280 N. E.		51,896	1783
Connecticut,	81	57	41,19	1,56 E.	New-Haven.	181 N. E.		209,150	1782
New-York,	350	300	40,40	1,5 E.	New-York.	95 N. E.		238,897	1786
New-Jersey,	160	52	40,15	0,23 E.	Trenton.	30 N. E.		149,435	1784
Pennsylvania,	288	156	39,56	00,00	Philadelphia.			360,000*	1787
Delaware,	92	16	39,10	00,25 W.	Dover.	2 S.		37,000*	1787
Maryland,	134	110	39,2	1,37 W.	Annapolis.	32 S. S. W.		253,630	1782
Virginia,	758	224	37,40	3,42 W.	Richmond.	276 S. S. W.		567,614	1782
North-Carolina,	758	110	36,04	1,52 W.	Edenton.	442 S. S. W.		270,000	1787
South-Carolina,	200	125	32,35	5,00 W.	Charleston.	814 S. S. W.		180,000*	1787
Georgia.	600	250	33,39	7,00 W.	Augusta.	934 S. W.		98,000*	1787
Vermont,	155	60	42,42	1,44 E.	Bennington.	299 N. E.	} Seperate gov'ts. in the Unit. States.	100,000*	1785
Western-territory,	1000	450	39,34	6,30 W.	Adelphi.	492 W.		6,000	1788
Kentucky.	includedinVirg.		38,25	10,00 W.	Lexington.	947 by water. W.		100,000*	1788
Province of Quebec	750	200	46,55	4,56 E.	Quebec.	690 N. N. E.	GreatBritain.	unknown	
Nova-Scotia,	300	250	44,56	14,29 E.	Halifax.	925 N. N. E.	do.	unknown	
E. and W. Floridas.	300	130	29,51	6,30 W.	Augustine.	1146 S. S. W.	Spain.	unknown	
Louisiana,	indefinite.		29,57	14,40 W.	New Orleans.	1646 S. W.	do.	unknown	
New-Mexico,	indefinite.		36,45	3,32 W.	St. Fee.	2190 W.	do.	unknown	
California,	765	212	26,5	39 W.	St. Juan.	3396 W. S. W.	do.	unknown	
Old-Mexico.	2700	250	20.0	26 W.	Mexico.	3021 S. W.	do.	unknown	

N. B. In the column containing the number of inhabitants, the numbers marked (*) are as reckoned in the Convention at Philadelphia in 1787, excepting North-Carolina, Vermont, Western-Territory, and Kentucky; the others are taken from actual enumeration.

The distances of the several capitals from Philadelphia, are reckoned as the roads run.

E   *The*

The UNITED STATES.

SITUATION and EXTENT.

Length 1250 miles } Between { 31° and 46° North Latitude.
Breadth 1040 } { 8° E. and 24° W. Long. from Philadelphia.

Boundaries.] IN the treaty of peace, concluded in 1783, the limits of the United States are thus defined. "And that all disputes which might arise in future on the subject of the boundaries of the said United States may be prevented, it is hereby agreed and declared, that the following are and shall be their boundaries, viz. From the north west angle of Nova-Scotia, viz. That angle which is formed by a line drawn due north from the source of St. Croix River to the Highlands, along the said Highlands, which divide those rivers that empty themselves into the river St. Lawrence, from those which fall into the Atlantic Ocean, to the north-westernmost head of Connecticut river; thence down along the middle of that river to the forty-fifth degree of north latitude; from thence by a line due west on said latitude, until it strikes the river Iroquois or Cataraquy; thence along the middle of the said river into Lake Ontario, through the middle of said Lake, until it strikes the communication by water between that lake and Lake Erie; thence along the middle of said communication into Lake Erie, through the middle of said lake, until it arrives at the water communication between that lake and Lake Huron; thence through the middle of said lake to the water communication between that lake and Lake Superior; thence through Lake Superior northward of the Isles Royal and Phillipeaux to the Long Lake; thence through the middle of said Long Lake, and the water communication between it and the Lake of the Woods to the said Lake of the Woods; thence through the said lake to the most northwestern point thereof, and from thence, on a due west course, to the River Mississippi; thence by a line to be drawn along the middle of said River Mississippi, until it shall intersect the northernmost part of the thirty-first degree of north latitude. South, by a line to be drawn due east from the determination of the line last mentioned, in the latitude of thirty-one degrees north of the equator, to the middle of the River Apalachichola, or Catahouche; thence along the middle thereof to its junction with the Flint River; thence strait to the head of St. Mary's River; and thence down along the middle of St. Mary's River to the Atlantic Ocean; east, by a line to be drawn along the middle of the River St. Croix, from its mouth in the Bay of Fundy to its source, and from its source directly north, to the aforesaid Highlands, which divide the rivers that fall into the Atlantic Ocean, from those which fall into the River St. Lawrence, comprehending all islands within twenty leagues of any part of the shores of the United States, and lying between lines to be drawn due east from the points where the aforesaid boundaries between Nova-Scotia on the one part, and East-Florida on the other, shall respectively touch the Bay of Fundy and the Atlantic Ocean, excepting such islands as now are, or heretofore have been, within the limits of the said province of Nova-Scotia."

The

The UNITED STATES. 35

The following calculations were made from actual measurement of the best maps, by THOMAS HUTCHINS, *Esquire, geographer to the United States.*

The territory of the United States contains by computation a million of square miles, in which are 640,000,000 of acres.
Deduct for water 51,000,000

Acres of land in the United States, 589,000,000

That part of the United States comprehended between the west temporary line of Pennsylvania on the east, the boundary line between Britain and the United States extending from the river St. Croix to the north-west extremity of the Lake of the Woods on the north, the river Mississippi to the mouth of the Ohio on the west, and the river Ohio on the south to the aforementioned bounds of Pennsylvania, contains by computation about four hundred and eleven thousand square miles, in which are
263,040,000 acres.
Deduct for water 43,040,000

To be disposed of by order of Congress. 220,000,000 of acres.

The whole of this immense extent of unappropriated western territory, containing, as above stated, 220,000,000 of acres, has been, by the cession of some of the original thirteen states, and by the treaty of peace, transferred to the federal government, and is pledged as a fund for sinking the continental debt. It is in contemplation to divide it into new states, with republican constitutions similar to the old states near the Atlantic ocean.

Estimate of the number of acres of water, north and westward of the river Ohio, within the territory of the United States.

	Acres.
In lake Superior,	21,952,780
Lake of the Woods,	1,133,800
Lake Rain, &c.	165,200
Red lake,	551,000
Lake Michigan,	10,368,000
Bay Puan,	1,216,000
Lake Huron,	5,009,920
Lake St. Clair,	89,500
Lake Erie, western part,	2,252,800
Sundry small lakes and rivers,	301,000
	43,040,000

Estimate of the number of acres of water within the thirteen United States.

In lake Erie, westward of the line extended from the north-west corner of Pennsylvania, due north to the boundary between the British territory and the United States, - 410,000

The UNITED STATES.

Brought forward,		43,040,000
Brought forward,	410,000	
In lake Ontario,	2,390,000	
Lake Champlain,	500,000	
Chesapeek bay,	1,700,000	
Albemarle bay,	330,000	
Delaware bay,	630,000	
All the rivers within the thirteen states including the Ohio,	2,000,000	
		7,960,000
Total,		51,000,000

Lakes and Rivers.] It may in truth be said, that no part of the world is so well watered with springs, rivulets, rivers, and lakes, as the territory of the United States. By means of these various streams and collections of water, the whole country is checkered into islands and peninsulas. The United States, and indeed all parts of North America, seem to have been formed by nature for the most intimate union. The facilities of navigation, render the communication between the ports of Georgia and New-Hampshire, infinitely more expeditious and practicable, than between those of Provence and Picardy in France; Cornwall and Caithness, in Great-Britain; or Gallicia and Catalonia, in Spain. The canals proposed at South-Key, Susquehannah, and Delaware, will open a communication from the Carolinas to the western counties of Pennsylvania and New-York. The improvements of the Patomak, will give a passage from the southern States, to the western parts of Virginia, Maryland, Pennsylvania, and even to the Lakes. From Detroit, on Lake Erie, to Alexandria, on the Patomak, six hundred and seven miles, are but two carrying places, which together do not exceed the distance of forty miles. The canals of Delaware and Chesapeek, will open the communication from South-Carolina to New-Jersey, Delaware, the most populous parts of Pennsylvania, and the midland counties of New-York. These important works might be effected, an accurate and well informed computer supposes, for two hundred thousand guineas; and North-America would thereby be converted into a clutter of large and fertile islands, communicating with each other with ease and little expence, and in many instances without the uncertainty or danger of the sea.

There is nothing in other parts of the globe, which resembles the prodigious chain of lakes in this part of the world. They may properly be termed inland seas of fresh water; and even those of the second or third class in magnitude, are of larger circuit than the greatest lake in the eastern continent. The best account of these lakes that I have seen, is in Carver's Travels in North-America. This book is my authority for the descriptions which follow.

The Lake of the Woods is so called from the large quantities of wood growing on its banks; such as oaks, pines, firs, spruce, &c. This lake lies nearly east of the south end of Lake Winnepeek, and is the source or conductor of one branch of the river Bourbon. Its length from east to west is is about feventy miles, and in fome places it is forty miles wide. The Killiftince Indians encamp on its borders to fifh and hunt. This lake is the communication between the Lakes Winnepeck and Bourbon, and Lake Superior.

Rainy or Long Lake lies eaft of the Lake of the Woods, and is nearly an hundred miles long, and in no part more than twenty miles wide.

Eaftward of this lake, lie feveral fmall ones which extend in a ftring to the great carrying place, and thence into Lake Superior. Between thefe little lakes are feveral carrying places, which render the trade to the north weft difficult, and exceedingly tedious, as it takes two years to make one voyage from Michillimackinac to thefe parts.

Lake Superior, formerly termed the Upper Lake from its northern fituation, is fo called from its magnitude, it being the largeft on the continent. It may juftly be termed the Cafpian of America, and is fuppofed to be the largeft body of frefh water on the globe. According to the French charts it is fifteen hundred miles in circumference; Carver fuppofes that if the utmoft extent of every bay was taken, it would exceed fixteen hundred. A great part of the coaft is bounded by rocks and uneven ground. The water is pure and tranfparent, and appears generally, throughout the lake, to lie upon a bed of huge rocks. It is worthy of remark, in regard to the waters of this lake, that although their furface, during the heat of fummer, is impregnated with no fmall degree of warmth, yet on letting down a cup to the depth of about a fathom, the water drawn from thence is fo exceffively cold, that, when taken into the mouth, it has the fame effect as ice.

The fituation of this lake from the moft accurate obfervations which have yet been made, lies between forty-fix and fifty degrees of north latitude, and between nine and eighteen degrees of weft longitude from the meridian of Philadelphia.

There are many iflands in this lake, two of them have each land enough, if proper for cultivation, to form a confiderable province; efpecially Ifle Royal, which is not lefs than an hundred miles long, and in many places, forty broad. The natives fuppofe thefe iflands are the refidence of the Great Spirit.

Two very large rivers empty themfelves into this lake, on the north and northeaft fide; one is called the Nipegon, which leads to a tribe of the Chipeways, who inhabit a lake of the fame name, and the other is the Michipicooton river, the fource of which is towards James' Bay, from whence there is but a fhort portage to another river, which empties itfelf into that bay.

Not far from the Nipegon is a fmall river, that, juft before it enters the lake, has a perpendicular fall from the top of a mountain, of more than fix hundred feet. It is very narrow, and appears at a diftance like a white garter fufpended in the air. There are upwards of thirty other rivers, which empty into this lake, fome of which are of a confiderable fize. On the fouth fide of it is a remarkable point or cape of about fixty miles in length, called point Chegomegan. About an hundred miles weft of this cape, a confiderable river falls into the lake, the head of which is compofed of a great affemblage of fmall ftreams. This river is remarkable for the abundance of virgin copper that is found on and near its banks.

Many

Many small islands, particularly on the eastern shores, abound with copper ore lying in beds, with the appearance of copperas. This metal might be easily made a very advantageous article of commerce, as it costs nothing on the spot, and requires but little expence to get it on board boats or canoes, in which it might be conveyed through the falls of St. Marie to the Isle of St. Joseph, which lies at the bottom of the straits near the entrance into Lake Huron, thence into Lake Ontario, from which it may be conveyed by water into the Mohawks river, except two portages, one of twenty yards and the other of about a mile ; down Mohawks river in the Hudson, except the portage at the Cohoes ; thence to New-York. The cheapness and ease with which any quantity of the ore may be procured, will make up for the distance and expence of transportation. This lake abounds with fish, particularly trout and sturgeon; the former weigh from twelve to fifty pounds, and are caught almost any season of the year in great plenty. Storms affect this lake as much as they do the Atlantic Ocean; the waves run as high, and the navigation is equally dangerous. It discharges its waters from the south east corner through the Straits of St. Marie, which are about forty miles long. Near the upper end of these Straits is a rapid, which, though it is impossible for canoes to ascend, yet, when conducted by careful pilots, may be descended without danger.

Though Lake Superior is supplied by near forty rivers, many of which are large, yet it does not appear that one tenth part of the waters which are conveyed into it by these rivers, is discharged by the abovementioned strait. How such a superabundance of water can be disposed of, remains a secret. They doubtless have a passage through some subterraneous cavities, deep, unfathomable, and never to be explored. The entrance into this lake from the straits of St. Marie, affords one of the most pleasing prospects in the world. On the left may be seen many beautiful little islands that extend a considerable way before you ; and on the right, an agreeable succession of small points of land, that project a little way into the water, and contribute, with the islands, to render this delightful bason calm, and secure from those tempestuous winds, by which the adjoining lake is frequently troubled.

Lake Huron, into which you enter through the straits of St. Marie, is next in magnitude to lake Superior. It lies between forty-two and forty-six degrees of north latitude, and between four and ten degrees west longitude. Its shape is nearly triangular, and its circumference about one thousand miles. On the north side of this lake is an island one hundred miles in length, and no more than eight miles broad. It is called Manataulin, signifying a place of spirits, and is considered as sacred by the Indians. About the middle of the southwest side of this lake is Saganaum Bay, about eighty miles in length, and about eighteen or twenty miles broad. Thunder Bay, so called from the continual thunder that is heard here, lies about half way between Saganaum Bay and the northwest corner of the lake. It is about nine miles across either way. The fish are the same as in lake Superior. The promontory that separates this lake from Lake Michigan, is a vast plain, more than one hundred miles long, and varying from ten to fifteen miles in breadth. This plain is about equally divided between the Ottowaw and Chipeway Indians. At the northeast corner, this lake communicates with Lake Michigan, by the Straits of Michillimackinac. It is remarkable, that although

The UNITED STATES.

though there is no diurnal flood or ebb to be perceived in the waters of these ſtraits, yet from an exact attention to their ſtate, a periodical alteration in them has been diſcovered. It has been obſerved that they riſe by gradual, but almoſt imperceptible degrees, till in ſeven years and an half they had reached the height of about three feet ; and in the ſame ſpace of time, they gradually fell to their former ſtate, ſo that in fifteen years they had completed this inexplicable revolution.

The Chipeway Indians live ſcattered around this lake ; particularly near Saganaum Bay. On its banks are found amazing quantities of ſand cherries.

Lake St. Claire lies about half way between Lake Huron and Lake Erie, and is about ninety miles in circumference. It receives the waters of the three great lakes, Superior, Michigan and Huron, and diſcharges them through the river or ſtrait, called Detroit, (which is in French the Strait) into Lake Erie. This lake is of a circular form, and navigable for large veſſels, except a bar of ſand towards the middle, which prevents loaded veſſels from paſſing. The cargoes of ſuch as are freighted, muſt be taken out and carried acroſs the bar in boats, and re-ſhipped. The town of Detroit is ſituated on the weſtern bank of the river of the ſame name, about nine miles below Lake St. Claire.

Lake Erie is ſituated between forty-one and forty-three degrees of north latitude, and between three and eight degrees weſt longitude. It is nearly three hundred miles long, from eaſt to weſt, and about forty in its broadeſt part. A point of land projects from the north ſide into this lake, ſeveral miles, towards the ſoutheaſt. The iſlands and banks towards the weſt end of the lake are ſo infeſted with rattle-ſnakes, as to render it dangerous to land on them. The lake is covered near the banks of the iſlands with the large pond lily ; the leaves of which lie on the ſurface of the water ſo thick, as to cover it entirely for many acres together ; on theſe, in the ſummer ſeaſon, lie myriads of water-ſnakes baſking in the ſun. Of the venomous ſerpents which infeſt this lake, the hiſſing ſnake is the moſt remarkable. It is about eighteen inches long, ſmall and ſpeckled. When you approach it, it flattens itſelf in a moment, and its ſpots, which are of various colours, become viſibly brighter through rage ; at the ſame time it blows from its mouth, with great force, a ſubtile wind, ſaid to be of a nauſeous ſmell ; and if drawn in with the breath of the unwary traveller, will infallibly bring on a decline, that in a few months muſt prove mortal. No remedy has yet been found to counteract its baneful influence. This lake is of a more dangerous navigation than any of the others, on account of the craggy rocks which project into the water, in a perpendicular direction, many miles together, affording no ſhelter from ſtorms. This lake at its northeaſt end, communicates with Lake Ontario, by the river Niagara, which runs from ſouth to north about thirty miles. At the entrance of this river, on its eaſtern ſhore, is fort Niagara, which is at preſent, contrary to the treaty of 1783, in poſſeſſion of the Britiſh government, as are moſt of our north-weſtern poſts. About eighteen miles north of this fort, are thoſe remarkable falls which are reckoned one of the greateſt natural curioſities in the world. The waters which ſupply the river Niagara riſe near two thouſand miles to the northweſt, and paſſing through the lakes Superior, Michigan, Huron and Erie, receiv-

ing

The UNITED STATES.

ing in their courfe, conftant accumulations, at length, with aftonifhing grandeur, rufh down a ftupendous precipice of one hundred and forty feet perpendicular; and in a ftrong rapid, that extends to the diftance of eight or nine miles below, fall near as much more: the river then lofes itfelf in Lake Ontario. The noife of thefe falls, (called the *Niagara Falls*) in a clear day and fair wind, may be heard, between forty and fifty miles. When the water ftrikes the bottom, it bounds to a great height in the air, occafioning a thick cloud of vapours, on which the fun, when he fhines, paints a beautiful rainbow.

Lake Ontario is fituated between forty-three and forty-five degrees of latitude, and between one and four weft longitude. Its form is nearly oval. Its greateft length is from fouthweft to northeaft, and its circumference about fix hundred miles. It abounds with fifh of an excellent flavor, among which are the Ofwego bafs, weighing three or four pounds. Near the foutheaft part, it receives the waters of the Ofwego river, and on the northeaft it difcharges itfelf into the river Cataraqui, or as it is now more commonly called, Iroquois. This river, at Montreal, takes the name of St. Lawrence, and paffing by Quebec, empties into the Gulf of the fame name.

Lake Champlain is next in fize to Lake Ontario, and lies nearly eaft from it, dividing the State of New-York from that of Vermont. It is about eighty miles in length from north to fouth, and in its broadeft part, fourteen. It is well ftored with fifh, and the land on its borders, and on the banks of its rivers, are good. Crown Point and Ticonderoga, are fituated on the bank of this lake, near the fouthern part of it.

Lake George lies fouth weft of Lake Champlain, and is about thirty-five miles long from north eaft to fouth weft, but narrow.—The adjacent country is mountainous; the vallies are tolerably good.

The Miffiffippi is the great refervoir of the waters of the Ohio and Illinois, and their numerous branches from the eaft; and of the Miffouri and other rivers from the weft. Thefe mighty ftreams united, are borne down with increafing majefty, through vaft forefts and meadows, and difcharged into the Gulf of Mexico. For an ingenious, beautiful and authentic defcription of this river, take the following, given by Mr. Hutchins, geographer to the United States. The great length and uncommon depth of this river, and the exceffive muddinefs and falubrious quality of its waters, after its junction with the Miffouri, are very fingular.* The direction of the channel is fo crooked, that from New Orleans to the mouth of the Ohio, a diftance which does not exceed four hundred and fixty miles in a ftrait line, is about eight hundred and fifty-fix by water. It may be fhortened at leaft two hundred and fifty miles, by cutting acrofs eight or ten necks of land, fome of which are not thirty yards wide. Charlevoix relates that in the year 1722, at Point Coupee or Cut Point, the

---

* *In a half pint tumbler of this water has been found a fediment of two inches of flime. It is, notwithftanding, extremely wholefome and well tafted, and very cool in the hotteft feafons of the year; the rowers, who are there employed, drink of it when they are in the ftrongeft perfpiration, and never receive any bad effects from it. The inhabitants of New Orleans ufe no other water than that of the river, which, by being kept in jars, becomes perfectly clear.*

the river made a great turn, and some Canadians, by deepening the channel of a small brook, diverted the waters of the river into it. The impetuosity of the stream was so violent, and the soil of so rich and loose a quality, that, in a short time, the point was entirely cut through, and travellers saved fourteen leagues of their voyage. The old bed has no water in it, the times of the periodical overflowings only excepted. The new channel has been since sounded with a line of thirty fathoms, without finding bottom.

In the spring floods the Mississippi is very high, and the current so strong that with difficulty it can be ascended; but that disadvantage is compensated by eddies or counter-currents, which always run in the bends close to the banks of the river, with nearly equal velocity against the stream, and assist the ascending boats. The current at this season descends at the rate of about five miles an hour. In autumn, when the waters are low, it does not run faster than two miles, but it is rapid in such parts of the river, as have clusters of islands, shoals and sand-banks. The circumference of many of these shoals being several miles, the voyage is longer and in some parts more dangerous than in the spring. The merchandize necessary for the commerce of the upper settlements on or near the Mississippi, is conveyed in the spring and autumn in batteaux, rowed by eighteen or twenty men, and carrying about forty tons. From New Orleans to the Illinois, the voyage is commonly performed in eight or ten weeks. A prodigious number of islands, some of which are of great extent, intersperse that mighty river. Its depth increases as you ascend it. Its waters, after overflowing its banks below the river Ibberville, never return within them again. These singularities distinguish it from every other known river in the world. Below New Orleans, the land begins to be very low on both sides of the river across the country, and gradually declines as it approaches nearer to the sea. This point of land, which in the treaty of peace in 1762, was mistaken for an island, is to all appearance of no long date; for in digging ever so little below the surface, you find water and great quantities of trees. The many beeches and breakers, as well as inlets, which arose out of the channel within the last half century, at the several mouths of the river, are convincing proofs that this peninsula was wholly formed in the same manner. And it is certain that when La Salle sailed down the Mississippi to the sea, the opening of that river was very different from what it is at present.

The nearer you approach to the sea, this truth becomes more striking. The bars that cross most of these small channels, opened by the current, have been multiplied by means of the trees carried down with the streams; one of which stopped by its roots or branches in a shallow part, is sufficient to obstruct the passage of thousands more, and to fix them at the same place. Such collections of trees are daily seen between the Balize and the Missouri, which singly would supply the largest city in America with fuel for several years. No human force being sufficient for removing them, the mud carried down by the river serves to bind and cement them together. They are gradually covered, and every inundation not only extends their length and breadth, but adds another layer to their height. In less than ten years time, canes and shrubs grow on them, and form points and islands, which forcibly shift the bed of the river.

F   Nothing

Nothing can be afferted with certainty, refpecting its length. Its fource is not known, but fuppofed to be upwards of three thoufand miles from the fea as the river runs. We only know, that from St. Anthony's falls, it glides with a pleafant clear ftream, and becomes comparatively narrow before its junction with the Miffouri, the muddy waters of which immediately difcolor the lower part of the river to the fea. Its rapidity, breadth, and other peculiarities then begin to give it the majeftic appearance of the Miffouri, which affords a more extenfive navigation, and is a longer, broader and deeper river than the Miffiffippi. It is in fact, the principal river, contributing more to the common ftream than does the Miffiffippi, even after its junction with the Illinois. It has been afcended by French traders about twelve or thirteen hundred miles, and from the depth of water, and breadth of the river at that diftance, it appeared to be navigable many miles further.

From the Miffouri river, to nearly oppofite the Ohio, the weftern bank of the Miffiffippi is (fome few places excepted) higher than the eaftern. From Mine au fer, to the Ibberville, the eaftern bank is higher than the weftern, on which there is not a fingle difcernible rifing or eminence, the diftance of feven hundred and fifty miles. From the Ibberville to the fea, there are no eminences on either fide, though the eaftern bank appears rather the higheft of the two, as far as the Englifh turn. Thence the banks gradually diminifh in height to the mouths of the river, where they are not more than two or three feet higher than the common furface of the water.

The flime which the annual floods of the river Miffiffippi leaves on the furface of the adjacent fhores, may be compared with that of the Nile, which depofits a fimilar manure, and for many centuries paft has infured the fertility of Egypt. When its banks fhall have been cultivated as the excellency of its foil and temperature of the climate deferve, its population will equal that of any other part of the world. The trade, wealth and power of America, will, at fome future period, depend, and perhaps centre upon the Miffiffippi. This alfo refembles the Nile in the number of its mouths, all iffuing into a fea that may be compared to the Mediterranean, which is bounded on the north and fouth by the two continents of Europe and Africa, as the Mexican bay is by North and South America. The fmaller mouths of this river might be eafily ftopped up, by means of thofe floating trees with which the river, during the floods, is always covered. The whole force of the channel being united, the only opening then left would probably grow deep as well as the bar.

Mr. Carver has travelled higher up this river, and appears to be better acquainted with its northern parts and fource, than any European or American, who has publifhed his obfervations. He is my authority for what follows.

The falls of St. Anthony, in about latitude 44° 30', received their name from Father Lewis Hennipin, a French miffionary, who travelled into thefe parts about the year one thoufand fix hundred and eighty, and was the firft European ever feen by the natives. The whole river, which is more than two hundred and fifty yards wide, falls perpendicularly about thirty feet, and forms a moft pleafing cataract. The rapids below, in the fpace of three hundred yards, render the defcent confiderably greater; fo
that

that when viewed at a diftance, they appear to be much higher than they really are. In the middle of the falls is a fmall ifland, about forty feet broad, and fomewhat longer, on which grow a few cragged hemlock and fpruce trees; and about half way between this ifland and the eaftern fhore, is a rock, lying at the very edge of the fall, in an oblique pofition, five or fix feet broad, and thirty or forty long. Thefe falls are peculiarly fituated, as they are approachable without the leaft obftruction from any intervening hill or precipece, which cannot be faid of any other confiderable fall, that I know of in the world. The country around is exceedingly beautiful. It is not an uninterrupted plain where the eye finds no relief, but compofed of many gentle afcents, which in the fpring and fummer, are covered with verdure, and interfperfed with little groves, that give a pleafing variety to the profpect.

A little diftance below the falls, is a fmall ifland of about an acre and an half, on which grow a great number of oak trees, almoft all the branches of which, able to bear the weight, are, in the proper feafon of the year, loaded with eagles nefts. Their inftinctive wifdom has taught them to choofe this place, as it is fecure, on account of the rapids above, from the attacks either of man or beaft.

The Miffiffippi has never been explored higher up than the river St. Francis; fo that we are obliged to the Indians, for all the intelligence relative to the more northern parts.

Mr. Carver relates, that from the beft accounts he could obtain from the Indians, together with his own obfervations, he had learned that the four moft capital rivers on the continent of North America, viz. The St. Lawrence, the Miffiffippi, the river Bourbon, and the Oregon, or the river of the Weft, have their fources in the fame neighbourhood. The waters of the three former, are within thirty miles of each other; the latter is rather farther weft.

This fhews that thefe parts are the higheft lands in North America; and it is an inftance not to be paralleled in the other three quarters of the globe, that four rivers of fuch magnitude fhould take their rife together, and each, after running feparate courfes, difcharge their waters into different oceans, at the diftance of more than two thoufand miles from their fources. For in their paffage from this fpot to the bay of St. Lawrence, eaft; to the bay of Mexico, fouth; to Hudfon's Bay, north; and to the bay at the ftraits of Annian, weft; where the river Oregon is fuppofed to empty, each of them traverfes upwards of two thoufand miles.

Mr. Jefferfon, whofe extenfive and accurate information, ranks him among the firft authorities, in his notes on Virginia, has given a defcription of the river Ohio, and annexed fuch remarks on the fituation of the weftern waters as will throw great light on this part of our fubject, and may not be omitted. His obfervations, together with thofe already made, will afford the reader a comprehenfive and pretty complete view of the internal navigation of the United States.

'The Ohio is the moft beautiful river on earth. Its current gentle, waters clear, and bofom fmooth and unbroken by rocks and rapids, a fingle inftance only excepted. It is one quarter of a mile wide at Fort Pitt: five hundred yards at the mouth of the Great Kanhaway: one mile and twenty-five poles at Louifville: one quarter of a mile on the rapids, three

or

44   The UNITED STATES.

or four miles below Louisville: half a mile where the low country begins, which is twenty miles above Green river: one mile and a quarter at the receipt of the Tanissee: and a mile wide at the mouth.
Its length, as measured according to its meanders by Capt. Hutchins, is as follows:

From Fort Pitt	Miles.		Miles.
To Log'sTown	18 1/2	To Little Miami	126 1/4
Big Beaver Creek	10 3/4	Licking Creek	8
Little Beaver Creek	13 1/2	Great Miami	26 3/4
Yellow Creek	11 3/4	Big Bones	32 1/4
Two Creeks	21 1/4	Kentucky	44 1/4
Long Reach	53 3/4	Rapids	77 1/2
End Long Reach	16 1/2	Low Country	155 1/4
Muskingum	25 1/2	Buffalo River	64 1/2
Little Kanhaway	12 1/4	Wabash	97 1/4
Hockhocking	16	Big Cave	42 3/4
Great Kanhaway	82 1/2	Shawanee River	52 1/2
Guiandot	43 3/4	Cherokee River	13
Sandy Creek	14 1/2	Massac	11
Sioto	48 3/4	Mississippi	46
			1188

In common winter and spring tides it affords fifteen feet water to Louisville, ten feet to La Tarte's rapids, forty miles above the mouth of the great Kanhaway, and a sufficiency at all times for light batteaux and canoes to Fort Pitt. The rapids are in latitude 38° 8′. The inundations of this river begin about the last of March, and subside in July. During these a first rate man of war may be carried from Louisville to New Orleans, if the sudden turns of the river and the strength of its current will admit a safe steerage. The rapids at Louisville descend about thirty feet in a length of a mile and a half. The bed of the river there is a solid rock, and is divided by an island into two branches, the southern of which is about two hundred yards wide, and is dry four months in the year. The bed of the northern branch is worn into channels by the constant course of the water, and attrition of the pebble stones carried on with that, so as to be passable for batteaux through the greater part of the year. Yet it is thought that the southern arm may be the most easily opened for constant navigation. The rise of the waters in these rapids does not exceed ten or twelve feet. A part of this island is so high as to have been never overflowed, and to command the settlement at Louisville, which is opposite to it. The fort, however, is situated at the head of the falls. The ground on the south side rises very gradually.

At Fort Pitt the river Ohio loses its name, branching into the Monongahela and Allegany.

The Monongahela is four hundred yards wide at its mouth. From thence is twelve or fifteen miles to the mouth of Yohogany, where it is three hundred yards wide. Thence to Redstone by water is fifty miles, by land thirty. Then to the mouth of Cheat river by water forty miles, by land twenty-eight, the width continuing at three hundred yards, and
the

the navigation good for boats. Thence the width is about two hundred yards to the weftern fork, fifty miles higher, and the navigation frequently interrupted by rapids; which however with a fwell of two or three feet become very paffable for boats. It then admits light boats, except in dry feafons, fixty-five miles further to the head of Tygarts valley, prefenting only fome fmall rapids and falls of one or two feet perpendicular and leffening in its width to twenty yards. The Weftern fork is navigable in the winter ten or fifteen miles towards the northern of the Little Kanhaway, and will admit a good waggon road to it. The Yohogany is the principal branch of this river. It paffes through the Laurel mountain, about thirty miles from its mouth; is fo far from three hundred to one hundred and fifty yards wide, and the navigation much obftructed in dry weather by rapids and fhoals. In its paffage through the mountain it makes very great falls, admitting no navigation for ten miles to the Turkey foot. Thence to the great croffing, about twenty miles, it is again navigable, except in dry feafons, and at this place is two hundred yards wide. The fources of this river are divided from thofe of the Patomak by the Allegany mountain. From the falls, where it interfects the Laurel mountain, to Fort Cumberland, the head of the navigation on the Patomak, is forty miles of very mountainous road. Wills's creek, at the mouth of which was Fort Cumberland, is thirty or forty yards wide, but affords no navigation as yet. Cheat river, another confiderable branch of the Monongahela, is two hundred yards wide at its mouth, and one hundred yards at the Dunkard's fettlement, fifty miles higher. It is navigable for boats, except in dry feafons. The boundary between Virginia and Pennfylvania croffes it about three or four miles above its mouth.

The Allegany river, with a flight fwell, affords navigation for light batteaux to Venango, at the mouth of French creek, where it is two hundred yards wide; and it is practifed even to Le Bœuf, from whence there is a portage of fifteen miles to Prefque Ifle on Lake Erie.

The country watered by the Miffiffippi and its eaftern branches, conftitutes five-eighths of the United States; two of which five-eighths are occupied by the Ohio and its waters: the refiduary ftreams which run into the Gulf of Mexico, the Atlantic, and the St. Lawrence water, the remaining three-eighths.

Before we quit the fubject of the weftern waters, we will take a view of their principal connections with the Atlantic. Thefe are three; the Hudfon's river, the Patowmak, and the Miffiffippi itfelf. Down the laft will pafs all the heavy commodities. But the navigation through the Gulf of Mexico is fo dangerous, and that up the Miffiffippi fo difficult and tedious, that it is thought probable that European merchandize will not return through that channel. It is moft likely that flour, timber, and other heavy articles will be floated on rafts, which will themfelves be an article for fale as well as their loading, the navigators returning by land or in light batteaux. There will therefore be a competition between the Hudfon and the Patomak rivers for the refidue of the commerce of all the country weftward of Lake Erie, on the waters of the lakes, of the Ohio, and upper parts of Miffiffippi. To go to New-York, that part of the trade which comes from the lakes or their waters muft firft be brought

into

into Lake Erie. Between Lake Superior and its waters and Huron are the rapids of St. Mary, which will permit boats to pafs, but not larger veffels. Lakes Huron and Michigan afford communication with Lake Erie by veffels of eight feet draught. That part of the trade which comes from the waters of the Miffiffippi muft pafs from them through fome portage into the waters of the lakes. The portage from the Illinois river into a water of Michigan is of one mile only. From the Wabafh, Miami, Mufkingum, or Allegany, are portages into the waters of Lake Erie, of from one to fifteen miles. When the commodities are brought into, and have paffed through Lake Erie, there is between that and Ontario an interruption by the falls of Niagara, where the portage is of eight miles; and between Ontario and the Hudfon's river are portages of the falls of Onondago, a little above Ofwego, of a quarter of a mile; from Wood creek to the Mohawks river two miles; at the little falls of the Mohawks river half a mile, and from Schenectady to Albany fixteen miles. Befides the increafe of expence occafioned by frequent change of carriage, there is an increafed rifk of pillage produced by committing merchandize to a greater number of hands fucceffively. The Patomak offers itfelf under the following circumftances. For the trade of the lakes and their waters weftward of Lake Erie, when it fhall have entered that lake, it muft coaft along its fouthern fhore, on account of the number and excellence of its harbours, the northern, though fhorteft, having few harbours, and thefe unfafe. Having reached Cayahoga, to proceed on to New-York it will have eight hundred and twenty-five miles and five portages: whereas it is but four hundred and twenty-five miles to Alexandria, its emporium on the Patomak, if it turns into the Cayahoga, and paffes through that, Bigbeaver, Ohio, Yohoganey, (or Monongalia and Cheat) and Patomak, and there are but two portages; the firft of which between Cayahoga and Beaver may be removed by uniting the fources of thefe waters, which are lakes in the neighbourhood of each other, and in a champaign country; the other from the waters of Ohio to Patomak will be from fifteen to forty miles, according to the trouble which fhall be taken to approach the two navigations. For the trade of the Ohio, or that which fhall come into it from its own waters or the Miffiffippi, it is nearer through the Patomak to Alexandria than to New-York by five hundred and eighty miles, and it is interrupted by one portage only. There is another circumftance of difference too. The lakes themfelves never freeze, but the communications between them freeze, and the Hudfon's river is itfelf fhut up by the ice three months in the year; whereas the channel to the Chefapeek leads directly into a warmer climate. The fouthern parts of it very rarely freeze at all, and whenever the northern do, it is fo near the fources of the rivers, that the frequent floods to which they are there liable break up the ice immediately, fo that veffels may pafs through the whole winter, fubject only to accidental and fhort delays. Add to all this, that in cafe of a war with our neighbours the Anglo-Americans or the Indians, the route to New-York becomes a frontier through almoft its whole length, and all commerce through it ceafes from that moment.—But the channel to New-York is already known to practice; whereas the upper waters of the Ohio and the Patomak, and the great falls of the latter, are yet to be cleared of their fixed obftructions.

Particular

Particular defcriptions of the other rivers in the United States, are referved to be given in the geographical account of the ftates, through which they refpectively flow. One general obfervation refpecting the rivers will, however, be naturally introduced here, and that is, that the entrances into almoft all the rivers, inlets and bays, from New-Hampfhire to Georgia, are from foutheaft to northweft.

Bays.] The coaft of the United States is indented with numerous bays, fome of which are equal in fize to any in the known world. Beginning at the northeafterly part of the continent, and proceeding fouthwefterly, you firft find the bay or gulf of St. Lawrence, which receives the waters of the river of the fame name. Next is Chebukto Bay, in Nova-Scotia, diftinguifhed by the lofs of a French fleet in a former war between France and Great Britain. The Bay of Fundy, between Nova Scotia and New-England, is remarkable for its tides, which rife to the height of fifty or fixty feet, and flow fo rapidly as to overtake animals which feed upon the fhore. Penobfcot, Broad and Cafco Bays, lie along the coaft of the Province of Main. Maffachufetts Bay fpreads eaftward of Bofton, and is comprehended between Cape Ann on the north, and Cape Cod on the fouth. The points of the harbour are Wahant and Alderton points. Paffing by Narraganfet and other bays in the ftate of Rhode Ifland, you enter Long Ifland found, between Montauk point and the Main. This *Sound*, as it is called, is a kind of inland fea, from three to twenty-five miles broad, and about one hundred and forty miles long, extending the whole length of the ifland, and dividing it from Connecticut. It communicates with the ocean at both ends of Long Ifland, and affords a very fafe and convenient inland navigation.

The celebrated ftrait, called *Hell-Gate*, is near the weft end of this found, about eight miles eaftward of New-York city, and is remarkable for its whirlpools which make a tremendous roaring at certain times of tide. Thefe whirlpools are occafioned by the narrownefs and crookednefs of the pafs, and a bed of rocks which extend quite acrofs it ; and not by the meeting of the tides from eaft and weft, as has been conjectured, becaufe they meet at Frogs point, feveral miles above. A fkilful pilot may with fafety, conduct a fhip of any burden through this ftrait with the tide, or, at ftill water, with a fair wind.

Delaware Bay is fixty miles long, from the Cape to the entrance of the river Delaware at Bombay-hook ; and fo wide in fome parts, as that a fhip, in the middle of it, cannot be feen from the land. It opens into the Atlantic northweft and foutheaft, between Cape Henlopen on the right, and Cape May on the left. Thefe Capes are eighteen miles apart.

The Chefapeek is one of the largeft bays in the known world. Its entrance is between Cape Charles and Cape Henry in Virginia, twelve miles wide, and it extends two hundred and feventy miles to the northward, dividing Virginia and Maryland. It is from feven to eighteen miles broad, and generally as much as nine fathoms deep ; affording many commodious harbours, and a fafe and eafy navigation. It receives the waters of the Sufquehannah, Patomak, Rappahannok, York and James rivers which are all large and navigable.

Face

THE UNITED STATES.

Face of the Country.] The tract of country belonging to the United States, is happily variegated with plains and mountains, hills and vallies. Some parts are rocky, particularly New England, the north parts of New York, and New Jersey, and a broad space, including the several ridges of the long range of mountains which run southwestward through Pennsylvania, Virginia, North Carolina, and part of Georgia, dividing the waters which flow into the Atlantic, from those which fall into the Mississippi. In the parts east of the Allegany mountains in the southern states, the country for several hundred miles in length, and sixty or seventy, and sometimes more, in breadth, is level and entirely free of stone. It has been a question agitated by the curious, whether the extensive tract of low, flat country which fronts the several states south of New York, and extends back to the hills, has remained in its present form and situation ever since the flood or whether it has been made by the particles of earth which have been washed down from the adjacent mountains, and by the accumulation of soil from the decay of vegetable substances; or by earth washed out of the bay of Mexico by the Gulf stream, and lodged on the coast; or by the recess of the ocean, occasioned by a change in some other part of the earth. Several phænomena deserve consideration in forming an opinion on this question.

1 It is a fact, well known to every person of observation who has lived in, or travelled through the southern states, that marine shells and other substances which are peculiar to the sea shore, are almost invariably found by digging eighteen or twenty feet below the surface of the earth. A gentleman of veracity told me, that in sinking a well many miles from the sea, he found, at the depth of twenty feet, every appearance of a salt marsh; that is, marsh grass, marsh mud, and brackish water. In all this flat country until you come to the hilly land, wherever you dig a well, you find the water, at a certain depth, fresh and tolerably good; but if you exceed that depth two or three feet, you come to a saltish or brackish water that is scarcely drinkable, and the earth dug up, resembles, in appearance and smell, that which is dug up on the edges of the salt marshes.

2 On and near the margin of the rivers are frequently found sand hills, which appear to have been drifted into ridges by the force of water. At the bottom of some of the banks in the rivers, fifteen or twenty feet below the surface of the earth, are washed out from the solid ground, logs branches and leaves of trees; and the whole bank from bottom to top, appears streaked with layers of logs, leaves and sand. These appearances are seen far up the rivers, from eighty to one hundred miles from the sea, where, when the rivers are low, the banks are from fifteen to twenty feet high. As you proceed down the rivers toward the sea, the banks decrease in height, but still are formed of layers of sand, leaves, and logs, some of which are intirely sound, and appear to have been suddenly covered to a considerable depth.

3 It has been observed that the rivers in the southern States, frequently vary their channels; that the swamps and low grounds are constantly filling up, and that the land, in many places, annually infringes upon the ocean. It is an authenticated fact, that no longer ago than 1771, at Cape Lookout on the coast of North-Carolina, in about latitude 34° 50′, there was an excellent harbour, capacious enough to receive an
hundred

hundred fail of shipping at a time, in a good depth of water. It is now entirely filled up, and is solid ground. Instances of this kind are frequent along the coast.

It is observable, likewise, that there is a gradual descent of about eight hundred feet, by measurement, from the foot of the mountains to the sea board. This descent continues, as is demonstrated by soundings, far into the sea.

IV. It is worthy of observation, that the soil on the banks of the rivers is proportionably coarse or fine according to its distance from the mountains. When you first leave the mountains, and for a considerable distance, it is observable that the soil is coarse, with a large mixture of sand and shining heavy particles. As you proceed towards the sea, the soil is less coarse, and so on in proportion as you advance the soil is finer and finer, until, finally, is deposited a soil so fine, that it consolidates into perfect clay; but a clay of a particular quality, for a great part of it has intermixed with it reddish streaks and veins like a species of *ochre*, brought probably from the *red-lands* which lie up towards the mountains. This clay, when dug up and exposed to the weather, will dissolve into a fine mould without the least mixture of sand or any gritty substance whatever. Now we know that running waters, when turbid, will deposit, first, the coarsest and heaviest particles, mediately, those of the several intermediate degrees of fineness, and ultimately, those which are the most light and subtle; and such in fact is the general quality of the soil on the banks of the southern rivers.

V. It is a well known fact, that on the banks of Savannah river, about ninety miles from the sea in a direct line, and one hundred and fifty or two hundred as the river runs, there is a very remarkable collection of oyster shells of an uncommon size. They run in a northeast and southwest direction, nearly parallel with the sea coast, in three distinct ridges, which together occupy a space of seven miles in breadth. The ridges commence at Savannah river, and have been traced as far south as the northern branches of the Altamaha river. They are found in such quantities, as that the indigo planters carry them away in large boat loads, for the purpose of making lime water, to be used in the manufacture of indigo. There are thousands and thousands of tons still remaining. The question is, how came they here? It cannot be supposed that they were carried by land. Neither is it probable that they were conveyed in canoes, or boats, to such a distance from the place where oysters are now found. The uncivilized natives, agreeably to their roving manner of living, would rather have removed to the sea shore, than have been at such immense labor in procuring oysters. Besides, the difficulties of conveying them would have been insurmountable. They would not only have had a strong current in the river against them, an obstacle which would not have been easily overcome by the Indians, who have ever had a great aversion to labour, but could they have surmounted this difficulty, oysters, conveyed such a distance either by land or water in so warm a climate, would have spoiled on the passage and have become useless. The circumstance of these shells being found in such quantities, at so great a distance from the sea, can be rationally accounted for in no other way, than by supposing that the sea shore was formerly near this bed of shells, and

The UNITED STATES.

that the ocean has since, by the operation of certain causes not yet fully investigated, receded. These phænomena, it is presumed, will authorize this conclusion, That a great part of the flat country which spreads easterly of the Allegany mountains, had, in some past period, a superincumbent sea; or rather that the constant accretion of soil from the various causes before hinted at, has forced it to retire.

Mountains.] The tract of country east of Hudson's river, comprehending part of the State of New-York, the four New-England States, and Vermont, is rough, hilly, and in some parts mountainous; but the mountains are comparatively small, in few instances more than five or six hundred yards in height, and generally less. These mountains will be more particularly described under New-England. In all parts of the world, and particularly on this western continent, it is observable, that as you depart from the ocean, or from a river, the land gradually rises; and the height of land, in common, is about equally distant from the water on either side. The *Andes* in South-America form the height of land between the Atlantic and Pacific Oceans.

That range of mountains, of which the Shining mountains are a part, begins at Mexico, and continuing northward on the east of California, separates the waters of those numerous rivers that fall into the Gulf of Mexico or the Gulf of California. Thence continuing their course still northward, between the sources of the Mississippi and the rivers that run into the South-Sea, they appear to end in about 47 or 48 degrees of north latitude; where a number of rivers rise, and empty themselves either into the South Sea, into Hudson's Bay, or into the waters that communicate between these two seas.

The Highlands between the Province of Main and the Province of Quebec, divide the rivers which fall into the St. Lawrence north, and into the Atlantic south. The Green Mountains, in Vermont, divide the waters which flow easterly into Connecticut river, from those which fall westerly into Lake Champlain and Hudson's River.

Between the Atlantic, the Mississippi, and the Lakes, runs a long range of mountains, made up of a great number of ridges. These mountains extend northeasterly and southwesterly, nearly parallel with the sea coast, about nine hundred miles in length, and from sixty to one hundred and fifty, and two hundred miles in breadth. Mr. Evans observes, with respect to that part of these mountains which he travelled over, viz. in the back parts of Pennsylvania, that scarcely one acre in ten is capable of culture. This, however, is not the case in all parts of this range. Numerous tracts of fine arable and grazing land intervene between the ridges. The different ridges which compose this immense range of mountains, have different names in different States.

As you advance from the Atlantic, the first ridge in Pennsylvania, Virginia, and North-Carolina, is the the Blue Ridge or South Mountain; which is from one hundred and thirty, to two hundred miles from the sea. This is about four thousand feet high, measuring from its base. Between this and the North Mountain, spreads a large fertile vale; next lies the Allegany ridge; next beyond this is the Long Ridge, called the Laurel Mountains, in a spur of which, about latitude 36°, is a spring of water, fifty feet deep, very cold, and blue as indigo. From these several ridges

proceed

proceed innumerable namelefs branches or fpurs. The Kittatinny mountains run through the northern parts of New-Jerfey and Pennfylvania. All thefe ridges, except the Allegany, are feparated by rivers, which appear to have forced their paffages through folid rocks.

The principal ridge is the Allegany, which has been defcriptively called the *back bone* of the United States. The general name for thefe mountains, taken collectively, feems not yet to have been determined. Mr. Evans calls them the *Endlefs Mountains:* others have called them the Appalachian mountains, from a tribe of Indians, who live on a river which proceeds from this mountain, called the Appalachikola. But the moft common, and without doubt the moft proper, name is the *Allegany Mountains*, fo called from the principal ridge of the range. Thefe mountains are not confufedly fcattered and broken, rifing here and there into high peaks overtopping each other, but ftretch along in uniform ridges, fcarcely half a mile high. They fpread as you proceed fouth, and fome of them terminate in high perpendicular bluffs. Others gradually fubfide into a level country, giving rife to the rivers which run foutherly into the Gulf of Mexico.

They afford many curious phœnomena, from which naturalifts have deduced many theories of the earth. Some of them have been whimfical enough; Mr. Evans fuppofes that the moft obvious of the theories which have been formed of the earth is, that it was originally made out of the ruins of another. "Bones and fhells which efcaped the fate of fofter annimal fubftances, we find mixed with the old materials, and elegantly preferved in the loofe ftones and rocky bafes of the higheft of thefe hills." But with deference to Mr. Evans's opinion, thefe appearances have been much more rationally accounted for by fuppofing the reality of the flood, of which Mofes has given us an account. But Mr. Evans thinks this too great a miracle to obtain belief. But whether is it a greater miracle for the Creator to alter a globe of earth by a deluge when made, or to create one new from the ruins of another? The former certainly is not lefs credible than the latter. "Thefe mountains," fays our author, "exifted in their prefent elevated height before the deluge, but not fo bare of foil as now." How Mr. Evans came to be fo circumftantially acquainted with thefe pretended facts, is difficult to determine, unlefs we fuppofe him to have been an Antediluvian, and to have furveyed them accurately before the convulfions of the deluge; and until we can be fully affured of this, we muft be excufed in not affenting to his opinion, and in adhering to the old philofophy of Mofes and his advocates. We have every reafon to believe that the primitive ftate of the earth was totally metamorphofed by the firft convulfion of nature, at the time of the deluge; that *the fountains of the great deep were indeed broken up*, and that the various *ftrata* of the earth were diffevered, and thrown into every poffible degree of confufion and diforder. Hence thofe vaft piles of mountains which lift their craggy cliffs to the clouds, were probably thrown together from the floating ruins of the earth: and this conjecture is remarkably confirmed by the vaft number of foffils and other marine *exuviæ*, which are found imbeded on the tops of mountains, in the interior parts of continents remote from the fea, in all parts of the world hitherto explored. The various circumftances attending thefe marine bodies, leave us to conclude, that they were actually
generated,

The UNITED STATES.

generated, lived, and died in the very beds wherein they are found, and therefore these beds must have originally been at the bottom of the ocean, though now in many instances elevated several miles above its surface. Hence it appears that mountains and continents were not primary productions of nature, but of a very distant period of time from the creation of the world; a time long enough for the *strata* to have acquired their greatest degree of cohesion and hardness; and for the testaceous matter of marine shells to become changed to a stony substance; for in the fissures of the lime-stone and other strata, fragments of the same shell have been frequently found adhering to each side of the cleft, in the very state in which they were originally broken; so that if the several parts were brought together, they would apparently tally with each other exactly. A very considerable time therefore must have elapsed between the chaotic state of the earth and the deluge, which agrees with the account of Moses, who makes it a little upwards of sixteen hundred years. These observations are intended to shew, in one instance out of many others, the agreement between revelation and reason, between the account which Moses gives us of the creation and deluge, and the present appearances of nature. Those who wish to have this agreement more fully and satisfactorily stated, are referred to a very learned and ingenious " *Inquiry into the original state and formation of the earth,*" by John Whitehurst, F. R. S. to whom I acknowledge myself indebted for some of the foregoing observations.

Soil and productions, vegetable and animal.] The soil of the United States, though so various that few general observations will apply, may be said to be equal to that of any country in the known world. Among the great variety of its productions are the following:

Indian corn, which is a native grain of America, from whence all the other parts of the world have been supplied. It agrees with all climates from the equator to latitude 45°. It flourishes best however between the latitudes 30° and 40°. The bunched Guinea corn, is a small grain cultivated by the Negroes in the southern states, and affords a fine food for poultry. The spiked indian corn is of a similar kind.

Rice, which was brought into Carolina first by Sir Nathaniel Johnson, 1688; and afterwards by a ship from Madagascar, in 1696; till which time it was not much cultivated. It flourishes only in Georgia, and the Carolinas. Several unsuccessful attempts have been made to cultivate it in Virginia.

The Wild Rice is a grain which grows in the greatest plenty in some of the interior parts of North America; and is the most valuable of all the spontaneous productions of the country. It is of a very sweet and nutritious quality, and in future periods may be of great service to infant colonies, in affording them a support until, in the course of cultivation, other supplies may be obtained. This useful grain grows in the water where it is about two feet deep, and in a rich muddy soil. In its stalk, ears, and manner of growing it very much resembles oats. It is gathered by the Indians in the following manner: About the time that it begins to turn from its milky state and to ripen, they run their canoes into the midst of it, and tying bunches of it together just below the ears, they leave it in this situation for three or four weeks, till it is perfectly ripe. At the end of this time, commonly about the last of September, they

return

The UNITED STATES. 53

return to the river, and placing their canoes close to the bunches of rice in such position as to receive the grain when it falls, they beat it out with pieces of wood formed for that purpose. Having done this they dry it with smoke, and then tread or rub off the outside husk, after which it is fit for use.

Wheat, rye, barley and oats, are cultivated throughout the states, some few parts excepted. In Pennsylvania is a kind of grain called spelts, which grows much like wheat. The grain, however, is better covered; and is good food for horses. The flour made from it is very white, and is frequently mixed with wheat flour for bread. This grain might probably be successfully introduced into the New England states.

Potatoes are said to be aboriginal of America. They are of many kinds, and are raised in great quantities. The sweet, or Carolina potatoe, does not thrive well in northern climates, nor do the other kinds in the lower parts of the southern states.

The culinary roots and plants are beets, carrots, parsnips, turneps, radishes, peas, beans, cabbage, cauliflowers, endive, cellery, angelica, lettuce, asparagus, peppergrafs, leeks, onions, watermelons, muskmelons, cantelopes, which are a species of the muskmelon, but much superior in richness and flavor, cucumbers, mandrakes, pumpkins, squashes, &c. Besides these are several other roots and plants of a medicinal kind, such as elecampane, spikenard or petty-morrell, sarsaparilla, ginseng, liquorice, snake-root, gold-thread, solomon's-seal, devil's-bit, horse-radish and blood-root.

The gold-thread is of the vine kind, and grows in swamps. The roots spread themselves just under the surface of the morass, and are easily drawn out by handfuls. They resemble a large entangled skein of silk, and are of a bright yellow. It is exceedingly bitter in taste, and is an excellent remedy for a soreness in the mouth.

Devil's-bit, is a wild plant that has the print of teeth in its roots. The indians have a tradition, that this root was once an universal remedy for all diseases; but some evil spirit, envying mankind the possession of so efficacious a medicine, gave the root a bite, which deprived it of a great part of its virtue: Hence its name.

Blood-root is a sort of plantain, that springs out of the ground in six or seven long rough leaves, the veins of which are red; the root of it is like a small carrot; when broken, the inside is of a deeper color than the outside, and distills several drops of juce that looks like blood. This juice is a strong, but dangerous emetic.

Of the various aromatic and other kinds of herbs are balm, savory, thyme, sage, balsam, sweet-marjorum, hyssop, tansey, mint, penny-royal, fennel, yarrow, may-weed, gargit, skunk-cabbage, or poke, wake-robin, bittany, scabious, mullen, wild pease, mouse-ear, wild indigo, cat-mint or as it is sometimes called, catnip, nettles, cinque-foil, eye-bright, sanikle, plantain of several kinds, maiden-hair, burr-dock, field-dock, rock-liverwort, noble-liverwort, blood-wort, mother-wort, wild beans, ground-ivy, water-cresses, &c. &c.

Mr. Catesbey observes that the aromatic herbs in the southern states, are more highly flavored, and more volatile, than in Europe.

Apples

The UNITED STATES.

Apples are the most common fruit in the United States. They grow in the greatest plenty and variety in the northern and middle states, and in the interior, but not in the maritime, parts of the southern. In the low country of Georgia the Carolinas and some other states, grows a sort of wild crab-apple. The blossoms are fragrant, the fruit is small and sour, and makes an exellent preserve, or sweet-meat.

Besides apples, are pears, peaches, quinces, apricots, nectarines, plums, cherries of many kinds, currants, goosberries, rasberries, blackberries, billberries, whortleberries, strawberries, mulberries, cranberries, &c. Of the nuts are chesnuts, black walnuts, hiccory nuts, butternuts, beech-nuts, hazlenuts, filberts and Illinois nuts, or pecannuts. These fruits grow in great abundance and perfection, in almost every part of North America.

The Illinois or pecannut is of the walnut kind, about the size of an acorn, and of an oval form; the shell is easily cracked and the kernel shaped like that of a walnut. The trees which bear this fruit grow principally on the Illinois river. The butter or oil nut is much longer and larger than the walnut. Its shell is furrowed, and contains a large quantity of kernel, which is very oily, and of a rich and agreeable flavor. An oil, equal to that of olives, might be extracted from this nut. The inside bark of this tree is much used in dyes. A decoction of its bark or buds is a safe and powerful cathartic; and is frequently used in the country instead of a more costly medicine. Filberts are of the hazlenut kind, but larger and more richly flavored.

Figs, oranges, lemons, and pomgranetes, are not natural to any state north of the Carolinas. The pomgranate requires salt water. Grapes of several sorts grow spontaneously from latitude 25° to 45° north. The various kinds of trees, shrubs, and flowers, so many of them as are worthy of notice, will be mentioned in the description of the several states.

The late Count de Buffon has advanced the opinion, that the animals in America are inferior, in almost every respect, to those on the eastern continent. Mr. Jefferson, in a very learned and elaborate manner, has confuted this opinion, and proved that the animals of America are, in most instances equal, and in many respects superior, to those of the old world; and has shewn that out of two hundred species of animals, which M. de Buffon supposes is the whole number existing on the earth, one hundred species are aboriginal of America.

The following catalogue of animals is collected principally from Catesby, Jefferson and Carver.

Beasts common to North America.

Mammoth	Moose Deer	Grey Fox Squirrel
Buffalo	Stag	Black Squirrel
Panther	Carrabou	Red Squirrel
Carcajou	Fallow Deer	Ground Squirrel
Wild cat	Greenland Deer	Flying Squirrel
Bear	Rabbit	Black Fox
Elk	Bahama Coney	Red Fox
White Bear	Monax	Grey Fox
Wolf	Grey Squirrel	Racoon
		Woodchuck

The UNITED STATES.

Woodchuck	Beaver	Field Mouse
Skunk	Mufquash	Moles
Opoffum	Otter	Quickhatch
Pole Cat	Fisher	Morfe
Weafle	Water Rat	Porcupine
Marten	Mufkrat	Seal.
Minx	Houfe Moufe	

These are divided into three claffes;

1. Beafts of different *genus* from any kown in the old world; of which are the Opoffum, the Racoon, the Quickhatch, &c.

2. Beafts of the fame genus, but of different fpecies from the eaftern continent, of which are

The Panther	Fallow Deer	Ground Squirrel
Wild Cat	Grey Fox	Flying Squirrel
Buffalo	Grey Squirrel	Pole Cat
Moofe Deer	Grey Fox Squirrel	Porcupine &c.
Stag	Black Squirrel	

3. Beafts which are the fame on both continents, viz.

The Bear	Otter	Field Moufe
White Bear	Water Rat	Mole
Wolf	Houfe Rat	Morfe
Weafle	Mufk Rat	Seal, &c.
Beaver	Houfe Moufe	

The MAMMOTH is not found in the civilized parts of America. It is conjectured, however, that he was carniverous, and that he ftill exifts on the north of the Lakes. Their tufks, grinders, and fkeletons of uncommon magnitude, have been found at the falt licks, on the Ohio, in New-Jerfey, and other places. The Indians have a tradition handed down from their fathers refpecting thefe animals, 'That in antient times a herd of them came to the Big-bone licks, and began an univerfal deftruction of the bears, deer, elks, buffaloes, and other animals which had been created for the ufe of the Indians: that the Great Man above, looking down and feeing this, was fo enraged that he feized his lightning, defcended to the earth, feated himfelf upon a neighbouring mountain, on a rock, on which his feat and the print of his feet are ftill to be feen, and hurled his bolts among them till the whole were flaughtered, except the big bull, who prefenting his forehead to the fhafts, fhook them off as they fell; but at length miffing one, it wounded him in the fide; whereon, fpringing round, he bounded over the Ohio, the Wabafh, the Illinois, and finally over the great lakes where he is living at this day.'

European naturalifts have fuppofed from the bones of this remarkable animal, that it is the fame with the Elephant; others that it anfwers to the hippopotamus or river horfe; the tufk and fkeletons have been afcribed to the former, while the grinders have been given to the latter. But Mr. Jefferfon obferves, that the fkeleton of the Mammoth (for fo the incognitum has been called) befpeaks an animal of five or fix times the cubic volume of the elephant, as Monfieur de Buffon has admitted; and that the grinders are five times as large as thofe of the elephant and quite of a different

ferent fhape, and adds that the elephant is a native only of the torrid zone and its vicinities, and that no bones of the mammoth have ever been found further fouth than the falines of Holfton river, a branch of the Taniffee, about the latitude 36° 30′ north, and as far north as the arctic circle. The mammoth, then, cannot be the fame animal as the elephant.

The Opossum is an animal of a diftinct genus, and therefore has little refemblance to any other creature. It is about the fize of a common cat, which it refembles in fome degree as to its body; its legs are fhort, the feet are formed like thofe of a rat, as are its ears; the fnout and head are long like the hog's; the teeth like thofe of a dog; its body is covered thinly with long briftly whitifh hair; its tail is long, fhaped like that of a rat without hair. But what is moft remarkable in this creature, and which diftinguifhes it from all others, is its falfe belly, which is formed by a fkin or membrane, (inclofing the dugs) which it opens and clofes at will. In this falfe belly, the young are concealed in time of danger. Though contrary to the laws of nature, it is believed by many, that thefe animals are bred at the teats of their dams. It is a fact, that the young ones have been many times feen, not larger than the head of a large pin, faft fixed and hanging to the teats in the falfe belly. In this ftate, their members are diftinctly vifible; they appear like an embryo clinging to the teats. By conftant obfervation, they have been found to grow into a perfect fœtus; and in proper time they drop off into the falfe belly, where they remain fecure, till they are capable of providing for themfelves. From thefe circumftances, it feems that the opoffum is produced, in a manner, out of the common courfe of nature. But it appears from the diffection of one of them by Dr. Tyfon, that their ftructure is fuch as is fitted for generation, like that of other animals; and of courfe he fuppofes that they muft neceffarily be bred and excluded in the fame way as other quadrupeds. But by what method the dam, after exclufion, fixes them on her teats, if this be the manner of production, is a fecret yet unknown.

The Buffalo is larger than an ox; high on the fhoulders; and deep through the breaft. The flefh of this animal is equal in goodnefs to beef; its fkin makes good leather, and its hair, which is of a woolly kind, is manufactured into a tolerably good cloth.

The Tyger of America refembles, in fhape, thofe of Afia and Africa, but is confiderably fmaller; nor does it appear to be fo fierce and ravenous as they are. The colour of it is a darkifh yellow, and is entirely free from fpots.

The Cat of the Mountain refembles a common cat, but is of a much larger fize. Its hair is of a reddifh or orange colour, interfperfed with fpots of black. This animal is exceedingly fierce, though it will feldom attack a man.

The Elk is fhaped like a deer, but is confiderably larger, being equal in bulk to a horfe. The horns of this creature grow to a prodigious fize, extending fo wide, that two or three perfons might fit between them at the fame time. But what is ftill more remarkable is, that thefe horns are fhed every year, in the month of February, and by Auguft, the new ones are nearly at their full growth.

The

The UNITED STATES.

The Moose is about the size of the elk, and its horns almost as large. Like the elk, it sheds its horns annually. Though this creature is of the deer kind, it never herds as do deer in general. Its flesh is exceedingly good food, easy of digestion, and very nourishing. Its skin, as well as that of the elk, is valuable, making when dressed, good leather.

The Carrabou is something like the moose in shape, though not nearly so tall. Its flesh is exceedingly good; its tongue in particular is in high esteem. Its skin, being smooth and free from veins, is valuable.

The Carcajou is a creature of the cat kind, and is a terrible enemy to the elk, and to the carrabou, as well as to the deer. He either comes upon them unperceived from some concealment; or climbs up into a tree, and taking his station on some of the branches, waits till one of them takes shelter under it; when he fastens upon his neck, and opening the jugular vein, soon brings his prey to the ground. The only way of escape is flying immediately to the water, for as the carcajou has a great dislike to that element, he will leave his prey rather than enter it.

The Skunk is the most extraordinary animal the American woods produce. It is of the same species with the pole-cat, for which, though different from it in many respects, and particularly in being of a less size, it is frequently mistaken. Its hair is long and shining, of a dirty white, mixed in some places with black. Its tail is long and bushy like that of the fox. It lives chiefly in woods and hedges; and is possessed of extraordinary powers, which however are exerted only when it is pursued. On such an occasion, it ejects from behind a small stream of water, of so subtle a nature, and so powerful a smell, that the air is tainted with it to a surprizing distance. On this account the animal is called by the French *Enfant du Diable*, the Child of the Devil, or *Bête Puante*, the Stinking Beast. The water which this creature emits in its defence, is generally supposed by naturalists to be its urine; but Mr. Carver, who shot and dissected many of them, declares that he found, near the urinal vessels, a small receptacle of water, totally distinct from the bladder, from which, he was satisfied, the horrid stench proceeded. The fat of the skunk, when externally applied, is a powerful emollient, and its flesh, when dressed without being tainted by its fetid water, is sweet and good.

The Porcupine or Hedge-Hog is about the size of a small dog, though it is neither so long nor so tall. Its shape resembles that of a fox, excepting its head, which is something like the head of a rabbit. Its body is covered with quills of about four inches in length, most of which are, excepting at the point, of the thickness of a straw. These quills the porcupine darts at his enemy, and if they pierce the flesh in the least degree, they will sink quite through it, and are not to be extracted without incision. The indians use these quills for boring their ears and noses to insert their jewels, and also by way of ornament to their stockings, hair, &c.

The Wood-Chuck is a ground animal of the fur kind, about fifteen inches long; its body is round, and its legs short; its fore paws are broad, and constructed for the purpose of digging holes in the ground, in which it burrows; its flesh is tolerably food.

The UNITED STATES.

The RACOON is an animal of a genus different from any known on the eastern continent. Its head is much like a fox's, only its ears are shorter, more round, and more naked. It also resembles that animal in its hair, which is thick, long and soft; and in its body and legs, excepting that the former is larger, and the latter both larger and shorter. Across its face runs a broad stripe including its eyes, which are large. Its snout is black, and roundish at the end like that of a dog; its teeth also are similar to those of the dog, both in number and shape; the tail is long and round, with annular stripes on it; the feet have five long slender toes, armed with sharp claws, by which it is enabled to climb trees, and run to the extremities of the boughs. Its fore feet serve it instead of hands, like those of the monkey.

The last quadruped which shall be particularly described, is the BEAVER. This is an amphibious animal, which cannot live for any long time in the water, and it is said can exist without it, provided it has the convenience of sometimes bathing itself. The largest beavers are nearly four feet in length, about fourteen or fifteen inches in breadth over the haunches, and weigh fifty or sixty pounds. The head of this animal is large; its snout long; its eyes small; its ears short, round, hairy on the outside, and smooth within; of its teeth, which are long, broad, strong and sharp, the under ones stand out of its mouth about the breadth of three fingers, and the upper about half a finger. Besides these teeth, which are called *incisors*, beavers have sixteen grinders, eight on each side, four above and four below, directly opposite to each other. With the former they are able to cut down trees of a considerable size, with the latter to break the hardest substances. Their legs are short, particularly the fore legs, which are only four or five inches long. The toes of the fore feet are separate; those of the hind feet have membranes between them. In consequence of this they can walk, though but slowly, while they swim as easily as any aquatic animals. Their tails somewhat resemble those of fish, and these, and their hind feet, are the only parts in which they do not resemble land animals. Their colour is different according to the different climates which they inhabit. In the most northern parts, they are generally quite black; in more temperate, brown; their colour becoming lighter and lighter as they approach towards the south. Their fur is of two sorts all over their bodies. That which is longest is generally about an inch long, though on the back it sometimes extends to two inches, gradually shortening towards the head and tail. This part is coarse and of little use. The other part of it consists of a very thick and fine down, of about three quarters of an inch long, so soft that it feels like silk, and is that which is commonly manufactured. Castor, so useful in medicine, is produced from the body of the beaver. It was formerly believed to be his testicles, but late discoveries have shewn that it is contained in four bags in the lower belly.

The ingenuity of the beavers in building their cabins, and in providing themselves subsistence, is truly wonderful. When they are about to choose a habitation, they assemble in companies, sometimes of two or three hundred, and after mature deliberation, fix on a place where plenty of provisions, and all necessaries are to be found. Their houses are always situated in the water, and when they can find neither lake nor
pond

pond convenient, they supply the defect by stopping the current of some brook or small river. For this purpose they select a number of trees, carefully taking those above the place where they intend to build that they may swim down with the current, and placing themselves by threes or fours round each tree, soon fell them. By a continuation of the same labour, they cut the trees into proper lengths, and rolling them into the water, navigate them to the place where they are to be used. After this they construct a dam with as much solidity and regularity as the most experienced workman could do. The formation of their cabins is no less remarkable. These cabins are built either on piles in the middle of the pond they have formed, on the bank of a river, or at the extremity of some point of land projecting into a lake. The figure of them is round or oval. Two thirds of each of them rises above the water, and this part is large enough to contain eight or ten inhabitants. They are contiguous to each other, so as to allow an easy communication. Each beaver has his place assigned him, the floor of which he curiously strews with leaves, rendering it clean and comfortable. The winter never surprizes these animals before their business is completed; for their houses are generally finished by the last of September, and their stock of provisions laid in, which consists of small pieces of wood disposed in such manner as to preserve its moisture.

Upwards of one hundred and thirty American BIRDS have been enumerated, and many of them described by Catesby, Jefferson and Carver. The following catalogue is inserted to gratify the curious, to inform the inquisitive, and to shew the astonishing variety in this beautiful part of creation.

The Blackbird	Crane or blue Heron	Flamingo
Razorbilled do.	Yellow-breasted Chat	Fieldfare of Carolina
Baltimore bird	Cormorant	or Robin
Bastard Baltimore	Hooping Crane	Purple Finch
Blue bird	Pine Creeper	Bahama Finch
Buzzard	Yellow throated Creeper	American Gold-Finch
Blue Jay	Dove	Painted Finch
Blue Grosbeak	Ground Dove	Crested Fly-catcher
Brown Bittern	Duck	Black-cap do.
Crested Bittern	Ilathera Duck	Little brown do.
Small Bittern	Round crested do.	Red-eyed do.
Booby	Sheldrach or Canvass do.	Finch creeper
Great Booby	Buffels head do.	Storm Finch
Blue Peter	Spoonbill do.	Goat Sucker of Carolina
Bullfinch	Summer do.	lina
Bald Coot	Blackhead do.	Gull
Cut Water	Blue winged Shoveller	Laughing Gull
White Curlew	Little brown Duck	Goose
Cat bird	Sprigtail	Canada Goose
Cuckow	Whitefaced Teal	Hawk
Crow	Blue winged Teal	Fishing Hawk
Cowpen bird	Pied bill Dobchick	Pigeon Hawk
Chattering Plover	Eagle	Night Hawk
or Kildee	Bald Eagle	Swallow-tailed do.
	Hangbird	Heron

The Heron	Pelican	Bahama Titmouse
Little white Heron	Water Pelican	Hooded do.
Heath cock	Pigeon of passage	Yellow rump
Hummingbird	White crowned pigeon	Towhe bird
Purple Jackdaw or	Parrot of Paradise	Red Thrush
Crow Blackbird	Paroquet of Carolina	Fox coloured Thrush
King bird	Raven	Little Thrush
Kingfisher	Rice bird	Tropic bird
Loon	Red bird	Turtle of Carolina
Lark	Summer Red bird	Water wagtail
Large Lark	Swan	Water hen
Blue Linnet	Soree	Water witch
Mock bird	Snipe	Wakon bird
Mow bird	Red Start	Whetsaw
Purple Martin	Red winged Starling	Large whitebilled wood-
Nightingale	Swallow	pecker
Noddy	Chimney do.	Large red crested do.
Nuthatch	Snow bird	Gold winged do.
Oyster catcher	Little Sparrow	Red bellied do.
Owl	Bahama do.	Hairy do.
Scretch Owl	Stork	Red headed do.
American Partridge	Turkey	Yellow bellied do.
or Quail	Wild Turkey	Smallest spotted do.
Pheasant or moun-	Tyrant	Wren
tain Partridge	Crested Titmouse	
Water Pheasant	Yellow do.	

Catesby observes, that the birds of America generally exceed those of Europe in the beauty of their plumage, but are much inferior to them in the melody of their notes.

The WATER PELICAN inhabits the Mississippi. Its pouch holds a peck.

The LARK is a lofty bird, and soars as high as any of the inhabitants of the airy region: Hence the old proverb, ' When the sky falls we shall catch larks.'

The WHIP-POOR-WILL, is remarkable for the plaintive melody of its notes. It acquires its name from the noise it makes, which to the people of the states sounds Whip-poor-will, to the Indians Muck-a-wiss. A striking proof how differently the same sounds impress different persons!

The LOON is a water fowl, of the same species of the Dobchick. It is an exceedingly nimble bird, and so expert at diving, that it is with great difficulty killed.

The PARTRIDGE. In some parts of the country there are three or four different kinds of Partridges, all of them larger than the Partridges of Europe. What is called the Quail in New-England, is denominated Partridge in the southern states, where the true Partridge is not to be found.

The WAKON-BIRD, which probably is of the same species with the bird of Paradise, receives its name from the ideas the Indians have of its superior excellence; the Wakon-bird being in their language the bird of the Great Spirit. It is nearly the size of the swallow, of a brown colour, shaded about the neck with a bright green. The wings are of a darker
brown

The UNITED STATES. 61

brown than the body. Its tail is compofed of four or five feathers, which are three times as long as its body, and which are beautifully fhaded with green and purple. It carries this fine length of plumage in the fame manner as the peacock does his, but it is not known whether like him, it ever raifes it to an erect pofition.

The WHETSAW is of the cuckow kind, being like that a folitary-bird, and fcarcely ever feen. In the fummer months it is heard in the groves, where it makes a noife like the filing of a faw, from which circumftance it has received its name.

The HUMMING-BIRD is the fmalleft of all the feathered inhabitants of the air. Its plumage furpaffes defcription. On its head is a fmall tuft of jetty black: its breaft is red; its belly white; its back, wings and tail of the fineft pale green: fmall fpecks of gold are fcattered over it with inexpreffible grace: and to crown the whole, an almoft imperceptible down, foftens the feveral colours and produces the moft pleafing fhades.

Of the Snakes which infeft the United States, are the following, viz.

The Rattle Snake	Corn do.
Small Rattle Snake	Hognofe do.
Yellow Rattle Snake	Houfe do.
W ter Viper	Green do.
Black Viper	Wampum do.
Brown Viper	Glafs do.
Copper-bellied Snake	Bead do.
Bluifh-green Snake	Wallor Houfe Adder
Black Snake	Striped or Garter Snake
Ribbon do.	Water Snake
Spotted Ribbon do	Hiffing do.
Chain do.	Thorn-tailed do.
Joint do.	Speckled do.
Green fpotted do.	Ring do.
Coachwhip do.	Two-headed do.

The THORN-TAIL SNAKE is of a middle fize, and of a very venomous nature. It receives its name from a thorn, like dart, in its tail, with which it inflicts its wounds.

The JOINT SNAKE is a great curiofity. Its fkin is as hard as parchment, and as fmooth as glafs. It is beautifully ftreaked with black and white. It is fo ftiff, and has fo few joints, and thofe fo unyielding, that it can hardly bend itfelf into the form of a hoop. When it is ftruck, it breaks like a pipe ftem; and you may, with a whip, break it from the tail to the bowels into pieces not an inch long, and not produce the leaft tincture of blood. It is not venomous.

The TWO-HEADED SNAKE. Whether this be a diftinct fpecies of fnakes intended to propagate its kind, or whether it be a monftrous production, is uncertain. The only ones I have known or heard of in this country, are, one taken near Champlain in 1762, and one preferved in the Mufeum of Yale College, in New-Haven.

The fnakes are not fo numerous nor fo venomous in the northern as in the fouthern ftates. In the latter, however, the inhabitants are furnifhed
with

with a much greater variety of plants and herbs, which afford immediate relief to perfons bitten by thefe venomous creatures. It is an obfervation worthy of perpetual and grateful remembrance, that wherever venomous animals are found, the GOD of nature has kindly provided fufficient antidotes againft their poifon.

Of the aftonifhing variety of INSECTS found in America, we will mention. The

Glow Worm	Sheep Tick	Butter Fly
Earth Worm	Loufe	Moth
Leg or Guinea do.	Wood Loufe	Ant
Naked Snail	Forty Legs or Centipes	Bee
Shell Snail	Caterpillar	Humble Bee
Tobacco Worm	Adder bolt	Black Wafp
Wood Worm	Cicada or Locuft	Yellow Wafp
Silk Worm	Man-gazer	Hornet
Wall Loufe or Bug	Cock Roche	Fly
Sow Bug	Cricket	Sand Fly
Horn Bug	Beetle	Mufketo
Flea	Fire Fly or Bug	Spider
Gnat		

To thefe may be added the infect, which of late years has proved fo deftructive to the wheat in many parts of the middle and New-England States, commonly, but erroneoufly, called the Heffian Fly.

The ALLIGATOR is a fpecies of the crocodile, and in appearance one of the uglieft creatures in the world. They are amphibious, and live in, and about creeks, fwamps and ponds of ftagnant water. They are very fond of the flefh of dogs and hogs, which they voracioufly devour when they have opportunity. They are alfo very fond of fifh, and devour vaft quantities of them. When tired with fifhing, they leave the water to bafk themfelves in the fun, and then appear more like logs of half rotten wood thrown afhore by the current, than living creatures; but upon perceiving any veffel or perfon near them, they immediately throw themfelves into the water. Some are of fo monftrous a fize as to exceed five yards in length. During the time they lie bafking on the fhore, they keep their huge mouths wide open, till filled with mufketoes, flies, and other infects, when they fuddenly fhut their jaws and fwallow their prey.

The alligator is an oviparous creature. The female makes a large hole in the fand near the brink of a river, and there depofits her eggs, which are as white as thofe of a hen, but much larger and more folid. She generally lays about an hundred, continuing in the fame place till they are all depofited, which is a day or two. She then covers them with the fand, and the better to conceal them, rolls herfelf not only over her precious *depofitum*, but to a confiderable diftance. After this precaution, fhe returns to the water and tarries until natural inftinct informs her that it is time to deliver her young from their confinement; fhe then goes to the fpot, attended by the male, and tearing up the fand, begins to break the eggs; but fo carefully that fcarce a fingle one is injured, and a whole fwarm of little alligators is feen crawling about. The female then takes them on her

her neck and back, in order to remove them into the water; but the watchful birds of prey make use of this opportunity to deprive her of some, and even the male alligator, who indeed comes for no other end, devours what he can, till the female has reached the water with the few remaining; for all those which either fall from her back, or do not swim, she herself eats; so that of such a formidable brood, happily not more than four or five escape.

These alligators are the great destroyers of the fish in the rivers and creeks, it being their most safe and general food: nor are they wanting in address to satisfy their desires. Eight or ten, as it were by compact, draw up at the mouth of a river or creek, where they lie with their mouths open, whilst others go a considerable distance up the river, and chace the fish downward, by which means none of any bigness escape them. The alligators being unable to eat under water, on seizing a fish, raize their heads above the surface, and by degrees draw the fish from their jaws, and chew it for deglutition.

Before the setting in of winter, it is said, not without evidence to support the assertion, that they swallow a large number of pine knots, and then creep into their dens, in the bank of some creek or pond, where they lie in a torpid state through the winter without any other sustenance than the pine knots.

The GUANA, the GREEN LIZARD of Carolina, the BLUE-TAILED LIZARD, and the LION LIZARD are found in the southern states, and are thought to be species of the same *genus*, with the crocodile and alligator.

In the little brooks, and swamps in the back parts of North Carolina, is caught a small amphibious lobster, in the head of which is found the eye stone.

Population, Character, &c.] From the best accounts that can at present be obtained, there are, within the limits of the United States, three millions, eighty three thousand, and six hundred souls. This number, which is rapidly increasing both by emigrations from Europe, and by natural population, is composed of people of almost all nations, languages, characters and religions. The greater part, however, are descended from the English; and, for the sake of distinction, are called Anglo-Americans.

The natural genius of Americans, not through prejudice we would charitably suppose, but through want of information, has suffered in the descriptions of some ingenious and eloquent European writers.

The Count de Buffon, has endeavoured to support the theory, 'That on this side the Atlantic, there is a tendency in nature to belittle her productions.' This new and unsupported theory, has been applied, by the Abbe Raynal, to the race of whites transplanted from Europe. Mr. Jefferson has confuted this theory; and by the ingenuity and abilities which he has shewn in doing it, has exhibited an instance of its falsehood.*

The

---

* Although the Abbe, in a later edition of his works, has withdrawn his censure from that part of America inhabited by Federo-Americans; yet he has left it in its full force on the other parts, where it is equally inapplicable, if we
consider

The UNITED STATES.

The affertion of the Abbe Raynal's that ' America has not yet produced one good poet, one able mathematician, one man of genius in a fingle art or a fingle fcience,'* produced the following reply from Mr. Jefferfon.

'When we fhall have exifted as a people as long as the Greeks did before they produced a Homer, the Romans a Virgil, the French a Racine and Voltaire, the Englifh a Shakefpeare and Milton, fhould this reproach be ftill true, we will enquire from what unfriendly caufes it has proceeded, that the other countries of Europe, and quarters of the earth fhall not have infcribed any name in the roll of poets. In war we have produced a WASHINGTON, whofe memory will be adored while liberty fhall have votaries, whofe name will triumph over time, and will in future ages affume its juft ftation among the moft celebrated worthies of the world, when that wretched philofophy fhall be forgotten which would arrange him among the degeneracies of nature. In Phyfics we have produced a FRANKLIN, than whom no one of the prefent age has made more important difcoveries, nor has enriched philofophy with more, or more ingenious folutions of the phænomena of nature. We have fuppofed Mr. RITTENHOUSE fecond to no aftronomer living : that in genius he muft be the firft, becaufe he is felf-taught. As an artift he has exhibited as great proofs of mechanical genius as the world has ever produced. He has not indeed made a world ; but he has by imitation approached nearer its Maker than any man who has lived from the creation to this day. As in philofophy and war, fo in government, in oratory, in painting, in the plaftic art, we might fhew that America, though but a child of yefterday, has already given hopeful proofs of genius, as well of the nobler kinds, which aroufe the beft feelings of man, which call him into action, which fubftantiate his freedom, and conduct him to happinefs, as of the fubordinate, which ferve to amufe him only. We therefore fuppofe, that this reproach is as unjuft as it is unkind ; and that, of the geniufes which adorn the prefent age, America contributes its full fhare. For comparing it with thofe countries, where genius is moft cultivated, where are the moft excellent models for art, and fcaffoldings for the attainment of fcience, as France and England for inftance, we calculate thus. The United States contain three millions of inhabitants ; France twenty millions ; and the Britifh iflands ten. We produce a Wafhington, a Franklin, a Rittenhoufe. France then fhould have half a dozen in each of thefe lines, and Great-Britain half that number, equally eminent. It may be true, that France has : we are but juft becoming acquainted with her, and our acquaintance fo far gives us high ideas of the genius of her inhabitants. It would be injuring too many of them to name particularly a Voltaire, a Buffon, the conftellation of Encyclopedifts, the Abbe Raynal himfelf, &c. &c. We therefore have reafon to believe fhe can produce her full quota of genius.

The confider the accumulated preffure of flavery, fuperftition and ignorance, under which the inhabitants are held. Whenever they fhall be able to throw off their fhackles, and act themfelves, they will doubtlefs fhew that they are like the reft of the world.

* Hift. Philof. P. 92. ed. Meaftrich, 1774.

THE UNITED STATES.

The present war having so long cut off all communication with Great-Britain, we are not able to make a fair estimate of the state of science in that country.

The Literature of the United States is very flourishing. Their progress in the art of war, in the science of government, in philosophy and astronomy, in poetry, and the various liberal arts and sciences, has, for so young a country, been astonishing. Colleges are instituted in all the states north of North Carolina, excepting Delaware; and liberal provision is making for their establishment in the others. These colleges are generally well furnished with libraries, apparatus, instructors and students.

The two late important revolutions in America which have been scarcely exceeded since the memory of man, I mean that of the declaration and establishment of independence, and that of the adoption of a new form of government without blood-shed, have called to historic fame many noble and distinguished characters who might otherwise have slept in oblivion.

But while we exhibit the fair side of the character of Federo-Americans, we would not be thought blind to their faults.

A European writer has justly observed that ' If there be an object truly ridiculous in nature, it is an American patriot, signing resolutions of independency with the one hand, and with the other brandishing a whip over his affrighted slaves.'

Much has been written, of late, to shew the injustice and iniquity of enslaving the Africans; so much as to render it unnecessary here to say any thing on that part of the subject. We cannot, however, forbear introducing a few observations respecting the influence of slavery upon policy, morals and manners. From repeated and accurate calculations, it has been found, that the expence of maintaining a slave, especially if we include the purchase money, is much greater than that of maintaining a free man; and the labour of the freeman, influenced by the powerful motive of gain, is, at least, twice as profitable to the employer as that of the slave. Besides, slavery is the bane of industry. It renders labour, among the whites, not only unfashionable, but disreputable. Industry is the offspring of necessity rather than of choice. Slavery precludes this necessity; and indolence, which strikes at the root of all social and political happiness, is the unhappy consequence.

These observations, without adding any thing upon the injustice of the practice, shew that slavery is impolitic. Its influence on manners and morals is equally pernicious. The negro wenches in many, perhaps I may say in most instances, are nurses to their mistresses children. The infant babe, as soon as it is born, is delivered to its black nurse, and perhaps seldom or never tastes a drop of its mother's milk. The children, by being brought up, and constantly associating with the negroes, too often imbibe their low ideas, and vitiated manners and morals; and contract a *negroish* kind of accent and dialect, which they often carry with them through life. A mischief common, in a greater or less degree, in all the southern states, at which humanity and decency blush, is the criminal intercourse between the whites and blacks. ' The enjoyment of a negro or mulatto woman,' says a traveller of observation, ' is spoken of as quite a common thing. No reluctance, delicacy, or shame, appear about the

matter.

matter. It is far from being uncommon to fee a gentleman at dinner, and his reputed offspring a flave, waiting at the table. 'I myfelf,' fays this writer, ' faw two inftances of this kind; and the company would very facetioufly trace the features of the father and mother in the child, and very accurately point out the more characteriftic refemblances. The fathers neither of them blufhed, nor feemed difconcerted. They were called men of worth, politenefs, and humanity. Strange perverfion of terms and language! The Africans are faid to be inferior in point of fenfe, underftanding, fentiment and feeling to white people: Hence the one infers a right to enflave the other. The African labours night and day to collect a fmall pittance to purchafe the freedom of his child: The whiteman begets his likenefs, and with much indifference and dignity of foul, fees his offspring in bondage and mifery, and makes not one effort to redeem his own blood. Choice food for fatire! wide field for burlefque! noble game for wit! fad caufe for pity to bleed, and for humanity to weep! unlefs the enkindled blood inflame refentment, and vent itfelf in execrations!'

To thefe I fhall add the obfervations of a native* of a ftate which contains a greater number of flaves than any of the others. For although his obfervations upon the influence of flavery were intended for a particular ftate, they will apply equally well to all places where this pernicious practice in any confiderable degree prevails.

' There muft doubtlefs' he obferves ' be an unhappy influence on the manners of our people produced by the exiftence of flavery among us. The whole commerce between mafter and flave is a perpetual exercife of the moft boifterous paffions, the moft unremitting defpotifm on the one part, and degrading fubmiffions on the other. Our children fee this, and learn to imitate it; for man is an imitative animal. This quality is the germ of all education in him. From his cradle to his grave he is learning to do what he fees others do. If a parent could find no motive either in his philanthropy or his felf-love, for reftraining the intemperance of paffion towards his flave, it fhould always be a fufficient one that his child is prefent. But generally it is not fufficient. The parent ftorms, the child looks on, catches the lineaments of wrath, puts on the fame airs in the circle of fmaller flaves, gives a loofe to his worft of paffions, and thus nurfed, educated, and daily exercifed in tyranny, cannot but be ftamped by it with odious peculiarities. The man muft be a prodigy who can retain his manners and morals undepraved by fuch circumftances. And with what execration fhould the ftatefman be loaded, who permitting one half the citizens thus to trample on the rights of the other, transforms thofe into defpots, and thefe into enemies, deftroys the morals of the one part, and the *amor patriæ* of the other. For if a flave can have a country in this world, it muft be any other in preference to that in which he is born to live and labour for another: in which he muft lock up the faculties of his nature, contribute as far as depends on his individual endeavours to the evanifhment of the human race, or entail his own miferable condition on the endlefs generations proceeding from him. With the morals of the people, their induftry alfo is deftroyed. For in a warm climate, no man will labour for himfelf who can make another labour for him. This is

fo

* Mr. Jefferfon,

The UNITED STATES.

so true, that of the proprietors of slaves a very small proportion indeed are ever seen to labour. And can the liberties of a nation be thought secure when we have removed their only firm basis, a conviction in the minds of the people that these liberties are the gift of God? That they are not to be violated but with his wrath? Indeed I tremble for my country when I reflect that God is just: that his justice cannot sleep forever: that considering numbers, nature and natural means only, a revolution of the wheel of fortune, an exchange of situation, is among possible events: that it may become probable by supernatural interference!—The Almighty has no attribute which can take side with us in such a contest. But it is impossible to be temperate and to pursue this subject through the various considerations of policy, of morals, of history natural and civil. We must be contented to hope they will force their way into every one's mind. I think a change already perceptible, since the origin of the present revolution. The spirit of the master is abating, that of the slave rising from the dust, his condition mollifying, the way I hope preparing, under the auspices of heaven, for a total emancipation, and that this is disposed, in the order of events, to be with the consent of the masters, rather than by their extirpation.'

Under the Fœderal government which is now established, we have reason to believe that all slaves in the United States, will in time be emancipated, in a manner most consistent with their own happiness, and the true interest of their proprietors. Whether this will be effected by transporting them back to Africa; or by colonizing them in some part of our own territory, and extending to them our alliance and protection until they shall have acquired strength sufficient for their own defence; or by incorporation with the whites; or in some other way, remains to be determined. All these methods are attended with difficulties. The first would be cruel; the second dangerous; and the latter disagreeable and unnatural. Deep-rooted prejudices entertained by the whites; ten thousand recollections, by the blacks, of the injuries they have sustained; new provocations; the real distinction which nature has made; besides many other circumstances which would tend to divide them into parties, and produce convulsions, are objections against retaining and incorporating the blacks with the citizens of the several states. But justice and humanity demand that these difficulties should be surmounted.

In the middle and northern States, there are comparatively but few slaves; and of course there is less difficulty in giving them their freedom. Societies for the manumission of slaves, have been instituted in Philadelphia and New-York; and laws have been enacted, and other measures taken in the New-England states to accomplish the same purpose. The Friends, (commonly called Quakers,) have evinced the propriety of their name, by their goodness in originating, and their vigorous exertions in executing, this truly humane and benevolent design.

The English language is the one which is universally spoken in the United States, in which business is transacted, and the records kept. It is spoken with great purity, and pronounced with propriety in New-England, by persons of education; and, excepting some few corruptions in pronunciation, by all ranks of people. In the middle and southern States, where they have had a great influx of foreigners, the language in many instances is corrupted, especially in pronunciation. Attempts are making to introduce a uniformity of pronunciation throughout the States, which for political, as well as other reasons, it is hoped will meet the approbation and encouragement of all literary and influential characters.

Intermingled with the Anglo-Americans, are the Dutch, Scotch, Irish, French, Germans, Swedes and Jews; all these, except the Scotch and Irish, retain, in a greater or less degree, their native language, in which they perform their public worship, converse and transact their business with each other.

The time, however, is anticipated when all distinctions between master and slave shall be abolished; and when the language, manners, customs, political and religious sentiments of the mixed mass of people who inhabit the United States, shall have become so assimilated, as that all nominal distinctions shall be lost in the general and honourable name of AMERICANS.

Government.] Until the fourth of July, 1776, the present Thirteen States were British colonies. On that memorable day, the Representatives of the United States of America, in Congress assembled, made a solemn declaration, in which they assigned their reasons for withdrawing their allegiance from the king of Great Britain. Appealing to the Supreme Judge of the world for the rectitude of their intentions, they did, in the name and by the authority of the good people of the colonies, solemnly publish and declare, That these United Colonies were, and of right ought to be FREE and INDEPENDENT States; that they were absolved from all allegiance to the British crown, and that all political connection between them and Great Britain was, and ought to be totally dissolved; and that as Free and Independent States, they had full power to levy war, conclude peace, contract alliances, establish commerce and do all other acts and things which Independent States may of right do. For the support of this declaration, with a firm reliance on the protection of divine providence, the delegates then in Congress, fifty-five in number, mutually pledged to each other their lives, their fortunes, and their sacred honor.

At the same time they published articles of Confederation and Perpetual Union between the States, in which they took the style of " THE UNITED STATES OF AMERICA," and agreed that each state should retain its sovereignty, freedom, and independence, and every power, jurisdiction and right not expressly delegated to Congress by the confederation. By these articles the thirteen United States severally entered into a firm league of friendship with each other for their common defence, the security of their liberties, and their mutual and general welfare; and bound themselves to assist each other, against all force offered to, or attacks that might be made upon all, or any of them on account of religion, sovereignty, commerce or any other pretence whatever. But for the more convenient management of the general interests of the United States, it was determined that Delegates should be annually appointed, in such manner as the Legislature of each State should direct, to meet in Congress the first Monday in November of every year, with a power reserved to each state to recall its delegates or any of them at any time within the year, and to

send

The UNITED STATES.

send others in their stead for the remainder of the year. No state was to be represented in Congress by less than two, or more than seven members; and no person could be a delegate for more than three years, in any term of six years; nor was any person, being a delegate, capable of holding any office under the United States, for which he, or any other for his benefit, should receive any salary, fees, or emolument of any kind. In determining questions in Congress, each state was to have one vote. Every state was bound to abide by the determination of Congress, in all questions which were submitted to them by the confederation. The articles of confederation were to be invariably observed by every state, and the union to be perpetual; nor was any alteration at any time hereafter to be made in any of the articles, unless such alterations be agreed to in Congress, and be afterwards confirmed by the legislatures of every state. The articles of confederation were ratified by Congress, July 9, 1778.

These articles of confederation, after eleven years experience, being found inadequate to the purposes of a fœderal government, for reasons hereafter mentioned, delegates were chosen in each of the United States, to meet and fix upon the necessary amendments. They accordingly met in convention at Philadelphia, in the summer of 1787, and agreed to propose the following constitution for the consideration of their constituents:

WE, the People of the United States, in order to form a more perfect union, establish justice, insure domestic tranquility, provide for the common defence, promote the general welfare, and secure the blessings of liberty to ourselves and our posterity, do ordain and establish this Constitution for the United States of America.

ARTICLE I.

Sect. 1. ALL legislative powers herein granted shall be vested in a Congress of the United States, which shall consist of a Senate and house of Representatives.

Sect. 2. The House of Representatives shall be composed of members chosen every second year by the people of the several states, and the electors in each state shall have the qualifications requisite for electors of the most numerous branch of the state legislature.

No person shall be a representative who shall not have attained to the age of twenty-five years, and been seven years a citizen of the United States, and who shall not, when elected, be an inhabitant of that state in which he shall be chosen.

Representatives and direct taxes shall be apportioned among the several states which may be included within this Union, according to their respective numbers, which shall be determined by adding to the whole number of free persons, including those bound to service for a term of years, and excluding Indians not taxed, three fifths of all other persons. The actual enumeration shall be made within three years after the first meeting of the Congress of the United States, and within every subsequent term of ten years, in such manner as they shall by law direct. The number of representatives shall not exceed one for every thirty thousand, but each state shall have at least one representative; and until such enumeration shall be made, the state of New-Hampshire shall be entitled to

choose

choose three, Massachusetts eight, Rhode Island and Providence Plantations one, Connecticut five, New-York six, New-Jersey four, Pennsylvania eight, Delaware one, Maryland six, Virginia ten, North-Carolina five, South-Carolina five, and Georgia three.

When vacancies happen in the representation from any state, the Executive authority thereof shall issue writs of election to fill such vacancies.

The House of Representatives shall choose their Speaker and other officers; and shall have the sole power of impeachment.

Sect. 3. The Senate of the United States shall be composed of two senators from each state, chosen by the legislature thereof, for six years; and each senator shall have one vote.

Immediately after they shall be assembled in consequence of the first election, they shall be divided as equally as may be into three classes. The seats of the senators of the first class shall be vacated at the expiration of the second year, of the second class at the expiration of the fourth year, and of the third class at the expiration of the sixth year, so that one third may be chosen every second year; and if vacancies happen by resignation, or otherwise, during the recess of the legislature of any state, the executive thereof may make temporary appointments until the next meeting of the legislature which shall then fill such vacancies.

No person shall be a senator who shall not have attained to the age of thirty years, and been nine years a citizen of the United States, and who shall not, when elected, be an inhabitant of that state for which he shall be chosen.

The vice-president of the United States shall be president of the senate, but shall have no vote, unless they be equally divided.

The senate shall choose their other officers, and also a president pro tempore, in the absence of the vice-president, or when he shall exercise the office of president of the United States.

The senate shall have the sole power to try all impeachments. When sitting for that purpose, they shall be on oath or affirmation. When the president of the United States is tried, the chief justice shall preside: And no person shall be convicted without the concurrence of two thirds of the members present.

Judgment in cases of impeachment shall not extend further than to removal from office, and disqualification to hold and enjoy any office of honor, trust or profit under the United States; but the party convicted shall nevertheless be liable and subject to indictment, trial, judgment and punishment, according to law.

Sect. 4. The times, places and manner of holding elections for senators and representatives, shall be prescribed in each state by the legislature thereof; but the Congress may at any time by law make or alter such regulations, except as to the places of chusing senators.

The Congress shall assemble at least once in every year, and such meeting shall be on the first Monday in December, unless they shall by law appoint a different day.

Sect. 5. Each house shall be the judge of the elections, returns and qualifications of its own members, and a majority of each shall constitute a quorum to do business; but a smaller number may adjourn from day to day, and may be authorised to compel the attendance of absent members,

members, in such manner, and under such penalties as each house may provide.

Each house may determine the rules of its proceedings, punish its members for disorderly behaviour, and, with the concurrence of two-thirds, expel a member.

Each house shall keep a journal of its proceedings, and from time to time publish the same, excepting such parts as may in their judgment require secrecy; and the yeas and nays of the members of either house on any question shall, at the desire of one-fifth of those present, be entered on the journal.

Neither house, during the session of Congress, shall, without the consent of the other, adjourn for more than three days, nor to any other place than that in which the two houses shall be sitting.

Sect. 6. The senators and representatives shall receive a compensation for their services, to be ascertained by law, and paid out of the treasury of the United States. They shall in all cases, except treason, felony and breach of peace, be privileged from arrest during their attendance at the session of their respective houses, and in going to and returning from the same; and for any speech or debate in either house, they shall not be questioned in any other place.

No senator or representative shall, during the time for which he was elected, be appointed to any civil office under the authority of the United States, which shall have been created, or the emoluments whereof shall have been encreased during such time; and no person holding any office under the United States, shall be a member of either house during his continuance in office.

Sect. 7. All bills for raising revenue shall originate in the house of representatives; but the senate may propose or concur with amendments as on other bills.

Every bill which shall have passed the house of representatives and the senate, shall, before it becomes a law, be presented to the president of the United States; if he approve he shall sign it, but if not he shall return it, with his objections to that house in which it shall have originated, who shall enter the objections at large on their journal, and proceed to re-consider it. If after such re-consideration two-thirds of that house shall agree to pass the bill, it shall be sent, together with the objections, to the other house, by which it shall likewise be re-considered, and if approved by two-thirds of that house it shall become a law. But in all such cases the votes of both houses shall be determined by yeas and nays, and the names of the persons voting for and against the bill shall be entered on the journal of each house respectively. If any bill shall not be returned by the President within ten days, (Sundays excepted) after it shall have been presented to him, the same shall be a law, in like manner as if he had signed it, unless the Congress by their adjournment prevent its return, in which case it shall not be a law.

Every order, resolution, or vote to which the concurrence of the Senate and House of Representatives may be necessary (except on a question of adjournment) shall be presented to the President of the United States; and before the same shall take effect, shall be approved by him, or, being disapproved by him, shall be re-passed by two-thirds of the Senate and House

of

The UNITED STATES.

of Reprefentatives, according to the rules and limitations prefcribed in the cafe of a bill.

Sect. 8. The Congrefs fhall have power

To lay and collect taxes, duties, impofts and excifes; to pay the debts and provide for the common defence and general welfare of the United States; but all duties, impofts and excifes fhall be uniform throughout the United States;

To borrow money on the credit of the United States;

To regulate commerce with foreign nations, and among the feveral ftates, and with the Indian tribes;

To eftablifh an uniform rule of naturalization, and uniform laws on the fubject of bankruptcies throughout the United States;

To coin money, regulate the value thereof, and of foreign coin, and fix the ftandard of weights and meafures;

To provide for the punifhment of counterfeiting the fecurities and current coin of the United States;

To eftablifh poft offices and poft roads;

To promote the progrefs of fcience and ufeful arts, by fecuring for limited times to authors and inventors the exclufive right to their refpective writings and difcoveries;

To conftitute tribunals inferior to the fupreme court;

To define and punifh piracies and felonies committed on the high feas, and offences againft the law of nations;

To declare war, grant letters of marque and reprifal, and make rules concerning captures on land and water;

To raife and fupport armies, but no appropriation of money to that ufe fhall be for a longer term than two years;

To provide and maintain a navy;

To make rules for the government and regulation of the land and naval forces;

To provide for calling forth the militia to execute the laws of the union, fupprefs infurrections, and repel invafions;

To provide for organizing, arming, and difciplining the militia, and for governing fuch part of them as may be employed in the fervice of the United States, referving to the ftates refpectively, the appointment of the officers, and the authority of training the militia according to the difcipline prefcribed by Congrefs;

To exercife exclufive legiflation in all cafes whatfoever, over fuch diftrict (not exceeding ten miles fquare) as may, by ceffion of particular ftates, and the acceptance of Congrefs, become the feat of government of the United States, and to exercife like authority over all places purchafed by the confent of the legiflature of the ftate in which the fame fhall be, for the erection of forts, magazines, arfenals, dockyards, and other needful buildings;—And

To make all laws which fhall be neceffary and proper for carrying into execution the foregoing powers, and all other powers vefted by this conftitution in the government of the United States, or in any department or officer thereof.

Sect. 9. The migration or importation of fuch perfons as any of the ftates now exifting fhall think proper to admit, fhall not be prohibited by
the

the Congress prior to the year one thousand eight hundred and eight, but a tax or duty may be imposed on such importation, not exceeding ten dollars for each person.

The privilege of the writ of habeas corpus shall not be suspended, unless when in cases of rebellion or invasion the public safety may require it.

No bill of attainder or ex post facto law shall be passed.

No capitation, or other direct tax, shall be laid, unless in proportion to the census or enumeration herein before directed to be taken.

No tax or duty shall be laid on articles exported from any state.—No preference shall be given by any regulation of commerce or revenue to the ports of one state over those of another: nor shall vessels bound to, or from, one state, be obliged to enter, clear, or pay duties in another.

No money shall be drawn from the treasury, but in consequence of appropriations made by law; and a regular statement and account of the receipts and expenditures of all public money shall be published from time to time.

No title of nobility shall be granted by the United States:—And no person holding any office of profit or trust under them, shall, without the consent of the Congress, accept of any present, emolument, office or title, of any kind whatever, from any king, prince, or foreign state.

Sect. 10. No state shall enter into any treaty, alliance, or confederation; grant letters of marque and reprisal; coin money; emit bills of credit; make any thing but gold and silver coin a tender in payment of debts; pass any bill of attainder, ex post facto law, or law impairing the obligation of contracts, or grant any title of nobility.

No State shall, without the consent of the Congress, lay any imposts or duties on imports or exports, except what may be absolutely necessary for executing its inspection laws; and the net produce of all duties and imposts, laid by any state on imports or exports, shall be for the use of the Treasury of the United States; and all such laws shall be subject to the revision and controul of the Congress. No state shall, without the consent of Congress, lay any duty of tonnage, keep troops, or ships of war in time of peace, enter into any agreement or compact with another state, or with a foreign power, or engage in war, unless actually invaded, or in such imminent danger as will not admit of delay.

A R T I C L E II.

Sect. 1. The executive power shall be vested in a president of the United States of America. He shall hold his office during the term of four years, and, together with the vice-president, chosen for the same term, be elected as follows:

Each state shall appoint, in such manner as the legislature thereof may direct, a number of electors equal to the whole number of senators and representatives to which the state may be entitled in the Congress: but no senator or representative, or person holding an office of trust or profit under the United States, shall be appointed an elector.

The electors shall meet in their respective states, and vote by ballot for two persons of whom one at least shall not be an inhabitant of the same state with themselves. And they shall make a list of all the persons voted for,

for, and of the number of votes for each; which list they shall sign and certify, and transmit sealed to the seat of the government of the United States, directed to the president of the senate. The president of the senate shall, in the presence of the senate and house of representatives, open all the certificates, and all the votes shall then be counted. The person having the greatest number of votes shall be the president, if such number be a majority of the whole number of electors appointed; and if there be more than one who have such majority, and have an equal number of votes, then the house of representatives shall immediately choose by ballot one of them for president; and if no person have a majority, then from the five highest on the list the said house shall in like manner choose the president. But in choosing the president, the votes shall be taken by states, the representations from each state having one vote; a quorum for this purpose shall consist of a member or members from two-thirds of the states, and a majority of all the states shall be necessary to a choice. In every case, after the choice of the president, the person having the greatest number of votes of the electors shall be the vice-president. But if there should remain two or more who have equal votes, the senate shall choose from them by ballot the vice-president.

The Congress may determine the time of choosing the electors, and the day on which they shall give their votes; which day shall be the same throughout the United States.

No person except a natural born citizen, or a citizen of the United States, at the time of the adoption of this constitution, shall be eligible to the office of president; neither shall any person be eligible to that office who shall not have attained to the age of thirty-five years, and been fourteen years a resident within the United States.

In case of the removal of the president from office, or of his death, resignation, or inability to discharge the powers and duties of the said office, the same shall devolve on the vice-president, and the Congress may by law provide for the case of removal, death, resignation or inability, both of the president and vice-president, declaring what officer shall then act as president, and such officer shall act accordingly, until the disability be removed, or a president shall be elected.

The president shall, at stated times, receive for his services, a compensation, which shall neither be encreased nor diminished during the period for which he shall have been elected, and he shall not receive within that period any other emolument from the United States, or any of them.

Before he enter on the execution of his office, he shall take the following oath or affirmation:

"I do solemnly swear (or affirm) that I will faithfully execute the office of president of the United States, and will to the best of my ability, preserve, protect and defend the constitution of the United States."

Sect. 2. The president shall be commander in chief of the army and navy of the United States, and of the militia of the several states, when called into the actual service of the United States; he may require the opinion in writing, of the principal officer in each of the executive departments upon any subject relating to the duties of their respective offices, and he shall have power to grant reprieves and pardons for offences against the United States, except in cases of impeachment.

He

The UNITED STATES. 75

He shall have power, by and with the advice and consent of the senate, to make treaties, provided two-thirds of the senators present concur; and he shall nominate, and by and with the advice and consent of the senate shall appoint ambassadors, other public ministers and consuls, judges of the supreme court, and all other officers of the United States, whose appointments are not herein otherwise provided for, and which shall be established by law. But the Congress may by law vest the appointment of such inferior officers, as they think proper, in the president alone, in the courts of law, or in the heads of departments.

The president shall have power to fill up all vacancies that may happen during the recess of the senate, by granting commissions which shall expire at the end of their next session.

Sect. 3. He shall from time to time give to the Congress information of the state of the union, and recommend to their consideration such measures as he shall judge necessary and expedient; he may, on extraordinary occasions, convene both houses, or either of them, and in case of disagreement between them, with respect to the time of adjournment, he may adjourn them to such time as he shall think proper; he shall receive ambassadors and other public ministers; he shall take care that the laws be faithfully executed, and shall commission all the officers of the United States.

Sect. 4. The president, vice-president and all civil officers of the United States, shall be removed from office on impeachment for, and conviction of, treason, bribery, or other high crimes and misdemeanors.

Article III.

Sect. 1. The Judicial power of the United States shall be vested in one supreme court, and in such inferior courts as the Congress may from time to time ordain and establish. The judges, both of the supreme and inferior courts, shall hold their offices during good behaviour, and shall, at stated times, receive for their services, a compensation, which shall not be diminished during their continuance in office.

Sect. 2. The Judicial power shall extend to all cases, in law and equity, arising under this constitution, the laws of the United States, and treaties made, or which shall be made, under their authority; to all cases affecting ambassadors, other public ministers and consuls; to all cases of admiralty and maritime jurisdiction; to controversies to which the United States shall be a party; to controversies between two or more states, between a state and citizens of another state, between citizens of different states, between citizens of the same state claiming lands under grants of different states, and between a state, or the citizens thereof, and foreign states, citizens or subjects.

In all cases affecting ambassadors, other public ministers and consuls, and those in which a state shall be party, the supreme court shall have original jurisdiction. In all the other cases before mentioned, the supreme court shall have appellate jurisdiction, both as to law and fact, with such exceptions, and under such regulations as the Congress shall make.

The trial of all crimes, except in cases of impeachment, shall be by jury; and such trial shall be held in the state where the said crime shall have been committed; but when not committed within any state, the trial shall be at such place or places as the Congress may by law have directed.

Sect.

Sect. 3. Treason against the United States, shall consist only in levying war against them, or in adhering to their enemies, giving them aid and comfort. No person shall be convicted of treason unless on the testimony of two witnesses to the same overt act, or on confession in open court.

The Congress shall have power to declare the punishment of treason, but no attainder of treason shall work corruption of blood, or forfeiture, except during the life of the person attainted.

Article IV.

Sect. 1. Full faith and credit shall be given in each state to the public acts, records, and judicial proceedings of every other state. And the Congress may by general laws prescribe the manner in which such acts, records and proceedings shall be proved, and the effect thereof.

Sect. 2. The citizens of each state shall be entitled to all privileges and immunities of citizens in the several states.

A person charged in any state with treason, felony, or other crime, who shall flee from justice, and be found in another state, shall on demand of the executive authority of the state from which he fled be delivered up, to be removed to the state having jurisdiction of the crime.

No person held to service or labour in one state, under the laws thereof, escaping into another, shall in consequence of any law or regulation therein, be discharged from such service or labour, but shall be delivered up on claim of the party to whom such service or labour may be due.

Sect. 3. New states may be admitted by the Congress into this union, but no new state shall be formed or erected within the jurisdiction of any other state; nor any state be formed by the junction of two or more states, or parts of states, without the consent of the legislatures of the states concerned as well as of the Congress.

The Congress shall have power to dispose of and make all needful rules and regulations respecting the territory or other property belonging to the United States; and nothing in this constitution shall be so construed as to prejudice any claims of the United States, or of any particular state.

Sect. 4. The United States shall guarantee to every state in this union a republican form of government, and shall protect each of them against invasion; and on application of the legislature, or of the executive (when the legislature cannot be convened) against domestic violence.

Article V.

The Congress, whenever two thirds of both houses shall deem it necessary, shall propose amendments to this constitution, or, on the application of the legislatures of two thirds of the several states, shall call a convention for proposing amendments, which, in either case, shall be valid to all intents and purposes, as part of this constitution, when ratified by the legislatures of three fourths of the several states, or by conventions in three fourths thereof, as the one or the other mode of ratification may be proposed by the Congress: Provided, that no amendment which may be made prior to the year one thousand eight hundred and eight, shall in any manner affect the first and fourth clauses in the ninth section of the first article; and that no state, without its consent, shall be deprived of its equal suffrage in the Senate. Article

THE UNITED STATES.

ARTICLE VI.

All debts contracted and engagements entered into, before the adoption of this constitution, shall be as valid against the United States under this constitution, as under the confederation.

This constitution, and the laws of the United States which shall be made in pursuance thereof; and all treaties made, or which shall be made, under the authority of the United States, shall be the supreme law of the land; and the judges in every state shall be bound thereby, any thing in the constitution or laws of any state to the contrary notwithstanding.

The senators and representatives before mentioned, and the members of the several state legislatures, and all executive and judicial officers, both of the United States and of the several states, shall be bound by oath or affirmation, to support this constitution; but no religious test shall ever be required as a qualification to any office or public trust under the United States.

ARTICLE VII.

The ratification of the conventions of nine states, shall be sufficient for the establishment of this constitution between the states so ratifying the same.

DONE in Convention, by the unanimous consent of the states present, the seventeenth day of September, in the year of our Lord One Thousand Seven Hundred and Eighty-seven, and of the Independence of the United States of America the Twelfth. In Witness whereof, we have hereunto subscribed our names.

GEORGE WASHINGTON, *President.*
Signed also by all the Delegates which were present from twelve States.
Attest. WILLIAM JACKSON, *Secretary.*

In CONVENTION, Monday September 17, 1787.
PRESENT,
The States of New-Hampshire, Massachusetts, Connecticut, Mr. Hamilton from New-York, New-Jersey, Pennsylvania, Delaware, Maryland, Virginia, North-Carolina, South-Carolina and Georgia.

Resolved,

THAT the preceding constitution be laid before the United States in Congress assembled, and that it is the opinion of this Convention, that it should afterwards be submitted to a convention of Delegates, chosen in each state by the people thereof, under the recommendation of its Legislature, for their assent and ratification; and that each convention assenting to, and ratifying the same, should give notice thereof to the United States in Congress assembled.

RESOLVED, That it is the opinion of this convention, that as soon as the conventions of nine states shall have ratified this constitution, the United States in Congress assembled, should fix a day on which Electors should be appointed by the states which shall have ratified the same, and a day on which the Electors should assemble to vote for the President, and the time and place for commencing proceedings under this constitution. That after such publication, the Electors should be appointed, and

the

The UNITED STATES.

the senators and representatives elected: That the electors should meet on the day fixed for the election of the President, and should transmit their votes certified, signed, sealed and directed, as the constitution requires, to the Secretary of the United States in Congress assembled; that the senators and representatives should convene at the time and place assigned; that the senators should appoint a President of the senate, for the sole purpose of receiving, opening and counting the votes for President; and, that after he shall be chosen, the Congress, together with the President, should, without delay, proceed to execute this Constitution.

By the unanimous order of the Convention,
GEORGE WASHINGTON, *President.*
WILLIAM JACKSON, *Secretary.*

In CONVENTION, *September* 17, 1787.

SIR,

WE have now the honour to submit to the consideration of the United States in Congress assembled, that constitution which has appeared to us the most advisable.

The friends of our country have long seen and desired, that the power of making war, peace and treaties, that of levying money and regulating commerce, and the correspondent executive and judicial authorities should be fully and effectually vested in the general government of the union; but the impropriety of delegating such an extensive trust to one body of men is evident.—Hence results the necessity of a different organization.

It is obviously impracticable in the federal government of these states, to secure all rights of independent sovereignty to each, and yet provide for the interest and safety of all.—Individuals entering into society, must give up a share of liberty to preserve the rest. The magnitude of the sacrifice must depend as well on situation and circumstances, as on the object to be obtained. It is at all times difficult to draw with precision the line between those rights which must be surrendered, and those which may be reserved; and on the present occasion this difficulty was encreased by a difference among the several states as to their situation, extent, habits and particular interests.

In all our deliberations on this subject, we kept steadily in our view, that which appears to us the greatest interest of every true American, the consolidation of our union, in which is involved our prosperity, felicity, safety, perhaps our national existence. This important consideration, seriously and deeply impressed on our minds, led each state in the convention to be less rigid on points of inferior magnitude, than might have been otherwise expected; and thus the constitution, which we now present, is the result of a spirit of amity, and of that mutual deference and concession which the peculiarity of our political situation rendered indispensible.

That it will meet the full and entire approbation of every state is not perhaps to be expected; but each will doubtless consider that had her interests been alone consulted, the consequences might have been particularly disagreeable or injurious to others: That it is liable to as few exceptions as could reasonably have been expected, we hope and believe: That it it may promote the lasting welfare of that country so dear to us all, and secure her freedom and happiness, is our most ardent wish.

With great respect, we have the honour to be, Sir, Your Excellency's most obedient, and humble servants,

GEORGE WASHINGTON, *President*.
By unanimous order of the Convention.

His Excellency the President of Congress.

ELEVEN states having already ratified the above constitution, Congress, agreeably to the seventh article, have taken the proper measures for its organization and establishment between the ratifying states.

Society of the Cincinnati.] This society has made so much noise both in Europe and America, and has derived such dignity and importance from the characters who compose it, that it is thought proper to insert the institution at large, for the information of the uninformed, and for the gratification of the respectable members of the Cincinnati, who wish to have their friendly and charitable intentions fully understood by all classes of their fellow citizens.

The INSTITUTION of the SOCIETY of the CINCINNATI, as altered and amended at their first general meeting at Philadelphia, May, 1784.

' IT having pleased the supreme governor of the universe to give success to the arms of our country, and to establish the United States free and independent : Therefore, gratefully to commemorate this event,— to inculcate to the latest ages the duty of laying down in peace, arms assumed for public defence, by forming an institution which recognizes that most important principle,—to continue the mutual friendships which commenced under the pressure of common danger, and to effectuate the acts of beneficence, dictated by the spirit of brotherly kindness, towards those officers and their families, who unfortunately may be under the necessity of receiving them ; the officers of the American army do hereby constitute themselves into *A society of friends* : and, possessing the highest veneration for the character of that illustrious Roman, *Lucius Quintius Cincinnatus*, denominate themselves THE SOCIETY OF THE CINCINNATI.

Sect. I. ' The persons who constitute this society, are all the commissioned and brevet officers of the army and navy of the United States, who have served three years, and who left the service with reputation ; all officers who were in actual service at the conclusion of the war ; all the principal staff officers of the continental army ; and the officers who have been deranged by the several resolutions of Congress, upon the different reforms of the army.

Sect. II. ' There are also admitted into this society, the late and present ministers of his most christian majesty to the United States ; all the generals and colonels of regiments and legions of the land forces ; all the admirals and captains of the navy, ranking as colonels, who have co-operated with the armies of the United States in their exertions for liberty; and such other persons as have been admitted by the respective state-meetings.

Sect.

Sect. III. 'The society shall have a president, vice-president, secretary, and assistant-secretary.

Sect. IV. 'There shall be a meeting of the society, at least once in three years, on the first Monday in May, at such place as the president shall appoint.

'The said meeting shall consist of the aforesaid officers (whose expences shall be equally borne by the state funds) a representation from each state.

'The business of this general meeting shall be,—to regulate the distribution of surplus funds;—to appoint officers for the ensuing term—and to conform the bye-laws of state-meetings to the general objects of the institution.

Sect. V. 'The society shall be divided into state-meetings: each meeting shall have a president, vice-president, secretary and treasurer, respectively to be chosen by a majority of votes annually.

Sect. VI. 'The state meetings shall be on the anniversary of independence. They shall concert such measures as may conduce to the benevolent purposes of the society; and the several state-meetings shall, at suitable periods, make application to their respective legislatures for grants of charters.

Sect. VII. 'Any member removing from one state to another, is to be considered, in all respects, as belonging to the meeting of the state in which he shall actually reside.

Sect. VIII. 'The state-meeting shall judge of the qualification of its members, admonish, and (if necessary) expel any one who may conduct himself unworthily.

Sect. IX. 'The secretary of each state-meeting shall register the names of the members resident in each state, and transmit a copy thereof to the secretary of the society.

Sect. X. 'In order to form funds for the relief of unfortunate members, their widows and orphans, each officer shall deliver to the treasurer of the state-meeting, one month's pay.

Sect. XI. 'No donation shall be received but from the citizens of the United States.

Sect. XII. 'The funds of each state-meeting shall be loaned to the state, by permission of the legislature, and the interest only, annually to be applied for the purposes of the society; and if, in process of time, difficulties should occur in executing the intentions of this society, the legislatures of the several states shall be entitled to make such equitable disposition as may be most correspondent with the original design of the constitution.

Sect. XIII. 'The subjects of his most Christian majesty, members of this society, may hold meetings at their pleasure, and form regulations for their police, conformable to the objects of the institution, and to the spirit of their government.

Sect. XIV. 'The society shall have an order; which shall be a bald eagle of gold, bearing on its breast the emblems described in the note,* suspended

---

* 'The principal figure to be Cincinnatus, three senators presenting him with

THE UNITED STATES.

suspended by a deep blue riband edged with white, descriptive of the union of America and France.

The motives which originally induced the officers of the American army to form themselves into a society of friends, are summed up in a masterly manner in their circular letter. 'Having,' say they, 'lived in the strictest habits of amity through the various stages of a war, unparalleled in many of its circumstances; having seen the objects for which we have contended, happily attained; in the moment of triumph and separation, when we were about to act the last pleasing melancholy scene in our military drama—pleasing, because we were to leave our country possessed of independence and peace—melancholy, because we were to part, perhaps never to meet again; while every breast was penetrated with feelings which can be more easily conceived than described; while every little act of tenderness recurred fresh to the recollection, it was impossible not to wish our friendships should be continued; it was extremely natural to desire they might be perpetuated by our posterity to the remotest ages. With these impressions, and with such sentiments, we candidly confess we signed the institution.—We know our motives were irreproachable.'

They rest their institution upon the two great pillars of FRIENDSHIP and CHARITY. Their benevolent intentions are, to diffuse comfort and support to any of their unfortunate companions who have seen better days, and merited a milder fate; to wipe the tear from the eye of the widow, who must have been consigned, with her helpless infants, to indigence and wretchedness, but for this charitable institution—to succour the fatherless—to rescue the female orphan from destruction, and to enable the son to emulate the virtues of the father. 'Let us then,' they conclude, 'prosecute with ardor what we have instituted in sincerity; let Heaven and our own consciences approve our conduct; let our actions be our best comment on our words; and let us leave a lesson to posterity, THAT THE GLORY OF SOLDIERS CANNOT BE COMPLETED WITHOUT ACTING WELL THE PART OF CITIZENS.'

Agriculture, Commerce and Manufactures.] The two important objects of attention in the United States, are agriculture and commerce. The richness of the soil, which amply rewards the industrious husbandman; the temperature of the climate, which admits of steady labour; the cheapness of land, which tempts the foreigner from his native home, lead us to fix on agriculture as the great leading interest of this country. This furnishes outward cargoes not only for all our own ships, but for those also which foreign nations send to our ports; or in other words, it pays for all our importations; it supplies a great part of the clothing of the inhabitants, and food for them and their cattle. What is consumed at home,

with a sword and other military ensigns: On a field in the back ground his wife standing at the door of their cottage; near it a plough and other instruments of husbandry. Round the whole omnia reliquit servare rempublicam. *On the reverse, the sun rising, a city with open gates, and vessels entering the port; fame crowning* Cincinnatus *with a wreath, inscribed,* virtutis præmium. *Below, hands joining, supporting a heart; with the motto,* esto perpetua. *Round the whole,* societas Cincinnatorum, instituta, A. D. 1783.

home, including the materials for manufacturing, is four or five times the value of what is exported.

The number of people employed in agriculture, is at least nine parts in ten of the inhabitants of the United States. It follows of course that they form the body of the militia, who are the bulwark of the nation. The value of the property occupied by agriculture, is many times greater than the property employed in every other way. The settlement of waste lands, the subdivision of farms, and the numerous improvements in husbandry, annually increase the pre-eminence of the agricultural interest. The resources we derive from it, are at all times certain and indispensibly necessary. Besides, the rural life promotes health, by its active nature, and morality, by keeping people from the luxuries and vices of the populous towns. In short, agriculture is the spring of our commerce, and the parent of our manufactures.

The vast extent of sea coast, which spreads before these confederated states; the number of excellent harbours and sea-port towns; the numerous creeks and immense bays, which indent the coast; and the rivers, lakes and canals, which peninsulate the whole country; added to its agricultural advantages and improvements, give this part of the world superior advantages for trade. Our commerce, including our exports, imports, shipping, manufactures and fisheries, may properly be considered as forming one interest. This has been considered as the great object, and the most important interest of the New England states; but erroneously, for according to the best calculations which have been made the proportion of property, and the number of men employed in manufactures, fisheries, navigation and trade, do not, even in this commercial part of the union, amount to one eighth of the property and people occupied in agriculture. In this estimate suitable deductions are made from the value and population of the large towns, for the idle and dissipated, for those who live upon their incomes, and for supernumerary domestic servants. But taking the union at large, the disproportion is much greater. The timber, iron, cordage, and many other articles necessary for building ships to fish or trade; nine parts in ten of their cargoes; the subsistence of the manufacturers, and a great part of their raw materials, are the produce of our lands.

Since commerce has ever been considered as the handmaid of agriculture, particularly in this country, where the agricultural interest so greatly predominates; and since neither can flourish without the other, policy and interest point out the necessity of such a system of commercial and agricultural regulations, as will originate and effectually preserve a proper connection and balance between them.

The consumption of fish, oil, whale-bone and other articles, obtained through the fisheries, in the towns and counties that are convenient to navigation, has become much greater than is generally supposed. It is computed that no less than five thousand barrels of mackarel, salmon, and pickled codfish, are vended annually in the city of Philadelphia: Add to them the dried fish, oil, spermaceti candles, whale-bone, &c. and it will be found that a little fleet of sloops and schooners are employed in the business. The number of coasting vessels entered at the custom-house of Philadelphia in the year 1785, was five hundred and sixty-seven; all the

other

The UNITED STATES.

other entries of sea veffels in the fame year were five hundred and one. The demand for the forementioned articles is proportionably great in other parts of the union, (efpecially in Bofton and the large commercial towns that lie along the coaft north-eaftward, which enter largely into the fifhing trade,) and the veffels employed in tranfporting them proportionably numerous. The increafe of our towns and manufactures will increafe the demand for thefe articles, and of courfe the number of coafting veffels. In the prefent ftate of our navigation, we can be in no doubt of procuring thefe fupplies by means of our own veffels. This will afford encouragement to the bufinefs of fhip-building, and increafe the number of our feamen, who muft hereafter form an important part of the defence of our country. Add to thefe our profpects from the fur trade of Canada. The vaft fettlements which are making at Pittfburg and in other parts in the neighbourhood of Canada; the advantages of our inland navigation, by means of the lakes, the northern branches of the Ohio, the Patomak, the Sufquehannah and the Hudfon, with many other circumftances, depending not only on the fituation, but likewife on the climate, proximity, &c. muft in a few years put a large fhare of this fur trade into our hands, and procure us at leaft, our proportionable fhare of the large profits thence arifing, which Canada, fince the year 1763, has enjoyed almoft exclufively. Thefe advantages, however, are ftill but in profpect; and muft remain fo until the Britifh, agreeably to treaty, fhall have evacuated the forts at Niagara, the large fettlements of the Heights, and that of Michillimakinak. Although the Britifh, by the treaty of peace, are to enjoy with us the portages of the navigation of the lakes, yet fhould a difpute arife, it will not be convenient for them to contend with us; for the northern and north-eaftern parts of the continent included in the Britifh limits, are much colder, more mountainous, and poorer than the United States; and have no rivers, but fuch as are full of rapids and falls; confequently, this trade cannot be carried on by the Canadians with the fame facility nor advantage as by us. Still they will have left the exclufive right to the communication from Montreal, with the high-lands, through the large river of the Owtawas which flows into the river St. Lawrence at the lake of the two mountains, nine miles from that city; but its rapids, or rather its furies, and everlafting falls, will render this way, if not impracticable, at leaft always very expenfive and precarious.

The quantity of fur exported from the northern parts of America to Great Britain, have amounted yearly to about forty-one thoufand pounds fterling, eftimated from the freight during the years 1768, 1769 and 1770. The export of buck-fkins amounted to upwards of thirty-three thoufand pounds. The fales of fur, which take place in London every fpring, produced, in 1782, four thoufand feven hundred pounds. It was a little increafed in 1783, and in 1784 it exceeded two hundred and forty-five thoufand pounds. All this fur is paid for by Englifh manufactures; and a fourth part of it is worked in England, where its worth is doubled. This valuable trade, which is carried on through Quebec, muft unavoidably fall into our hands, as foon as the fortifications which the Britifh ftill poffefs in our northern territories fhall be reftored to us. To this confideration, rather than to the pretended compaffion for the Royalifts, may be be attributed the delay of that reftitution. The period when this reftitution *muft* be made, the Britifh anticipate with forrow. Such are fome of the commercial refources and profpects of this country.

But for various reafons, the advantages for trade which nature has fo liberally given us, have never yet been properly improved. Before the revolution, Great-Britain claimed an exclufive right to the trade of her American colonies. This right, which fhe inflexibly maintained, enabled her to fix her own price, as well on the articles which fhe purchafed from us, as upon thofe of her own manufactures exported for our confumption. The carrying trade too, was preferved almoft exclufively in her own hands, which afforded a temptation to the carriers, that was often too powerful to be withftood, to exact exorbitant commiffions and freights. Although we will not even hazard a conjecture how much Great-Britain enriched herfelf by this exclufive trade with her colonies, yet this we may fay, that by denying us the privilege of carrying our produce to foreign markets, fhe deprived us of the opportunity of realizing, in their full extent, the advantages for trade which nature has given us.

The late war, which brought about our feparation from Great-Britain, threw our commercial affairs into great confufion. The powers of our national government have hitherto been unequal to the complete execution of any meafures, calculated effectually to recover them from their deranged fituation. Through want of power in Congrefs to collect a revenue for the difcharge of our foreign and domeftic debt, our credit is deftroyed, and trade of confequence greatly embarraffed. Each ftate, hitherto, in her defultory regulations of trade, has regarded her own intereft, while that of the union has been neglected. And fo different are the interefts of the feveral ftates, that their laws refpecting trade, have often clafhed with each other, and been productive of unhappy confequences. The large commercial ftates have had it in their power to opprefs their neighbours; and in fome inftances this power has been directly or indirectly exercifed. Thefe impolitic and unjuftifiable regulations, formed on the impreffion of the moment, and proceeding from no uniform or permanent principles, have excited unhappy jealoufies between the clafhing ftates, and occafioned frequent ftagnations in their trade, and in fome inftances, a fecrecy in their commercial policy. This laft mentioned circumftance, together with the inconvenience in fome ftates, want of proper regulations in others, and impoffibility in the reft of preferving complete accounts of their annual exports and imports, render it impoffible, at prefent, to give fuch an accurate ftatement of the trade of the United States, as to determine on which fide the balance lies; whether for or againft us.

The Britifh parliament, too well acquainted with our deranged and defencelefs fituation, have improved the favourable juncture to fhackle our trade with every poffible embarraffment. In their late act for regulating the trade between the United States and the Weft-India Iflands, they have enacted, ' That no goods or commodities whatever fhall be imported or brought from any of the territories of the faid United States of America, into any of his majefty's Weft-India Iflands, (in which defcription the Bahama Iflands, and the Bermuda, or Somer's Iflands, are included) under penalty of the forfeiture thereof, and alfo of the fhip or veffel, in which

the

The UNITED STATES. 85

the fame fhall be fo imported or brought, together with all her guns, furniture, ammunition, tackle and apparel, except tobacco, pitch, tar, turpentine, hemp, flax, mafts, yards, bowfprits, ftaves, heading, boards, timber, fhingles, and lumber of any fort; horfes, neat cattle, fheep, hogs, poultry and live ftock of any fort; bread, bifcuit, flour, beans, peas, potatoes, wheat, rice, oats, barley, and grain of any fort; fuch commodities refpectively being the growth or production of any of the territories of the faid United States of America.'

None of thefe commodities enumerated, according to the act, are to be imported into any of the faid iflands from the United States, under the like forfeiture as above-mentioned, 'except by Britifh fubjects, in Britifh built fhips, owned by his majefty's fubjects, and navigated according to law.'

All fuch goods or commodities, as are not by law prohibited to be exported to any foreign country, may, by virtue of this act, be exported from the Weft-India Iflands, in Britifh veffels only, to any part of the United States. Salt from Turks Iflands is the only exception. This article may be brought away by American veffels going in ballaft, not otherwife, on paying a tonnage duty of two fhillings and fix-pence fterling for every ton.

This act alfo prohibits the importation of any of the forementioned articles, fuch as tobacco, pitch, tar, &c. into any ifland, under the dominion of his majefty, in the Weft-Indies, from any ifland in the Weft-Indies, under the dominion of any foreign European fovereign, or ftate, upon the penalty of the forfeiture of the veffel and cargo; except in cafes of public emergency and diftrefs.

The trade of the United States, carried with the provinces of Nova-Scotia, New-Brunfwick, the Iflands of Cape Breton, St. Johns, Newfoundland, and the province of Quebec, is fubject to the forementioned regulations and reftrictions. In regard to the province of Quebec, however, it muft be here obferved, that Lord.Dorchefter, in an ordinance iffued April 17, 1788, has enacted, ' That all goods, wares, and merchandifes (beaver, peltries and furs excepted) of the growth and manufacture or product of this province, or of any other the dominions of Great-Britain, and fuch as may lawfully be imported into this province by fea, may be exported therefrom by land or inland navigation, to any of the neighbouring ftates, free from duty, impoft or reftraint. And there fhall be the like freedom of importation from the faid ftates into this province, if the fame be made by the route or, communication of Lake Champlain and the river Sorel or Richelieu, and not otherwife, of the following enumerated articles, that is to fay, mafts, yards, bowfprits, fpars, plank, boards, knees, futtocks, or any kind of fhip-timber; hoops, ftaves, fhingles, clapboards, trees, wood, lumber, pitch, tar, turpentine, tallow, hemp, flax, and any kind of naval ftores; feeds, wheat, rye, indian corn, beans, peas, potatoes, rice, oats, barley, and all other grains; butter, cheefe, honey, horfes, neat cattle, fheep, hogs, poultry, and other live ftock, and live provifions, and frefh fifh; and whatfoever is of the growth of the faid ftates; and gold or filver coin or bullion.'

In this ordinance it is further enacted, ' That the importation by land or by inland navigation into this province, of rum, fpirits, copper coin,

and

and all other goods, wares and merchandifes not enumerated, be prohibited, and such articles fiezed and forfeited, together with every of the above enumerated articles, if the fame fhall not have been imported by the route or communication aforefaid.'

As a further embarraffment of our trade, Great Britain, in direct violation of the treaty of 1783, in which it was agreed, ' That his Britannic Majefty fhall, with all convenient fpeed, withdraw all his armies, garrifons and fleets, from the United States, and from every poft, place and harbour within the fame,' ftill retains our northern pofts, and thereby effectually deprives us of the large profits arifing from the fur trade.

This view of the prefent embarraffed ftate of our internal and foreign trade, points out the abfolute need we have of a government, invefted with powers adequate to the formation and execution of fuch a fyftem of commercial regulations, as will enable us to meet the oppofers of our trade upon their own ground; a fyftem which will render us refpectable at home and abroad; which will place our commerce upon a uniform and intelligible footing, and promote the general interefts of the union, with the fmalleft injury to the interefts of individual ftates. Such a fyftem may be hoped for, and rationally expected as one happy confequence of the newly eftablifhed Fœderal Government.

Our good and faithful allies and friends, the French, have been more liberal in their policy. In the arret, paffed in council December 29, 1787, for encouraging the commerce of France with the United States of America, it is ordained, That whale oil and fpermaceti, the produce of the fifheries of the United States, brought directly into France in French or American bottoms, fhall be fubject to a duty only of feven livres ten fols (equal to fix fhillings and three pence fterling,) the barrel of five hundred and twenty weight; and whale fins fhall be fubject to a duty of only fix livres thirteen fols and four deniers (equal to five fhillings and fix pence half penny,) the quintal, with ten fols per livre on each of the faid duties; which ten fols per livre fhall ceafe on the laft day of December, 1790.

The other fifh oils and dry falted fifh produced and imported as aforefaid, are not liable to pay any other or greater duties, than the moft favoured nations, are or fhall be fubject in the fame cafe.

Corn, wheat, rye, rice, peas, beans, lentils, flax-feed and other feeds, flour, trees and fhrubs, pot and pearl afhes, fkins, and fur of beaver, raw hides, furs and peltry, and timber carried from the United States to France in French or American bottoms, are fubject to a duty of one eighth per cent on their value. Veffels, proved to have been built in the United States, and fold in France, or purchafed by Frenchmen, are exempted from duties. Turpentine, tar and pitch, are liable to a duty of two and a half per cent on their value. Arms may be imported into the United States, in French or American veffels, on paying a duty of one eighth per cent. on their value; and gunpowder duty free by giving a cautionary bond. Books and papers of all forts imported as aforefaid, are to be exempted from all duties, and entitled to a reftitution of the fabrication duties on paper and pafte-board. Permiffion is given to ftore all productions and merchandize of the United States, for fix months, in all the ports of France open to the commerce of her colonies, fubject to a duty only of

one

one eighth per cent. His majesty reserves to himself the power of granting encouragement to favor the exportation of arms, hard ware, jewellery, bonnetry, wool, cotten, coarse woollens, small draperies and stuffs of cotton of all sorts, and other merchandize of French fabric, which may be sent to the United States.

As to other merchandizes not enumerated in this act, imported and exported in French or American vessels, and with respect to all commercial conventions whatever, his majesty ordains, ' That the citizens of the United States enjoy in France, the same rights, privileges and exemptions, with the subjects of his majesty ; saving what is provided in the ninth article hereof.*

' His majesty grants to the citizens and inhabitants of the United States all the advantages which are enjoyed, or which may be hereafter enjoyed by the most favoured nations in his colonies of America : and moreover his majesty ensures to the said citizens and inhabitants of the United States all the privileges and advantages which his own subjects of France enjoy or shall enjoy in Asia, and in the scales leading thereto, provided always, that their vessels shall have been fitted out and dispatched in some port of the United States.'

Such is the state of our commerce with France ; on which I would only observe, that the advantages which might naturally be expected to flow to the United States from their liberal privileges granted in the abovementioned act, are greatly lessened, in consequence of the same privileges having been granted to all foreigners.

In reviewing our agricultural and commercial advantages, those of manufactures must not be overlooked. Though it is confessed, that the United States have full employment for all their citizens in the extensive field of agriculture, yet since we have a valuable body of manufacturers already here, and many more will probably emigrate from Europe to enjoy the blessings of life, in this land of civil and religious liberty ; and since we have some poor citizens who are unable to make settlements on our waste lands, good policy, no doubt, will encourage these men to improve the great *natural powers* which this country possesses, for carrying on the manufacturing business.

These are the people to be employed in managing those factories which can be carried on by water mills, windmills, fire, horses, and ingeniously contrived machines ; which, as they require but few hands, do not divert

people

---

* The article referred to ordains that, ' The admiralty duties on the vessels of the United States entering into, or going out of the ports of France, shall not be levied but conformably with the edict of the month of June last, in the cases therein provided for, and with the letters patent of the tenth of January, 1770, for the objects for which no provision shall have been made by the said edict : his majesty reserving to himself moreover, to make known his intentions as to the manner in which the said duties shall be levied, whether in proportion to the tonnage of the vessels, or otherwise, as also to simplify the said duties of the admiralty, and to regulate them as far as shall be possible on the principles of reciprocity, as soon as the orders shall be completed, which were given by his majesty according to the twenty-sixth article of the said act of the month of June last.'

The UNITED STATES.

people from agriculture, and are not burdened with any heavy expence of boarding, lodging, cloathing and paying workmen. By wind and water machines we can make pig and bar iron, hallow ware and cannon shot, nail rods, tire, sheet-iron, sheet-copper, sheet-brafs and sheet-lead, anchors, meal of all kinds, gun-powder, writing, printing and hanging paper, snuff, linseed oil, boards plank and scantling; and they assist us in finishing scythes, sickles and woollen cloths. In the European factories, they also card, spin and weave by water. By means of water likewise, our bleaching and tanning businesses are carried on.

Breweries, which we cannot estimate too highly, distilleries, salt and pot-ash works, sugar houses, potteries, casting and steel furnaces, works for animal and vegetable oils and refining drugs, steam engines, and several other works are, or may be carried on by means of that powerful and useful element fire, and be attended with the same savings, that were particularized in speaking of water machines.

Horses grind the tanners bark, and potters clay; they work the brewers and distillers pumps; and, by an inventive mind, might be applied as the moving principle of many kinds of mills.

Machines ingenuously constructed will give us immense assistance. The cotton and silk manufacturers in Europe are possessed of some, that are invaluable to them. One instance has been precisely ascertained, which employs a few hundreds of women and children, and performs the work of TWELVE THOUSANDS of carders, spinners, and winders. They have been so curiously improved of late years, as to weave the most complicated manufactures. We may certainly borrow some of their inventions, and may strike out others of the same nature ourselves; for on the subject of mechanics, America may justly pride herself.

A very useful machine has lately been invented and made in Connecticut,[*] for the purpose of cutting and bending wire for card teeth; which will make thirty-six thousand in an hour. By a small improvement it may be made to cut double that number with equal ease. With this machine in its present form, a man, though blind, with a boy to tend the wire, might easily cut an hundred pounds of wire in a day. Consequently with the proposed improvement, they might cut two hundred pounds. The inventor of this, has several other useful manufacturing machines partly completed.

In short, every combination of machinery may be expected from a country, a NATIVE SON[*] of which, reaching this inestimable object in its highest point, has epitomised the motions of the spheres that roll throughout the universe.

The advantages which nature has given us for these manufactural improvements, have not been neglected; but in some states, particularly in Pennsylvania, New Jersey, Connecticut and Massachusetts, have been lately much improved. Still our manufactures will admit of being further pushed without interfering with the general interests of commerce

or

---

[*] By Mr. Ebenezer Chittendon of New Haven, an obscure mechanic, whose ingenuity and originality of genius entitle him to public notice and encouragement.

[*] David Rittenhouse, Esq; of Pennsylvania.

The UNITED STATES.

or agriculture; provided they are judiciously apportioned to, and encouraged in those states, which from nature, population and their internal resources, are best fitted to pursue them to advantage. In Georgia, South Carolina, North Carolina, Virginia and Maryland, where the people, considering the extensive territory which they inhabit, are comparatively few, tillage profitable, and provisions dear, must manufacture to an evident loss; while the advancement of this business in most of the northern states, which are full of inhabitants, and where provisions are cheap, and land dear, will afford the means of subsistence to many good citizens, whose occupations have been rendered unprofitable by the consequences of the revolution. In the former, full scope may be given to agriculture, leaving the benefits of manufacturing (so far as they are within our reach) to the latter. The produce of the southern states might be exchanged for such manufactures as can be made by the northern, to mutual advantage.

Some of our manufactories too, are made highly subservient to the interests of agriculture. The workers in leather of every kind, in flax and hemp, in iron, wood, stone and clay, in furs, horn, and many other articles employ either the spontaneous productions of the earth or the fruits of cultivation. Malt liquors too, if generally used, and it is a happy circumstance that they are becoming fashionable, linseed oil, starch, and corn spirits, were they not a poison to our morals and constitutions, would require more grain to make them than has been exported in any year since the revolution. And as grapes are the spontaneous production of all the United States, and by culture might be raised in any quantities, and in great perfection, particularly in the southern states, we may not omit to anticipate the time as not far distant, when we shall have it in our power to make wines of such quality, and in such quantities as to preclude all foreign importations. I cannot omit to observe here the impolicy, and I may add, immorality of importing and consuming such amazing quantities of spiritous liquors. They impair the estates, debilitate the bodies, and occasion the ruin of the morals of thousands of the citizens of America. They kill more people than any one disease, perhaps than all diseases besides. It cannot be then but that they are ruinous to our country.

It appears from the best calculations that can be obtained, that in the course of the years 1785, 1786, and 1787, TWELVE MILLIONS of dollars were expended by the United States, in purchasing West India spiritous liquors; and perhaps nearly half that sum for spirits distilled at home.

The expenditure of this immense sum, a sum which would well nigh cancel our whole national debt, so far from benefitting us, has entailed diseases, idleness, poverty, wretchedness and debt on thousands, who might otherwise have been healthy, independent in their circumstances and happy.

Experience has proved that spiritous liquors, except for certain medicinal uses, are altogether unnecessary. In the moderate use of wine, which is a generous and cheering liquor, and may be plentifully produced in our own country; of beer, which strengthens the arm of the labourer without debauching him; of cider, which is wholesome and palatable, and of molasses and water, which has become a fashionable drink, in the

M use

use of these liquors, labourers, and other people who have made the experiment, have been found to enjoy more health and better spirits than those who have made only a moderate use of spiritous liquors. The reason of this is made obvious by a careful calculation lately made, from which it appears that malt liquors, and several of the imported wines, are much more nourishing and cheaper than spirits. In a pint of beer, or half a pint of Malaga or Teneriffe wine, there is more strength than in a quart of rum. The beer and the wine abound with nourishment, whereas the rum has no more nourishment in it than a pound of air. These considerations point out the utility, may I not add, the necessity of confining ourselves to the use of our own home made liquors, that in this way we might encourage our own manufactures, promote industry, preserve the morals and lives of our citizens, and save our country from the enormous annual expence of four millions of dollars.

Another encouragement to promote regular factories of many kinds in suitable parts of the union, arises from the heavy charges of bringing European goods into our markets. The merchants commissions for shipping and the f me for selling, cost of packages, custom house papers in Europe, and the same with a duty of five per cent. here, porterages, freight, insurance, damage, interest of money, waste and loss on exchange; these may be rated at twenty-five per cent. on the finest and least bulky of our manufactures. This twenty-five per cent. which would be much greater on articles of a more bulky and weighty kind, is a solid premium, operating like a bounty to our manufacturers to encourage their business. This substantial advantage over European manufacturers they always must have, so long as the broad Atlantic divides us.

These are some of our numerous internal resources and advantages for the encouragement of factories in those parts of the union where they can be attended to in perfect consistency with the highest interests of commerce and agriculture.

After having indulged in the enumeration of some of our manufactural advantages and prospects, which I am sensible is deviating from the common track of Geographers, whose business it is to relate things as they are, and not to anticipate what they might be, we will now proceed to take a general view of the present state of our manufactures.

Of the long list of articles which we now make ourselves, we will mention, meal of all kinds, ships and boats, malt and distilled liquors, potash, gunpowder, cordage, loaf-sugar, pasteboard, cards and paper of every kind, books in various languages, snuff, tobacco, starch, cannon, musquets, anchors, nails, and very many other articles of iron, bricks, tiles, potters ware, mill-stones, and other stone work, cabinet work, trunks and Windsor chairs, carriages and harness of all kinds, corn-fans, ploughs and many other implements of husbandry, sadlery and whips, shoes and boots, leather of various kinds, hosiery, hats and gloves, wearing apparel, coarse linens, and woollens, and some cotten goods, linseed and fish-oil, wares of gold, silver, tin, pewter, lead, brass and copper, bells, clocks and watches, wool and cotten cards, printing types, glass and stone ware, candles, soap and several other valuable articles. These are tending to greater perfection, and will soon be sold so cheap as to throw foreign goods of the same kind entirely out of the market.

Pennsylvania

The UNITED STATES.

Pennsylvania has confessedly taken the lead of all her sister states in manufactural improvements. A society for the encouragement of manufactures and the useful arts, was instituted at Philadelphia in the summer of 1787. Several ingenious, well written pamphlets were published at the time, representing our numerous resources and advantages for promoting manufactures, and pointing out the principles upon which they ought to be established.* These publications had a salutary effect; and have no doubt had their due share of influence in cherishing that spirit of industry and attention to home manufactures, which of late has greatly prevailed in the eastern and middle states.

A cotton manufactory has lately been established at Philadelphia, at which are made jeans, fustians, velvets, velverets and corduroys, equal in goodness to those imported, and much cheaper. Cotton enough might be raised in the southern states, and manufactured in the northern, to clothe all their citizens. A flourishing woollen manufactory has lately been established at Hartford in Connecticut, with a capital of four thousand dollars, which is increasing. It is computed that in East Jersey, more than eight times the quantity of linen and woollen cloth has been manufactured the present year, than in any one year since the peace. In several other states the increase has been equally great.

New England, the seat of the fisheries, has the great advantage of being the cheapest and most populous part of America. Its inhabitants are healthy, active and intelligent, and can be frugal; and have produced their share of mechanical inventions. These circumstances render it probable that factories of various kinds, which are now numerous and flourishing, will soon be greatly increased in this part of the union.

An extravagant and wasteful use of foreign manufactures, has been too just a charge against the people of America, since the close of the war. They have been so cheap, so plenty, and so easily obtained on credit, that the consumption of them has been absolutely wanton. To such an excess has it been carried, that the importation of the finer kind of coat, vest and sleeve buttons, buckles, broaches, breast pins, and other trinkets into the port of Philadelphia only, is supposed to have amounted in a single year to ten thousand pounds sterling; which cost the wearers above sixty thousand dollars. A proportionable quantity of these expensive and shewy trinkets, it is presumed, have been imported into the other states. Our farmers, in most parts of the union, to their great honor and advantage, have been long in the excellent œconomical practice of domestic manufactures for their own use. It is chiefly in large towns that this madness for foreign finery rages and destroys. There, unfortunately, it has been and is still epidemical.

These general observations on the agriculture, commerce and manufactures of the union at large, are introductory to a more particular account of them in the descriptions of the several states.

Military

---

* *Two of these Pamphlets were written by Tench Coxe, Esq; of Philadelphia. It is wished they could be read by every citizen of the United States. To extend the influence of the valuable information, and patriotic sentiments which they contain, I have made a very free use them in the foregoing observations, on the subjects of which they treat.*

Military and Marine strength.] On these two heads, as we have no accurate estimate of the number of inhabitants in some of the states, and no official returns of the militia; and as we have in fact no marine strength, we are left to the field of conjecture and anticipation. The following estimate may serve until a better one can be made. Suppose the number of inhabitants in the United States to be three millions, eighty-three thousand. Deduct from this five hundred and sixty thousand, the supposed number of negroes; the remainder will be two millions, five hundred and twenty-three thousand, the number of whites. Suppose one sixth part of these capable of bearing arms, it will be found that the number of fencible men in the United States are four hundred and twenty thousand. This, it is conceived, is but a moderate estimate. In Virginia, according to Mr. Jefferson's calculation, the number of whites is two hundred and ninety-six thousand, eight hundred and fifty-two; and the militia forty-nine thousand nine hundred and seventy-one, which is very nearly one sixth part. In Connecticut there are thirty-nine thousand three hundred and eighty-eight males between sixteen and fifty years of age, who are supposed capable of bearing arms; and the whole number of whites is two hundred and two thousand eight hundred and seventy-seven; the proportion of fighting men therefore is about one in five. In Rhode Island, Massachusetts and New Hampshire, the proportion is about the same. In Vermont, Kentucky, the Western territory and Georgia, which have been newly settled by a young and thrifty race of husbandmen from the older states, there is, without doubt, a much greater proportion of soldiers. So that in estimating our military strength, we may safely venture to reckon upon four hundred and twenty thousand men. A great proportion of these are well disciplined, veteran soldiers, whose bravery and expertness in war have been tried and honourably approved. And Europe will acknowledge, that no part of the world can bring into the field an army, of equal numbers, more formidable than can be raised in the United States,

As to marine strength we have none. All then that can be said on this subject must be by way of anticipation. I mentioned marine strength, only that I might have opportunity of introducing the excellent observations of Mr. Jefferson on this head. After having estimated the pecuniary abilities of Virginia and finding that it could, without distress, contribute one million of dollars annually towards supporting a federal army, paying the federal debt, building a federal navy, &c. &c. he proceeds to make an application of these abilities, if, unhappily, we should come hereafter to measure force with any European power.

' Such an event,' he observes, ' is devoutly to be deprecated. Young as we are, and with such a country before us to fill with people and with happiness, we should point in that direction the whole generative force of nature, wasting none of it in efforts of mutual destruction. It should be our endeavor to cultivate the peace and friendship of every nation, even of that which has injured us most, when we shall have carried our point against her. Our interest will be to throw open the doors of commerce, and to knock off all its shackles, giving perfect freedom to all persons for the vent of whatever they may choose to bring into our ports, and asking the same in theirs. Never was so much false arithmetic employed on any
subject,

subject, as that which has been employed to purſuade nations that it is
their intereſt to go to war. Were the money which it has coſt to gain, at
the cloſe of a long war, a little town, or a little territory, the right to cut
wood here, or to catch fiſh there, expended in improving what they already poſſeſs, in making roads, opening rivers, building ports, improving
the arts, and finding employment for their idle poor, it would render them
much ſtronger, much wealthier and happier. This I hope will be our
wiſdom. And, perhaps, to remove as much as poſſible the occaſions of
making war, it might be better for us to abandon the ocean altogether,
that being the element whereon we ſhall be principally expoſed to joſtle
with other nations : to leave to others to bring what we ſhall want, and to
carry what we can ſpare. This would make us invulnerable to Europe,
by offering none of our property to their prize, and would turn all our citizens to the cultivation of the earth ; and, I repeat it again, cultivators of
the earth are the moſt virtuous and independent citizens. It might be
time enough to ſeek employment for them at ſea, when the land no longer
offers it. But the actual habits of our countrymen attach them to commerce. They will exerciſe it for themſelves. Wars then muſt ſometimes
be our lot; and all the wiſe can do, will be to avoid that half of them
which would be produced by our own follies, and our acts of injuſtice ;
and to make for the other half the beſt preparations we can. Of what
nature ſhould theſe be ? A land army would be uſeleſs for offence, and
not the beſt nor ſafeſt inſtrument of defence. For either of theſe purpoſes,
the ſea is the field on which we ſhould meet an European enemy. On
that element it is neceſſary we ſhould poſſeſs ſome power. To aim at
ſuch a navy as the greater nations of Europe poſſeſs, would be a fooliſh and
wicked waſte of the energies of our countrymen. It would be to pull on
our own heads that load of military expence, which makes the European
labourer go ſupperleſs to bed, and moiſtens his bread with the ſweat of brows.
It will be enough if we enable ourſelves to prevent inſults from thoſe nations of Europe which are weak on the ſea, becauſe circumſtances exiſt,
which render even the ſtronger ones weak as to us. Providence has placed
their richeſt and moſt defenceleſs poſſeſſions at our door; has obliged their
moſt precious commerce to paſs as it were in review before us. To protect this, or to aſſail us, a ſmall part only of their naval force will ever be
riſked acroſs the Atlantic. The dangers to which the elements expoſe
them here are too well known, and the greater dangers to which they
would be expoſed at home, were any general calamity to involve their
whole fleet. They can attack us by detachment only; and it will ſuf-
fice to make ourſelves equal to what they may detach. Even a ſmaller
force than they may detach will be rendered equal or ſuperior by the quick-
neſs with which any check may be repaired with us, while loſſes with
them will be irreparable till too late. A ſmall naval force then is ſufficient for us, and a ſmall one is neceſſary. What this ſhould be, I will not
undertake to ſay. I will only ſay, it ſhould by no means be ſo great as
we are able to make it. Suppoſe the million of dollars, or three hundred
thouſand pounds, which Virginia could annually ſpare without diſtreſs,
to be applied to the creating a navy. A ſingle year's contribution would
build, equip, man, and ſend to ſea a force which ſhould carry three hundred guns. The reſt of the confederacy, exerting themſelves in the ſame proportion,

portion, would equip in the same time fifteen hundred guns more. So that one year's contributions would set up a navy of eighteen hundred guns. The British ships of the line average seventy-six guns; their frigates thirty-eight. Eighteen hundred guns then would form a fleet of thirty ships, eighteen of which might be of the line, and twelve frigates. Allowing eight men, the British average for every gun, their annual expence, including subsistence, cloathing, pay, and ordinary repairs, would be about twelve hundred and eighty dollars for every gun, or two million three hundred and four thousand dollars for the whole. I state this only as one year's possible exertion, without deciding whether more or less than a year's exertion should be thus applied.'

History.] In addition to what we have already written of the discovery and settlement of North-America, we shall give a brief history of the late war with Great-Britain, with a sketch of the events which preceded and prepared the way for the revolution. This general view of the history of the United States, will serve as a suitable introduction to the particular histories of the several states, which will be given in their proper places.

America was originally peopled by uncivilized nations, which lived mostly by hunting and fishing. The Europeans, who first visited these shores, treating the natives as wild beasts of the forest, which have no property in the woods where they roam, planted the standard of their respective masters where they first landed, and in their names claimed the country by *right of discovery.** Prior to any settlement in North-America numerous titles of this kind were acquired by the English, French, Spanish, and Dutch navigators, who came hither for the purposes of fishing and trading with the natives. Slight as such titles were, they were afterwards the causes of contention between the European nations. The subjects of different princes often laid claim to the same tract of country, because both had discovered the same river or promontary; or because the extent of their respective claims was indeterminate.

While the settlements in this vast uncultivated country were inconsiderable and scattered, and the trade of it confined to the bartering of a few trinkets for furs, a trade carried on by a few adventurers, the interfering of claims produced no important controversy among the settlers or the nations of Europe. But in proportion to the progress of population, and the growth of the American trade, the jealousies of the nations, which had made early discoveries and settlements on this coast, were alarmed; ancient claims were revived; and each power took measures to extend and secure its own possessions at the expence of a rival.

By the treaty of Utrecht in 1713, the English claimed a right of cutting log-wood in the Bay of Campeachy, in South-America. In the exercise of this right, the English merchants had frequent opportunities of carrying on a contraband trade with the Spanish settlements on the continent. To remedy this evil, the Spaniards resolved to annihilate a claim, which, though

---

* *As well may the New Zealanders, who have not yet discovered Europe, fit out a ship, land on the coast of England or France, and, finding no inhabitants but poor fishermen and peasants, claim the whole country by right of discovery.*

The UNITED STATES. 95

though often acknowledged, had never been clearly afcertained. To effect this defign, they captured the Englifh veffels, which they found along the Spanifh Main, and many of the Britifh fubjects were doomed to work in the mines of Potofi.

Repeated feverities of this kind at length (1739) produced a war between England and Spain. Porto Bello was taken from the Spaniards, by Admiral Vernon. Commodore Anfon, with a fquadron of fhips, failed to the South Seas, diftreffed the Spanifh fettlements on the weftern fhore of America, and took a Galleon laden with immenfe riches. But in 1741 a formidable armament, deftined to attack Carthagena, under the command of Lord Cathcart, returned unfuccefsful, with the lofs of upwards of twelve thoufand Britifh foldiers and feamen, and the defeat of the expedition, raifed a clamour againft the minifter, Sir Robert Walpole, which produced a change in the adminiftration. This change removed the fcene of war to Europe, fo that America was not immediately affected by the fubfequent tranfactions; except that Louifburgh, the principal fortrefs of Cape Breton, was taken from the French by General Pepperell, affifted by Commodore Warren and a body of New-England troops.

This war was ended in 1748 by the treaty of peace figned at Aix la Chapelle, by which reftitution was made on both fides of all places taken during the war.

Peace however was of fhort duration. The French poffeffed Canada, and had made confiderable fettlements in Florida, claiming the country on both fides of the Miffiffippi, by right of difcovery. To fecure and extend their claims, they eftablifhed a line of forts, on the Englifh poffeffions, from Canada to Florida. They had fecured the important pafs at Niagara, and erected a fort at the juction of the Allegany and Monongahela rivers, called Fort Du Quefne. They took pains to fecure the friendfhip and affiftance of the natives, encroachments were made upon the Englifh poffeffions, and mutual injuries fucceeded. The difputes among the fettlers in America, and the meafures taken by the French to command all the trade of the St. Lawrence river on the north, and of the Miffiffippi on the fouth, excited a jealoufy in the Englifh nations, which foon broke forth in open war.

In 1756, four expeditions were undertaken in America againft the French. One was conducted by General Monckton, who had orders to drive the French from the encroachments on the province of Nova-Scotia. This expedition was attended with fuccefs. General Johnfon was ordered, with a body of troops, to take poffeffion of Crown Point, but he did not fucceed. General Shirly commanded an expedition againft the fort at Niagara, but loft the feafon by delay. General Braddock marched againft fort Du Quefne, but in penetrating through the wildernefs, he incautioufly fell into an ambufcade and fuffered a total defeat. General Braddock was killed, but a part of his troops were faved by the prudence and bravery of General Wafhington, at this time a Colonel, who then began to exhibit proofs of thofe military talents, by which he afterwards conducted the armies of America to victory, and his country to independence. The ill fuccefs of thefe expeditions left the Englifh fettlements in America expofed to the depredations of both the French and Indians. But the war now raged in Europe and the Eaft Indies, and engaged the attention of both nations in thofe quarters. It

It was not until the campaign in 1758 that affairs assumed a more favorable aspect in America. But upon a change of administration, Mr. Pitt was appointed prime minister, and the operations of war became more vigorous and successful. General Amherst was sent to take possession of Cape Breton; and after a warm siege, the garrison of Louisburg surrendered by capitulation. General Forbes was successful in taking possession of Fort Du Quesne, which the French thought fit to abandon. But General Abercrombie, who commanded the troops destined to act against the French at Crown Point and Ticonderoga, attacked the lines at Ticonderoga, where the enemy were strongly entrenched, and was defeated with a terrible slaughter of his troops. After his defeat, he returned to his camp at Lake George.

The next year, more effectual measures were taken to subdue the French in America. General Prideaux and Sir William Johnson began the operations of the campaign by taking the French fort near Niagara.* General Amherst took possession of the forts at Crown Point and Ticonderoga, which the French had abandoned.

But the decisive blow, which proved fatal to the French interests in America, was the defeat of the French army, and the taking of Quebec, by the brave General Wolfe. This hero was slain in the beginning of the action, on the plains of Abram, and Monsieur Montcalm, the French commander, likewise lost his life. The loss of Quebec was soon followed by the capture of Montreal by General Amherst, and Canada has remained ever since in possession of the English.

Colonel Grant, in 1761, defeated the Cherokees in Carolina and obliged them to sue for peace. The next year, Martinico was taken by Admiral Rodney and General Monckton; and also the island of Grenada, St. Vincents and others. The capture of these was soon followed by the surrender of the Havanna, the capital of the island of Cuba.

In 1763, a definitive treaty of peace was concluded at Paris between Great Britain, France and Spain, by which the English ceded to the French several islands in the West Indies, but were confirmed in the possession of all North America on this side the Mississippi, except New Orleans, and a small district of the neighbouring country.

But this war, however brilliant the successes and glorious the event, proved the cause of great and unexpected misfortunes to Great Britain. Engaged with the combined powers of France and Spain, during several years, her exertions were surprizing and her expence immense. To discharge the debts of the nation, the parliament was obliged to have recourse to new expedients for raising money. Previous to the last treaty in 1763, the Parliament had been satisfied to raise a revenue from the American Colonies by monopoly of their trade.

It will be proper here to observe that there were three kinds of government established in the British American Colonies. The first was a charter government, by which the powers of legislation were vested in a governor, council and assembly, chosen by the people. Of this kind were the governments of Connecticut and Rhode-Island. The second was a proprietary

* *General Prideaux was killed by the bursting of a mortar, before the surrender of the French.*

proprietary government, in which the proprietor of the province, was governor; although he generally refided abroad, and adminiftered the government by a deputy of his own appointment; the affembly only being chofen by the people. Such were the governments of Pennfylvania and Maryland; and originally of New Jerfey and Carolina. The third kind was that of royal government, where the governor and council were appointed by the crown, and the affembly by the people. Of this kind were the governments of New Hampfhire, Maffachufetts, New York, New Jerfey, after the year 1702, Virginia, the Carolinas, after the refignation of the proprietors, in 1728; and Georgia. This variety of governments created different degrees of dependence on the crown. To render laws valid, it was conftitutionally required that they fhould be ratified by the king; but this formality was often difpenfed with, efpecially in the charter governments.

At the beginning of the laft war with France, commiffioners from many of the colonies had affembled at Albany, and propofed that a great council fhould be formed by deputies from the feveral colonies, which, with a general governor to be appointed by the crown, fhould be empowered to take meafures for the common fafety, and to raife money for the execution of their defigns. This propofal was not relifhed by the Britifh miniftry; but in place of this plan, it was propofed, that the governors of the colonies, with the affiftance of one or two of their council, fhould affemble and concert meafures for the general defence; erect forts, levy troops, and draw on the treafury of England for monies that fhould be wanted; but the treafury to be reimburfed by a tax on the colonies, to be laid by the Englifh parliament. To this plan, which would imply an avowal of the rightof parliament to tax the colonies, the provincial affemblies objected with unfhaken firmnefs. It feems therefore that the Britifh parliament, *before* the war, had it in contemplation to exercife the right they claimed of taxing the colonies at pleafure, without permitting them to be reprefented. Indeed it is obvious that they laid hold of the alarming fituation of the colonies about the year 1754, and 1755, to force them into an acknowledgment of the right, or to the adoption of meafures that might afterwards be drawn into precedent. The colonies however, with an uncommon forefight and firmnefs, defeated all their attempts. The war was carried on by requifitions on the colonies for fupplies of men and money, or by voluntary contributions.

But no fooner was peace concluded, than the Englifh parliament refumed the plan of taxing the colonies; and to juftify their attempts, faid, that the money to be raifed, was to be appropriated to defray the expence of defending them in the late war.

The firft attempt to raife a revenue in America appeared in the memorable *ftamp act*, paffed March 22, 1765; by which it was enacted that certain inftruments of writing, as bills, bonds, &c. fhould not be valid in law, unlefs drawn on ftamped paper, on which a duty was laid. No fooner was this act publifhed in America, than it raifed a general alarm. The people were filled with apprehenfions at an act which they fuppofed an attack on their conftitutional rights. The colonies petitioned the king and parliament for a redrefs of the grievance, and formed affociations for the purpofe of preventing the importation and ufe of Britifh manufactures, until the act fhould be repealed. This fpirited and unanimous

The UNITED STATES.

opposition of the Americans produced the desired effect, and on the 18th of March, 1766, the stamp act was repealed. The news of the repeal was received in the colonies with universal joy, and the trade between them and Great Britain was renewed on the most liberal footing.

The parliament, by repealing this act, so obnoxious to their American brethren, did not intend to lay aside the scheme of raising a revenue in the colonies, but merely to change the mode. Accordingly the next year, they passed an act, laying a certain duty on glass, tea, paper and painters colors; articles which were much wanted, and not manufactured, in America. This act kindled the resentment of the Americans, and excited a general opposition to the measure; so that parliament thought proper in 1770, to take off these duties, except three pence a pound on tea. Yet this duty, however trifling, kept alive the jealousy of the colonists, and their opposition to parliamentary taxation continued and increased.

But it must be remembered that the inconvenience of paying the duty was not the sole, nor principal cause of the opposition, it was the *principle* which, once admitted, would have subjected the colonies to unlimited parliamentary taxation, without the privilege of being represented. The *right*, abstractly considered, was denied; and the smallest attempt to establish the claim by precedent, was uniformly resisted. The Americans could not be deceived as to the views of parliament; for the repeal of the stamp act was accompanied with an unequivocal declaration, ' that the parliament had a right to make laws of sufficient validity to bind the colonies in all cases whatsoever.'

The colonies therefore entered into measures to encourage their own manufactures, and home productions, and to retrench the use of foreign superfluities; while the importation of tea was prohibited. In the royal and proprietary governments, the governors and people were in a state of continual warfare. Assemblies were repeatedly called, and suddenly dissolved. While sitting, the assemblies employed the time in stating grievances and framing remonstrances. To inflame these discontents, an act of parliament was passed, ordaining that the governors and judges should receive their salaries of the crown; thus making them independent of the provincial assemblies, and removeable only at the pleasure of the king.

These arbitrary proceedings, with many others not here mentioned,* could not fail of producing a rupture. The first act of violence, was the Massacre at Boston, on the evening of the fifth of March, 1770. A body of British troops had been stationed in Boston to awe the inhabitants and inforce the measures of parliament. On the fatal day, when blood was to be shed, as a prelude to more tragic scenes, a riot was raised among some soldiers and boys; the former aggressing by throwing snow-balls at the latter. The bickerings and jealousies between the inhabitants and soldiers, which had been frequent before, now became serious. A multitude was soon collected, and the controversy became so warm, that to disperse the people, the troops were embodied
and

---

* *See an enumeration of grievances in the ' act of independence,' and in a variety of petitions to the king and parliament.*

The UNITED STATES.

and ordered to fire upon the inhabitants. This fatal order was executed and several persons fell a sacrifice. The people restrained their vengeance at the time; but this wanton act of cruelty and military despotism fanned the flame of liberty; a flame that was not to be extinguished but by a total separation of the Colonies from their oppressive and hostile parent.

In 1773 the spirit of the Americans broke out into open violance. The Gaspee, an armed schooner belonging to his Britannic Majesty, had been stationed at Providence in Rhode-Island, to prevent smuggling. The vigilance of the commander irritated the inhabitants to that degree, that about two-hundred armed men entered the vessel at night, compelled the officers and men to go a shore, and set fire to the schooner. A reward of five hundred pounds, offered by government for apprehending any of the persons concerned in this daring act, poduced no effectual discovery.

About this time, the discovery and publication of some private confidential letters, written by the royal officers in Boston, to persons in office in England, served to confirm the apprehensions of the Americans, with respect to the designs of the British government. It was now made obvious that more effectual measures would be taken to establish the supremacy of the British Parliament over the Colonies. The letters recommended decisive measures, and the writers were charged, by the exasperated Americans, with betraying their trust and the people they governed.

As the resolutions of the Colonies not to import or consume tea, had, in a great measure, deprived the English government of a revenue from this quarter, the parliament formed a scheme of introducing tea into America, under cover of the East India Company. For this purpose an act was passed, enabling the company to export all sorts of teas, duty free, to any place whatever. The company departed from their usual mode of business and became their own exporters. Several ships were freighted with teas, and sent to the American colonies, and factors were appointed to receive and dispose of their cargoes.

The Americans, determined to oppose the revenue-system of the English parliament in every possible shape, considered the attempt of the East India Company to evade the resolutions of the colonies, and dispose of teas in America, as an indirect mode of taxation, sanctioned by the authority of Parliament. The people assembled in various places, and in the large commercial towns, took measures to prevent the landing of the teas. Committees were appointed, and armed with extensive powers to inspect merchants books, to propose tests, and make use of other expedients to frustrate the designs of the East India Company. The same spirit pervaded the people from New Hampshire to Georgia. In some places, the consignees of the teas were intimidated so far as to relinquish their appointments, or to enter into engagements not to act in that capacity. The cargo sent to South Carolina was stored, the consignees being restrained from offering the tea for sale. In other provinces, the ships were sent back without discharging their cargoes.

But in Boston the tea shared a more violent fate. Sensible that no legal measures could prevent its being landed, and that if once landed, it would be disposed of; a number of men in disguise, on the 18th of December 1773, entered the ships and threw overboard three hundred and forty chests of it, which was the proportion belonging to the East India

Company,

The UNITED STATES.

Company. No sooner did the news of this destruction of the tea reach Great Britain, than the parliament determined to punish that devoted town. On the king's laying the American papers before them, a bill was brought in and passed, 'to discontinue the landing and discharging, lading and shipping of goods, wares and merchandizes at the town of Boston, or within the harbour.'

This act, passed March 25, 1774, called the Boston Port Bill, threw the inhabitants of Massachusetts into the greatest consternation. The town of Boston passed a resolution, expressing their sense of this oppressive measure, and a desire that all the colonies would concur to stop all importation from Great Britain. Most of the colonies entered into spirited resolutions, on this occasion, to unite with Massachusets in a firm opposition to the unconstitutional measures of the parliament. The first of June, the day on which the Port Bill was to take place, was appointed to be kept as a day of humiliation, fasting and prayer throughout the colonies, to seek the divine direction and aid, in that critical and gloomy juncture of affairs.

It ought here to be observed, that this rational and pious custom of observing fasts in times of distress and impending danger, and of celebrating days of public thanksgiving, after having received special tokens of divine favor, has ever prevailed in New England since its first settlement, and in some parts of other states. These public supplications and acknowledgments to heaven, at the commencement of hostilities, and during the whole progress of the war, were more frequent than usual, and were attended with uncommon fervor and solemnity. They were considered by the people, as an humble appeal to heaven for the justness of their cause, and designed to manifest their dependence on the God of Hosts for aid and success in maintaining it against their hostile brethren. The prayers and public discourses of the Clergy who were friends to their suffering country (and there were very few who were not) breathed the spirit of patriotism; and as their piety and integrity had generally secured to them the confidence of the people, they had great influence and success in encouraging them to engage in its defence. In this way, that venerable class of citizens, aided the cause of their country; and to their pious exertions, under the GREAT ARBITER of human affairs, has been justly ascribed no inconsiderable share of the success and victory that crowned the American arms.

During the height of the consternation and confusion which the Boston Port Bill occasioned; at the very time when a town meeting was sitting to consider of it, General Gage, who had been appointed to the government of Massachusetts, arrived in the harbour. His arrival however did not allay the popular ferment, or check the progress of the measures then taking, to unite the Colonies in opposition to the oppressive act of parliament.

But the port bill was not the only act that alarmed the apprehensions of the Americans. Determined to compel the province of Massachusetts to submit to their laws, parliament passed an act for 'the better regulating government in the province of Massachusetts Bay.' The object of this act was to alter the government, as it stood on the charter of king William, to take the appointment of the executive out of the hands of the people,

THE UNITED STATES.

people, and place it in the crown; thus making even the judges and sheriffs dependent on the king, and removeable only at his pleasure.

This act was soon followed by another, which ordained that any person, indicted for murder, or other capital offence, committed in aiding the magistrates in executing the laws, might be sent by the governor either to another colony, or to Great Britain for his trial.

This was soon followed by the Quebec Bill; which extended the bounds of that province, and granted many privileges to the Roman Catholics. The object of this bill was, to secure the attachment of that province to the crown of England, and prevent its joining the colonies in their resistance of the laws of parliament.

But these measures did not intimidate the Americans. On the other hand they served to confirm their former apprehensions of the evil designs of government, and to unite the colonies in their opposition. A correspondence of opinion with respect to the unconstitutional acts of parliament, produced a uniformity of proceedings in the colonies. The people generally concurred in a proposition for holding a congress by deputation from the several colonies, in order to concert measures for the preservation of their rights. Deputies were accordingly appointed, and met at Philadelphia, on the 26th of October, 1774.

In this first congress, the proceedings were cool, deliberate and loyal; but marked with unanimity and firmness. Their first act was a declaration, or state of their claims as to the enjoyment of all the rights of British subjects, and particularly that of taxing themselves exclusively, and of regulating the internal police of the colonies. They also drew up a petition to the king, complaining of their grievances and praying for a repeal of the unconstitutional and oppressive acts of Parliament. They signed an association to suspend the importation of British goods, and the exportation of American produce, until their grievances should be redressed. They sent an address to the inhabitants of Great-Britain, and another to the people of America; in the former of which they enumerated the oppressive steps of parliament, and called on their British brethren not to aid the ministry in enslaving their American subjects; and in the latter, they endeavoured to confirm the people in a spirited and unanimous determination to defend their constitutional rights.

In the mean time, every thing in Massachusetts wore the appearance of opposition by force. A new council for the governor had been appointed by the crown. New judges were appointed and attempted to proceed in the execution of their office. But the juries refused to be sworn under them; in some counties, the people assembled to prevent the courts from proceeding to business; and in Berkshire they succeeded, setting an example of resistance that has since been followed, in violation of the laws of the State.

In this situation of affairs, the day for the annual muster of the militia approached. General Gage, apprehensive of some violence, had the precaution to seize the magazines of ammunition and stores at Cambridge and Charleston, and lodged them in Boston. This measure, with the fortifying of that neck of land which joins Boston to the main land at Roxbury, caused a universal alarm and ferment. Several thousand people assembled, and it was with difficulty they could be restrained from falling upon the British troops.

On

On this occasion, an assembly of delegates from all the towns in Suffolk county, was called; and several spirited resolutions were agreed to. These resolutions were prefaced with a declaration of allegiance; but they breathed a spirit of freedom that does honor to the delegates. They declared that the late acts of parliament and the proceedings of General Gage, were glaring infractions of their rights and liberties, which their duty called them to defend by all lawful means.

This assembly remonstrated against the fortification of Boston Neck, and against the Quebec bill; and resolved upon a suspension of commerce, an encouragement of arts and manufactures, the holding of a provincial congress, and a submission to the measures which should be recommended by the continental congress. They recommended that the collectors of taxes should not pay any money into the treasury, without further orders; they also recommended peace and good order, as they meant to act merely upon the defensive.

In answer to their remonstrance, General Gage assured them that he had no intention to prevent the free egress and regress of the inhabitants to and from the town of Boston, and that he would not suffer any person under his command to injure the person or property of any of his majesty's subjects.

Previous to this, a general assembly had been summoned to meet; and notwithstanding the writs had been countermanded by the governor's proclamation, on account of the violence of the times and the resignation of several of the new counsellors, yet representatives were chosen by the people who met at Salem, resolved themselves into a provincial congress and adjourned to Concord.

This congress addressed the governor with a rehearsal of their distresses, and took the necessary steps for defending their rights. They regulated the militia, made provision for supplying the treasury, and furnishing the people with arms; and such was the enthusiasm and union of the people that the recommendations of the provincial congress had the force of laws.

General Gage was incensed at these measures—he declared, in his answer to the address, that Britain could never harbour the black design of enslaving her subjects and published a proclamation in which he insinuated that such proceedings amounted to rebellion. He also ordered barracks to be erected for the soldiers; but he found difficulty in procuring labourers, either in Boston or New-York.

In the beginning of 1775, the fishery bills were passed in parliament, by which the colonies were prohibited to trade with Great-Britain, Ireland or the West-Indies, or to take fish on the banks of Newfoundland.

In the distresses to which these acts of parliament reduced the town of Boston, the unanimity of the colonies was remarkable, in the large supplies of provision, furnished by the inhabitants of different towns from New Hampshire to Georgia, and shipped to the relief of the sufferers.

Preparations began to be made, to oppose by force, the execution of these acts of parliament. The militia of the country were trained to the use of arms—great encouragement was given for the manufacture of gunpowder, and measures were taken to obtain all kinds of military stores.

In February, Colonel Leslie was sent with a detachment of troops from Boston, to take possession of some cannon at Salem. But the people had
intelligence

intelligence of the design—took up the draw bridge in that town, and prevented the troops from passing, until the cannon were secured; so that the expedition failed.

In April Colonel Smith, and Major Pitcairn were sent with a body of about nine hundred troops, to destroy the military stores which had been collected at Concord, about twenty miles from Boston. It is believed, that another object of this expedition, was to seize on the persons of Messrs. Hancock and Adams, who by their spirited exertions, had rendered themselves very obnoxious to General Gage. At Lexington, the militia were collected on a green, to oppose the incursion of the British forces. These were fired upon by the British troops, and eight men killed on the spot.

The militia were dispersed, and the troops proceeded to Concord; where they destroyed a few stores. But on their return, they were incessantly harrassed by the Americans, who, inflamed with just resentment, fired upon them from houses and fences, and pursued them to Boston. The loss of the British in this expedition, in killed, wounded and prisoners, was two hundred and seventy-three men.

Here was spilt the *first blood* in the late war; a war which severed America from the British empire. *Lexington* opened the first scene of this great drama, which, in its progress, exhibited the most illustrious characters and events, and closed with a revolution, equally glorious for the actors, and important in its consequences to mankind.

This battle roused all America. The militia collected from all quarters, and Boston, in a few days was besieged by twenty thousand men. A stop was put to all intercourse between the town and country, and the inhabitants were reduced to great want of provisions. General Gage promised to let the people depart, if they would deliver up their arms. The people complied, but when the general had obtained their arms, the perfidious man, refused to let the people go.

This breach of faith, and the consequences that attended it, were justly and greatly complained of; and although many, at different times, were permitted to leave the town, they were obliged to leave all their effects behind; so that many who had been used to live in ease and affluence, were at once reduced to extreme indigence and misery. A circumstance peculiarly and wantonly aggravating, and which was the ground of the bitterest complaints of congress, was that passports were granted or retained in such a manner, as that families were broken, and the dearest connections separated; part being compelled to quit the town, and part cruelly retained against their inclination.

In the mean time, a small number of men, to the amount of about two hundred and forty, under the command of Colonel Allen, and Colonel Easton, without any public orders, surprized and took the British garrisons at Ticonderoga and Crown Point, without the loss of a man on either side.

During these transactions, the Generals Howe, Burgoyne, and Clinton, arrived at Boston from England, with a number of troops. In June following, our troops attempted to fortify Bunker's hill, which lies near Charlestown, and but a mile and an half from Boston. They had, during the night, thrown up a small breast-work, which sheltered them from

the

the fire of the British cannon. But the next morning, the British army was sent to drive them from the hill, and landing under cover of their cannon, they set fire to Charlestown, which was consumed, and marched to attack our troops in the entrenchments. A severe engagement ensued, in which the British, according to their own accounts, had seven hundred and forty killed, and eleven hundred and fifty wounded. They were repulsed at first, and thrown into disorder; but they finally carried the fortification, with the point of the bayonet. The Americans suffered a small loss, compared with the British; the whole loss in killed, wounded and prisoners being but about four hundred and fifty.

The loss most lamented on this bloody day, was that of Dr. Warren. who was at this time a major-general, and commanded the troops on this occasion. He died like a brave man, fighting valiantly at the head of his party, in a little redoubt at the right of our lines.

General Warren, who had rendered himself conspicuous by his universal merit, abilities, and eloquence, had been a delegate to the first general congress, and was at this time president of the provincial congress of Massachusetts. But quitting the humane and peaceable walk of his profession as a physician, and breaking through the endearing ties of family connections, he proved himself equally calculated for the field, as for public business or private study.

About this time, the Continental Congress appointed George Washington Esq; a native of Virginia, to the chief command of the American army.* This gentleman had been a distinguished and successful officer in the preceeding war, and he seemed destined by heaven to be the savior of his country. He accepted the appointment with a diffidence which was a proof of his prudence and his greatness. He refused any pay for eight years laborious and arduous service; and by his matchless skill, fortitude and perseverance, conducted America through indescribeable difficulties, to independence and peace

While true merit is esteemed, or virtue honored, mankind will never cease to revere the memory of this Hero; and while gratitude remains in the human breast, the praises of WASHINGTON shall dwell on every American tongue.

General Washington, with other officers appointed by congress, arrived at Cambridge, and took command of the American army in July. From this time, the affairs of America began to assume the appearance of a regular and general opposition to the forces of Great Britain.

In Autumn, a body of troops, under the command of General Montgomery, besieged and took the garrison at St. John's, which commands the entrance into Canada. The prisoners amounted to about seven hundred. General Montgomery pursued his success, and took Montreal; and designed to push his victories to Quebec.

A body of troops, commanded by General Arnold, was ordered to march to Canada, by the river Kennebek, and through the wilderness. After suffering every hardship, and the most distressing hunger, they arrived in Canada, and were joined by General Montgomery, before Quebec. This city, which was commanded by Governor Carleton, was immediately besieged. But there being little hope of taking the town by a siege, it was determined to storm it.

The

* See Note (A) at the close of this history.

The attack was made on the laſt day of December, but proved unſucceſsful, and fatal to the brave General;* who, with his aid, was killed in attempting to ſcale the walls.

Of the three diviſions which attacked the town, one only entered, and that was obliged to ſurrender to ſuperior force. After this defeat, Gen. Arnold, who now commanded the troops, continued ſome months before Quebec, although his troops ſuffered incredibly by cold and ſickneſs. But the next ſpring, the Americans were obliged to retreat from Canada.

About this time, the large and flouriſhing town of Norfolk in Virginia, was wantonly burnt by order of lord Dunmore, the then royal governor of that province.

General Gage went to England in September, and was ſucceeded in the command, by General Howe.

Falmouth, a conſiderable town in the province of Main in Maſſachuſetts, ſhared the fate of Norfolk; being laid in aſhes by order of the Britiſh admiral.

The Britiſh king entered into treaties with ſome of the German Princes for about ſeventeen thouſand men, who were to be ſent to America the next year, to aſſiſt in ſubduing the colonies. The parliament alſo paſſed an act, forbidding all intercourſe with America; and while they repealed the Boſton-port and fiſhery bills, they declared all American property on the high ſeas, forfeited to the captors. This act induced Congreſs to change the mode of carrying on the war; and meaſures were taken to annoy the enemy in Boſton. For this purpoſe, batteries were opened on ſeveral hills, from whence ſhot and bombs were thrown into the town. But the batteries which were opened on Dorcheſter point had the beſt effect, and ſoon obliged general Howe to abandon the town. In March 1776, the Britiſh troops embarked for Halifax, and General Waſhington entered the town in triumph.

In the enſuing ſummer, a ſmall ſquadron of ſhips commanded by Sir Peter Parker, and a body of troops under the generals Clinton and Cornwallis, attempted to take Charleſton, the capital of South Carolina. The ſhips made a violent attack upon the fort on Sullivan's Iſland, but were repulſed with great loſs, and the expedition was abandoned.

In July, Congreſs publiſhed their declaration of independence, which ſeparated America from Great Britain. This great event took place two hundred and eighty-four years after the firſt diſcovery of America by Columbus—one hundred and ſixty-ſix, from the firſt effectual ſettlement in Virginia—and one hundred and fifty-ſix from the firſt ſettlement of Plymouth in Maſſachuſetts, which were the earlieſt Engliſh ſettlements in America.

Juſt after this declaration, General Howe with a powerful force arrived near New York; and landed the troops upon Staten Iſland. General Waſhington was in New York with about thirteen thouſand men, who were encamped either in the city or the neighbouring fortifications.

The operations of the Britiſh began by the action on Long Iſland, in the month of Auguſt. The Americans were defeated, and general Sullivan and lord Sterling, with a large body of men, were made priſoners. The night after the engagement, a retreat was ordered, and executed with ſuch

* See Note (B)

such silence, that the Americans left the island without alarming their enemies, and without loss.

In September, the city of New York was abandoned by the American army, and taken by the British. In November, Fort Washington on York Island was taken, and more than two thousand men made prisoners. Fort Lee, opposite to Fort Washington, on the Jersey shore, was soon after taken, but the garrison escaped.

About the same time, general Clinton was sent with a body of troops to take possession of Rhode Island; and succeeded. In addition to all these losses and defeats, the American army suffered by desertion, and more by sickness, which was epidemic, and very mortal.

The northern army at Ticonderoga, was in a disagreeable situation, particularly, after the battle on Lake Champlain, in which the American force, consisting of a few light vessels, under the command of generals Arnold and Waterbury, was totally dispersed. But general Carleton, instead of pursuing his victory, landed at Crown Point, reconnoitered our posts at Ticonderoga and Mount Independence, and returned to winter quarters in Canada.

The American army might now be said to be no more. All that now remained of an army, which at the opening of the campaign, amounted to at least twenty-five thousand men, did not now exceed three thousand. The term of their engagements being expired, they returned, in large bodies, to their families and friends; the few, who from personal attachment, local circumstances, or superior perseverance and bravery, continued with the Generals Washington and Lee, were too inconsiderable to appear formidable in the view of a powerful and victorious enemy.

In this alarming and critical situation of affairs, General Lee, through an imprudent carelessness, which ill became a man in his important station, was captured by a party of the British light horse commanded by Col. Harcourt; this unfortunate circumstance gave a severe shock to the remaining hopes of the little army, and rendered their situation truly distressing.

While these things were transacting in New-Jersey, General Washington, far from being discouraged by the loss of General Lee, and always ready to improve every advantage to raise the drooping spirits of his handful of men, had made a stand on the Pennsylvania side of the Delaware. Here he collected his scattered forces, called in the assistance of the Pennsylvania militia, and on the night of the 25th of December (1776) when the enemy were lulled into security by the idea of his weakness, and by the inclemency of the night which was remarkably boisterous, as well as by the fumes of a Christmas eve, he crossed the river, and at the breaking of day, marched down to Trenton, and so completely surprized them, that the greater part of the detachment which were stationed at this place, surrendered after a short resistance. The horsemen and a few others made their escape at the opposite end of the town. Upwards of nine hundred Hessians were taken prisoners at this time.

This successful expedition first gave a favorable turn to our affairs, which, after this, seemed to brighten through the whole course of the war. Soon after, General Washington attacked the British troops at Princeton,
and

and obtained a complete victory; not, however, without being bravely oppofed by Colonel Mawhood.

The addrefs in planning and executing thefe enterprizes, reflected the higheft honor on the commander, and the fuccefs revived the defponding hopes of America. The lofs of general Mercer, a gallant officer, at Princeton, was the principal circumftance that allayed the joys of victory.

The following year, 1777, was diftinguifhed by very memorable events, in favor of America. On the opening of the campaign, governor Tryon was fent with a body of troops, to deftroy the ftores at Danbury, in Connecticut. This plan was executed, and the town moftly burnt. The enemy fuffered in their retreat, and the Americans loft general Woofter, a brave and experienced officer.

General Prefcot was taken from his quarters, on Rhode Ifland, by the addrefs and enterprize of colonel Barton, and conveyed prifoner to the continent.

General Burgoyne, who commanded the northern Britifh army, took poffeffion of Ticonderoga, which had been abandoned by the Americans. He pufhed his fucceffes, croffed Lake George, and encamped upon the banks of the Hudfon, near Saratoga. His progrefs however was checked, by the defeat of colonel Baum, near Bennington, in which the undifciplined militia of Vermont, under general Stark, difplayed unexampled bravery, and captured almoft the whole detachment.

The militia affembled from all parts of New England, to ftop the progrefs of general Burgoyne.

Thefe, with the regular troops, formed a refpectable army, commanded by general Gates. After two fevere actions, in which the generals Lincoln and Arnold, behaved with uncommon gallantry, and were wounded, general Burgoyne found himfelf enclofed with brave troops, and was forced to furrender his whole army, amounting, according to fome, to ten thoufand, and according to others to five thoufand feven hundred and fifty-two men, into the hands of the Americans. This memorable event happened on the 17th of October, 1777; and diffufed an univerfal joy over America, and laid a foundation for the treaty with France.

But before thefe tranfactions, the main body of the Britifh forces had embarked at New York, failed up the Chefapeek, and landed at the head of Elk river. The army foon began their march for Philadelphia. General Wafhington had determined to oppofe them, and for this purpofe made a ftand, firft at Red Clay Creek, and then upon the heights, near Brandywine creek. Here the armies engaged, and the Americans were overpowered, and fuffered great lofs. The enemy foon purfued their march, and took poffeffion of Philadelphia, towards the clofe of September.

Not long after, the two armies were again engaged at Germantown, and in the beginning of the action, the Americans had the advantage; but by fome unlucky accident, the fortune of the day was turned in favor of the Britifh. Both fides fuffered confiderable loffes; on the fide of the Americans, was general Nafh.

In an attack upon the forts at Mud-Ifland and Red-Bank, the Heffians were unfuccefsful, and their commander, colonel Donop, killed. The
Britifh

British also lost the Augusta, a ship of the line. But the forts were afterwards taken, and the navigation of the Delaware opened. General Washington was reinforced, with part of the troops, which had composed the northern army, under general Gates; and both armies retired to winter quarters.

In October, the same month in which general Burgoyne was taken at Saratoga, general Vaughan, with a small fleet, sailed up Hudson's river, and wantonly burnt Kingston, a beautiful Dutch settlement, on the west side of the river.

The beginning of the next year, 1778, was distinguished by a treaty of alliance between France and America; by which we obtained a powerful and generous ally. When the English ministry were informed that this treaty was on foot, they dispatched commissioners to America, to attempt a reconciliation. But America would not now accept their offers. Early in the spring, Count de Estaing, with a fleet of fifteen sail of the line, was sent by the court of France to assist America.

General Howe left the army, and returned to England; the command then devolved upon Sir Henry Clinton.

In June the British army left Philadelphia, and marched for New-York. On their march they were annoyed by the Americans; and at Monmouth, a very regular action took place, between part of the armies; the enemy were repulsed with great loss, and had General Lee obeyed his orders, a signal victory must have been obtained. General Lee, for his ill conduct that day, was suspended, and was never afterwards permitted to join the army.

General Lee's conduct, at several times before this, had been very suspicious. In December 1776, he lay at Chatham, about eleven miles from Elizabeth-Town, with a brigade of troops, when a great quantity of baggage was stored at Elizabeth-Town, under a guard of only five hundred Hessians. General Lee was apprized of this, and might have surprized the guard and taken the baggage. But he neglected the opportunity, and after several marches and counter-marches between Troy, Chatham and Morris-Town, he took up his quarters at, or near White's tavern, where he was surprized and taken prisoner by a party of the British horse. He was heard to say repeatedly that General Washington would ruin a fine army. It was suspected that he had designs to supplant the General, and his friends attempted to place him at the head of the army. General Washington's prudent delays and cautious movements afforded General Lee's friends many opportunities to spread reports unfavourable to his character. It was insinuated, with some success, that General Washington wanted courage and abilities. Reports of this kind, at one time, rendered General Lee very popular, and it is supposed he wished to frustrate General Washington's plans, in order to increase the suspicions already entertained of his Generalship, and turn the public clamour in his own favour. His conduct at Monmouth, must have proceeded from such a design; for he commanded the flower of the American army, and was not destitute of courage.

In August general Sullivan, with a large body of troops, attempted to take possession of Rhode-Island, but did not succeed. Soon after, the stores and shipping at Bedford in Massachusetts, were burnt by a party

The UNITED STATES.

of the British troops. The same year, Savannah, then the capital of Georgia, was taken by the British, under the command of colonel Campbell. In the following year (1779) general Lincoln was appointed to the command of the southern army.

Governor Tryon and Sir George Collier made an incursion into Connecticut, and burnt, with wanton barbarity, the towns of Fairfield and Norwalk. But the American arms were crowned with success, in a bold attack upon Stoney Point, which was surprized and taken by general Wayne, in the night of the 15th of July. Five hundred men were made prisoners, with little loss on either side.

A party of British forces attempted this summer, to build a fort on Penobscot river, for the purpose of cutting timber in the neighbouring forests. A plan was laid by Massachusetts to dislodge them, and a considerable fleet collected for the purpose. But the plan failed of success, and the whole marine force fell into the hands of the British, except some vessels which were burnt by the Americans themselves.

In October, general Lincoln and Count de Estaing made an assault upon Savannah; but they were repulsed with considerable loss. In this action, the celebrated Polish Count Pulaski, who had acquired the reputation of a brave soldier, was mortally wounded.

In this summer, general Sullivan marched with a body of troops, into the Indians country, and burnt and destroyed all their provisions and settlements that fell in their way.

On the opening of the Campaign, the next year, (1780) the British troops left Rhode-Island. An expedition under general Clinton and Lord Cornwallis, was undertaken against Charleston, South-Carolina, where general Lincoln commanded. This town, after a close siege of about six weeks, was surrendered to the British commander; and general Lincoln, and the whole American garrison, were made prisoners.

General Gates was appointed to the command in the southern department, and another army collected. In August, Lord Cornwallis attacked the American troops at Camden, in South-Carolina, and routed them with considerable loss. He afterwards marched through the southern states, and supposed them entirely subdued.

The same summer, the British troops made frequent incursions from New York into the Jersies; ravaging and plundering the country.

In June, a large body of the enemy, commanded by General Kniphausen, landed at Elizabeth Town point, and proceeded into the country. They were much harrassed in their progress by Colonel Dayton and the troops under his command. When they arrived at Connecticut Farms, according to their usual but sacrilegious custom, they burnt the Presbyterian church,* parsonage house and a considerable part of the village. But the most cruel and wanton act that was perpetrated during this incursion, was the murder of Mrs. Caldwell, the wife of the Reverend Mr. Caldwell of Elizabeth Town.

The

* *Presbyterian Churches were called* nests *of* rebellion; *and it appears by the number that were burnt in every part of this continent where the British had access, that they were particularly obnoxious.*

This amiable woman, feeing the enemy advancing, retired with her houfe-keeper, a child of three years old, an infant of eight months, and a little maid, to a room fecured on all fides by ftone walls, except at a window oppofite the enemy. She prudently took this precaution to avoid the danger of tranfient fhot, fhould the ground be difputed near that place, which happened not to be the cafe; neither was there any firing from either party near the houfe until the fatal moment, when Mrs. Caldwell, unfufpicious of any immediate danger, fitting on the bed with her little child by the hand, and her nurfe, with her infant babe by her fide, was inftantly fhot dead by an unfeeling Britifh foldier, who had come round to the unguarded part of the houfe, with an evident defign to perpetrate the horrid deed. Many circumftances attending this inhuman murder, evince, not only that it was committed by the enemy with defign, but alfo, that it was by the permiffion, if not by the command, of general Kniphaufen, in order to intimidate the populace to relinquifh their caufe. A circumftance which aggravated this piece of cruelty, was, that when the Britifh officers were made acquainted with the murder, they did not interfere to prevent the corpfe from being ftripped and burnt, but left it half the day, ftripped in part, to be tumbled about by the rude foldiery; and at laft it was removed from the houfe, before it was burned, by the aid of thofe who were not of the army.

Mrs. Caldwell was an amiable woman, of a fweet and even temper, difcreet, prudent, benevolent, foft and engaging in her manners, and beloved by all her acquaintance. She left nine promifing children.

Mrs. Caldwell's death was foon followed by that of her hufband's. In November, 1781, Mr. Caldwell, hearing of the arrival of a young lady at Elizabeth Town point, whofe family in New York, had been peculiarly kind to the American prifoners, rode down to efcort her up to town. Having received her into his chair, the fentinel obferving a little bundle tied in the lady's handkerchief, faid it muft be feized for the ftate. Mr. Caldwell inftantly left the chair, faying he would deliver it to the commanding officer who was then prefent; and as he ftepped forward with this view, another foldier impertinently told him to ftop, which he immediately did; the foldier notwithftanding, without further provocation, fhot him dead on the fpot. Such was the untimely fate of Mr. Caldwell. His public difcourfes were fenfible, animated and perfuafive; his manner of delivery agreeable and pathetic. He was a very warm patriot, and greatly diftinguifhed himfelf in fupporting the caufe of his fuffering country. As a hufband he was kind; as a citizen given to hofpitality. The villain who murdered him was feized and executed.

In July, a French fleet, under Monfieur d'Ternay, with a body of land forces, commanded by Count de Rochambeau, arrived at Rhode-Ifland, to the great joy of the Americans.

This year was alfo diftinguifhed by the infamous treafon of general Arnold. General Wafhington having fome bufinefs to tranfact at Wethersfield in Connecticut, left Arnold to command the important poft of Weftpoint; which guards a pafs in Hudfon's river, about fixty miles from New York. Arnold's conduct in the city of Philadelphia, the preceding winter, had been cenfured; and the treatment he received in confequence, had given him offence.

He

He determined to take revenge ; and for this purpofe, he entered into a negociation with Sir Henry Clinton, to deliver Weftpoint, and the army, into the hands of the Britifh. While General Wafhington was abfent, he difmounted the cannon in fome of the forts, and took other fteps to render the taking of the poft eafy for the enemy.

But by a providential difcovery, the whole plan was defeated. Major Andre, aid to general Clinton, a brave officer, who had been fent up the river as a fpy, to concert the plan of operations with Arnold, was taken, condemned by a court martial, and executed. Arnold made his efcape, by getting on board the Vulture, a Britifh veffel, which lay in the river. His conduct has ftamped him with infamy ; and, like all traitors, he is defpifed by all mankind. General Wafhington arrived in camp juft after Arnold had made his efcape, and reftored order in the garrifon.

After the defeat of general Gates in Carolina, general Greene was appointed to the command in the fouthern department.* From this period, things in that quarter wore a more favorable afpect. Colonel Tarleton, the active commander of the Britifh legion, was defeated by general Morgan, the intrepid commander of the rifle men.

After a variety of movements, the two armies met at Guilford, in Carolina. Here was one of the beft fought actions during the war. General Greene and Lord Cornwallis exerted themfelves at the head of their refpective armies ; and although the Americans were obliged to retire from the field of battle, yet the Britifh army fuffered an immenfe lofs, and could not purfue the victory. This action happened on the 15th March 1781.

In the fpring, Arnold, the traitor, who was made a brigadier-general in the Britifh fervice, with a fmall number of troops, failed for Virginia, and plundered the country. This called the attention of the French fleet to that quarter; and a naval engagement took place between the Englifh and French, in which fome of the Englifh fhips were much damaged, and one entirely difabled.

After the battle of Guilford, general Greene moved towards South-Carolina, to drive the Britifh from their pofts in that ftate. Here Lord Rawdon obtained an inconfiderable advantage over the Americans, near Camden. But general Greene more than recovered this difadvantage, by the brilliant and fuccefsful action at the Eutaw Springs ; where general Marian diftinguifhed himfelf, and the brave colonel Wafhington was wounded and taken prifoner.

Lord Cornwallis, finding general Greene fuccefsful in Carolina, marched to Virginia, collected his forces, and fortified himfelf in Yorktown. In the mean time Arnold made an incurfion into Connecticut, burnt a part of New London, took Fort Grifwold by ftorm, and put the garrifon to the fword. The garrifon confifted chiefly of men fuddenly collected from the little town of Groton, which, by the favage cruelty of the Britifh officer who commanded the attack, loft, in one hour, almoft all its heads of families. The brave colonel Ledyard, who commanded the fort, was flain with his own fword, after he had furrendered.

The

* Note (C)

The UNITED STATES.

The marquis de la Fayette, the brave and generous nobleman, whose services command the gratitude of every American, had been difpatched with about two thoufand light infantry, from the main army, to watch the motions of lord Cornwallis in Virginia. He profecuted this expedition with the greateft military ability. Although his force was much inferior to that of the enemy, he obliged them to leave Richmond, and Williamfburgh, and to feek protection under their fhipping.

About the laft of Auguft, count de Graffe arrived with a large fleet in the Chefapeek, and blocked up the Britifh troops at Yorktown. Admiral Greaves, with a Britifh fleet, appeared off the Capes, and an action fucceeded; but it was not decifive.

General Wafhington had before this time moved the main body of his army, together with the French troops, to the fouthward; and as foon as he heard of the arrival of the French fleet in the Chefapeek, he made rapid marches to the head of Elk, where embarking, the troops foon arrived at Yorktown.

A clofe fiege immediately commenced, and was carried on with fuch vigour, by the combined forces of America and France, that lord Cornwallis was obliged to furrender. This glorious event which took place on the 19th of October, 1781, decided the conteft in favor of America; and laid the foundation of a general peace.

A few months after the furrender of Cornwallis, the Britifh evacuated all their pofts in South Carolina and Georgia, and retired to the main army in New York.

On the night of the 3d of March, 1783, Major William Crane, Captain Thomas Quigley, and fix others, embarked from Elizabeth Town point in a whale-boat, and proceeded for New York, where they boarded and took poffeffion of a twenty-four gun fhip, called the Eagle, then lying under the old battery. This expedition was conducted with fo much gallantry and addrefs, that no oppofition was attempted by the crew; on the contrary, every individual fought a place of fecurity; but their endeavours for that purpofe were rendered abortive by the unprecedented valour and vigilance of thofe heroic men, who conducted the enterprize.—After having captured three naval Captains, and eighteen men, they fecured them on board the floop, which then lay along fide the Eagle; and which was laden with one hundred and nineteen puncheons of Jamaica fpirits, moft of the fhips fails, with twelve nine pounders, loaded and mounted, befides mufquets, &c.—The floop they brought off, and paffed through the Kills, without moleftation for Elizabeth Town point; where, having lightened the veffel, they conducted her in triumph to the landing.

The next fpring (1782) Sir Guy Carleton arrived in New York, and took the command of the Britifh army in America. Immediately on his arrival, he acquainted general Wafhington and Congrefs, that negociations for a peace had been commenced at Paris.

On the 30th of November, 1782, the provifional articles of peace were figned at Paris; by which Great Britian acknowledged the independence and fovereignty of the United States of America; and thefe articles were afterwards ratified by a definitive treaty.

Thus ended a long and arduous conflict, in which Great-Britain expended near an hundred millions of money, with an hundred thoufand
lives,

lives, and won nothing. America endured every cruelty and distress from her enemies; lost many lives and much treasure; but delivered herself from a foreign dominion, and gained a rank among the nations of the earth.

Holland acknowledged the independence of the United States on the 19th of April 1782; Sweden, February 5th 1783; Denmark, the 25th of February; Spain, in March, and Russia in July 1783.

No sooner was peace restored by the definitive treaty, and the British troops withdrawn from the country, than the United States began to experience the defects of their general government. While an enemy was in the country, fear, which had first impelled the colonies to associate in mutual defence, continued to operate as a band of political union. It gave to the resolutions and recommendations of congress the force of laws, and generally commanded a ready acquiescence on the part of the state legislatures. Articles of confederation and perpetual union had been framed in congress, and submitted to the consideration of the states, in the year 1778. Some of the states immediately acceded to them; but others, which had not unappropriated lands, hesitated to subscribe a compact, which would give an advantage to the states which possessed large tracts of unlocated lands, and were thus capable of a great superiority in wealth and population. All objections however had been overcome, and by the accession of Maryland in March 1781, the articles of confederation were ratified, as the frame of government for the United States.

These articles however were framed during the rage of war, when a principle of common safety supplied the place of a coercive power in government; by men who could have had no experience in the art of governing an extensive country, and under circumstances the most critical and embarrassing. To have offered to the people, at that time, a system of government armed with the powers necessary to regulate and controul the contending interests of thirteen States, and the possessions of millions of people, might have raised a jealousy between the states or in the minds of the people at large, that would have weakened the operations of war, and perhaps have rendered a union impracticable. Hence the numerous defects of the confederation.

On the conclusion of peace, these defects began to be felt. Each state assumed the right of disputing the propriety of the resolutions of congress, and the interest of an individual state was placed in opposition to the common interest of the union. In addition to this source of division, a jealousy of the powers of congress began to be excited in the minds of people.

This jealousy of the privileges of freemen, had been roused by the oppressive acts of the British parliament; and no sooner had the danger from this quarter ceased, than the fears of people changed their object, and were turned against their own rulers.

In this situation, there were not wanting men of industry and talents, who had been enemies to the revolution, and who embraced the opportunity to multiply the apprehensions of people and encrease the popular discontents. A remarkable instance of this happened in Connecticut. A soon as the tumults of war had subsided, an attempt was made to convince the people, that the act of congress passed in 1778, granting to the officers of the army, half pay for life, was highly unjuft and tyrannical; and that it was but the firft ftep towards the eftablifhment of penfions and an uncontrolable defpotifm. The act of congrefs, paffed in 1783, commuting half pay for life for five years full pay, was defigned to appeafe the apprehenfions of people, and to convince them that this gratuity was intended merely to indemnify the officers for their loffes by the depreciation of the paper currency; and not to eftablifh a precedent for the granting of penfions. This act however did not fatisfy the people, who fuppofed that the officers had been generally indemnified for the lofs of their pay, by the grants made them from time to time by the legiflatures of the feveral ftates. Befides the act, while it gave five years full pay to the officers, allowed but one year's pay to the privates; a diftinction which had great influence in exciting and continuing the popular ferment, and one that turned a large fhare of the public rage againft the officers themfelves.

The moment an alarm was raifed refpecting this act of congrefs, the enemies of our independence became active in blowing up the flame, by fpreading reports unfavourable to the general government, and tending to create public diffenfions. Newfpapers, in fome parts of the country, were filled with inflammatory publications; while falfe reports and groundlefs infinuations were induftrioufly circulated to the prejudice of congrefs and the officers of the late army. Among a people feelingly alive to every thing that could affect the rights for which they had been contending, thefe reports could not fail of having a powerful effect; the clamour foon became general; the officers of the army, it was believed, had attempted to raife their fortunes on the diftreffes of their fellow citizens, and Congrefs become the tyrants of their country.

Connecticut was the feat of this uneafinefs; although other ftates were much agitated on the occafion. But the inhabitants of that ftate, accuftomed to order and a due fubordination to the laws, did not proceed to outrages; they took their ufual mode of collecting the fenfe of the ftate—affembled in town-meetings—appointed committees to meet in convention, and confult what meafures fhould be adopted to procure a redrefs of their grievances. In this convention, which was held at Middletown, fome nugatory refolves were paffed, expreffing a difapprobation of the half-pay act, and the fubfequent commutation of the grant for five years whole pay. The fame fpirit alfo difcovered itfelf in the affembly at their October feffion, in 1783. A remonftrance againft the acts in favor of the officers, was framed in the houfe of reprefentatives, and notwithftanding the upper houfe refufed to concur in the meafure, it was fent to Congrefs.

During this fituation of affairs, the public odium againft the officers, was augmented by another circumftance. The officers, juft before the difbanding of the army, had formed a fociety, called by the name of the *Cincinnati*, after the Roman Dictator, Cincinnatus, which, it was faid, was intended to perpetuate the memory of the revolution, the friendfhip of the officers, and the union of the ftates; and alfo to raife a fund for the relief of poor widows and orphans, whofe hufbands and fathers had fallen during the war, and for their defcendants. The fociety was divided into ftate focieties, which were to meet on the 4th of July, and with other bufinefs, depute a number of their members to convene annually in general meeting. The members of the inftitution were to be diftinguifhed

guished by wearing a medal, emblematical of the defign of the fociety, and the honors and advantages were to be hereditary in the eldeft male heirs, and in default of male iffue, in the collateral male heirs. Honorary members were to be admitted, but without the hereditary advantages of the fociety, and provided their number fhould never exceed the ratio of one to four of the officers or their defcendants.

Whatever were the real views of the framers of this inftitution, its defign was generally underftood to be harmlefs and honorable. The oftenfible views of the fociety could not however fkreen it from popular jealoufy. A fpirited pamphlet appeared in South Carolina, the avowed production of Mr. Burke, one of the Judges of the fupreme court in that ftate, in which the author attempted to prove that the principles, on which the fociety was formed, would, in procefs of time, originate and eftablifh an order of nobility in this country, which would be repugnant to the genius of our republican governments and dangerous to liberty. This pamphlet appeared in Connecticut, during the commotions raifed by the half pay and commutation acts, and contributed not a little to fpread the flame of oppofition. Nothing could exceed the odium which prevailed at this time, againft the men who had hazarded their perfons and properties in the revolution.

Notwithftanding the difcontents of the people were general, and ready to burft forth in fedition, yet men of information, viz. the officers of government, the clergy, and perfons of liberal education, were moftly oppofed to the unconftitutional fteps taken by the committees and convention at Middletown. They fupported the propriety of the meafures of Congrefs, both by converfation and writing, proved that fuch grants to the army were neceffary to keep the troops together, and that the expence would not be enormous nor oppreffive. During the clofe of the year 1783, every poffible exertion was made to enlighten the people, and fuch was the effect of the arguments ufed by the minority, that in the beginning of the following year, the oppofition fubfided, the committees were difmiffed, and tranquillity reftored to the ftate. In May, the legiflature were able to carry feveral meafures which had before been extremely unpopular. An act was paffed granting the impoft of five per cent. to Congrefs; another giving great encouragement to commerce, and feveral towns were incorporated with extenfive privileges, for the purpofe of regulating the exports of the ftate, and facilitating the collection of debts.

The oppofition to the congreffional acts in favor of the officers, and to the order of the cincinnati, did not rife to the fame pitch in the other ftates as in Connecticut; yet it produced much difturbance in Maffachufetts, and fome others. Jealoufy of power had been univerfally fpread among the people of the United States. The deftruction of the old forms of governments, and the licentioufnefs of war had, in a great meafure, broken their habits of obedience; their paffions had been inflamed by the cry of defpotifm; and like centinels, who have been fuddenly furprized by the approach of an enemy, the ruftling of a leaf was fufficient to give them an alarm. This fpirit of jealoufy, which has not yet fubfided, and which will probably continue vifible during the prefent generation, operated with other caufes to relax the energy of our federal operations.

During

The UNITED STATES.

During the war, vast sums of paper currency had been emitted by Congress, and large quantities of specie had been introduced, towards the close of the war, by the French army, and the Spanish trade. This plenty of money enabled the states to comply with the first requisitions of Congress; so that during two or three years, the federal treasury was, in some measure, supplied. But when the danger of war had ceased, and the vast importations of foreign goods had lessened the quantity of circulating specie, the states began to be very remiss in furnishing their proportion of monies. The annihilation of the credit of the paper bills had totally stopped their circulation, and the specie was leaving the country in cargoes, for remittances to Great Britain; still the luxurious habits of the people, contracted during the war, called for new supplies of goods, and private gratification seconded the narrow policy of state-interest in defeating the operations of the general government.

Thus the revenues of Congress were annually diminishing; some of the states wholly neglecting to make provision for paying the interest of the national debt; others making but a partial provision, until the scanty supplies received from a few of the rich states, would hardly satisfy the demands of the civil list.

This weakness of the federal government, in conjunction with the flood of certificates or public securities, which Congress could neither fund nor pay, occasioned them to depreciate to a very inconsiderable value. The officers and soldiers of the late army were obliged to receive for wages these certificates, or promissary notes, which passed at a fifth, or eighth or a tenth of their nominal value; being thus deprived at once of the greatest part of the reward due for their services. Some indeed profited by speculations in these evidences of the public debt; but such as were under a necessity of parting with them, were robbed of that support which they had a right to expect and demand from their countrymen.

Pennsylvania indeed made provision for paying the interest of her debts, both state and federal; assuming her supposed proportion of the continental debt, and giving the creditors her own state notes in exchange for those of the United States. The resources of that state are immense, but she has not been able to make punctual payments, even in a depreciated paper currency.

Massachusetts, in her zeal to comply fully with the requisitions of Congress, and satisfy the demands of her own creditors, laid a heavy tax upon the people. This was the immediate cause of the rebellion in that state, in 1786. But a heavy debt lying on the state, added to burdens of the same nature, upon almost every incorporation within it; a decline, or rather an extinction of public credit; a relaxation and corruption of manners, and a free use of foreign luxuries; a decay of trade and manufactures, with a prevailing scarcity of money; and, above all, individuals involved in debt to each other—these were the real, though more remote causes of the insurrection. It was the tax which the people were required to pay, that caused them to feel the evils which we have enumerated—this called forth all their other grievances; and the first act of violence committed, was the burning or destroying of a tax bill. This sedition threw the state into a convulsion which lasted about a year; courts of justice were

were violently obstructed; the collection of debts was suspended; and a body of armed troops, under the command of General Lincoln, was employed during the winter of 1786, to disperse the insurgents. Yet so numerous were the latter in the counties of Worcester, Hampshire and Berkshire, and so obstinately combined to oppose the execution of law by force, that the governor and council of the state thought proper not to intrust general Lincoln with military powers, except to act on the offensive, and to repel force with force, in case the insurgents should attack him. The leaders of the rebels however were not men of talents; they were desperate, but without fortitude; and while they were supported with a superior force, they appeared to be impressed with that conscioufness of guilt, which awes the most daring wretch, and makes him shrink from his purpose. This appears by the conduct of a large party of the rebels before the magazine at Springfield; where general Shepard with a small guard, was stationed to protect the continental stores. The insurgents appeared upon the plain, with a vast superiority of numbers, but a few shot from the artillery made the multitude retreat in disorder with the loss of four men. This spirited conduct of general Shepard, with the industry, perseverance and prudent firmness of general Lincoln, dispersed the rebels, drove the leaders from the state, and restored tranquillity. An act of indemnity was passed in the legislature for all the insurgents, except a few leaders, on condition they should become peaceable subjects and take the oath of allegiance. The leaders afterwards petitioned for pardon, which, from motives of policy, was granted by the legislature.

But the loss of public credit, popular disturbances, and insurrections were not the only evils which were generated by the peculiar circumstances of the times. The emissions of bills of credit and tender laws, were added to the black catalogue of political disorders.

The expedient of supplying the deficiencies of specie, by emissions of paper bills, was adopted very early in the colonies. The expedient was obvious and produced good effects. In a new country, where population is rapid, and the value of lands increasing, the farmer finds an advantage in paying legal interest for money; for if he can pay the interest by his profits, the increasing value of his lands will, in a few years, discharge the principal.

In no colony was this advantage more sensibly experienced than in Pennsylvania. The emigrations to that province were numerous—the natural population rapid—and these circumstances combined, advanced the value of real property to an astonishing degree. As the first settlers there, as well as in other provinces, were poor, the purchase of a few foreign articles drained them of specie. Indeed for many years, the balance of trade must have necessarily been greatly against the colonies.

But bills of credit, emitted by the state and loaned to the industrious inhabitants, supplied the want of specie, and enabled the farmer to purchase stock. These bills were generally a legal tender in all colonial or private contracts, and the sums issued did not generally exceed the quantity requisite for a medium of trade, they retained their full nominal value in the purchase of commodities. But as they were not received by the British merchants, in payment for their goods, there was a great demand

for

for specie and bills, which occasioned the latter at various times to appreciate. Thus was introduced a difference between the English sterling money and the currencies of the colonies which remains to this day.*

The advantages the colonies had derived from bills of credit, under the British government, suggested to Congress, in 1775, the idea of issuing bills for the purpose of carrying on the war. And this was perhaps their only expedient. Money could not be raised by taxation—it could not be borrowed. The first emissions had no other effect upon the medium of commerce, than to drive the specie from circulation. But when the paper substituted for specie, had, by repeated emissions, augmented the sum in circulation, much beyond the usual sum of specie, the bills began to lose their value. The depreciation continued in proportion to the sums emitted, until seventy, and even one hundred and fifty nominal paper dollars, were hardly an equivalent for one Spanish milled dollar. Still from the year 1775 to 1781, this depreciating paper currency was almost the only medium of trade. It supplied the place of specie, and enabled Congress to support a numerous army; until the sum in circulation amounted to two hundred millions of dollars. But about the year 1780, specie began to be plentiful, being introduced by the French army, a private trade with the Spanish islands, and an illicit intercourse with the British garrison at New York. This circumstance accelerated the depreciation of the paper bills, until their value had sunk almost to nothing. In 1781, the merchants and brokers in the southern states, apprehensive of the approaching fate of the currency, pushed immense quantities of it suddenly into New England—made vast purchases of goods in Boston—and instantly the bills vanished from circulation.

The whole history of this continental paper is a history of public and private frauds. Old specie debts were often paid in a depreciated currency—and even new contracts for a few weeks or days were often discharged with a small part of the value received. From this plenty and fluctuating state of the medium, sprung hosts of speculators and itinerant traders, who left their honest occupations for the prospect of immense gains, in a fraudulent business, that depended on no fixed principles; and the profits of which could be reduced to no certain calculations.

To increase these evils, a project was formed to fix the prices of articles, and restrain persons from giving or receiving more for any commodity than the price stated by authority. These regulating acts were reprobated by every man acquainted with commerce and finance; as they were intended to prevent an effect without removing the cause. To attempt to fix the value of money, while streams of bills were incessantly flowing from the treasury of the United States, was as ridiculous as an attempt to restrain the rising of water in rivers amidst showers of rain.

Notwithstanding

---

* A Dollar, in Sterling money, is 4/6. But the price of a Dollar rose in New-England currency to 6/. in New York to 8/. in New Jersey Pennsylvania and Maryland to 7/6; in Virginia to 6/. in North Carolina to 8/. in South Carolina and Georgia to 4/8. This difference, originating between paper and specie, or bills, continued afterwards to exist in the nominal estimation of gold and silver. *Franklin's Miscel. Works, P. 217.*

The UNITED STATES.

Notwithstanding all opposition, some states framed and attempted to enforce these regulating acts. The effect was, a momentary apparent stand in the price of articles; innumerable acts of collusion and evasion among the dishonest; numberless injuries done to the honest; and finally a total disregard of all such regulations, and the consequential contempt of laws and the authority of the magistrate.

During these fluctuations of business, occasioned by the variable value of money, people lost sight, in some measure, of the steady principles which had before governed their intercourse with each other. Speculations followed and relaxed the rigour of commercial obligations.

Industry likewise had suffered by the flood of money which had deluged the states. The prices of produce had risen in proportion to the quantity of money in circulation, and the demand for the commodities of the country. This made the acquisition of money easy, and indolence and luxury with their train of desolating consequences, spread themselves among all descriptions of people.

But as soon as hostilities between Great-Britain and America were suspended, the scene was changed. The bills emitted by congress had long before ceased to circulate; and the specie of the country was soon drained off to pay for foreign goods, the importations of which exceeded all calculation. Within two years from the close of the war, *a scarcity of money* was the general cry. The merchants found it impossible to collect their debts, and make punctual remittances to their creditors in Great-Britain; and the consumers were driven to the necessity of retrenching their superfluities in living and of returning to their antient habits of industry and œconomy.

This change was however progressive and slow. In many of the states which suffered by the numerous debts they had contracted, and by the distresses of war, the people called aloud for emissions of paper bills to supply the deficiency of a medium. The depreciation of the continental bills, was a recent example of the ill effects of such an expedient, and the impossibility of supporting the credit of paper, was urged by the opposers of the measure as a substantial argument against adopting it. But nothing would silence the popular clamor; and many men of the first talents and eminence, united their voices with that of the populace. Paper money had formerly maintained its credit, and been of singular utility; and past experience, notwithstanding a change of circumstances, was an argument in its favor that bore down all opposition.

Pennsylvania, although one of the richest states in the union, was the first to emit bills of credit, as a substitute for specie. But the revolution had removed the necessity of it, at the same time, that it had destroyed the means by which its former credit had been supported. Lands, at the close of the war, were not rising in value—bills on London could not so readily be purchased, as while the province was dependent on Great Britain— the state was split into parties, one of which attempted to defeat the measures most popular with the other—and the depreciation of continental bills, with the injuries which it had done to individuals, inspired a general distrust of all public promises.

Notwithstanding a part of the money was loaned on good landed security, and the faith of that wealthy state pledged for the redemption of

the

the whole at its nominal value, yet the advantages of specie as a medium of commerce, especially as an article of remittance to London, soon made a difference of ten per cent. between the bills of credit and specie. This difference may be considered rather as an appreciation of gold and silver, than a depreciation of paper; but its effects, in a commercial state, must be highly prejudicial. It opens the door to frauds of all kinds, and frauds are usually practised on the honest and unsuspecting, especially upon all classes of labourers.

This currency of Pennsylvania is receivable in all payments at the custom house, and for certain taxes, at its nominal value; yet it has sunk to two-thirds of this value, in the few commercial transactions where it is received.

North Carolina, South Carolina, and Georgia had recourse to the same wretched expedient to supply themselves with money; not reflecting that industry, frugality, and good commercial laws are the only means of turning the balance of trade in favour of a country, and that this balance is the only permanent source of solid wealth and ready money. But the bills they emitted shared a worse fate than those of Pennsylvania; they expelled almost all the circulating cash from the states; they lost a great part of their nominal value, they impoverished the merchants, and embarrassed the planters.

The state of Virginia had too much wisdom to emit bills; but tolerated a practice among the inhabitants of cutting dollars and smaller pieces of silver, in order to prevent it from leaving the state. This pernicious practice prevailed also in Georgia.*

Maryland escaped the calamity of a paper currency. The house of delegates brought forward a bill for the emission of bills of credit to a large amount; but the senate firmly and successfully resisted the pernicious scheme. The opposition between the two houses was violent and tumultuous; it threatened the state with anarchy; but the question was carried to the people, and the good sense of the senate finally prevailed.

New-Jersey is situated between two of the largest commercial towns in America, and consequently drained of specie. This state also emitted a large sum in bills of credit, which served to pay the interest of the public debt; but the currency depreciated, as in other states.

Rhode-Island exhibits a melancholy proof of that licentiousness and anarchy which always follows a relaxation of the moral principles. In a rage for supplying the state with money and filling every man's pocket without obliging him to earn it by his diligence, the legislature passed an act for making one hundred thousand pounds in bills; a sum much more than sufficient for a medium of trade in that state, even without any specie. The merchants in Newport and Providence opposed the act with firmness; their opposition added fresh vigor to the resolution of the assembly, and induced them to enforce the scheme by a legal tender of a most extraordinary nature. They passed an act, ordaining that if any creditor should refuse to take their bills, for any debt whatever, the debtor might lodge

the

---

* *A dollar was usually cut in five pieces, and each passed by tale for a quarter; so that the man who cut it gained a quarter, or rather a fifth. If the state should re-coin this silver, it must lose a fifth.*

the sum due, with a justice of the peace, who should give notice of it in the public papers; and if the creditor did not appear and receive the money within six months from the first notice, his debt should be forfeited. This act astonished all honest men; and even the promoters of paper moneymaking in other states, and on other principles, reprobated this act of Rhode-Island, as wicked and oppressive. But the state was governed by faction. During the cry for paper money, a number of boisterous ignorant men, were elected into the legislature, from the smaller towns in the state. Finding themselves united with a majority in opinion, they formed and executed any plan their inclination suggested; they opposed every measure that was agreeable to the mercantile interest; they not only made bad laws to suit their own wicked purposes, but appointed their own corrupt creatures to fill the judicial and executive departments. Their money depreciated sufficiently to answer all their vile purposes in the discharge of debts—business almost totally ceased, all confidence was lost, the state was thrown into confusion at home and was execrated abroad.

Massachusetts Bay had the good fortune, amidst her political calamities, to prevent an emission of bills of credit. New Hampshire made no paper; but in the distresses which followed her loss of business after the war, the legislature made horses, lumber and most articles of produce a legal tender in the fulfilment of contracts. It is doubtless unjust to oblige a creditor to receive any thing for his debt, which he had not in contemplation at the time of the contract. But as the commodities which were to be a tender by the law of New Hampshire, where of an intrinsic value, bearing some proportion to the amount of the debt, the injustice of the law was less flagrant, than that which enforced the tender of paper in Rhode Island. Indeed a similar law prevailed for some time in Massachusetts; and in Connecticut it is a standing law, that a creditor shall take land on an execution, at a price to be fixed by three indifferent freeholders; provided no other means of payment shall appear to satisfy the demand. In a state, that has but little foreign commerce, and but little money in circulation, such a law may not only be tolerable; but, if people are satisfied with it, may produce good effects. It must not however be omitted, that while the most flourishing commercial states introduced a paper medium, to the great injury of honest men, a bill for an emission of paper in Connecticut, where there is very little specie, could never command more than one eighth of the votes of the legislature. The movers of the bill have hardly escaped ridicule; so generally is the measure reprobated as a source of frauds and public mischief.

The legislature of New York, a state that had the least necessity and apology for making paper money, as her commercial advantages always furnish her with specie sufficient for a medium, issued a large sum in bills of credit, which support their value better than the currency of any other state. Still the paper has raised the value of specie, which is always in demand for exportation, and this difference of exchange between paper and specie, exposes commerce to most of the inconveniencies resulting from a depreciated medium.

Such is the history of paper money thus far; a miserable substitute for real coin, in a country where the reins of government are too weak to compel

compel the fulfilment of public engagements; and where all confidence is public faith is totally destroyed.

While the states were thus endeavoring to repair the loss of specie, by empty promises, and to support their business by shadows, rather than by reality, the British ministry formed some commercial regulations that deprived them of the profits of their trade to the West Indies and to Great Britain. Heavy duties were laid upon such articles as were remitted to the London merchants for their goods, and such were the duties upon American bottoms, that the states were almost wholly deprived of the carrying trade. A prohibition, as has been mentioned, was laid upon the produce of the United States, shipped to the English West India Islands in American built vessels, and in those manned by American seamen. These restrictions fell heavy upon the eastern states, which depended much upon ship-building for the support of their trade; and they materially injured the business of the other states.

Without a union that was able to form and execute a general system of commercial regulations, some of the states attempted to impose restraints upon the British trade that should indemnify the merchant for the losses he had suffered, or induce the British ministry to enter into a commercial treaty and relax the rigor of their navigation laws. These measures however produced nothing but mischief. The states did not act in concert, and the restraints laid on the trade of one state operated to throw the business into the hands of its neighbour. Massachusetts, in her zeal to counteract the effect of the English navigation laws, laid enormous duties upon British goods imported into that state; but the other states did not adopt a similar measure; and the loss of business soon obliged that state to repeal or suspend the law. Thus when Pennsylvania laid heavy duties on British goods, Delaware and New Jersey made a number of free ports to encourage the landing of goods within the limits of those states; and the duties in Pennsylvania served no purpose, but to create smuggling.

Thus divided, the states began to feel their weakness. Most of the legislatures had neglected to comply with the requisitions of Congress for furnishing the federal treasury; the resolves of Congress were disregarded; the proposition for a general impost to be laid and collected by Congress was negatived first by Rhode Island, and afterwards by New-York. The British troops continued, under pretence of a breach of treaty on the part of America, to hold possession of the forts on the frontiers of the states, and thus commanded the fur trade. Many of the states individually were infested with popular commotions or iniquitous tender laws, while they were oppressed with public debts; the certificates or public notes had lost most of their value, and circulated merely as the objects of speculation; Congress lost their respectability, and the United States, their credit and importance.

In the midst of these calamities, a proposition was made in 1785, in the house of delegates in Virginia, to appoint commissioners, to meet such as might be appointed in the other states, who should form a system of commercial regulations for the United States, and recommend it to the several legislatures for adoption. Commissioners were accordingly appointed, and a request was made to the legislatures of the other states to accede to the proposition. Accordingly several of the states appointed commissioners who met at Annapolis in the summer of 1786, to consult what mea-

sures

fures should be taken to unite the states in some general and efficient commercial system. But as the states were not all represented, and the powers of the commissioners were, in their opinion, too limited to propose a system of regulations adequate to the purposes of government, they agreed to recommend a general convention to be held at Philadelphia the next year, with powers to frame a general plan of government for the United States. This measure appeared to the commissioners absolutely necessary. The old confederation was essentially defective. It was destitute of almost every principle necessary to give effect to legislation.

It was defective in the article of legislating over states, instead of individuals. All history testifies that recommendations will not operate as laws, and compulsion cannot be exercised over states, without violence, war and anarchy. The confederation was also destitute of a sanction to its laws. When resolutions were passed in Congress, there was no power to compel obedience by fine, by suspension of privileges or other means. It was also distitute of a guarantee for the state governments. Had one state been invaded by its neighbour, the union was not constitutionally bound to assist in repelling the invasion, and supporting the constitution of the invaded state. The confederation was further deficient in the principle of apportioning the quotas of money to be furnished by each state; in a want of power to form commercial laws, and to raise troops for the defence and security of the union; in the equal suffrage of the states, which placed Rhode Island on a footing in Congress with Virginia; and to crown all the defects, we may add the want of a judiciary power, to define the laws of the union, and to reconcile the contradictory decisions of a number of independent judicatories.

These and many inferior defects were obvious to the commissioners, and therefore they urged a general convention, with powers to form and offer to the consideration of the states, a system of general government that should be less exceptionable. Accordingly in May, 1787, delegates from all the states, except Rhode Island, assembled at Philadelphia; and chose General Washington for their president. After four months deliberation, in which the clashing interests of the several states, appeared in all their force, the convention agreed to recommend the plan of federal government which we have already recited.

As soon as the plan of the federal constitution was submitted to the legislatures of the several states, they proceeded to take measures for collecting the sense of the people upon the propriety of adopting it. In the small state of Delaware, a convention was called in November, which, after a few days deliberation, ratified the constitution, without a dissenting voice.

In the convention of Pennsylvania, held the same month, there was a spirited opposition to the new form of government. The debates were long and interesting. Great abilities and firmness were displayed on both sides; but, on the 13th of December, the constitution was received by two-thirds of the members. The minority were dissatisfied, and with an obstinacy that ill became the representatives of a free people, published their reasons of dissent, which were calculated to inflame a party already violent, and which, in fact produced some disturbances in the western parts of the state. But the opposition has since gradually subsided. In

In New-Jerfey, the convention which met in December, were unanimous in adopting the conftitution; as was likewife that of Georgia.

In Connecticut there was fome oppofition; but the conftitution was, on the 9th of January 1788, ratified by three-fourths of the votes in convention, and the minority peaceably acquiefced in the decifion.

In Maffachufetts, the oppofition was large and refpectable. The convention, confifting of more than three hundred delegates, were affembled in January, and continued their debates, with great candor and liberality about five weeks. At length the queftion was carried for the conftitution by a fmall majority, and the minority, with that manly condefcenfion which becomes great minds, fubmitted to the meafure, and united to fupport the government.

In New-Hampfhire, the federal caufe was, for fome time doubtful. The greateft number of the delegates in convention, were at firft on the fide of the oppofition; and fome, who might have had their objections removed by the difcuffion of the fubject, inftructed to reject the conftitution. Although the inftructions of conftituents cannot, on the true principles of reprefentation, be binding upon a deputy, in any legiflative affembly, becaufe his conftituents are but a *part* of the ftate, and have not heard the arguments and objections of the *whole*, whereas his act is to affect the *whole* ftate, and therefore is to be directed by the fenfe or wifdom of the whole, collected in the legiflative affembly; yet the delegates in the New-Hampfhire convention conceived, very erroneoufly, that the fenfe of the freemen in the towns, thofe little diftricts, where no act of legiflation can be performed, impofed a reftraint upon their own wills.* An adjournment was therefore moved, and carried. This gave the people opportunity to gain a farther knowledge of the merits of the conftitution, and at the fecond meeting of the convention, it was ratified by a refpectable majority.

In Maryland, feveral men of abilities appeared in the oppofition, and were unremitted in their endeavours to perfuade the people, that the propofed plan of government was artfully calculated to deprive them of their deareft rights; yet in convention it appeared that five-fixths of the voices were in favour of it.

In South Carolina, the oppofition was refpectable; but two-thirds of the convention appeared to advocate and vote for the conftitution.

In Virginia, many of the principal characters oppofed the ratification of the conftitution with great abilities and induftry. But after a full difcuffion of the fubject, a fmall majority, of a numerous convention, appeared for its adoption.

In New-York, two-thirds of the delegates in convention were, at their firft meeting, determined to reject the conftitution. Here therefore the debates were the moft interefting, and the event extremely doubtful. The argument was managed with uncommon addrefs and abilities on both fides of the queftion. But during the feffion, the ninth and tenth ftates had acceded to the propofed plan, fo that by the conftitution, Congrefs were empowered to iffue an ordinance for organizing the new government. This event placed the oppofition on new ground; and the expediency of

uniting

---

* *This pernicious opinion has prevailed in all the ftates, and done infinite mifchief.*

uniting with the other states—the generous motives of conciliating all differences, and the danger of a rejection, influenced a respectable number, who were originally opposed to the constitution, to join the federal interest. The constitution was accordingly ratified by a small majority; but the ratification was accompanied here, as in Virginia, with a bill of rights, declaratory of the sense of the convention, as to certain great principles, and with a catalogue of amendments, which were to be recommended to the consideration of the new Congress, and the several state legislatures.

North Carolina met in convention in July, to deliberate on the new constitution. After a short session they rejected it by a majority of one hundred and seventy six, against seventy six. This is the first state that has, in a formal manner, rejected the constitution. Upon what principle they did it, it is difficult to tell, and delicate to conjecture. The miseries that will probably arise from their separation from the union, and their internal divisions may eventually occasion a reconsideration. It is certain that their rejection of the new plan of government, will have no effect in impeding its organization and establishment between the ratifying states.

Rhode Island was doomed to be the sport of a blind and singular policy. The legislature, in consistency with the measures which had been before pursued, did not call a convention, to collect the sense of the state upon the proposed constitution; but in an unconstitutional and absurd manner, submitted the plan of government to the consideration of the people. Accordingly it was brought before town meetings, and in most of them rejected. In some of the large towns, particularly in Newport and Providence, the people collected and resolved, with great propriety, that they could not take up the subject; and that the proposition for embracing or rejecting the federal constitution, could come before no tribunal but that of the *State* in convention or legislature.

It is hoped, that the very respectable minority, who have ever strenuously opposed the proceedings of the infatuated majority, will, by their prudent and persevering exertions, effect the salvation of the state. New York rejected the proceedings of the first Congress, and Georgia refused to send delegates; yet in two years after they were both among the foremost in supporting our independence. In two years North Carolina and Rhode Island, may be as warmly engaged in supporting, as they are now in opposing the constitution. If we may judge from their present situations, they have more need of an efficient government than any state in the union.

From the moment the proceedings of the general convention at Philadelphia transpired, the public mind was exceedingly agitated, and suspended between hope and fear, until nine states had ratified their plan of a federal government. Indeed the anxiety continued until Virginia and New York had acceded to the system. But this did not prevent the demonstrations of their joy, on the accession of each state.

On the ratification in Massachusetts, the citizens of Boston, in the elevation of their joy, formed a procession in honor of the happy event, which was novel, splendid and magnificent. This example was afterwards followed and in some instances improved upon, in Baltimore, Charleston, Philadelphia,

The UNITED STATES.

Philadelphia, New Haven, Portfmouth and New-York fucceffively. Nothing could equal the beauty and grandeur of thefe exhibitions. A fhip was mounted upon wheels, and drawn through the ftreets; mechanics erected ftages, and exhibited fpecimens of labour in their feveral occupations, as they moved along the road; flags with emblems, defcriptive of all the arts and of the federal union, were invented and difplayed in honor of the government; multitudes of all ranks in life affembled to view the majeftic fcenes; while fobriety, joy and harmony marked the brilliant exhibitions, by which the Americans celebrated the eftablifhment of their Empire.

NOTES.

NOTE (A) for Page 104.

NOTWITHSTANDING it has often been afferted with confidence, that General Wafhington was a native of England, certain it is his anceftors came from thence to this country fo long ago as the year 1657. He, in the third defcent after their migration, was born on the 11th of February, (old ftyle) 1732, at the parifh of Wafhington, in Weftmoreland county, in Virginia. His father's family was numerous, and he was the firft fruit of a fecond marriage. His education having been principally conducted by a private tutor, at fifteen years old he was entered a midfhipman on board of a Britifh veffel of war ftationed on the coaft of Virginia, and his baggage prepared for embarkation: but the plan was abandoned on account of the reluctance his mother expreffed to his engaging in that profeffion.

Previous to this tranfaction, when he was but ten years of age, his father died, and the charge of the family devolved on his eldeft brother. His eldeft brother, a young man of the moft promifing talents, had a command in the colonial troops employed againft Carthagena, and on his return from the expedition, named his new patrimonial manfion MOUNT VERNON, in honour of the admiral of that name, from whom he had received many civilities. He was afterwards made Adjutant General of the militia of Virginia, but did not long furvive. At his deceafe (notwithftanding there are heirs of an elder branch who poffefs a large moiety of the paternal inheritance) the eldeft fon by the fecond marriage, inherited this feat and a confiderable landed property. In confequence of the extenfive limits of the colony, the vacant office of Adjutant General was divided into three diftricts, and the *future Hero of America*, before he attained his twentieth year, began his military fervice by a principal appointment in that department, with the rank of major.

When he was little more than twenty one years of age, an event occurred which called his abilities into public notice. In 1753, while the government of the colony was adminiftered by lieutenant governor Dinwiddie, encroachments were reported to have been made by the French, from Canada, on the territories of the Britifh colonies, at the weftward. Young Mr. Wafhington, who was fent with plenary powers to afcertain the facts, treat with the favages and warn the French to defift from their aggreffions, performed the duties of his miffion, with fingular induftry, intelligence

and

and addrefs. His journal, and report to governor Dinwiddie, which were published, announced to the world that correctnefs of mind, manlinefs in ftyle and accuracy in the mode of doing bufinefs, which have fince characterifed him in the conduct of more arduous affairs. But it was deemed, by fome, an extraordinary circumftance that fo juvenile and inexperienced a perfon fhould have been employed on a negociation, with which fubjects of the greateft importance were involved : fubjects which fhortly after became the origin of a war between England and France, that raged for many years throughout every part of the globe.

As the troubles ftill fubfifted on the frontiers, the colony of Virginia raifed, the next year, a regiment of troops for their defence. Of this corps, Mr. Fry, one of the profeffors of the college, was appointed Colonel, and Major Wafhington receivd the commiffion of Lieutenant Colonel. But Colonel Fry died the fame fummer, without ever having joined; and of courfe left his regiment and rank to the fecond in command. Colonel Wafhington made indefatigable efforts to form the regiment, eftablifh magazines, and open roads fo as to pre-occupy the advantageous poft at the confluence of the Allegany and Monongahela rivers, which he had recommended for that purpofe in his report the preceding year. He was to have been joined by a detachment of independent regulars from the fouthern colonies, together with fome companies of provincials from North Carolina and Maryland. But he perceived the neceffity of expedition, and without waiting for their arrival, commenced his march in the month of May. Notwithftanding his precipitated advance, on his afcending the Laurel hill, fifty miles fhort of his object, he was advifed that a body of French had already taken poffeffion and erected a fortification, which they named fort *du Quefne*. He then fell back to a place known by the appellation of *the Great Meadows*, for the fake of forage and fupplies. Here he built a temporary ftockade, merely to cover his ftores; it was from its fate called fort *Neceffity*. His force when joined by Captain M'Kay's regulars, did not amount to four hundred effectives. Upon receiving information from his fcouts that a confiderable party was approaching to reconnoitre his poft, he fallied and defeated them. But in return he was attacked by an army, computed to have been fifteen hundred ftrong, and after a gallant defence, in which more than one third of his men were killed and wounded, was forced to capitulate. The garrifon marched out with the honours of war, but were plundered by the Indians, in violation of the articles of capitulation. After this difafter, the remains of the Virginia regiment returned to Alexandria to be recruited and furnifhed with neceffary fupplies.

In the year 1755, the Britifh government fent to this country general Braddock, who, by the junction of two veteran regiments from Ireland, with the independent and provincial corps in America, was to repel the French from the confines of the Englifh fettlements. Upon a royal arrangement of rank, by which " no officer who did not *immediately* derive his commiffion from the king, could command one who did," Col. Wafhington relinquifhed his regiment and went as an extra aid de camp into the family of general Braddock. In this capacity, at the battle of Monongahela, he attended that general, whofe life was gallantly facraficed in attempting to extricate his troops from the fatal ambufcade into

which

which his over-weening confidence had conducted them. Braddock had several horses shot under him, before he fell himself; and there was not an officer, whose duty obliged him to be on horseback that day, excepting Colonel Washington, who was not either killed or wounded. This circumstance enabled him to display greater abilities in covering the retreat and saving the wreck of the army, than he could otherwise have done. As soon as he had secured their passage over the ford of the Monongahela, and found they were not pursued, he hastened to concert measures for their further security with Colonel Dunbar, who had remained with the second division and heavy baggage at some distance in the rear. To effect this, he travelled with two guides, all night, through an almost impervious wilderness, notwithstanding the fatigues he had undergone in the day, and notwithstanding he had so imperfectly recovered from sickness that he was obliged in the morning to be supported with cushions on his horse. The public accounts in England and America were not parsimonious of applause for the essential service he had rendered on so trying an occasion.

Not long after this time, the regulation of rank, which had been so injurious to the Colonial officers, was changed to their satisfaction, in consequence of the discontent of the officers and the remonstrance of Colonel Washington; and the supreme authority of Virginia, impressed with a due sense of his merits, gave him, in a new and extensive commission, the command of all the troops raised and to be raised in that colony.

It would not comport with the intended brevity of this sketch, to mention in detail the plans he suggested or the system he pursued for defending the frontiers, until the year 1758, when he commanded the van brigade of General Forbes's army in the capture of Fort Du Quesne. A similar reason will preclude the recital of the personal hazards and atchievments which happened in the course of his service. The tranquillity on the frontiers of the middle colonies having been restored by the success of this campaign, and the health of Colonel Washington having become extremely debilitated by an inveterate pulmonary complaint, in 1759 he resigned his military appointment. Authentic documents are not wanting to shew the tender regret which the Virginia line expressed at parting with their commander, and the affectionate regard which he entertained for them.

His health was gradually re-established. He married Mrs. Custis,* a handsome and amiable young widow, possessed of an ample jointure; and settled as a planter and farmer on the estate where he now resides in Fairfax county. After some years he gave up planting tobacco, and went altogether into the farming business. He has raised seven thousand bushels of wheat, and ten thousand of Indian corn in one year. Athough he has confined his own cultivation to this domestic tract of about nine thousand acres, yet he possesses excellent lands, in large quantities, in several other counties. His judgment in the quality of soils, his command of money to avail himself of purchases, and his occasional employment in early life as a surveyor, gave him opportunities of making advantageous locations; many of which are much improved.

After he left the army, until the year 1775, he thus cultivated the arts of peace. He was constantly a member of assembly, a magistrate of his
R   county,

* *General and Mrs. Washington were both born in the same year.*

county, and a judge of the court. He was elected a delegate to the first Congress in 1774; as well as to that which assembled in the year following. Soon after the war broke out, he was appointed by Congress commander in chief of the forces of the United Colonies.

It is the less necessary to particularize, in this place, his transactions in the course of the late war, because the impression which they made is yet fresh in every mind. But it is hoped posterity will be taught, in what manner he transformed an undisciplined body of peasantry into a regular army of soldiers. Commentaries on his campaigns would undoubtedly be highly interesting and instructive to future generations. The conduct of the first campaign, in compelling the British troops to abandon Boston by a bloodless victory, will merit a minute narration. But a volume would scarcely contain the mortifications he experienced and the hazards to which he was exposed in 1776 and 1777, in contending against the prowess of Britain, with an inadequate force. His good destiny and consummate prudence prevented want of success from producing want of confidence on the part of the public; for want of success is apt to lead to the adoption of pernicious counsels through the levity of the people or the ambition of their demagogues. Shortly after this period, sprang up the only cabal, that ever existed during his public life, to rob him of his reputation and command. It proved as impotent in effect, as it was audacious in design. In the three succeeding years the germ of discipline unfolded; and the resouces of America having been called into co-operation with the land and naval armies of France, produced the glorious conclusion of the campaign in 1781. From this time the gloom began to disappear from our political horizon, and the affairs of the union proceeded in a meliorating train, until a peace was most ably negociated by our ambassadors in Europe, in 1783.

No person, who had not the advantage of being present when general Washington received the intelligence of peace, and who did not accompany him to his domestic retirement, can describe the relief which that joyful event brought to his labouring mind, or the supreme satisfaction with which he withdrew to private life. From his triumphal entry into New York, upon the evacuation of that city by the British army, to his arrival at Mount Vernon, after the resignation of his commission to Congress, festive crowds impeded his passage through all the populous towns, the devotion of a whole people pursued him with prayers to Heaven for blessings on his head, while their gratitude sought the most expressive language of manifesting itself to him, as their common father and benefactor. When he became a private citizen he had the unusual felicity to find that his native state was among the most zealous in doing justice to his merits; and that stronger demonstrations of affectionate esteem (if possible) were given by the citizens of his neighbourhood, than by any other description of men on the continent. But he has constantly declined accepting any compensation for his services, or provision for the augmented expences which have been incurred by him in consequence of his public employment, although proposals have been made in the most delicate manner, particularly by the states of Virginia and Pennsylvania.

The virtuous simplicity which distinguishes the private life of General Washington, though less known than the dazzling splendor of his military

tary atchievments, is not lefs edifying in example, or worthy the attention of his countrymen. The confpicuous character he has acted on the theatre of human affairs, the uniform dignity with which he fuftained his part amidft difficulties of the moft difcouraging nature, and the glory of having arrived through them at the hour of triumph, have made many official and literary perfons, on both fides of the ocean, ambitious of a correfpondence with him. Thefe correfpondencies unavoidably engrofs a great portion of his time; and the communications contained in them, combined with the numerous periodical publications and news papers which he perufes, render him, as it were, the *focus of political intelligence for the new world*. Nor are his converfations with well-informed men lefs conducive to bring him acquainted with the various events which happen in different countries of the globe. Every foreigner of diftinction, who travels in America, makes it a point to vifit him. Members of Congrefs and other dignified perfonages do not pafs his houfe, without calling to pay their refpects. As another fource of information it may be mentioned, that many literary productions are fent to him annually by their authors in Europe; and that there is fcarcely one work written in America on any art, fcience, or fubject, which does not feek his protection, or which is not offered to him as a token of gratitude. Mechanical inventions are frequently fubmitted to him for his approbation, and natural curiofities prefented for his inveftigation. But the multiplicity of epiftolary applications, often on the remains of fome bufinefs which happened when he was commander in chief, fometimes on fubjects foreign to his fituation, frivolous in their nature, and intended merely to gratify the vanity of the writers by drawing anfwers from him, is truly diftrefling and almoft incredible. His benignity in anfwering, perhaps, encreafes the number. Did he not hufband every moment to the beft advantage, it would not be in his power to notice the vaft variety of fubjects that claim his attention. Here a minuter defcription of his domeftic life may be expected.

To apply a life, at beft but fhort, to the moft ufeful purpofes; he lives as he ever has done, in the unvarying habits of regularity, temperance and induftry. He rifes, in winter as well as fummer, at the dawn of day; and generally reads or writes fome time before breakfaft. He breakfafts about feven o'clock, on three fmall indian hoe-cakes and as many difhes of tea. He rides immediately to his different farms, and remains with his labourers until a little paft two o'clock, when he returns and dreffes. At three he dines, commonly on a fingle difh, and drinks from half a pint to a pint of Madeira wine. This, with one fmall glafs of punch, a draught of beer, and two difhes of tea (which he takes half an hour before fun-fetting) conftitutes his whole fuftenance until the next day. Whether there be company or not, the table is always prepared by its elegance and exuberance for their reception; and the General remains at it for an hour after dinner, in familiar converfation and convivial hilarity. It is then that every one prefent is called upon to give fome abfent friend as a toaft; the name not unfrequently awakens a pleafing remembrance of paft events, and gives a new turn to the animated colloquy. General Wafhington is more chearful than he was in the army. Although his temper is rather of a ferious caft and his countenance commonly carries the impreffion of thoughtfulnefs, yet
he

he perfectly relishes a pleasant story, an unaffected sally of wit, or a burlesque description which surprises by its suddenness and incongruity with the ordinary appearance of the object described. After this sociable and innocent relaxation, he applies himself to business; and about nine o'clock retires to rest. This is the *rotine*, and this the hour he observes, when no one but his family is present; at other times he attends politely upon his company until they wish to withdraw. Notwithstanding he has no offspring, his actual family consists of eight persons.* It is seldom alone. He keeps a pack of hounds, and in the season indulges himself with hunting once in a week; at which diversion the gentlemen of Alexandria often assist.

AGRICULTURE is the favourite employment of General Washington, in which he wishes to pass the remainder of his days. To acquire and communicate practical knowledge, he corresponds with Mr. Arthur Young, who has written so sensibly on the subject, and also with many agricultural gentlemen in this country. As improvement is known to be his passion, he receives envoys with rare seeds and results of new projects from every quarter. He likewise makes copious notes, relative to his own experiments, the state of the seasons, the nature of soils, the effects of different kinds of manure, and such other topics as may throw light on the farming business.

On Saturday in the afternoon, every week, reports are made by all his overseers, and registered in books kept for the purpose: so that at the end of the year, the quantity of labour and produce may be accurately known. Order and œconomy are established in all the departments within and without doors. His lands are inclosed in lots of equal dimensions, and crops are assigned to each for many years. Every thing is undertaken on a great scale: but with a view to introduce or augment the culture of such articles as he conceives will become most beneficial in their consequence to the country. He has, this year, raised two hundred lambs, sowed twenty seven bushels of flax-seed, and planted more than seven hundred bushels of potatoes. In the mean time, the public may rest persuaded that there is manufactured, under his roof, linen and woollen cloth, nearly or quite sufficient for the use of his numerous household.

NOTE (B) for Page 105.

GENERAL Montgomery descended from a respectable family in the North of Ireland, and was born in the year 1737. His attachment to liberty was innate, and matured by a fine education and an excellent understanding. Having married a wife, and purchased an estate in New-York, he was, from these circumstances, as well as from his natural love

---

* *The family of General Washington, in addition to the General and his Lady, consists of* Major George Washington, *(Nephew to the General and late Aid de Camp to the Marquis de la Fayette) with his wife, who is a niece to the General's Lady*—Col. Humphreys, *formerly Aid de Camp to the General*—Mr. Lear, *a gentleman of liberal education, private secretary to the General—and two Grand Children of Mrs. Washington.*

love of freedom, and from a conviction of the juftnefs of her caufe, induced to confider himfelf as an American. From principle, he early embarked in her caufe, and quitted the fweets of eafy fortune, the enjoyment of a loved and philofophical rural life, with the higheft domeftic felicity, to take an active fhare in all the hardfhips and dangers that attend the foldiers life.

Before he came over to America, he had been an officer in the fervice of England, and had fuccefsfully fought her battles with the immortal Wolfe at Quebec, in the war of 1756, on the very fpot, where, when fighting under the ftandard of freedom, he was doomed to fall in arms againft her. No one who fell a martyr to freedom in this unnatural conteft, was more fincerely, or more univerfally lamented. And what is extraordinary, the moft eminent fpeakers in the Britifh parliament, forgetting for the moment, that he had died in oppofing their cruel and oppreffive meafures, difplayed all their eloquence in praifing his virtues and lamenting his fate. A great orator, and a veteran fellow-foldier of his in the French war of 1756, fhed abundance of tears, while he expatiated on their faft friendfhip and mutual exchange of tender fervices in that feafon of enterprize and glory.

All enmity to this veteran foldier expired with his life; and refpect to his private character prevailed over all other confiderations. By the orders of General Carleton, his dead body received every poffible mark of diftinction from the victors, and was interred in Quebec, on the firft day of January 1776, with all the honors due to a brave foldier.

Congrefs were not unmindful of the merit of this amiable and brave officer, nor remifs in manifefting the efteem and refpect they entertained for his memory. Confidering it not only as a tribute of gratitude juftly due to the memory of thofe who have peculiarly diftinguifhed themfelves in the glorious caufe of liberty, to perpetuate their names by the moft durable monuments erected to their honor, but greatly conducive to infpire pofterity with emulation of their illuftrious actions, that honourable body

" *Refolved*, That to exprefs the veneration of the United Colonies for their late General, RICHARD MONTGOMERY, and the deep fenfe they entertain of the many fignal and important fervices of that gallant officer, who, after a feries of fuccefses, amidft the moft difcouraging difficulties, fell at length in a gallant attack upon Quebec, the capital of Canada; and to tranfmit to future ages, as examples truly worthy of imitation, his patriotifm, conduct, boldnefs of enterprize, infuperable perfeverance, and contempt of danger and death; a monument be procured from Paris, or other part of France, with an infcription facred to his memory, and expreffive of his amiable character, and heroic atchievments, and that the continental treafurers be directed to advance a fum not exceeding 300l. fterling, to Dr. Benjamin Franklin, who is defired to fee this refolution properly executed, for defraying the expence thereof."

This refolve was carried into execution at Paris, by that ingenious artift, Mr. Caffiers, fculptor to the king of France, under the direction of Dr. Franklin. The monument is of white marble, of the moft beautiful fimplicity, and inexpreffible elegance, with emblematical devices, and the following truly claffical infcription, worthy of the modeft, but great mind of a Franklin.

To

To the GLORY of
RICHARD MONTGOMERY, Major General
of the armies of the United States of America,
Slain at the siege of Quebec,
the 31st of December, 1775, aged 38 years.

This elegant monument has lately been erected in front of St. Paul's church in New York.

There is a remarkable circumstance connected with the fall of this brave officer, that merits to be recorded, because the fact is of a very interesting nature, and will serve to perpetuate the memory of a very amiable and deserving character, who was also a martyr in the cause of his country. The circumstance is this:

One of General Montgomery's Aides de Camp, was Mr. Macpherson, a most promising young man, whose father resided at Philadelphia, and was greatly distinguished in privateering in the war of 1756. This gentleman had a brother in the 16th regiment, in the British service, at the time of Montgomery's expedition into Canada, and who was as violent in favour of the English government, as this General's Aide de Camp was enthusiastic in the cause of America; the latter had accompanied his General a day or two previous to the attack in which they both lost their lives, to view and meditate on the spot where Wolfe had fallen; on his return he found a letter from his brother, the English officer, full of the bitterest reproaches against him, for having entered into the American service, and containing a pretty direct wish, that if he would not abandon it, he might meet with the deserved fate of a rebel. The Aid de Camp immediately returned him an answer, full of strong reasoning in defence of his conduct, but by no means attempting to shake the opposite principles of his brother, and not only free from acrimony, but full of expressions of tenderness and affection; this letter he dated, " from the spot where Wolfe lost his life, in fighting the cause of England, *in friendship with America.*" This letter had scarcely reached the officer at New York, before it was followed by the news of his brother's death. The effect was instantaneous, nature, and perhaps reason prevailed; a thousand, not unworthy sentiments rushed upon his distressed mind; he quitted the English service, entered into that of America, and fought every occasion of distinguishing himself in her service!

NOTE (C) for Page 111.

GENERAL GREENE was born at Warwick in the state of Rhode Island, about the year 1741, of reputable parents, belonging to the society of *Friends*. He was endowed with an uncommon degree of judgment and penetration, his disposition was benevolent and his manners affable. At an early period of life, he was chosen a member of the assembly, and he discharged his trust to the entire satisfaction of his constituents.

After the battle of Lexington, three regiments of troops were raised in Rhode Island, and the command of them given to Mr. Greene, who was nominated

nominated a Brigadier General. His merit and abilities both in council and in the field, were foon noticed by General Wafhington, and in Auguft 1776, he was appointed Major General. In the furprife at Trenton, and the battle of Princeton, General Greene diftinguifhed himfelf; and in the action of Germantown, in 1777, he commanded the left wing of the American army, where he exerted himfelf to retrieve the fortune of the day.

At the battle of Brandywine, General Greene, diftinguifhed himfelf by fupporting the right wing of the American army, when it gave way, and judicioufly covering the whole, when routed and retreating in confufion; and their fafety from utter ruin, was generally afcribed to his fkill and exertions, which were feconded by the troops under his command.

In March, 1778, he was appointed Quarter-mafter General, an office he accepted on condition of not lofing his rank in the line, and his right to command in action according to his feniority. In the execution of this office, he fully anfwered the expectations formed of his abilities; and enabled the army to move with additional celerity and vigor.

At the battle of Monmouth, the commander in chief, difgufted with the behaviour of General Lee, depofed him in the field of battle, and appointed General Greene to command the right wing, where he greatly contributed to retrieve the errors of his predeceffor, and to the fubfequent event of the day.

He ferved under General Sullivan in the attack on the Britifh Garrifon at Rhode Ifland, where his prudence and abilities were difplayed in fecuring the retreating army.

In 1780 he was appointed to the command of the fouthern army, which was much reduced by a feries of ill fortune. By his amazing diligence, addrefs and fortitude, he foon collected a refpectable force and revived the hopes of our fouthern brethren.

Under his management, General Morgan gained a complete victory over Colonel Tarleton. He attacked Lord Cornwallis at Guilford, in North Carolina, and although defeated, he checked the progrefs and difabled the army of the Britifh General. A fimiliar fate attended Lord Rawdon, who gained an advantage over him at Camden.

His action with the Britifh troops at Eutaw Springs was one of the beft conducted, and moft fuccefsful engagements that took place during the war. For this General Greene was honored by Congrefs with a Britifh ftandard and a gold medal. As a reward for his particular fervices in the fouthern department, the ftate of Georgia prefented him with a large and valuable tract of land on an ifland near Savannah.

After the war, he returned to his native ftate; the contentions and bad policy of that ftate, induced him to leave it and retire to his eftate in Georgia.

He removed his family in October 1785; but in June the next fummer, the extreme heat, and the fatigue of a walk brought on a diforder that put a period to his life, on the 19th of the fame month. He lived univerfally loved and refpected, and his death was as univerfally lamented.

His body was interred in Savannah, and the funeral proceffion attended by the Cincinnati.

Immediately

Immediately after the interment of the corpſe, the members of the Cincinnati held a meeting in Savannah, and reſolved, 'That in token of the high reſpect and veneration in which the ſociety hold the memory of their late illuſtrious brother, Major General Greene, deceaſed, George Waſhington Greene, his eldeſt ſon, be admitted a member of this ſociety, to take his ſeat on his arrriving at the age of eighteen years.' This ſon of the General's lately embarked for France, to receive his education with George Waſhington, ſon of the Marquis de la Fayette, that active and illuſtrious friend of America.

General Greene left behind him a wife and five children, the eldeſt of whom, who has been juſt mentioned, is about thirteen years old.

On Tueſday, the 12th of Auguſt, the United States in Congreſs aſſembled came to the following reſolution : ' That a monument be erected to the memory of Nathaniel Greene, Eſq. at the ſeat of federal government, with the following inſcription ;

Sacred to the Memory of
NATHANIEL GREENE, Eſquire,
who departed this Life,
on the nineteenth of June, MDCCLXXXVI ;
late MAJOR GENERAL
in the Service of the United States,
and
Commander of their Army
in the
Southern Department :
The United States in Congreſs aſſembled,
in Honour of his
Patriotiſm, Valour, and Ability,
have erected this Monument.

NOTE (D) for Page 112.

THE enthuſiaſtic zeal and great ſervices of the Marquis de la Fayette, merit a particular detail. At the age of nineteen he eſpouſed the cauſe of America, with all the ardor which the moſt generous philanthropy could inſpire. At a very early period of the war, he determined to embark from his native country, for the United States. Before he could complete his intention, intelligence arrived in Europe, that the American inſurgents, reduced to two thouſand men, were flying through Jerſey before a Britiſh force of thirty thouſand regulars. This news ſo effectually extinguiſhed the little credit which America had in Europe, in the beginning of the year 1777, that the commiſſioners of Congreſs at Paris, though they had previouſly encouraged his project, could not procure a veſſel to forward his intentions. Under theſe circumſtances they thought it but honeſt to diſſuade him from the preſent proſecution of his perilous enterpriſe. It was in vain they acted ſo candid a part. The flame which America had kindled in his breaſt, could not be extinguiſhed by her misfortunes.

misfortunes. 'Hitherto,' said he, in the true spirit of patriotism, 'I have only cherished your cause—now I am going to serve it. The lower it is in the opinion of the people, the greater will be the effect of my departure; and since you cannot get a vessel, I shall purchase and fit out one to carry your dispatches to Congress and myself to America.' He accordingly embarked and arrived in Charleston early in the year 1777. Congress soon conferred on him the rank of major-general. He accepted the appointment, but not without exacting two conditions, which displayed the elevation of his spirit: the one, that he should serve on his own expence; the other, that he should begin his services as a volunteer.

He was soon appointed to command an expedition to Canada. The plan was to cross the lakes on the ice; the object, to seize Montreal and St. Johns. He was now at the age of twenty, and must have keenly experienced the allurements of independent command; but his cool judgment, and honest heart, restrained him from indulging a passion for military fame, under circumstances that might have injured the cause which he had so zealously espoused. He found that, in case of his proceeding, the army under his command would be in danger of experiencing a fate similar to that of the unfortunate Burgoyne. With a boldness of judgment that would have done honor to the most experienced general, and without advancing beyond Albany, he relinquished the expedition. Soon after he received the thanks of Congress for his prudence.

In the four campaigns which succeeded the arrival of the marquis de la Fayette in America, he gave repeated proofs of his military talents in the middle and eastern states; but the events that took place under his command in Virginia, deserve particular notice.

Early in the year 1781, while the war raged to the southward of Virginia, the marquis de la Fayette was detached on an expedition against Portsmouth; but here his active zeal received a check, no less fatal to his hopes than when he was obliged to relinquish the expedition to Canada. The engagement near the capes of the Chesapeek, between the French chief d'escadre d'Estouches, and the British admiral Arbuthnot, which took place on the fifth of March, 1781, defeated the enterprise. Upon this event he marched back to the Head of Elk, where he received an order from General Washington to return to Virginia, to oppose general Philips, who had joined general Arnold at Portsmouth. Although the troops under his command were in want of almost every thing, he nevertheless proceeded with them to Baltimore. Here he learned that general Philips was urging preparations to embark at Portsmouth, with upwards of three thousand men. With the marquis de la Fayette it was a moment of extreme distress and embarrasment. In his whole command there was not one pair of shoes; but the love and confidence he had universally excited, enabled him to obtain a loan of money which procured him some necessaries for his troops, and gave renewed vigor to his march. He supposed Richmond to be the object of general Philips, and therefore marched thither with so great expedition, that he arrived at that place the evening before general Philips. He was joined the first night after his arrival by major-general baron Steuben, with a corps of militia. In this manner was the capital of Virginia, at that time filled with almost

all

all the military stores of the state, saved from the most imminent danger. The British appeared the next morning at Manchester, just opposite to Richmond. The two armies surveyed each other for some time, and then general Philips, apprehending it to be too hazardous to attack the marquis de la Fayette in his strong position, very prudently retired.

Such was the great superiority of numbers by the combination of the forces under general Arnold, general Philips and lord Cornwallis—so fatal to all the southern states would have been the conquest of Virginia—that the marquis de la Fayette had before him a labour of the last consequence, and was pressed on all sides by innumerable difficulties.

In the first moments of the rising tempest, and until he could provide against its utmost rage, he began to retire with his little army, which consisted of about a thousand regulars, two thousand militia, and sixty dragoons. Lord Cornwallis, exulting in the prospect of success, which he thought to be heightened by the youth of his opponent, incautiously wrote to Great Britain, 'that the boy could not escape him.' The engagement, however, which was to confirm his promise, was sedulously avoided. Finding it impossible to force an action, he next endeavoured to cut off the communication of the marquis de la Fayette with general Wayne, who, with eight hundred Pennsylvanians, was advancing from the northward. The junction however, was effected at Rackoon Ford without loss. The next object of lord Cornwallis, was to get possession of the American stores, which, for their greater security, had been removed from Richmond to Albemarle old court-house above the Point of Fork. While the troops commanded by the marquis de la Fayette and general Wayne were forming a junction, lord Cornwallis had gotten between them and their public stores. The possession of these was a principal object with both armies. The marquis de la Fayette, by forced marches, got within a few miles of the British army, when they were yet distant two days march from Albemarle old court-house. Once more the British general considered himself sure of his adversary. To save the stores he knew was his design, but to accomplish that object, his lordship saw no practical way but by a road, in passing which, the American army might be attacked to great advantage. It was a critical moment, but the marquis de la Fayette had the good fortune to extricate himself. He opened in the night, by part of his army, a nearer road to Albemarle, which, having been many years disused, was much embarrassed, and, to the astonishment of lord Cornwallis, posted himself in a strong position the next day between the British army and the American stores.

His lordship, finding all his schemes frustrated, fell back to Richmond whither he was followed by the marquis de la Fayette. The main American army in Virginia was now reinforced by the troops under major-general baron Steuben, and by volunteer corps of Virginia and Maryland gentlemen. And the marquis de la Fayette had the address to impress lord Cornwallis with an idea, that his force was much greater than he actually commanded. His lordship, therefore, retreated to Williamsburg.

After a series of manœuvres, which it is not necessary to relate, and in which the British general displayed the boldness of enterprize, and the young marquis the sound judgment of age, blended with the ardour of youth,

youth, the former fixed himself and his army in York-town. The latter, under various pretences, sent the Pennsylvania troops to the south side of James River; collected a force in Gloucester county, and made sundry arrangements subservient to the grand design of the whole campaign, which was the capture of lord Cornwallis, and the British army under his command.

Sometime after the capture of Cornwallis, the marquis de la Fayette went to France, where he successfully used his endeavours to promote the commercial and political interest of these states.

Pennsylvania, in order to show her esteem for this gallant nobleman, has lately erected part of her western territory into a separate county, and named it FAYETTE.

NEW ENGLAND.

THE states east of New York, were formerly called the *New England Colonies:* They are still known by the general name of New England. Several things are common to them all. Their religion, manners, customs, and character; their climate, soil, productions, natural history, &c. are in many respects similar. Many of the historical events which took place in their settlement, and in their progress until the year 1692, are intimately connected. These considerations have led to the following general description of New England.

As the territory of Vermont was included in some of the original patents granted by the Plymouth Company, and was settled wholly from New England, it is considered as a part of it, and included in the following account.

SITUATION and EXTENT.

Length 350 miles ⎱ Between ⎰ 41° and 46° North Latitude.
Breadth 140   ⎰   ⎱ 1° 30' and 8° East Longitude.

Boundaries.] New England is bounded, north by Canada; east by Nova Scotia and the Atlantic ocean; south by the Atlantic and Long Island Sound, and west by New York. It lies in the form of a quarter of a circle. Its west line, beginning at the mouth of Byram river which empties into Long Island Sound at the south west corner of Connecticut, latitude 41°, runs a little east of north, until it strikes the 45th degree of latitude, and then curves to the eastward almost to the Gulf of St. Lawrence.

Civil divisions.] New England is divided into five states, viz. New Hampshire, Massachusetts, Rhode Island, Connecticut and Vermont. These states are subdivided into counties, and the counties into townships.

Face of the country, mountains, &c.] New England is a high, hilly, and in some parts a mountainous country, formed by nature to be inhabited by a hardy race of free, independent republicans.—The mountains are comparatively small, running nearly north and south in ridges parallel to each other. Between these ridges, flow the great rivers in majestic meanders, receiving the innumerable rivulets and larger streams which proceed from the mountains on each side. To a spectator on the top of a neighbouring mountain, the vales between the ridges, while in a state of nature, exhibit a romantic appearance. They seem an ocean of woods, swelled and depressed in its surface like that of the great ocean itself. A richer though less romantic view is presented, when the vallies, by industrious husbandmen, have been cleared of their natural growth; and the fruit of their labour appears in loaded orchards, extensive meadows, covered

with

NEW ENGLAND. 141

with large herds of sheep and neat cattle, and rich fields of flax, corn and the various kinds of grain.

These vallies, which have received the expressive name of *interval lands*, are of various breadths, from two to twenty miles; and by the annual inundations of the rivers which flow through them, there is frequently an accumulation of rich, fat soil, left upon their surface when the waters retire.

There are four principal ranges of mountains, passing nearly from north-east to south-west, through New-England. These consist of a multitude of parallel ridges, each having many spurs, deviating from the course of the general range; which spurs are again broken into irregular, hilly land. The main ridges terminate, sometimes in high bluff heads, near the sea coast; and sometimes by a gradual descent in the interior part of the country. One of the main ranges runs between Connecticut and Hudson's rivers. This range branches, and bounds the vales through which flows the Housatonick river. The most eastern ridge of this range terminates in a bluff head at Meriden. A second ends in like manner at Willingford, and a third at New Haven.

In Lyme, on the east side of Connecticut river, another range of mountains commences, forming the eastern boundary of Connecticut vale. This range trends northerly, at the distance, generally, of about ten or twelve miles east from the river, and passes through Massachusetts, where the range takes the name of Chicabee mountain; thence crossing into New-Hampshire, at the distance of about twenty miles from the Massachusetts line, it runs up into a very high peak, called *Monadnick*, which terminates this ridge of the range. A western ridge continues, and in about latitude 43° 20′, runs up into *Sunipee* mountains. About fifty miles further, in the same ridge, is *Moosecoog* mountain.

A third range begins near Stonington in Connecticut. It takes its course northeasterly, and is sometimes broken and discontinued; it then rises again, and ranges in the same direction into New Hampshire, where, in latitude 43° 25′, it runs up into a high peak, called *Cowsawaskoog*.

The fourth range has a humble beginning about Hopkinton, in Massachusetts. The eastern ridge of this range runs north, by Watertown and Concord, and crosses Merrimack river at Pantucket Falls. In New Hampshire, it rises into several high peaks, of which the White mountains is the principal. From these White mountains, a range continues north east, crossing the east boundary of New Hampshire, in latitude 44° 30′, and forms the height of land between Kennebek and Chaudiere rivers.

These ranges of mountains are full of lakes, ponds and springs of water, that give rise to numberless streams of various sizes, which, interlocking each other in every direction, and falling over the rocks in romantic cascades, flow meandering into the rivers below. No country on the globe is better watered than New England.

On the sea coast the land is low, and in many parts level and sandy. In the vallies, between the forementioned ranges of mountains, the land is generally broken, and in many places rocky, but of a strong rich soil, capable of being cultivated to good advantage, which also is the case with many spots even on the tops of the mountains.

Rivers.]

Rivers.] The only river which will be described under New England is Connecticut river. It rises in a swamp on the height of land, in latitude 45° 10′, longitude 4 east. After a sleepy course of eight or ten miles, it tumbles over four separate falls, and turning west keeps close under the hills which form the northern boundary of the vale through which it runs. The Amonoosuck, and Israel rivers, two principal branches of Connecticut river, fall into it from the east, between the latitudes 44° and 45°. Between the towns of Walpole on the east, and Westminster on the west side of the river, are the great Falls. The whole river, compressed between two rocks scarcely thirty feet asunder, shoots with amazing rapidity into a broad bason below. Over these falls, a bridge one hundred and sixty feet in length, was built in 1784, under which the highest floods may pass without detriment. This is the first bridge that was ever erected over this noble river. Above Deerfield in Massachusetts, it receives Deerfield river from the west, and Millers river from the east, after which it turns westerly in a sinuous course to Fighting falls, and a little after tumbles over Deerfield falls, which are impassable by boats. At Windsor, in Connecticut, it receives Farmington river from the west; and at Hartford, meets the tide. From Hartford it passes on in a crooked course, until it falls into Long Island sound, between Saybrook and Lyme.

The length of this river, in a straight line, is nearly three hundred miles. Its general course is several degrees west of south. It is from eighty, to one hundred rods wide, one hundred and thirty miles from its mouth.

At its mouth is a bar of sand which considerably obstructs the navigation. Ten feet water at full tides is found on this bar, and the same depth to Middleton. The distance of the bar from this place, as the river runs, is thirty-six miles. Above Middleton are several shoals which stretch quite across the river. Only six feet water is found on the shoal at high tide, and here the tide ebbs and flows but about eight inches. About three miles below Middleton, the river is contracted to about forty rods in breadth, by two high mountains. Almost every where else the banks are low, and spread into fine extensive meadows. In the spring floods, which generally happen in May, these meadows are covered with water. At Hartford the water sometimes rises twenty feet above the common surface of the river, and having all to pass through the above-mentioned streight, it is sometimes two or three weeks before it returns to its usual bed. These floods add nothing to the depth of water on the bar at the mouth of the river; this bar lying too far off in the sound to be affected by them.

On this beautiful river, whose banks are settled almost to its source, are many pleasant, neat, well-built towns. On its western bank, from its mouth northward, are the towns of Saybrook, Haddam, Middleton, Weathersfield, Hartford, Windsor, and Suffield, in Connecticut; West Springfield, Northampton, Hatfield, and Deerfield, in Massachusetts; Guilford, Brattleborough, in which is Fort Dummer, Westminster, Windsor, Hartford, Fairlee, Newbury, Brunswick, and many others in Vermont. Crossing the river into New Hampshire, and travelling on the eastern bank, you pass through Woodbury nearly opposite to Brunswick, Northumberland, the Coos country, Lyman, Orford, Lyme, Hanover, in

which

NEW ENGLAND.

which is Dartmouth College, Lebanon, Cornish, Clermont, Charleston, or No. 4, Chesterfield, and many others in New Hampshire, Sunderland, Hadley, Springfield, Long-meadow, in Massachusetts; and in Connecticut, Enfield, East Windsor, East Hartford, Glastenbury, East Haddam, and Lyme.

This river is navigable to Hartford, upwards of fifty miles from its mouth, and the produce of the country for two hundred miles above is brought thither in boats. The boats which are used in this business are flat-bottomed, long and narrow, for the convenience of going up stream, and of so light a make as to be portable in carts. They are taken out of the river at three different carrying places, all of which make fifteen miles.

Sturgeon, salmon, and shad are caught in plenty, in their season, from the mouth of the river upwards, excepting sturgeon, which do not ascend the upper falls; besides a variety of small fish, such as pike, carp, pearch, &c.

From this river are employed three brigs of one hundred and eighty tons each, in the European trade; and about sixty sail, from sixty to one hundred and fifty tons, in the West India trade; besides a few fishermen, and forty or fifty coasting vessels.

Natural Growth.] The soil, as may be collected from what has been said, must be very various. Each tract of different soil, is distinguished by its peculiar vegetation, and is pronounced good, middling, or bad, from the species of trees which it produces; and one species generally predominating in each soil, has originated the descriptive names of oak land—birch, beach and chesnut lands—pine barren—maple, ash, and cedar swamps, as each species happens to predominate. Intermingled with these predominating species are walnut, firs, elm, hemlock, magnolia, or moose wood, sassafrass, &c. &c. The best lands produce walnut and chesnut; the next, beach and oak; lands of the third quality produce fir and pitch pine; the next, whortleberry and barberry bushes; and the poorest produces nothing but poor marshy imperfect shrubs, which is the lowest kind (if you will allow me to use a hard word) of *suffrutex* vegetation.

Among the flowering trees and shrubs in the forests, are the red flowering maple, the sassafrass, the locust, the tulip tree, the chesnut, the wild cherry, prune, crab, sloe, pear, honey-suckle, wild rose, dogwood, elm, leather tree, laurel, hawthorn, &c. which in the spring of the year give the woods a most beautiful appearance, and fill them with a delicious fragrance.

Among the fruits which grow wild, are the several kinds of grapes, which are small, four and thick skinned. The vines on which they grow are very luxuriant, often overspreading the highest trees in the forests. These wild vines, without doubt, might be greatly meliorated by proper cultivation, and a wine be produced from the grapes equal, if not superior, to the celebrated wines of France. Besides these, are the wild cherries, white and red mulberries, cranberries, walnuts, hazelnuts, chesnuts, butter nuts, beech nuts, wild plums and pears, whortleberries, bilberries, goosberries, strawberries, &c.

Productions.

NEW ENGLAND.

Productions.] The foil in the interior country is calculated for the culture of Indian corn, rye, oats, barley, flax, and hemp, for which the foil and climate are peculiarly proper, buck-wheat, beans, peas, &c. In many of the inland parts wheat is raifed in large quantities; but on the fea coaft it has never been cultivated with fuccefs, being fubject to blafts. Various reafons have been affigned for this. Some have fuppofed that the blafts were occafioned by the faline vapours of the fea; others have attributed them to the vicinity of Barberry bufhes; but perhaps the fandinefs and poverty of the foil, may be as efficacious a caufe as either of the others.

The fruits which the country yields from culture, are, apples in the greateft plenty; of thefe cyder is made which conftitutes the principal drink of the inhabitants; alfo, pears of various forts, quinces, peaches, from which is made peach brandy, plums, cherries, apricots, &c. The culinary plants are fuch as have already been enumerated.

New England is a fine grazing country; the vallies, between the hills, are generally interfected with brooks of water, the banks of which are lined with a tract of rich meadow or interval land. The high and rocky ground is, in many parts, covered with honey fuckle, and generally affords the fineft of pafture. It will not be a matter of wonder, therefore, that New England boafts of raifing fome of the fineft cattle in the world; nor will fhe be envied, when the labour of raifing them is taken into view. Two months of the hotteft feafon in the year, the farmers are employed in procuring food for their cattle; and the cold winter is fpent in dealing it out to them. The pleafure and profit of doing this, is however a fatisfying compenfation to the honeft and induftrious farmer.

Population, Military Strength, Manners, Cuftoms and Diverfions.] New England is the moft populous part of the United States. It contains at leaft, eight hundred and twenty-three thoufand fouls. One fifth of thefe are fencible men. New England then, fhould any great and fudden emergency require it, could furnifh an army of one hundred and fixty-four thoufand fix hundred men. The great body of thefe are land-holders and cultivators of the foil. The former attaches them to their country; the latter, by making them ftrong and healthy, enables them to defend it. The boys are early taught the ufe of arms, and make the beft of foldiers. Few countries on earth, of equal extent and population, can furnifh a more formidable army than this part of the union.

New England may, with propriety, be called a nurfery of men, whence are annually tranfplanted, into other parts of the United States, thoufands of its natives. The State of Vermont, which is but of yefterday, and contains about one hundred thoufand fouls, has received more inhabitants from Connecticut, than from any other ftate; and yet between the years 1774 and 1782, notwithftanding her numerous emigrations to Vermont, Sufquehannah and other places, and the depopulation occafioned by a feven years bloody war, it is found, from actual cenfus of the inhabitants in the years before mentioned, that they have increafed from one hundred and ninety-feven thoufand eight hundred and fifty-fix, their number in 1774, to two hundred and nine thoufand one hundred and fifty, their number in 1782. Vaft numbers of the New Englanders, fince the war, have emigrated into the northern parts of New-York, into Kentucky and the

Weftern

Western Territory, and into Georgia; and some are scattered into every State, and every town of note in the union.

The inhabitants of New-England are almost universally of English descent; and it is owing to this circumstance, and to the great and general attention that has been paid to education, that the English language has been preserved among them so free of corruption. It is true, that from laziness, inattention and want of acquaintance with mankind, many of the people in the country have accustomed themselves to use some peculiar phrases, and to pronounce certain words in a flat drawling manner. Hence foreigners pretend they know a New Englandman from his manner of speaking. But the same may be said with regard to a Pennsylvanian, a Virginian, or a Carolinian; for all have some phrases and modes of pronunciation peculiar to themselves, which distinguish them from their neighbours. Men of eminence in the several learned professions, and colleges, ought to be considered as forming the standard of pronunciation for their respective states; and not that class of people who have imbibed the habit of using a number of singular and ridiculous phrases, and who pronounce badly.

The New Englanders are generally tall, stout, and well built. They glory, and perhaps with justice, in possessing that spirit of freedom, which induced their ancestors to leave their native country, and to brave the dangers of the ocean and the hardships of settling a wilderness. Their education, laws and situation, serve to inspire them with high notions of liberty. Their jealousy is awakened at the first motion toward an invasion of their rights. They are indeed often jealous to excess; a circumstance which is a fruitful source of imaginary grievances, and of innumerable groundless suspicions, and unjust complaints against government. But these ebullitions of jealousy, though censurable, and productive of some political evils, shew that the essence of true liberty exists in New England; for jealousy is the guardian of liberty, and a characteristic of free republicans. A law, respecting the descent of estates which are generally held in fee simple, which for substance is the same in all the New England States, is the chief foundation and protection of this liberty. By this law, the possessions of the father are to be equally divided among all the children, excepting the eldest son, who has a double portion. In this way is preserved that happy mediocrity among the people, which, by inducing œconomy and industry, removes from them temptations to luxury, and forms them to habits of sobriety and temperance. At the same time, their industry and frugality exempt them from want, and from the necessity of submitting to any encroachment on their liberties.

In New England, learning is more generally diffused among all ranks of people than in any other part of the globe; arising from the excellent establishment of schools in every township.

Another very valuable source of information to the people is the News papers, of which not less than thirty thousand are printed every week in New England, and circulated in almost every town and village in the country.

A person of mature age, who cannot both read and write, is rarely to be found. By means of this general establishment of schools, the extensive circulation of News papers, and the consequent spread of learning, every township throughout the country, is furnished with men capable of conducting the affairs of their town with judgment and discretion. These men are the channels of political information to the lower class of people; if such a class may be said to exist in New England, where every man thinks himself at least as good as his neighbour, and believes that all mankind are, or ought to be equal. The people from their childhood form habits of canvassing public affairs, and commence politicians. This naturally leads them to be very inquisitive. It is with knowledge as with riches, the more a man has, the more he wishes to obtain; his desire has no bound. This desire after knowledge, in a greater or less degree, prevails throughout all classes of people in New England: and from their various modes of expressing it, some of which are blunt and familiar, bordering on impertinence, strangers have been induced to mention *impertinent inquisitiveness* as a distinguishing characteristic of New England people. But this is true only with regard to that class of people who have confined themselves to domestic life, and have not had opportunity of mingling with the world; and such people are not peculiar to New England—they compose a great part of the citizens of every State. This class, it is true, is large in New England, where agriculture is the principle employment. But will not a candid and ingenuous mind, ascribe this inquisitiveness in these honest and well meaning people, to a *laudable* rather than to a censurable disposition?

A very considerable part of the people have either too little, or too much learning to make peaceable subjects. They know enough, however, to think they know a great deal, when in fact they know but little. "A little learning is a dangerous thing." Each man has his independent system of politics; and each assumes a dictatorial office. Hence originates that restless, litigious, complaining spirit, which forms a dark shade in the character of New Englandmen.

This litigious temper is the genuine fruit of republicanism—but it denotes a corruption of virtue, which is one of its essential principles. Where a people have a great share of freedom, an equal share of virtue is necessary to the peaceable enjoyment of it. Freedom, without virtue or honour, is licentiousness.

Before the late war, which introduced into New England a flood of corruptions, with many improvements, the sabbath was observed with great strictness; no unnecessary travelling, no secular business, no visiting, no diversions were permitted on that sacred day. They considered it as consecrated to divine worship, and were generally punctual and serious in their attendance upon it. Their laws were strict in guarding the sabbath against every innovation. The supposed severity with which these laws were composed and executed, together with some other traits in their religious character, have acquired, for the New Englanders, the name of a superstitious, bigotted people. But superstition and bigotry are so indefinite in their significations, and so variously applied by persons of different principles and educations, that it is not easy to determine whether they ever deserved that character. Leaving every person to enjoy his own opinion in regard to this matter, we will only observe, that, since the war, a catholic tolerant spirit, occasioned by a more enlarged intercourse with mankind, has greatly increased, and is becoming universal; and if they do not break
the

the proper bound, and liberalize away all true religion, of which there is much danger, they will counteract that strong propensity in human nature, which leads men to vibrate from one extreme to its opposite.

There is one distinguishing characteristic in the religious character of this people, which we must not omit to mention ; and that is, the custom of annually celebrating Fasts and Thanksgivings. In the spring, the several governors issue their proclamations, appointing a day to be religiously observed in fasting, humiliation and prayer throughout their respective states, in which the predominating vices, that particularly call for humiliation, are enumerated. In autumn, after harvest, that gladsome æra in the husbandman's life, the governors again issue their proclamations appointing a day of public thanksgiving, enumerating the public blessings received in the course of the foregoing year.

This pious custom originated with their venerable ancestors, the first settlers of New England ; and has been handed down as sacred, through the successive generations of their posterity. A custom so rational, and so happily calculated to cherish in the minds of the people a sense of their dependence on the GREAT BENEFACTOR of the world for all their blessings, it is hoped will ever be sacredly preserved.

There is a class of people in New England of the baser sort, who, averse to honest industry, have recourse to knavery for subsistence. Skilled in all the arts of dishonesty, with the assumed face and frankness of integrity, they go about, like wolves in sheep's clothing, with a design to defraud. These people, enterprizing from necessity, have not confined their knavish tricks to New England. Other states have felt the effects of their villiany. Hence they have characterized the New Englanders, as a knavish, artful, and dishonest people. But that conduct which distinguishes only a small class of people in any nation or state, ought not to be indiscriminately ascribed to all, or be suffered to stamp their national character. In New England, there is as great a proportion of honest and industrious citizens, as in any of the United States.

The people of New England, generally obtain their estates by hard and persevering labour : They of consequence know their value, and spend with frugality. Yet in no country do the indigent and unfortunate fare better. Their laws oblige every town to provide a competent maintenance for their poor, and the necessitous stranger is protected, and relieved from their humane institutions. It may in truth be said, that in no part of the world are the people happier, better furnished with the necessaries and conveniencies of life, or more independent than the farmers in New England. As the great body of the people are hardy, independent freeholders, their manners are, as they ought to be, congenial to their employment, plain, simple, and unpolished. Strangers are received and entertained among them with a great deal of artless sincerity, and friendly, unformal hospitality. Their children, those imitative creatures, to whose education particular attention is paid, early imbibe the manners and habits of those around them ; and the stranger, with pleasure, notices the honest and decent respect that is paid him by the children as he passes through the country.

As the people, by representation, make their own laws and appoint their own officers, they cannot be oppressed ; and living under governments, which

which have few lucrative places, they have few motives to bribery, corrupt canvaſſings or intrigue. Real abilities and a moral character unblemiſhed, are the qualifications requiſite in the view of moſt people, for officers of public truſt. The expreſſion of a wiſh to be promoted, is the direct way to be diſappointed.

The inhabitants of New England, are generally fond of the arts, and have cultivated them with great ſucceſs. Their colleges have flouriſhed beyond any others in the United States. The illuſtrious characters they have produced, who have diſtinguiſhed themſelves in politics, law, divinity, the mathematics and philoſophy, natural and civil hiſtory, and in the fine arts, particularly in poetry, evince the truth of theſe obſervations.

Many of the women in New England are handſome. They generally have fair, freſh and healthful countenances, mingled with much female ſoftneſs and delicacy. Thoſe who have had the advantages of a good education (and they are conſiderably numerous) are genteel, eaſy, and agreeable in their manners, and are ſprightly and ſenſible in converſation. They are early taught to manage domeſtic concerns with neatneſs and œconomy. Ladies of the firſt rank and fortune, make it a part of their daily buſineſs to ſuperintend the affairs of the family. Employment at the needle, in cookery, and at the ſpinning wheel, with them is honourable. Idleneſs, even in thoſe of independent fortunes, is univerſally diſreputable. The women in the country manufacture the greateſt part of the clothing of their families. Their linen and woollen cloths are ſtrong and decent. Their butter and cheeſe is not inferior to any in the world.

Dancing is the principal and favourite amuſement in New England; and of this the young people of both ſexes are extremely fond. Gaming is practiſed by none but thoſe who cannot, or rather will not find a reputable employment. The gameſter, the horſe-jockey, and the knave, are equally deſpiſed, and their company is avoided by all who would ſuſtain fair and irreproachable characters. The odious and inhuman practices of duelling, gouging, cock-fighting and horſe-racing, are ſcarcely known here.

The athletic and healthy diverſions of cricket, foot-ball, quoits, wreſtling, jumping, hopping, foot races, and priſon-baſs are univerſally practiſed in the country, and ſome of them in the moſt populous places, and by people of almoſt all ranks. Squirrel hunting is a noted diverſion in country places, where this kind of game is plenty. Some divert themſelves with fox hunting, and others with the more profitable ſports of fiſhing and duck hunting: and in the frontier ſettlements where deer and fur game abound, the inhabitants make a lucrative ſport of hunting them.

In the winter ſeaſon, while the ground is covered with ſnow, which is commonly two or three months, ſleighing is the general diverſion. A great part of the families throughout the country are furniſhed with horſes and ſleighs. The young people collect in parties, and with a great deal of ſociability, reſort to a place of rendezvous, where they regale themſelves for a few hours, with dancing and a ſocial ſupper, and then retire. Theſe diverſions, as well as all others, are many times carried to exceſs. To theſe exceſſes, and a ſudden expoſure to extreme cold after the exerciſe of

dancing,

dancing, phyficians have afcribed the confumptions, which are fo frequent among the young people in New England.

Trade.] New England has no one ftaple commodity. The ocean and the forefts afford the two principal articles of export. Codfifh, mackarel, fhad, falmon, and other fifh—whale oil, and whale bone—mafts, boards, fcantling, ftaves, hoops, and fhingles, have been, and are ftill exported in large quantities. The annual amount of cod and other fifh, for foreign exportation, including the profits arifing from the whale fifhery, is eftimated at upwards of half a million.

Befides the articles enumerated, they export from the various parts of New England, fhips built for fale, horfes, mules, live ftock—pickled beef and pork, pot-afh, pearl-afh, flax feed, butter and cheefe—New England diftilled rum, and other articles which will be mentioned in their proper places. The balance of trade, as far as imperfect calculations will enable us to judge, has generally been againft New England; not from any unavoidable neceffity, but from her extravagant importations. From a view of the annual imports into New England, it appears that the greateft part of them confifts of the luxuries, or at beft the difpenfable conveniences of life; the country affords the neceffaries in great abundance.

The paffions, for the gratification of which, thefe articles of luxury are confumed, have raged fince the peace of 1783, and have brought a heavy debt upon the confumers. Neceffity, that irrefiftible governnefs of mankind, has of late, in a happy degree checked the influence of thefe paffions, and the people begin to confine themfelves more to the neceffaries of life. It is wifhed that the principles of induftry and frugality, may gain fuch ftrength, as to make thofe wants, which at firft may be painful, become fo familiar as to be no longer felt.

Hiftory.] New England owes its firft fettlement to religious perfecution. Soon after the commencement of the reformation* in England, which was not until the year 1534, the Proteftants were divided into two parties, one the followers of Luther, and the other of Calvin. The former had chofen gradually, and almoft imperceptibly, to recede from the church of Rome; while the latter, more zealous, and convinced of the importance of a thorough

---

* *The reformation was begun by* Martin Luther, *a native of* Saxony, *born in the year* 1483. *He was educated in the Roman Catholic religion, and was an Auguftin Friàr, when, in* 1517, *having written ninety-five Thefes againft the Pope's indulgencies, he exhibited them to public view on the church door at* Wirtenburgh, *in* Saxony, *and thus began the reformation in* Germany. *In* 1528, *the reformed religion was introduced into* Switzerland *by* Zuinglius, Oecolampadius, *and others.*

The year following, the Diet *of the* German Empire *affembled at* Spire, *and iffued a decree againft the reformation. Againft this decree, the* Elector *of* Saxony, George, Marquis *of* Brandenburg, Erneft, *and* Francis, Duke *of* Lunenburg, *the* Landgrave *of* Hefs, *and the* Count *of* Anhalt, *who were joined by feveral of the cities, publicly read their* Protest, *and in this way, acquired for themfelves and their fucceffors down to the prefent time, the name of* Protestants. Calvin,

NEW ENGLAND.

rough reformation, and at the same time possessing much firmness and high notions of religious liberty, were for effecting a thorough change at once. Their consequent endeavours to expunge from the church all the inventions which had been brought into it since the days of the Apostles, and to introduce the 'Scripture purity,' derived for them the name of PURITANS. From these the inhabitants of New England descended.

During the successive reigns of Henry VIII, Mary, Elizabeth, and James the first, the Protestants, and especially the Puritans, were the objects of bloody persecution; and thousands of them were either inhumanly burnt, or left more cruelly to perish in prisons and dungeons.

In 1602, a number of religious people in the North of England, finding their ministers urged with *subscription*, or silenced, and themselves greatly oppressed with the commissary courts and otherwise, entered into a solemn covenant with each other 'to walk with God and one another, in the enjoyment of the ordinances of God according to the primitive pattern,' whatever it might cost them.

Among the ministers who entered into this association, was Mr. Robinson, a man of eminent piety and learning, and the Father of New England.

In 1608, Mr. Robinson's church removed to Amsterdam, in Holland; and the next year to Leyden, where they lived in great friendship and harmony among themselves and their neighbours, until they removed to New England.

As early as 1617, Mr. Robinson and his church meditated a removal to America. Their motives for this were, to preserve the morals of their youth—to prevent them, through want of employment, from leaving their parents and engaging in business unfriendly to religion—to avoid the inconveniencies of incorporating with the Dutch, and to lay a foundation for propagating the gospel in remote parts of the world: Such were the true reasons of their removal.

These reasons having been proposed and maturely considered by the church, after seeking divine direction by humiliation and prayer, they agreed to come over to America, and settle in a distinct body, under the general government of Virginia; they also agreed that their pastor, Mr. Robinson, should remain with the greatest part of the Church, whether they chose to tarry at Leyden, or to come over to America.

In consequence of this agreement, they sent Messrs. R. Cushman, and J. Carver, to treat with the Virginia company upon the subject of settling within

CALVIN, *another celebrated reformer, was born at* Noyon, *in* France, *in the year* 1509. *He improved upon* Luther's *plan—expunged many of the Romish ceremonies which he had indulged—entertained different ideas concerning some of the great doctrines of Christianity, and set the Protestant, at a greater remove from the Roman Catholic religion. The followers of* Luther *have been distinguished by the name of* LUTHERANS; *and the followers of* Calvin *by the name of* CALVINISTS.

Such was the rapid growth of the Protestant interest, that in 1563, *only* 46 *years after the commencement of the reformation by* Luther, *there were in France* 2150 *assemblies of Protestants.*

within the limits of their patent, and to enquire whether, in cafe of their removal, the king would grant them liberty of confcience.

The agents were fuccefsful in their application. The company affured them that they would do every thing in their power to forward fo good a defign, and were willing to grant them a patent with ample privileges. But fuch was the bigotry of the times, that the king, though felicited by fome of the firft men in the kingdom, could not be prevailed upon to grant them *liberty in religion*. He did, however, at laft agree to connive at them, and to permit them to live unmolefted, provided they behaved peaceably; but to tolerate them by his public authority under his feal, was inadmiffible.

This was indeed difcouraging to the pious people at Leyden; yet with an humble confidence in divine providence, they determined to purfue their original defign.

Accordingly they fent their agents to England, where, in September 1619, after a long attendance, they obtained of the Virginia company a patent of the northern parts of Virginia.* This patent, with propofals from Mr. Wefton, and feveral other refpectable merchants and friends, refpecting their migration, were tranfmitted to the people at Leyden, for their confideration. Thefe were accompanied with a requeft that they would immediately commence their preparations for the voyage. On receiving this intelligence, the people, agreeably to their pious cuftom previous to their engaging in any important affair, appointed a day of folemn prayer, on which occafion, Mr. Robinfon, in a fermon from 1 Sam. xxiii. chap. 3, 4 ver. endeavoured to difpel their fears, and encourage their refolutions. As it was not convenient for them all to go at firft, not even for all who were willing, they improved this religious opportunity to determine who fhould firft embark. After canvafing the matter, it was found convenient for the greater number to remain, for the prefent, at Leyden; and of courfe Mr. Robinfon, according to agreement, was to tarry with them. The other part, with Mr. Brewfter for their elder and teacher, agreed to be the firft adventurers. The neceffary preparations were now to be made. A fmall fhip of fixty tons was purchafed, and fitted out in Holland; and another of about one hundred and eighty tons, hired in London. The former was called the *Speedwell*, and the latter the *May-flower*. All other matters being prepared, a large concourfe of friends from Leyden and Amfterdam, accompanied the adventurers to the fhip, which lay at Delf Haven; and the night preceding their embarkation was fpent in tearful prayers, and in the moft tender and friendly intercourfe. The next day fair wind invited their departure. The parting fcene is more eafily felt than defcribed. Their mutual good wifhes—their affectionate and cordial embraces, and other endearing expreffions of chriftian love and friendfhip, drew tears even from the eyes of the ftrangers who beheld the fcene. When the time arrived that they muft part, they all, with their beloved paftor, fell on their knees, and with eyes, and hands, and hearts lifted to Heaven, fervently commended their adventuring brethern

* *This patent was taken out in the name of John Wincob, who providentially never came to America, and fo all their trouble and expence in obtaining it were loft, as they never made any ufe of it.*

brethren to the Lord and his blessing. Thus, after mutual embraces, accompanied with many tears, they bid a long, and many of them, a last farewell.

This was on the 22d. of July, 1620. The same day they sailed before a fair wind for Southampton, where they found the other ship from London, with the rest of the adventurers.

After they had made the necessary preparations for embarkation, they divided themselves into two companies, one for each ship, and with the approbation of the captains, each company chose a governor, and two or three assistants to preserve order among the people, and to distribute the provisions. On the 5th of August they sailed; but the smallest ship proved so leaky, that they were obliged to return and refit. On the 21st of August, they sailed again, and proceeded about one hundred leagues from land, when they found their little ship totally unfit for the voyage, and returned.

It was not until the 6th of September that they put to sea again, leaving their little ship, and part of their company behind. On the 9th of November, after a dangerous voyage, they arrived at Cape Cod, and the next day anchored in the harbour which is formed by the hook of the Cape. This was not the place of their destination, neither was it within the limits of their patent.

It was their intention to have settled at the mouth of Hudson's river; but the Dutch, intending to plant a colony there of their own, privately hired the master of the ship to contrive delays in England, and then to conduct them to these northern coasts, and there, under pretence of shoals and winter, to discourage them from venturing to the place of destination. This is confidently asserted by the historians of that time. Although the harbour in which they had anchored was good, the country around was sandy and barren. These were discouraging circumstances; but the season being far advanced, they prudently determined to make the best of their present situation.

As they were not within the limits of their patent, and consequently not under the jurisdiction of the Virginia company, they concluded it necessary to establish a separate government for themselves. Accordingly, before they landed, having on their knees devoutly given thanks to God for their safe arrival, they formed themselves into a body politic, by a SOLEMN CONTRACT,* to which they all subscribed, thereby making it the basis of their government. They chose Mr. John Carver, a gentleman of piety and approved abilities, to be their governor for the first year. This was on the 11th of November.

Their

---

* *The following is an authentic copy of this contract*—" *In the Name of* God Amen : *We whose Names are under-written, the LoyalSubjects of our dread Sovereign Lord King* JAMES *by the grace of* GOD, *of* Great-Britain, France, *and* Ireland, *King, Defender of the Faith, &c.*

" *Having undertaken for the Glory of* God, *and advancement of the Christian Faith, and Honour of our King and Country, a Voyage to Plant the* first Colony *in the* Northern Parts *of* Virginia ; *Do by these Presents solemnly and mutually in the Presence of God, and one o another,* Covenant *and* Combine *ourselves*

NEW ENGLAND.

Their next object was to fix on a convenient place for settlement. In doing this they were obliged to encounter numerous difficulties, and to suffer incredible hardships. Many of them were sick in consequence of the fatigues of a long voyage—their provisions were bad—the season was uncommonly cold—the Indians, though afterwards friendly, were now hostile—and they were unacquainted with the coast. These difficulties they surmounted; and on the 31st of December they were all safely landed at a place, which, in grateful commemoration of Plymouth in England, the town which they last left in their native land, they called PLYMOUTH. This is the first English town that was settled in New England.

In some of their excursions in search of a suitable place for settlement, they found buried several baskets of Indian corn, to the amount of ten bushels, which fortunately, served them for planting the next spring, and perhaps was the means of preserving them from perishing with hunger. They made diligent enquiry for the owners, whom they found, and afterwards paid the full value of the corn.

Before the end of November, Susanna, the wife of William White, was delivered of a son, whom they called PEREGRINE. He is supposed to have been the first child of European extract, born in New England.

The whole company that landed consisted of but 101 souls. Their situation was distressing and their prospect truly dismal and discouraging. Their nearest neighbours, except the natives, were a French settlement at Port Royal, and one of the English at Virginia. The nearest of these was 500 miles from them, and utterly incapable of affording them relief in a time of famine or danger. Wherever they turned their eyes, distress was before them. Persecuted for their religion in their native land—grieved for the profanation of the holy sabbath, and other licentiousness in Holland—fatigued by their long and boisterous voyage—disappointed, through the treachery of their commander, of their expected country—forced on a dangerous and unknown shore, in the advance of a cold winter—surrounded with hostile barbarians, without any hope of human succour—denied the aid or favour of the court of England—without a patent—without a public promise of the peaceable enjoyment of their religious liberties—worn out with toil and sufferings—without convenient shelter from the rigours of the weather.—Such were the prospects, and such the situation of these pious, solitary christians. To add to their distresses, a general and very mortal sickness prevailed among them, which swept off forty-six of their number before the opening of the next spring.

ourselves together unto a Civil Body Politic, for our better Ordering and Preservation, and Furtherance of the Ends aforesaid; and by Virtue hereof to enact, constitute and frame such just and equal Laws, Ordinances, Acts, Constitutions and Offices from Time to Time, as shall be thought most meet and convenient for the General Good of the Colony; unto which we Promise all due Submission and Obedience: In witness whereof we have hereunder subscribed our Names at Cape Cod, the 11th of November, in the Year of the Reign of our Sovereign Lord King JAMES of England, France, and Ireland the Eighteenth and of Scotland the Fifty-fourth, Anno Domini, 1620."

This instrument was signed by 41 heads of families, with the number in their respective families annexed, making in the whole 101 souls.

NEW ENGLAND.

To support them under these trials, they had need of all the aids and comforts which christianity affords; and these were sufficient. The free and unmolested enjoyment of their religion, reconciled them to their humble and lonely situation---they bore their hardships with unexampled patience, and persevered in their pilgrimage of almost unparalleled trials, with such resignation and calmness, as gave proof of great piety and unconquerable virtue.

On the 3d of November, 1620, king James signed a patent incorporating the duke of Lenox, the marquisses of Buckingham and Hamilton, the earls of Arundel and Warwick, Sir Francis Gorges, with thirty-four others, and their successors, styling them, 'The council established at Plymouth in the county of Devon, for the planting, ruling, ordering and governing of New England in America.' To this council he granted all that part of America which lies between the 40th and 48th degrees of north latitude. This patent is the great *civil basis* of all the grants and patents by which New England was afterwards divided.

The Plymouth council retained the power vested in them by the crown until the year 1635, when they resigned their charter. Previous to this, however, the council had made several grants of land to adventurers, who proposed to settle in New England.—They granted New Hampshire to Capt. John Mason in 1621—the Province of Main, to Sir R. Gorges in 1622, and Massachusetts Bay to Sir Henry Rosewell and five others in 1627.

As early as March 1621, Masassoit,* one of the most powerful Sagamores of the neighbouring Indians, with sixty attendants, made a visit to the Plymouth settlers, and entered into a formal and very friendly treaty with them, wherein they agreed to avoid injuries on both sides—to punish offenders—to restore stolen goods—to assist each other in all justifiable wars —to promote peace among their neighbours, &c.—Masassoit and his successors for fifty years, inviolably observed this treaty. The English are much indebted to him for his friendship; and his memory will ever be respected in New England.

The Narragansetts, disliking the conduct of Masassoit, declared war against him, which occasioned much confusion and fighting among the Indians. The Plymouth colony interposed in favour of Masassoit, their good ally, and terminated the dispute, to the terror of their enemies. Even CANONICUS himself the terrific Sachem of the Narragansetts, sued for peace.

The prudent, friendly and upright conduct of the Plymouth colony toward their neighbours, the Indians, secured their friendship and alliance. On the 13th of September 1621, no less than nine Sachems declared allegiance to king James; and Masassoit with many of his Sub-Sachems, who lived around the bays of Patuxent and Massachusetts, subscribed a writing acknowledging the king of England their master. These transactions are so many proofs of the peaceful and benevolent disposition of the Plymouth settlers; for had they been otherwise disposed they never could have introduced and maintained a friendly intercourse with the natives.

On

* *The seat of Masassoit was at Pakanokit, on Namasket river, which empties into Narraganset Bay.*

On the 10th of Sept. this year, the king granted to Sir William Alexander a patent of all the tract of country bounded by a line drawn from Cape Sables to the Bay of St. Mary; thence to the river St. Croix, thence north to Canada river—down the river to Gachepe; thence southeast to Cape Breton Island and Cape Breton; thence round to Cape Sables; with all seas and islands within six leagues of the western and eastern parts, and within forty leagues southward of Cape Breton and Cape Sables; to be called *Nova-Scotia*.

The first *duel* in New England, was fought with sword and dagger between two servants. Neither of them was killed, but both were wounded. For this disgraceful offence, they were formally tried before the whole company, and sentenced to have 'their heads and feet tied together, and so to be twenty-four hours without meat or drink.' Such, however, was the painfulness of their situation, and their piteous intreaties to be released, that, upon promise of better behaviour in future, they were soon released by the governor. Such was the origin, and such, I may almost venture to add, was the termination of the odious practice of duelling in New England, for there have been very few duels fought there since. The true method of preventing crimes is to render them disgraceful. Upon this principle, can there be invented, a punishment better calculated to exterminate this criminal practice, than the one already mentioned?

In 1622, Mr. Weston sent over a colony, which attempted a settlement at Weymouth. But they being a set of rude, profane fellows, regardless of justice, provoked the Indians by stealing their corn and other abuses, to become their enemies, and occasioned much trouble both to themselves and the Plymouth settlers. At length the Indians entered into a conspiracy to destroy the settlement, and would have effected it, had it not been for the interposition of their Plymouth friends. Such, however, was the reduced state of the colony, and their danger from the natives, that they thought it prudent to break up the settlement; which they did in March 1623, and afterwards returned to England.

This year (1622) died *Squanto* the friend of the English, who merits to have his name perpetuated in history. Squanto was one of the twenty Indians whom Hunt perfidiously carried to Spain;[*] whence he came to London, and afterwards to his native country with the Plymouth colony. Forgetting the perfidy of those who made him a captive, he became a warm friend to the English, and continued so to the day of his death. A few days before he died, he desired the governor to pray that he might go to the Englishman's God in heaven. He gave the few articles he possessed to several of his English friends as remembrances of his love.

We have already mentioned that Mr. Carver was elected governor of the colony immediately after their arrival. He died the 5th of April following. His loss was most sensibly felt and sincerely lamented. He was a man of great piety, and indefatigable in his endeavors to advance the interest and happiness of the colony. Mr. William Bradford was soon after chosen to succeed him in office. This gentleman, by renewed elections, was continued in office until he died in 1657, except in 1633, 1636 and 1644, when Edward Winslow was chosen, and 1634 when Thomas Prince was

---

[*] *See Page* 28.

was elected, who also succeeded Governor Bradford and was annually elected, until his death in 1673, when Josias Winslow succeeded and continued until he died in 1680, and was succeeded by Thomas Hinkley, who held the place, except in the interruption by Andrew, until the junction with the Massachusetts in 1692.

In March 1624 Mr. Winslow, agent for the colony, arrived in the ship Charity, and, together with a good supply of clothing, brought a *bull and three heifers*, which were the first cattle of the kind in this part of America. From these, and others that were afterwards brought over from England, sprang the present multitudes of cattle in the northern states. None of the domestic animals were found in America by the first European settlers.

This year Lyford and Oldham, two treacherous intriguing characters, influenced the factious part of the adventurers, to join them in opposing the church and government of the colony. Their artful designs got vent, and occasioned much disturbance. Oldham was detected and banished. Lyford, who afterwards proved to be a villain, was, upon apparent repentance, pardoned and received.

At the close of this year, (1624) the plantation at New Plymouth, consisted of 180 persons, who lived in thirty-two dwelling houses. Their stock was a few cattle and goats, and a plenty of swine and poultry. Their town was impaled about half a mile in compass. On a high mount in the town, they had erected a fort of wood, lime and stone, and a handsome watch-tower. This year they were able to freight a ship of 180 tons. Such was the healthfulness of the place or of the seasons, that, notwithstanding their frequent destitution of the necessaries of life, not one of the first planters died for three years.

However rigid the New Plymouth colonists may have been at their first separation from the church of England, yet they never discovered that persecuting spirit which we have seen in Massachusetts. When Mrs. Hutchinson and her adherents were banished from that colony, they applied to the colony of Plymouth, for leave to settle upon Aquidnick or Rhode Island, which was then acknowledged to be within Plymouth patent, and it was readily granted, although their tenets were no more approved by Plymouth than by the Massachusetts. Some of the Quakers also fled to Plymouth bounds, and probably saved their lives, for although they made laws severe enough against erroneous opinions, yet in no case capital; and the Baptists were still more favourably received, the town of Swanzey being principally settled by Baptist refugees from the Massachusetts colony, and when one of their ministers settled in the church of Plymouth, they were content that he should baptize by immersion or dipping any who desired it, provided he took no exception to the other minister's sprinkling such for whom immersion was not judged necessary.

About this time several ineffectual attempts were made to settle Weymouth, Dorchester, Cape Ann and Nantasket.

The year 1625 is distinguished by the death of the Rev. Mr. Robinson. He died at Leyden in March, in the 50th year of his age. He was truly a great and good man, and lived in great love and harmony with his people. He was held in high estimation by all his acquaintance, for his learning, piety, moderation and excellent accomplishments. His death was lamented as a public loss, and felt by none more than by his beloved

and

and far diftant people at Plymouth. His fon Ifaac came over to Plymouth, where he lived to the age of 90 years. His defcendants ftill live in Barnftable county in Maffachufetts.

After the death of Mr. Robinfon, the remaining part of his congregation were extremely defirous of coming over to their friends at Plymouth, and meafures were taken for the purpofe; yet it was not until feveral years after, that they effected their defign.

In Auguft, 1629, thirty-five of the Leyden congregation with their families, and many more pious people from England, arrived in a fhip from London, to the great joy of their friends at Plymouth. The next fpring, another company of Leydeners came over. Whether thefe were the whole that remained, or whether others came over after them, is not certain.

From this time New England began to flourifh. Sir Henry Rofwell and others, had received a patent of Maffachufetts from the Council of New England. Settlements were fuccefsfully enterprized at Salem, Charleftown, Bofton, Dorchefter and other places, fo that in forty years from this time (1629) 120 towns were fettled, and forty churches were gathered.

The Laudian perfecution was conducted with unrelenting feverity; and while it caufed the deftruction of thoufands in England, proved to be a principle of life and vigor to the infant fettlements in America. Several men of eminence in England, who were the friends and protectors of the Puritans, entertained a defign of fettling in New England, if they fhould fail in the meafures they were purfuing for the eftablifhment of the liberty, and the reformation of the religion of their own country. They folicited and obtained grants in New England, and were at great pains in fettling them. Among thefe patentees were the Lords Brook, Say and Seal, the Pelhams, the Hampdens and the Pyms; names which afterwards appeared with great eclat. Sir Matthew Boyntow, Sir William Conftable, Sir Arthur Haflerig, and Oliver Cromwell, were actually upon the point of embarking for New England, when Archbifhop Laud, unwilling that fo many objects of his hatred fhould be removed out of the reach of his power, applied for, and obtained, an order from the court to put a ftop to thefe tranfportations. However, he was not able to prevail fo far as to hinder New England from receiving vaft additions, as well of the clergy, who were filenced and deprived of their living and for non-conformity, as of the laity who adhered to their opinions.

New Plymouth, until this time, had remained without a patent. Several attempts were made, agents were fent and much money was expended, with a view to obtain one, but all hitherto had proved abortive. On the 13th of January, 1630, the council of New England fealed a patent to William Bradford, Efq; and his heirs, of 'all that part of New England lying between Cohaffet rivulet towards the north, and Narraganfett river towards the fouth, the weftern ocean towards the eaft, and between and within a ftrait line directly extending up the main land towards the weft from the mouth of Narraganfett river, to the utmoft bound of a country in New England, called Pokanoket, alias Sawamfett weftward, and another like ftrait line extending directly from the mouth of Cohaffet river toward

ward the weft fo far up into the main land as the utmoft limits of the faid Pokanoket extend:' Alfo, 'all that part of New England between the utmoft limits of Caperfecont which adjoineth to the river Kennebek, and the falls of Negumke, with the faid river itfelf, and the fpace of fifteen miles on each fide between the bounds above faid,' with all the rights, jurifdictions, privileges, &c. &c. ufual and neceffary.

This patent paffed the King's hand, and would no doubt have now been finifhed, had not the agents, without the notice or advice of the colony, inferted a claufe to free the colony from cuftoms feven years inward, and twenty-one outward. But in confequence of this claufe the patent was never finifhed, and they remained without a charter, until they were incorporated with Maffachufetts in 1691 or 1692. Notwithftanding this, New Plymouth was a government *de facto*, and confidered as fuch by king Charles in his letters and orders which were fent them at various times previous to their incorporation with Maffachufetts.

It was in the fpring of 1630, that the GREAT CONSPIRACY was entered into by the Indians in all parts, from the Narraganfetts round to the eaftward, to extirpate the Englifh. The colony at Plymouth was the principal object of this confpiracy. They well knew that if they could effect the deftruction of Plymouth, the infant fettlement at Maffachufetts, would fall an eafy facrifice. They laid their plan with much art. Under colour of having fome diverfion at Plymouth, they intended to have fallen upon the inhabitants, and thus to have effected their defign. But their plot was difclofed to the people at Charlefton, by John Sagamore, an Indian, who had always been a great friend to the Englifh. This treacherous defign of the Indians alarmed the Englifh, and induced them to erect forts and maintain guards, to prevent any fuch fatal furprize in future. Thefe preparations, and the firing of the *great guns*, fo terrified the Indians that they difperfed, relinquifhed their defign, and declared themfelves the friends of the Englifh.

Such was the vaft increafe of inhabitants in New England by natural population, and particularly by emigrations from Great Britain, that in a few years, befides the fettlements in Plymouth and Maffachufetts, very flourifhing colonies were planted in Rhode Ifland, Connecticut, New Haven and New Hampfhire. The dangers to which thefe colonies were expofed from the furrounding Indians, as well as from the Dutch, who, although very friendly to the infant colony at Plymouth, were now likely to prove troublefome neighbours, firft induced them to think of an alliance and confederacy for their mutual defence. Accordingly in 1643, the four colonies of Plymouth, Maffachufetts, Connecticut and New-Haven, agreed upon articles of confederation, whereby a congrefs was formed, confifting of two commiffioners from each colony, who were chofen annually, and when met were confidered as the reprefentatives of 'The united colonies of New England.' The powers delegated to the commiffioners, were much the fame as thofe vefted in Congrefs by the articles of confederation, agreed upon by the United States in 1778. The colony of Rhode Ifland would gladly have joined in this confederacy, but Maffachufetts, for particular reafons, refufed to admit their commiffioners. This union fubfifted, with fome few alterations, until the year 1686,

NEW ENGLAND.

1686, when all the charters, except that of Connecticut, were in effect vacated by a commission from James the II.

I shall close this general history of New England with a few remarks respecting the Indians.

We cannot even hazard a conjecture respecting the Indian population of New England at the time of its settlement by the English. Captain Smith, in a voyage to this coast in 1614, supposed, that on the Massachusetts Island, there were about 3,000, Indians. All accounts agree that the sea coast and the neighbouring islands were thickly inhabited.

Three years before the arrival of the Plymouth colony, a very mortal sickness, supposed to have been the *plague*, raged with great violence among the Indians in the eastern parts of New England. Whole towns were depopulated. The living were not able to bury the dead ; and their bones were found lying above ground, many years after. The Massachusetts Indians are said to have been reduced from 30,000 to 300 fighting men. In 1633, the small pox swept off great numbers of the Indians in Massachusetts.

In 1763, on the Island of Nantucket, in the space of four months, the Indians were reduced by a mortal sickness, from 320 to 85 souls. The hand of providence is noticeable in these surprising instances of mortality, among the Indians, to make room for the English. Comparatively few have perished by wars. They waste and moulder away—they, in a manner unaccountable, disappear.

The number of Indians in the state of Connecticut in 1774, was 1363. Their number was again taken in 1782, but was not kept separate from that of the Negroes. Their number is doubtless much lessened. The principal part of their present population in this state is at Mohegan in New London county.

The number of Indians in Rhode Island in 1783, was only 525. More than half of these live in Charleston, in the county of Washington. In 1774, the number of Indians in Rhode Island, was 1482 ; so that in nine years the decrease was 957. I have not been able to ascertain the exact state of the Indian population in Massachusetts and New Hampshire. In 1784, there was a tribe of about forty Indians at Norridgewalk in the Province of Main, with some few other scattering remains of tribes in other parts ; and a number of towns thinly inhabited round Cape Cod.

When the English first arrived in America, the Indians had no times nor places set apart for religious worship. The first settlers in New England, were at great pains to introduce among them the habits of civilized life, and to instruct them in the christian religion. A few years intercourse with the Indians, induced them to establish several good and natural regulations. They ordained that if a man be idle a week, or at most a fortnight, he shall pay five shillings. Every young man, not a servant, shall be obliged to set up a wigwam, and plant for himself. If an unmarried man shall lie with an unmarried woman, he shall pay twenty shillings. If any woman shall not have her hair tied up she shall pay five shillings, &c.

NEW ENGLAND.

The Rev. Mr. Elliott of Roxbury, near Bofton, who has been ftyled the *great Indian Apoftle*, with much labour, learned the Natic dialect of the Indian languages. He publifhed an Indian grammar, and preached in Indian to feveral tribes, and in 1664, tranflated the Bible, and feveral religious books into the Indian language. He relates feveral pertinent queries of the Indians refpecting the Chriftian religion. Among others; whether JESUS CHRIST, the mediator or interpreter, could underftand prayers in the Indian language? If the father be bad and the child good, why fhould God in the fecond commandment be offended with the child? How the Indians came to differ fo much from the Englifh in the knowledge of GOD and JESUS CHRIST, fince they all fprang from one father. Mr. Elliott was indefatigable in his labours, and travelled through all parts of Maffachufetts and Plymouth colonies as far as Cape Cod. The colony had fuch a veneration for him, that in an act of the general affembly relating to the Indians, they exprefs themfelves thus, ' By the advice of faid magiftrates, and of Mr. Elliott.' Mr. Mayhew, who alfo learned the Indian language, was very active in propagating the knowledge of chriftianity among the Indians at Nantucket, Martha's Vineyard and Elizabeth Ifland.

Mr. Brainard, was a truly pious and fuccefsful miffionary among the Indians on the Sufquehannah and Delaware rivers. In 1744, he rode about 4000 miles among the Indians; fometimes five or fix weeks together without feeing a white perfon. The Rev. Mr. Kirtland, of Stockbridge, has been laborioufly engaged, and greatly ferviceable in civilizing and chriftianizing the Oneida and other Indians.

Concerning the religion of the untaught natives of America, Mr. Brainard, who was well acquainted with it, informs us that after the coming of the white people, the Indians in New-Jerfey, who once held a plurality of Deities, fuppofed there were only three, becaufe they faw people of three kinds of complexions, viz.—Englifh, Negroes and themfelves.

It is a notion pretty generally prevailing among them, that it was not the fame God made them who made us; but that they were created after the white people: and it is probable they fuppofe their God gained fome fpecial fkill by feeing the white people made, and fo made them better: for it is certain they look upon themfelves, and their methods of living, which they fay their God exprefly prefcribed for them, vaftly preferable to the white people, and their methods.

With regard to a future ftate of exiftence, many of them imagine that the *chichung*, i. e. the fhadow, or what furvives the body, will, at death, go fouthward, and in an unknown but curious place—will enjoy fome kind of happinefs, fuch as hunting, feafting, dancing, and the like. And what they fuppofe will contribute much to their happinefs in the next ftate is, that they fhall never be weary of thofe entertainments.

Thofe who have any notion about rewards and punifhments in a future ftate, feem to imagine that moft will be happy, and that thofe who are not fo, will be punifhed only with privation, being only excluded from the walls of the good world where happy fpirits refide.

Thefe rewards and punifhments, they fuppofe to depend entirely upon their behaviour towards mankind; and have no reference to any thing which relates to the worfhip of the Supreme Being.

The

NEW HAMPSHIRE. 161

The natives of New England, according to Mr. Neal, believed not only a plurality of Gods, who made and governed the feveral nations of the world, but they made Deities of every thing they imagined to be great, powerful, beneficial, or hurtful to mankind; yet, they conceived one Almighty Being, who dwells in the fouthweft region of the heavens, to be fuperior to all the reft: this Almighty Being they call Kichtan, who at firft, according to their tradition, made a man and woman out of a ftone, but upon fome diflike deftroyed them again; and then made another couple out of a tree, from whom defcended all the nations of the earth; but how they came to be fcattered and difperfed into countries fo remote from one another they cannot tell. They believed their Supreme God to be a good Being, and paid a fort of acknowledgment to him for plenty, victory and other benefits.

But there is another power which they called Hobbamocko, in Englifh the Devil, of whom they ftood in greater awe, and worfhipped merely from a principle of fear.

The immortality of the foul was univerfally believed among them; when good men die they faid their fouls went to Kichtan, where they meet their friends, and enjoy all manner of pleafures; when wicked men die, they went to Kichtan alfo, but were commanded to walk away; and fo wander about in reftlefs difcontent and darknefs forever.

NEW HAMPSHIRE.

SITUATION and EXTENT.

miles.
Length 180 } Between { 2° 40' and 4° 20' Eaft Longitude.
Breadth 60 } { 42° 50' and 45° North Latitude.

Boundaries.] BOUNDED northwardly by the Britifh province of Quebec; northeaft by the old Province of Main; foutheaft by the Atlantic ocean; fouth by the ftate of Maffachufetts; weft and northweft by the weftern bank of Connecticut river, which forms the line of divifion between New Hampfhire and Vermont. The fhape of New Hampfhire, refembles an open fan, Connecticut river being the curve, the fouthern line the fhorteft, and the eaftern line the longeft fide.

Civil Divifions.] New Hampfhire is divided into counties* and townfhips; of the former are the five following, viz.
X Counties.

* *The firft act for dividing New Hampfhire into counties was paffed as late as* 1769.

NEW HAMPSHIRE.

Counties.	Chief Towns.
Rockingham,	Portsmouth and Exeter,
Stafford,	Dover and Durham,
Hillsborough,	Amherst,
Cheshire,	Keen and Charlestown,
Grafton.	Haveril and Plymouth.

In 1776, there were 165 settled townships in this state. Since that time the number has been greatly increased; and as a confiderable part of the state is unlocated, the number will continue to increase. Those townships which were laid out in the infancy of the state are large and differ in their size; but those of later date are uniformly six miles square.

Chief Towns.] Portsmouth is much the largest town in this state. It stands on the southeast side of Pifcataqua river, about two miles from the sea, and contains about 600 houses, and 4400 inhabitants. The town is handsomely built, and pleasantly situated. Its public buildings are a court house, two churches for Congregationalists, one for Epifcopalians, and one other house for public worship.

Its harbour is one of the finest on the continent, having a sufficient depth of water for vessels of any burthen. It is defended against storms by the adjacent land, in such a manner, as that ships may securely ride there in any season of the year. Besides, the harbour is so well fortified by nature, that very little art will be necessary to render it impregnable. Its vicinity to the sea renders it very convenient for naval trade. A light house, with a single light, stands at the entrance of the harbour.

Exeter is a pretty town, fifteen miles south westerly from Portsmouth, on the south side of Exeter river. It has a harbour of eight and an half feet water, and was formerly famous for ship building.

Dover Neck, which makes a part of the town of Dover, is situated between two branches of Pifcataqua river, and is a fine dry and healthy situation; so high as to command the neighbouring shores, and afford a very extensive and delightful prospect.

There are many confiderable and flourishing towns on Connecticut river, in the western parts of this state.

Rivers, bays and lakes.] The Pifcataqua river has four branches, Berwick, Cochechy, Exeter and Derham, which are all navigable for small vessels and boats, some fifteen, others twenty miles from the sea. These rivers unite about eight miles from the mouth of the harbour, and form one broad, deep, rapid stream, navigable for ships of the largest burden. This river forms the only port of New Hampshire. Its principal branch called Nywichwannot, springs from the southernmost of Lovel's ponds, and tumbling over several falls, in its southerly course, meets the other streams, which uniting form Pifcataqua river. A line drawn from the northern head of this river, until it meets the boundary of the province of Quebec, divides New Hampshire from the Province of Main.

The Merrimak bears that name from its mouth to the confluence of Pemigewaffet and Winipifiokee rivers, the latter has its source in the lake of the same name; one branch of the former rises in Squam Pond, latitude 43° 50'. Their junction is in about latitude 43° 30'

NEW HAMPSHIRE. 163

In its courfe, it receives numberlefs fmall ftreams iffuing from ponds and fwamps in the vallies. It tumbles over two confiderable falls, Amafkäëg, twenty-fix feet perpendicular, and Pantucket great falls, which has two pitches, and the ftream fhoots with an inconceiveable rapidity between the upper and lower pitches. The upper fall is ten feet perpendicular; the rapid, between the two falls defcends ten feet in the courfe of its fhot; the latter falls twenty-four feet in fixty-five rods. In the whole the water falls forty feet. From Haverhill the river runs winding along, through a pleafant rich vale of meadow—and paffing between Newbury Port and Salifbury, empties into the ocean.

Great Bay, fpreading out from Pifcataqua river, between Portfmouth and Exeter, is the only one that deferves mentioning.

There are feveral remarkable ponds or Lakes in this ftate. *Umbagog* is a large lake, quite in the northeaft corner of the ftate. *Winnifipiokee* lake, is nearly in the centre of the ftate, and is about twenty miles long, and from three to eight broad.

Face of the Country.] The land next to the fea, is generally low, but as you advance into the country the land rifes into hills. Some parts of the ftate are mountainous.

Mountains.] The *White mountains* are the higheft part of a ridge, which extends northeaft and fouthweft, to a length not yet afcertained. The whole circuit of them is not lefs than fifty miles. The height of thefe mountains above an adjacent meadow, is reckoned, from obfervations made by the Rev. Mr. Cutler of Ipfwich, in 1784, to be about 5500 feet, and the meadow is 3500 feet above the level of the fea. The fnow and ice, cover them nine or ten months in the year, during which time, they exhibit that bright appearance from which they are denominated the *White mountains*. From this fummit, in clear weather, is exhibited a noble view, extending fixty or feventy miles in every direction. Although they are more than feventy miles within land, they are feen many leagues off at fea, and appear like an exceeding bright cloud in the horifon. Thefe immenfe heights, being copioufly replenifhed with water, afford a variety of beautiful cafcades. Three of the largeft rivers in New England, receive a great part of their waters from thefe mountains. Amanoofuck and Ifrael Rivers, two principal branches of Connecticut, fall from their weftern fides. Peabody river, a branch of the Amarifcogen, falls from the northeaft fide, and almoft the whole of the Saco, defcends from the fouthern fide. The higheft fummit of thefe mountains, is in about latitude 44°.

The *Monadnik* is a very high mountain, in Chefhire county, in the fouth weftern parts of the ftate.

Climate.] The air in New Hampfhire is ferene and healthful. The weather is not fo fubject to change as in more fouthern climates. This ftate, embofoming a number of very high mountains, and lying in the neighbourhood of others, whofe towering fummits are covered with fnow and ice three quarters of the year, is intenfly cold in the winter feafon. The heat of fummer is great, but of fhort duration. The cold braces the conftitution, and renders the labouring people healthful and robuft.

Soil

NEW HAMPSHIRE.

Soil and Productions.] On the sea coast, and many places inland, the soil is sandy, but affords good pasturage. The intervals at the foot of the mountains are greatly enriched by the freshets which bring down the soil upon them, forming a fine mould, and producing corn, grain and herbage in the most luxuriant plenty. The back lands, which have been cultivated, are generally very fertile, and produce the various kinds of grain, fruits, and vegetables, which are common to the other parts of New England. The uncultivated lands are covered with extensive forests of pine, fir, cedar, oak, walnut, &c.

Mnaufactures.] As this state is the living magazine of masts and naval timber, and affords every other material necessary for ship building, that business may here be carried on extensively, and to very great advantage. Indeed much was done in this way before the war. A number of merchant vessels, and some frigates were built annually, and sold in Europe; and in the time of the war, a seventy-four gun ship was built at Portsmouth. Since the peace, this business has been revived.

Trade.] The principal trade of New Hampshire was formerly to the West India sugar islands, to which they exported all the various kinds of lumber—horses, cattle, sheep, poultry, salted provisions, pot and pearl ashes, dried fish, &c. and received in return, rum, sugar, molasses, cocoa, &c. Their ships were usually sent to the West India islands for freight to Europe, or to the Bay of Honduras, for logwood; and from thence to Europe, where they were sold. They also exported masts, yards and spars for the royal navy of Great Britain.

Population, Character, &c.] No actual census of the inhabitants has been lately made. In the Convention at Philadelphia, in 1787, they were reckoned at 102,000.

There is no characteristical difference between the inhabitants of this and the other New England States. The ancient inhabitants of New Hampshire were emigrants from England. Their posterity, mixed with emigrants from Massachusetts, fill the lower and middle towns.

Emigrants from Connecticut compose the largest part of the inhabitants of the western towns, adjoining Connecticut river. Slaves there are none. Negroes, who were never numerous in New Hampshire, are all free by the first article of the bill of rights.

Islands.] The Isles of Shoals are the only Islands in the sea, belonging to New Hampshire. They are convenient for the Codfishery, which was formerly carried on there to great advantage, but the people are now few and poor.

Indians.] There are no Indians in the State. The scattered remains of former tribes, retired to Canada many years since.

Constitution.] The Constitution of the State which was adopted in 1784, is taken almost verbatim, from that of Massachusetts. The principal differences, except such as arise from local circumstances, are the following; The stiles of the Constitutions, and of the supreme magistrates in each state, are different. In one it is ' GOVERNOR of the COMMONWEALTH of Massachusetts,' in the other ' PRESIDENT of the STATE of New Hampshire.''

NEW HAMPSHIRE.

shire." In each State the supreme magistrate has the title of His Excellency."

The President of New Hampshire, like the Governor of Massachusetts, has not the power of negativing all bills and resolves of the senate and house of representatives, and of preventing their passing into laws, unless approved of by two thirds of the members present. In New Hampshire 'the President of the State presides in the senate,' in Massachusetts the senate choose their own President.

There are no other differences worth mentioning, except it be in the mode of appointing militia officers, in which New Hampshire has greatly the advantage of Massachusetts. *See Massachusetts.*

Colleges, Academies, &c.] In the township of Hanover, in the western part of this State, is Dartmouth College, situated on a beautiful plain, about half a mile east of Connecticut River, in latitude 43° 33′ It was named after the Right Honorable William Earl of Dartmouth, who was one of its principal benefactors. It was founded by the late pious and benevolent Dr. Eleazer Wheelock, who, in 1769, obtained a royal charter, wherein ample privileges were granted, and suitable provision made for the education and instruction of youth, of the Indian tribes, in reading, writing, and all parts of learning which should appear necessary and expedient for civilizing and christianizing the children of Pagans, as well as in all liberal arts and sciences, and also of English youths and any others. The very humane and laudable attempts which have been made to christianize and educate the Indians, have not, through their native untractableness, been crowned with that success which was hoped and expected. Its situation, in a frontier country, exposed it during the late war to many inconveniencies, which prevented its rapid progress. It flourished, however, amidst all its embarrassments, and is now one of the most growing seminaries in the United States. It has, in the four classes, about 130 students under the direction of a President, two Professors, and two Tutors. It has twelve Trustees, who are a body corporate, invested with the powers necessary for such a body. The library is elegant, containing a large collection of the most valuable books. Its apparatus consists of a competent number of useful instruments, for making mathematical and philosophical experiments. There are three buildings for the use of the students; one of which was erected in 1786, and is not yet finished. It is one hundred and fifty feet in length, and fifty in breadth, three stories high and handsomely built. It has a broad passage running through its centre from end to end, intersected by three others. In front is a large green encircled with a number of handsome houses. Such is the salubrity of the air, that no instance of mortality has happened among the students since the first establishment of the College.

At Exeter, there is a flourishing Academy, under the instruction of Mr. William Woodbridge; and at Portsmouth a Grammar School. All the towns are bound by law to support schools; but the grand jurors, whose business it is to see that these laws are executed, are not so careful as they ought to be in presenting sins of *omission.*

Churches, &c.] The churches in New Hampshire are principally for congregationalists; some for Presbyterians and Baptists, and one for Episcopalians.

lians. Ministers contract with their parishes for their support. No parish is obliged to have a minister; but if they make a contract with one, they are obliged by law to fulfil it. Liberty is ever given to any individual of a parish to change their denomination; and in that case they are liberated from their part of the parish contract.

Damage sustained in the late war.] The enemy never entered New Hampshire. This is the only state that escaped their ravages. Their losses of men and ships, damage by depreciation of money and loss of business, were felt in proportion as in other states.

History.] The first discovery made by the English of any part of New Hampshire, was in 1614, by Capt. John Smith, who ranged the shore from Penobscot to Cape Cod; and in this route, discovered the river Piscataqua. On his return to England, he published a description of the country, with a map of the coast, which he presented to Prince Charles, who gave it the name of NEW ENGLAND.

In 1621, Capt. John Mason, obtained from the council of Plymouth, a grant of all the land from the river *Naumkeag* (new Salem) round Cape Ann, to the river Merrimak, up each of those rivers, and from a line connecting the furthest sources of them inclusively, with all islands within three miles of the coast. This district was called *Mariana*. The next year, another grant was made to Sir Ferdinando Gorges and Mason jointly, of all the lands between the Merrimak and Sagadahok, extending back to the great lakes of Canada. This grant, which includes a part of the other, was called *Laconia*.

Under the authority of this grant, in 1623, a settlement was made at Little Harbour, near the mouth of the Piscataqua.

In 1629, some planters from Massachusetts Bay, wishing to form a settlement in the neighbourhood of Piscataqua, procured a general meeting of the Indians, at Squamscot falls, where, *with the universal consent of their subjects*, they purchased of the Indian chiefs, for a valuable consideration, a tract of land comprehended between the rivers Piscataqua and Merrimak, and a line connecting these rivers, drawn at the distance of about thirty miles from the sea coast, and obtained a deed of the same, witnessed by the principal persons of Piscataqua and the Province of Main.

The same year, Mason procured a new patent under the common seal of the council of Plymouth, of all lands included within lines drawn from the mouths and through the middle of Piscataqua and Merrimak rivers, until sixty miles were completed, and a line crossing over land connecting those points, together with all islands within five leagues of the coast. This tract of land was called New Hampshire. It comprehended the whole of the abovementioned Indian purchace; and what is singular and unaccountable, the same land which this patent covered, and much more, had been granted to Gorges and Mason jointly seven years before.

In 1635, the Plymouth company resigned their charter to the king, but this resignation, did not materially affect the patentees under them, as the several grants to companies and individuals were mostly confirmed at some subsequent period by charters from the crown.

In 1640 four distinct governments had been formed on the several branches of Piscataqua. The people under these governments, unprotected by England,

NEW HAMPSHIRE. 167

England, in consequence of her own internal distractions, and too much divided in their opinions to form any general plan of government which could afford any prospect of permanent utility, thought best to solicit the protection of Massachusetts. That government readily granted their request, and accordingly, in April, 1641, the principal settlers of Piscataqua, by a formal instrument, resigned the jurisdiction of the whole to Massachusetts, on condition that the inhabitants should enjoy the same liberties with their own people, and have a court of justice erected among them. The property of the whole patent of Portsmouth, and of one third of that of Dover, and of all the improved lands therein, was reserved to the lords and gentlemen proprietors and their heirs forever. These reservations were acceded to on the part of Massachusetts, and what is extraordinary, and manifested the fondness of the government for retaining them under their jurisdiction, a law, of Massachusetts, declaring that none but church members should sit in the general court, was dispensed with in their favour. While they were united with Massachusetts, they were governed by the general laws of the colony, and the conditions of the union were strictly observed. During this period however, they had to struggle with many difficulties. One while involved together with Massachusetts in a bloody war with the Indians; and repeatedly disturbed, with the warm disputes occasioned by the ineffectual efforts of Mason's heirs to recover the property of their ancestor. These disputes continued until 1679, when Mason's claim, though never established in law, was patronized by the crown, and New Hampshire was erected into a separate government. Massachusetts was directed to recall all her commissions for governing in that province, which was accordingly done. The first commission for the government of New Hampshire, was given to Mr. Cutt, as president of the province on the 18th of September 1679.

In the year 1691, Mason's heirs sold their title to their lands in New England to Samuel Allen of London, for £2750. This produced new controversies, concerning the property of the lands, which embroiled the province for many years.

In 1692, Colonel Samuel Allen was commissioned governor of New Hampshire. Eight years after he came over to America to prosecute his claim, but died before the affair was concluded.

The inhabitants about this time suffered extremely from the cruel barbarity of the Indians; Exeter, Dover, and the frontier settlements, were frequently surprized in the night—the houses plundered and burnt—the men killed and scalped—and the women and children either inhumanly murdered, or led captives into the wilderness. The first settlers in other parts of New England were also, about this time, harrassed by the Indians, and it would require volumes to enumerate their particular sufferings.

In 1737, a controversy, which had long subsisted between the two governments of Massachusetts and New Hampshire, respecting their divisional line, was heard by commissioners appointed by the crown for that purpose. These commissioners determined that the northern boundaries, of Massachusetts should be a line three miles north from the river Merrimak as far as Pantucket falls, then to run west 10° north, until it meets New York line. Although Massachusetts felt themselves aggrieved by this decision, and attempted several ways to obtain redress, the line has never

never been altered, but is, at prefent, the divifional line between the two ftates. Douglafs mentions, 'That the governor of Maffachufetts, for many years, was alfo governor of New Hampfhire, with a diftinct commiffion.' This muft have been many years after New Hampfhire had been erected into a feparate government in 1679. He adds that New Hampfhire entered a complaint to the king in council againft the joint governor, relative to fettling the boundaries between the two provinces. This complaint was judged by the king to have been well founded, and ' therefore a feparate governor for New Hampfhire was commiffioned anno. 1740.'

Although New Hampfhire was under the jurifdiction of the governor of Maffachufetts, yet they had a feparate legiflature. They ever bore a proportionable fhare of the expences and levies in all enterprizes, expeditions and military exertions, whether planned by the colony or the crown. In every ftage of the oppofition that was made to the encroachments of the Britifh parliament, the people, who ever had a high fenfe of liberty, cheerfully bore their part. At the commencement of hoftilities, indeed, while their council was appointed by royal *mandamus*, their patriotic ardour was checked by thefe crown officers. But when freed from this reftraint, they flew eagerly to the American ftandard when the voice of their country declared for war, and their troops had a large fhare of the hazard and fatigue, as well as of the glory of accomplifhing the late revolution.

MASSACHUSETTS.

SITUATION and EXTENT.

Length 150 miles, Breadth 60 } Between { 41° 20' and 42° 50' North Latitude. 2° and 5° 30' Eaft Longitude.

Boundaries.] BOUNDED northwardly by New Hampfhire and Vermont; weft by New-York; fouthwardly by Connecticut, Rhode Ifland and the Atlantic; eaft by the Atlantic, and Maffachufetts Bay.

Rivers.] Merrimak river before defcribed, runs through the northeaftern part of this ftate. Charles river rifes from five or fix fources, on the fouth eaft fide of Hopkinton and Hollifton ridge. The main ftream runs northeaft, then north and north eaftwardly, round this ridge, until, in Natick townfhip, it mingles with Mother-Brook, which is a confiderable branch of Charles river. The river thus formed, runs weftward, tumbling

MASSACHUSETTS.

in falls acrofs the fouthweft end of Brooklyn hills, and paffing near Framingham pond, runs northeaft to Cambridge; hence winding round in a finuous courfe falls into Bofton harbour. Taunton river, rifes in the Blue Mountains, which lie back of Milton and Braintree, and forms the principal drain of the country lying eaft of thefe mountains—the river runs nearly a ftraight courfe fouthweft, under the foot of the mountains, to Tiverton on Narraganfett Bay. Concord river, is formed by three branches, one iffuing from Framingham Pond, and the other two from the mountains about Marlborough. Thefe ftreams united run north and fall into the Merrimak river a little below Pantucket falls.

Myftic and Medford rivers, run from north to fouth into Bofton harbour. Ipfwich river, rifing in Wilmington in Middlefex county, runs eaft and then northeaft into the Atlantic, at Ipfwich. Weftfield river, from the northweft, empties into Connecticut river at Springfield. A little above, the Chicabee from the northeaft empties into the fame river. Deerfield river rifes in Vermont and running fouthwardly through Wilmington, Charlemont, and between Shelburn and Conway, enters and paffes through a large tract of the fineft meadow in the world. In thefe meadows it receives Green River, from the mountains, which is about four rods wide; hence they pafs on together, in a broad fmooth ftream, about three miles into Connecticut river.

Capes.] The only Capes of note on the coaft of Maffachufetts, are Cape Ann on the north fide of Bofton Bay, and Cape Cod on the fouth. The latter is the terminating hook of a promontory, which extends far into the fea; and is remarkable for having been the firft land which was made by the firft fettlers of Plymouth on the American coaft in 1620. In the barb of the hook, which is made by the Cape, is Cape Cod harbour. This promontory, circumfcribes Barnftable Bay, and forms Barnftable county. This County is almoft an ifland. The ifthmus which connects it to the Continent, is between Sandwich bay on the north, and Buzzards bay on the fouth. The diftance between them is but fix or feven miles. Herring brook almoft croffes this neck or ifthmus, fo that a canal of about one mile only would infulate the county, and fave feveral hundred miles dangerous navigation in paffing from Newport to Bofton, and be otherwife of immenfe advantage to trade. Such a canal has been *talked* of for more than an hundred years paft. The eaftern coaft of this promontory is fubject to continual changes. Large tracts of fand bank, in the courfe of forty or fifty years, by the conftant accumulation of fand and mud occafioned by the coil and recoil of the tides, have been transformed into folid marfh land. The fand banks extend two hundred miles into the fea forming dangerous fhoals.

Iflands.] Among other iflands which border upon this coaft, are Kappawak, Martha's Vineyard and Nantucket. Kappawak, now Dukes county, and the neighbouring ifles, were difcovered as early as 1602, by Bartholomew Gofnold. In honour of Queen Elizabeth, he called a clufter of fmall iflands near the cape, Elizabeth ifles. To another neighbouring ifland he gave the name of Martha's Vineyard. Dukes county is twenty miles in length, and about four in breadth. It contains feven parifhes.

rishes. Edgarton, which includes the island Chabaquidick, is the shire town. This little island is about half a mile from the harbour, and renders it very secure. This county is full of inhabitants, who, like their neighbours at Nantucket, subsist principally by fishing. They send three representatives to the general assembly, and one senator.

Nantucket lies south of Cape Cod, and is considerably less than Dukes county. It contains, according to Douglass, 23,000 acres, including the beach. No mention is made of the discovery and settlement of this island, under its present name, by any of our historians. It is more than probable that this is the island which is usually called Nautican by ancient voyagers. It formerly had the most considerable whale fishery on the coast; but the war almost ruined them. They are now beginning to revive their former business. Most of the inhabitants are whalers and fishermen. As the island is low, sandy and barren, it is calculated only for those people who are willing to depend almost entirely on the watry element for subsistence. The island of itself constitutes one county by the name of Nantucket. It has but one town, called Sherburne, and sends one representative to the general assembly.

Light-Houses.] Within the State of Massachusetts are the following Light-Houses; on Plumb island, near Newbury, are two, which must be brought to bear in a line with each other in order to pass the bar in safety. On Thatchers island, off Cape Ann, two lights of equal height. Another stands on a rock on the north side of the entrance of Boston harbour, with one single light. On the north point of Plymouth harbour are two lights one over the other. On a point at the entrance of the harbour on the island of Nantuckett is one with a single light. This light may be seen as far as Nantucket shoals extend. The island being low, the light appears over it.

Religion.] The religion of this commonwealth is established, by their excellent constitution, on a most liberal and tolerant plan. All persons, of whatever religious profession or sentiments, may worship God agreeably to the dictates of their own consciences, unmolested, provided they do not disturb the public peace. The legislature are empowered to require of the several towns, parishes, &c. to provide, at their own expence, for the public worship of God, and to require the attendance of the subject on the same. The people have liberty to choose their own teachers, and to contract with them for their support.

The body of the churches in this state are established upon the congregational plan. Their rules of church discipline and government are, in general, founded upon the Cambridge platform, as drawn up by the synod of 1648. The churches claim no jurisdiction over each other, and the power of ecclesiastical councils is only advisory.

The following statement, shews what are the several religious denominations in this state, and their proportional numbers.

Denominations.

MASSACHUSETTS.

Denominations.	Number of Congregations.	Supposed number of each denomination.
Congregationalists,	400	277,600
Baptists,	84	58,296
Episcopalians,	16	11,104
Friends or Quakers,	10	6,940
Presbyterians,	4	2,776
Universalists,	1	694
Total.	515	357,410

In this statement it is supposed that all the inhabitants in the state consider themselves as belonging to one or the other of the religious denominations mentioned; and that each religious society, of every denomination, is composed of an equal number of souls; that is, each is supposed to contain 694, which, if we reckon the number of inhabitants in the state at 357,511, will be the proportion for each congregation. Although this may not be an exact apportionment of the different sects, yet it is perhaps as accurate as the nature of the subject will allow, and sufficient to give a general idea of the proportion which the several denominations bear to each other.

The number of congregational churches in 1749 was 250.

In 1760, the number of inhabitants in this state, was about 268,850. The proportion of the sects then was nearly as follows, viz.

Sects.	Congregations.	Supposed number of souls of each sect.
Congregationalists,	306	225,426
Friends meetings,	22	16,192
Baptists,	20	14,723
Episcopalians,	13	9,568
Presbyterians,	4	2,944
Total.	365	268,850

The congregational ministers in this state, have an annual meeting at Boston, the Thursday following the last Wednesday in May, on which occasion a sermon is preached, and a collection made for the relief and support of such of their society as are in needy circumstances. This collection is chiefly applied to the support of the widows of deceased ministers.

Civil Divisions.] The Commonwealth of Massachusetts is divided into fourteen counties, and sub-divided into 355 townships. The following table exhibits a comparative view of the population—agricultural improvements—military strength, &c. of the several counties, together with their sea ports and principal trading towns.

TABLE.

MASSACHUSETTS.
TABLE.

Counties.	Number of Inhabitants.	Acres of improved Land.	Ditto unimproved	Number of Horses of all ages.*	Number of horned cattle of all kinds.*	Number of fighting men.†
Suffolk,	36,783	105,635 ½	77,556	3729	19,271	7356
Essex,	48,723	171,893 ¾	47,801	4195	28,317	9744
Middlesex,	34,823	163,834 ¾	199,548	5217	32,675	6964
Hampshire,	43,143	142,375	671,344	8442	39,904	8628
Plimouth,	25,016	92,513 ¾	129,191	2784	20,552	5003
Barnstable,	13,353	39,202 ¼	45,720	930	8071	2670
Dukes, (island)	3110	18,198	42,172	312	2043	622
Nantucket, (an island)	4269	16,092	1431	219	583	Chiefly quakers
Bristol,	25,640	97,360	130,767	2958	17,860	5130
York,	20,500	66,142	264,931	2101	18,710	4102
Worcester,	47,614	207,430	510,236	8321	51,369	9523
Cumberland,	14,714	53,865	260,693	1635	14,588	2943
Lincoln,	15,270	45,803	799,970	1712	15,699	3054
Berkshire,	24,544	87,028	234,497	6762	18,348	4909
Total	357,511	1,087,372	3.185,857	49,417	286,999	70,648

* *This valuation was taken in* 1784, *and supposed to be* less *than the reality.*

† *This estimate is very imperfect—No account having been taken for near twelve years.*

Number

MASSACHUSETTS.

Number of townships.	Number of congregational place of worship.	Do. baptiſt.	Ditto other denominations.	Sea-Ports and principal trading towns.	Towns where the courts are held.
23	32		3	Boſton.	Boſton.
22	54	2	8	Salem, Newbury Port. Marblehead, Beverly. Glouceſter or C. Ann. Haverhill, Ipſwich.	Salem, Ipſwich and Newbury Port.
40	47	2	1	Charleſtown.	Cambridge, Concord.
60	58	11	4	An inland county.	Springfield, Northampton, Hadley & Deerfield.
14	27	4	1	Plymouth, Rocheſter.	Plymouth.
10	14	2	1	The C. of Barnſtable is ſurrounded by the ſea, therefore every T. has a ſmall port and trade.	Barnſtable.
3	5	2		Edgartown.	Edgartown, Tiſbury.
1	1		1	Sherburne.	Sherburne.
14	13	20	4	New Bedford, Dighton	Taunton.
21	23	4	1	York, Pepperelſboro, Biddeford.	York, Biddeford.
49	53	13	3	(Inland.)	Worceſter.
20	20	3	2	Portland.	Portland.
53	29	2	1	Bath, Boothbay Goldſboro, Paſſamaquady, Machias, Penobſcot, Wiſcaſſet.	Pownalboro, Waldoboro' and Hallowell.
25	24	10	1	(Inland.)	Lenox.
355	400	84	31		

Population, Character, &c.] The above table exhibits an accurate account of the population of this ſtate. The moſt populous parts of the ſtate are included between the ſea coaſt, and a line drawn parallel to it at the diſtance of ten or twelve miles; and between two lines drawn parallel to Connecticut river on each ſide, at the diſtance of five or ſix miles.
Character, &c. ſee New England.
Literary

174 MASSACHUSETTS.

Literary and humane Societies.] The literary, humane and charitable inſtitutions in Maſſachuſetts, exhibit a fair trait in the character of the inhabitants. Among the firſt literary inſtitutions in this ſtate, is the AMERICAN ACADEMY OF ARTS AND SCIENCES, incorporated May 4th 1780. It is declared in the act, that the end and deſign of the inſtitution, is to promote and encourage the knowledge of the antiquities of America, and of the natural hiſtory of the country, and to determine the uſes to which the various natural productions of the country may be applied. Alſo to promote and encourage medical diſcoveries, mathematical diſquiſitions, philoſophical enquiries and experiments ; aſtronomical, meteorological and geographical obſervations ; improvements in agriculture, arts, manufacture, commerce, and the cultivation of every ſcience that may tend to advance a free, independent, and virtuous people. There are never to be more than two hundred members, nor leſs than forty. This ſociety has four ſtated annual meetings.

The MASSACHUSETTS CHARITABLE SOCIETY, incorporated December 16, 1779, is intended for the mutual aid of themſelves and families, who may be diſtreſſed by any of the adverſe accidents of life, and for the comforting and relieving of widows and orphans of their deceaſed members. The members of this ſociety meet annually, and are not to exceed an hundred in number.

The BOSTON EPISCOPAL CHARITABLE SOCIETY, firſt inſtituted in 1724, and incorporated February 12, 1784, has for its object, charity to ſuch as are of the epiſcopal church, and to ſuch others as the ſociety ſhall think fit ; but more eſpecially the relief of thoſe who are members of, and benefactors to the ſociety, and afterwards become ſuitable objects of its charity. The members of this ſociety meet annually, and are not to exceed one hundred in number.

The MASSACHUSETTS MEDICAL SOCIETY, was incorporated November 1, 1781. The deſign of this inſtitution is, to promote medical and ſurgical knowledge ; enquires into the animal œconomy, and the properties and effects of medicine, by encouraging a free intercourſe with the gentlemen of the faculty throughout the United States of America, and a friendly correſpondence, with the eminent in thoſe profeſſions throughout the world ; as well as to make a juſt diſcrimination between ſuch as are duly educated and properly qualified for the duties thereof, and thoſe who may ignorantly, and wickedly adminiſter medicine, whereby the health and lives of many valuable individuals may be endangered, and perhaps loſt to community.

Further to evidence their humanity and benevolence, a number of the medical and other gentlemen, in the town of Boſton, in 1785, formed a ſociety, by the name of the HUMANE SOCIETY, for the purpoſe of recovering perſons apparently dead, from drowning, ſuffocation, ſtrangling, and other accidents. This humane ſociety have erected three huts, furniſhed with wood, tinder boxes, blankets, &c. one on Lovel's Iſland in Boſton harbour, one on Nantaſket beach, and another on Situate beach near Marſhfield, for the comfort of ſhip-wrecked ſeamen. Huts of the ſame kind are erected on Plumb Iſland, near Newbury, by the marine ſociety of that place ; and there are alſo ſome contiguous to Hampton and Saliſbury beach.

At

MASSACHUSETTS.

At their semiannual meetings, a public discourse is delivered by some person appointed by the trustees for that purpose, on some medical subject connected with the principal object of the society; and as a stimulus to investigation, and a reward of merit, a medal is adjudged annually by the president and trustees, to the person who exhibits the most approved dissertation.

The SOCIETY FOR PROPAGATING THE GOSPEL among the Indians and others in North-America, was incorporated November 19, 1787. They are enabled to receive subscriptions of charitably disposed persons, and may take any personal estate in succession. All donations to the society either by subscriptions, legacy or otherwise, excepting such as may be differently appropriated by the donors, to make a part of, or be put into the capital stock of the society, which is to be put out on interest on good security, or otherwise improved to the best advantage, and the income and profits are to be applied to the purposes aforesaid, in such manner as the society shall judge most conducive to answer the design of their institution.

This Society is formed into a board of commissioners from the Scot's Society for promoting Christian knowledge among the Indians in America.

Next to Pennsylvania, this State has the greatest number of societies for the promotion of useful knowledge and human happiness; and as they are founded on the broad basis of *benevolence* and *charity*, they cannot fail to prosper. These institutions which are fast encreasing in almost every state in the union, are so many evidences of the advanced and advancing state of civilization and improvement in this country. They prove likewise that a free republican government, like ours, is, of all others, the most happily calculated to promote a general diffusion of useful knowledge, and the most favourable to the benevolent and humane feelings of the human heart.

Literature, Colleges, Academies, &c.] According to the laws of this Commonwealth, every town having fifty housholders or upwards, is to be constantly provided with a school-master to teach children and youth to read and write; and where any town has 100 families, there is also to be a grammar school set up therein, and some discreet person, well instructed in the language, procured to keep the same, and be suitably paid by the inhabitants.

These laws respecting schools, are not so well regarded in many parts of the State, as the wise purposes which they were intended to answer, and the happiness of the people require.

Next in importance to the Grammar Schools are the Academies, in which, as well as in the Grammar schools, young gentlemen are fitted for admission to the University.

DUMMER ACADEMY, at Newbury, was founded many years since, by means of a liberal donation from the Honorable William Dummer, formerly Lieutenant Governor, and a worthy man, whose name it has ever since retained. It was incorporated in 1782, and is under the superintendence of fourteen respectable trustees.

PHILLIPS's ACADEMY, at Andover, owes its existence to the benefactions of the Honourable Samuel Phillips, Esq; of Andover, in the county

county of Effex, and State of Maffachufetts Bay, and the Honourable John Phillips, Efq; of Exeter, in the county of Rockingham, and State of New Hampſhire. It was incorporated October 4, 1780, and has twelve truſtees.

LEICESTER ACADEMY, in the townſhip of Leicefter, was incorporated in 1784. For the encouragement of this inſtitution, Ebenezer Crafts and Jacob Davis, Efqr's. generoufly gave a large and commodious manfion houfe, lands and appurtenances, in Leicefter, for that ufe.

At Williams-town, in Berkſhire county, is another Academy, which is yet in its infancy. Colonel Ephraim Williams, has made a handfome donation, in lands, for its encouragement and fupport.

At Hingham is a well endowed fchool, or Academy, which in honor of its principal donor and founder, is called DERBY SCHOOL.

Thefe Academies have very handfome funds, and are flourifhing. The defigns of the truftees are, to diffeminate virtue and true piety, to promote the education of youth in the Englifh, Latin, Greek, and French languages, to encourage their inſtruction in writing, arithmetic, oratory, geography, practical geometry, logic, philofophy, and fuch other of the liberal arts and fciences, or languages, as may be thought expedient.

HARVARD COLLEGE (now UNIVERSITY) takes its date from the year 1638. Two years before, the general court gave four hundred pounds for the fupport of a public fchool at Newtown, which has fince been called Cambridge. This year (1638) the Rev. Mr. John Harvard, a worthy miniſter refiding in Charlefton, died, and left a donation of £779 for the ufe of the forementioned public fchool. In honour to the memory of fo liberal a benefactor, the general court the fame year, ordered that the fchool fhould take the name of HARVARD COLLEGE.

In 1642, the College was put upon a more refpectable footing, and the governor, deputy governor, and magiftrates, and the minifters of the fix next adjacent towns, with the prefident, were erected into a corporation for the ordering and managing its concerns. This year nine young gentlemen received the degree of Batchelor of Arts. It received its firſt charter in 1650.

Cambridge, in which the univerfity is fituated, is a pleafant village, four miles weftward from Bofton, containing a number of gentlemen's feats which are neat and well built. The univerfity confifts of four elegant brick Edifices, handfomely enclofed. They ftand on a beautiful green which fpreads to the north weft, and exhibit a pleafing view.

The names of the feveral buildings are, Harvard Hall, Maffachufetts Hall, Hollis Hall, and Holden Chapel. Harvard Hall is divided into fix appartments; one of which is appropriated for the library, one for the mufeum, two for the philofophical apparatus, one is ufed for a chapel, and the other for a dining hall. The library, in 1787, confifted of 12,000 volumes; and will be continually increafing from the intereft of permanent funds, as well as from cafual benefactions. The philofophical apparatus belonging to this univerfity, coft between 1400 and £1500 lawful money, and is the moft elegant and complete of any in America.

Agreeably to the prefent conftitution of Maffachufetts, his excellency the governor, lieutenant governor, the council and fenate, the prefident of the univerfity, and the minifters of the congregational churches in the towns

MASSACHUSETTS.

towns of Boston, Charlestown, Cambridge, Watertown, Roxbury, and Dorchester, are, *ex officiis*, overseers of the University.

The corporation is a distinct body, consisting of seven members, in whom is vested the property of the university.

The instructors in the university, are a president, Hollisian professor of divinity, Hollisian professor of the mathematics and natural philosophy, Hancock professor of oriental languages, professor of anatomy and surgery, professor of the theory and practice of physic, professor of chymistry and materia medica, and four tutors.

This university as to its library, philosophical apparatus and professorships, is at present the first literary institution on this continent. Since its first establishment, 3146 students have received honorary degrees from its successive officers; 1002 of whom have been ordained to the work of the gospel ministry. It has generally from 120 to 150 students.

Chief towns.] BOSTON is the capital, not only of Massachusetts, but of New England. It is built on a Peninsula of an irregular form, at the bottom of Massachusetts Bay. The neck or isthmus which joins the Peninsula to the continent, is at the south end of the town, and leads to Roxbury. The length of the town, including the neck, is about three miles; the town itself is not quite two miles. Its breadth is various. At the entrance from Roxbury, it is narrow. The greatest breadth is one mile and 139 yards. The buildings in the town cover about 1000 acres. It contains near 1800 dwelling houses.

By a late computation, the number of inhabitants was found to be 14,640, of these 6,570 were males, and 8,070 females. This number is exclusive of strangers and transient persons, who make nearly one third of the whole number of souls in Boston. The ratable polls, at the time of the census, were about 2,620. In this town, there are seventy-nine streets, thirty-eight lanes, and twenty-one alleys, exclusive of squares and courts; and about eighty wharves and quays, very convenient for vessels. The principal wharf extends 600 yards into the sea, and is covered on the north side with large and convenient stores. It far exceeds any other wharf in the United States.

In Boston are sixteen houses for public worship; of which nine are for congregationalists, three for episcopalians, two for baptists, one for the friends, and one for universalists, or independents. There is one old meeting house desolate and in ruins, in school street.

The other public buildings are the state house, faneuil hall, an alms house, a workhouse, and a bridewell. That building which was formerly the governor's house, is now occupied in its several apartments, by the council, the treasurer, and the secretary; the two latter hold their offices in it. The public granary is converted into a store, and the linen manufactory house, is now occupied by the bank. Most of the public buildings are handsome, and some of them are elegant. The town is irregularly built, but, as it lies in a circular form around the harbour, it exhibits a very handsome view as you approach it from the sea. On the west side of the town is the mall, a very beautiful public walk, adorned with rows of trees, and in view of the common, which is always open to refreshing breezes. Beacon hill, which overlooks the town from the west, affords a fine variegated prospect.

The harbour of Boston is safe, and large enough to contain 500 ships

MASSACHUSETTS.

at anchor, in a good depth of water; while the entrance is so narrow as scarcely to admit two ships abreast. It is diversified with many islands, which afford rich pasturing, hay and grain. About three miles from the town is the Castle, which commands the entrance of the harbour. Here are mounted about forty pieces of heavy artillery, besides a large number of a smaller size. The fort is garrisoned by a company of about fifty soldiers, who also guard the convicts that are sentenced, and sent here to labour. These are all employed in the nail manufactory.

In Boston there are two grammar schools, and four for writing, &c. whose masters are supported by the town: besides twelve or fourteen private schools.

It has been computed, that during the siege in 1775, as many houses were destroyed in Boston by the British troops, as were burnt in Charlestown. Since the peace, a spirit of repairs and improvement has diffused itself among the inhabitants. A few years may render the metropolis of Massachusetts as famed for arts, manufactures, and commerce, as any city in the United States.

The town next to Boston, in point of numbers and commercial importance, is Salem. This town was settled as early as 1628, by Mr. Endicot, afterwards governor, and a colony under his direction. It is the oldest town in the state, except Plymouth, which was settled eight years before. In 1786, it contained 646 dwelling houses, and 6700 inhabitants. In this town are five churches for congregationalists, one for episcopalians, and a meeting house for the friends. Its harbour is inferior to that of Boston. The inhabitants, notwithstanding, carry on a large foreign trade. Salem is fifteen miles northeastward of Boston, and is considered as the metropolis of the county of Essex.

Newbury Port, forty-five miles eastward from Boston, is situated on the southwest side of Merrimak river, about two miles from the sea. The town is about a mile in length, and a fourth of a mile in breadth, and contains 450 dwelling houses, and 4113 natural inhabitants. It has one episcopal, one presbyterian, and two congregational churches. The business of ship building is largely carried on here. These towns, with Marblehead, Gloucester or Cape Ann, and Beverly, carry on the fishery, which furnishes the principal article of exportation from Massachusetts.

Worcester is one of the largest inland towns in New England. It is the shire town of Worcester county, and is about forty-seven miles westward of Boston.

On Connecticut river, in the county of Hampshire, are a number of very pleasant towns. Of these Springfield is the oldest and largest. It stands on the east side of Connecticut river about ninety-six miles westward of Boston. The courts are held here and at Northampton alternately. Within its ancient limits, are about 700 families, who are divided into eight worshipping assemblies. The original township has been divided into six parishes, some of which have been incorporated into distinct townships. The settlement of Springfield was begun in 1636, by William Pychon, Esq; whose descendants are still living in the place. He called the place Springfield, in remembrance of his native place in England, which bore that name.

Hadley is a neat little town on the opposite side of the river from Northampton. Northampton,

MASSACHUSETTS. 179

Northampton, Hatfield, and Deerfield are all pleasant, flourishing towns, succeeding each other as you travel northerly on the west side of the river.

Constitution.] The Constitution of the Commonwealth of Massachusetts established in 1780, contains a declaration of rights and a frame of government. The declaration asserts the natural freedom and equality of men—Liberty of conscience—Freedom of the Press—Trial by jury—Sovereignty and independence—that all power is derived from the people—that hereditary honours and emoluments are inadmissible—that every subject is entitled to protection of life, liberty, and property—and, in return, must obey the laws and pay his proportion of the common expence—that he shall not be obliged to accuse himself; but may be heard in his own defence—that he may keep arms; but standing armies shall not be maintained in time of peace—that no tax shall be levied without the consent of the people by their representatives—that no ex post facto law shall be made—that the martial law shall extend only to men in actual military service—that the legislative, executive, and judiciary powers shall be kept distinct, &c. By the frame of government, the power of legislation is lodged in a general court, consisting of two branches, viz. a senate and a house of representatives, each having a negative upon the other. They meet annually on the last Tuesday in May. No act can be passed without the approbation of the governor, unless two-thirds of both branches are in favour of it. Either branch, or the governor and council, may require the opinion of the justices of the supreme judicial court, upon important questions. Senators are chosen by districts, of which there cannot be less than thirteen. The number of counsellors and senators, for the whole Commonwealth, is forty; the number of each district is in proportion to their public taxes; but no district shall be so large, as to have more than six. Sixteen senators make a quorum. The representatives are chosen by the several towns, according to their numbers of rateable polls. For 150 polls one is elected; and for every addition of 225, an additional one. Their travelling expences, to and from the general court, are defrayed by the public, but their wages for attendance are paid by their own towns. Impeachments, for misconduct in office, are made by the representatives, and tried by the senate; but the judgment can go only to removal from office and future disqualification. Money bills originate in the house of representatives, but may be altered by the senate. Representatives are privileged from arrests on mesne process. Sixty members make a quorum. The supreme executive authority is vested in a governor, who is elected annually by the people, and has a council consisting of the lieutenant governor, and nine gentlemen chosen out of the forty, who are returned for counsellors and senators. Five counsellors make a quorum. The governor is commander of all the military force of the Commonwealth. He may convene the general court, may adjourn them, when the two branches disagree about the time, and in their recess, may prorogue them from time to time, not exceeding ninety days—may pardon convicts, but the legislature alone can grant pardons, before conviction. He commissions all officers, and with advice of council, appoints all judicial officers. Military officers are thus appointed; the respective companies choose their captain and subalterns, who choose their regimental officers, who choose
their

their brigadiers. The major-generals are appointed by the general court. Justices of the peace are commissioned for seven years; all other judicial, and all executive and military officers, continue during good behaviour, yet are removeable by the governor, upon address of the legislature. The salaries of governor and justices of the supreme court, cannot be diminished, although they may be enlarged. Official qualifications are as follows—for a voter, twenty one year's age, one year's residence, a freehold of three pounds annual value or sixty pounds of any other estate—for a representative, £.100 freehold or £.200 other estate, and one year's residence in the town—for a senator, £.300 freehold or £.600 other estate in the Commonwealth, and five years residence in the district—for governor or lieutenant governor, £.1000 freehold, and seven years residence. Every governor, lieutenant governor, counsellor, senator, or representative, must declare that he believes the Christian religion, and has the legal qualifications. A governor, lieutenant governor, or justice of the supreme court can hold no other office. No man shall hold two of these offices, judge of probates, sheriff, register. No justices of the supreme court, secretary, attorney-general, treasurer, judge of probate, instructor of Harvard College, clerk, register, sheriff or custom officer can have a seat in the legislature. The privilege of Habeas Corpus cannot be suspended more than a year at one time. In 1795, if two-thirds of the qualified voters desire it, a convention shall be called to revise the constitution.

Bridges.] The principal bridge in this State, or in any of the United States, is that which was built over Charles river, between Boston and Charlestown, in 1786.

The following is an accurate description of this convenient and handsome structure:

		Feet.
	The abuttment at Charlestown, from the old landing, is	100
	Space to the first pier,	16 ½
36	Piers at an equal distance, to draw,	522 ½
	Width of the draw,	30
39	Piers at equal distance,	672
75	the whole number of piers,	
	Spaces to the abuttment at Boston,	16 ¼
	Abuttment at Boston to the old landing,	45 ½
	Whole length,	1503

Each pier is composed of seven sticks of oak timber, united by a cap-piece, strong braces and girts, and afterwards driven into the bed of the river, and firmly secured by a single pile on each side, driven obliquely to a solid bottom. The piers are connected to each other by large string pieces, which are covered with four-inch plank. The bridge is 43 feet in width, and on each side is accommodated with a passage six feet wide, railed in for the safety of people on foot. The bridge has a gradual rise from each end, so as to be two feet higher in the middle than at the extremities. Forty elegant lamps are erected, at a suitable distance from each other,

MASSACHUSETTS.

other to illuminate it when neceſſary. There are four ſtrong ſtone wharves, connected with three piers each, funk in various parts of the river.

The draw is conſtructed on the moſt approved plan; the machinery is very ſimple; and it is deſigned to require the ſtrength of two men only in raiſing it. The floor on the bridge at the higheſt tides, is four feet above the water, which generally riſes about twelve or fourteen feet.

This bridge was completed in thirteen months: and while it exhibits the greateſt effect of private enterprize within the United States, is a moſt pleaſing proof, how certainly objects of magnitude may be attained by ſpirited exertions.

Another bridge, of a ſimilar conſtruction, has been erected over Myſtic river at Malden; and another is now building at Beverly, which will connect that flouriſhing little town with Salem. Theſe are works of much enterprize, ingenuity and public ſpirit; and ſerve to ſhew that architecture, in this State, has ariſen to a high pitch of improvement. It is a conſideration not unworthy of being here noticed, that while many other nations are waſting the brilliant efforts of genius, in monuments of ingenious folly, to perpetuate their pride; the Americans, according to the true ſpirit of republicaniſm, are employed almoſt entirely in works of public and private utility.

Trade, Manufactures and Agriculture.] In the year 1787, the exports from this State exceeded their imports; and it is more than probable that from the rapid increaſe of manufactural and agricultural improvements, and the prevailing ſpirit of induſtry and œconomy, the balance in favour of the State will be annually increaſed. The exports from the port of Boſton, the year paſt, (Auguſt 1788) conſiſting of fiſh, oil, New England rum, lumber of various kinds, pot and pearl-aſhes, flax-feed, furs, pork, beef, corn, flour, butter, cheeſe, beans, peas, bar-iron, hallow ware, bricks, whale-bone, tallow and ſpermaceti candles, ſoap, loaf-ſugar, wool-cards, leather, ſhoes, naval ſtores, ginſeng, tobacco, boats duck, hemp, cordage, nails, &c. amount to upwards of £.345.000 lawful money. New England rum, pot-aſh, lumber, fiſh, and the produce of the fiſhery, are the principal articles of export. No leſs than 4783 hogſheads of New England rum were diſtilled and exported from this State laſt year, beſides the home conſumption, which was not inconſiderable.*

New

---

* New England rum is diſtilled from molaſſes imported from the Weſt Indies. It may be a queſtion worthy of conſideration, whether the molaſſes which is annually diſtilled in New England, by being mixed with water, would not afford a drink cheaper, more palatable, and more nouriſhing, than that which is made from the rum diſtilled from it, and treble in quantity? If ſo, all the labour and expence of diſtillation might be ſpared, and converted to more uſeful, and perhaps to more lucrative manufactural or agricultural purpoſes. New England rum is by no means a wholeſome liquor. Dr. Douglaſs has aſſerted 'That it has killed more Indians than their wars and ſickneſſes. It does not ſpare white people, eſpecially when made into flip, which is rum mixed with ſmall beer, and muſcovado ſugar.'

MASSACHUSETTS.

New markets for the produce of this, and the other states, are continually increasing. The Cape of Good Hope, the Isle of France, Surat, Batavia and Canton, have lately opened their ports to receive the articles of beef, pork, bacon, butter, cheese, timber, ginseng, and several others. To Great-Britain are sent pot and pearl-ashes, staves, flax seed, bees wax, &c. To the West Indies, lumber, fish, pork, beef, flour, &c. The whale, cod and mackarel fisheries, employ a great number of hands, and yield a handsome profit. The *Negro* trade is totaily prohibited in Massachusetts by an act passed in the winter of 1788.

Annual improvements are made in agriculture, chiefly by gentlemen of fortune. The common husbandmen in the country, generally choose to continue in the old track of their forefathers. The Academy of Arts and Sciences have a committee, by the name of the 'Agricultural Committee,' whose business it is to receive and communicate any useful information upon that subject.

In this state, are manufactured pot and pearl ashes, linseed oil, bar and cast iron, cannon, cordage, spermaceti oil and candles, and many smaller articles, such as linen, woollen and cotten cloth, hosiery, hats, shoes, tools and instruments of husbandry, wool cards, snuff, clocks, cutlery, muskets, cabinet work, &c. The town of Lynn is particularly famous for the manufacture of womens silk and stuff shoes. It is computed that they make 170,000 pair of them annually. These are exported to various parts of the union.

A cotton manufactory has lately been established at Beverly, which bids fair to be productive of advantages to the town.

An association of the tradesmen and manufacturers of the town of Boston, has lately been formed, consisting of a representative from each branch. In this body the whole manufacturing interest of that patriotic town is combined. By a circular letter of August 20th, they have strongly recommended the same procedure to their brethren in the several sea-ports in the union. This association will doubtless be productive of happy effects.

Ship building, after a long stagnation since the peace, now begins to revive in various maratime parts of the state. Preparations are making for a glass house in Boston.

Mr. Joseph Pope, of Boston, has constructed a large, complete and elegant *Planetarium*, six feet in diameter. This is entirely a work of original genius and assiduous application, as Mr. Pope never saw any machine of the kind but his own. It exhibits a proof of great strength of mind, and really does him much honour.

Revenue and Taxes] The principal sources of revenue are land and poll taxes, imposts, excises and the sales of new lands. Taxes are levied on all males between sixteen and fifty except such as are exempted by law—also on the number of acres of improved and unimproved land---on dwelling houses and barns, ware-houses, stores, &c. these are all valued, and upon this valuation taxes are laid, so many pounds for every £.1000.

Mines and minerals.] In Attleborough is a magnetic iron ore ; it yields a red shot iron, not good. In Attleborough Gore, is some copper ore, but so intermixed with the iron rock ore, as to render both unprofitable.
Allum

MASSACHUSETTS. 183

Allum flate, or ftone, has been found in fome parts; alfo ruddle, or red earth, which ferves to mark fheep, and may be ufed as a ground color for priming, inftead of Spanifh brown. Several mines of black lead, have been difcovered in Brimfield, and the neighbouring places; and white pipe clay, and yellow and red ochre, at Martha's Vineyard. There is a valuable copper mine at Leverett, in the county of Hampfhire, lately difcovered; and at Newbury are beds of lime ftone and afbeftos.

Hiftory.] On the 19th of March, 1627, the Plymouth council fealed a patent to Sir Henry Rofwell, and five others, of all that part of New England, included between a line drawn three miles fouth of Charles river, and another three miles north of Merimak river, from the Atlantic to the fouth fea.* This patent gave a good right to the foil, but no powers of government. A royal charter was neceffary. This paffed the feals March 4th, 1628. Until this year, a few fcattering fettlements only, had been made in Maffachufetts Bay. In the fummer of 1627, Mr. Endicot, one of the original planters, with a fmall colony, was fent over to begin a plantation at Naumkeag, (now Salem.) The June following, about 200 perfons, furnifhed with four minifters,† came over and joined Mr. Endicot's colony; and the next year they formed themfelves into a regular church. This was the firft church gathered in Maffachufetts, and the fecond in New England. The church at Plymouth had been gathered eight years before. In 1629, a larger embarkation was projected by the company in England; and at the requeft of a number of refpectable gentlemen, moft of whom afterwards came over to New England, the general confent of the company was obtained, that the government and patent fhould be transferred and fettled in Maffachufetts.

In 1630, feventeen fhips from different ports in England, arrived in Maffachufetts,

* This tract of country was called MASSACHUSETTS BAY. The Maffachufetts tribe of Indians, lived around, and gave their name to the large bay at the bottom of this tract, hence the name Maffachufetts Bay. The Indian word is *Mais Tchufaeg,* fignifying the country this fide the hills.

The following Extract from the Epiftle dedicatory to a Sermon preached at Plymouth, in 1620, will fhew the ideas then entertained, refpecting the fituation of the *South Sea.*

" New England, fo call'd, not only (to avoid novelties) becaufe Captain Smith hath fo entituled it in his Defcription, but becaufe of the Refemblance that is in it, of *England* the native foil of Englifhmen: It being much what the fame for heat and cold in Summer and Winter, it being Champion Ground, but not high Mountains, fomewhat like the Soil in *Kent* and *Effex*; full of Dales, and meddow Ground, full of Rivers and fweet Springs, as *England* is. But principally, fo far as we can yet find it is an Ifland, and near about the Quantity of *England*, being cut out from the maine land in *America*, as *England* is from the mai neof *Europe*, by a great arm of the Sea, which entreth in forty degrees, and runneth up North Weft and by Weft, and goeth out either into the South Sea, or elfe into the Bay of *Canada.*"

† Meffrs. Higginfon, Skelton, Bright and Smith.

Massachusetts, with more than 1500 passengers, among whom were many persons of distinction. Incredible were the hardships they endured. Exposed to the relentless cruelties of the Indians, who, a few months before, had entered into a general conspiracy to extirpate the English—reduced to a scanty pittance of provisions, and that of a kind to which they had not been accustomed, and destitute of necessary accomodations, numbers sickened and died; so that before the end of the year, they lost 200 of their number. About this time settlements were made at Charlestown, Boston, Dorchester, Cambridge, Roxbury and Medford. The first general court of Massachusetts was held on the 19th of October, 1631, not by representation, but by the freemen of the corporation at large. At this court, they agreed that in future, the freemen should choose the assistants, and that the assistants should choose, from among themselves, the governor and deputy governor. The court of assistants were to have the power of making laws and appointing officers. This was a departure from their charter. One hundred and nine freemen were admitted this court. At the next general court of election, in the same year, the freemen, notwithstanding their former vote, resolved to choose their own governor, deputy, and assistants, and passed a most extraordinary law, ' that none but church members should be admitted to the freedom of the body politic.' This law continued in force until the dissolution of the government; with this alteration, however, that instead of being church members, the candidates for freedom, must have a certificate from the minister, that they were of orthodox principles, and of good lives and conversations.

In the years 1632 and 1633, great additions were made to the colony. Such was the rage for emigration to New England, that the King in council thought fit to issue an order, (February 7, 1633,) to prevent it. This order, however, was not strictly obeyed; for this year, came over Messrs. Cotton, Hooker and Stone, three of the most famous pillars of the church. Mr. Cotton settled at Boston, and the other two at Cambridge. Mr. Hooker, and 100 others, removed in 1636, and settled at Hartford, on Connecticut river.

In 1634, twenty four of the principal inhabitants appeared in the general court for elections, as the representatives of the body of freemen, and resolved, ' That none but the general court had power to make and establish laws—to elect officers—to raise monies, and confirm proprieties;' and determined that four general courts be held yearly, to be summoned by the governor, and not be dissolved without the consent of the major part of the court---that it be lawful for the freemen of each plantation, to choose two or three persons as their representatives, to transact, on their behalf, the affairs of the commonwealth, &c. Thus was settled the legislative body, which, except an alteration of the number of general courts, which were soon reduced to two only in a year, and other not very material circumstances, continued the same as long as the charter lasted.

In 1636 Mrs. Hutchinson, a very extraordinary woman who came to New England with Mr. Cotton, made great disturbances in the churches. Two capital errors with which she was charged, were, ' That the Holy Ghost dwells personally in a justified person; and that nothing of sanctification,

fication, can help to evidence to believers their justification.' Disputes ran high about the covenant of works, and the covenant of grace, and involved both the civil and religious affairs of the colony in great confusion. The final result was, a synod was appointed to be held at Cambridge, in August, 1637, where were present, both ministers and messengers of churches and magistrates, who after three weeks disputing, condemned, as erroneous, above eighty points or opinions, said to have been maintained by some or other in the country. The result was signed by all the members but Mr. Cotton. In consequence of this, Mrs. Hutchinson and some of her principal followers were sentenced to banishment. She, with her husband and family, shortly after removed to Aquidnick (Rhode Island) where, in 1642, Mr. Hutchinson died. She being dissatisfied with the people or place, removed to the Dutch country beyond New Haven, and the next year, she and all her family, being sixteen souls, were killed by the Indians, except one daughter who was carried into captivity.

The year 1637, was distinguished by the Pequot wars, in which were slain five or six hundred Indians, and the tribe almost wholly destroyed. This struck such terror into the Indians, that for forty years succeeding, they never openly commenced hostilities with the English.

The year 1638, was rendered memorable by a very great earthquake throughout New England.

In 1640, the importation of settlers ceased. The motives for emigrating to New England were removed by a change in the affairs of England. They who then professed to give the best account, say that in 298 ships, which were the whole number from the beginning of the colony, there arrived 21,200 passengers, men, women and children, perhaps about 4000 families. Since then more persons have removed from New England to other parts of the world, than have arrived from thence hither. The present inhabitants therefore of New England, are justly to be estimated a natural increase, by the blessing of Heaven, from the first 21,000 that arrived by the year 1640. It was judged that they had, at this time, 12,000 neat cattle, and 3000 sheep. The charge of transporting the families and their substance, was computed at £.192,000 sterling.

In 1641, many discouragements were given to the settlers by their former benefactors, who withheld their assistance from them, and endeavoured, though without success, to persuade them to quit their new establishments. The following year, the Indians confederated under Miantinomo, a leader of the Narraganset Indians, for the exterpation of the English. The confederacy was fortunately discovered in its infancy and produced no mischief.

This year (1643) great disturbance was made in the colony by a sect which arose from the ashes of Antinomianism. The members of it, by their imprudence, exposed themselves to the intolerant spirit of the day, and Gorton, the leader of the party, was sentenced to be confined to Charlestown, there to be kept at work, and to wear such bolts and irons as might hinder his escape, and was threatened with severer punishment in case of a repetition of his crime. The rest were confined to different towns, one in a town, upon the same conditions with Gorton. These sentences were cruel and unjustifiable; yet much of the apparent severity is removed, when the character and conduct of Gorton is taken into view.

All who have published any thing concerning him, except Mr. Calender, have represented him as an infamous character.

About this time the French of Acadie or Nova-Scotia, who had differed among themselves repeatedly, and engaged the English occasionally with them, awakened the fears of the colony. But these were soon happily composed. The Indians were this year (1644) and the following at war among themselves.

In 1646, the colony was disturbed by some of its principal inhabitants, who had conceived a dislike of some of the laws, and the government. Several of these disaffected persons were imprisoned, and the rest compelled to give security for their future good behaviour.

An epidemical sickness passed through the country the next year, and swept away many of the English, French and Dutch.

In 1648, we have the first instance of the credulity and infatuation respecting witchcraft, which, for some time, prevailed in this colony. Margaret Jones, of Charlestown, was accused of having so malignant a quality, as to cause vomiting, deafness and violent pains by her touch. She was accordingly tried, condemned and executed. Happy would it have been, if this had been the only instance of this infatuation. But why shall we wonder at the magistrates of New England, when we find the celebrated Lord Chief Justice Hale and others of high rank, in Old England, shortly after chargeable with as great delusion. The truth is, it was the spirit of the times; and the odium of the witchcraft and other infatuations, ought never to have been mentioned as peculiar to New England, or ascribed to their singular bigotry and superstition, as has been injuriously done by many European historians. The same spirit prevailed at this time in England, and was very probably brought from thence, as were most of the laws and customs of the first settlers in America. The same infatuation sprang up in Pennsylvania soon after its settlement.*

The

---

* *The following extracts from the records of Pennsylvania, shew that the method of proceeding with supposed witches, was equally ridiculous in the infancy of that colony as in New England.*

"   " 7th 12th Mo. 1683.
" Council Book A. } Margaret Mattson and Yethro Hendrickson ex-
      Page 43.   } amined and about to be proved Witches, whereup-
on this Board ordered that Neels Mattson should enter into a Recognizance of fifty pounds for his Wife's appearance before this bord the 27th instant.

" Hendrick Jacobson doth the same for his Wife.
                                                " 27th of the 12th Month.
Page 44. " Margaret Matson's Indictment was read and she pleads not guilty and will be tryed by the Country.

Page 45. " The Jury went forth and upon their Returne brought her in guilty of having the Common fame of a Witch, but not guilty in manner and form as she stands indicted.

Page 46. " Neels Mattson and Antho Neelson enters into a Recognizance of fifty pounds a piece for the good behaviour of Margaret Mattson for six months.

" Jacob Hendrickson enters into a Recognizance of fifty pounds for the good behaviour of Getro Hendrickson for six Months."   The

'The scrupulousness of the people appears to have arisen to its height in 1649, and was indeed ridiculous. The custom of wearing long hair, 'after the manner of ruffians and barbarous Indians,' as they termed it, was deemed contrary to the word of God, 'which says it is a shame for a man to wear long hair.' This expression of the Apostle Paul, induced these pious people to think this custom criminal in all ages and nations. In a clergyman it was peculiarly offensive, as they were required in an especial manner to go *patentibus auribus*, with open ears.

The use of tobacco was prohibited under a penalty; and the smoke of it, in some manuscripts, is compared to the smoak of the bottomless pit. The sickness frequently produced by smoaking tobacco was considered as a species of drunkenness, and hence what we now term smoaking, was then often called 'drinking tobacco.' At length some of the clergy fell into the practice of smoaking, and tobacco, by an act of government, 'was set at liberty.'

In 1650, a corporation in England, constituted for propagating the gospel among the Indians, began a correspondence with the commissioners of the colonies, who were employed as agents for the corporation as long as the union of the colonies continued. In consequence of this correspondence, the colonists, who had too long neglected their duty, renewed their attempts to instruct the Indians in the knowledge of the Christian religion. These attempts were attended with little success.

While the English and Dutch were at war in Europe, in 1653, information was given to the governor of Massachusetts, that the Dutch governor had been endeavouring to engage the Indians in a confederacy against the English, to expel or destroy them. This created an alarm through the colonies. An examination was made, and preparations for a war ensued, which the pacification at home prevented.

In 1655, a distemper, like to that of 1647, went through the plantations.

In 1656 began what has been generally called the persecution of the quakers. The first who openly professed the principles of this sect in this colony, were Mary Fisher and Ann Austin, who came from Barbadoes in July of this year. A few weeks after, nine others arrived in the ship Speedwell of London. On the 8th of September they were brought before the court of Assistants. It seems they had before affirmed that they were sent by God to reprove the people for their sins; they were accordingly questioned how they could make it appear that God sent them? After pausing they answered that they had the same call that Abraham had to go out of his country. To other questions they gave rude and contemptuous answers, which is the reason assigned for committing them to prison. A great number of their books which they had brought over

with

The author of the European settlements in America, among many errors as to historical facts, judiciously observes on the subject of the New England persecutions, 'Such is the manner of proceeding of religious parties towards each other, and in this respect the New England people are not worse than the rest of mankind; nor was their severity any just matter of reflection upon that mode of religion which they profess. No religion whatsoever, true or false, can excuse its own members, or accuse those of any other upon the score of persecution.'

with intent to scatter them about the country, were seized and reserved for the fire. Soon after this, as the governor was going from public worship on the Lord's day to his own house, several gentlemen accompanying him, Mary Prince called to him from a window of the prison, railing at and reviling him, saying, Woe unto thee, thou art an oppressor; and denouncing the judgments of God upon him. Not content with this, she wrote a letter to the governor and magistrates filled with opprobrious stuff. The governor sent for her twice from the prison to his house and took much pains to persuade her to desist from such extravagancies. Two of the ministers were present, and with much moderation and tenderness endeavoured to convince her of her errors, to which she returned the grossest railings, reproaching them as hirelings, deceivers of the people, Baal's priests, the seed of the serpent, of the brood of Ishmael and the like.

At this time there was no special provision made in the laws for the punishment of the Quakers. But in virtue of a law which had been made against heretics in general, the court passed sentence of banishment upon them all. Afterwards other severe laws were enacted, among which were the following; any quaker, after the first conviction, if a man, was to lose one ear, and for the second offence, the other—a woman to be each time severely whipped—and the third time, whether man or woman, to have their tongues bored through with a red hot iron.

The persecution of any religious sect ever has had, and ever will have a tendency to increase their number. Mankind are compassionate beings; and from a principle of pity they will often advocate a cause which their judgment disowns. Thus it was in the case of the Quakers; the spectators compassionated their sufferings, and then adopted their sentiments. Their growing numbers induced the legislature in their October session, to pass a law to punish with death all Quakers who should return into the jurisdiction after banishment. Under this impolitic as well as unjust law, four persons only suffered death, and these had, in the face of prudence as well as of law, returned after having been banished. That some provision was necessary against these people so far as they were disturbers of civil peace and order, every one will allow; but such sanguinary laws against particular doctrines or tenets in religion are not to be defended. The most that can be said for our ancestors is that they tried gentler means at first, which they found utterly ineffectual, and that they followed the examples of the authorities in most other states and in most ages of the world, who with the like absurdity have supposed every person could and ought to think as they did, and with the like cruelty have punished such as appeared to differ from them. We may add that it was with reluctance that these unnatural laws were carried into execution.

The laws in England at this time were very severe against the Quakers; and though none were actually put to death by public execution, yet many were confined in prisons where they died in consequence of the rigor of the law. King Charles the second also, in a letter to the colony of Massachusetts approved of their severity.* The conduct of the quakers, at several

---

* *Extract from the King's Letter dated the 28th June 1662.*

"We

MASSACHUSETTS.

several times, was such as rendered them proper subjects of a mad-house, or a house of correction; and it is to be lamented that ever any greater severities were used. I will mention one or two instances of their conduct, which clearly manifest a species of madness. 'Thomas Newhouse went into the meeting-house at Boston with a couple of glass bottles and broke them before the congregation, and threatened, *Thus will the Lord break you in pieces.* Another time M. Brewster came in with her face smeared as black as a coal. Deborah Wilson went through the streets of Salem, naked as she was born.' While we condemn the severity with which the Quakers were treated on the one part, we cannot, at the same time, avoid censuring their imprudent, indelicate and infatuated conduct on the other.

These unhappy disturbances continued, until the friends of the Quakers in England interposed, and obtained an order from the king, September 9th 1661, requiring that a stop should be put to all capital or corporal punishments of his subjects called Quakers. This order was prudently complied with, and the disturbances by degrees subsided. From this time the Quakers became in general an orderly, peaceable people, and have submitted to the laws of the governments under which they have resided, except such as relate to the militia and the support of the ministry, and in their scruples as to these, they have from time to time wisely been indulged. They are a moral, friendly, and benevolent people, and have much merit as a body for their strict discipline, regular correspondence, for their hospitality, and particularly for their engagedness in the abolition of the slavery of the Negroes. In this land of civil and religious freedom, it is hoped, that persecution will never again lift its direful head against any religious denomination of people, whose sentiments and conduct are consistent with the peace and happiness of society.

Soon after the restoration of Charles the II, in 1660, many complaints were made to his majesty respecting the colony, and, agreeably to a requisition from him, agents were sent over to answer to them. These were favourably received, and returned in a short time with letters from the king, commanding the alteration of some of the laws and customs, and directing the administration of justice to be in his name. The letters not being strictly obeyed, and new complaints coming to the king's ears, four commissioners were dispatched in 1665, to the colony, with absolute authority to hear and determine every cause. This authority met with merited opposition. The colonists adhered to what they imagined to be their just rights and privileges, and though somewhat culpable for their obstinate defence of a few unwarrantable peculiarities, deserve commendation for their general conduct. The commissioners left the colony dissatisfied and enraged.

Their report, however, occasioned no trouble from England, on account

---

'We cannot be understood hereby to direct or wish that any indulgence should be granted to those persons commonly called Quakers, whose principles being inconsistent with any kind of government, we have found it necessary by the advice of our parliament here, to make a sharp law against them, and are well contented that you do the like there.'

count of the jealousies of government which then prevailed there, and the misfortunes of the plague and fire of London.

The colony now attained a more prosperous condition than it had hitherto known. A spirit of industry and œconomy pervaded the people, and many of the magistrates and merchants became opulent. The civil and ecclesiastical parts of the constitution had, from the beginning, been harmoniously united, and continued to be until 1670; when a division, which had been made some years before in the church, originated a dispute, in which the civil authority interposed, and claimed a superiority to the ecclesiastical. The clergy notwithstanding, continued to have great influence in government, until the dissolution of the charter.

The war, commonly called Philips war, occasioned the next disturbances in the colony. This war lasted several years. Many Indians were engaged in it. They meditated the general destruction of the English, and much cruelty was exercised by both parties, until a period was put to hostilities by the death of Philip, the Indian chief, in 1676.

In the height of the distress of the war, and while the colony was contending for the possession of the soil with the natives, complaints were renewed in England, which struck at the powers of government, and an enquiry was set on foot, and followed from time to time, until 1684, when a judgment was given against the charter.

The succeeding year, the legislature, expecting every day to be superseded, paid little attention to public affairs.

In 1686, May 15th, a commissioner arrived appointing a president, and divers gentlemen of the council, to take upon them the administration of government. This administration was short, and productive of no grievances.

On the 19th of December, the same year, arrived Sir Edmund Andros, with a commission from king James, for the government of New England. Connecticut however, was not included in his commission. His kind professions encouraged, for a while, the hopes of the people, who from his character expected a different treatment from him. He soon acted out himself, and, together with his council, did many arbitrary acts to the oppression of the people, and the enrichment of himself and followers.

The press was restrained—public thankfgiving, without an order from the crown, was prohibited—fees of all officers were encreased, and the people compelled to petition for new patents of their lands, for which they were obliged to pay exorbitant prices.

The colony was greatly disquieted by these and similar tyrannical proceedings; and when news arrived of the declaration of the prince of Orange, in 1689, the governor and about fifty others were seized and confined, and afterwards sent home, and the old magistrates reinstated in their offices.

The affairs of the colony were conducted with prudence, and liberty being granted to the people by the crown, to exercise for the present their former government, they proceeded with regularity according to the old charter, striving in vain to get it confirmed, until, in 1692, they received and adopted a new one. The new charter comprehended all the territory of the old one, together with the colony of new Plymouth,

the

MASSACHUSETTS. 191

the Province of Main and Nova Scotia, and all the country between the Province of Main and Nova Scotia, as far northward as the River St. Lawrence*; alfo Elizabeth Iflands, and the iflands of Nantucket and Martha's Vineyard.

By the new charter, the appointment of the governor was in the crown, and every freeholder of forty fhillings fterling a year, and every inhabitant of forty pounds fterling perfonal eftate, was a voter for reprefentatives.

The French of Quebec inftigating the Indians and joining with them to plunder and kill the Englifh, and the French of Acadie infefting the coafts, and taking many veffels, the general court in the winter of 1689, meditated an attack upon Port Royal, now called Annapolis Royal, and upon Quebec. Forces were fent out and took Port Royal and the whole fea coaft from that to Penobfcot, and the New England fettlements.

The fuccefs of this expedition, and the ravage of the French and Indians at the opening of the fpring, determined the general court to profecute their defign upon Quebec. But the feafon was fo far advanced when the troops arrived at Canada—the French fo fuperior in number—the weather fo tempeftuous, and the ficknefs fo great among the foldiers, that this expedition was attended with great lofs.

A truce was concluded with the neighbouring Indians, while the troops were gone out of the colony, but hoftilities were foon renewed.

The French and Indians molefted the inhabitants of the frontiers daily. Acadie fell again into the hands of the French, and was afterwards retaken by the Englifh. The inhabitants of this territory experienced the greateft fufferings at every change of their mafter.

A new expedition was planned againft Canada, and affiftance from England folicited year after year, for the reduction of the French, who were endeavouring by the aid of the favages to ruin entirely the Britifh fettlements.

In 1692, the fpirit of infatuation refpecting witchcraft was again revived in New England, and raged with uncommon violence. Several hundreds were accufed, many were condemned, and fome executed. Various have been the opinions refpecting the delufion which occafioned this tragedy. Some pious people have believed there was fomething fupernatural in it, and that it was not all the effect of fraud and impofture. Many are willing to fuppofe the accufers to have been under bodily diforders which affected their imaginations. This is kind and charitable, but fcarcely probable. It is very poffible that the whole was a fcene of fraud and impofture, began by young girls, who at firft perhaps thought of nothing more than exciting pity and indulgence, and continued by adult perfons, who were afraid of being accufed themfelves. The one and the other, rather than confefs their fraud, fuffered the lives of fo

many

---

* Since the treaty of Utrecht, in 1713, Nova Scotia was arbitrarily taken from Maffachufetts, and erected into a feparate government. And by the treaty of 1783, the territory between the Highlands which form a part of the northern boundary of the United States, and the river St Lawrence, was ceded to Great Britain.

MASSACHUSETTS.

many innocents to be taken away, through the credulity of judges and juries.

That the odium of this tragic conduct might not rest upon the New Englanders alone, it ought here to be observed, that the same infatuation was at this time current in England. The law by which witches were condemned, was a copy of the statute in England; and the practice of the courts was regulated by precedents there afforded. Some late instances prove that England is not entirely cured of that delusion.

In 1711, some ships and troops being sent over, the colony troops joined them, and an attempt was made upon Canada, in which the greater part of them perished. This disaster was very grievous to the people of New England, and many persons, in consequence of it, abandoned every expectation of conquering Canada.

Frequent excursions on the frontiers immediately followed; but as soon as the peace of Utrecht was known, the Indians of the various tribes requested to be at peace with the English—asked pardon for their violation of former treaties, and engaged for the future to demean themselves as good subjects of the crown of Great-Britain. Articles of a general treaty were drawn up and signed by both parties.

From 1675, when Philip's war began, to the present time, 1713, five or six thousand of the youth of the country had perished by the enemy, or by distempers contracted in the service of their country. The colonies, which usually doubled their inhabitants in five and twenty years, had not at this time double the number which they had fifty years before. The prospect of a long peace which the general treaty afforded, was interrupted by the machinations of one Ralle, a French Jesuit, who instigated the Indians to make fresh incursions on the borders of the colony in 1717. After several ineffectual attempts to persuade the Indians to desist from their operations, forces were sent out by government from time to time, who destroyed several parties of the Indians, but there was no cessation of hostilities until the death of Ralle in 1724.

In 1725, a treaty was made with the Indians, and a long peace succeeded it. The length of the peace is in a great measure to be attributed to the favourable acts of government, made soon after its commencement, respecting the Indian trade.

In 1721, the small pox made great havock in Boston and the adjacent towns. Of 5889 who took it in Boston, 844 died. Innoculation was introduced on this occasion, contrary however to the minds of the inhabitants in general. Dr. C. Mather, one of the principal ministers of Boston, had observed, in the philosophical transactions, a letter from Timonious from Constantinople, giving a favourable account of the operation. He recommended it to the physicians of Boston to make the experiment, but all declined but Dr. Boyhston. To shew his confidence of success, he began with his own children and servants. Many pious people were struck with horror at the idea, and were of opinion that if any of his patients should die, he ought to be treated as a murderer.

All orders of men in a greater or less degree, condemned a practice which is now universally approved and to which thousands owe the preservation of their lives.

In

PROVINCE OF MAIN.

In 1745, according to a propofal and plan of the governor of this colony, Louifburg was befieged and taken. The poffeffion of this place appeared neceffary for the fecurity of the Englifh fifhery, and prevented an attack upon Nova Scotia, which the French had meditated and threatened.

The reduction of Louifburg by a Britifh colony, furprized Great Britain and France, and occafioned both powers to form important plans for the next year. Great Britain had in view the reduction of Canada, and the extirpation of the French from the northern continent. France, the recovery of Louifburg, the conqueft of Nova Scotia, and the deftruction of the Englifh fea coaft from Nova Scotia to Georgia. Great preparations were accordingly made by both monarchs. A very formidable French fleet failed for the American coaft; a Britifh fquadron was long expected to oppofe them, and to protect the colonies; but expected in vain. The colonies were in immediate and imminent danger. Fortunately for them, the French fleet was rendered unfit to accomplifh their defign, by a violent ftorm, which damaged moft of the fhips fo much as that they were obliged to return to France, or retire to the Weft Indies to refit.

Pious men faw the immediate hand of divine providence in the protection, or rather refcue of the Britifh colonies this year, as they had done in the almoft miraculous fuccefs of the Cape Breton expedition, the year before.

By the time the fears of the colonies, which had been excited by the French fleet, were removed, the feafon was too far advanced to profecute the Canada expedition. The inactive profecution of the war in Europe on both fides, indicated peace to be near, which the next year was effected.

Here governor Hutchinfon ends his hiftory of Maffachufetts. It belongs to the profeffed hiftorian to relate the important events which have happened fince. Several of them, however, may be found in the foregoing hiftory of the United States. It ought in juftice here to be obferved, that in point of military, political, and literary importance, Maffachufetts is inferior to none, and fuperior to moft, of the ftates in the union.

PROVINCE OF MAIN,

Including the lands which lie eaft, as far as Nova Scotia.
(Belonging to Maffachufetts.)

SITUATION and EXTENT.

miles.
Length 300 } Between { 43° and 46° North Latitude,
Breadth 104 } { 4° and 8° Eaft Longitude.

Boundaries.] BOUNDED northweftwardly by the highlands, which feparate the rivers which fall into the St. Lawrence, from thofe which fall into the Atlantic ocean; eaftwardly by the river St. Croix, and a line drawn due north from its fource to the faid high lands, which divides this territory from Nova Scotia; foutheaftwardly by the Atlantic ocean; and weftwardly by New Hampfhire.

The Old Province of Main (included in the limits prefcribed above) is bounded on the fouthweft and weft by New Hampfhire; foutheaft by the Atlantic ocean, and north and northeaft by the land, called in fome maps Sagadahok. It was fuppofed at the time of its being made a province, to have been 120 miles fquare; but by a fettlement of the line, in 1737, on the part, or fide adjoining New Hampfhire, the form of the land was reduced from a fquare to that of a diamond. The Province of Main contains, according to Douglafs, about 9,600 fquare miles.

Civil divifion.] The whole Province of Main, and the territory to the eaft of it as far as the weftern boundary of Nova Scotia, were formerly in one county, by the name of Yorkfhire. In 1761, this extenfive county was divided into three counties. The eafternmoft, called LINCOLN, contains all lands eaft of Sagadahok, and fome part of Main, viz. Georgetown, on the fea coaft, and all the lands between the rivers Kennebek and Amerafcoggin. This county is faid to be 150 miles fquare. It has been in agitation for feveral years to divide it into three, but for various reafons the divifion has hitherto been delayed. For the accommodation of the inhabitants, it is at prefent divided into three diftricts, in each of which is a judge, a regifter of probate, and a regifter of deeds. A great part of this county is yet in a ftate of nature. It is however rapidly fettling. The frontier inhabitants on each fide of the Canada line, are but a few miles apart.

Next to Lincoln is CUMBERLAND county, of which Portland is the county town, and capital of the whole territory. This county contains nearly half the Old Province of Main. The reft of the Province of Main is included in YORK county. Thefe three counties are fubdivided into ninety-four townfhips, of which Lincoln contains fifty-three, Cumberland twenty, and York twenty one. Thefe counties in 1778, had fix regiments of militia.

In 1778, a ftate tax of £.254,718:16:11, was affeffed on the polls and eftates, within the Commonwealth of Maffachufetts, by their general court. The following apportionment of that tax to the three counties abovementioned, will ferve to fhew the proportion which they bear to the whole ftate.

York county, - £.11,102:16:8
Cumberland, do. - 6,428: 6:2   } Which is nearly one thirteenth
Lincoln, do. - 1,782: 7:8   } part of the whole fum.
Total, £.19,313:10:6

Rivers.] St. Croix is a fhort and inconfiderable river, forming the eaftern boundary of the United States.* It falls into Paffamaquody bay.

Penobfcot

* *Governor Pownal fuppofes that Paffamaquody river, which is fifteen or twenty*

PROVINCE of MAIN.

Penobscot river rises in some ponds in the heart of the country, and passing through several small lakes, it tumbles for near two miles over falls, which effectually prevent any further marine navigation. To these falls, which are about fifty* miles from the sea, this river is navigable for vessels of an hundred tons. It empties into Penobscot bay.

Kennebek river rises from a little pond in the height of land, in north latitude 45° 20′ and about 5° 10′ east longitude. Its general course is from north to south. It is navigable for vessels of an hundred tons, to Hallowell, fifty miles from Small point, at the mouth of the river.

Sagadahok or Amerascoggin river, which, properly speaking, is but the main western branch of the Kennebek, rises in latitude 44° 50′ northeastward of the *White Hills*, in lake Umbagoog. Peabody river, and another branch fall into this main stream from the east side of the White Hills. Its course is south about twenty-six miles, then east northeast sixty, when it meets a second main stream from the northeast, thirty-four miles from its source. Hence the river runs south forty miles. In this course it passes within two miles of the sea coast, then turns north, and runs over Pejepskaeg falls into Merry Meeting bay; from thence, with the waters of Kennebek, which likewise fall into this bay, with several other small streams, it passes off to the sea, sixteen miles, by the name of *Kennebek*, or Sagadahok river.

The Dutch formerly had a settlement at the place that is now called Newcastle, which was under the jurisdiction of the then governor of New York, then called Manhadoes. The town was built on a beautiful neck of land, where rows of old cellars, near each other, are now to be seen.

Saco river has two sources, one in Ossipee pond, near Ossipee mountain; the other, which is its principal branch, falls from the south side of the White Hills. The former is called Ossipee, and the latter Pigwaket river. (Ossipee pond, and Ossipee mountain are in New Hampshire, as are the White Hills.) These soon unite, and the river, keeping in a general southeastern course for sixty or seventy miles, passes between Pepperillborough and Biddeford townships into Saco bay, near Winter Harbour. Marine navigation is stopped by Saco falls, seven or eight miles from the sea. At these falls, which are about twenty feet in height, are the greatest board-works in this part of the country. The river here is broken by small islands in such a manner as to afford a number of fine saw-mill seats. Before the war, 4,000,000 feet of pine boards were annually sawed by the mills at this place. Logs are floated down the river from sixty or seventy miles above the mills; and vessels can come up quite to the mills to take in their lading.

Besides these are a number of smaller rivers. Steven's, a salt water river; Presumscut and Royal rivers run into Casco Bay. Kennebunk and

---

twenty miles east of St. Croix, is the real eastern boundary of New England. For, said he, 'The French, according to their mode of taking possession, always fixed a cross in every river they came to. Almost every river on the coast of Sagadahok has, in its turn, been deemed by them La Riviere de St. Croix. Under equivocation of this general appellative, they have amused our negotiators on every occasion.'

* *Governor Pownal says, thirty-five.*

and Moufom rivers, extend fome diftance into the country, and empty into Wells bay. Webhannet river is the principal entrance by water in to the town of Wells, and has a barred harbour. York river runs up feven or eight miles, and has a tolerable harbour for veffels under 200 tons. Its rocks render it fomewhat hazardous for ftrangers. Spurwing river runs through Scarborough to the weftward of Cape Elizabeth, and is navigable a few miles for veffels of an hundred tons. Sheepfcut is navigable twenty or thirty miles, and empties into the ocean at the fame mouth with Kennebek. On this river is an excellent port called Wifcaffet, in the townfhip of Pownalborough. At the head of navigation on this river is Newcaftle, which extends from Sheepfcut to Damarifcotta river. Pemaquid and Damarifcotta are fmall rivers; the former has a beautiful harbour, but is not navigable above its mouth.

Bays and Capes.] The fea coaft is indented with innumerable bays. Thofe worth noticing are Penobfcot bay, at the mouth of Penobfcot river, which is long and capacious. Its eaft fide is lined with a clufter of fmall iflands. On a fine peninfula in this bay, the Britifh, in the late war, built a fort and made a fettlement, which is now a townfhip of Maffachufetts, and a commodious fituation for the lumber trade. It has been called hitherto by its old Indian name Majabagadufe, or for the fake of brevity, Bagadufe. At the diftance of about four leagues weftwardly, is Broad Bay, on the weftern fhore of which, Pemaquid point or Cape projects into the fea. Cafco Bay is between Cape Elizabeth, and Cape Small Point. It is twenty-five miles wide, and about fourteen in length. It is a moft beautiful bay, interfperfed with fmall iflands, and forms the entrance into Sagadahok. It has a fufficient depth of water for veffels of any burden. Wells bay lies between Cape Neddik, and Cape Porpoife.

Ponds or lakes.] Sabago pond is about twenty miles northweft of Falmouth. Cobefeiconti ponds are between Amarafcoggin and Kennebek rivers. Befides thefe there are Moufom and Lovel's ponds, and feveral others.

Mountains.] Agamemticus, a noted landmark for failors, is about eight miles from the fea, in latitude 43° 16', and lies in the townfhip of York, a few miles weftward of Wells.

Chief towns.] Portland is a peninfula that was formerly part of Falmouth. In July, 1786, the compact part of the town, and the port were incorporated by the name of Portland. It has an excellent, fafe and capacious harbour, but incapable of defence, except by a navy, and carries on a foreign trade, and the fifhery, and builds fome fhips. The town is growing, and capable of great improvments. The old town of Falmouth, which included Portland, was divided into three parifhes, which contained more than 700 families, in flourifhing circumftances, when the Britifh troops burnt it in 1775. It is now chiefly rebuilt.

Kittery is a pretty little town on the eaft fide of the mouth of Pifcataqua river, and is famous for fhip-building. One of its prefent inhabitants* is one of the firft geniufes in that line, in America. York, Wells, Berwick.

* Mr. Peck.

PROVINCE of MAIN. 197

Berwick, Arundel, Biddeford and Scarborough, are all considerable towns.

Climate.] The heat in summer is intense, and the cold in winter equally extreme. All fresh water lakes, ponds and rivers are usually passable on ice, from Christmas, until the middle of March. The longest day is fifteen hours and sixteen minutes, and the shortest eight hours and forty-four minutes. The climate is very healthful. Many of the inhabitants live ninety years.

Face of the country, Soil and Produce.] The face of the country, in regard to evenness or roughness, is similar to the rest of the New England states. About Casco Bay, it is level and sandy, and the soil thin and poor. Throughout this country, there is a greater proportion of dead swamps than in any other part of New England. The tract lying between Passamaquody and Penobscot rivers is white pine land, of a strong moist soil, with some mixture of oaks, white ash, birch and other trees, and the interior parts, are interspersed with beech ridges. The sea coast is generally barren. In many towns the land is good for grazing. Wells and Scarborough have large tracts of salt marsh. The inland parts of Main are fertile, but newly and thinly settled. The low swamps are useless.

The grain raised here is principally Indian corn—little or no wheat—some rye, barley, oats and peas. The inhabitants raise excellent potatoes, in large quantities, which are frequently used instead of bread. Their butter has the preference to any in New England, owing to the goodness of the grass, which is very sweet and juicy. Apples, pears, plums, peaches and cherries grow here very well. Plenty of cyder, and some perry is made in the southern and western parts of Main. The perry is made from choak pears, and is an agreeable liquor, having something of the harshness of claret wine, joined with the sweetness of metheglin.

Timber.] On the high lands are oak in some places, but not plenty, maple, beech and white birch. The white birch in this part of the country, is unlike that which grows in other parts. It is a large sightly tree, fit for many uses. Its bark, which is composed of a great number of thicknesses, is, when separated, smoother and softer than any paper. The clay-lands produce fir. The timber of this tree is unfit for use, but it yields the balsam which is so much admired. This balsam is contained in small protuberances, like blisters, under the smooth bark of the tree. The fir tree is an evergreen resembling the spruce, but very tapering, and not very large or tall.

Trade, Manufactures, &c.] From the first settlement of Main until the year 1774 or 1775, the inhabitants generally followed the lumber trade to the neglect of agriculture. This afforded an immediate profit. Large quantities of corn and other grain were annually imported from Boston and other places, without which it was supposed the inhabitants could not have subsisted. But the late war, by rendering these resources precarious, put the inhabitants upon their true interest, i. e. the cultivation of their lands, which, at a little distance from the sea, are well adapted for raising grain. The inhabitants now raise a sufficient quantity for their own consumption; though too many are still more fond of the axe than of the plough.

plough. Their wool and flax are very good—hemp has not been sufficiently tried. Almost every family manufacture wool and flax into cloth, and make husbandry utensils of every kind for their own use.

Mines and Minerals.] Iron and Bog ore are found in many places in great plenty, and works are erected to manufacture it into iron. There is a stone in Lebanon, which yields copperas and sulphur.

Exports.] This country abounds with lumber of the various kinds, such as masts, which of late, however, have become scarce, white-pine boards, ship timber, and every species of split lumber manufactured from pine and oak; these are exported from Quamphegon in Berwick, Saco falls in Biddeford, and Pepperillborough, Presumscut falls in Falmouth, and Amerascoggin falls in Brunswick. The rivers abound with salmon in the Spring season. On the sea coast fish of various kinds are caught in plenty. Of these the cod fish are the principal. Dried fish furnishes a capital article of export.

Animals.] In this country are deer, moose, beaver, otters, sables, brown squirrils, white-rabbits, bears, which have frequently destroyed cornfields, wolves, which are destructive to sheep, mountain-cats, porcupines or hedge hogs—patridges, but no quails, wild-geese and ducks, and other water fowls, abound on the sea coast in their seasons. No venomous serpents are found east of Kennebek river.

Character and Religion.] The inhabitants are a hardy robust set of people. The males are early taught the use of the musquet, and from their frequent use of it in fowling, are expert marks-men. The people in general are humane and benevolent. The common people ought, by law, to have the advantage of a school education, but there is here, as in other parts of New England, too visible a neglect.

In March 1788, the general court ordered that a tract of land, six miles square, should be laid out between Kennebek and Penobscot rivers, to the northward of Waldo patent, to be appropriated for the foundation of a college.

As to religion, the people are moderate Calvinists. Notwithstanding Episcopacy was established by their former charter, the churches are principally on the congregational plan; but are candid, catholic and tolerant towards those of other persuasions.

In 1785, they had seventy-two religious assemblies, to supply which were thirty-four ministers.

History.] The first attempt to settle this country was made in 1607, on the west side of Sagadahok, near the sea. No permanent settlement however was at this time effected. It does not appear that any further attempts were made until between the years 1620 and 1630.

In 1636, Courts were held at Saco and other places, of which some records are extant. From these records it appears that the courts acted both in a legislative and judicial capacity. Very few of their orders and laws are to be found. They proceeded in a summary method, attending more to substance than form, making the laws of England their general rule.

In

In 1635, Sir Ferdinando Gorges obtained a grant from the council of Plymouth, of the tract of country between the rivers Pifcataqua and Sagadahok, which is the mouth of Kennebek; and up Kennebek fo far as to form a fquare of 120 miles. It is fuppofed that Sir Ferdinand firft inftituted government in this Province.

In 1639, Gorges obtained from the crown a charter of the foil and jurifdiction, containing as ample powers perhaps as the King of England ever granted to any fubject.

In the fame year he appointed a governor and council, and they adminiftered juftice to the fettlers until about the year 1647, when, hearing of the death of Gorges, they fuppofed their authority ceafed, and the people on the fpot univerfally combined and agreed to be under civil government, and to elect their officers annually.

Government was adminiftered in this form until 1652, when the inhabitants fubmitted to the Maffachufetts, who, by a new conftruction of their charter which was given to Roffwell and others, in 1628, claimed the foil and jurifdiction of the Province of Main as far as the middle of Cafco Bay. Main then firft took the name of Yorkfhire; and county courts were held in the manner they were in Maffachufetts, and the towns had liberty to fend their deputies to the general court at Bofton.

In 1664, Charles II. granted to his brother the Duke of York, all that part of New England which lies between St. Croix and Pemaquid rivers on the fea coaft; and up Pemaquid river, and from the head thereof to Kennebek river, and thence the fhorteft courfe north to St. Lawrence river. This was called the Duke of York's property and annexed to the government of New-York. The Duke of York, on the death of his brother Charles II, became James II, and upon James' abdication, thefe lands reverted to the crown.

At prefent, the territory of the Sagadahok is fuppofed to contain all lands lying between the river St. Croix eaft, and Kennebek weft, and from the Atlantic to the highlands in the northern boundary of the United States.

Upon the reftoration of Charles II, the heirs of Gorges complained to the crown of the Maffachufetts ufurpation; and in 1665, the King's commiffioners who vifited New England, came to the province of Main, and appointed magiftrates and other officers independent of Maffachufetts Bay. The magiftrates, thus appointed, adminiftered government according to fuch inftructions as the king's commiffioners had given them, until about the year 1668, when the Maffachufetts general court fent down commiffioners and interrupted fuch as acted by the authority derived from the king's commiffioners. At this time public affairs were in confufion; fome declaring for Gorges and the magiftrates appointed by the king's commiffioners, and others for Maffachufetts. The latter however prevailed, and courts of pleas and criminal jurifdiction were held as in other parts of the Maffachufetts Bay.

About the year 1674, the heirs of Gorges complained again to the king and council of the ufurpation of Maffachufetts Bay, and they were called upon to anfwer for their conduct. The refult was, they ceafed for a time to exercife their jurifdiction, and Gorges, grandfon of Ferdinando, fent over inftructions. But in 1677, the Maffachufetts, by their

agent,

200   PROVINCE OF MAIN.

agent, John Usher, Esq; afterwards governor of New Hampshire, purchased the right and interest of the patent for £.1200 sterling. The Massachusetts now supposed they had both the jurisdiction and the soil, and accordingly governed in the manner the charter of Main had directed, until 1684, when the Massachusetts charter was vacated.

In 1691, by charter from William and Mary, the Province of Main and the large territory eastward, extending to Nova-Scotia, was incorporated with the Massachusetts Bay; since which it has been governed, and courts held as in other parts of the Massachusetts.

This country, from its first settlement, has been greatly harrassed by the Indians.

In 1675, all the settlements were in a manner broken up and destroyed. From about 1692 until about 1702, was one continued scene of killing, burning and destroying. The inhabitants suffered much for several years preceding and following the year 1724. And so late as 1744 and 1748, persons were killed and captivated by the Indians in many of the towns next the sea.

Since this period, the inhabitants have lived in peace, and have increased to upwards of 50,000 souls. This number is daily and rapidly increasing. To facilitate intercourse between the inhabitants, the legislature have lately adopted measures for opening roads in different parts of the country. Such is their growing importance and their ardent desire for independence, that their political separation from Massachusetts may be supposed not far distant.

RHODE-ISLAND.

SITUATION and EXTENT.

miles.
Length 68 } Between { 3° and 4° East Longitude.
Breadth 40   { 41° and 42° North Latitude.

Boundaries. BOUNDED north and east by the Commonwealth of Massachusetts; south by the Atlantic; west by Connecticut. These limits comprehend what has been called Rhode-Island and Providence Plantations.

Civil

RHODE-ISLAND.

Civil Divisions and Population.] This State is divided into five counties, which are subdivided into twenty-nine townships, as follows:

Counties.	Townships.	No. of Inhabitants.
Newport,	Newport,	5530
	Portsmouth,	1350
	Foster,	1763
	Jamstown,	345
	Middletown,	674
	Tiverton,	1959
	Little Compton	1341
Washington,	Westerly,	1720
	North Kingston	2328
	South-Kingston	2675
	Charlstown,	1523
	Exeter,	2058
	Richmond,	1094
	Hopkinton.	1735
Kent,	East Greenwich	1609
	West Greenw.	1698
	Coventry.	2107
Providence,	Providence,	4310
	Warwick,	2112
	Smithfield,	2217
	Scituate,	1628
	Gloucester,	2791
	Cumberland,	1548
	Cranston,	1589
	Johnston,	996
	North Provid.	698
Bristol,	Bristol,	1032
	Warren,	905
	Barrington.	534
Total five.	Twenty-nine.	51,896

A census of the inhabitants was made in 1774, when they amounted to 59,103. The diminution of inhabitants in the State in nine years, 7623. In Newport, 3679, almost half the whole number. Some Towns have gained 389.
The number of inhabitants in Rhode-Island and Providence Plantations was in the year 1730 { 15,302 Whites. 2,633 Blacks. | 1748 { 29,755 Whites. 4,373 Blacks. | 1761 { 35,939 Whites. 4,697 Blacks. | 1774 { 54,435 Whites. 5,243 Blacks. | 1783 { 48,538 Whites. 3,361 Blacks.

The civil dissentions in which this State has for some time past been involved, have occasioned many emigrations. Until these dissentions are composed, the number will no doubt continue to decrease.

The inhabitants are chiefly of English extraction. The original settlers migrated from Massachusetts.

Bays, Harbours and Islands.] Narraganfett Bay makes up from fouth to north, between the main land on the east and weft. It embofoms many fertile iflands, the principal of which are Rhode-Iiland, Canonnicut, Prudence, Patience, Hope, Dyer's and Hog iflands. The harbours are Newport, Providence, Wickford, Patuxet, Warren and Briftol.

Rhode-Ifland is thirteen miles long from north to fouth, and four miles wide, and is divided into three townfhips, Newport, Portfmouth, and Middleton. It is a noted refort for invalids from fouthern climates.

The Ifland is exceedingly pleafant and healthful; and is celebrated for its fine women. Travellers, with propriety, call it the *Eden* of America. It fuffered much by the late war. Some of its moft ornamental country feats were deftroyed, and their fine groves, orchards, and fruit trees, wantonly cut down. The foil is of a fuperior quality. Before the war 30,000 fheep commonly fed upon this ifland; and one year there were 37,000. Two years ago there were not 3000 fheep upon the ifland. They have probably increafed fince.

Canonnicut lies weft of Rhode-Ifland, and is fix miles in length, and about one mile in breadth. It was purchafed of the Indians in 1657, and incorporated by act of affembly by the name of Jameftown, in 1678.

Block Ifland, called by the Indians Maniffes, is about forty-three miles fouthweft from Newport, and is the foutheremoft land belonging to the State. It was erected into a townfhip, by the name of New-Shoreham, in 1672.

Prudence Ifland is nearly or quite as large as Canonnicut, and lies north of it.

Rivers.] Providence and Taunton rivers both fall into Narraganfett Bay, the former on the weft, the latter on the eaft fide of Rhode-Ifland. Providence river rifes in Maffachufetts, and is navigable as far as Providence, thirty miles from the fea. One branch of Taunton river proceeds from Winifimoket ponds; the other rifes within about a mile of Charles river. In its courfe, foutherly, it paffes by the town of Taunton, from which it takes its name. It is navigable for fmall veffels to Taunton. Common tides rife about four feet.

Climate.] Rhode-Ifland is as healthful a country as any part of North America. The winters, in the maritime parts of the State, are milder than in the inland country; the air being foftened by a fea vapour, which alfo enriches the foil. The fummers are delightful, efpecially on Rhode-Ifland, where the extreme heats, which prevail in other parts of America, are allayed by cool and refrefhing breezes from the fea.

The diforders moft prevalent, are confumptions and the diffentary. Thefe are not fo much owing to the climate, as to intemperance and imprudence.

Soil and Productions.] This State, generally fpeaking, is a country for pafture and not for grain. It however produces corn, rye, barley, oats and flax, and culinary plants and roots in great variety and abundance. Its natural growth is the fame as in the other New England States. The weftern and northweftern parts of the State are but thinly inhabited, and are barren and rocky. In the Narraganfett country the land is fine for grazing.

The

RHODE-ISLAND. 203

The people are generally farmers, and raife great numbers of the fineft and largeft neat cattle in America; fome of them weighing from 16 to 1800 weight. They keep large dairies, and make butter and cheefe of the beft quality, and in large quantities for exportation. Narraganfett is famed for an excellent breed of pacing horfes. They are ftrong, and remarkable for their fpeed, and for their excellency in enduring the fatigues of a long journey.

Trade.] Before the war, the merchants in Rhode-Ifland imported from Great-Britain, dry goods—from Holland, money—from Africa, flaves—from the Weft-Indies, fugars, coffee and molaffes—and from the neighbouring colonies, lumber and provifions. With the money which they obtained in Holland, they paid their merchants in England; their fugars they carried to Holland; the flaves from Africa, they carried to the Weft-Indies, together with the lumber and provifions procured from their neighbors; the rum diftilled from molaffes, was carried to Africa to purchafe negroes; with their dry goods from England they trafficked with the neighbouring colonies. By this kind of circuitous commerce, they fubfifted and grew rich. But the war, and fome other events have had a great, and in moft refpects, an injurious effect upon the trade of this State. The flave trade, which was a fource of wealth to many of the people in Newport, and in other parts of the State, has happily been abolifhed. The legiflature have paffed a law prohibiting fhips from going to Africa for flaves, and felling them in the Weft-India iflands; and the oath of one feaman, belonging to the fhip, is fufficient evidence of the fact. This law is more favourable to the caufe of humanity, than to the temporal interefts of the merchants who had been engaged in this inhuman trade. The prohibition of the flave trade, and the iniquitous and deftructive influence of paper money, combined with the devaftations of a cruel war, have occafioned a ftagnation of trade in Newport, which is truly melancholy and diftreffing. The falutary influences of a wife and efficient government, it is hoped will revive the defponding hopes of the people in this beautiful city, and place them in their former affluent and refpectable fituation.

The prefent exports from the State are flax-feed, lumber, horfes, cattle, fifh, poultry, onions, cheefe and barley. The imports, confifting of European and Weft-India goods, and logwood from the Bay of Honduras, exceed the exports. About 600 veffels enter and clear annually at the different ports in this State.

Light-Houfe.] For the fafety and convenience of failing into the harbour of Newport, a *light-houfe* was erected, in 1749, in Beavertail at the fouth end of Canonnicut ifland.

Dr. Douglafs, in his SUMMARY, &c. publifhed in 1753, has given a particular defcription of it. As I know not that any material alteration has taken place refpecting it, fince that time, I fhall infert it from him.

' The diameter at the bafe, is 24 feet, and at the top 13 feet. The height from the ground to the top of the cornice is 58 feet, round which is a gallery, and within that ftands the lanthorn, which is about 11 feet high, and 8 feet diameter.

The ground the light-houfe ftands on, is about 12 feet above the furface of the fea at high water.

The following are the bearings (by the compass) of several remarkable places from the light-house, viz.

Point Judith	S. W.	3 Degrees.	S.
Block-Island N. W. Point,	S. W.	8 ————	S.
Ditto S. E. Point,	S. W. by S.	5 ————	S.
Whale Rock	W.	9 ————	S.
Brenton's Reaf	E. S. E.	4 ————	E.
Seal Rock	E. S. E.	10 ————	E.
S. Point of Rhode-Island	E.	7 ————	S.
Watch House on Castle-Hill	E. N. E.	4 ————	E.
Brenton's Point	E. N. E.	4 ————	N.
Fort on Goat-Island	E. N. E.	5 ————	N.
S. Easternmost of the Dumplins	N. E. by E.		
Kettle Bottom Rock	N. E.	4 ————	E.
Anchoring place between the town of Newport and coaster's harbour.	N. E. by E.		

There is a small sunken rock lies off due S. and at the distance of about 200 yards from the light-house.'

Mountains.] In the town of Bristol is Mount Hope, or as some, Mont Haup, which is remarkable only on account of its having been the seat of King Philip, and the place where he was killed. It is now the seat of governor Bradford.

Indians.] There are about 500 Indians in this State. The greater part of them reside at Charlestown. They are peaceable and well disposed towards government, and speak the English language.

Chief Towns.] Newport and Providence are the two principal towns in the State. Newport lies in lat. 41° 35′ This town was first settled by Mr. William Coddington, afterwards governor, and the father of Rhode-Island, with seventeen others, in 1639. Its harbour, which is one of the finest in the world, spreads westward before the town. The entrance is easy and safe, and a large fleet may anchor in it and ride in perfect security. The town lies north and south upon a gradual ascent as you proceed eastward from the water, and exhibits a beautiful view from the harbour, and from the neighbouring hills which lie westward upon the Main. West of the town is Goat Island, on which is a fort. Between this island and the town is the harbour. Front or Water Street is a mile in length, and level.

Newport contains about 1000 houses, built chiefly of wood, and 5530 inhabitants. It has nine houses for public worship: three for the Baptists, two for Congregationalists, one for Episcopalians, one for Quakers, one for Moravians, and a synagogue for the Jews. The other public buildings are a State-house, and an Edifice for the public library. The situation, form and architecture of the State-house, give it the preference to most public buildings in America. It stands sufficiently elevated, and a long wharf and paved parade lead up to it from the harbour.

The building for the Library consists of one large room, thirty-six feet long, twenty-six feet broad and nineteen feet high, where the books are kept, with two small offices adjoining. The principal or west front is a pediment

pediment and portico of four columns, of the Dorick order; the whole *entablature* of which, runs quite round the building. The two offices are placed as wings, one on each fide the portico, and connected with the body of the building fo as to form two half-pediments proceeding from the lower part of the *entablature*. The eaft front confifts of a plain Dorick pediment, fupportrd by a ruftic arcade of three arches, in the receffes of which, are placed three Venetian windows after the Dorick order. The outfide of the whole building is ruftick work, and ftands on a bafe five feet from the ground, and the entrance is by a flight of fteps the whole width of the portico.

In the year 1747, Abraham Redwood, Efq; gave 1294 volumes, valued at £.500 fterling, as the foundation of a library in Newport. Several other valuable donations were afterwards given. Thefe books were depofited in the above-defcribed edifice, which was erected for the purpofe of receiving them. A number of gentlemen were incorporated into a body politic by the name of the 'Company of the Redwood Library,' with power to choofe annually eight directors, a treafurer, fecretary and librarian. This elegant building is now much out of repair, and one third of the books in the library were either carried off or deftroyed by the Britifh during the war.

Providence is fituated on Providence river, about thirty miles northweft of Newport, in latitude 41° 51' north. It is at prefent by far the moft flourifhing town in the State. It contains 700 houfes, and upwards 4300 inhabitants. Its public buildings are a college, an elegant church for Baptifts, two for Congregationalifts, befides others for other denominations. This town carries on a large foreign trade, and an extenfive and gainful traffic with the furrounding country. The town is fituated on both fides of the river, and is connected by a commodious bridge.

The inhabitants of Providence, the laft year, manufactured 100,000 yards of cloth more than in any year fince the peace. This cloth, at a moderate valuation, will amount to 20,000 Dollars.

This town, and Newport, and a few others, have, from the firft, firmly oppofed the late iniquitous meafures of their infatuated legifiature.

Briftol is a pleafant little town, about fixteen miles north of Newport, on the Main. It has an excellent foil, and is almoft as remarkable for the production of onions, as Wethersfield in Connecticut.

Fifhes.] In the rivers and bays are plenty of fheeps-head, black-fifh, herring, fhad, lobfters, oyfters and clams; and around the fhores of Rhode Ifland, befides thofe already mentioned, are cod, halibut, mackerel, bafs, haddock, &c. &c. to the amount of more than feventy different kinds, fo that in the feafons of fifh, the markets are alive with them. Travellers are agreed that Newport furnifhes the beft fifh market in the world.

Religion.] The conftitution of the ftate admits of no religious eftablifhments, any further than depends upon the voluntary choice of individuals. All men profeffing one Supreme Being, are equally protected by the laws, and no particular fect can claim pre-eminence. This unlimited liberty in religion is one principal caufe why there is fuch a variety of religious fects in Rhode Ifland. The baptifts are the moft numerous of any denomination in the ftate. In 1784 they had thirty congregations. Thefe, as well as the other baptists in New England, are chiefly upon the Calvinistic plan as to doctrines, and independents in regard to church government. There are, however, some who profess the Arminian tenets, and are called Arminian baptists. Others observe the Jewish or Saturday Sabbath, from a persuasion that it was one of the ten commandments, which they plead are all in their nature moral, and were never abrogated in the New Testament, and must at least be deemed of equal validity for public worship as any day particularly set apart by Jesus Christ and his apostles. These are called sabbatarian, or seventh-day baptists. There are others who are called separate baptists. The baptists in general refuse to communicate with other denominations; for they hold that immersion is necessary to baptism, and that baptism is necessary to communion. Therefore they suppose it inconsistent for them to admit unbaptised persons (as others are in their view) to join with them in this ordinance. The baptists are increasing in New England; but their increase is much more rapid in Kentucky and the southern states. The number of their congregations in New England in 1784, was 155. Of these seventy-one were in Massachusetts; twenty-five in New Hampshire; thirty in Rhode Island, and twenty-nine in Connecticut.*

The other religious denominations in Rhode Island are congregationalists, friends or quakers, episcopalians, moravians and jews. There is also a small number of the universal friends, the disciples of Jemima Wilkinson. Besides these there is a considerable number of the people who can be reduced to no particular denomination, and are, as to religion, strictly *Nothingarians*.

In some parts of this state, public worship is attended with punctuality and propriety, in others they make the sabbath a day of visiting and festivity; and in others they esteem every day alike, having no place of meeting for the purpose of religious worship. They pay no taxes for the support of ecclesiastics of any denomination; and a peculiarity which distinguishes this state from every other protestant country in the known world is, that no contract formed by the minister with his people, for his salary, is valid in law: So that ministers are dependent wholly on the integrity of the people for their support, since their salaries are not recoverable by law. It ought in justice, however, to be observed, that the clergy in general are liberally maintained, and none who merit it have reason to complain for want of support.

Literature.] The literature of this state is confined principally to the towns of Newport and Providence. There are men of learning and abilities scattered through other towns, but they are rare. The bulk of the inhabitants in other parts of the state, are involved in greater ignorance perhaps than in any other part of New England. An impartial history of their transactions since the peace, would evince the truth of the above observations.

At Providence, is Rhode Island college. The charter for founding this Seminary of Learning was granted by the general assembly of the state, An. 1764, in consequence of the petition of a large number of the most

* See Backus's *Church Hist. of New England.*

RHODE-ISLAND.

most respectable characters in the state. By the charter, the corporation of the college consists of two separate branches by the name of the Trustees and Fellows of Rhode island college,* with distinct, separate and respective powers. The number of trustees is thirty-six, of whom twenty-two are of the denomination called baptists, five of the denomination of friends, five episcopalians, and four congregationalists. The same proportion of the different denominations to continue *in perpetuum*. The number of the fellows (inclusive of the president, who is a fellow *ex officio*) is twelve, of whom eight are baptists, the others chosen indiscriminately from any denomination of protestants. The concurrence of both branches, by a majority of each, is necessary for the validity of any act, except adjudging and conferring degrees, which exclusively belongs to the fellowship as a learned faculty. The president must be a baptist, professors and other officers of instruction are not limited to any particular denomination. There is annually a general meeting of the corporation, on the first Wednesday in September, at which time the public commencement is held.

This institution was first founded at Warren, in the county of Bristol, and the first commencement held there in 1769, at which time seven persons, alumni of the college, received the degrees of Bachelor of Arts.

In the year 1770, the college was removed to Providence, where a large, elegant building was erected for its accommodation, by the generous donations of individuals, mostly from the town of Providence. It is situated on a hill to the east of the town; and while its elevated situation renders it delightful, by commanding an extensive, variegated prospect, it furnishes it with a pure, salubrious air. The edifice is of brick, four stories high, 150 feet long, and 46 wide, with a projection of ten feet each side. It has an entry lengthwise with rooms on each side. There are forty eight rooms for the accommodation of students, and eight larger ones for public uses. The roof is covered with slate.

From December 1776, to June 1782, the college edifice was used by the French and American troops for an hospital and barracks, so that the course of education was interrupted during that period. No degrees were conferred from 1776 to 1786. From 1786 the college again became regular, and is now very flourishing, containing upwards of sixty students.

This institution is under the instruction of a president, a professor of natural and experimental philosophy, a professor of mathematics and astronomy, a professor of natural history, and three tutors. The several classes are instructed in the learned languages, and the various arts and sciences. The studies of the freshman year, are the Latin and Greek languages, English grammar and rhetoric. Of the sophimore, Guthrie's geography, Ward's arithmetic, Hammond's algebra, Sheridan's rhetorical grammar and lectures on elocution, Watts' logick, and Cicero de Oratore. Of the junior, Horace, Kaim's elements of criticism, Euclid's elements, Atkinson's epitome, Love's surveying, Martin's grammar, Philosophia Britannica, and Ferguson's astronomy. Of the senior, Lucian's

* *This name to be altered when any generous Benefactor arises, who by his liberal donation shall entitle himself to the honour of giving the college a name.*

cian's dialogues, Lock's essays on the human understanding, Hutchinson's moral philosophy, Bolingbrooke on history, and a review of all the studies of the several years. Every year are frequent exercises in speaking, and the various kinds of composition. There are two examinations, several public exhibitions for speaking, and three vacations annually. The institution has a library of between two and three thousand volumes, containing a valuable collection of ancient and modern authors. Also a small, but very valuable philosophical apparatus. Nearly all the funds of the college are at interest in the treasury of the state, and amount to almost two thousand pounds.

At Newport there is a flourishing academy, under the direction of a rector and tutors, which teach the learned languages, English grammar, geography, &c.

Societies.] A marine society was established at Newport in 1752, for the purpose of relieving distressed widows and orphans of maritime brethren, and of such of their society as may need assistance.

Curiosities.] About four miles northeast of Providence lies a small village, called Pawtucket, a place of some trade, and famous for lamprey eels. Through this village runs Pawtucket river, which empties into Providence river two miles east of the town. In this river is a beautiful fall of water, directly over which a bridge has been built, which divides the Commonwealth of Massachusetts from the state of Rhode Island. The fall, in its whole length, is upwards of fifty feet. The water passes through several chasms in a rock which runs diametrically across the bed of the stream, and serves as a dam to the water. Several mills have been erected upon these falls; and the spouts and channels which have been constructed to conduct the streams to their respective wheels, and the bridge, have taken very much from the beauty and grandeur of the scene; which would otherwise have been indescribably charming and romantic.

Constitution.] The constitution of this state is founded on the charter granted by Charles II. in the fourteenth year of his reign; and the frame of government was not essentially altered by the revolution. The legislature of the state consists of two branches—a senate or upper house, composed of ten members, called in the charter *assistants*—and a house of representatives, composed of deputies from the several towns. The members of the legislature are chosen twice a year; and there are two sessions of this body annually, viz. on the first Wednesday of May, and the last Wednesday in October.

The supreme executive power is vested in a governor, or in his absence, in the deputy governor, who are chosen annually in May by the suffrages of the people. The governor presides in the upper house, but has only a single voice in enacting laws.

There is one supreme judicial court, composed of five judges, whose jurisdiction extends over the whole state, and who hold two courts annually in each county.

In each county, there is an inferior court of common pleas and general sessions of the peace, held twice a year for the trial of causes not capital, arising within the county, from which an appeal lies to the supreme court.

The

RHODE-ISLAND.

The justices of the peace, as in other States, have cognizance of small causes; and since the revolution, their powers have been enlarged to an uncommon, if not to a dangerous extent.

History.] This State was first settled from Massachusetts. Motives of the same kind with those which are well known to have occasioned the settlement of most of the other United States, gave birth to this. The emigrants from England who came to Massachusetts, though they did not perfectly agree in religious sentiments, had been tolerably united by their common zeal against the ceremonies of the church of England. But as soon as they were removed from Ecclesiastical courts, and possessed of a patent allowing liberty of conscience, they fell into disputes and contentions among themselves. And notwithstanding all their sufferings and complaints in England, excited by the principle of uniformity, (such is human nature) the majority here were as fond of this principle, as those from whose persecution they had fled.

The true grounds of religious liberty were not embraced or understood at this time by any sect. While all disclaimed persecution for the sake of conscience, a regard for the public peace, and for the preservation of the church of Christ from infection, together with the obstinacy of the Hereticks, was urged in justification of that, which, stripped of all its disguises, the light of nature and the laws of Christ, in the most solemn manner condemn.

Mr. Roger Williams, a minister, who came over to Salem in 1630, was charged with holding a variety of errors, and was at length banished from the then colony of Massachusetts, and afterwards from Plymouth, *as a disturber of the peace of the Church and Commonwealth*; and, as he says, ' a bull of excommunication was sent after him.' He had several treaties with Myantonomo and Canonicus, the Narragansett Sachems, in 1634 and 1635; who assured him he should not want for land. And in 1634-5 he and twenty others, his followers, who were voluntary exiles, came to a place called by the Indians Mooshausick, and by him *Providence.*

Here they settled, and though secured from the Indians by the terror of the English, they for a considerable time greatly suffered through fatigue and want.

The unhappy divisions and contentions in Massachusetts still prevailed. And in the year 1636, governor Winthrop strove to exterminate the opinions which he disapproved. Accordingly a Synod was called at Newtown (now Cambridge) on the 30th of August, when eighty erroneous opinions were presented, debated, and condemned; and a court holden in October following, at the same place, banished a few leading persons of those who were accused of these errors, and censured several others; not, it seems, for holding these opinions, but for seditious conduct. The disputes which occasioned this disturbance, were about the same points as the five questions debated between the Synod and Mr. Cotton, which are thus described by Dr. Mather: They were ' about the order of things in our union to our Lord Jesus Christ; about the influence of our faith in the application of his righteousness; about the use of our sanctification in evidencing our justification; and about the consideration of our Lord Jesus Christ by men yet under a covenant of works; briefly, they were about the

D d points

points whereon depend the grounds of our affurance of bleffednefs in a better world.'*

The whole colony of Maffachufetts, at this time, was in a violent ferment. The election of civil officers was carried by a party fpirit, excited by religious differ.fion. Thofe who were banifhed by the court, joined by a number of their friends, went in queft of a new fettlement, and came to Providence, where they were kindly entertained by Mr. R. Williams; who, by the affiftance Sir Henry Vane, jun. procured for them, from the Indians, Aquidnick, now Rhode-Ifland. Here, in 1638, the people, eighteen in number, formed themfelves into a body politic, and chofe Mr. Coddington, their leader, to be their judge or chief magiftrate. This fame year the fachems figned the deed or grant of the ifland. For which *Indian gift*, it is faid, they paid very dearly by being obliged to make repeated purchafes of the fame lands from feveral claimants.

The other parts of the State were purchafed of the natives at feveral succeffive periods.

In the year 1643, the people being deftitute of a patent or any legal authority, Mr. Williams went to England as agent, and by the affiftance of Sir Henry Vane, jun. obtained of the Earl of Warwick (then governor and admiral of all the plantations) and his council, ' a free and abfolute charter of civil incorporation, by the name of the incorporation of Providence Plantations in Narraganfett Bay.' This lafted until the charter granted by Charles II, in 1663, by which the incorporation was ftiled, ' The Englifh colony of Rhode-Ifland and Providence Plantations in New England.' This charter, without any effential alteration, has remained the foundation of their government ever fince.

As the original inhabitants of this State were perfecuted, at leaft in their own opinion, for the fake of confcience, a moft liberal and free toleration was eftablifhed by them. So little has the civil authority to do with religion here, that, as has been already hinted, no contract between a minifter and a fociety (unlefs incorporated for that purpofe) is of any force. It is probably for thefe reafons that fo many different fects have ever been found here; and that the Sabbath and all religious inftitutions, have been more neglected in this, than in any other of the New England States. Mr. Williams is faid to have become a Baptift in a few years after his fettling at Providence, and to have formed a church of that perfuafion; which, in 1653, difagreed about the rite of laying on of hands; fome holding it neceffary to church communion, and others judging it indifferent; upon which the church was divided into two parts. At Newport Mr. John Clark and fome others formed a church, in 1644, on the priciples of the Baptifts; which church was afterwards divided like that at Providence.

In 1720, there was a Congregational church gathered at Newport, and the Reverend Nathaniel Clap was ordained as paftor. Out of this church another was formed in 1728. The worfhip of God according to the rites of the church of England was inftituted here in 1706, by the fociety for propagating the gofpel in foreign parts. And in 1738, there were feven worfhipping

Mag. E. 7. P. 17.

RHODE-ISLAND.

worshipping assemblies in this town, and a large society of Quakers at Portsmouth at the other end of the island.

In 1730, the colony was filled with inhabitants; and chiefly by the natural increase of the first settlers. The number of souls in the State at this time was 17,935; of which no more than 985 were Indians, and 1648 negroes.

In 1738, there were above one hundred sail of vessels belonging to Newport.

The colony of Rhode-Island, from its local situation, has ever been less exposed to the incursions of the neighbouring Indians, and from the French from Canada, than their neighbours in Massachusetts and Connecticut. Many of the colony have, from its first establishment, professed the principles of the Quakers, which forbad them to fight. For these reasons, the colony has been very little concerned in the old wars with the French and Indians. In the expedition against Port Royal in 1710, and in the abortive attempt against Canada in 1711, they had some forces. Towards the intended expedition against Canada in 1746, they raised 300 men, and equipped a sloop of war with 100 seamen; but in their voyage to Nova-Scotia, they met with misfortunes and returned. Soon after, the design was dropped.

Through the whole of the late unnatural war with Great-Britain, the inhabitants of this State have manifested a patriotic spirit; their troops have behaved gallantly, and they are honoured in having produced the second general in the field.

The rage for paper money in Rhode-Island is not peculiar to the present time. From 1710 to 1750, Dr. Douglass observes that the most beneficial business of the colony was, ' Banking or negociating a *base fraudulent paper money currency*, which was so contrived that amongst themselves it came out at about two and an half per cent. interest, and they lent it to the neighbouring colonies at ten per cent. a most bare-faced cheat. The interest of these public iniquitous frauds went, one quarter to the several townships to defray their charges; the other three quarters were lodged in the treasury to defray the government charges of the colony.'*

In 1744, there was an emission of £.160,000 O.T. in paper bills of credit, under pretence of the Spanish and impending French war. But it was distributed among the people by way of loan at four per cent. interest for the first ten years, after which the principal was to be paid off by degrees, in ten years more without interest. This soon depreciated.

In 1750, the current bills amounted to £.525,335 O. T. which in its depreciated state, was then supposed by the wise and honest, sufficient for all the purposes of the colony; yet it was then meditated to emit £.200,000 O. T. more, upon loan. This Dr. Douglass supposes could not have been designed as ' a further medium of trade, but a *knavish device of fraudulent debtors of the loan of money*, to pay off their loans at a very depreciated value.'† He again observes,‖ ' Their design is by quantity to depreciate the value of their bills; and lands mortgaged for public bills
will

---

* Douglass Sum. V. II. p. 99.
† Ibid. P. 107.
‖ P. 87.

will be redeemed in thefe *minorated* bills, at a very inconfiderable real value.' Were this writer living, would he not now fpeak the fame language refpecting the prefent ftate of Rhode-Ifland?

But enough has already been faid* upon the paper-money injuftice and political confufion which pervade this unhappy State. I will only obferve that thefe meafures have deprived the ftate of great numbers of its worthy and moft refpectable inhabitants; they have had a moft pernicious influence upon the morals of the people, by legally depriving the widow and the orphan of their juft dues, and otherwife eftablifhing iniquity by law, and have occafioned a ruinous ftagnation of trade. It is hoped the time is not far diftant, when a wife and efficient government will abolifh thefe iniquitous laws, and reftore tranquility to the State.

CONNECTICUT.

SITUATION and EXTENT.

miles.

Length 82 } Between. { $41°$ and $42° \ 2'$ North Latitude.
Breadth 57 } { $1° \ 50'$ and $3° \ 20'$ Eaft Longitude.

Boundaries.] BOUNDED north, by Maffachufetts; eaft, by Rhode-Ifland; fouth, by the found, which divides it from Long Ifland; weft, by the ftate of New York.

The divifional line between Connecticut and Maffachufetts, as fettled in 1713, was found to be about feventy-two miles in length. The line dividing Connecticut from Rhode-Ifland, was fettled in 1728, and found to be about forty-five miles. The fea coaft, from the mouth of Paukatuk river, which forms a part of the eaftern boundary of Connecticut, in a direct fouthweftwardly line to the mouth of Byram river, is reckoned at about ninety miles. The line between Connecticut and New York, runs from latitude $41°$ to latitude $42° \ 2'$; 72 miles.‡ Connecticut contains about 4,674 fquare miles; equal to about 2,960,000 acres.

Rivers.] The principal rivers in this ftate are Connecticut, defcribed under New England, Houfatonik, the Thames, and their branches. One branch of the Houfatonik† rifes in Lanefborough, the other in Windfor, both in Berkfhire county in Maffachufetts. It paffes through

---

* See Hift. of United States, P. 120, &c.
‡ Douglafs.
† An Indian name, fignifying *Over the Mountain*.

a number of pleasant towns, and empties into the sound between Stratford, and Milford. It is navigable twelve miles, to Derby. A bar of shells, at its mouth, obstructs its navigation for large vessels. In this river, between Salisbury and Canaan, is a cataract, where the water of the whole river, which is 150 yards wide, falls about sixty feet perpendicularly, in a perfectly white sheet. A copious mist arises, in which floating rainbows are seen in various places at the same time, exhibiting a scene exceedingly grand and beautiful.

Naugatuk is a small river, which rises in Torrington, and empties into the Housatonik at Derby. Farmington river rises in Becket, in Massachusetts, and after a very crooked course, part of which is through the fine meadows of Farmington, it empties into Connecticut river in Windsor.

The Thames empties into Long Island sound at New London. It is navigable fourteen miles, to Norwich Landing. Here it loses its name, and branches into Shetucket, on the east, and Norwich or Little river, on the west. The city of Norwich stands on the tongue of land between these rivers. Little river, about a mile from its mouth, has a remarkable and very romantic cataract. A rock ten or twelve feet in perpendicular height, extends quite across the channel of the river. Over this the whole river pitches, in one entire sheet upon a bed of rocks below. Here the river is compressed into a very narrow channel between two craggy cliffs, one of which towers to a considerable height. The channel descends gradually, is very crooked and covered with pointed rocks. Upon these the water swiftly tumbles, foaming with the most violent agitation, fifteen or twenty rods, into a broad bason which spreads before it. At the bottom of the perpendicular falls, the rocks are curiously excavated by the constant pouring of the water. Some of the cavaties, which are all of a circular form, are five or six feet deep. The smoothness of the water above its descent—the regularity and beauty of the perpendicular fall—the tremendous roughness of the other, and the craggy, towering cliff which impends the whole, present to the view of the spectator a scene indescribably delightful and majestic. On this river are some of the finest mill seats in New England, and those immediately below the falls, occupied by Lathrop's mills, are perhaps not exceeded by any in the world. Across the mouth of this river is a broad, commodious bridge in the form of a wharf, built at a great expence.

Shetucket river, the other branch of the Thames, four miles from its mouth, receives Quinnabog, which has its source in Brimfield in Massachusetts; thence passing through Sturbridge and Dudley in Massachusetts, it crosses into Connecticut, and divides Pomfret from Killingly, Canterbury, from Plainfield and Lisbon, from Preston, and then mingles with the Shetucket. In passing through this hilly country, it tumbles over many falls, and affords a vast number of mill seats. The source of the Shetucket is not far from that of the Quinnabog. It has the name of Willamantik while passing through Stafford, and between Tolland and Willington, Coventry and Mansfield. Below Windham it takes the name of Shetucket, and empties as above. These rivers are fed by numberless brooks from every part of the adjacent country. At the mouth of Shetucket, is a bridge of timber 124 feet in length, supported

at

at each end by pillars, and held up in the middle by braces on the top, in the nature of an arch.

East, or North Haven river rises in Southington, not far from a bend in Farmington river, and passing through Wallingford and North Haven, falls into New-Haven harbour. It has been meditated to connect the source of this river with Farmington river.

Mill river and West river are inconsiderable streams, bounding the city of New-Haven on the east and west.

West of the Housatonik, are a number of small rivers which fall into the sound. Among these is Byram river, noticeable as forming a part of the boundary between New-York and Connecticut. But neither this, nor any of the others, are considerable enough to merit particular descriptions.

Harbours] The two principal harbours are at New-London and New-Haven. The former opens to the south. From the light-house, which stands at the mouth of the harbour, to the town, is about three miles; the breadth is three quarters of a mile, and in some places more. The harbour has from five to six fathom water—a clear bottom—tough oze, and as far as one mile above the town is entirely secure, and commodious for large ships.

New-Haven harbour is greatly inferior to that of New-London. It is a bay which sets up northerly from the sound, about four miles. Its entrance is about half a mile wide. It has very good anchorage, and two and an half fathom at low water, and three fathom and four feet at common tides.

The whole of the sea coast is indented with harbours, many of which are safe and commodious, but are not sufficiently used to merit a description.

Climate, soil and productions.] Connecticut, though subject to the extremes of heat and cold in their seasons, and to frequent sudden changes, is very healthful. As many as one in forty-six of the inhabitants of Connecticut, who were living in 1774, were upwards of seventy years old. From accurate calculation it is found that about one in eight live to the age of seventy years and upwards, one in thirteen, to the age of eighty years, and one in about thirty to the age of ninety.*

In the maritime towns the weather is variable, according as the wind blows from the sea or land. As you advance into the country, the sea breezes have less effect upon the air, and consequently the weather is less variable. The shortest day is eight hours and fifty-eight minutes, and the

---

* *The following was extracted from the minutes of the Rev. Dr. Wales, formerly minister of Milford, now professor of divinity in Yale College.*

'*From January 1, 1771, to January 1, 1777, 239 persons died at Milford; of which 33, or about one seventh part, were upwards of 70 years old; and 84, or about one third part of the whole, were under 10 years.*

'*From January 1, 1771, to June 3, 1782, died at Milford, 417 persons; of which 31, or about one thirteenth part of the whole number, were 80 years old and upward.*'

Other calculations of a similar kind, made in different parts of the state from the bills of mortality, confirm the justness of the above proportion.

CONNECTICUT.

the longest fifteen hours. The northwest winds, in the winter season, are often extremely severe and piercing, occasioned by the great body of snow which lies concealed from the dissolving influence of the sun in the immense forests north and northwest. The clear and serene temperature of the sky, however, makes amends for the severity of the weather, and is favorable to health and longevity. Connecticut is generally broken land, made up of mountains, hills and vallies; and is exceedingly well watered. Some small parts of it are thin and barren. It lies in the fifth and sixth northern climates, and has a strong, fertile soil. Its principal productions are Indian corn, rye, wheat in many parts of the state, oats and barley, which are heavy and good, and of late buck-wheat—flax in large quantities—some hemp, potatoes of several kinds, pumpkins, turnips, peas, beans, &c. &c. fruits of all kinds, which are common to the climate. The soil is very well calculated for pasture and mowing, which enables the farmers to feed large numbers of neat cattle and horses. Actual calculation has evinced, that any given quantity of the best mowing land in Connecticut, produces about twice as much clear profit, as the same quantity of the best wheat land in the state of New York. Many farmers, in the eastern part of the state, have lately found their advantage in raising mules, which are carried from the ports of Norwich and New London, to the West India Islands, and yield a handsome profit. The beef, pork, butter and cheese of Connecticut, are equal to any in the world.

Trade.] The trade of Connecticut is principally with the West India Islands, and is carried on in vessels from sixty to one hundred and forty tons. The exports consist of horses, mules, oxen, oak staves, hoops, pine boards, oak plank, beans, Indian corn, fish, beef, pork, &c. Horses, live cattle and lumber, are permitted in the Dutch, Danish and French ports. Beef and fish are liable to such heavy duties in the French islands, as that little profit arises to the merchant who sends them to their ports. Pork and flour are prohibited. As the ordinance making free ports in the French West India Islands extends to all foreigners, the price of molasses and other articles, has been greatly enhanced by the English purchases for Canada and Nova Scotia; so that the trade of Connecticut with the French West India Islands is not profitable. Cotton, cocoa, indigo and sugars, are not permitted to be brought away by Americans. The severity with which these prohibitory laws are administered is such, as that these articles cannot be smuggled.

Connecticut has a large number of coasting vessels employed in carrying the produce of the state to other states.—To Rhode-Island, Massachusetts and New Hampshire they carry pork, wheat, corn and rye.—To North and South Carolinas and Georgia, butter, cheese, salted beef, cyder, apples, potatoes, hay, &c. and receive in return rice, indigo and money. But as New York is nearer, and the state of the markets always well known, much of the produce of Connecticut, especially of the western parts, is carried there; particularly pot and pearl ashes, flax-feed, beef, pork, cheese and butter, in large quantities. Most of the produce of Connecticut river from the parts of Massachusetts, New Hampshire and Vermont, as well as of Connecticut, which are adjacent, goes to the same market. Considerable quantities of the produce of the eastern parts of the state, are marketted at Boston and Providence. The

CONNECTICUT.

The value of the whole exported produce and commodities from this state, before the year 1774, was then estimated at about £.200,000 lawful money, annually. Since this time no accurate estimate has been made, so that it is impossible to tell whether the amount has since been increased or diminished.

In 1774, the number of shipping in Connecticut, was 180; their tonnage, 10,317; seafaring men 1162; besides upwards of twenty sail of coasting vessels, which employed about ninety seamen. This State has not yet fully recovered the confusion in which it was involved by the late war; so that the number of shipping, &c. has not, at any period since 1774, been ascertained with accuracy. It is probable, however, considering the losses sustained by the war, the decay of the ship building business, and the number of unfortunate ship wrecks, and losses by hurricanes in the West-Indies, that the shipping and seamen are not now so numerous as in 1774.

The number of shipping from the port of New London, employed last year in the European and West India trade was, four ships, one snow, fifty-four brigantines, thirty-two schooners, and forty-five sloops. The number of horses and cattle exported from the district round New London, from the 10th of January 1787, to the 10th of January 1788, was 6917; besides jack-asses imported and exported, not included. From 1786 to 1787, the number was 6671, so that the last year exceeded the other 246. From March 1787 to January 1788, 1454 horses, 700 oxen and 23 cows, were exported from the port of Middleton.

Manufactures.] The farmers in Connecticut and their families, are mostly clothed in plain, decent homespun cloth. Their linens and woollens are manufactured in the family way; and although they are generally of a coarser kind, they are of a stronger texture, and much more durable than those imported from France and Great Britain. Many of their cloths are fine and handsome.

The woollen manufactory at Hartford has already been mentioned. The legislature of the state have encouraged it, and it bids fair to grow into importance. We have also mentioned Mr Chittendon's useful machine for bending and cutting card teeth. This machine is put in motion by a manderil twelve inches in length, and one inch in diameter. Connected with the manderil are six parts of the machine, independent of each other; the first, introduces a certain length of wire into the chops of the *corone*; the second, shuts the chops and holds fast the wire in the middle until it is finished; the third, cuts off the wire; the fourth, doubles the tooth in proper form; the fifth, makes the last bend; and the sixth, delivers the finished tooth from the machine. The manderil is moved by a band wheel, five feet in diameter, turned by a crank. One revolution of the manderil makes one tooth; ten are made in a second, and 36.000 in an hour, &c. as has been already observed (P. 88.) With one machine like this, teeth enough might be made to fill cards sufficient for all the manufacturers in New England. In New Haven is a linen manufactory, which flourishes; and one for cotton is about to be established. In East Hartford is a glass work, a snuff and powder mill, and an iron work and slitting mill. Iron works are established also at Salisbury, Norwich, and other parts of the state. At Stafford is a furnace at which is made

large

large quantities of hollow ware, and other ironmongery, sufficient to supply the whole state. Paper is manufactured at Norwich, Hartford, New Haven and in Litchfield county. Nails, of every size, are made in almost every town and village in Connecticut; so that considerable quantities can be exported to the neighbouring states, and at a better rate than they can be had from Europe. Ironmongery, hats of the best kind, candles, leather, shoes and boots, are manufactured in this state. We must not omit to mention wooden dishes, and other wooden ware, which are made in vast quantities in Suffield, and some few other places, and sold in almost every part of the eastern states. Oil mills, of a new and very ingenious construction, have been erected in several parts of the state.

It appears from experiments made formerly in this state, that a bushel of sun-flower seed yields a gallon of oil, and that an acre of ground planted with the seed at three feet apart, will yield between forty and fifty bushels of the seed. This oil is as mild as sweet oil, and is equally agreeable with sallads, and as a medicine. It may moreover be used with advantage in paints, varnishes and ointments. From its being manufactured in our own country, it may always be procured and used in a fresh state. The oil is pressed from the seed in the same manner that cold drawn linseed oil is obtained from flax-seed, and with as little trouble. Sweet olive oil sells for six shillings a quart. Should the oil of the sun-flower sell for only two thirds of that price, the produce of an acre of ground, supposing it to yield only forty bushels of the seed, will be thirty two pounds, a sum far beyond the product of an acre of ground in any kind of grain. The seed is raised with very little trouble, and grows in land of moderate fertility: It may be gathered and shelled, fit for the extraction of the oil, by women and children.

Civil divisions and population.] Connecticut is divided into eight counties, viz. Hartford, New Haven, New London, Fairfield, Windham, Litchfield, Middlesex and Tolland. The counties are subdivided into upwards of eighty townships, each of which is a corporation, invested with power to hold lands, choose their own town officers, to make prudential laws, the penalty of transgression not to exceed twenty shillings, and to choose their own representatives to the general assembly. The townships are generally divided into two or more parishes, in each of which is one or more places for public worship.

The following table exhibits a view of the population, &c. of this state in 1782. Since this time the counties of Middlesex and Tolland have been constituted, and a number of new townships, made up of divisions of the old ones, have impoliticly* been incorporated.

E e   TABLE.

---

* *The multiplication of townships increases the number of representatives, which is already too great for the most democratical government, and unnecessarily enhances the expence of maintaining civil government in the state.*

CONNECTICUT.

TABLE.

Counties.	Towns where the Courts are held.	Number of Townships.	Males between 16 & 50.	Total whites	Total Blacks Ind.&Negr.
Hartford.	Hartford Middlesex and Tolland†	21	10,815	55,647	1320
New Haven.	New Haven.	9	4,776	25,092	885
New London.	New London and Norwich,	8	5,884	31,13	1920
Fairfield.	Fairfield and Danbury.	10	5,755	29,722	1134
Windham.	Windham.	12	5,361	28,185	485
Litchfield.	Litchfield.	19	6,797	33,127	529
	Total.	79	39,388	202,877	6273

Number of Females in the state 103,735. Population for every square mile about 45.

Connecticut is the most populous, in proportion to its extent, of any of the thirteen states. It is laid out in small farms from fifty to three or four hundred acres each, which are held by the farmers in fee simple; and are generally cultivated as well as the nature of the soil will admit. The state is chequered with innumerable roads or high ways, crossing each other in every direction. A traveller, in any of these roads, even in the most unsettled parts of the state, will seldom pass more than two or three miles without finding a house or cottage, and a farm under such improvments as to afford the necessaries for the support of a family. The whole state resembles a well cultivated garden, which, with that degree of industry that is necessary to happiness, produces the necessaries and conveniencies of life in great plenty.

In 1756 the number of inhabitants in Connecticut was 130,611. In 1774, there were 197,856 souls. In 18 years the increase was 67,245. From 1774 to 1782, the increase was but 11,294 persons. This comparatively small increase of inhabitants may be satisfactorily accounted for from the destruction of the war, and the numerous emigrations to Vermont, the western parts of New Hampshire, and other states.

The

---

† *Middleton and Tolland, are now the shire towns of Middlesex and Tolland counties. Courts are also held at Haddam, which is the half shire town of Middlesex county.*

CONNECTICUT.

The inhabitants are almost entirely of English descent. There are no Dutch, French, or Germans, and very few Scotch or Irish people in any part of New England.

Character, Manners, &c.] In addition to what has been already said on these particulars, under New England, it may be observed, that the people of Connecticut are remarkably fond of having all their disputes, even those of the most trivial kind, settled *according to law.* The prevalence of this litigious spirit, affords employment and support for a numerous body of lawyers. The number of actions entered annually upon the several dockets in the State, justifies the above observations. That party spirit, however, which is the bane of political happiness, has not raged with such violence in this State as in Massachusetts and Rhode-Island. Public proceedings have been conducted, generally, and especially of late, with much calmness and candor. The people are well informed in regard to their rights, and judicious in the methods they adopt to secure them. The State was never in greater political tranquility than at present.

The clergy, who are numerous, and, as a body, very respectable, have hitherto preserved a kind of aristocratical balance in the very democratical government of the State; which has happily operated as a check upon the overbearing spirit of republicanism. It has been lamented that the unhappy religious disputes which have too much prevailed among some of the clergy; and the too great attention that others have paid to their temporal concerns, to the neglect of their flocks; and an inattention to the qualifications of those who have been admitted to the sacred office, have, heretofore, considerably diminished their influence. It is a pleasing circumstance that the rage for Theological disputation is abating; and greater strictness is observed in the admission of candidates to the ministry. Their influence is on the increase; and it is no doubt to be attributed, in part, to their increasing influence, that an evident reformation in the manners of the people of this State, has taken place since the peace. In regard to learning and abilities, the clergy at the present day, are equal to their predecessors at any former period.

Religion.] The best in the world, perhaps, for a republican government. As to the mode of exercising church government and discipline, it might not improperly be called a republican religion. Each church is a separate jurisdiction, and claims authority to choose their own minister, to exercise government, and enjoy gospel ordinances within itself. The churches, however, are not independent of each other; they are associated for mutual benefit and convenience. The associations have power to licence candidates for the ministry, to consult for the general welfare, and to recommend measures to be adopted by the churches, but have no authority to enforce them. When disputes arise in churches, councils are called, by the parties, to settle them; but their power is only advisory. There are as many associations in the State as there are counties; and they meet twice in a year. These are all combined in one general association, who meet annually.

All religions that are consistent with the peace of society, are tolerated in Connecticut; and a spirit of liberality and Catholicism is increasing. There are very few religious sects in this State. The bulk of the people are congregationalists. Besides these there are Episcopalians and Baptists; and

and formerly there was a society of Sandimanians at New Haven; but they are now reduced to a very small number. The Episcopalian churches are respectable, and are under the superintendence of a Bishop. There were twenty-nine congregations of the Baptists in 1784. These congregations, with those in the neighbouring states, meet in associations, by delegation, annually. These associations consist of messengers chosen and sent by the churches. Some of their principles are ' The imputation of Adam's sin to his posterity—the inability of man to recover himself—effectual calling by sovereign grace—justification by imputed righteousness—immersion for Baptism, and that on profession of faith and repentence—congregational churches, and their independency—reception into them upon evidence of sound conversion.' The Baptists, during the late war, were warm and active friends to their country; and by their early approbation of the new form of government,* have manifested the continuance of their patriotic sentiments.

Damages sustained in the late war.] After the establishment of the peace in 1783, a number of gentlemen were appointed by the general assembly to estimate the damage done by the British troops, in the several towns which they ravaged. The following is the result of their enquiries.

Amount of Losses.

	£	s	d
New London, (burnt by Benedict Arnold, September 6, 1781,)	145,788	15	6
Groton, do. do.	23,217	6	
Scattering towns, do. do.	9,806	9	2
	£. 178,812	10	8
Norwalk, (burnt by the British, 1779)	£. 34,867	9	2
———— confiscated property and other losses	2,077	0	0
	£. 36,944	9	2
Greenwich,	£. 6,365	11	8
———— Losses of men not on oath,	369	17	7
	£. 6,735	9	3
Fairfield, (burnt in 1779)	£. 40,807	2	10
New-Haven, ravaged by governor Tryon July 1779	£. 24,893	7	6
East-Haven, do. do.	4,882	16	4
West-Haven, do. do.	474	0	3
Other losses not before-computed,	586	0	1
	£. 30,836	4	2
Amount of the losses in the whole State, in money valued as in 1774,	£. 294,235	16	1

Chief

* In their association at New-York October 1787.

CONNECTICUT.

Chief Towns.] There are a great number of very pleasant towns, both maritime and inland, in Connecticut. It contains five incorporated towns or cities. Two of these, Hartford and New Haven, are the capitals of the State. The general assembly is holden at the former in May, and at the latter in October, annually.

HARTFORD (city) is situated at the head of navigation on the west side of Connecticut river, about fifty miles from its entrance into the sound. Its buildings are a State House—two churches for congregationalists—a distillery, besides upwards of 300 dwelling houses, a number of which are handsomely built with brick.

The town is divided by a small river, with high romantic banks. Over this river is a bridge connecting the two divisions of the town. Hartford is advantageously situated for trade, has a very fine back country, enters largely into the manufacturing business, and is a rich flourishing commercial town.

NEW HAVEN (city) lies round the head of a bay, which makes up about four miles north from the sound. It covers part of a large plain, which is circumscribed on three sides by high hills or mountains. Two small rivers bound the city east and west. The town was originally laid out in squares of sixty rods. Many of these squares have been divided by cross streets. Four streets run northwest and southeast, these are crossed by others at right angles—Near the centre of the city is the public square; on and around which are the public buildings, which are a State House, College and Chapel, three churches for Congregationalists and one for Episcopalians. These are all handsome and commodious buildings. The college, chapel, state house, and one of the churches are of brick. The public square is encircled with rows of trees, which render it both convenient and delightful. Its beauty, however, is greatly diminished by the burial ground, and several of the public buildings, which occupy a considerable part of it.

Many of the streets are ornamented with two rows of trees, one on each side, which give the city a rural appearance. The prospect from the steeples is greatly variegated, and extremely beautiful. There are about 500 dwelling houses in the city, principally of wood, and well built, and some of them elegant. The streets are sandy, but neat and cleanly. Within the limits of the city, are between 3 and 4000 souls. About one in seventy die annually; this proves the healthfulness of its climate. Indeed as to pleasantness of situation and salubrity of air, New Haven is not exceeded by any city in America. It carries on a considerable trade with New York and the West-India Islands, and is flourishing.*

NEW LONDON (city) stands on the west side of the river Thames, near its entrance into the sound, in latitude 41° 25′. It has two places for public worship, one for Episcopalians and one for Congregationalists, and about 300 dwelling houses. Its harbour is the best in Connecticut, and as good as any in the United States; and is defended by fort Trumbull

and

* The following account of the number of inhabitants in the city of
New

and fort Grifwold, the one in New London, the other in Groton. A confiderable part of the town was burnt by the infamous Benedict Arnold, in 1781. It has fince been rebuilt.

NORWICH (city) ftands at the head of Thames river, 12 or 14 miles north from New London. It is a commercial city, has a rich and extenfive back country, and avails itfelf of its natural advantages at the head of navigation. Its fituation upon a river which affords a great number of convenient feats for mills and water machines of all kinds, render it very eligible in a manufactural view.

The inhabitants are not neglectful of the advantages which nature has fo liberally given them. They manufacture paper of all kinds, ftockings, clocks,

---

New Haven, and their different ages, together with the number of buildings of different kinds, is the refult of an accurate enumeration, September 20th 1787. As it may furnifh fufficient date from which, at any future enumeration, feveral valuable and inftructive calculations may be made, it is thought proper to preferve it.

Age	No.	Age	No.	Age	No.	Age	No.
1	173	23	58	45	28	67	3
2	113	24	55	46	22	68	5
3	100	25	66	47	34	69	3
4	119	26	51	48	9	70	6
5	107	27	55	49	12	71	1
6	100	28	50	50	35	72	2
7	87	29	40	51	17	73	2
8	96	30	66	52	14	74	2
9	89	31	45	53	16	75	3
10	85	32	42	54	12	76	1
11	70	33	38	55	17	77	5
12	80	34	33	56	18	78	2
13	86	35	49	57	10	79	3
14	95	36	50	58	11	80	4
15	71	37	31	59	7	81	
16	103	38	31	60	28	82	
17	62	39	36	61	11	83	1
18	84	40	52	62	8	84	1
19	62	41	29	63	9	85	
20	74	42	33	64	10	86	1
21	77	43	29	65	13	87	1
22	57	44	18	66	8	90	1

Total number of fouls 3339   Number of Families 614
Seventeen years and under 1636   Dwelling houfes 466
Upwards of feventeen 1703   Stores 103
Number of ftudents 176   Barns and Shops 324
    Males 1645   Total buildings of all kinds 893
    Females 1694

In 1724 there were 163 buildings of all kinds, from which we may conclude, the number of fouls and buildings, has doubled, fince that time, in periods of about twenty years.

CONNECTICUT.

clocks and watches, chaises, buttons, stone and earthern ware, wire, oil, chocolate, bells, anchors, and all kinds of forge work. The city contains about 450 dwelling houses, a court house, and two churches for congregationalists, and one for episcopalians. The city is in three detached, compact divisions; viz. Chelsea, at the landing, the town, and Bean-hill; in the latter division is a flourishing academy; and in the town is a school supported by a donation from Dr. Daniel Lathrop, deceased. The executive courts of law are held alternately at New London and Norwich.

MIDDLETON (city) is pleasantly situated on the western bank of Connecticut river, fifteen miles south of Hartford. It is the principal town in Middlesex county—has about 300 houses—a court house—one church for congregationalists—one for episcopalians—a naval office—and carries on a large and increasing trade.

Four miles south of Hartford is WETHERSFIELD, a very pleasant town of between two and three hundred houses situated on a fine soil, with an elegant brick church for congregationalists. A Fair is held here twice a year. This town is noted for raising onions.

Windsor, Farmington, Litchfield, Milford, Stratford, Fairfield and Guilford, are all considerable and very pleasant towns.

Curiosities.] Two miles west of New Haven is a mountain, on the top of which is a cave, remarkable for having been the residence of generals Whaley and Goffe, two of the judges of Charles I. who was beheaded. They arrived at Boston, July 27th 1660, and came to New Haven the March following. May 11th 1661, they retired and concealed themselves behind West mountain, three miles from New Haven; and the 19th of August, they removed to Milford, where they lived concealed until the 13th of October, 1664; when they returned to New Haven, and immediately proceeded to Hadley, where they remained concealed for about ten years, in which time Whaley died. Goffe soon after abdicated. In 1665, John Dixwell, Esq. another of the kings judges, visited them while at Hadley, and afterwards proceeded to New Haven, where he lived many years, and was known by the name of John Davis. Here he died, and was buried in the public burying place, where his grave stone is standing to this day, with this inscription, ' J. D. Esq. deceased March 18th in the 82d. year of his age, 1688.'

In the town of Pomfret is a cave rendered remarkable by the humorous adventure of General Putnam. This cave is described and the story elegantly told by Colonel Humphreys in his life of that hero. The story and the description I shall insert in his own words.

Soon after Mr. Putnam removed to Connecticut, the wolves, then very numerous, broke into his sheep fold and killed seventy fine sheep and goats, besides wounding many lambs and kids. ' This havoc was committed by a she-wolf, which, with her annual whelps, had for several years infested the vicinity. The young were commonly destroyed by the vigilance of the hunters, but the old one was too sagacious to come within reach of gun-shot: upon being closely pursued she would generally fly to the western woods, and return the next winter with another litter of whelps.

This

This wolf, at length, became such an intolerable nuisance, that Mr. Putnam entered into a combination with five of his neighbours to hunt alternately until they could destroy her. Two, by rotation, were to be constantly in pursuit. It was known, that, having lost the toes from one foot, by a steel trap, she made one track shorter than the other. By this vestige, the pursuers recognized, in a light snow, the route of this pernicious animal. Having followed her to Connecticut river and found she had turned back in a direct course towards Pomfret, they immediately returned, and by ten the next morning the blood-hounds had driven her into a den, about three miles distant from the house of Mr. Putnam: the people soon collected with dogs, guns, straw, fire and sulphur to attack the common enemy. With this apparatus several unsuccessful efforts were made to force her from the den. The hounds came back badly wounded and refused to return. The smoke of blazing straw had no effect. Nor did the fumes of burnt brimstone, with which the cavern was filled, compel her to quit the retirement. Wearied with such fruitless attempts (which had brought the time to ten o'clock at night) Mr. Putnam tried once more to make his dog enter, but in vain; he proposed to his negro man to go down into the cavern and shoot the wolf: the negro declined the hazardous service. Then it was that their master, angry at the disappointment, and declaring that he was ashamed to have a coward in his family, resolved himself to destroy the ferocious beast, least she should escape through some unknown fissure of the rock. His neighbours strongly remonstrated against the perilous enterprize: but he, knowing that wild animals were intimidated by fire, and having provided several strips of birch-bark, the only combustible material which he could obtain, that would afford light in this deep and darksome cave, prepared for his descent. Having, accordingly, divested himself of his coat and waistcoat, and having a long rope fastened round his legs, by which he might be pulled back, at a concerted signal, he entered head foremost, with the blazing torch in his hand.

The aperture of the den, on the east side of a very high ledge of rocks, is about two feet square; from thence it descends obliquely fifteen feet, then running horizontally about ten more, it ascends gradually sixteen feet towards its termination. The sides of this subterraneous cavity are composed of smooth and solid rocks, which seem to have been divided from each other by some former earthquake. The top and bottom are also of stone, and the entrance, in winter, being covered with ice, is exceedingly slippery. It is in no place high enough for a man to raise himself upright: nor in any part more than three feet in width.

Having groped his passage to the horizontal part of the den, the most terrifying darkness appeared in front of the dim circle of light afforded by his torch. It was silent as the house of death. None but monsters of the desert had ever before explored this solitary mansion of horror. He, cautiously proceeding onward, came to the ascent; which he slowly mounted on his hands and knees until he discovered the glaring eye-balls of the wolf, who was sitting at the extremity of the cavern. Started at the sight of fire, she gnashed her teeth and gave a sullen growl. As soon as he had made the necessary discovery, he kicked the rope as a signal for pulling him out. The people, at the mouth of the den, who had

listened

CONNECTICUT.

listened with painful anxiety, hearing the growling of the wolf, and supposing their friend to be in the most imminent danger, drew him forth with such celerity that his shirt was stripped over his head and his skin severely lacerated. After he had adjusted his cloaths and loaded his gun with nine buck-shot, holding a torch in one hand and the musquet in the other, he descended a second time. When he drew nearer than before, the wolf, assuming a still more fierce and terrible appearance, howling, rolling her eyes, snapping her teeth, and dropping her head between her legs, was evidently in the attitude and on the point of springing at him. At the critical instant he levelled and fired at her head. Stunned with the shock and suffocated with the smoak, he immediately found himself drawn out of the cave. But having refreshed himself and permitted the smoke to dissipate, he went down the third time. Once more he came within sight of the wolf, who appearing very passive, he applied the torch to her nose: and perceiving her dead, he took hold of her ears, and then kicking the rope (still tied round his legs) the people above, with no small exultation, dragged them both out together.

Another bold and almost presumptuous deed, in this veteran hero, has rendered remarkable, a precipice at Horseneck, in this state. The story is this. ' About the middle of the winter 1778, general Putnam was on a visit to his out-post at Horseneck, he found governor Tryon advancing upon that town with a corps of fifteen hundred men—to oppose these, general Putnam had only a picket of one hundred and fifty men and two iron field-pieces without horse or drag-ropes. He, however, planted his cannon on the high ground by the meeting-house, and retarded their approach by firing several times, until, perceiving the horse (supported by the infantry) about to charge, he ordered the picket to provide for their safety by retiring to a swamp inaccessible to horse; and secured his own by plunging down the steep precipice at the church upon a full trot. This precipice is so steep, where he descended, as to have artificial stairs composed of nearly one hundred stone steps for the accommodation of foot passengers. There the dragoons, who were but a swords length from him, stopped short. For the declivity was so abrupt that they ventured not to follow: and, before they could gain the valley by going round the brow of the hill in the ordinary road, he was far enough beyond their reach.'

Tetoket mountain in Branford, latitude 41° 20', on the northwest part of it, a few feet below the surface, has ice in large quantities in all seasons of the year.

Colleges, Academies, and Schools.] In no part of the world is the education of all ranks of people more attended to than in Connecticut. Almost every town in the state is divided into districts, and each district has a public school kept in it a greater or less part of every year. Somewhat more than one third of the monies arising from a tax on the polls and ratable estate of the inhabitants, is appropriated to the support of schools, in the several towns, for the education of children and youth. The law directs that a grammar school shall be kept in every county town throughout the state.

There is a grammar school at Hartford, and another at New Haven, supported by a donation of governor Hopkins. This venerable and benevolent

F f

nevolent gentleman, in his laft will, dated 1657, left, in the hands of Theophilus Eaton Efq. and three others, a legacy of £.1324 'as an encouragement, in thefe foreign plantations, of breeding up hopeful youths both at the grammar fchool and college.' In 1664, this legacy was equally divided between New Haven and Hartford ; and grammar fchools were erected, which have been fupported ever fince.

At Greenfield there is a refpectable academy, under the care and inftruction of the Rev. Dr. Dwight. At Plainfield is another, under the care of the Rev. Mr. Benedict. This academy has flourifhed for feveral years, and furnifhed a number of ftudents for Yale and Dartmouth colleges. At Norwich and Windham, likewife, are academies furnifhed with able inftructors ; each of thefe academies have fixty or feventy fcholars.

YALE COLLEGE was founded in 1700, and remained at Killingworth until 1707—then at Saybrook, until 1716, when it was removed and fixed at New Haven. Among its principal benefactors was governor Yale, in honor of whom, in 1718, it was named YALE COLLEGE. Its firft building was erected in 1717, being 170 feet in length, and 22 in breadth, built of wood. This was taken down in 1782. The prefent college edifice, which is of brick, was built in 1750, under the direction of the Rev. Prefident Clap, and is 100 feet long, and 40 feet wide, three ftories high, and contains thirty-two chambers, and fixty-four ftudies, convenient for the reception of a hundred ftudents. The college chapel, which is alfo of brick, was built in 1761, being fifty feet by forty, with a fteeple 125 feet high. In this building is the public library, confifting of about 2500 volumes ; and the philofophical apparatus, which is at prefent incomplete. It contains, however, the principal machines neceffary for exhibiting moft of the experiments in the whole courfe of experimental philofophy and aftronomy. The fum of £.500, collected by fubfcriptions, is now in readinefs to be expended in the purchafe of fuch other inftruments and machines, as will render the philofophical apparatus complete.

The college mufeum, to which additions are conftantly making, contains fome great natural curiofities.

This literary inftitution was incorporated by the general affembly of Connecticut. The firft charter of incorporation was granted to eleven minifters, under the denomination of truftees, 1701. The powers of the truftees were enlarged by the additional charter, 1723. And by that of 1745, the truftees were incorporated by the name of 'The Prefident and Fellows of Yale college, New Haven.' The corporation are empowered to hold eftates, continue their fucceffion, make academic laws, elect and conftitute all officers of inftruction and government, ufual in univerfities, and confer all learned degrees. The ordinary executive government is in the hands of the prefident and tutors. The prefent officers of the college are, a prefident, who is alfo profeffor of ecclefiaftical hiftory, a profeffor of divinity, and three tutors. The number of ftudents for feveral years paft has been from 150 to 250, divided into four claffes. The prefent number is about 140. It is worthy of remark, that as many as five fixths of thofe who have received their educations at this univerfity, were natives of Connecticut.

In 1732, the Rev. George Berkley, D. D. then dean of Derry, and afterwards bifhop of Cloyne, in Ireland, made a generous donation of 880
volumes

CONNECTICUT.

volumes of books, and an estate in Rhode-Island, that rents yearly for 100 ounces of silver—which is divided into three parts, and annually appropriated to the three best scholars in the latin and greek classics. This has proved a great incentive among the students to excel in classical learning. The first donation to the college in land, consisting of about 600 acres, was made by major James Fitch, in 1701. The general assembly, in 1732, gave 1500 acres within the state. Dr. Daniel Lathrop, of Norwich, added a donation of £.500 to the college funds in 1781. The course of education, in this university, comprehends the whole circle of literature. The three learned languages are taught, together with so much of the sciences as can be communicated in four years. Great attention is paid to oratory and the belles lettres.

In May and September, annually, the several classes are critically examined in all their classical studies. As incentives to improvement in composition and oratory, quarterly exercises are appointed by the president and tutors to be exhibited by the respective classes in rotation. A public commencement is held annually, on the second Wednesday in September, which calls together a more numerous and brilliant assembly, than are convened by any other anniversary in the state.

Two thousand and eighty have received the honours of this university; of whom 633 have been ordained to the work of the gospel ministry.

Accessus. A. D.	Presidents.	Exitus. A. D.
1701	Abraham Pierson,	1707
1719	Timothy Cutler, S. T. D.	1722
1726	Elisha Williams,	1739
1739	Thomas Clap,	1766
1777	Ezra Stiles, S. T. D. L. L. D.	

Mines, minerals and fossils.] On the bank of Connecticut river, two miles from Middleton, is a lead mine, which was wrought during the war, at the expence of the state, and was productive. It is too expensive to work in time of peace. Copper mines have been discovered and opened in several parts of the state, but have proved unprofitable, and are much neglected. Iron mines are numerous and productive. Steel ore has been found in the mountains between Woodbury and New Milford. Talks of various kinds, white, brown and chocolate coloured crystals, zink or spelter, a semi-metal, and several other fossils and metals have been found in Connecticut.

Mode of levying taxes.] All free-holders in the state are required by law, to give in lists of their polls and rateable estate,* to persons appointed in the respective towns to receive them, on or before the 20th of August annually. These are valued according to law, arranged in proper order, and sent to the general assembly annually in May.

The

---

* *In Connecticut, horses, horned cattle, improved and unimproved land, houses, shipping, all sorts of riding carriages, clocks and watches, silver plate and money at interest, are rateable estate. All males between sixteen and seventy years of age, unless exempted by law, are subjects of taxation.*

CONNECTICUT.

The sum total of the list of the polls and rateable estate of the inhabitants of Connecticut, as brought into the general assembly in May, 1787, was as follows ;

Sum total of the single list,	£.1,484,901:6:4:¼
Assessments,	47,790:2:9
One quarter of the four-folds,	1,176:9:4
Total,	£.1,533,867:18:5:¼

On this sum taxes are levied, so much on the pound, according to the sum proposed to be raised. A tax of two pence on the pound, would raise £.12,782:4s.

The ordinary annual expences of government before the war, amounted to near £.4000 sterling, exclusive of that which was appropriated to the support of schools. The expences have since increased.

Mineral springs.] At Stafford is a medicinal spring, which is said to be a sovereign remedy for scorbutic, cutaneous and other disorders. At Guilford is a spring, whose water, it is said, when separated from the fountain, will evaporate even when put into a bottle and tightly corked.

Constitution and Courts of Justice.] It is difficult to say what is the constitution of this state. Contented with the form of government which originated from the charter of Charles II. granted in 1662, the people have not been disposed to run the hazard of framing a new constitution since the declaration of independence. They have tacitly adopted their old charter as the ground of civil government, so far as it is applicable to an independent people.

Agreeably to this charter, the supreme legislative authority of the state is vested in a governor, deputy governor, twelve assistants or counsellors, and the representatives of the people, styled the *General Assembly.* The governor, deputy governor and assistants, are annually chosen by the freemen in the month of May. The representatives (their number not to exceed two from each town) are chosen by the freemen twice a year, to attend the two annual sessions, on the second Thursdays of May and October. This assembly has power to erect judicatories, for the trial of causes civil and criminal, and to ordain and establish laws for settling the forms and ceremonies of government. By these laws the general assembly is divided into two branches, called the upper and lower houses. The upper house is composed of the governor, deputy governor and assistants. The lower house, of the representatives of the people. No law can pass without the concurrence of both houses. The judges of the superior court hold their offices during the pleasure of the general assembly. The judges of the county courts, and justices, are annually appointed. Sheriffs are appointed by the governor and council, without limitation of time. The governor is captain general of the militia, the deputy governor, lieutenant general. All other military officers are appointed by the assembly and commissioned by the governor.

The mode of electing the governor, deputy governor, assistants, treasurer and secretary, is as follows: The freemen in the several towns meet on the Monday next after the first Tuesday in April, annually, and give

give in their votes for the persons they choose for the said offices respectively, with their names written on a piece of paper, which are received and sealed up by a constable in open meeting, the votes for each office by themselves, with the name of the town and office written on the outside. These votes, thus sealed, are sent to the general assembly in May, and there counted by a committee from both houses. All Freemen are eligible to any office in government. In choosing assistants, twenty persons are nominated, by the vote of each freeman, at the freeman's meeting for choosing representatives in September annually. These votes are sealed up, and sent to the general assembly in October, and are there counted by a committee of both houses, and the twenty persons who have the most votes stand in nomination; out of which number the twelve who have the greatest number of votes, given by the freemen at their meeting in April, are, in May, declared assistants in the manner above mentioned. The qualifications of freemen are, maturity in years—quiet and peaceable behaviour —a civil conversation, and freehold estate to the value of forty shillings per annum, or forty pounds personal estate in the list, certified by the select men of the town ; it is necessary, also, that they take the oath of fidelity to the state. Their names are enrolled in the town clerk's office, and they continue freemen for life, unless disfranchised by sentence of the superior court, on conviction of misdemeanor.

The courts are as follows : The justices of the peace, of whom a number are annually appointed in each town by the general assembly, have authority to hear and determine civil actions, where the demand does not exceed four pounds. If the demand exceeds forty shillings, an appeal to the county is allowed. They have cognizance of small offences, and may punish by fine, not exceeding forty shillings, or whipping not exceeding ten stripes, or sitting in the stocks. There are eight county courts in the state, held in the several counties by one judge and four justices of the quorum, who have jurisdiction of all criminal cases, arising within their respective counties, where the punishment does not extend to life, limb, or banishment. They have original jurisdiction of all civil actions which exceed the jurisdiction of a justice. Either party may appeal to the superior court, if the demand exceeds twenty pounds, except on bonds or notes vouched by two witnesses.

There are several courts of probate, in each county, consisting of one judge. The peculiar province of this court, is the probate of wills, granting administration on intestate estates, ordering distribution of them, and appointing guardians for minors, &c. An appeal lies from any decree of this court to the superior court.

The superior court consists of five judges. It has authority in all criminal cases extending to life, limb or banishment, and other high crimes and misdemeanors, to grant divorces, and to hear and determine all civil actions brought by appeal from the county courts, or the court of probate, and to correct the errors of all inferior courts. This is a circuit court, and has two stated sessions in each county annually. The superior and county courts try matters of fact by a jury, or without if the parties will agree.

There is a supreme court of errors, consisting of the deputy governor and the twelve assistants. Their sole business is to determine writs of
error

error, brought on judgments of the superior court, where the error complained of appears on the record. They have two stated sessions annually, viz. on the Tuesdays of the weeks preceding the stated sessions of the general assembly.

The county court is a court of chancery, empowered to hear and determine cases in equity, where the matter in demand does not exceed one hundred pounds. The superior court has cognizance of all cases where the demand exceeds that sum. Error may be brought from the county, to the superior court, and from the superior court to the supreme court of errors, on judgment in cases of equity as well as of law.

The general assembly, only, have power to grant pardons and reprieves —to grant commissions of bankruptcy—or protect the persons and estates of unfortunate debtors.

The common law of England, so far as it is applicable to this country, is considered as the common law of this state. The reports of adjudication in the courts of king's bench, common pleas and chancery, are read in the courts of this State as authorities; yet the judges do not consider them as conclusively binding, unless founded on solid reasons which will apply in this State, or sanctioned by concurrent adjudications of their own courts.*

The feudal system of descents was never adopted in this State. All the real estate of intestates is divided equally among the children, males and females, except that the eldest son has a double portion. And all estates given in tail, must be given to some person then in being or to their immediate issue, and shall become fee simple estates to the issue of the first donee in tail. The widow of an intestate is entitled to a third part of the personal estate forever, and to her dower, or third part of the houses and lands belonging to the intestate at the time of his death, during her life.

Practice of law.] The practice of law in this State has more simplicity, but less precision, than in England. Assistants and judges are impowered to issue writs through the state, and justices, through their respective counties. In these writs, the substance of the complaints or the declarations must be contained, and if neither of the parties shew good reason for delay, the causes are heard and determined the same term to which the writs are returnable. Few of the fictions of law, so common in the English practice, are known in this State. The plaintiff always has his election to attach or summon the defendant. Attornies are admitted and qualified by the county courts. Previous to their admission to the bar, they must study two years with a practising attorney in the State, if they have had a college education, and three years if they have not; their morals must be good, and their characters unblemished, and they must sustain an examination by the attornies of the court of the county where they are admitted, and be by them recommended to the court. When admitted to the county court, they can practice, without other qualifications, in any court in the State. There are upon an average, about thirteen attornies to each county, one hundred and four in the State; a very great proportion for the real exigencies of the people. Yet from the litigious spirit of the citizens, the most

---

* A volume of reports of adjudications of the superior court, it is expected will soon be published by a gentlemen of abilities, in the profession of law, under the inspection of the court.

moſt of them find employment and fupport. There is no attorney general, but there is one attorney to the State in each county.

New Inventions.] Early in the war, David Buſhnel, A. M. of Saybrook, invented a machine for *fubmarine* navigation, altogether different from any thing hitherto deviſed by the art of man. This machine was ſo conſtructed as that it could be rowed horizontally, at any given depth, under water, and could be raiſed or depreſſed at pleaſure. To this machine, called the *American Turtle*, was attached a magazine of powder, which was intended to be faſtened under the bottom of a ſhip with a driving ſcrew, in ſuch a way as that the ſame ſtroke which diſengaged it from the machine ſhould put the internal clock work in motion. This being done, the ordinary operation of a gun-lock, at the diſtance of half an hour, or any determinate time, would cauſe the powder to explode and leave the effects to the common laws of nature. The ſimplicity, yet combination diſcovered in the machaniſm of this wonderful machine, have been acknowledged by thoſe ſkilled in phyſics, and particularly Hydraulics, to be not leſs ingenious than novel. Mr. Buſhnel invented ſeveral other curious machines for the annoyance of the Britiſh ſhipping, but from accidents, not militating againſt the philoſophical principles, on which their ſucceſs depended, they but partially ſucceeded. He deſtroyed a veſſel in the charge of commodore Symmonds. One of his kegs alſo demoliſhed a veſſel near the Long Iſland ſhore. About Chriſtmas 1777, he committed to the Delaware river a number of kegs, deſtined to fall among the Britiſh fleet at Philadelphia; but his ſquadron of kegs, having been ſeparated and retarded by the ice, demoliſhed but a ſingle boat. This cataſtrophe, however, produced an alarm, unprecedented in its nature and degree; which has been ſo happily deſcribed by the Hon. Francis Hopkinſon, in a ſong, ſtiled ' The Battle of the Kegs,'* that the event it celebrates will not be forgotten, ſo long as mankind ſhall continue to be delighted with works of humour and taſte.

Mr. Hanks, of Litchfield, has invented a method of winding up clocks by means of Air or Wind only, which is new and ingenious.

Mr. Culver, of Norwich, has conſtructed (whether he was the inventor I know not) a Dock-Drudge, which is a boat for clearing docks and removing bars in rivers; a very ingenious and uſeful machine. Its good effects have already been experienced in the navigation of the river Thames, the channel of which has been confiderably deepened. This machine will no doubt be productive of very great advantages to navigation throughout the United States.

A machine for drawing wire was invented ſometime ſince at Norwich, by the Hon. N. Niles, now in Vermont.

The Rev. Joſeph Badger, while a member of Yale College in 1785, conſtructed an ingenious *planetarium*, (without ever having ſeen one of the kind) which is depoſited in the library of that univerſity.

Hiſtory.] The preſent territory of Connecticut, at the time of the firſt arrival of the Engliſh, was poſſeſſed by the Pequot, the Mohegan, Podunk, and many other ſmaller tribes of Indians.

The

* See Col. Humphrey's life of General Putnam, P. 123.

CONNECTICUT.

The Pequots were numerous and warlike. Their country extended along the fea coaft from Paukatuk, to Connecticut river. About the year 1630, this powerful tribe extended their conquefts over a confiderable part of Connecticut, over all Long Ifland and part of Narraganfett. Sassacus, who was the Grand Monarch of the whole country, was king of this nation. The feat of his dominion was at New London; the ancient Indian name of which was Pequot.

The Mohegans were a numerous tribe, and their territory extenfive. Their ancient claim, which was furveyed and fettled by commiffioners from Queen Ann, in 1705, comprehended all New London county, except a narrow ftrip of about eight miles wide, on the fea coaft, almoft the whole of the county of Windham, and a part of the counties of Tolland and Hartford. Uncus, diftinguifhed for his friendfhip to the Englifh, was the Sachem of this tribe.

The Podunks inhabited Eaft Hartford, and the circumjacent country. The firft Sachem of this tribe, of whom the Englifh had any knowledge, was Tatanimoo. He was able to bring into the field more than 200 fighting men.

The firft grant of Connecticut was made, by the Plymouth council, to the Earl of Warwick, in 1630, and confirmed by his majefty in council the fame year. This grant comprehended 'all that part of New England which lies weft from Narraganfett river, 120 miles on the fea coaft, from thence, in latitude and breadth aforefaid, to the fouth fea.' The year following, the Earl affigned this grant to Lord Say and Seal, Lord Brook and nine others.

No Englifh fettlements were attempted in Connecticut until the year 1633, when a number of Indian traders, having purchafed of Zequaffon and Natawanute, two principal Sachems, a tract of land at the mouth of Little river in Windfor, built a houfe and fortified it, and ever after maintained their right of foil upon the river.

The fame year, a little before the arrival of the Englifh, a company of Dutch traders came to Hartford, and built a houfe which they called the *Hirfe of Good Hope*, and erected a fmall fort, in which they planted two cannon. The remains of this fettlement are ftill vifible on the bank of Connecticut river. This was the only fettlement of the Dutch in Connecticut in thefe ancient times. The Dutch, and after them the Province of New York, for a long time claimed as far eaft as the weftern bank of Connecticut river. It belongs to the profeffed hiftorian to prove or difprove the juftice of this claim. Douglafs fays, ' The partition line between New York and Connecticut as eftablifhed December 1, 1664, run from the mouth of Memoroncok river, (a little weft from Byram river,) N. N, W. and was the *ancient eafterly limits of New York*, until Nov. 23, 1683, when the line was run nearly the fame as it is now fettled.'* If Douglafs is right, the New York claim could not have been well founded.

In 1634, Lord Say and Seal, &c. fent over a fmall number of men, who built a fort at Saybrook, and held a treaty with the Pequot Indians, who, in a formal manner, gave to the Englifh their right to Connecticut river and the adjacent country.

In

---

* Douglafs Sum. Vol. II. P. 161.

CONNECTICUT.

In 1635, the Plymouth council granted to the Duke of Hamilton, all lands between Narraganfett and Connecticut rivers, and back into the country as far as Maffachufetts fouth line. This covered a part of the Earl of Warwick's patent, and occafioned fome difputes in the colony. There were feveral attempts to revive the Hamilton claim, but were never profecuted.

In Oct. of this year, about fixty perfons, from Newtown, Dorchefter, and Watertown, in Maffachufetts, came and fettled Hartford, Wetherf- field and Windfor, in Connecticut; and the June following the famous Mr. Hooker, and his company came and fettled at Hartford, and was a friend and father to the colony to the day of his death.

The firft court held in Connecticut was at Hartford, April 26th, 1636.

The year 1637 was diftinguifhed by the war with the Pequots. This warlike nation had, for fome time, been troublefome neighbours. They folicited the Narraganfetts to join them in extirpating the Englifh. They had furprized and killed feveral of the Englifh upon Connecticut river. Thefe threatning appearances and actual hoftilities, induced the three colonies of Maffachufetts, Plymouth and Connecticut, to combine their forces, to carry the war into their country, and to attempt the entire deftruction of the whole tribe. Myantonomo, the Narragan- fett Sachem, and Uncas, Sachem of the Mohegans, fent to the Englifh and offered their fervice to join with them againft the Pequots. Forces were accordingly raifed in all the colonies; but thofe of Connecticut, on account of their vicinity to the enemy, were firft in action. Captain Mafon, with 80 Englifh and 100 Indians from Connecticut river, proceeded by water to the Narraganfett's country, where 200 of that tribe joined him. On the 24th of May, they began their march for Saffacus' fort on Pequot, now Thames, river. They afterwards determined firft to affault Myftic fort, which was fituated between them and Pequot river. On the morn- ing of the 26th of May the attack was made. The Indians, after a mid- night revel, were buried in a deep fleep. At the moment of their approach, the centinel happened to be gone into a wigwam to light his pipe. The barking of a dog gave the alarm. The Indians awoke, feized their arrows, and began their hedious yell. They were joined in their tremendous noife by the Indians in the Englifh army, who were in the rear and afraid to ap- proach. The battle was warm and bloody, and the victory compleat. The fort was taken—about 70 wigwams were burnt—50 or 60 of the Indians were killed—many were wounded and taken, and the reft efcaped. Saffacus and his wariors at Pequot, ftruck with terror at the news of this defeat, de- molifhed their principal fort, burnt their wigwams, and fled to the weftward. Capt. Stoughton, with 160 men from Maffachufetts, had by this time arrived at Saybrook. He with his forces joined Captain Mafon and purfued the Indians, and overtook and furrounded them in a great fwamp near Fair- field. A Sachem and ninety-nine women and children came out and de- livered themfelves up to their purfuers. Terms of peace were offered to the reft. But after a fhort parley they determined, that ' as they had lived they would die together.' There were about eighty who made this refolution. Part of thefe efcaped by means of the darknefs of the night. The reft were either killed or taken. In this action the Indians had guns,

G g which

which is the first account of their having used them. Saffacus fled to the Mohawks, by whom it is reported he was murdered; but it is more probable that he and his company incorporated with them. Many of the Indian captives were *unjustifiably* sent to Bermudas and sold for slaves. The Pequot tribe was wholly extinguished. This succesful expedition struck the Indians that remained with such terror, as restrained them from open hostilities for near forty years after.

The English thus obtained the country east of the Dutch settlements, by right of conquest. The pursuit of the Indians led to an acquaintance with the lands on the sea coast, from Saybrook to Fairfield. It was reported to be a very fine country. This favourable report induced Messrs. Eaton and Hopkins, two very respectable London merchants, and Mr. Davenport, a man of distinguished piety and abilities, with their company, who arrived this year (1637) from London, to think of this part of the country as the place of their settlement. Their friends in Massachusetts, sorry to part with so valuable a company, dissuaded them from their purpose. Influenced, however, by the promising prospects which the country afforded, and flattering themselves that they should be out of the jurisdiction of a general governor, with which the country was from time to time threatened, they determined to proceed. Accordingly, in March 1638, with the consent of their friends on Connecticut river, they settled at New Haven, and laid the foundation of a flourishing colony, of which Quinnipiak, now New Haven, was the chief town. The first public worship, in this new plantation, was attended on Lord's day, April 18th, 1638, under a large spreading oak. The Rev. Mr. Davenport, preached from Matt. iii. 1. on the temptations of the wildernefs. Both colonies, by voluntary compact, formed themselves into distinct commonwealths, and remained so until their union in 1665.

In 1639, the three towns on Connecticut river, already mentioned, finding themselves without the limits of any jurisdiction, formed themselves into a body politic, and agreed upon articles of civil government. These articles were the foundation of Connecticut charter, which was granted in 1662. The substance of the articles, so far as they respect the holding of assemblies, the time and manner of electing magistrates and other civil officers, (except that in the old confederation no person was to be chosen governor more than once in two years) and the extent of legislative powers, was transferred into, and established in said charter.

The first church was gathered in New Haven this year, and consisted of seven members. These were chosen by the settlers after Mr. Davenport had preached from the words of Solomon, ' Wisdom hath builded her house, she hath hewed out her seven pillars.' These men were indeed the pillars of the church, to whom the rest were added as they became qualified. They were. also, the court to try all civil actions.

The first settlers in New Haven had all things common; all purchases were made in the name and for the use of the whole plantation, and the lands were apportioned out to each family, according to their number and original stock.

At their first election, in October 1639, Mr. Theophilus Eaton was chosen governor for the first year. Their elections, by agreement, were to be annual; and the Word of God their only rule in conducting the affairs of government in the plantation. In

CONNECTICUT.

In 1643, the articles of confederation between the four New England colonies, mentioned p. 158, were unanimously adopted by the colonies of New Haven and Connecticut.

The English settlement on Delaware, which was under the jurisdiction of New Haven, was surprized by the Swedes, and the people put in irons under a false pretence that they were entering into a conspiracy with the Indians to extirpate the Swedes.

The general court of New Haven, this year, established it as a fundamental article not to be disputed, That none be admitted as free Burgesses but church members, and that none but such should vote at elections. They also ordained, That each town choose from among themselves judges (church members) to be a court, to have cognizance of all civil actions not exceeding twenty pounds; and of criminal causes, where the punishment was, sitting in the stocks, whipping and fining not exceeding five pounds. There was liberty of appeal from this to the court of magistrates. The court of magistrates consisted of all the magistrates throughout the colony; who were to meet twice a year, at New Haven, for the trial of all capital causes. Six made a quorum.

The general court was to consist of the governor, deputy-governor, magistrates and two representatives from each town. The annual election of officers of government was at this time established, and has ever since continued.

The unsettled state of the colony, had hitherto prevented their establishing a code of laws. To supply this defect, the general court ordered, ' That the judicial laws of God as they were delivered to Moses, and as they are a fence to the moral, being neither typical nor ceremonial, nor having any reference to Canaan, shall be accounted of moral equity and generally bind all offenders, and be a rule to all the courts in this jurisdiction in their proceedings against offenders, until they be branched out into particulars hereafter.'

About this time a war broke out between the Mohegan and Narragansett Indians. A personal quarrel between Myantonomo, sachem of the Narragansetts, and Uncas sachem of the Mohegans, was the foundation of the war. Myantonomo raised an army of 900 warriors and marched towards the Mohegan country. Uncas by his spies received timely notice of their approach. His seat of residence was in some part of Norwich. He quickly collected 600 of his bravest warriors, and told them, ' The Narragansetts must not come into our town, we must meet them.' They accordingly marched about three miles to a large plain, where the two armies met, and halted within bow shot of each other. A parley was proposed by Uncas, and agreed to by Myantonomo. The sachems met, and Uncas addressed his enemy as follows. ' You have a great many brave men—so have I—You and I have quarrelled, but these warriors, what have they done? Shall they die to avenge a private quarrel between us? No. Come like a brave man, as you pretend to be, and let us fight. If you kill me, my men shall be yours, if I kill you, your men shall be mine.' Myantonomo replied, ' My men came to fight, and they shall fight.' Uncas, like an experienced warrior, aware of the result of the conference from the superior force of his enemy, had previously signified to his men, that if Myantonomo refused to fight him in single combat, he would

immediately

immediately fall, which was to be the signal for them to begin the attack. As soon therefore as Myantonomo had finished his laconic speech, Uncas dropped—his men instantly obeyed the signal, and poured in a shower of arrows upon the unsuspecting Narragansetts, and rushing on with their horrid yells and savage fierceness, put them to flight. Many were killed on the spot—the rest were closely pursued, and some were precipitately driven down craggy precipices, and dashed in pieces. At a place called, from this event, Sachem's Plain, Uncas overtook and seized Myantonomo by the shoulder. They sat down together; and Uncas with a hoop, called in his men, and the battle ceased. Doubtful what to do with the Royal prisoner, Uncas and his warriors, in council, determined to carry him to the governor and council at Hartford, and be advised by them. Thither he was accordingly conducted. The governor having advised with his council, told Uncas, That the English were not then at war with the Narragansetts, and of course that it was not proper for them to intermeddle in the matter. Uncas was left to do with him as he pleased. Myantonomo was conducted back to the plain where he was taken, and put to death by Uncas himself. The tragic scene did not end with his death. Uncas, after the manner of the Indians, with his tomahawk, cut off a large piece of flesh from the shoulder of his slaughtered enemy, broiled and ate it, saying, with an air of savage triumph, 'It is the sweetest meat I ever ate—It makes me have a stout heart.' His body was afterwards buried, and a pillar erected over it, the remains of which are visible to this day.

Some historians have insinuated that the governor and council secretly advised Uncas to put Myantonomo to death—and others, more bold, have declared that they '*ordered* him (Myantonomo) to be carried out of their jurisdiction and to be slain;' but that they 'kindly added that he should not be tortured; and sent some persons to see execution done, who had the satisfaction to see the captive king murdered in cool blood.'* I know of no foundation for this unfavourable representation of the affair.

Myantonomo was one of the most potent Indian Princes in New England. Seven years before this he had assisted the English in their wars with the Pequots.

The Narragansetts were greatly enraged at the death of their prince, and resolved to take vengeance on the Mohegans. The united colonies interposed to prevent a war between them, but in vain. The Narragansetts resolutely declared, they would continue the war until they had Uncas' head. But as Uncas had ever been a friend to the English, they joined him against his enemies, and were victorious. Such, however, was the enmity of the Narragansetts to the English, that they afterwards sent some of their men to Uncas, with large presents, to induce him to join with them in a war with the colonies. Uncas replied, 'Go tell your king that I will go to Norwich, and advise with Major John Mason and Mr. Fitch; if they tell me to join him and fight against the English, I will join him.' In the war that happened soon after, Uncas assisted the English, and the Narragansetts were subdued, and never after were formidable.

In

* Hist. of Providence. &c. published in the Providence Gazette, 1765, No. 128.

In confideration of the fuccefs and increafe of the New England colonies, and that they had been of *no charge* to the nation, and in profpect of their being in future very ferviceable to it, the Englifh parliament, March 10th, 1643, granted them an exemption from all cuftoms, fubfidies and other duties, until further order.

To write a connected, progreffive hiftory of any of the ftates, is not within the limits of my defign. This, as I have before obferved, is left to the profeffed hiftorian.* Some of the moft remarkable and interefting events, related in a detached and fummary manner, is all that muft be expected.

In 1644, the Connecticut adventurers purchafed of Mr. Fenwick, agent for lord Say and Seal, and lord Brook, their right to the colony of Connecticut, for £1600.

The hiftory of Connecticut is marked with traces of the fame fpirit, which has been mentioned as characteriftic of the Maffachufetts, in different ftages of their hiftory. Indeed, as Maffachufetts was the ftock whence Connecticut proceeded, this is to be expected.

The colony of Connecticut expreffed their difapprobation of the ufe of tobacco, in an act of their general affembly at Hartford, in 1647, wherein it was ordered ' That no perfon under the age of twenty years, nor any other that hath already accuftomed himfelf to the ufe thereof, fhall take any tobacco, until he fhall have brought a certificate, from under the hand of fome who are approved for knowledge and fkill in phyfic, that it is ufeful for him ; and alfo that he hath received a licence from the court for the fame. All others who had addicted themfelves to the ufe of tobacco were, by the fame court, prohibited taking it in any company, or at their labours, or on their travels, unlefs they were ten miles at leaft *from any houfe*,† (I fuppofe) or more than once a day, though not in company, on pain of a fine of *fix-pence* for each time ; to be proved by one fubftantial evidence. The conftable in each town to make prefentment of fuch tranfgreffions to the particular court, and upon conviction, the fine to be paid without gainfaying.

Nor were the Connecticut fettlers behind their brethren in Maffachufetts in regard to their feverity againft the Quakers; and they have the fame apology.‡ The general court of New Haven, 1658, paffed a fevere law againft the Quakers. They introduced their law with this preamble.

' Whereas there is a curfed fect of hereticks lately fprung up in the world, commonly called Quakers, who take upon them that they are immediately fent from God, and infallibly affifted by the fpirit, who yet fpeak and write blafphemous opinions, defpife government, and the order of God in church and commonwealth, fpeaking evil of dignities, &c.

' Ordered

---

* *The Rev. Mr. Benjamin Trumbull of North Haven, has for feveral years, with indefatigable induftry, been making collections for a hiftory of Connecticut. His abilities as a writer, and his accuracy as a hiftorian the public already know. It is hoped the public will fhortly be favoured with his hiftory. Through his indulgence in permitting me to felect from his manufcripts, I am enabled to publifh moft of the above facts.*

† *There is a defect in the copy.*

‡ *See Hift. Maffachufetts, P. 188.*

'Ordered—That whofoever fhall bring, or caufe to be brought, any known Quaker or Quakers, or other blafphemous hereticks, fhall forfeit the fum of £50.' Alfo,

If a Quaker come into this jurifdiction on civil bufinefs, the time of his ftay fhall be limited by the civil authority, and he fhall not ufe any means to corrupt or feduce others. On his firft arrival, he fhall appear before the magiftrate, and from him have licence to pafs on his bufinefs. And (for the better prevention of hurt to the people) have one or more to attend upon them at their charge, &c. The penalties in cafe of difobedience were whipping, imprifonment, labour, and a deprivation of all converfe with any perfon.

For the fecond offence, the perfon was to be branded in the hand with the letter H—to fuffer imprifonment—and be put to labour. For the third, to be branded in the other hand, imprifoned, &c. as before. For the fourth, the offender was to have his tongue bored through with a red hot iron—imprifoned—and kept to labour, until fent away at their own charge.

Any perfon who fhould attempt to defend the fentiments of the Quakers, was, for the third offence, to be fentenced to banifhment.

Had the pious framers of thefe laws paid a due attention to the excellent advice of that fagacious doctor of the law, Gamaliel, they would, perhaps, have been prevented from the adoption of fuch fevere and unjuftifiable meafures. This wife man, when his countrymen were about to be outrageous in perfecuting the apoftles, addreffed them in the following words, which merit to be engraved in letters of gold ; 'REFRAIN FROM THESE MEN, AND LET THEM ALONE : FOR IF THIS COUNSEL OR THIS WORK BE OF MEN, IT WILL COME TO NOUGHT : BUT IF IT BE OF GOD, YE CANNOT OVERTHROW IT ; LEST HAPLY YE BE FOUND EVEN TO FIGHT AGAINST GOD.'[*] This divine maxim was but little attended to in times of perfecution. Our anceftors feem to have left it to pofterity to make the important difcovery, that perfecution is the direct method to multiply its objects.

But thefe people, who have been fo much cenfured and ridiculed, had, perhaps, as many virtues as their pofterity ; and had they an advocate to defend their caufe, he no doubt might find as broad a field for ridicule, and as juft a foundation for cenfure, in the furvey of modern manners, as has been afforded in any period fince the fettlement of America. It would be wife, then, in the moderns, who ftand elevated upon the fhoulders of their anceftors, with the book of *their* experience fpread before them, to improve their virtues and veil their faults.

The colonies of Connecticut and New Haven, from their firft fettlement, increafed rapidly ; tracts of land were purchafed of the Indians, and new towns fettled from Stamford to Stonington, and far back into the country, when, in 1661, Major John Mafon, as agent for the colony, bought of the natives all lands which had not before been purchafed by particular towns, and made a public furrender of them to the colony, in the prefence of the general affembly. Having done thefe things, the colonifts petitioned king Charles II. for a charter, and their petition was granted. His majefty

---

[*] Acts v. Chap.

CONNECTICUT.

jesty on the 23d of April 1662, issued his letters patent under the great seal, ordaining that the colony of Connecticut, should forever hereafter be one body corporate and politic, in fact and in name, confirming to them their ancient grant and purchase, and fixing their boundaries as follows, (viz.) 'All that part of his Majesty's dominions in New England, in America, bounden east by Narragansett river, commonly called Narragansett bay, where the river falleth into the sea; and on the north by the line of Massachusetts plantation, and on the south by the sea, and in longitude as the line of the Massachusetts colony, running from east to west, that is to say, from the said Narragansett bay on the east, to the south sea on the west part, with the islands thereunto belonging.' This charter has ever since remained the basis of the government of Connecticut.

Such was the ignorance of the Europeans, respecting the geography of America, when they first assumed the right of giving away lands which the God of nature had long before given to the Indians, that their patents extended they knew not where, many of them were of doubtful construction, and very often covered each other in part, and have produced innumerable disputes and mischiefs in the colonies, some of which are not settled to this day. It is not my business to touch upon these disputes. I have only to observe, that Connecticut construed her charter literally, and passing over New York, which was then in possession of the subjects of a christian Prince, claimed, in latitude and breadth mentioned therein, to the south sea. Accordingly purchases were made of the Indians, on the Delaware river, west of the western bounds of New York, and within the supposed limits of Connecticut charter, and settlements were made thereon by people from, and under the jurisdiction of, Connecticut. The charter of Pennsylvania, granted to William Penn, in 1681, covered these settlements. This laid the foundation for a dispute, which, for a long time, was maintained with warmth on both sides. The matter was at last submitted to gentlemen chosen for the purpose, who decided the dispute in favor of Pennsylvania. Many however still assert the justice of the Connecticut claim.

The state of Connecticut, has lately ceded to Congress all their lands west of Pennsylvania, except a reserve of twenty miles square. This cession, Congress have accepted, and thereby indubitably established the right of Connecticut to the *reserve*.

But to return. The colony of New Haven, though unconnected with the colony of Connecticut, was comprehended within the limits of their charter, and, as they concluded, within their jurisdiction. But New Haven remonstrated against their claim, and refused to unite with them, until they should hear from England. It was not until the year 1665, when it was believed that the king's commissioners had a design upon the New England charters, that these two colonies formed a union, which has ever since amicably subsisted between them.

In 1672, the laws of the colony were revised, and the general court ordered them to be printed; and also, that 'every family should buy one of the law books—such as pay in silver, to have a book for twelve pence, such as pay in wheat, to pay a peck and a half a book; and such as pay in pease, to pay two shillings a book, the pease at three shillings the bushel.' Perhaps it is owing to this early and universal spread of law books, that the people of Connecticut are, to this day, so fond of the law.

In 1750, the laws of Connecticut were again revised, and published in a small folio volume, of 258 pages. Dr. Douglass observes, that they were the most natural, equitable, plain and concise *code* of laws, for plantations, hitherto extant.' There has been a revision of them since the peace, in which they were greatly and very judiciously simplified.

The years 1675 and 1676, were distinguished by the wars with Philip and his Indians, and with the Narragansetts, by which the colony was thrown into great distress and confusion. The inroads of the enraged savages were marked with cruel murders, and with fire and devastation.

In 1684, the charter of Massachusetts Bay and Plymouth were taken away, in consequence of *Quo warrantos* which had been issued against them. The charter of Connecticut would have shared the same fate, had it not been for ———— Wadsworth, Esq. who, having very artfully procured it when it was on the point of being delivered up, buried it under an oak tree in Hartford, where it remained until all danger was over, and then was dug up and reassumed.

Connecticut has ever made rapid advances in population. There have been more emigrations from this, than from any of the other States, and yet it is at present full of inhabitants. This increase, under the divine Benediction, may be ascribed to several causes. The bulk of the inhabitants are industrious sagacious husbandmen. Their farms furnish them with all the necessaries, most of the conveniencies, and but few of the luxuries of life. They of course must be generally temperate, and, if they choose, can subsist with as much independence as is consistent with happiness. The subsistence of the farmer is substantial, and does not depend on incidental circumstances, like that of most other professions. There is no necessity of serving an apprenticeship to the business, nor of a large stock of money to commence it to advantage. Farmers, who deal much in barter, have less need of money than any other class of people. The ease with which a comfortable subsistence is obtained, induces the husbandman to marry young. The cultivation of his farm makes him strong and healthful. He toils cheerfully through the day—eats the fruit of his own labour with a gladsome heart—at night devoutly thanks his bounteous God for his daily blessings—retires to rest, and his sleep is sweet. Such circumstances as these have greatly contributed to the amazing increase of inhabitants in this state.

Besides, the people live under a free government, and have no fear of a tyrant. There are no overgrown estates, with rich and ambitious landlords, to have an undue and pernicious influence in the election of civil officers. Property is equally enough divided, and must continue to be so, as long as estates descend as they now do. No person is prohibited from voting, or from being elected into office, on account of his poverty. He who has the most merit, not he who has the most money, is generally chosen into public office. As instances of this, it is to be observed, that many of the citizens of Connecticut, from the humble walks of life, have arisen to the first offices in the state, and filled them with dignity and reputation.

tion. That base business of electioneering, which is so directly calculated to introduce wicked and designing men into office, is yet but little known in Connecticut. A man who wishes to be chosen into office, acts wisely, for that end, when he keeps his desires to himself.

A thirst for learning prevails among all ranks of people in the State. More of the young men in Connecticut, in proportion to their numbers, receive a public education, than in any of the states. Dr. Franklin and other literary characters, have honoured this state by saying, that it is the *Athens of America*.

Some have believed, and with reason, that the fondness for academic and collegiate education is too great—that it induces too many to leave the plough. If men of liberal education would return to the farm, and use their knowledge in improving agriculture, and encouraging manufactures, there could not be too many men of learning in the state; but this is too seldom the case.

Connecticut had but few citizens who did not join in opposing the oppressive measures of Great-Britain, and was active and influential, both in the field and in the cabinet, in bringing about the revolution. Her soldiers were applauded by the commander in chief, for their bravery and fidelity.

What has been said in favour of Connecticut, though true when generally applied, needs to be qualified with some exceptions. Dr. Douglass spoke the truth when he said, that 'some of the meaner sort are villains.' Too many are idle and dissipated, and much time is unprofitably and wickedly spent in lawsuits and petty arbitrations. The public schools, in some parts of the state, have been too much neglected, and in procuring instructors, too little attention is paid to their moral and literary qualifications.

The revolution, which so essentially affected the governments of most of the colonies, produced no very perceptible alteration in the government of Connecticut. While under the jurisdiction of Great-Britain, they elected their own governors, and all subordinate civil officers, and made their own laws, in the same manner, and with as little controul as they now do. Connecticut has ever been a republic, and perhaps as perfect and as happy a republic as has ever existed. While other states, more monarchical in their government and manners, have been under a necessity of undertaking the difficult task of altering their old, or forming new, constitutions, and of changing their monarchical for republican manners, Connecticut has uninterruptedly proceeded in her old track, both as to government and manners; and, by these means, has avoided those convulsions which have rent other states into violent parties.

At the anniversary election of the governor and other public officers, which is held yearly at Hartford on the second Wednesday in May, a sermon is preached, which is published at the expence of the state.* On these occasions a vast concourse of respectable citizens, particularly of the clergy, are

* *Would it not answer many valuable purposes, if the gentlemen, who are annually appointed to preach the election sermons, would furnish a sketch of the history of the state for the current year, to be published at the close of their sermons? Such*

are collected from every part of the state; and while they add dignity and solemnity to the important and joyful transactions of the day, serve to exterminate party spirit and to harmonize the civil and religious interests of the state.

Connecticut has been highly distinguished in having a succession of governors, eminent both for their religious and political accomplishments. With the following list of their venerable names, I shall conclude my account of Connecticut.

Colony of Connecticut.

Accessus.	Names.	Exitus.
1639	John Haynes,	1640
1640	Edward Hopkins,	1641
1641	John Haynes,	1642
1642	George Wyllis,	1643
1643	John Haynes,	1644
1644	Edward Hopkins,	1645
1645	John Haynes,	1646
1646	Edward Hopkins,	1647
1647	John Haynes,	1648
1648	Edward Hopkins,	1649
1649	John Haynes,	1650
1650	Edward Hopkins,	1651
1651	John Haynes,	1652
1652	Edward Hopkins,	1653
1653	John Haynes,	1653 died.
1654	Edward Hopkins,	1655
1655	Thomas Wells,	1656
1656	John Webster,	1657

(Esquires.)

Colony of New Haven.

Accessus.	Names.	Exitus.
1639	Theop. Eaton,	1658 died*
1659	Fra. Newman,	1661 died.
1662	William Leet,	1665.

(Esquires.)

This year (1665) the colonies of New Haven and Connecticut united, and governor Winthrop was governor of both, and governor Leet deputy-governor.

1657 John

Such a sketch, which might easily be made, would render election sermons much more valuable. They would then be a very authentic depositum for future historians of the state, they would be more generally and more eagerly purchased and read—they would serve to disseminate important knowledge, that of the internal affairs of the state, which every citizen ought to know, and might, if judiciously executed, operate as a check upon party spirit, and upon ambitious and designing men.

---

* Governor Eaton was buried in New Haven. The following inscription is upon his tomb stone.

' EATON so meek, so fam'd, so wise, so just,
' The Phœnix of our world, here hides his dust.
' This name forget, New England never must.

† ' T' attend you, Sir, under these framed stones,
' Are come your honour'd Son,‡ and daughter Jones,
' On each hand to repose their weary bones.'

† These lines seem to have been added afterwards.
‡ The Governor's Son-in-law.

1657 John Winthrop,		1658
1658 Thomas Wells,		1659
1659 John Winthrop,		1676
1676 William Leet,		1680
1680 Robert Treat,		1696
1696 John Winthrop,		1707
1707 Gurdon Saltonstall,	Esquires.	1724
1724 John Talcott,		1741
1741 Jonathan Law,		1751
1751 Roger Woolcot,		1754
1754 Thomas Fitch,		1766
1766 William Pitkin,		1770
1770 Jonathan Trumbull,		1784
1784 Matthew Grifwold,		1785
1785 Samuel Huntington.		

NEW YORK.

SITUATION and EXTENT.

Length 350 miles } Between { 40° 40' and 45° North Latitude.
Breadth 300 } { 5° W. and 1° 30' East Longitude.

Boundaries.] BOUNDED southeastwardly, by the Atlantic ocean; east, by Connecticut, Massachusetts and Vermont; north, by the 45th degree of latitude, which divides it from Canada; northwestwardly, by the river Iroquois, or St. Lawrence, and the Lakes Ontario and Erie; southwest and south, by Pennsylvania and New Jersey. The whole state contains about 44,000 square miles, equal to 28,160,000 acres.

Rivers.] Hudson's river is one of the largest and finest rivers in the United States. It rises in the mountainous country between the Lakes Ontario and Champlain. Its length is about 250 miles. In its course southward, it approaches within a few miles of the Mohawks river, at Saucondauga. Thence it runs north and northeast towards Lake George, and is but six or eight miles from it. The course of the river thence to New York, where it empties into York bay, is very uniformly south, 12 or 15° west. From Albany to Lake George, is sixty-five miles. This distance, the river is navigable only for batteaux, and has two portages, occasioned by falls, of half a mile each. It was one of these falls that General Putnam so miraculously descended, in the year 1758, to the astonishment of the Indians who beheld him.*

The

---

* See Col. Humphrey's life of Gen. Putnam, P. 60.

The banks of Hudson's river, especially on the western side, are chiefly rocky cliffs. The passage through the Highlands, which is sixteen miles, affords a wild, romantic scene. In this narrow pass, on each side of which the mountains tower to a great height, the wind, if there be any, is collected and compressed, and blows continually as through a bellows. Vessels, in passing through it, are often obliged to lower their sails. The bed of this river, which is deep and smooth to an astonishing distance, through a hilly, rocky country, and even through ridges of some of the highest mountains in the United States, must undoubtedly have been produced by some mighty convulsion in nature. The tide flows a few miles above Albany, which is 160 miles from New York. It is navigable for sloops of 80 tons to Albany, and for ships, to Hudson. About 60 miles above New York the water becomes fresh. The river is stored with a variety of fish, which renders a summer passage to Albany, delightful and amusing to those who are fond of angling.

The advantages of this river for carrying on the fur trade with Canada, by means of the lakes, have already been mentioned. Its convenience for internal commerce are singularly great. The produce of the remotest farms is easily and speedily conveyed to a certain and profitable market, and at the lowest expence. In this respect, New York has greatly the advantage of Philadelphia. A great proportion of the produce of Pennsylvania is carried to market in waggons, over a great extent of country, some of which is rough; hence it is that Philadelphia is crouded with waggons, carts, horses and their drivers, to do the same business that is done in New York, where all the produce of the country is brought to market by water, with much less shew and parade. But Pennsylvania has other advantages, which will be mentioned in their proper place, to compensate for this natural defect. The increasing population of the fertile lands upon the northern branches of the Hudson, must annually increase the amazing wealth that is conveyed by its waters to New York.

The river St. Lawrence divides this state from Canada. It rises in Lake Ontario, runs northeastward—embosoms Montreal, which stands upon an island—passes by Quebec, and empties, by a broad mouth, into the bay of St. Lawrence. Among a variety of fish in this river are salmon. They are found as far up as the falls of Niagara, which they cannot pass.

Onondago river rises in the lake of the same name, runs westwardly into Lake Ontario at Oswego. It is boatable from its mouth, to the head of the lake, (except a fall which occasions a portage of twenty yards) thence batteaux go up Wood-creek almost to Fort Stanwix; whence there is a portage of a mile to Mohawks river. Toward the head waters of this river salmon are caught in great quantities.

Mohawks river rises to the northward of Fort Stanwix, and runs southwardly to the fort, then eastward 110 miles, into the Hudson. The produce that is conveyed down this river is landed at Skenectady, and is thence carried by land sixteen miles, over a barren, shrub plain, to Albany. Except a portage of about a mile, occasioned by the little falls, sixty miles above Skenectady, the river is passable for boats, from Skenectady, nearly or quite to its source. The Cohoez, in this river, are a great curiosity. They are about two miles from its entrance into the Hudson.

Hudson. The river is about 100 yards wide—the rock over which it pours as over a mill-dam, extends almost in a line from one side of the river to the other, and is about thirty feet perpendicular height. Including the descent above, the fall is as much as sixty or seventy feet. The rocks below, in some places, are worn many feet deep by the constant friction of the water. The view of this tremendous cataract is diminished by the height of the banks on each side of the river. About a mile below the falls, the river branches and forms a large island; but the two mouths may be seen at the same time from the opposite bank of the Hudson. The branches are fordable at low water, but are dangerous.

Delaware river rises in Lake Utstayantho, and takes its course southwest, until it crosses into Pennsylvania in latitude 42°. Thence southwardly, dividing New York from Pennsylvania, until it strikes the northwest corner of New Jersey, in latitude 41° 24′; and then passes off to sea, through Delaware bay, having New Jersey on the east side, and Pennsylvania and Delaware on the west.

Susquehannah river has its source in lake Otsego, from which it takes a southwest course. It crosses the line, which divides New York and Pennsylvania, three times, the last time near Tyoga point, where it receives Tyoga river. Batteaux pass to its source—thence to Mohawks river is but twenty miles.

Tyoga river rises in the Allegany mountains, in about latitude 42°, runs eastwardly, and empties in the Susquehannah at Tyoga point, in latitude 41° 57′. It is boatable about fifty miles.

Seneca river rises in the Seneca country, and runs eastwardly, and in its passage receives the waters of the Seneca and Cayoga lakes, (which lie north and south, ten or twelve miles apart, each is between thirty and forty miles in length, and about a mile in breadth) and empties into the Onondago river, a little above the falls. It is boatable from the lakes downwards.

Cheneffee river rises near the source of the Tyoga, and runs northwardly by the Cheneffee castle and flats, and empties into Lake Ontario eighty miles east of Niagara fort.

The northeast branch of the Allegany river, heads in the Allegany mountains, near the source of the Tyoga, and runs directly west until it is joined by a larger branch from the southward, which rises near the west branch of the Susquehannah. Their junction is on the line between Pennsylvania and New York. From this junction, the river pursues a northwest course, leaving a segment of the river of about fifty miles in length, in the state of New York, thence it proceeds in a circuitous southwest direction, until it crosses into Pennsylvania. From thence to its entrance into the Miffiffippi, it has already been described, (Page 45.)

There are few fish in the rivers, but in the brooks are plenty of trout; and in the Lakes, yellow perch, sunfish, salmon trout, catfish, and a variety of others.

From this account of the rivers, it is easy to conceive of the excellent advantages for conveying produce to market from every part of the state.

The settlements already made in this state, are chiefly upon two narrow oblongs, extending from the city of New York, east and north.

The

The one eaft, is Long Ifland, which is 140 miles long, and narrow, and furrounded by the fea. The one extending north is about forty miles in breadth, and bifected by the Hudfon. And fuch is the interfection of the whole ftate, by the branches of the Hudfon, the Delaware, the Sufquehannah, and other rivers which have been mentioned, that there are few places, throughout its whole extent, that are more than fifteen or twenty miles from fome boatable or navigable ftream.

Bays and Lakes.] York bay, which is nine miles long and four broad, fpreads to the fouthward before the city of New York. It is formed by the confluence of the Eaft and Hudfon's rivers, and embofoms feveral fmall iflands, of which Governor's ifland is the principal. It communicates with the ocean through the *Narrows*, between Staten and Long Iflands, which are fcarcely two miles wide. The paffage up to New York, from Sandy Hook, the point of land that extends fartheft into the fea, is fafe, and not above twenty miles in length. The common navigation is between the eaft and weft banks, in about twenty-two feet water. There is a light houfe at Sandy Hook, on Jerfey fhore.

South Bay, is the fouthern branch or head of Lake Champlain. It commences at the falls of a creek, which is navigable feveral miles into the country, and forms moft excellent meadows. From the falls to Ticonderoga, is thirty miles. The bay is generally half a mile wide near the head, but in feveral places below, a mile. Its banks are fteep hills or cliffs of rocks, generally inacceffable. At Ticonderoga, this bay unites with Lake George, which comes from the fouthweft, towards the Hudfon, and is about thirty-five miles long, and one mile broad. After their union, they are contracted to a fmall breadth, between Ticonderoga, on the weft, and Mount Independence, on the eaft. They then open into Lake Champlain before defcribed.

Oneida Lake lies about twenty miles weft of Fort Stanwix, and extends weftward about 25 miles.

Salt Lake is fmall, and empties into Seneca river, foon after its junction with the Onondago river. This lake is ftrongly impregnated with faline particles, which circumftance gave rife to its name. The Indians make their falt from it.

Lake Otfego, at the head of Sufquehannah river is about nine miles long, and narrow.

Caniaderago Lake is nearly as large as Lake Otfego, and fix miles weft of it. A ftream, by the name, of Oaks Creek, iffues from it, and falls into the Sufquehannah river, about five miles below Otfego. The beft cheefe in the ftate of New York is made upon this creek.

Chatoque Lake is the fource of Conawongo river, which empties into the Allegany. The lower end of it, whence the river proceeds, is in latitude 42° 10′ from thence to its head, is about twenty-five miles. From the northweft part of this lake to Lake Erie, is nine miles, and was once a communication ufed by the French.

On the north fide of the mountains, in Orange county, is a very valuable tract called the *Drowned Lands*, containing about 40 or 50,000 acres. The waters, which defcend from the furrounding hills, being but flowly difcharged by the river iffuing from it, cover thefe vaft meadows every winter, and render them extremely fertile; but they expofe the inhabitants

tants in the vicinity to intermittents. The Wallkill river, which passes through this extensive *amphibious* tract, and empties into Hudson's river, is, in the spring, stored with very large eels in great plenty. The bottom of this river is a broken rock ; and it is supposed, that for £. 2000, the channel might be deepened so as to let off all the waters from the meadows, and thereby redeem from the floods a large tract of rich land, for grafs, hemp, and indian corn.

Face of the country, Soil and Productions.] The state, to speak generally, is intersected by ridges of mountains running in a northeast and southwest direction. Beyond the Allegany mountains, however, the country is a dead level, of a fine, rich soil, covered in its natural state, with maple, beach, birch, cherry, black walnut, locust, hickory, and some mulberry trees. On the banks of Lake Erie, are a few chesnut and oak ridges. Hemlock swamps are interspersed thinly through the country. All the creeks that empty into Lake Erie, have falls, which afford many excellent mill seats.

East of the Allegany mountains, the country is broken into hills with rich intervening vallies. The hills are clothed thick with timber, and when cleared afford fine pasture—the vallies, when cultivated, produce, wheat, hemp, flax, peas, grafs, oats, indian corn.

Besides the trees already mentioned, there are, in various parts of the state, the several kinds of oak, such as white, red, yellow, black and chesnut oak ; white, yellow, spruce and pitch pines ; cedar, balsam, or fir tree, butternut, aspin, commonly called poplar, white wood, which in Pennsylvania is called poplar, and in Europe the tulip tree, sugar and rock maple, the linden tree, which, with the whitewood, grows on the low rich ground. the buttonwood or sycamore, shrub cranberry, the fruit of which hangs in clusters like grapes as large as cherries ; this shrub too grows on low ground. Besides these is the sumach which bears clusters of red berries ; the Indians chew the leaves instead of tobacco ; the berries are used in dyes. Of the commodities produced from culture, wheat is the staple, of which immense quantities are raised, and exported. Indian corn and peas are likewise raised for exportation ; and rye, oats, barley, &c. for home consumption.

In some parts of the state large dairies are kept which furnish for the market butter and cheese. The best lands in this state, which lie along the Mohawks river, and west of the Allegany mountains, are yet in a state of nature, or are just beginning to be settled.

Civil Divisions, Population, Character, &c.] This state, agreeably to an act of their legislature, passed in March 1788, is divided into sixteen counties ; which, by another act passed at the same time, were divided into townships, as in the following table.

TABLE

NEW YORK.

TABLE.

Counties.	Chief Towns.	Total No. of Inhabit'ts.	Blacks.	Apportionment of a tax of £. 24,000	Number of townships.
NEW YORK.	New York, City.	23,614	2103	£. 6,100	‡
Albany,	Albany,	72,360	4690	2950	15
Suffolk,	East Hampton, Huntington,	13,793	1068	2000	8
Queens,	Jamaica,	13,084	2183	2000	6
Kings,	Flatbush, Brooklyn,	3,986	1317	900	6
Richmond,	Richmond,	3,152	693	450	4
West Chester,	Bedford, Whiteplains,	20,554	1250	1700	21
Orange,	Goshen, Orange,	14,062	858	1200	6
Ulster,	Kingston,	22,143	2662	1700	13
Dutchefs,	Poughkeepsie,	32,636	1645	2550	12
*Columbia,	Hudson, Kinderhook,			1250	7
Washington,	Salem,	4,456	15	400	9
*Clinton,	Plattsburgh,				4
Montgomery,	Johnstown,	15,657	405	800	9
†Cumberland,					
†Gloucester.					
Total sixteen.		238,897	18,889	£. 24,000	120

* *These two counties were not constituted in 1786, when the above enumeration was made, and were included in some of the other counties.*
† *These Counties are claimed by New York, but are within the limits and under the jurisdictions of Vermont.*
‡ *Not mentioned in the act.*

In

NEW YORK.

In the above mentioned acts the limits of the counties and townships are defined. These townships are corporations invested with certain privileges. The act directs, that the freeholders in the several townships shall assemble in town meetings, on the first Tuesday in April annually, and choose their town officers, viz. one supervisor, one town clerk, from three to seven assessors, one or more collectors, two overseers of the poor, commissioners of highways, constables, fence viewers, pound-matters, &c. These are to hold their respective offices one year, or until others be chosen. This act, which appears to have originated from a spirit of pure republicanism, is to be in force after the first day of April 1789. I cannot but notice, with pleasure, the happy tendency of this act, to disseminate through the state such information and such principles as are calculated to cherish the spirit of freedom, and to support our republican government. The frequent collection of people in town-meetings makes them acquainted with each other, and assimilates their ideas and their manners: Their being invested with power, makes them feel their importance, and rouses their ambition—Their town-meetings will be a school, in which all the free citizens of the state may learn how to transact public business with propriety, and in which they may qualify themselves for the higher offices of the state.—The number of public offices will be increased, without increasing the expences of the state; and as the desire of promotion is innate in human nature, and as ambition to possess the requisite qualifications commonly accompanies this desire, the probability is, that the number of persons qualified for public office will be increased, and of course the number of good citizens proportionably multiplied, and the subordinate civil affairs of the state more faithfully and more regularly transacted.

The number of Inhabitants in this state, in 1786, was 238,897; of which 18,889 were negroes. In 1756, there were 83,233 whites, and 13,542 blacks, 96,775 in the whole. In 1771, there were 148,124 whites, and 19,883 blacks, total 168,007. The blacks, since this enumeration, have decreased 1000, which is a happy circumstance. From the humane exertions that are making, in this state, for their emancipation, it is probable that they will continue to decrease. From the above enumerations it appears, that the average increase of inhabitants, from 1756 to 1786, has been 4554. A considerable part of these, however, have immigrated from Europe and the New England states. These immigrations have been very numerous, particularly from Rhode Island, Connecticut and Massachusetts, since the peace of 1783.

The population for every square mile, including the whole state, is only five, so that this state is but a ninth part as populous as Connecticut. But it is to be considered that Connecticut has no waste lands, and not half the state of New York is settled. The state of Connecticut, however, throughout is at least three times as thickly populated as the settled parts of New York. For if we suppose only one third of the state settled, the population for every square mile will then be only sixteen. From these calculations, one of these conclusions will follow, either first, That the soil of Connecticut is preferable to that of New York; or secondly, That the settled parts of New York would support a number of inhabitants treble to their present number; or, thirdly, That the people in Connecticut are better farmers and œconomists, or are less affluent and live poorer than the people of New York. The reader is left to adopt which of these conclusions he pleases.

Previous to the year 1756, Mr. Smith, the historian of New York, observes, that the colony met with many discouragements in regard to its settlement. 'The French and Indian irruptions,' said he, ' to which we have always been exposed, have driven many families into New Jersey. At home, the British acts for the transportation of felons, have brought all the American colonies into discredit with the industrious and honest poor, both in the kingdoms of Great Britain and Ireland.'—' The bigotry and tyranny of some of our governors, together with the great extent of their grants, may also be considered among the discouragements against the full settlement of this province. Most of these gentlemen, coming over with no other view than to raise their own fortunes, issued extravagant patents, charged with small quit-rents, to such as were able to serve them in the assembly ; and these patentees, being generally men of estates, have rated their lands so exorbitantly high, that very few poor persons could either purchase or lease them. Add to all these, that the New England planters have always been disaffected to the Dutch ; nor was there, after the surrender, any foreign accession from the Netherlands.'* Such were the discouragements which this state had to encounter, in regard to its settlement, so long as it remained a British province. But the revolution has removed most of these obstructions, and produced essential alterations in favor of this state. The few Indians who remain are, in general, friendly. Cargoes of thieves, burglars, pick-pockets, cut-purses and other villains and flagitious banditti, from Great Britain, who had forfeited their lives to society, are not now forced upon this or any of the other states, as they were before the revolution. They have no royal governors, independent of the people, to tyranize over, and oppress their subjects ; and to enrich themselves and their particular friends at the expence of the essential interests of the state. The overgrown estates, which have heretofore proved an effectual bar to population, and are opposed to every principle of democracy, are diminishing, or are put upon such a footing as in some measure to prevent these inconveniencies. The unhappy spirit of disaffection and jealousy, which formerly subsisted, in a high degree between the province of New York, and the New England colonies, has, since the revolution, in a great measure subsided, and would perhaps have now been extinct, had it not been unfortunately revived, of late, by some political and commercial differences. But the growing liberality of both parties, and a wise and harmonizing government, will, it is hoped, soon rise superior to all local prejudices, compose all differences, whether they are of a political, commercial or national kind, and form the whole into one band of affectionate BROTHERS.

The effects of the revolution have been as greatly, and as happily felt by this, as by any of the United States. The accession of inhabitants within a few years, has been great, and so long as New York is the seat of the general government, will continue to increase. The new settlements that are forming in the northern and western parts of the state, are principally by people from New England. It is remarkable that the Dutch
enterprize

---

* Smith's Hist. New York, P. 207. 210.

enterprize few or no settlements. Among all the new townships that have been settled since the peace, (and they have been astonishingly numerous) it is not known that one has been settled by the Dutch. Although they are as 'intent upon gain' as other people, they had rather rest secure of what they possess, than hazard all or even a part, in uncertain attempts to increase it.

The English language is generally spoken throughout the state, but is not a little corrupted by the Dutch dialect, which is still spoken in some counties. But as Dutch schools are almost, if not wholly discontinued, that language, in a few generations, will probably cease to be used at all. And the increase of English schools has already had a perceptible effect in the improvement of the English language.

The manners of the people differ as well as their language. The ancestors of the inhabitants in the southern and middle parts of Long Island, were either natives of England, or the immediate descendents of the first settlers of New England, and their manners and customs are similar to those of their ancestors. The counties inhabited by the Dutch, have adopted the English manners in a great degree, but still retain many modes, particularly in their religion, which are peculiar to the Hollanders. They are industrious, neat and œconomical in the management of their farms and their families. Whatever business they pursue, they generally follow the old track of their forefathers, and seldom invent any new improvements in agriculture, manufactures or mechanics. They were the first settlers of this state, and were particularly friendly to the English colony that settled at Plymouth in New England, in 1620; and continued to be amicably disposed towards the English colonies east of them, until the unhappy dispute arose concerning the lands on Connecticut river.

A celebrated traveller* through this state, some years since, has given the following account of the Dutch; 'They are every where well known for their avarice and selfishness. They are unhospitable, and never disposed to oblige beyond a prospect of interest.' A commentator on this passage remarks 'Such inward feelings (if it be true that they exist) we may well suppose would produce disagreeable consequences, when united with the natural effects of their situation in a conquered country; for the prejudice arising from this circumstance still remains, though the event long since took place. As the New England people were operative in producing this event, their first and greatest malice is against them; while the difference in their natural dispositions, and the peculiarities in the manners and customs of both parties, render them obnoxious each to the other, and afford an infinite fund to a genius for the malevolent burlesque.

The design of the Dutch in coming to this country was not to improve their minds, nor to erect public seminaries of science, but to increase their fortunes. Thus did their darling passion, and the unhappy circumstance of their situation, debar them from eminence, or even progress in the field of science. A want of schools and seminaries furnished with able instructors of their own nation—their unacquaintedness with the English language, and their national pride, have all conspired to keep them

in

* Kalm.

in their native ignorance of every mental improvement. This will account for many unfavourable peculiarities in their manners and customs.'

'It is not to be doubted,' continues this writer, 'that there are many bright geniuses among them, who, through the difficulties of obtaining an education, have remained unpolished and unimproved. There are many, indeed, who, by their assiduous application, surmount every obstacle, burst through the cloud that overshadows them, and shine with distinguished lustre in the first offices of church and state; and their lustre is brightened by being contrasted with the total darkness in which others are involved; for to be sure, from the causes already assigned, no people are so ignorant as the lower class.

Another cause of their unsociability and apparent reserve in encourageing and associating with strangers, is their want of enterprize. Their neighbours, more enterprizing, immigrate and reap the fruit of those advantages which their local situation puts in their own power. This excites jealousy and rivalship. The balance of this rivalship they see is against them. The preservation of their interest and of their dignity, calls them to unite in opposing their rivals. But it is evident that their union and friendship, in this regard, have too often their prime source in interest, are continued through interest, and have interest for their ultimate object. The intended effect of this union, is in a great measure lost, through the natural jealousies and clashing interests of heads of families and their parties; for although they are all combined by the general bond of national prejudice and national customs, and national religion, they are split into numerous and warm parties. And among them, he who has the greatest interest and the strongest party, not he who has the most merit, is the greatest man, the most honourable man, and the best qualified for public office. In their meetings, they are ever led to think and say the worst of their opponents, and recal all the little circumstances of burlesque, malice, or mistake in them, which persons of more liberal sentiments would wish charitably to veil and bury in oblivion. Thus it is that the practice of slandering and injuring .ach others characters, becomes common, and furnishes a great part of their daily conversation; while that sweet and friendly intercourse, which mends the heart, and that dignified and sensible conversation which improves the mind, are almost wholly neglected.' Thus this commentator.

However true these observations may have been in regard to that part of the people with which this writer was more immediately acquainted, (and it is presumed he never meant to have them generally applied) they will admit only of a partial application to the Dutch inhabitants throughout the state; and even in this case it ought in justice to be observed, that the revolution and its consequences, have had a very perceptible influence in diffusing a spirit of liberality among them, and in dispelling the clouds of ignorance and national prejudice. Schools, academies and colleges are established and establishing for the education of their children, in the English and learned languages, and in the arts and sciences, and a literary and scientific spirit is evidently increasing. If such are the buddings of improvement in the dawn of our empire, what a rich harvest may we expect in its meridian. The

NEW YORK.

The city of New York is inhabited principally by merchants, mechanics, shop-keepers and tradesmen, composed of almost all nations and religions. They are generally respectable in their several professions, and sustain the reputation of honest, punctual, fair dealers.

The manners and character of the inhabitants of every colony or state, will take their colouring, in a greater or less degree, from the peculiar manners of the first settlers. It is much more natural for immigrants to a settlement to adopt the customs of the original inhabitants, than the contrary, even though the immigrants should, in a length of time, become the most numerous. Hence it is that the neatness, parsimony and industry of the Dutch were early immitated by the first English settlers in the province, and, until the revolution, formed a distinguishing trait in their provincial character. It is still discernible, though in a much less degree, and will probably continue visible many years to come.

Besides the Dutch and English already mentioned, there are in this state many immigrants from Scotland, Ireland, Germany, and some few from France. The principal part of these are settled in the city of New York; and retain the manners, the religion, and some of them, the language of their respective countries.

Chief Towns.] There are three incorporated cities in this state; New York, Albany and Hudson. New York is the capital of the state, and, so long as it continues to be the seat of the general government, must be considered as the capital of the United States.

This city stands on the southwest point of an island, at the confluence of the Hudson and East River. The principal part of the city lies on the east side of the island, although the buildings extend from one river to the other. The length of the city on East River is about two miles; but falls much short of that distance on the banks of the Hudson. Its breadth on an average, is nearly three-fourths of a mile: and its circumference may be four miles. The plan of the city is not perfectly regular, but is laid out with reference to the situation of the ground. The principal streets run nearly parallel with the rivers. These are intersected, though not at right angles, by streets running from river to river. In the width of the streets there is a great diversity. Water-street and Queen-street, which occupy the banks of East River, are very conveniently situated for business, but they are low and too narrow; not admitting, in some places, of walks on the sides for foot passengers. Broad-street, extending from the Exchange to City-hall, is sufficiently wide. This was originally built on each side of the creek, which penetrated almost to the City-hall. This street is low, but pleasant; and that part which did not suffer by the fire during the war, is generally well built; the other is recovering from its ruins.

But the most convenient and agreeable part of the city is Broadway. This street runs upon the height of land between the two rivers, beginning at the fort near the south end of the city and extending to the Hospital, in front of which it opens into an extensive plain or common. This street is wide, and elevated so as to command a delightful prospect of the town, and the Hudson.

Wall-street is generally wide and elevated, and the buildings elegant. Hanover-square and Dock-street are conveniently situated for business,
and

and the houses well built. William-street is also elevated and convenient, and is the principal market for retailing of dry goods. Many of the other streets are pleasant, but most of them are irregular and narrow.

The houses are generally built of brick, and the roofs tiled. There are remaining a few houses built after the old Dutch manner; but the English taste has prevailed, almost a century.

Upon the southwest point of the land stands the fort, which is a square with four bastions; within the walls of which the governors used formerly to reside. Below the fort, near the water, there is a line of fortifications of considerable extent, designed to command the entrance into both rivers. But it is questionable, whether any number of cannon would prevent ships from passing with a favourable wind and tide; and indeed whether New York is capable of defence *by land* against a powerful marine force. The battery however, in the summer season, furnishes the citizens with an agreeable walk, which is open to refreshing breezes from the bay.

The City-hall is a brick building, more strong than elegant. It is three stories in height, with wings at each end, and fronts Broad-street, which affords an extensive prospect. The first floor is an open walk, except two small apartments for the door-keeper and city watch. In the second story of the eastern wing, is the assembly chamber, now occupied by Congress, and adorned with the following paintings: The portrait of the great Columbus, belonging to the assembly of this state; a painting valuable only for its antiquity and the character of the man—The likenesses of the King and Queen of France, as large as the life, executed in a masterly manner, and presented to Congress by his Most Christian Majesty; equally valuable for the richness of the paintings, the dignity of the personages whom they represent, and as pledges of royal friendship—The likeness of General Washington, presented by a gentleman in England; a likeness dear to every American, and destined to grace the walls of every council chamber in the New World.

The western wing contains a room for the council or senate, now occupied by the secretary of Congress, and another for the Mayor's court. In the body of the house is a spacious hall for the supreme judicial court. Large additions are now making to this building for the accommodation of Congress, under the direction of the ingenious Mon. Le Enfant.

There are three houses of public worship belonging to the reformed Protestant Dutch Church, one is called the Old Dutch Church which was built in the year 1693, and rebuilt in the year 1766; another is called the North Church, which was founded in the year 1767, and dedicated to the service of God in the year 1769. This last church being ruined by the British during the late war, was repaired in the year 1784, and has since been used with the old church for the performance of divine service. The middle church, generally called the New Dutch Church, was built in the year 1729; it is the most spacious of the three, but was also ruined in the war, and is not yet fully repaired.

The people of this denomination were the first settlers of this state, and make a respectable part of the citizens. The church in the city is considered as one church or congregation, though worshipping in different places. The charter, or act of incorporation, was granted by William

the

the Third, in the year 1696, when Benjamin Fletcher, Efq; was governor of the province. The minifters, elders and deacons, are the body corporate, and hold confiderable property. Many years before the war, they found it neceffary, by reafon of the decline of the Dutch language, to have fervice performed in Englifh, and had then two Dutch and two Englifh minifters. Since the war it has been performed chiefly in Englifh, and they have at prefent only two minifters.

There are four Prefbyterian churches in the city of New York. The firft was erected in the year 1719, built of ftone, and rebuilt and enlarged in the year 1748—it is eighty feet long and fixty wide, with a cupola and bell; and ftands in the upper end of Wall-ftreet, the north fide of the ftreet, near the Broadway. The fecond was erected in the year 1767, is a genteel brick building, eighty-three feet long, and fixty-five feet wide, with a fteeple not finifhed; it ftands on the eaft fide of the green, at the head of Beekman and Naffau-ftreets.

The congregations worfhipping in thefe churches are connected with each other, under the care of the fame minifters, who preach alternately in them, and having the fame elders and deacons; their temporalities alfo are managed by the fame truftees, incorporated under the law of the ftate, paffed in April 1784, capacitating religious focieties of every denomination to incorporate themfelves, for the purpofes therein mentioned.

The third Prefbyterian Church was erected in the year 1768, is a genteel ftone building, fixty-five and an half feet long, and fifty-five and an half feet wide, and ftands in Little-Queen-ftreet, not far from the Broadway. This church is alfo incorporated agreeably to the fame law.

Thefe three churches were occupied by the Britifh troops during the late war, as hofpitals and barracks, and were left by them in a moft ruinous fituation—and have been repaired with great neatnefs, and at a very great expence, by their refpective congregations, fince the peace.

The fourth Prefbyterian Church was erected in the year 1787, is a neat frame building, fifty feet long and twenty-four wide, and ftands in Naffau-ftreet.

The clergy of the Prefbyterian Churches in this city are maintained by the revenues arifing from the rents of their pews.

There are three Epifcopal Churches in New York, under one charter, which was granted the 6th of May, 1697. Trinity church was built in the year 1696, and at feveral times afterwards improved and enlarged. It was fituated on the weft fide of Broadway, in view of the Hudfon, with a fpacious cemetary on each fide; including the tower and chancel, it was about 148 feet in length and 72 in breadth—and the fteeple 173 feet in height. This was fuppofed to be the moft ftately building of the kind in America, but was deftroyed in the fire which happened juft after the Britifh troops entered the city in 1776. It is now rebuilding; and feveral thoufand pounds have already been fubfcribed for that purpofe.

St. George's Chapel, in Beekman-ftreet, was finifhed in 1750. This is a neat building, formed with hewn ftone, and the roof tiled.

St. Paul's Chapel, in Broadway, was completed in 1766. This building, which is in itfelf elegant, is embellifhed with a fuperb monument, erected, by order of Congrefs and at the expence of the United States, to the memory of the brave General Montgomery, who fell in the attack of Quebec, December 31, 1775.

To the foregoing may be added the following churches:

German, Lutheran and Calvinists,	2	Moravians,	1
Roman Catholic,	1	Methodists,	1
Friends Meeting,	1	Jews Synagogue,	1
Baptists,	2	French Protestant Church, (out of repair)	1

The government of the city (which was incorporated in 1696) is now in the hands of a Mayor, Aldermen and Common Council. The city is divided into seven wards, in each of which there is chosen annually by the people an Alderman and an assistant, who, together with the Mayor and Recorder, form the Common Council. The Mayor and Recorder are appointed annually by the council of appointment.

The Mayor's court, which is held from time to time by adjournment, is in high reputation, as a court of law.

A court of sessions is likewise held for the trial of criminal causes.

The situation of the city is both healthy and pleasant. Surrounded on all sides by water, it is refreshed with cool breezes in summer, and the air in winter is more temperate than in other places under the same parallel. York island is fifteen miles in length, and hardly one in breadth. It is joined to the main by a bridge called *King's bridge*. The channels between Long and Staten Islands, and between Long and York Islands are so narrow as to occasion an unusual rapidity of the tides, which is increased by the confluence of the waters of the Hudson and East River. This rapidity in general prevents the obstruction of the channel by ice—so that the navigation is clear, except for a few days in seasons when the weather is uncommonly severe. There is no bason or bay for the reception of ships; but the road where they lie in East river, is defended from the violence of the sea by the islands which interlock with each other; so that except that of Rhode Island, the harbour of New York, which admits ships of any burthen, is the best in the United States.

This city is esteemed the most eligible situation for commerce in the United States. It almost necessarily commands the trade of one half New Jersey, most of that of Connecticut, and part of that of Massachusetts; besides the whole fertile interior country, which is penetrated by one of the largest rivers in America. This city imports most of the goods consumed between a line of thirty miles east of Connecticut river, and twenty miles west of the Hudson, which is 130 miles, and between the ocean and the confines of Canada, about 250 miles; a considerable portion of which is the best peopled of any part of the United States, and the whole territory contains at least half a million people, or one sixth of the inhabitants of the union. Besides, some of the other states are partially supplied with goods from New York. But in the staple commodity flour, Pennsylvania and Maryland have rivalled it—the superfine flour of those states commanding a higher price than that of New York.

In the manufacture likewise of iron, paper, cabinet works, &c. Pennsylvania exceeds not only New York, but all her sister states. In times of peace, however, New York will command more commercial business than any town in the United States. In time of war it will be insecure,

# NEW YORK.							257

insecure, without a marine force; but a small number of ships will be able to defend it from the most formidable attacks by sea.

A want of good water is a great inconvenience to the citizens; there being few wells in the city. Most of the people are supplied every day with fresh water, conveyed to their doors in casks, from a pump near the head of Queen-street, which receives it from a pond, almost a mile from the city. Several proposals have been made by individuals to supply the citizens by pipes; but none have yet been accepted.

New York is the gayest place in America. The ladies, in the richness and brilliancy of their dress, are not equalled in any city in the United States; not even in Charleston, (S.C.) which has heretofore been called the centre of the *Beau Monde*. The ladies, however, are not solely employed in attentions to dress. There are many who are studious to add to their brilliant external accomplishments, the more brilliant and lasting accomplishments of the mind. Nor have they been unsuccessful; for New York can boast of great numbers of refined taste, whose minds are highly improved, and whose conversation is as inviting as their personal charms. Tinctured with a Dutch education, they manage their families with good œconomy and singular neatness.

In point of sociability and hospitality, New York is hardly exceeded by any town in the United States. If, however, in regard to these agreeable characteristics, the preference must be given to any one place, it decidedly belongs to Charleston. Some travellers have, in these respects, given Boston and Newport the preference to New-York. Several causes have operated to diminish the sociability of the citizens of New-York—particularly the change of inhabitants, by immigrations from Europe—the loss of property during the ravages of the war—and the unfavourable state of business a great part of the time since the peace. These causes have operated equally unfavourably in some other parts of the union.

An enquirer, who would wish to acquaint himself with the true state of the people of New York, their manners, and government, would naturally ask the citizens for their societies for the encouragement of sciences, arts, manufactures, &c? For their public libraries? For the patrons of literature? Their well regulated academies? For their female academy for instructing young ladies in geography, history, belles lettres, &c.? Such enquiries might be made with propriety, but could not, at present, be answered satisfactorily.

On a general view of this city, as described thirty years ago, and in its present state, the comparison is flattering to the present age; particularly the improvements in taste, elegance of manners, and that easy unaffected civility and politeness which form the happiness of social intercourse.

It is found, by a memorandum in one of the old registers, that the number of inhabitants in the city, taken by order of the King in the year 1697, was as follows:

Whites.	Men,	946
	Women,	1018
	Young men and boys,	864
	Young women and girls,	899
Negroes.	Men,	209
	Women,	205
	Boys and girls,	161
K k	Total,	4302

Num-

Number of inhabitants in the city and county of New York, in 1756, 10,881—1771, 21,863—1786, 23,614.*

The city of Albany is situated upon the west side of Hudson's river, 160 miles north of the city of New York, in latitude 42°, 36′, and is by charter† one mile upon the river, and 16 miles back. It contains about 600 houses, built mostly by trading people on the margin of the river. The houses stand chiefly upon Pearl, Market and Water streets, and six other streets or lanes which cross them nearly at right angles. They are built in the Old Dutch Gothic stile, with the gable end to the street, which custom the first settlers brought with them from Holland. The gable end is commonly of brick, with the heavy moulded ornament of slanting with notches, like stairs, and an iron horse, for a weather cock, on the top. There is one little appendage to their houses, which the people, blind to the inconveniences of it, still continue, and that is the water gutters or spouts which project from every house, rendering it almost dangerous to walk the streets in a rainy day. Their houses are seldom more than one story and an half high, and have but little convenience, and less elegance; but they are kept very neat, being rubbed with a mop almost every day, and scoured every week. The same neatness, however, is not observed in the streets, which are very muddy most of the year, except those which are paved; and these are seldom swept and very rough.

The city of Albany contains about 4000 inhabitants, collected from almost all parts of the northern world. As great a variety of languages are spoken in Albany, as in any town in the United States. Adventurers, in pursuit of wealth, are led here by the advantages for trade which this place affords. Situated on one of the finest rivers in the world, at the head of sloop navigation, surrounded with a rich and extensive back country, and the store-house of the trade to and from Canada, and the Lakes, it must flourish, and the inhabitants cannot but grow rich. Hudson, however, is their rival. Other rivals may spring up.

Albany is said to be an unsociable place. This is naturally to be expected. A heterogeneous collection of people, invested with all their national prejudices, eager in the pursuit of gain, and jealous of a rivalship, cannot expect to enjoy the pleasures of social intercourse or the sweets of an intimate and refined friendship.

A gentleman of observation and discernment, who resided some time in Albany, has made the following observations, which, though of general application, I beg leave to introduce under this particular head, " To form a just idea of the manners and customs of the inhabitants, we must confine ourselves to the Dutch, who being much the most numerous, give the *tone* to the manners of the place. Two things unite more particularly to render these disagreeable to foreigners; first, a natural prejudice which we all possess in favor of our own, and against the manners of an other place or nation : secondly, their close union, like the Jews of old, to prevent the innovation of foreigners, and to keep the balance of interest always in their own hands. It

* *This account of the city of New York is taken principally from* Mr. Webster's *valuable Magazine, for March* 1788.

† Albany was incorporated by Col. Dongan, in 1686. *Smith.*

It is an unhappy circumstance when an infant nation adopt the vices, luxuries and manners of an old one; but this was in a great measure the case with the first settlers of Albany, most of whom were immediately from Amsterdam. Their diversions are walking and sitting in mead-houses, and in mixed companies they dance. They know nothing of the little plays and amusements common to small social circles. The gentlemen who are lively and gay, play at cards, billiards, chess, &c. others go to the tavern, mechanically, at 11 o'clock—stay until dinner, and return in the evening. It is not uncommon to see forty or fifty at these places of resort, at the same time; yet they seldom drink to intoxication, unless in company, or on public occasions, when it is thought to be no disgrace.

They seldom admit many spectators to their marriages; but the day after, the groom prepares a cold collation, with punch, wine, &c. to partake of which, he expects all his friends will come, at 11 o'clock, without any invitation. A dictator, with absolute power, is then appointed to preside at each table, or in each room, and it seldom happens that any are suffered to leave the house, until the whole circle exhibits a shocking specimen of human depravity.

Their funeral ceremonies are equally singular. None attend them without a previous invitation. At the appointed hour, they meet at the neighbouring houses or stoops, until the corps is brought out. Ten or twelve persons are appointed to take the bier all together, and are not relieved. The clerk then desires the gentlemen (for ladies never walk to the grave, nor even attend the funeral, unless of a near relation) to fall into the procession. They go to the grave, and return to the house of mourning in the same order. Here the tables are handsomely set and furnished with cold and spiced wine, tobacco and pipes, and candles, paper, &c. to light them. The conversation turns upon promiscuous subjects, however improper, and unsuitable to the solemnity of the occasion, and the house of mourning is soon converted into a house of feasting.

The best families live extremely well, enjoying all the conveniences and luxuries of life; but the poor have scarcely the necessaries for subsistence.

The ground covered by the city charter, is of a thin, poor soil. In the river before the city is a beautiful little island, which, were it properly cultivated, would afford a faint resemblance of Paradise.

The well-water in this city is extremely bad, scarcely drinkable by those who are not accustomed to it. Indeed all the water for cooking is brought from the river, and many families use it to drink. The water in the wells, if Kalm was well informed, is unwholsome, being full of little insects, resembling, except in size, those which we frequently see in stagnated rain water.

The public buildings are a Low Dutch church, one for Presbyterians, one for Germans or High Dutch, one for episcopalians—a hospital and the City-Hall.

The city of Hudson has had the most rapid growth of any place in America, if we except Baltimore, in Maryland. It is situated on the east side of Hudson's river, in latitude 42° 23' and is 130 miles north of New York; thirty miles south of Albany, and four miles west from old Claverack town. It is surrounded by an extensive and fertile back country, and in proportion to its size and population, carries on a large trade.

No

No longer ago than the autumn of 1783, Messrs. Seth and Thomas Jenkins, from Providence, in the state of Rhode-Island, having first reconnoitred all the way up the river, fixed on the unsettled spot where Hudson now stands, for a town. To this spot they found the river was navigable for vessels of any size. They purchased a tract of about a mile square, bordering on the river, with a large bay to the southward, and divided it into thirty parcels or shares. Other adventurers were admitted to proportions, and the town was laid out in squares, formed by spacious streets, crossing each other at right angles. Each square contains thirty lots, two deep, divided by a twenty feet alley; each lot is fifty feet in front and 120 feet in depth.

In the spring of 1784, several houses and stores were erected. The increase of the town from this period to the spring of 1786, two years only, was astonishingly rapid, and reflects great honour upon the enterprizing and persevering spirit of the original founders. In the space of time just mentioned, no less than 150 dwelling-houses, besides shops, barns, and other buildings, four ware houses, several wharves, spermaceti works, a covered rope-walk, and one of the best distilleries in America, were erected, and 1500 souls collected on a spot, which, three years before, was improved as a farm, and but two years before, began to be built. Its increase since has been equally rapid; a Printing-office has been established, and several public buildings have been erected, besides dwelling-houses, stores, &c. The inhabitants are plentifully and conveniently supplied with water brought to their cellars in wooden pipes, from a spring two miles from the town.

It stands on an eminence from which are extensive and delightful views, to the northwest, north, and round that way to the southeast, consisting of hills and vallies, variegated with woods and orchards, cornfields and meadows, with the river which is in most places a mile over, and may be seen a considerable distance to the northward, forming a number of bays and creeks. From the southeast to the southwest, the city is screened with hills at different distances, and west, afar off over the river and a large valley, the prospect is bounded by a chain of stupendous mountains, called the Katts-kill, running to the west-north-west, which add magnificence and sublimity to the whole scene.

Upwards of twelve hundred sleighs entered the city daily, for several days together, in Frebruary, 1786, loaded with grain of various kinds; boards, shingles, staves, hoops, iron ware, stone for building, firewood, and sundry articles of provision for the market, from which some idea may be formed of the advantage of its situation, with respect to the country adjacent, which is every way extensive and fertile, particularly to the westward.

Poughkeepsie is the shire town of Dutchess county, and is situated upon the east side of Hudson's river, and north of Wappingers-kill or creek. It is a pleasant little town, and has frequently been the seat of the state government.

Lansinburgh, formerly called the New City, stands on the east side of the Hudson, just opposite the south branch of Mohawks river, and nine miles north of Albany. It is a very flourishing place, containing upwards of a 100 houses, pleasantly situated on a plain at the foot of a hill.

Kingston

Kingston is the county town of Ulster. Before it was burnt by the British, in 1777, it contained about 200 houses, regularly built on an elevated dry plain, at the mouth of a little pleasant stream, called Eusopus Kill or creek, that empties into the Hudson; but is nearly two miles west from the river. The town has been rebuilt.

Skenectady is sixteen miles northwest of Albany, in Albany county, situated on the banks of the Mohawks river. The town is compact and regular, built principally of brick, on a rich flat of low land, surrounded with hills. The windings of the river through the town, and the fields, which are often overflowed in the spring, afford a beautiful prospect about harvest time. As it is at the foot of navigation on a long river, which passes through a very fertile country, and is the medium of all the western trade through the lakes, that comes down the Hudson, it must grow rich in proportion as the country west of it populates.

Agriculture and Manufactures.] New York is at least half a century behind her neighbours in New England, New Jersey, and Pennsylvania, in point of improvement in agriculture and manufactures. Among other reasons for this deficiency that of want of enterprize in the inhabitants is not the least. Indeed their local advantages have been such as that they have grown rich without enterprize. Besides, lands have hitherto been cheap, and farms of course large, and it requires much less ingenuity to raise 1000 bushels of wheat upon 60 acres of land, than to raise the same quantity upon 30 acres. So long therefore as the farmer in New York can have 60 acres of land, to raise 1000 bushels of wheat, he will never trouble himself to find out how he can raise the same quantity upon half the land. It is population alone that stamps a value upon lands, and lays a foundation for high improvements in agriculture. When a man is obliged to maintain a family upon a small farm, his invention is exercised to find out every improvement that may render it more productive. This appears to be the great reason why the lands on Delaware and Connecticut rivers, produce to the farmer twice as much clear profit as lands in equal quantity and of the same quality upon the Hudson. If the preceeding observations be just, improvements will keep pace with population and the increasing value of lands. Another cause which has heretofore operated in preventing agricultural improvements in this state, has been their government, which, in the manner it was conducted until the revolution, was extremely unfavourable to improvements of almost every kind, and particularly in agriculture. The governors were many of them land-jobbers, bent on making their fortunes; and being invested with power to do this, they either engrossed for themselves, or patented away to their particular favorites a very great proportion of the whole province. This, as has been before observed, proved an effectual bar to population, and of course, according to our present hypothesis, has kept down the price of lands, and so prevented improvements in agriculture. It ought to be observed, in this connection, that these overgrown estates could be cultivated only by the hands of tenants, who, having no right in the soil, and no certain prospect of continuing upon the farm which they hold at the will of their landlord, had no motives to make those expensive improvements, which, though not immediately productive, would prove very profitable in some future period. The tenant, dependent

dent on his landlord for his annual support, confines his views and improvements to the present year; while the independent freeholder, secure of his estate for himself and his successors, carries his views into futurity, and early lays the foundation for growing improvement. But these obstacles have been removed, in a great measure, by the revolution. The fine fertile country of the Mohawks, in Montgomery county, which was formerly possessed by Sir William Johnson, and other land-jobbers, who were enemies to their country, has been forfeited to the state, and is now split up into freehold estates, and settling with astonishing rapidity.

The foregoing observations will in a great measure account for the great neglect of manufactural improvements. Smith, whom I have so often quoted; thirty years ago, observed, 'It is much owing to the disproportion between the number of our inhabitants, and the vast tracts still remaining to be settled, that we have not as yet, entered upon scarcely any other manufactures, than such as are indispensibly necessary for our home convenience.' This same cause has operated ever since, in the same way.

Great improvements in agriculture cannot be expected (unless they are made by a few individuals who have a particular genius for that business) so long as lands are plenty and cheap; and improvements in manufactures never precede, but invariably follow improvements in agriculture. These observations apply more particularly to the country. The city of New York contains a great number of people, who are employed in the various branches of manufactures. Among many other articles manufactured in this city are the following, wheel carriages of all kinds, loaf sugar, bread, beer, shoes and boots, sadlery, cabinet work, cutlery, hats, clocks, watches, potters ware, umbrellas, all kinds of mathematical and musical instruments, ships and every thing necessary for their equipment. A glass work and several iron works have been established in different parts of the country, but they never have been very productive, owing solely to the want of workmen, and the high price of labour, its necessary consequence; for the internal resources and advantages for these manufactories, such as ore, wood, water, hearth-stone, proper situations for bloomeries, forges and all kinds of water works, are immense. There are several paper mills in the state, which are worked to advantage.

Trade.] The situation of New York, with respect to foreign markets, has decidedly the preference to any of the states. It has at all seasons of the year, a short and easy access to the ocean. We have already mentioned that it commands the trade of a great proportion of the best settled, and best cultivated parts of the United States. It has been supposed, by gentlemen well informed, that more wealth is conveyed down Connecticut river, and through the Sound to New York, than down the Hudson. This is not improbable, as the banks of Connecticut are more fertile, and much thicker, and more extensively settled than the banks of the Hudson. New York has not been unmindful of her superior local advantages, but has availed herself of them to their full extent. Some of her commercial regulations have been viewed as oppressive and injurious

to

to the interests of her neighbours, and been productive of many heavy complaints and unhappy jealousies, which have proved unfriendly to that political union which ever ought to subsist between confederated sister states. But as it is expected that the new government will remedy these evils, a bare mention of them is sufficient.

There appears to be a secrecy in the commercial policy of this state. An accurate account of their annual exports and imports, if known at all, is known to few. All therefore that can be expected under this head, in addition to what has already been observed, is simply an enumeration of the several articles exported and imported, without pretending to fix their amount. Mr. Smith* observes, ' In our trafic with other places, the balance is almost constantly in our favour.' This I believe has generally been the case. Their exports to the West Indies are, biscuit, pease, Indian corn, apples, onions, boards, staves, horses, sheep, butter, cheese, pickled oysters, beef and pork. But wheat is the staple commodity of the state, of which no less than 677,700 bushels were exported in the year 1775, besides 2,555 tons of bread, and 2,828 tons of flour. Inspectors of flour are appointed to prevent impositions, and to see that none is exported but that which is deemed by them merchantable. West India goods are received in return for these articles. Besides the above mentioned articles, are exported flax-seed, cotton-wool, farsaparilla, coffee, indigo, rice, pig iron, bar iron, pot ash, pearl ash, furs, deer skins, log wood, fustic, mahogany, bees wax, oil, Madeira wine, rum, tar, pitch, turpentine, whale fins, fish, sugars, molasses, salt, tobacco, lard, &c. but most of these articles are imported for re-exportation. In the year 1774, there were employed, in the trade of this state, 1075 vessels, whose tonnage amounted to 40,812.

Mountains.] The long range of Allegany mountains commences with the Katts Kill mountain upon Hudson's river. This range, which Mr. Jefferson calls the *Spine* of the United States, spreads through this state, in a northeast and southwest direction, in several distinct ridges, with different names.

Medicinal Springs.] The most noted springs in this state are those of Saratoga. They are eight or nine in number, situated in the margin of a marsh, formed by a branch of Kayadarossora Creek, about twelve miles west from the confluence of Fish-Creek and Hudson's River. They are surrounded by a rock of a peculiar kind and nature, formed by the petrefaction of the water. One of them, however, more particularly attracts the attention; it rises above the surface of the earth five or six feet, in the form of a pyramid. The aperture in the top, which discovers the water, is perfectly cylindrical, of about nine inches diameter. In this the water is about twelve inches below the top, except at the time of its annual discharge, which is commonly in the beginning of summer. At all times it appears to be in as great agitation as if boiling in a pot, although it is extremely cold. The same appearances obtain in the other Springs, except that the surrounding rocks are of different figures, and the water flows regularly from them.

By

* Hist. New York. p. 213.

By obfervation and experiment, the principal impregnation of the water is found to be a foffile acid, which is predominant in the tafte. It is alfo ftrongly impregnated with a faline fubftance, which is very difcernible in the tafte of the water, and in the tafte and fmell of the petrified matter about it. From the corrofive and diffolving nature of the acid, the water acquires a chalybeate property, and receives into its compofition a portion of calcareous earth, which, when feparated, refembles an impure magnefia. As the different fprings have no effential variance in the nature of their waters, but the proportions of the chylabeate impregnation, it is rendered probable that they are derived from one common fource, but flow in feparate channels, where they have connection with metalic bodies, in greater or lefs proportions.

The prodigious quantity of air contained in this water, makes another diftinguifhing property of it. This air, ftriving for enlargement, produces the fermentation and violent action of the water before defcribed. After the water has ftood a fmall time in an open veffel (no tight one will contain it) the air efcapes, becomes vapid, and loofes all that life and pungency which diftinguifh it when firft taken from the pool. The particles of diffolved earth are depofited as the water flows off, which, with the combination of the falts and fixt air, concrete and form the rocks about the fprings.

The effects it produces upon the human body are various; the natural operation of it when taken, is cathartick, in fome inftances an emetick. As it is drank, it produces an agreeable fenfation in paffing over the organs of tafte, but as foon as it is fwallowed, there fucceeds an unpleafant tafte and the eructations which take place afterwards, caufe a pungency very fimilar to that produced by a draught of cider or beer, in a ftate of fermentation.

The following curious experiments made on thefe waters, were extracted from Dr. Mitchell's Journal.

‘A young turkey held a few inches above the water in the crater of the lower fpring, was thrown into convulfions in lefs than half a minute, and gafping fhewed figns of approaching death; but on removal from that place and expofure to the frefh air, revived, and became lively. On immerfion again for a minute in the gas, the bird was taken out languid and motionlefs.

A fmall dog put into the fame cavity, and made to breathe the contained air, was, in lefs than one minute, thrown into convulfive motions—made to pant for breath, and laftly to lofe entirely the power to cry or move; when taken out, he was too weak to ftand, but foon, in the common air, acquired ftrength enough to rife and ftagger away.

A trout recently caught, and brifkly fwimming in a pail of brook water, was carefully put into a veffel juft filled from the fpring; the fifh was inftantly agitated with violent convulfions, gradually loft the capacity to move and poife itfelf, grew ftupid and infenfible, and in a few minutes was dead.

A candle repeatedly lighted and let down near the furface of the water, was fuddenly extinguifhed, and not a veftige of light or fire remained on the wick.

These experiments nearly correspond with those usually made in Italy, at the famous GROTTO DEL CANI, for the entertainment of travellers; as mentioned by Keysler, Addison and others.

A bottle filled with the water and shaken, emits suddenly a large quantity of ærial matter, that either forces out the cork, or makes a way beside or through it, or bursts the vessel.

A quantity of wheaten flour, moistened with this water and kneaded into dough, when made into cakes and put into a baking-pan, rose, during the application of heat, into light and spungy bread, without the aid of yeast or leaven.

From which it appears, that the air extricated from the water is precisely similar to that produced by ordinary fermentation.

Some lime-water, made of abalactiles brought from the subterranean cave at Rhinebec, became immediately turbid on mixture with the spring water, but when the water had been lately drawn, the precipitate was quickly re-dissolved.

Some of the rock surrounding the spring, on being put into the fire, calcined to quick-lime, and slacked very well.

When the ærial matter has evaporated, the water loses its transparency and lets fall a calcarious sediment.

Whence it is true, that the gas is ærial acid, that the rock is lime-stone, and that by means of the former, the water becomes capable of dissolving and conveying the latter.'

Minerals and fossils.] This state embosoms vast quantities of iron ore. Naturalists have observed that ore in swamps and pondy ground, vegetates and increases. There is a silver mine at Phillipsburg, which produces virgin silver. Spar, zink or spelter, a semi metal, magnez, used in glazings, peritus, of a golden hue, various kinds of copper ore, and lead and coal mines are found in this state. Also petrified wood, plaster of Paris, ising-glass in sheets, talks and chrystals of various kinds and colors, asbestos, and several other fossils. A small black stone has also been found, which vitrifies with a small heat, and makes excellent glass.

Literary and Humane Societies.] There are very few societies for improvement in knowledge or humanity in this state; and these few are in the city of New York. The first is ' The society for promoting useful knowledge.' This society is upon an establishment similar to other philosophical societies in Europe and America, but is not incorporated. The members meet once a month. Secondly, ' The society for the manumission of slaves and protecting such of them as have been or may be liberated.' This society meets once a quarter. Both these societies consist of gentlemen of the first character in the city, and of some in other parts of the state. Besides these, there is the ' Philological society,' instituted in 1788. This growing society has for its principal object the improvement of the English language.

Literature, Colleges, Academies, &c.] Until the year 1754, there was no college in the province of New York. The state of literature, at that time, I shall give in the words of their historian, ' Our schools are in the lowest order ; the instructors want instruction, and through a long and shameful neglect of all the arts and sciences, our common speech is extremely corrupt, and the evidences of a bad taste, both as to thought and language, are visible in all our proceedings, public and private. This was undoubtedly a just representation at the time when it was written; and although much attention has since been paid to education in some populous towns, the observations are now but too justly applicable to the country at large. There are many flourishing Academies and grammar schools, lately established in the state ; but many parts of the country are either unfurnished with schools, or the schools which they have are kept by low ignorant men, and are worse than none ; for children had better remain in ignorance than be ill taught. But a great proportion of the United States are in the same situation in regard to schools.

Kings-College, in the city of New York, was principally founded by the voluntary contributions of the inhabitants of the province, assisted by the general assembly, and the corporation of Trinity church, in the year 1754, a royal charter being then obtained, incorporating a number of gentlemen therein mentioned, by the name of " The governors of the college of the province of New York, in the city of New York, in America :" and granting to them and their successors for ever, amongst various other rights and privileges, the power of conferring all such degrees, as are usually conferred by either of the English universities.

By the charter it was provided that the president shall always be a member of the church of England, and that a form of prayer collected from the liturgy of that church, with a particular prayer for the college, shall be daily used, morning and evening, in the college-chapel ; at the same time, no test of their religious persuasion was required from any of the fellows, professors or tutors ; and the advantages of education were equally extended to students of all denominations.

The building (which is only one third of the intended structure) consists of an elegant stone edifice, three complete stories high, with four stair cases, twelve apartments in each, a chapel, hall, library, museum, anatomical theatre and a school for experimental philosophy.

All students, but those in medicine, before the revolution, were obliged to lodge and diet in the college, unless they were particularly exempted by the governors or president ; and for the security of their morals, &c. the edifice was surrounded by an high fence, which also encloses a large court and garden ; and a porter used constantly to attend at the front gate, which was locked at 10 o'clock each evening in summer, and at 9 in winter ; after which hours, the names of all that come in were delivered weekly to the president.

The college is situated on a dry gravelly soil, about 150 yards from the bank of Hudson's river, which it overlooks ; commanding a most extensive and beautiful prospect.

Since the revolution the literature of the state has engaged the attention of the legislature. In one of their late sessions an act passed constituting twenty-one gentlemen (of whom the governor and lieutenant governor, for the time being, are members *ex officiis*) a body corporate and politic, by the name and stile of ' The regents of the university of the state of New York.' They are entrusted with the care of literature in general in the state, and have power to grant charters of incorporation for erecting colleges and academies throughout the state—are to visit these institutions as often as they shall think proper, and report their state to the legislature once a year. All degrees above that of master of arts are to be conferred by the regents.

Kings college, which we have already described, is now called COLUMBIA COLLEGE. This college, by an act of the legislature passed in the spring of 1787, was put under the care of twenty-four gentlemen, who are a body corporate, by the name and style of 'The trustees of Columbia college, in the city of New York.' This body possesses all the powers vested in the governors of Kings college, before the revolution, or in the regents of the university, since the revolution, so far as their power respected this institution, except the conferring of the higher degrees. No regent can be a trustee of any particular college or academy in the state.

The college edifice has received no additions since the peace. The funds produce, annually, about £1000. The library and museum were destroyed during the war. The philosophical apparatus cost about 300 guineas. Until the revolution the college did not flourish. The plan upon which it was originally founded, was contracted, and its situation unfavourable. The former objection is removed, but the latter must remain. It has between thirty and forty students, in four classes. The number for several years has been increasing. The officers of instruction and immediate government are, a president, professor of languages, professor of mathematics, professor of logic and rhetoric, professor of natural philosophy, professor of geography, and a professor of moral philosophy. There are many other professors belonging to the university, but their professorships are merely honorary.

There are several academies in the state. One is at Flatbush, in Kings county, on Long Island, four miles from Brooklyn-ferry. It is situated in a pleasant, healthy village. The building is large, handsome and convenient, and is called *Erasmus Hall*. The academy is flourishing under the care of a principal and other subordinate instructors. The trustees of this institution have been incorporated by the regents of the university.

There is a very flourishing academy at East Hampton, on the east end of Long Island; to which also the regents have given a charter of incorporation by the name of CLINTON ACADEMY.

There are other academies, or more properly grammar schools, in different parts of the state. There are several in the city of New York, furnished with able instructors; one at Kingston, in Ulster county; one at Goshen, in the county of Orange; two at Albany; one at Skenectady; one at Lansingburgh, and another at West Chester. None of these have yet applied for charters. Besides these, in many parts of the state, there are schools erected, which are maintained by the voluntary contributions of the parents. A spirit for literary improvement, is evidently diffusing its influence throughout the state.

Religion.] The constitution of this state provides for 'the free exercise and enjoyment of religious profession and worship, without discrimination or preference, within the state, for all mankind. Provided that the
liberty

liberty of confcience hereby granted, fhall not be fo conftrued as to excufe acts of licentioufnefs, or juftify practifes inconfiftent with the peace and fafety of the ftate.

The various religious denominations in this ftate, with the number of their refpective congregations are as follows.

Denominations.	No. Congreg'ns.	Denominations.	No. Congreg'ns.
Eng. Prefbyterian,	87	German Lutheran,	12
Dutch Reformed,	66	Moravians,	2
(Including fix of the German language.)		Methodifts,	1
		Roman Catholic,	1
Baptifts,	30	Jews,	1
Epifcopalians,	26	Shakers,	unknown.
Friends, or Quakers.	20		

The prefbyterian churches are governed by congregational, prefbyterial and fynodical affemblies. Thefe affemblies poffefs no civil jurifdiction. Their power is wholly moral or fpiritual, and that only minifterial and declarative. They poffefs the right of requiring obedience to the laws of Chrift, and of excluding the difobedient from the privileges of the church; and the powers requifite for obtaining evidence and inflicting cenfure; but the higheft punifhment, to which their authority extends, is to exclude the contumacious and impenitent from the congregation of believers.

The *church feffion*, which is the congregational affembly, confifts of the minifter or minifters and elders of a particular congregation. This body is invefted with the fpiritual government of the congregation.

A *prefbytery* confifts of all the minifters, and one ruling elder from each congregation, within a certain diftrict. Three minifters and three elders, conftitutionally convened, are competent to do bufinefs. This body have cognizance of all things that regard the welfare of the particular churches within their bounds, which are not cognizable by the feffion. Alfo, they have a power of receiving and iffuing appeals from the feffions —of examining and licenfing candidates for the miniftry—of ordaining fettling, removing, or judging minifters—of refolving queftions of doctrine or difcipline, and whatever elfe pertains to the fpiritual concerns of the churches under their care.

A *Synod* is a convention of feveral prefbyteries. The fynod have power to admit and judge of appeals, regularly brought up from the prefbyteries—to give their judgment on all references made to them, of an ecclefiaftical kind—to correct and regulate the proceedings of prefbyteries, &c.

The higheft judicatory of the prefbyterian church is ftiled *The general council of the prefbyterian church in the United States of America*. This grand council is to confift of an equal delegation of bifhops and elders from each prefbytery within their jurifdiction, by the title of *commiffioners to the general council*. Fourteen commiffioners make a quorum. The Council conftitute the bond of union, peace, correfpondence, and mutual confidence among all their churches; and have power to receive and iffue all appeals and references which may regularly be brought before them from the inferior judicatories—to regulate and correct the proceedings of the synods, &c.—Thus the whole presbyterian interest is judiciously combined, and governed.

The Synods of New York and Philadelphia, during their session at Philadelphia in May, 1788, resolved themselves into four synods, viz. The synod of New York; the synod of Philadelphia; the synod of Virginia, and the synod of Carolina. These synods are to meet annually in their respective states, whence they take their names; and once a year, by their commissioners, in general council, at Philadelphia.

There are a number of Presbyterian churches, commonly called *Seceders*, who have a separate ecclesiastical jurisdiction. These, as well as the other presbyterians, and the Dutch reformed churches, hold the doctrines of the gospel upon the Calvinistic plan, without any essential differences.

The Dutch reformed churches in this state, are divided into four classes; viz. The classis of New York, comprehending eighteen churches; the classis of Kingston, twenty-three churches; the classis of Albany, twenty-three churches; a part of the classis of Hackinsak, four churches. These classes, together with the classes of Hackinsak and New Brunswick, in New Jersey, compose the Dutch reformed synod of New York and New Jersey. The classes consist of ministers and ruling elders; each classis delegates two ministers and an elder to represent them in synod. From the first planting of the Dutch churches in New York and New Jersey, they have, under the direction of the classis of Amsterdam, been formed exactly upon the plan of the established church of Holland, as far as that is ecclesiastical. A strict correspondence is maintained between the Dutch reformed synod of New York and New Jersey, and the synod of North Holland, and the classis of Amsterdam. The acts of their synods are mutually exchanged every year, and mutual advice is given and received in disputes respecting doctrinal points and church discipline.

The principles and constitution of the Baptist churches have already been mentioned.

The Episcopalian churches hold the same principles—have the same mode of worship and church government—and are in every other respect constituted upon the same plan with the church of the same denomination in England.

For an account of the Friends, and the Moravians, see Pennsylvania.

The Methodist interest, though small in this state, has greatly increased in the southern states since the revolution. They have estimated their number at 37,800. But their numbers are so various in different places, at different times, that it would be a matter of no small difficulty to find out their exact amount. The late famous Mr. John Wesley has been called the Father of this religious sect. They warmly oppose the Calvinistic doctrines of election and final perseverance, and maintain that sinless perfection is attainable in this life. Their mode of preaching is entirely extemporaneous, very loud and animated, bordering on enthusiasm. They appear studiously to avoid connection in their discourses, and are fond of introducing pathetic stories, which are calculated to affect the tender passions. Their manner is very solemn, and their preaching is frequently attended with a surprizing effect upon their audiences. Their churches are supplied by their preachers in rotation.

NEW YORK.

The Shakers are a sect who sprung up in Europe. A part of them came over from England to New York in 1774, and being joined by others, they settled at Nisqueaunia, above Albany, whence they spread their doctrines and increased to a considerable number; but their interest is now fast declining. The late *Anna Leese*, whom they stiled the *Elect Lady*, was the head of this sect. Her followers asserted, that she was the woman spoken of in the twelfth chapter of the Revelation, and that she spoke seventy-two tongues:—And although these tongues were unintelligible to the living, she conversed with the dead who understood her language. They alledged also that she was the mother of all the *Elect* :—that she travailed for the whole world—that no blessing could descend to any person but only by and through her, and that in the way of her being possessed of their sins, by their confessing and repenting of them, one by one, according to her direction. The Elect Lady used to assert that she was immortal—that the day of judgment had commenced, and that she and her followers, were already set to judge the world. But her death has indisputably proved that she was not immortal as to her bodily presence; and this circumstance no doubt, has created suspicions in the minds of some of her followers respecting some other of her assertions and doctrines, and occasioned them to renounce the scheme.

Their worship, if such extravagant conduct may be so called, consists principally in dancing, singing, leaping, clapping their hands, falling on their knees, and uttering themselves in groans and sighs, in a sound resembling that of the roaring of water; turning round on their heels with astonishing swiftness, to shew, as they say, the power of God. All these gesticulations are performed in the most violent and boisterous manner; and occasion, at intervals, a shuddering not unlike that of a person in a strong fit of the ague. Hence they are called, not improperly, *Shakers*.

Before we leave this head, we must mention, that in April 1784, the legislature of this state passed an act enabling all religious denominations to appoint trustees, not less than three or more than nine, who shall be a body corporate, for the purpose of taking care of the temporalities of their respective congregations, and for the other purposes therein mentioned.

The Ministers of every denomination in the state, are supported by the voluntary contributions of the people, raised generally by subscription, or by a tax upon the pews; except the Dutch Churches in New York, Albany, Skenectady and Kingston, which have, except the two last, large estates confirmed by a charter. The Episcopal church also in New York possess a very large estate, in, and near the city.

Constitution and Courts of Justice.] The present constitution of the state was established by convention authorized for the purpose, April 20, 1777.

The supreme legislative powers of the state are vested in two branches, a *Senate* and *Assembly*. The members of the senate are elected by the freeholders of the state, who possess freehold estates to the value of £.100, clear of debts. For the purpose of electing senators, the state is divided into four great districts, each of which chooses a certain number, viz.

Southern District, including the counties of { New York, Suffolk, West Chester, Kings, Queens, Richmond, } } Nine Senators. Middle District { Dutchess, Ulster, Orange, } Six.

Western

Western District { Albany, Montgomery, } Six.   Eastern District { Washington, Cumberland, Gloucester, } Three.

The senators are divided by lot into four classes, six in each class, and numbered, first, second, third, and fourth. The seats of the first class are vacated at the expiration of one year—the second, at the expiration of the next, &c. and their places filled by new elections. Thus a small change is made in the senate every year; but three fourths of the members remaining, preserve a knowledge of the business of a former session. A majority of the senate is necessary to do business, and each branch of the legislature has a negative upon the other.

The legislature can at any time alter this division of the state for the choice of senators; and an increase of electors in any district, to the amount of one-twenty-fourth of the electors in the whole state, entitles the district to another senator. But the number of senators can never exceed one hundred.

The assembly of the state is composed of representatives from the several counties, chosen annually in May, in the following proportion:

For the city and county of New York, nine.
For the city and county of Albany, seven.

For Dutchess,	7	For Richmond,	2
West Chester,	6	Montgomery,	6
Ulster,	6	Washington,)	
Suffolk,	5	and Clinton,)	4
Queens,	4	Columbia,	3
Orange,	4	Cumberland,	3
Kings,	2	Gloucester,	2

By the constitution, however, it is ordered, that at the end of seven years after the termination of the late war, a census of the electors and inhabitants shall be taken, and the representation apportioned according to the number of electors in each county.

Every male inhabitant of full age, who has resided in the state six months preceding the day of election, and possessing a freehold to the value of twenty pounds, in the county where he is to give his vote; or has rented a tenement therein of the yearly value of forty shillings, and has been rated and actually paid taxes, is entitled to vote for representatives in assembly. The freedom of the cities of New York and Albany, likewise entitles a person to the privilege of voting for members of assembly in the city or county where he resides. The method of voting is now by ballot, but subject to alteration by the legislature. The house of assembly, a majority of which is necessary to proceed to business, chooses its own speaker, and is a judge of its own privileges.

In all debates on great questions, the house resolves itself into a committee of the whole—the speaker leaves the chair, and a chairman is appointed for the occasion. After the business is completed, the committee rises—the speaker takes the chair—and the chairman reports to the house the proceedings of the committee. How far this imitation of the British house of commons is supported by good reasons, it may not be easy to determine. Certain it is, that in other legislatures, the proceedings are equally well conducted without this formality.

The number of representatives is limited to three hundred. The present number is sixty-five.

The supreme executive power of the state is vested in a governor, (in whose absence a deputy governor is appointed to serve) chosen once in three years by the freemen of the state. The lieutenant governor is, by his office, president of the senate; and, upon an equal division of voices, has a casting vote; but has no voice on other occasions. The governor has not a seat in the legislature; but as a member of the council of revision and council of appointment, he has a vast influence in the state.

The council of revision is composed of the chancellor, the judges of the supreme court or any of them, and the governor. This council is empowered to revise all bills which have passed the two houses of the legislature, and if it shall appear to the council that such bills ought not to pass into laws, they shall be returned to the house in which they originated, with the objections of the council. The house shall then proceed to reconsider the bills, with the objections, and if, notwithstanding, two-thirds of the house shall agree to the bills, they shall be sent to the other house, where they shall be reconsidered and the assent of two-thirds of the members pass them into laws. But if a bill is not returned in ten days, it becomes a law of course.

The subordinate officers of the state are appointed by the *council of appointment*, which is composed of one senator from each district, to be chosen annually by the legislature, with the governor or in his absence, the lieutenant governor or the president of the senate, who has a casting vote only.

All military officers hold their commissions during pleasure. The chancellor, the judges of the supreme court and the first judge of each county court, hold their offices during good behaviour. The officers can hold no other office at the same time, except that of delegate to congress.

Sheriffs and coroners are appointed annually, and can serve but four years successively.

A court of errors and impeachment is instituted, composed of the president of the senate, the senate, chancellor and judges of the supreme court, or the major part of them, under the regulation of the legislature. The power of impeachment is vested in the house of representatives, and the members on trial must be sworn.

Besides the court of errors and impeachment, there is first, a *Court of Chancery*, consisting of a chancellor, appointed by the council of appointment, who holds his office during good behaviour, or until he arrive at the age of sixty years. Secondly, a *Supreme Court*, the judges of which are appointed in the same manner and for the same time as the chancellor. This is a circuit court.—Thirdly, *County Courts*, held in each county, the judges of which are appointed in the manner above mentioned, and the first judge holds his office during good behaviour. Besides these there are the justices' courts, court of probates, court of admiralty, court of exchequer, a court of oyer and terminer and general gaol delivery, and courts of quarter sessions.

The practice in the supreme court, to which an appeal lies from the courts below, is in imitation of the courts of common pleas and king's bench in England.

NEW YORK.

All free governments abound with lawyers. Where men have the privilege of thinking and acting for themselves, they will involve themselves in debt, and quarrel with their neighbours. In proportion to the debts and disputes of the people, lawyers will multiply. Of these America furnishes a plentiful growth, and New York has its share, as it contains not less than 120 licenced Attornies. In this state, the practice of law is conformed to the English mode, and is perhaps better regulated than in the other States. The several degrees in the profession—the number of critical examinations that candidates are obliged to pass through before they can be admitted as Counsellers in the higher courts; together with the time of study required by the rules of admission, render an access to the first honors of the bar so difficult as to preclude ignorant pretenders to the important science of law. New York can boast of many men eminent in every liberal profession, and which has hitherto furnished America with some of her most able legislators. It is however to be feared that a too rigid adherence to the forms of legal process in England, has sometimes perplexed the road to justice, and prevented valuable improvements in the practice, not only of this, but of most of the States.

Mode of raising internal taxes.] The legislature fix upon the sum to be raised, and apportion it among the several counties. This being done, the supervisors, one from each township in the respective counties, assemble and assign to each township its proportion of the quota of the county. The supervisor and assessors in each township then apportion their quota among the individuals of the township according to the value of their real and personal estates. The tax, thus laid, is collected by the collector of the township, and lodged with the county treasurer, who transmits it to the treasurer of the state.

Indians.] The *Oneidas* inhabit on Oneida Creek, twenty-one miles west of Fort Stanwix. The tribe consists of about 400 men, women and children.

The *Tuscaroras* migrated from North-Carolina and the frontiers of Virginia, and were adopted by the Oneidas, with whom they have ever since lived, upon the supposition that they were originally of the same nation, because there is a similarity in their languages.

The *Senecas* inhabit on the Chenessee river at the Chenessee castle. The tribe consists of about 800 souls. They have two towns, of sixty or seventy souls each, on French Creek, in Pennsylvania; and another town on Buffaloe Creek, attached to the British; and two small towns on Allegany river, attached to the Americans. Obeil or Cornplanter, one of the Seneca chiefs resides here.

The *Mohawks* were acknowledged by the other tribes, to use their own expression, to be 'the true old heads of the confedracy;' and were formerly a powerful tribe, inhabiting on the Mohawks river. As they were strongly attached to the Johnson family, on account of Sir William Johnson, they emigrated to Canada, with Sir John Johnson, about the year 1776. There is now only one family of them in the state, and they live about a mile from fort Hunter. The father of this family was drowned in the winter of 1788.

All the confederated tribes, except the Oneidas and Tuscaroras sided with the British in the late war, and fought against the Americans.

The *Onondagas* live near the Salt or Onondaga Lake, about twenty-five miles from the Oneida Lake. In the spring of 1779, a regiment of men were sent from Albany, by general J. Clinton, against the Onondagas. This regiment surprized their town—took thirty-three prisoners—killed twelve or fourteen, and returned without the loss of a man. A party of the Indians were at this time, ravaging the American frontiers. There are very few of the *Delaware* tribe in this State.

The *Five* confederated *Nations* were settled along the banks of the Susquehannah, and in the adjacent country, until the year 1779, when general Sullivan, with an army of 4000 men, drove them from their country to Niagara, where, being obliged to live on salted provisions to which they were unaccustomed, great numbers of them died. Two hundred of them, it is said, were buried in one grave, where they had encamped. General Sullivan burnt several of their towns—destroyed their provisions, and defeated them in an engagement at Newton. Since this irruption into their country, their former habitations have been mostly deserted, and many of them have gone to Canada.

On the 13th of November, 1787, John Livingston, Esq; and four others obtained of the Six Nations of Indians a lease for 999 years, on a yearly rent reserved of 2000 dollars, of all the country included in the following limits, viz. Beginning at a place commonly known by the name of Canada Creek, about seven miles west of Fort Stanwix, now Fort Shuyler, thence northeastwardly to the line of the province of Quebec; thence along the said line to the Pennsylvania line, thence east on the said line or Pennsylvania line, to the line of property, so called by the state of New York, thence along the said line of property to Canada Creek aforesaid. And on the 8th Jan. 1788, the same persons obtained a lease, of the Oneida Indians, for 999 years, on a rent reserved for the first year, of 1200 dollars, and encreasing it at the rate of 100 dollars a year until it amount to 1500 dollars, of all the tract of land commonly called the Oneida country, except a reservation of several tracts specified in the lease. But these leases having been obtained without the consent of the legislature of the state, the senate and assembly, in their session, March 1788, resolved, "That the said leases are purchases of lands, and therefore that by the constitution of this state the said leases are not binding on the said Indians, and are not valid."—This very important and interesting dispute remains to be settled.

We shall conclude this account of the Indians, with an Indian speech to Sir William Johnson, superintendant of Indian affairs, at a treaty held with the Six Nations and others at Fort Stanwix, in October 1768, for the settlement of a boundary line between the Colonies and the Indians.

' We remember that on our first meeting you, when you came with your ships, we kindly received you—entertained you—entered into an alliance with you, though we were then great and numerous, and your people inconsiderable and weak. And we know that we entered into a covenant chain of bark with you, and fastened your ship therewith. But being apprehensive the bark would break and your ship be lost, we made one of iron and held it fast that it should not slip from us—but seeing the former chain was liable to rust, we made a silver one to guard against it.'

Islands.]

Islands.] There are three islands of note belonging to this state; viz. York Island, which has already been described, Long Island and Staten Island.

Long Island extends from the city of New York east, 140 miles, and terminates with Montauk point. It is not more than ten miles in breadth, on a medium, and is separated from Connecticut by Long Island sound. The island is divided into three counties; Kings, Queens and Suffolk.

Kings County lies at the west end of Long Island, opposite New York, and is not above ten miles long, and eight broad. The inhabitants are principally Dutch, and live well. It contains a number of pleasant villages, of which Flatbush, Brooklyn, or Breucklin and Bedford, are the principal.

Queens County lies next to Kings as you proceed eastward. It is about thirty miles long and twelve broad. Jamaica, Newtown, Hampstead, in which is a handsome court house, and Oysterbay are the principal villages in this county.

Suffolk County is about 100 miles long and ten broad, and comprehends all the eastern part of the island, and several little islands adjoining; viz. Shelter Island, Fishers Island, Plumb Island and the Isle of Wight. Its principal towns are Huntington, Southampton, Smithtown, Brook Haven, East Hampton, in which is the academy, Southhold and Bridge Hampton.

The south side of the island is flat land, of a light sandy soil, bordered on the sea coast with large tracts of salt meadow, extending from the west point of the island to Southampton. This soil, however, is well calculated for raising grain, especially Indian corn. The north side of the island is hilly, and of a strong soil—adapted to the culture of grain, hay and fruit. A ridge of hills extends from Jamaica to Southhold. Large herds of cattle feed upon Hampstead plain, and on the salt marshes upon the south side of the Island.

Hampstead plain, in Queens county, is a curiosity. It is sixteen miles in length, east and west, and seven or eight miles wide. The soil is black, and to appearance rich, and yet it was never known to have any natural growth, but a kind of wild grass, and a few shrubs. It is frequented by vast numbers of plover—Rye grows tolerably well on some parts of the plain. The most of it lies common for cattle, horses and sheep. As there is nothing to impede the prospect in the whole length of this plain, it has a curious but tiresome effect upon the eye, not unlike that of the ocean.

East of this plain, on the middle of the island, is a barren heath, overgrown with shrub oaks and pines, in which, it is supposed, there are several thousand deer. It is frequented also by a great number of growse or heath hens, a very delicious bird. Laws have been passed for the preservation of these birds and the deer.

It is remarkable that on Montauk point, at the east end of the island, there are no flies. Between this point and East Hampton is a beach, three quarters of a mile wide, in the centre of which was found, about fifty years ago, under a sand hill which was blown up by the wind, the entire skeleton of a large whale, nearly half a mile from the water.

There

There are very few rivers upon the Island. The largest is Peakonok, which rises about ten miles west of a place called River-head, where the court house stands, and runs easterly into a large bay dividing Southhold from Southampton. In this bay are Robin and Shelter Islands.

The south side of the island is indented with numerous streams of various sizes which fall into a large bay, two or three miles over, formed by a beach, about eighty rods wide, which appears like a border to the island, extending from the west end of it to Southampton. Through this beach, in various places, are inlets of such depth as to admit of vessels of sixty or seventy tons.

This bay was formerly fresh water. As evidences of this, the stumps of trees are to be seen in great numbers on the salt marsh, near the upland. Oysters, clams, and fish of various kinds, are caught with ease, and in great plenty in this bay, with seines, during the winter season. It is not uncommon to see forty or fifty vessels here loading with oysters at the same time. And what is almost incredible, though I was told of it by two gentlemen of truth, and who were well informed as to the matter, thirty waggon loads of bass have been caught in this bay at one draught.

Rockonkama pond, lies about the centre of the island, between Smithtown and Islip, and is about a mile in circumference. This pond has been found by observation, to rise gradually for several years, until it had arrived to a certain height, and then to fall more rapidly to its lowest bed; and thus it is continually ebbing and flowing. The cause of this curious phenomenon has never been investigated. Two miles to the southward of this pond is a considerable stream, called Connecticut river, which empties into the bay.

There are two whale fisheries; one from Sagg harbour which produces about 1000 barrels of oil annually. The other is much smaller, and is carried on by the inhabitants in the winter season, from the south side of the island. They commonly catch from three to seven whales in a season, which produce from twenty-five to forty barrels of oil. This fishery was formerly a source of considerable wealth to the inhabitants, but through a scarcity of whales, it has greatly declined of late years.

There is a considerable trade carried on from Sagg harbour, whence is exported to the West Indies and other places, whale oil, pitch-pine boards, horses, cattle, flax seed, beef, &c. The produce of the middle and western parts of the island, is carried to New York.

The island contains 30,863 inhabitants.

Staten Island lies nine miles southwest of the city of New York, and forms Richmond county. It is about eighteen miles in length, and, at a medium, six or seven in breadth, and contains 3,152 inhabitants. On the south side is a considerable tract of level, good land; but the island in general is rough, and the hills high. Richmond is the only town of any note on the island, and that is a poor, inconsiderable place. The inhabitants are principally Dutch and French.

History.] Hudson's River was first discovered in 1608, by Henry Hudson, an Englishman, who sold his claim to the Dutch.

In 1614, the States General granted a patent to several merchants for an exclusive trade on the river Hudson. The same year this company built a fort on the west side of the river, near Albany, and named it Fort Orange.

In 1615, a fort was built on the southwest point of Manhattan's, now York island; but the first settlers planted themselves about two miles from this fort and built a church there, the ruins of which, it is said, are still visible, near the two mile stone on the public road. In this situation, finding themselves insecure during the wars between the English and Dutch, they left this place and planted their habitations under the guns of the fort, which laid the foundation of the present city.

In 1614, Captain Argall, under Sir Thomas Dale, governor of Virginia, visited the Dutch on Hudson's river, who being unable to resist him, prudently submitted for the present, to the king of England, and under him to the governor of Virginia. Determined upon the settlement of a colony, the States general, in 1621, granted the country to the West India company; and in the year 1629, Wouter Van Twiller arrived at Fort Amsterdam, now New York, and took upon himself the government.

In August 27, 1664, governor Stuyvesant surrendered the colony to colonel Nicolls, who had arrived in the bay a few days before, with three or four ships and about 300 soldiers, having a commission from king Charles the II. to reduce the place, which then was called New Amsterdam, but was changed to New York, as was Fort Orange to Albany, in honour of his Royal Highness James Duke of York and Albany. Very few of the inhabitants thought proper to remove out of the country; and their numerous descendants are still in many parts of this state, and New Jersey.

In 1667, at the peace of Breda, New York was confirmed to the English, who in exchange ceded Surinam to the Dutch.

The English kept peaceable possession of the country until the year 1673, when the Dutch, with whom they were then at war, sent a small squadron, which arrived at Staten Island on the 30th of July. John Manning, a captain of an independent company, who had at that time the command of the fort, sent a messenger down to the commodore, and treacherously made his terms with him: on the same day the ships came up, moored under the fort, landed their men, and entered the garrison, without giving or receiving a shot. All the magistrates and constables from East Jersey, Long Island, Æsopus, and Albany, were summoned to New York; and the major part of them swore Allegiance to the States General and the Prince of Orange. The conquerors, however, did not long enjoy the fruits of their success, for on the 9th of February the year following, a treaty of peace between England and Holland was signed at Westminster; by the sixth article of which, this province was restored to the English, in whose hands it remained until the late revolution.

While New York remained in possession of the Dutch it was called New Netherlands, and governed by a Scout, Burgomasters and Schepens. From its surrender to the English in 1664, to 1683, the province was ruled by governors, appointed and commissioned by the Duke of York, and their council, whose rules and orders had the force of laws. From the last named period, the people were admitted to a share of the legislative authority.

The confederated Cantons of Indians, before the incorporation of the Tuscaroras, a people driven by the Carolinians from the frontiers of Virginia, consisted of five nations, viz. the Mohawks, Oneidas, Senecas, Onondagas,

Onondagas, and Cayugas. The alliance and trade of these six nations, inhabiting the territory west of Albany to the distance of more than 200 miles, though much courted by the French of Canada, have been almost uninterruptedly enjoyed by the English.

In 1684, the French attempted the destruction of these Indians, because they interrupted their trade with the more distant tribes, called the Far Nations. The Seneca Indians interrupted this trade, because the French supplied the Miamies, with whom they were then at war, with arms and amunition.

To effect the destruction of the Indians great preparations were made by the French. But famine and sickness prevailing among them the expedition proved fruitless. Four years after this, 1200 Indians attacked Montreal, burnt many houses and put 1000 of the inhabitants to the sword.

In 1689, Colonel Dongan, the governor, being called home by king James, and a general disaffection to government prevailing at New York, one Jacob Leisler took possession of the garrison, for king William and queen Mary, and assumed the supreme power over the province. His reduction of Albany, held by others for William, and the confiscation of the estates of his opponents, was an impolitic measure; and sowed the seeds of mutual animosity, which for a long time greatly embarrassed the public affairs.

The French, in 1689, in order to detach the six nations from the British interest, sent out several parties against the English colonies. One of the parties, consisting of about 200 French and some of the Caghnuaga Indians, commanded by D'Ailldebout, De Mantel and Le Moyne, was intended for New York. But by the advice of the Indians, they determined first to attack Skenectady.

For this place they accordingly directed their course, and after twenty days march, in the depth of winter, through the snow, carrying their provisions on their backs, they arrived in the neighbourhood of Skenectady, on the 8th of February, 1690. Such was the extreme distress to which they were reduced, that they had thoughts of surrendering themselves prisoners of war. But their scouts, who were a day or two in the village entirely unsuspected, returned with such encouraging accounts of the absolute security of the people, that the enemy determined on the attack. They entered, on Saturday night about eleven o'clock, at the gates, which were found unshut; and, that every house might be invested at the same time, divided into small parties of six or seven men. The inhabitants were in a profound sleep, and unalarmed, until their doors were broke open. Never were people in a more wretched consternation. Before they were risen from their beds, the enemy entered their houses, and began the perpetration of the most inhuman barbarities. No tongue can express the cruelties that were committed. The whole village was instantly in a blaze. Women with child ripped open, and their infants cast into the flames, or dashed against the posts of the doors. Sixty persons perished in the massacre, and twenty-seven were carried into captivity. The rest fled naked towards Albany, through a deep snow which fell that very night in a terrible storm; and 25 of the fugitives lost their limbs in the flight, through the severity of the frost. The news of this dreadful tragedy reached Albany, about break of day, and universal dread seized the inhabitants of that city,

the

NEW YORK.

the enemy being reported to be one thousand four hundred strong. A party of horse was immediately dispatched to Skenectady, and a few Mohawks then in town, fearful of being intercepted, were with difficulty sent to apprise their own castles.

The Mohawks were unacquainted with this bloody scene, until two days after it happened, our messengers being scarcely able to travel through the great depth of the snow. The enemy, in the mean time, pillaged the town of Skenectady until noon the next day; and then went off with their plunder, and about forty of their best horses. The rest, with all the cattle they could find, lay slaughtered in the streets.

Upon the arrival of a governor at New York, commissioned by the king, Leisler imprudently refused to surrender the garrison, for which he and his son were condemned to death, as guilty of high treason.

The whole province of New York was originally settled by non-episcopalians, chiefly by presbyterians, except a few episcopal families in the city of New York. In 1693, Col. Fletcher, then governor of the province, projected the scheme of a general tax for building churches and supporting episcopal ministers, and artfully effected his design in part. This overture laid the foundation for a dispute between the presbyterians and episcopalians, which, until the revolution, was maintained on both sides with great warmth and animosity. Several of the governors, particularly the infamous* Lord Cornbury, shewed great partiality to the episcopalians and persecuted the presbyterians.

To prevent the Roman Catholic missionaries from Canada from influencing the Indian allies of the province to renounce their allegiance to the British crown, under the pretext of religion, the legislature of the province, in July, 1700, passed a law, prohibiting Jesuits and Popish priests

---

* *The following extract from the history of New York, will fully justify this epithet. Speaking of Lord Cornbury, the Historian says, 'His Lordship's sense of honor and justice was as weak and indelicate, as his bigotry was rampant and uncontroulable: and hence we find him guilty of an act complicated of a number of vices, which no man could have perpetrated without violence to the very slightest remains of generosity and justice. When his excellency retired to Jamaica, on account of the Great Sickness in 1702, one Hubbard, the presbyterian minister, lived in the best house in the town. His lordship begged the loan of it for the use of his own Family, and the clergyman put himself to no small inconveniencies to favour the governor's request; but in return for the generous benefaction, his lordship perfidiously delivered the parsonage-house into the hands of the piscopal party, and encouraged one Cardwel, the sheriff, a mean fellow, who afterwards put an end to his own life, to seize upon the Glebe, which he surveyed into lots, and farmed for the benefit of the episcopal church. These tyrannical measures justly inflamed the indignation of the injured sufferers, and that again the more embittered his lordship against them. They resented, and he persecuted: nor did he confine his pious rage to the people of Jamaica. He detested all who were of the same denomination; nay, averse to every sect except his own, he insisted that neither the ministers nor schoolmasters of the Dutch, the most numerous persuasion in the province, had a right to preach or instruct without his gubernatorial licence; and some of them tamely submitted to his unauthoritative rule.'*

priests from exercising their office in the province, on pain of perpetual imprisonment. If any one should escape from prison and be afterwards taken, he was to be put to death. This law, however vindicable in a political view, is certainly to be condemned on the principle of religion, as it favoured as highly of persecution as any law ever passed in New England. The truth is, the legislators in both instances intended to prevent political evils, but their laws for this end were highly exceptionable. The offenders against the public peace ought to have been treated in a civil, not in a religious capacity. Civil and ecclesiastical power are entirely distinct, and never ought to be blended. The religious persecutions, which have proved the destruction of thousands of pious people, may, in a great measure, be ascribed to the undue interference of civil with ecclesiastical authority.

This law against the Roman Catholics, remained unrepealed (though it was never enforced) until the revolution.

In 1709, a vigorous expedition was meditated against Canada, in making preparation for which, this province expended above £.20,000; but the expected assistance from Britain failing, it was never prosecuted. Soon after, Col. Schuyler, who had been very influential with the Indians, went to England with five Sachems, who were introduced into the presence of Queen Anne. The object of this visit was to stimulate the ministry to the reduction of Canada.

In 1711, a considerable fleet was sent over for that purpose, but eight transports being cast away on the coast, the rest of the fleet and troops returned without making any attempt to reduce Canada.

In 1710, Governor Hunter brought over with him about 3000 Palatines, who, the year before, had fled to England from the rage of persecution in Germany. Many of these people settled in the city of New York; others settled on a tract of several thousand acres in the manor of Livingston, and some went to Pennsylvania, and were instrumental in inducing thousands of their countrymen to immigrate to that province.

The prohibition of the sale of Indian goods to the French, in 1720, excited the clamour of the merchants at New York, whose interest was affected by it. The measure was undoubtedly a politic one; and the reasons for it were these; The French by this trade were supplied with articles which were wanted by the Indians. This prevented the Indians from coming to Albany, and drew them to Montreal; and they being employed by the French, as carriers, became attached to them from interest. About the same time, a trading house was erected by the English at Oswego, on Lake Ontario; and another by the French at Niag a.

In 1729, the act prohibiting the trade between Albany and Montreal was imprudently repealed by the king. This naturally tended to undermine the trade at Oswego, and to advance the French commerce of Niagara; and at the same time to alienate the affections of the Indians from Britain. Not long after this, the French were suffered to erect a fortress at Lake Champlain. To prevent the ill consequences of this, a scheme was projected to settle the lands near Lake George, with loyal protestant Highlanders from Scotland. A tract of thirty thousand acres was accordingly promised to captain Campbell, who, at his own expence, transported

eighty-

eighty-three Proteſtant families to New York. But through the ſordid views of ſome perſons in power, who aimed at a ſhare in the intended grant, the ſettlement was never made.

We have already mentioned, in the hiſtory of the United States, ſome of the moſt important events that have taken place in this ſtate ſince the revolution. To be more particular is inconſiſtent with my deſign. I ſhall conclude this hiſtory, with a liſt of the governors of New York, after having mentioned that,

In 1787, the legiſlature of this ſtate, ceded to the Commonwealth of Maſſachuſetts, all the lands, within their juriſdiction, weſt of a meridian that ſhall be drawn from a point in the north boundary line of Pennſylvania, eighty-two miles weſt from the Delaware; (excepting one mile along the eaſt ſide of Niagara river) and alſo ten townſhips between the Chenengo and Owegy rivers, reſerving the juriſdiction to the ſtate of New York. This ſeſſion was made to ſatisfy a claim of Maſſachuſetts, founded upon their original charter.

A liſt of Governors *from the year* 1664 *to the preſent time.*

Names of Gov's.	Began to govern.	Names of Gov's.	Began to govern.
Nicolls	1664	Burnet	1720
Lovelace	1668	Montgomerie	1728
Androſs	1674	Vandam	1731
Brockhuſt	1682	Coſby	1732
Dongan	1683	Clarke	1735
Slaughter	1690	Clinton	1743
Ingoldſby	1691	Oſborn	1753
Fletcher	1692	De Lancey	1753
Bellemont	1698	Sir Charles Hardy	1755
Nanfan	1699	De Lancey	1757
Bellemont	1700	Colden (Preſident)	1760
Depeyſter	1700	Monckton	1761
Smith	1700	Colden	1761
Nanfan	1701	Monckton	1762
Cornbury	1702	Colden	1763
Lovelace	1708	Sir Henry Moore	1765
Schuyler	1709	Colden	1769
Ingoldſby	1709	Dunmore	1770
Beekman	1710	Tryon	1771
Hunter	1710	Clinton	1778

NEW JERSEY.

SITUATION and EXTENT.

Miles.

Length 160 } Between { 39° and 41° 24' North Latitude.
Breadth 52 } { The body of the state lies between the meridian of Philadelphia, and 1° East Longitude.

Boundaries.] BOUNDED east, by Hudson's river and the sea; south, by the sea; west, by Delaware bay and river, which divide it from the states of Delaware and Pennsylvania; north, by a line drawn from the mouth of Mahakkamak river, in latitude 41° 24' to a point on Hudson's river in latitude 41°. Containing about 8320 square miles, equal to 5,324,800 acres.

Bays, Ponds, Rivers, &c.] New Jersey is washed, on the east and southeast, by Hudson's river and the ocean; and on the west by the river Delaware.

The most remarkable bays are, Arthur Kull, or Newark bay, formed by the union of Posaik and Hakkensak rivers. This bay opens to the right and left and embraces Staten Island. There is a long bay, formed by a beach, four or five miles from the shore, extending along the coast northeast and southwest, from Manasquand river, in Monmouth county, almost to Cape May. Through this beach are a number of inlets, by which the bay communicates with the ocean.

On the top of a mountain, in Morris county, is a lake or pond, three miles in length, and from a mile to a mile and an half in breadth, from which proceeds a continual stream. It is in some places deep. The water is of a sea-green colour; but when taken up in a tumbler, is, like the water of the ocean, clear and of a crystaline colour.

The rivers in this state, though not large are numerous. A traveller, in passing the common road from New York to Philadelphia, crosses three considerable rivers, viz. the Hakkensak and Posaik between Bergen and Newark, and the Raritan by Brunswick. The Hakkensak rises in Bergen county, runs a southwardly course, and empties into Newark bay.—At the ferry, near its mouth, it is 460 yards wide, and is navigable fifteen miles.

Posaik is a very crooked river. It rises in a large swamp in Morris county. Its general course is from W. N. W. to E. S. E. until it mingles with the Hakkinsak at the head of Newark bay. It is navigable about ten miles, and is 230 yards wide at the ferry. The cataract in this river, is one of the greatest natural curiosities in the state. The river is about forty yards wide, and moves in a flow gentle current, until coming within a short distance of a deep cleft in a rock, which crosses the channel, it descends and falls above seventy feet perpendicularly, in one entire sheet. One end of the cleft, which was evidently made by some violent convulsion in nature, is closed; at the other, the water rushes out with
incredible

incredible swiftness, forming an accute angle with its former direction, and is received into a large bason, whence it takes a winding course through the rocks, and spreads into a broad, smooth stream. The cleft is from four to twelve feet broad. The falling of the water occasions a cloud of vapour to arise, which, by floating amidst the sun beams, presents to the view rainbows, that add beauty to the tremendous scene. The western bank of this river, between Newark and the falls, affords one of the pleasantest roads for a party of pleasure in New Jersey. The bank being high, gives the traveller an elevated and extensive view of the opposite shore, which is low and fertile, forming a landscape picturesque and beautiful. Many handsome country-seats adorn the sides of this river; and there are elegant situations for more. Gentlemen of fortune might here display their taste to advantage. The fish of various kinds with which this river abounds, while they would furnish the table with an agreeable repast, would afford the sportsman an innocent and manly amusement.

Raritan river is formed by two considerable streams called the north and south branches; one of which has its source in Morris, the other in Hunterdon county. It passes by Brunswick and Amboy, and mingles with the waters of the Arthur Kull Sound, and helps to form the fine harbour of Amboy. It is a mile wide at its mouth, 250 yards at Brunswick, and is navigable about sixteen miles. At Raritan Hills, through which this river passes, is a small cascade, where the water falls fifteen or twenty feet, very romantically between two rocks. Opposite the lower part of the town of Brunswick, is a remarkable declivity in the bed of the river, not perceptible however in its current. Below this declivity, a twenty gun ship may ride securely at any time of tide, while no farther up than opposite the main street of the town, the river is fordable with horses and carriages at low water. The tide, however, rises so high, that large shallops pass a mile above the ford; so that it is no uncommon thing to see vessels of considerable burden riding at anchor, and a number of large river craft lying above, some dry and others on their beems ends, for want of water, within gunshot of each other.

Besides these are Cesarea river, or Cohansey Creek, which rises in Salem county, and is about thirty miles in length, and navigable for vessels of an hundred tons to Bridgetown, twenty miles from its mouth.

Mullicas river divides the counties of Gloucester and Burlington, and is navigable twenty miles for vessels of sixty tons.

Maurice river rises in Gloucester county, runs southwardly about forty miles, and is navigable for vessels of an hundred tons, fifteen miles, and for shallops ten miles farther.

Alloway Creek, in the county of Salem, is navigable sixteen miles for shallops, with several obstructions of drawbridges. Ancocus creek in Burlington county is also navigable sixteen miles. These with many other smaller streams empty into the Delaware, and carry down the produce which their fertile banks and the neighbouring country afford.

That part of the state which borders on the sea, is indented with a great number of small rivers and creeks, such as Great Egg-harbour, and Little Egg-harbour rivers, Navesink, Shark, Matiticung, and forked rivers, which, as the country is flat, are navigable for small craft, almost to their sources.

Civil

NEW JERSEY.

Civil Divisions, Population, &c.] New Jersey is divided into 13 counties, which are subdivided into 94 townships or precincts, as follows.

TABLE.

	Counties.	Principal towns.	Length.	Breadth.	No. White Inhabitants.	Do. Black.
These seven counties lie from S. to N. on Delaware river. Cape May and Gloucester extend across to the sea.	Cape May.	None.	30	9	2093	138
	Cumberland	Bridgetown.	50	20	5000	100
	Salem,	Salem.				
	Gloucester.	Woodbury and Gloucester.	30	22		
	Burlington.	Burlington and Bordentown.	60	30	15,500	520
	Hunterdon.	Trenton.	37	12	17,130	1233
	Sussex.	Newtown.				
These four counties lie from N. to S. on the Eastern side of the State.	Bergen.	Hakkensak.				
	Essex.	Newark and Elizabeth-Town.				
	Middlesex.	Amboy and Brunswick.				
	Monmouth.	Shrewsbury and Freehold.	30	30	13,216	1492
Inland.	Somerset.	Boundbrook.				
	Morris.	Morristown.	25	20	12,925	491

Total

In 1784, a census of the inhabitants was made by order of the legislature, when they amounted to 140,435, of which 10,501 were blacks. Of these blacks, 1939 only were slaves; so that the proportion of slaves to the whole of the inhabitants in the state, is as one to seventy-six. The population for every square mile is eighteen. In

NEW JERSEY.

In 1738, the number of inhabitants in New Jersey was 47,369; of which 3,981 were slaves. In 1745, there were 61,403 inhabitants in the colony, of which 4606 were slaves. The average annual increase of inhabitants in New Jersey since the year 1738, has been 2219, exclusive of emigrations.

No. Slaves.	Acres of improved Land.	Do. unimproved.	No. Horses.	No. Cattle.	No. Militia.	No. Townships.	No. Presb. Con.	Do. Baptist.	Do. Friends.	Do. other deno.	No. dwelling houses.
33	36,160	28,023	508	2417	450	3	1	2	2		420
30	84,582	74,543	1736	5195	1000	7	3	4	1	2	1200
41	119,297	36,502	2922	6687		9		3			
46	156,979	134,049	3261	7736	2000	9	6		6	4	
53	194,600	55,425	4657	9820	3000	11	1	4	15	1	2600
263	267,192	16,116	7613	10952		10	9	2	2	5	
82	240,055	29,628	5460	9048		12		2			
317	130,848	14,398	4221	6400		6					
185	109,617	9,418	3985	8080		3	3				
210	166,149	10,792	4036	8308		7		4			
264	197,065	42,868	4505	11634	1600	6	6	4	3	5	
318	173,224	2,763	4707	7564		6		1			
117	156,809	30,429	4817	8374		5	9	1	1	3	
1959	2,032,587	484,954	52,488	102,221		94	30				

Since the peace of 1783, great numbers of the inhabitants have emigrated to the country west of the Allegany Mountains. The increase of inhabitants in the state must be small so long as these emigrations shall continue;

continue; and they will probably continue as long as there are unsettled lands within the limits of the United States, on which emigrants can more easily subsist by agriculture, than in their native state.

Face of the Country, Mountains, Soil and Productions.] The counties of Sussex, Morris, and the northern part of Bergen, are mountainous. The *South Mountain*, which is one ridge of the great *Allegany range*, crosses this state in about latitude 41°. This mountain embosoms such amazing quantities of iron ore, that it may not improperly be called the *Iron Mountain*. The Kittatinny ridge passes through this state north of the South mountain. Several spurs from these mountains, are projected in a southern direction. One passes between Springfield and Chatham. Another runs west of it, by Morristown, Baskinridge and Vealtown. The interior country is, in general, agreeable variegated with hills and vallies. The southern counties which lie along the sea coast, are pretty uniformly flat and sandy. The noted Highlands of Navesink and center Hill, are almost the only hills within the distance of many miles from the sea coast. The Highlands of Navesink are on the sea coast near Sandy Hook, in the township of Middletown, and are the first lands that are discovered by mariners as they come upon the coast. They rise about 600 feet above the surface of the water.

As much as five-eighths of most of the southern counties, or one-fourth of the whole state, is a sandy barren, unfit for cultivation. The land on the sea coast in this, like that in the more southern states, has every appearance of *made ground*. The soil is generally a light sand; and by digging, on an average, about fifty feet below the surface, (which can be done, even at the distance of twenty or thirty miles from the sea, without any impediment from rocks or stones) you come to salt marsh. The gentleman who gave this information adds, 'I have seen an oyster shell that would hold a pint, which was dug out of the marsh, at fifty feet deep in digging a well.' 'About seven years since,' continues my informer, 'at Long Branch, in the county of Monmouth, in the banks of the Atlantic, which were greatly torn by a great rise of the sea in a violent easterly storm, was discovered the skeleton of some huge carnivorous animal. The country people who first saw it had so little curiosity, as to suffer it to be wholly destroyed, except a jaw tooth which I saw. This was about two and an half inches wide, five inches long and as many deep. The person who helped to take it out of the bank, assured me there was one rib seven feet four inches, and another four feet long.'----To account for these curious phenomena is not my business. This is left for the ingenious naturalist, who has abilities and leisure to compare facts and appearances of this kind, and who probably may thence draw conclusions which may throw much light on the ancient history of this country.

This state has all the varieties of soil from the worst to the best kind. It has a greater proportion of *barrens* than any of the states, if we except North-Carolina; and even than this, if we include the *premature State of Franklin*. The good land in the southern counties lies principally on the banks of the rivers and creeks. The soil, on these banks, is generally a stiff clay; and while in a state of nature, produces various species of oak, hickory, poplar, chesnut, ash, gum, &c. The *barrens* produce little else but

but shrub oaks and white and yellow pines. There are large bodies of salt meadow along the Delaware, which afford a plentiful pasture for cattle in summer, and hay in winter; but the flies and musketoes frequent these meadows in large swarms, in the months of June, July and August, and prove very troublesome both to man and beast. In Gloucester and Cumberland counties are several large tracts of banked meadow. Their vicinity to Philadelphia renders them highly valuable. Along the sea coast the inhabitants subsist principally by feeding cattle on the salt meadows, and by the fish of various kinds, such as rock, drum, shad, perch, &c. black turtle, crabs and oysters, which the sea, rivers, and creeks afford in great abundance. They raise Indian corn, rye, potatoes, &c. but not for exportation. Their swamps afford lumber, which is easily conveyed to a good market.

In the hilly and mountainous parts of the state, which are not too rocky for cultivation, the soil is of a stronger kind, and covered in its natural state with stately oaks, hickories, chesnuts, &c. &c. and when cultivated produces wheat, rye, Indian corn, buck-wheat, oats, barley, flax, and fruits of all kinds common to the climate. The land in this hilly country is good for grazing, and the farmers feed great numbers of cattle for New York and Philadelphia markets; and many of them keep large dairies.

The orchards in many parts of the state equal any in the United states, and their cyder is said, and not without reason, to be the best in the world. It is pretty certain that it cannot be surpassed in goodness. It is only to be regretted that too many of the inhabitants make too free a use of it, to the injury not only of their healths but of their reputations; and that the pernicious practice of distilling it, and thereby rendering it still more prejudicial, is prevailing. It is pity that the blessings of bounteous heaven should thus, by their abuse, be turned into curses.

The markets of New York and Philadelphia receive a very considerable proportion of their supplies from the contiguous parts of New Jersey. And it is worthy of remark that these contiguous parts are exceedingly well calculated, as to the nature and fertility of their soils, to afford these supplies; and the intervention of a great number of navigable rivers and creeks renders it very convenient to market their produce. These supplies consist of vegetables of many kinds, apples, pairs, peaches, plumbs, strawberries, cherries, and other fruits—cyder in large quantities and of the best quality, butter, cheese, beef, pork, mutton and the lesser meats.

Trade.] The trade of this state is carried on almost solely with and from those two great commercial cities, New York on one side, and Philadelphia on the other; though it wants not good ports of its own. Several attempts have been made by the legislature, to secure to the state its own natural advantages, by granting extraordinary privileges to merchants, who would settle at Amboy and Burlington, two very commodious ports. But the people having long been accustomed to send their produce to the markets of Philadelphia and New York, and of course having their correspondencies established, and their mode of dealing fixed, they find it difficult to turn their trade from the old channel.

Besides, in these large cities, where are so many able merchants, and so many wants to be supplied, credits are more easily obtained, and a better and quicker market is found for produce, than could be expected in towns less populous and flourishing. These and other causes of the same kind, have, hitherto, rendered abortive the encouragements held out by the legislature.

New York and Pennsylvania, however, not contented with the privilege of being the factors and carriers for this state, charge it with the same duties they do their own citizens. This heavy and unreasonable tax upon the people, together with the loss they sustain in dealing with a depreciated paper currency, occasions the balance of trade to be against the state in almost every respect.

The articles exported, besides those already mentioned, are, wheat, flour, horses, live cattle, hams, which are celebrated as being the best in the world, lumber, flax-seed, leather, iron, in great quantities, in pigs and bars, and formerly copper ore was reckoned among their most valuable exports; but the mines have not been worked since the commencement of the late war.

The imports consist chiefly of dry and West India goods, and teas from the East Indies.

Manufactures and Agriculture.] The manufactures of this state have hitherto been very inconsiderable, not sufficient to supply its own consumption, if we except the articles of iron, nails and leather. A spirit of industry and improvement, particularly in manufactures, has however greatly increased in the two last years. Most of the families in the country, and many in the populous towns, are clothed in strong, decent homespun; and it is a happy circumstance for our country, that this plain AMERICAN dress is every day growing more fashionable, not only in this, but in all the eastern and middle states.

In Trenton and Newark, are several very valuable tanyards, where leather, in large quantities and of an excellent quality, is made and exported to the neighbouring markets. Steel was manufactured at Trenton in time of the war, but not considerably since. In Gloucester county is a glass house. Paper mills, and nail manufactories are erected and worked to good advantage in many parts of the state. Wheat also is manufactured into flour to good account, in the western counties, where wheat is the staple commodity. But the iron manufacture is, of all others, the greatest source of wealth to the state. Iron works are erected in Gloucester, Burlington, Morris and other counties. The mountains in the county of Morris, give rise to a number of streams necessary and convenient for these works, and at the same time furnish a copious supply of wood and ore of a superior quality. In this county alone are no less than seven rich iron mines, from which might be taken ore sufficient to supply the United States; and to work it into iron are two furnaces, two rolling and slitting mills, and about thirty forges, containing from two to four fires each. These works produce annually about 540 tons of bar iron, 800 tons of pigs, besides large quantities of hallow ware, sheet iron, and nail rods. In the whole state, it is supposed there is yearly made about 1200 tons of bar iron, 1200 do. of pigs, 80 do. of nail rods, exclusive of hallow ware, and various other castings, of which vast quantities are made.

Early

NEW JERSEY.

Early in the late war, a powder mill was erected in Morristown by Col. Ford, who was enabled, by the ample supply of saltpetre furnished by the patriotic inhabitants, to make a considerable quantity of that valuable and necessary article, at a time when it was most needed. And when the enemy were at the door, it afforded a timely supply.

Although the bulk of the inhabitants in this state are farmers, yet agriculture has not been improved (a few instances excepted) to that degree which from long experience, we might rationally expect, and which the fertility of the soil in many places, seems to encourage. A great part of the inhabitants are Dutch, who, although they are in general neat and industrious farmers, have very little enterprize, and seldom adopt any new improvements in husbandry, because, through habits and want of education to expand and liberalize their minds, they think their old modes of tilling the best. Indeed this is the case with the great body of the common people, and proves almost an insurmountable obstacle to agricultural improvements.

Mines and Minerals.] This state embosoms vast quantities of iron and copper ore. The iron ore is of two kinds; one is capable of being manufactured into malleable iron, and is found in mountains and in low barrens; the other, called *bog-ore*, grows* in rich bottoms; and yields iron of a hard, brittle quality, and is commonly manufactured into hallow ware, and used sometimes instead of stone in building.

A number of copper mines have been discovered in different parts of the state. One is in Bergen county, which when worked by the Schuylers, (to whom it belonged) were considerably productive; but they have for many years been neglected.

The following account of a copper mine at New Brunswick, is given by a gentleman of distinction, well informed upon the subject.

" About the years 1748, 1749, 1750, several lumps of virgin copper from five to thirty pounds weight, (in the whole upwards of 200 pounds) were plowed up in a field, belonging to Philip French, Esq; within a quarter of a mile of New Brunswick. This induced Mr. Elias Boudinot, of the city of Philadelphia, to take a lease of Mr. French of this land, for ninety-nine years, in order to search for copper ore, a body of which he concluded must be contained in this hill. He took in several partners, and about the year 1751 opened a pit in the low grounds, about 2 or 300 yards from the river. He was led to this spot by a friend of his, who, a little before, passing by at three o'clock in the morning, observed a body of flame arise out of the ground, as large as a common sized man, and soon after die away. He drove a stake on the spot. About fifteen feet deep, Mr. Boudinot came on a vein of bluish stone, about two feet thick, between two perpendicular loose bodies of red rock, covered with a sheet of pure virgin copper, a little thicker than gold leaf. This bluish stone was filled with sparks of virgin copper, very much like copper filings, and now and then a large lump of virgin copper from five to thirty pounds

---

* *Some persons perhaps will be surprized at my saying that ore grows, but that it does in fact grow is well known to many curious naturalists who have carefully observed it.*

pounds weight. He followed this vein almoft thirty feet, when, the water coming in very faft, the expence became too great for the company's capital. A ftumping mill was erected, when by reducing the bluifh ftone to a powder, and wafhing it in large tubs, the ftone was carried off and the fine copper preferved, by which means many tons of the pureft copper was fent to England without ever paffing through the fire; but labour was too high to render it poffible for the company to proceed. Sheets of copper about the thicknefs of two pennies, and three feet fquare, on an average, have been taken from between the rocks, within four feet of the furface, in feveral parts of the hill. At about fifty or fixty feet deep, they came to a body of fine folid ore, in the midft of this bluifh vein, but between rocks of a white flinty fpar, which, however, was worked out in a few days. Thefe works lie now wholly neglected, although the vein when left was richer than ever it had been. There was alfo a very rich vein of copper ore difcovered at rocky hill, in Somerfet county, which has alfo been neglected from the heavy expence attending the working of it. There have been various attempts made to fearch the hills beyond Boundbrook, known by the name of Van Horne's mountain, but for the fame reafon it is now neglected. This mountain difcovers the greateft appearance of copper ore, of any place in the ftate. It may be picked up on the furface of many parts of it. A fmelting furnace was erected, before the revolution, in the neighbourhood by two Germans, who were making very confiderable profit on their work, until the Britifh deftroyed it in the beginning of the war. The inhabitants made it worth their while, by collecting the ore from the furface, and by partially digging into the hill, to fupply the furnace. Befides a company opened a very large fhaft on the fide of the hill, from which alfo a great deal of valuable ore and fome virgin copper were taken. Two lumps of virgin copper were found here in the year 1754 which weighed 1900 pounds.

Curious Springs.] In the upper part of the county of Morris, is a cold mineral fpring, which is frequented by valetudinarians, and its waters have been ufed with very confiderable fuccefs. In the townfhip of Hanover, in this county, on a ridge of hills are a number of wells, which regularly ebb and flow about fix feet twice in every twenty-four hours. Thefe wells are nearly forty miles from the fea, in a ftreight line. In the county of Cape May, is a fpring of frefh water, which boils up from the bottom of a falt water creek, which runs nearly dry at low tide; but at flood tide, is covered with water directly from the ocean to the depth of three or four feet; yet in this fituation, by letting down a bottle well corked, through the falt water into the fpring, and immediately drawing the cork with a ftring prepared for the purpofe, it may be drawn up full of fine, untainted frefh water. There are fprings of this kind in other parts of the ftate. In the county of Hunterdon, near the top of Mufkonetkony mountain, is a noted medicinal fpring, to which invalids refort from every quarter. It iffues from the fide of the mountain in a very romantic manner, and is conveyed into an artificial refervoir for the accommodation of thofe who wifh to bathe in, as well as to drink, the waters. It is a ftrong calybeate and very cold. Thefe waters have been ufed with very confiderable fuccefs; but perhaps the exercife neceffary to get to them,

them, and the purity of the air in this lofty fituation, aided by a lively imagination, have as great efficacy in curing the patient as the waters.

Caves, Monuments, &c.] In the townſhip of Shrewſbury, in Monmouth county, on the ſide of a branch of Naveſink river, is a remarkable cave, in which there are three rooms. The cave is about thirty feet long, and fifteen feet broad. Each of the rooms is arched. The center of the arch is about five feet from the bottom of the cave; the ſides not more than two and an half. The mouth of the cave is ſmall; the bottom is a looſe ſand; and the arch is formed in a ſoft rock, through the pores of which, the moiſture is ſlowly exudated, and falls in drops on the ſand below.

On Sandy Hook, about a mile from the light houſe, is a monument, which was erected to commemorate a very melancholy event that took place juſt at the cloſe of the late war. The following inſcription, which is upon a marble plate on one ſide of the monument, will afford ſufficient information of the matter.

" Here lies the remains of the honourable Hamilton Douglaſs Halliburton, ſon of Sholto Charles Earl of Morton, and heir of the ancient family of Halliburton of Pitcurr in Scotland; who periſhed on this coaſt with twelve more young gentlemen, and one common ſailor, in the ſpirited diſcharge of duty, the 30th or 31ſt of December, 1783: Born October the 10th 1763; a youth who, in contempt of hardſhip and danger, though poſſeſſed of an ample fortune, ſerved ſeven years in the Britiſh navy with a manly courage. He ſeemed to be deſerving of a better fate. To his dear memory, and that of his unfortunate companions, this monumental ſtone is erected by his unhappy mother, Katharine, Counteſs Dowager of Morton.

JAMES CHAMPION, Lieutenant of Marines.

ALEXANDER JOHNSTON,
GEORGE PADDY,   } Midſhipmen.
ROBERT HEYWOOD,

CHARLES GASCOIGNE,   WILLIAM TOMLINSON,
ANDREW HAMILTON,   Young   JOHN M'CHAIR,
WILLIAM SCOTT,   gentlemen   WILLIAM SPRAY,
DAVID REDDIE,   ROBERT WOOD.

GEORGE TOWERS, Sailor.

Caſt away in purſuit of deſerters; all found dead; and buried in this grave.

Of his Britannic Majeſty's ſhip Aſſiſtance,
Mr. HALLIBURTON, Firſt Lieutenant."

Character, Manners and Cuſtoms.] Many circumſtances concur to render theſe various in different parts of the ſtate. The inhabitants are a collection of Low Dutch, Germans, Engliſh, Scotch, Iriſh, and New Englanders, or their deſcendants. National attachment, and mutual convenience have generally induced theſe ſeveral kinds of people to ſettle together in a body---and in this way their peculiar national manners, cuſtoms, and character, are ſtill preſerved, eſpecially among the lower claſs of people, who have little intercourſe with any but thoſe of their own nation. Religion, although its tendency is to unite people in thoſe things that are

eſſential

essential to happiness, occasions wide differences as to manners, customs, and even character. The Presbyterian, the Quaker, the Episcopalian, the Baptist, the German and Low Dutch Calvinist, the Methodist and the Moravian, have each their distinguishing characteristics, either in their worship, their discipline, or their dress. There is still another very perceptible characteristical difference, distinct from either of the others, which arises from the intercourse of the inhabitants with different states. The people in West Jersey trade to Philadelphia, and of course imitate their fashions, and imbibe their manners. The inhabitants of East Jersey trade to New York, and regulate their fashions and manners according to those of New York. So that the difference in regard to fashions and manners between East and West Jersey, is nearly as great as between New York and Philadelphia.—Add to all these the differences common in all countries, arising from the various occupations of men, such as the Civilian, the Divine, the Lawyer, the Physician, the Mechanic, the clownish, the decent, and the respectable Farmer, all of whom have different pursuits, or pursue the same thing differently, and of course must have a different set of ideas and manners;—When we take into view all these differences, (and all these differences exist in New Jersey, and many of them in all the other states) it cannot be expected that many general observations will apply. It may, however, in truth be said, that the people of New Jersey are generally industrious, frugal and hospitable. There are, comparatively, but few men of learning in the state, nor can it be said that the people in general have a taste for the sciences. The lower class, in which may be included three fifths of the inhabitants of the whole state, are ignorant, and are criminally neglectful in the education of their children. There are, however, a number of gentlemen of the first rank in abilities and learning in the civil offices of the state, and in the several learned professions.

It is not the business of a geographer to compliment the ladies; nor would we be thought to do it when we say, that there is at least as great a number of industrious, discreet, amiable, genteel and handsome women in New Jersey, in proportion to the number of inhabitants, as in any of the thirteen states. Whether an adequate degree of solid mental improvement, answering to the personal and other useful qualities we have mentioned, is to be found among the fair of this state, is a more weighty concern. Perhaps it may be said with justice, that in general, though there is not the same universal taste for knowledge, discernable among the ladies here, as in some other of the states, owing in a great measure to the state of society, and the means of improvement, there are, however, many signal instances of improved talents among them, not surpassed by those of their sisters in any of the other states.

Religion.] There are, in this state, about fifty Presbyterian congregations, subject to the care of three Presbyteries, viz. that of New York, of New Brunswick, and Philadelphia. A part of the charge of New York and Philadelphia Presbyteries lies in New Jersey, and part in their own respective states. To supply these congregations, there are at present about twenty-five ministers.

There

NEW JERSEY.

There are upwards of forty congregations of Friends, commonly called quakers; who are in general, sober, plain, industrious, good citizens. For an account of their religious tenets see Pennsylvania.

There are thirty associated congregations of Baptists, in New Jersey, whose religious tenets are similar to those already mentioned under Connecticut, (page 220.)

The Episcopalian interest consists of twenty-five congregations.

There are, in this state, two classes belonging to the Dutch Reformed Synod of New York and New Jersey. The classis of Hakkensak, to which belongs thirteen congregations; and the classis of New Brunswick, to which belong fifteen congregations. We have already given an account of their church government, discipline, &c. (page 269.)

The Moravians have a flourishing settlement at Hope, in Sussex county. This settlement was begun in 1771, and now consists of upwards of 100 souls.

The Methodist interest is small in this state. The Swedes have a church in Gloucester county: and there are three congregations of the Seventh-Day Baptists. All these religious denominations live together in peace and harmony; and are allowed, by the constitution of the state, to worship Almighty God agreeably to the dictates of their own consciences; and are not compelled to attend or support any worship contrary to their own faith and judgment. All Protestant inhabitants, of peaceable behaviour, are eligible to the civil offices of the state.

Colleges, Academies, and Schools.] There are two colleges in New Jersey; one at Princeton, called Nassau Hall, the other at Brunswick, called Queens College. The college at Princeton was first founded by charter from John Hamilton, Esq; President of the council, about the year 1738, and enlarged by governor Belcher in 1747. The charter delegates a power of granting to "the students of said college, or to any others thought worthy of them, all such degrees as are granted in either of our universities or any other college in Great-Britain." It has twenty-three trustees. The governor of the state, and the president of the college are, *ex officiis*, two of them. It has an annual income of about £.900 currency; of which £.200 arises from funded public securities and lands, and the rest from the fees of the students.

The president of the college, is also professor of eloquence, criticism, and chronology. The vice-president is also professor of divinity and moral philosophy. There is also a professor of mathematics, and natural philosophy, and two masters of languages. The four classes in college contain about seventy students. There is a grammar school, of about thirty scholars, connected with the college, under the superintendance of the president, and taught by two masters.

Before the war this college was furnished with a Philosophical apparatus, worth £.500, which (except the elegant Orrery constructed by Mr. Rittenhouse) was almost entirely destroyed by the British army in the late war, as was also the library, which now consists of between 2 and 3000 volumes.

The college edifice is handsomely built with stone, and is 180 feet in length, 54 in breadth, and 4 stories high; and is divided into forty-two convenient

convenient chambers for the accommodation of the students, besides a dining hall, chapel room, and a room for the library. Its situation is exceedingly pleasant and healthful. The view from the college balcony is extensive and charming.

This college has been under the care of a succession of Presidents eminent for piety and learning; and has furnished a number of Civilians Divines, and Physicians of the first rank in America. It is remarkable, that all the Presidents of this college, except Dr. Witherspoon, who is now President, were removed by death very soon after their election into office.*

The charter for Queens college, at Brunswick, was granted just before the war, in consequence of an application from a body of the Dutch church. Its funds, raised wholly by free donations, amounted, soon after its establishment, to four thousand pounds; but they were considerably diminished by the war. The students are under the care of President Hardenberg. The grammar school, which is connected with the college, consists of between thirty and forty students, under the care of the trustees. This college has lately increased both in numbers and reputation.

There are a number of flourishing academies in this state. One at Trenton, in which are about eighty students in the different branches. It has a fund of about one hundred and fifty pounds per annum, arising from the interest on public securities. Another in Hakkensak, in the county of Bergen, of upwards of an hundred scholars. Instruction and board are said to be cheaper here than in any part of the state. There is another flourishing academy at Orangedale, in the county of Essex, consisting of nearly as many scholars as either of the others, furnished with able instructors and good accommodations. Another has lately been opened at Elizabethtown, and consists of upwards of twenty students in the languages, and is increasing. There is also an academy in Burlington, in which young ladies and gentlemen are taught the English language grammatically, geography, and the learned languages. Besides these, there are grammar schools at Newark, Springfield, Morristown, Bordentown and Amboy. There are no regular establishments for common schools in the state. The usual mode of education is for the inhabitants of a village or neighbourhood to join in affording a temporary support for a schoolmaster, upon such terms as is mutually agreeable. But the encouragement which these occasional teachers meet with, is generally such, as that no person of abilities adequate to the business, will undertake it; and of course, little advantage is derived from these schools. The improvement in these common schools is generally in proportion to the wages of the teacher.

Chief

* Accessus.	Presidents.	Exitus.
1746,	Rev. Jonathan Dickinson,	1747,
1748,	Rev. Aaron Burr,	1757,
1758,	Rev. Jonathan Edwards,	1758,
1758,	Rev. Samuel Davies,	1760,
1761,	Rev. Samuel Finley, D. D.	1766.
1767,	Rev. John Witherspoon, D. D.	

NEW JERSEY.

Chief Towns.] There are a number of towns in this state, nearly of equal size and importance, and none that has more than two hundred houses, compactly built. TRENTON is the largest town in New Jersey. It is situated on the northeast side of the river Delaware, opposite the falls, nearly in the center of the state, from north to south, in lat. 40° 15', and about 20' east of the meridian of Philadelphia. The river is not navigable above these falls, except for boats, which will carry from five to seven hundred bushels of wheat. This town, with Lamberton, which joins it on the south, contains two hundred houses, and about fifteen hundred inhabitants. Here the legislature meets, the supreme court sits, and the public offices are all kept, except the secretary's, which is at Burlington. On these accounts, it is considered as the capital of the state. In the neighbourhood of this pleasant town, are several gentlemen's seats, finely situated on the banks of the Delaware, and ornamented with taste and elegance. This town, being a thoroughfare between the eastern parts of the state and Philadelphia, has a considerable inland trade.

BURLINGTON *(City)* extends three miles along the Delaware, and one mile back, at right angles, into the county of Burlington, and is twenty miles above Philadelphia by water, and seventeen by land. The island, which is the most populous part of the city, is a mile and a quarter in length, and three quarters of a mile in breadth. It has four entrances over bridges and causeways, and a quantity of bank meadow adjoining. On the island are one hundred and sixty houses, nine hundred white and one hundred black inhabitants. But few of the Negroes are slaves. The main streets are conveniently spacious, and mostly ornamented with trees in the fronts of the houses, which are regularly arranged. The Delaware, opposite the town, is about a mile wide; and, under shelter of Mittinnicunk and Burlington Islands, affords a safe and convenient harbour. It is commodiously situated for trade, but is too near the opulent city of Philadelphia to admit of any considerable increase. There are two houses for public worship in the town, one for the Friends or Quakers, who are the most numerous, and one for Episcopalians. The other public buildings are two market houses, a courthouse, and the best gaol in the state. Besides these, there is an academy, already mentioned, a free school, a nail manufactory, and an excellent distillery, if that can be called excellent, which produces a poison both of health and morals.

The city is a free port. The mayor, recorder, and aldermen hold a commercial court, when the matter in controversy is between foreigners and foreigners, or between foreigners and citizens. The island of Burlington was laid out, and the first settlements made as early as 1677. In 1682, the island Mittinnicunk, or Free-School island, was given for the use of the island of Burlington; the yearly profits arising from it (which amount to one hundred and eighty pounds) are appropriated for the education of poor children.

PERTH AMBOY *(City)* took its name from James Drummond, earl of Perth; and Ambo, the Indian word for point, and stands on a neck of land included between Raritan river and Arthur Kull sound. Its situation is high and healthy. It lies open to Sandy Hook, and has one of the best harbours on the continent. Vessels from sea may enter it in one tide, in almost any weather. Great efforts have been made, and legislative encouragements offered, to render it a place of trade, but without success. This town was early incorporated with city privileges, and continued to send two members to the general assembly until the revolution. Until this event, it was the capital of East-Jersey; and the legislature and supreme court used to sit here and at Burlington alternately.

Brunswick *(City)* was incorporated in 1784, and is situated on the southwest side of Raritan river, twelve miles above Amboy. It contains about two hundred houses, and sixteen hundred inhabitants, one half of which are Dutch. Its situation is low and unpleasant, being on the bank of the river, and under a high hill which rises back of the town. The ice, at the breaking up of the river in winter, frequently lodges on the shallow fording-place, just opposite the town, and forms a temporary dam, which occasions the water to rise many feet above its usual height, and sometimes to overflow the lower floors of those houses which are not guarded against this inconvenience, by having their foundations elevated. The water in the springs and wells is generally bad. The inhabitants are beginning to build on the hill above the town, which is very pleasant, and commands a pretty prospect. The citizens have a considerable inland trade, and several small vessels belonging to the port.

Princeton, is a pleasant, healthy village, of about eighty houses, fifty-two miles from New-York, and forty-three from Philadelphia. Its public buildings are a large college edifice of stone, already described, and a presbyterian church built of brick.

Elizabethtown *(City)* is fifteen miles from New York. Its situation is pleasant, and its soil is equal in fertility to any in the state. In the compact part of the town, there are about one hundred and fifty houses. The public buildings are a very handsome presbyterian brick church, lately built,* an episcopal church, also of brick, and an academy. Governor Livingston's seat is about a mile westward of the compact part of the town. Its fine situation—the elegance and convenience of the buildings—the arangement and variety of forest-trees—the gardens ---the artificial fish-ponds, &c. discover a refined and judicious taste. Ornament and utility are happily united. It is, indeed, a seat worthy of a Republican Patriot, and of the author of the ' Philosophical Solitude.'§

This is one of the oldest towns in the state. It was purchased of the Indians as early as 1664, and was settled soon after.

Newark is nine miles from New-York. It is a handsome, flourishing town, about the size of Elizabethtown, and has two presbyterian churches, one of which is of stone and unfinished, and is the largest and most elegant building in the state. Besides these there is an episcopal church, a court-house and goal. This town has the fame of making the best cyder in the world.

Shrewsbury

---

* *Their former church, which was very elegant, was burnt in 1780, by a refugee, who was a native, and an inhabitant of Elizabethtown.*

§ *A celebrated Ode, written by Governor Livingston in early life.*

NEW JERSEY.

SHREWSBURY is between thirty and forty miles southwest by south from New York, on the sea coast, and is the largest and most populous town in the county of Monmouth. The soil in this and the neighbouring towns of Freehold and Middletown, are remarkably fertile. The inhabitants, 4321 in number, in the whole township, are a mixture of friends, episcopalians, presbyterians and methodists. Each has a house of worship. The friends are the most numerous. Among the first settlers of this town, which is one of the oldest in the state, were a number of families from New England.

MIDDLETOWN is fifty miles east by north from Trenton, and thirty southwest by south from New York, adjoining Shrewsbury. Sandy-Hook (so called from its shape and soil) is included in this township. On the point of the Hook stands the light house, one hundred feet high, built by the citizens of New York.

Practice of Physic.] There is a ‘Medical Society’ in this state, consisting of about thirty of their most respectable physicians, who meet twice a year. No person is admitted to the practice of physic, without a licence from the supreme court, founded on a certificate from this society, or at least two of its members, testifying his skill and abilities. It is remarkable that in the county of Cape May, no regular physician has ever found support. Medicine has been administered by women, except in some extraordinary cases.

Practice of Law.] No person is permitted to practice as an attorney in any court without a licence from the governor. This cannot be obtained, unless the candidate shall be above twenty-one years of age, and shall have served a regular clerkship with some licenced attorney for four years, and have taken a degree in some public college, otherwise he must serve five years. He must also submit to an examination by three of the most eminent counsellors in the state, in the presence of the judges of the supreme court. After three years practice as an attorney, he becomes a candidate for a counsellor's licence, which is granted on a like examination. In consequence of these wise regulations, the practice of law in this state is respectable. Many of the people here, however, as in other states, think (because perhaps they are instruments in obliging them to pay their debts) that the lawyers know too much. But their knowlege will not injure those who are innocent, and who will let them alone. Experience has verified this observation in the county of Cape May. No lawyer lives within sixty miles of that county, and it is seldom that any attend their courts. The consequence is, that no person's landed estate was ever sold in this county, by a sheriff, for the payment of a debt. It is wished that this county may ever form this singular exception, perhaps, from all the counties in the United States.

Constitution.] The government of this state, agreeably to their constitution, is vested in a governor, legislative council, and general assembly. The governor is chosen annually, by the council and assembly jointly, and is stiled, "Governor and commander in chief in and over the state of New Jersey, and the territories thereunto belonging, chancellor and ordinary in the same." The legislative council is composed of one member from each county, chosen annually by the people. They must be worth one thousand pounds in real and personal estate within the county,

NEW JERSEY.

and have been freeholders and inhabitants of the counties they represent for one year. The general assembly is composed of three members from each county chosen as above; each of them must be worth five hundred pounds, in real and personal estate within the county, and have been freeholders and inhabitants as above. All these, on taking their seats in the legislature, must swear "that he will not assent to any law, vote or proceeding, WHICH SHALL APPEAR TO HIM injurious to the public welfare of the state, or that shall annul or repeal that part of the constitution which establishes annual elections, nor that part respecting trial by jury, nor that part which secures liberty of conscience."

The governor sits in, and presides over the legislative council, and has a casting vote in their debates. His privy or executive council, is composed of any three members of the legislative council; and the governor and any seven members of the council are a court of appeals in the last resort, as to points of law in civil cases, and possess a power of pardoning criminals in all cases whatsoever. The council chuse one of their members to be vice president, who, when the governor is absent from the state, possesses the supreme executive power. The council may originate any bills, excepting preparing and altering any money bill, which is the sole prerogative of the assembly. In every other respect their powers are equal. Every bill is read three times in each house. None of the judges of the supreme court, or other courts, sheriffs, or any person possessed of any post of profit under the governor, except justices of the peace, is entitled to a seat in the assembly. The estate of a suicide is not forfeited for his offence.

Courts of Justice, Laws, &c.] The courts of justice in this state are, First, *Justices courts.* A competent number of persons are appointed in each county by the council and assembly, in joint meeting, who are called justices of the peace, and continue in office five years, who, besides being conservators of the peace, agreeably to the English laws, are authorized to hold courts for the trial of causes under twelve pounds. From this court, persons aggrieved, may appeal to the quarter sessions. Secondly, *Courts of quarter sessions of the peace*, are held quarterly in every county, by at least three of the justices. This court takes cognizance of breaches of the peace, and is generally regulated by the rules of the English law.

Thirdly, *Courts of common pleas*, which are held quarterly, by judges appointed for that purpose, in the same manner as the justices of the peace, and who are commonly of their number, and hold their commissions five years. This court may be held by a single judge, and has cognizance of demands to any amount, and is constructed on, and governed by the principles of the English laws.

Fourthly, *Supreme courts*, which are held four times a year, at Trenton, by three judges appointed for that purpose, who hold their offices three years, but one judge only is necessary to the holding this court. This court has cognizance of all actions, both civil and criminal throughout the state, having the united authority of the courts of kings bench, common pleas and exchequer in England. The courts of oyer and terminer and nisi prius, commonly held once a year in each county, for the trial of causes arising in the county, and brought to issue in the supreme

supreme court, are properly branches of this court, and are held by one of the judges of it, except that in the courts of oyer and terminer, some of the gentlemen of the county are always added in the commission as assistants to the judge; but they cannot hold the court without him.

Fifthly, *Orphan's courts*, lately established by act of assembly, are held by the judges of the court of common pleas, *ex officio*, and have cognizance of all matters relating to wills, administrations, &c.

Sixthly, *Court of Chancery*, held by the governor *ex officio*, always open. It is a court of law and equity, founded on the same principles, and governed by the same rules as the court of chancery in England.

Seventhly, *High Court of Errors and Appeals*, composed of the governor, and seven of the council, and is a court of appeals in the last resort, in all cases of law.

All the English laws which had been practised upon in the state, and which were not repugnant to revolution principles, were adopted by the constitution, and very few alterations of consequence have since been made, except in the descent of real estates, which, instead of descending to the eldest son, agreeably to the old feudal system, as formerly, are now divided (where there is no will) equally among the children, both male and female, except that the oldest son has two shares; a mode of descent much more consistent with republican principles.

Military strength.] The military strength of New Jersey, consists only of the militia, about 30,000 in number, who have been too much neglected since the war.

Revenue.] About £10,000 are raised annually for the support of government, and for the payment of incidental charges, and of the pensions of those who were disabled in the public service during the war; and about £44,000 raised annually for the payment of the interest on the public debt of this state, and their quota of the debt of the United States. This revenue is raised by a tax on lands, iron works, mills, distilleries, breweries, ferries, fisheries, carriages, stages, taverns, horses, cattle, &c.

History.] It is a task of no small difficulty to give the reader a just view of the history of New Jersey. Dr. Douglass observes in great truth, that ' the affairs of this colony have always been in a confused state, which occasions an unavoidable confusion in its history.'

The first settlers of New Jersey, were a number of Dutch emigrants from New York, who came over between the years 1614, and 1620, and settled in the county of Bergen. Next after these, in 1627, came over a colony of Swedes and Finns, and settled on the river Delaware. They afterwards purchased of the Indians, the land on both sides New-Swedeland stream, (now called Delaware river) from Cape Henlopen to the falls; and, by presents to the Indian chiefs, obtained peaceable possession of it. The Dutch and Swedes, though not in harmony with each other, kept possession of the country many years. In 1683, the Dutch had a house devoted to religious worship at New Castle; the Swedes at the same time had three, besides one on the island of Tenecum, one at Christiana, and one at Wicoco. The present Swedish churches in Philadelphia and Gloucester county in New Jersey, are descendants of these first settlers.

In

In March, 1634, Charles II. granted all the territory, called by the Dutch New Netherlands, to his brother the duke of York: And in June, 1664, the duke granted that part now called New Jerſey, to Lord Berkley of Stratton, and Sir George Carteret jointly; who, in 1665, agreed upon certain conceſſions with the people for the government of the province, and appointed Philip Carteret, Eſq. their governor. He purchaſed conſiderable tracts of land from the Indians, for ſmall conſiderations, and the ſettlements increaſed.

The Dutch reduced the country in 1672; but it was reſtored by the peace of Weſtminſter, February 9th, 1674.

In conſequence of the conqueſt made by the Dutch, and to obviate any objections that might be made on account of it againſt the former grant, a new patent was iſſued, in 1674, to the duke of York, for the ſame country. In July of this year, New Jerſey was divided, and Weſt Jerſey was granted, by the duke of York, to the aſſigns of Lord Berkley; and Eaſt Jerſey to Sir G. Carteret. The diviſion line was to run from the ſoutheaſt point of Little Egg Harbour, on Barnegate Creek, being about the middle between Cape May and Sandy Hook, to a creek, a little below Ancocus creek, on Delaware river, thence about thirty-five miles, ſtrait courſe, along Delaware river up to 41° 40′ north latitude. This line has never been ſettled, but has ever ſince continued to be a ſubject of contention.

In 1675, Weſt Jerſey, which had been granted to Lord Berkley, was ſold to John Fenwick, in truſt for Edward Bylinge. Fenwick came over with a colony, and ſettled at Salem. Theſe were the firſt Engliſh ſettlers in Weſt Jerſey. In 1676, the intereſt of Bylinge in Weſt Jerſey was aſſigned to William Penn, Gavin Laurie, and Nicolas Lucas, as truſtees, for the uſe of his creditors. Mutual quit claims were executed between Sir George Carteret and the truſtees of Bylinge. This partition was confirmed in 1719, by an act of the general aſſembly of the Jerſeys.

In 1678, the duke of York made a new grant of Weſt Jerſey to the aſſigns of Lord Berkley.

Agreeably to Sir George Carteret's will, dated December 5, 1678, Eaſt Jerſey was ſold, in 1682, to twelve proprietors, who by twelve ſeparate deeds, conveyed one half of their intereſt to twelve other perſons, ſeparately, in fee ſimple. This grant was confirmed to theſe twenty-four proprietors, by the duke of York the ſame year. Theſe twenty-four ſhares, by ſales of ſmall parts of them, and by theſe ſmall parts being again divided among the children of ſucceſſive families, became at laſt ſubdivided in ſuch a manner, as that ſome of the proprietors had only one 40th part, of a 48th part of a 24th ſhare. Weſt Jerſey was in the ſame condition. This created much confuſion in the management of the general proprietors, particularly in regard to appointing governors. Theſe inconveniences, aided by other cauſes of complaint, which had been increaſing for ſeveral years, and were faſt advancing to a dangerous criſis, diſpoſed the proprietors to ſurrender the government to the crown; which was accordingly done, and accepted by queen Ann, on the 17th of April, 1702. Till this time the government of New Jerſey was proprietory; it now became royal, and ſo continued till the memorable fourth of July, 1776. This

NEW JERSEY. 301

This state was the seat of war for several years, during the bloody contest between Great Britain and America. Her losses both of men and property, in proportion to the population and wealth of the state, was greater than of any other of the thirteeen states. When General Washington was retreating through the Jersies, almost forsaken by all others, her militia were at all times obedient to his orders; and for a considerable length of time, composed the strength of his army. There is hardly a town in the state that lay in the progress of the British army, that was not rendered signal by some enterprize or exploit. At Trenton the enemy received a check which may be said with justice to have turned the tide of the war. At Princeton, the seat of the muses, they received another, which, united, obliged them to retire with precipitation, and to take refuge in disgraceful winter quarters. But whatever honour this state might derive from the relation, it is not our business to give a particular description of battles or sieges; we leave this to the pen of the historian, and only observe in general, that the many military atchievments performed by the Jersey soldiers, give this state one of the first ranks among her sisters in a military view, and entitle her to a share of praise that bears no proportion to her size, in the accomplishment of the late glorious revolution.

GOVERNORS of NEW JERSEY, *from the surrender of the Government by the Proprietors in 1702, to the present time.*

† Edward, viscount Cornbury, 1702 to 1708, removed and succeeded by
† John, lord Lovelace,   1708 to 1709, died and the government devolved to
  Lt. Gov. Richard Ingoldsby, 1709 to 1710, when came in
† Brigadier Robert Hunter,   1710 to 1720, who resigned in favour of
† William Burnet,   1720 to 1727, removed and succeeded by
† John Montgomery,   1728 to 1731, died and was succeeded by
† William Crosby,   1731 to 1736, died and the government devolved to
  John Anderson, *President of the Council* 1736, by whose death about two weeks after the government devolved to
  John Hamilton, *President of the Council* 1736 to 1738

Those marked † were Governors in chief, and down to this time were Governors of New York and New Jersey, but from 1738 forward, New Jersey has had a separate governor.

† Lewis Morris,   1738 to 1746, died and the government devolved to
  John Hamilton, *President,* 1746——— by whose death it devolved to
  John Reading, *President,* 1746 to 1747.
† Jonathan Belcher,   1747 to 1757, died and the government again devolved to
  John Reading, *President,* 1757 to 1758.

Thomas Pownall, then Governor of Massachusetts, being Lieutenant Governor, arrived on the death of Governor Belcher, but continued in the province a few days only.

† Francis Bernard,   1758 to 1760, removed to Boston and succeeded by

† Thomas

PENNSYLVANIA

‡ Thomas Boone,   1760 to 1761, removed to S. Carolina and succeeded by
‡ Josiah Hardy,   1761 to 1763, removed & succeeded by
‡ William Franklin,   1763 to 1776, removed & succeeded by
‡ William Livingston,   1776——

✣✣✣✣✣✣✣✣✣✣✣✣✣✣✣✣✣✣✣✣✣✣✣✣✣✣✣✣✣✣✣✣✣

PENNSYLVANIA.

SITUATION and EXTENT.

Miles.
Length 288 } Between { 39° 43 and 42° North Latitude.
Breadth 156 }   { 0° 20′ East, and 5° West Longitude.

Boundaries. BOUNDED east, by Delaware river; north, by the parallel of 42° north latitude, which divides it from the state of New York; south, by the parallel of 39° 43′ 18″ north latitude, which divides it from the states of Delaware, Maryland, and Virginia; west, by a meridian line, drawn from the termination of five degrees of longitude, from a point on Delaware river, near Wilmington, in the parallel of 39° 43 18″ to intersect the parallel of 42°. This line divides this state from a part of Virginia, the Western Territory, (so called) and from a tract of land, 20 miles square, which was confirmed to Connecticut by Congress. The northwest corner of Pennsylvania, extends about one mile and an half into Lake Erie, and is about twenty miles west of the old French fort at Presque Isle. The state lies in the form of a parallelogram, and contains about 44,900 square miles, equal to about 28,800,000 acres.

Mines and Minerals.] The following table exhibits the number, situation, and various kinds of mines and minerals in this state. On the west side of the mountains, vitriolic, aluminous, and other mineral earths are found in great abundance. Beds of coal, lying pretty deep, in a horizontal direction, are almost universal in this western country; but metallic ores of all kinds, especially that of iron, appear to be wanting; while they are found in great plenty eastward of the mountains. A very probable reason has been assigned why it should be so. It is this; The country eastward of the mountains, as hereafter mentioned, has evidently been torn to pieces by some violent convulsion, while that on the other side has remained undisturbed. During this convulsion, the iron ore was probably thrown up from very great depths, where, by its gravity, it was accumulated, and coal, which lay nearer the surface, was, by the same convulsion buried immensely deep.

Civil

PENNSYLVANIA.

Civil divisions.] Pennsylvania is divided into twenty counties, which, with their county towns, situation, &c. are mentioned in the following table.

TABLE.

Counties.	County Towns.	Situation.	Settl'd	Mines, &c.
Philadel. (City)	Philadelphia.	On Delaware R	All	
Chester.	West Chester.	On Susquehan. R	All	Iron ore.
Philadelphia.	Philadelphia.	On Delaware R	All	
Bucks.	Newton.	On Delaware R	All	Iron ore.
Montgomery.	Norriston.	On Schuylkill R	All	Iron ore.
Lancaster.	Lancaster.	On Susquehan. R	All	Iron ore.
Dauphin.	Louisburg.	On Susquehan. R	$\frac{3}{4}$	
Berks.	Reading.	On Schuylkill R	$\frac{3}{4}$	Coal mines &c
Northampton.	Easton.	On Delaware R	$\frac{3}{4}$	Iron ore.
Luzerne.	Wilksborough.	On Susquehan. R	$\frac{3}{4}$	Coal mines.
York.	York.	On Susquehan. R	$\frac{1}{2}$	Iron ore.
Cumberland.	Carlisle.	On Susquehan. R	$\frac{1}{2}$	Lead mines &c
Northumberland.	Sunbury.	On west branch S.	*$\frac{1}{12}$	
Franklin.	Chamberstown.	On Susquehan. R	$\frac{3}{4}$	
Bedford.	Bedford.	On Juniatta R	$\frac{1}{2}$	Iron mines &c
Huntingdon.	Huntingdon.	On Juniatta R	$\frac{1}{4}$	Coal mines.
Westmoreland.	Greensburg.	On Allegany R	$\frac{1}{4}$	Coal mines.
Fayette.	Union.	On Monongahela	$\frac{1}{2}$	
Washington.	Washington.	. W. corner state	$\frac{1}{4}$	
Allegany.	Pittsburg.	On Allegany R	$\frac{1}{4}$	

Rivers.

* A very large proportion of the vacant lands in the state are in this county, (Northumberland) to the amount of about eight millions of acres.

PENNSYLVANIA.

Rivers.] There are six considerable rivers which, with their numerous branches, peninsulate the whole state, viz. The Delaware, Schuylkill, Susquehannah, Yohoganey, Monongahela, and Allegany. We have already given an account of the rise and progress of Delaware river, until it crosses into Pennsylvania (page 245): From the mouth of Delaware bay, at Cape Henlopen, to Philadelphia, is reckoned one hundred and eighteen miles. So far there is a sufficient depth of water for a seventy-four gun ship. From Philadelphia to Trenton Falls is thirty-five miles. This is the head of sloop navigation. The river is navigable for boats that carry eight or nine tons, forty miles further, and for Indian canoes, except several small falls or portages, one hundred and fifty miles. At Easton, it receives the Lehigh from the west, which is navigable thirty miles. The tide sets up as high as Trenton Falls, and at Philadelphia rises generally about six feet. A north-east and east wind raises it higher.

On Cape Henlopen * stands the light house, with a few other houses. Opposite the light house on the Jersey shore, twelve miles, is Cape May. Between these Capes is the entrance into the Delaware bay. The entrance into the river is twenty miles further up, at Bombay Hook, where the river is four or five miles wide. From Bombay Hook to Reedy Island is twenty miles. This island is the rendezvous of outward bound ships in autumn and spring, waiting for a favourable wind. The course from this to the sea is S. S. E. so that a N. W. wind, which is the prevailing wind in these seasons, is fair for vessels to put out to sea. This river is generally frozen one or two months in the year so as to prevent navigation.

From Chester to Philadelphia, twenty miles, the channel of the river is narrowed by islands of marsh, which are generally banked and turned into rich and *immensely valuable* meadows.

Billingsport, twelve miles below Philadelphia, was fortified in the late war for the defence of the channel. Opposite this fort, several large frames of timber, headed with iron spikes, called chevaux de frizes, were sunk to prevent the British ships from passing. Since the peace, a curious machine has been invented in Philadelphia, to raise them.

The Schuylkill rises north west of the Kittatinny mountains, through which it passes, into a fine champaign country, and runs, from its source, upwards of one hundred and twenty miles in a south east direction, and falls into the Delaware three miles below Philadelphia. It is navigable from above Reading, eighty-five or ninety miles, to its mouth. There are three floating bridges thrown across it, made of logs fastened together, and lying upon the water.

The Susquehannah river rises in lake Otsego, in the state of New York, and runs in such a winding course as to cross the boundary line between New York and Pennsylvania three times. It receives Tyoga river, one of its principal branches, in lat. 41° 57', three miles south of the boundary line. The Susquehannah branch is navigable for batteaux to its source, whence, to Mohawks river, is but twenty miles. The Tyoga branch is navigable fifty miles, for batteaux; and its source is but a few miles from the Cheneffee, which empties into lake Ontario. From

Tyoga

---

* *Henlopen* is a Swedish word, signifying 'entering in.'

Tyoga point, the river proceeds southeast to Wyoming, without any obstruction by falls, and then southwest, over Wyoming falls, till at Sunbury, in about lat. 41° it meets the west branch of Susquehannah, which is navigable ninety miles from its mouth, and some of the branches of it are navigable fifty miles, and are said to approach very near some of the boatable branches of the Allegany river. From Sunbury the river is passable with boats to Louisburg and Middletown, on Swetara; and with rafts of boards and masts to Lancaster, but it is attended with difficulty and danger on account of the numerous falls below Middletown. About fifteen miles above Louisburg, it receives the Juniatta, from the north west, proceeding from the Allegany mountains, and flowing through a mountainous, broken country. It is navigable, however, eighty miles from its mouth.

The Swetara, which falls into the Susquehannah from the northeast, is navigable fifteen miles. It is in contemplation to cut a canal about twenty miles from the Swetara to the Tulpehocken, a branch of the Schuylkill. Should this be effected, a passage would be open to Philadelphia from the Juniatta, the Tyoga, and the east and west branches of the Susquehannah, which water at least 15,000,000 of acres. From this junction, the general course of the river is about southeast until it falls into the head of Chesapeek bay, just below Havre de Grace. It is about a mile wide at its mouth, and is navigable for sea vessels but about twenty miles, on account of its rapids. The banks of this river are very romantic, particularly where it passes through the mountains. This passage has every appearance of having been forced through by the pressure of the water, or of having been burst open by some convulsion in nature.

The several branches of Yohogany river rise on the west side of the Allegany mountains. After running a short distance, they unite and form a large beautiful river, which, in passing some of the most western ridges of the mountains, precipitates itself over a level ledge of rocks, lying nearly at right angles to the course of the river. These falls, called the Ohiopyle falls, are about twenty feet in perpendicular height, and the river is perhaps eighty yards wide. For a considerable distance below the falls, the water is very rapid, and boils and foams vehemently, occasioning a continual mist to rise from it, even at noon day, and in fair weather. The river at this place runs to the southwest, but presently winds round to the northwest, and continuing this course for thirty or forty miles, it loses its name by uniting with the Monongahela, which comes from the southward, and contains perhaps, twice as much water. These united streams, shortly after their junction, mingle with the waters of the Allegany at Pittsburgh, and together form the grand river Ohio.

The Monongahela has been particularly described, and some observations made on the navigation of the Allegany. (Page 44.) In addition it may be observed, that at the junction of French Creek (which comes from the northwest) with the Allegany, are the remains of a British fortification; and about a mile above is a fort, built in 1787, and then guarded by a company of about sixty American soldiers, under the command of Capt. Hart, from Connecticut. The Pennsylvania north line, crosses French Creek about three miles above Le Bœuf, where there was formerly a fort. From Le Bœuf to Presque-isle, fourteen or fifteen miles, is an old waggon road, cut by the French in the war of 1755. The lands on French Creek are very fertile, and mostly cleared, which is an evidence that its former Indian inhabitants were numerous. Fourteen miles from the mouth of this creek is a gentle rapid, thence to its mouth, it is slow, deep and smooth.

Before we leave this interesting head concerning rivers, we cannot omit inserting the observations of Mr. Charles Thomson, secretary of Congress. 'Besides the three channels mentioned (page 45) between the western waters, and the Atlantic, there are two others, to which the Pennsylvanians are turning their attention; one from Presque-isle, on Lake Erie, to Le Bœuf, down the Allegany to Kiskiminitas, then up the Kiskiminitas, and from thence, by a small portage, to Juniata, which falls into the Susquehanna: The other from Lake Ontario to the east branch of the Delaware, and down that to Philadelphia. Both these are said to be very practicable; and, considering the enterprising temper of the Pennsylvanians, and particularly of the merchants of Philadelphia, whose object is concentered in promoting the commerce and trade of one city, it is not improbable but one or both of these communications will be opened and improved.'*

There is said to be still another communication equally as practicable as either of the others; and that is between the southern branch of the Tyoga and a branch of the Allegany, the head waters of which, are but a short distance from each other. The Seneca Indians say they can walk four times in a day, from the boatable waters of the Ohio, to those of the Tyoga, at the place now mentioned. And between the Susquehannah, just before it crosses into Pennsylvania the first time, and the Delaware, is a portage of only twelve miles.

One remark must not be omitted here, and that is, that in all the back country, waters of this state, even in those high up in the mountains, marine petrefactions may be found in great abundance.

Swamps.] The only swamps worth noticing, are, the *Great Swamp*, between Northampton and Luzerne counties, and *Buffaloe swamp* in the northwestern parts of Northumberland county, near the head waters of the west branch of the Susquehannah. These swamps, on examination and survey, are found to be bodies of rich farm land, thickly covered with beach and sugar maple.

Mountains, face of the country, soil and productions.] As much as nearly one third of this state may be called mountainous; particularly the counties of Bedford, Huntingdon, Cumberland, part of Franklin, Dauphin, and part of Bucks and Northampton, through which pass, under various names, the numerous ridges and spurs, which collectively form what we chuse to call, for the sake of clearness, the GREAT RANGE OF ALLEGANY MOUNTAINS. The principal ridges in this range, in Pennsylvania, are the Kittatinny, or Blue mountain, which pass north of Nazareth in Northampton county, and pursue a southwest course, across the Lehigh, through Dauphin county, just above Louisburg, thence on the west side of the Susquehannah through Cumberland and Franklin counties. Back of these, and nearly parallel with them, are Peters, Tuscarora, and Nescopek mountains, on the east of the Susquehannah; and on the west,

Shareman's

* See Appendix to Mr. Jefferson's Notes on Virginia. No. I.

Shareman's hills, Sideling hills, Ragged, Great Warriors, Evits and Wills mountains; then the great Allegany ridge, which being the largeſt, gives its name to the whole range; weſt of this are the Laurel and Cheſnut ridges. Between the Juniatta and the weſt branch of the Suſquehannah are Jacks, Tuſſys, Nittiny and Bald Eagle mountains. The vales between theſe mountains are generally of a rich, black ſoil, ſuited to the various kinds of grain and graſs. Some of the mountains will admit of cultivation almoſt to their tops.

There is a remarkable difference between the country on the eaſt and weſt ſide of the range of mountains we have juſt been deſcribing. Between theſe mountains and the lower falls of the rivers which run into the Atlantic, not only in this but in all the ſouthern ſtates, are ſeveral ranges of ſtones, ſand, earths and minerals, which lie in the utmoſt confuſion. Beds of ſtone, of vaſt extent, particularly of limeſtone, have their ſeveral layers broken in pieces, and the fragments thrown confuſedly in every direction. Between theſe lower falls and the ocean, is a very extenſive collection of ſand, clay, mud and ſhells, partly thrown up by the waves of the ſea, partly brought down by floods from the upper county, and partly produced by the decay of vegetable ſubſtances. The country weſtward of the Allegany mountains, in theſe reſpects, is totally different. It is very irregular, broken and variegated, but there are no mountains; and when viewed from the moſt weſtern ridge of the Allegany, it appears to be a vaſt extended plain. All the various ſtrata of ſtone appear to have lain undiſturbed in the ſituation wherein they were firſt formed. The layers of clay, ſand and coal, are nearly horizontal. Scarcely a ſingle inſtance is to be found to the contrary. Detached rocks are indeed found here in all ſituations, as well as eaſtward of the mountains; but theſe are only ſuch as lie near the ſurface, and being undermined by the waters, have tumbled from their original places. Every appearance, in ſhort, tends to confirm the opinion, that the original cruſt, in which the ſtone was formed, has never been broken up on the weſt ſide of the mountains, as it evidently has been eaſtward of them. The irregularity and unevenneſs of the country weſtward of the mountains, appear to have been the effect of water deſcending in heavy ſhowers of rain. Many thouſands of ſquare miles are cut by innumerable deep drains for carrying off water, and nothing is left between them but high, ſteep and narrow ridges. The prodigious rains which produced this ſurprizing effect, probably filled up the intervals between the mountains, and the preſſure of the water in time, may have become ſo great as to have, at length, broken through the loweſt and weakeſt parts of them; and in ſuch places have carried away the rocks which formed the ridges, down nearly as low as the preſent beds of the rivers; part of the water running eaſtward, and part weſtward, ſo that the principal ridge, the proper Allegany, only was left unbroken. The rocks, thus torn from their beds, appear to have been lodged within a few miles of the mountains, where at this day we find them; and the gravel, ſand and earth, carried far below, and depoſited in the lower country, in ſucceſſion, according to their reſpective gravities.*

In

---

* See Col. Mag. Vol. I. P. 49.

In this connection, in confirmation of what we have now been saying, and also of what was observed, page 48, I beg leave to introduce the remarks of the secretary of Congress, whom we just now quoted, which were suggested on his reading Mr. Jefferson's description of the passage of the Patomak through the Blue ridge. 'The reflections I was led into on viewing this passage of the Patomak through the Blue ridge were, that this country must have suffered some violent convulsion, and that the face of it must have been changed from what it probably was some centuries ago; that the broken and ragged faces of the mountain on each side the river; the tremendous rocks, which are left with one end fixed in the precipice, and the other jutting out, and seemingly ready to fall for want of support; the bed of the river for several miles below obstructed, and filled with the loose stones carried from this mound; in short, every thing on which you cast your eye evidently demonstrates a disrupture and breach in the mountain, and that, before this happened, what is now a fruitful vale, was formerly a great lake or collection of water, which possibly might have here formed a mighty cascade, or had its vent to the ocean by the Susquehannah, where the Blue ridge seems to terminate. Besides this, there are other parts of this country which bear evident traces of a like convulsion. From the best accounts I have been able to obtain, the place where the Delaware now flows through the Kittatinny mountain, which is a continuation of what is called the North ridge, or mountain, was not its original course, but that it passed through what is now called 'the Wind-gap,' a place several miles to the westward, and above an hundred feet higher than the present bed of the river. This wind-gap is about a mile broad, and the stones in it such as seem to have been washed for ages by water running over them. Should this have been the case, there must have been a large lake behind that mountain, and by some uncommon swell in the waters, or by some convulsion of nature, the river must have opened its way through a different part of the mountain, and meeting there with less obstruction, carried away with it the opposing mounds of earth, and deluged the country below with the immense collection of waters to which this new passage gave vent. There are still remaining, and daily discovered, innumerable instances of such a deluge on both sides of the river, after it passed the hills above the falls of Trenton, and reached the champaign. On the New Jersey side, which is flatter than the Pennsylvania side, all the country below Crosswick hills seems to have been overflowed to the distance of from ten to fifteen miles back from the river, and to have acquired a new soil by the earth and clay brought down and mixed with the native sand. The spot on which Philadelphia stands evidently appears to be made ground. The different strata through which they pass in digging to water, the acorns, leaves, and sometimes branches, which are found above twenty feet below the surface, all seem to demonstrate this. I am informed that at York town in Virginia, in the bank of York river, there are different strata of shells and earth, one above another, which seem to point out that the country there has undergone several changes; that the sea has, for a succession of ages, occupied the place where dry land now appears; and that the ground has been suddenly raised at various periods. What a

change

change would it make in the country below, should the mountains at Niagara, by any accident, be cleft asunder, and a passage suddenly opened to drain off the waters of Erie and the Upper Lakes! While ruminating on these subjects, I have often been hurried away by fancy, and led to imagine, that what is now the bay of Mexico, was once a champaign country; and that from the point or cape of Florida, there was a continued range of mountains through Cuba, Hispaniola, Porto rico, Martinique, Gaudaloupe, Barbadoes, and Trinidad, till it reached the coast of America, and formed the shores which bounded the ocean, and guarded the country behind: That, by some convulsion or shock of nature, the sea had broken through these mounds, and deluged that vast plain, till it reached the foot of the Andes; that being there heaped up by the trade-winds, always blowing from one quarter, it had found its way back, as it continues to do, through the gulph between Florida and Cuba, carrying with it the loom and sand it may have scooped from the country it had occupied, part of which it may have deposited on the shores of North America, and with part formed the banks of Newfoundland.—But these are only the visions of fancy.*

In addition to what we have already said respecting the face of the country in Pennsylvania, it may be observed, that, except the Allegany range of mountains, which crosses the state in an oblique direction, and is from twenty to fifty miles wide, the state is generally level, or agreeably diversified with gentle hills and vales.

The soil is of the various kinds; in some parts it is barren; a great proportion of the state is good land; and no inconsiderable part is very good. Perhaps the proportion of first rate land is not greater in any of the thirteen states. The richest part of the state that is settled is Lancaster county. The richest that is unsettled, is between Allegany river and Lake Erie, in the northwest corner of the state. Of this fine tract, 100,000 acres, lying on, and near French Creek, are for sale by the state. The convenient communications through this creek into the Allegany, and from the Allegany, through various creeks and rivers to the Susquehannah and Patomak have already been mentioned.

The north side of Pennsylvania is the richest and the best settled land throughout, owing entirely to the circumstance of the western road having been run by the armies, prior to 1762, through the towns of Lancaster, Carlisle and Bedford, and thence to Pittsburg. For the purpose of turning the tide of settlers from this old channel into the unsettled and more fertile parts of the state, the government and landed interest of Pennsylvania have been, and are still busy in cutting convenient roads. During the last summer (1788) they run a road north, from the former roads beyond Bethlehem, to the north portage between Delaware and Susquehannah; and thence north 80 degrees west to the mouth of the Tyoga, the first seventy miles, and the last above sixty. It is now in contemplation to cut a road from Sunbury, at the forks of the east and west branches of Susquehannah; west, 150 miles, to the mouth of Toby's creek, which empties into the Allegany river, from the east. This road will be through a tract of rich land, now for sale by
the

* Jefferson's Notes on Virginia. Appendix No. II.

PENNSYLVANIA.

the state. A road is also cutting from the mouth of the Tyoga, southward, to the mouth of Loyal, a branch of the west branch of Susquehannah. Another road is cutting from Huntingdon town, on Franks town branch of the Juniatta, westward thirty miles, to a navigable branch of the Allegany.

Thus the well judged policy of this state, is paving the way for the settlement of all their waste lands. And to evidence their benevolence, and their wishes to have the advantages of education increased, and more extensively enjoyed, they have allotted 60,000 acres of these waste lands for the use of public schools; and above 60,000 more have been granted for that purpose, and to the societies established for the promotion of knowledge, the arts, religion, &c.

In addition to the common observation, that the natural growth of this state is similar to that of New Jersey, and New York, which is indeed the case in most respects, it may be said, that there are in Pennsylvania, great bodies of sugar maple, particularly in the counties of Northampton, Luzerne, Northumberland and Washington, which yield a well tasted and wholesome sugar, to profit.

Cumberland and Franklin valley is timbered principally with locust, black walnut, hickory and white oak. The mountainous parts are covered with pines, chesnuts, &c.

The produce from culture, consists of wheat, which is the staple commodity of the state, some rye, indian corn, buck wheat, oats, spletz,* barley, which is now raised in greater quantities than formerly, occasioned by the vast consumption of it by the breweries in Philadelphia, hemp, flax and vegetables of all the various kinds common to the climate. Pennsylvania is a good grazing country, and great numbers of cattle are fed, and large dairies are kept, but their beef, pork and cheese, are not reckoned so good as those of Connecticut and the other parts of New England; but their butter has been supposed superior.

Climate, diseases, longevity, &c.] Nothing different from that of Connecticut; except, that on the west side of the mountains, the weather is much more regular. The inhabitants never feel those quick transitions from cold to heat, by a change of the wind from north to south, as those so frequently experience, who live eastward of the mountains, and near the sea. The hot southwardly winds get chilled by passing over the long chain of Allegany mountains.

It has been observed that Pennsylvania is now more unhealthy than formerly; that bilious and remitting fevers, which a few years ago, appeared chiefly in the neighbourhood of rivers, creeks and mill ponds, now appear in parts remote from them all, and in the highest situations. This change has been traced to three causes; First, To the increase of mill ponds. Till these were established, intermittents, in several counties in Pennsylvania, were unknown. Secondly, To the clearing of the country. It has been remarked that intermittents on the shores of the Susquehannah, have kept an exact pace with the passages which have been opened for the propagation of marsh effluvia, by cutting down the wood which formerly grew in its neighbourhood. A distinction, however,

* See this kind of grain described, Page 53.

PENNSYLVANIA. 311

however, is to be made between clearing and cultivating a country. While clearing a country makes it sickly in the manner that has been mentioned, cultivating a country, that is, draining swamps, destroying weeds, burning brush, and exhaling the unwholsome and superfluous moisture of the earth, by means of frequent crops of grain, grasses and vegetables of all kinds, render it healthy. Several parts of the United States have pressed through the several stages that have been described. The first settlers received their country from the hand of nature, pure and healthy. Fevers soon followed their improvements, nor were they finally banished, until the higher degrees of cultivation took place. Nor even then, where the salutary effects of cultivation were rendered abortive by the neighbourhood of mill ponds.

As a third cause of this increase of fevers, the unequal quantities of rain which have fallen of late years, has been assigned. While the creeks and rivers were confined within steady bounds, there was little or no exhalation of febrile miasmata from their shores. But the dry summers of 1780, 1781, and 1782, by reducing the rivers and creeks far below their ancient marks; while the wet spring of 1784 and 1785, by swelling them, beyond their natural heights, have, when they have fallen, as in the former case, left a large and extensive surface of moist ground exposed to the action of the sun, and of course to the generation and exhalation of fabrile miasmata.*

This state, having been settled but little more than a hundred years, is not sufficiently old to determine from facts the state of longevity. Among the people called Quakers, who are the oldest settlers, there are instances of longevity, occasioned by their living in the old, cultivated counties, and the temperance imposed on them by their religion. There are fewer long-lived people among the Germans, than among other nations, occasioned by their excess of labour and low diet. They live chiefly upon vegetables and watery food, that affords too little nourishment to repair the waste of their strength by hard labour.

Nearly one half of the children born in Philadelphia, die under two years of age, and chiefly with a disease in the stomach and bowels. Very few die at this age in the country.

Population, character, manners, &c.] In the grand convention, which was held in Philadelphia, in the summer of 1787, the inhabitants in Pennsylvania, were reckoned at 60,000. It is probable they are now more numerous: perhaps 400,000. If we fix them at this, the population for every square mile will be only nine; by which it appears that Pennsylvania is only one fifth as populous as Connecticut.

But Connecticut was settled nearly half a century before Pennsylvania; so that in order to do justice to Pennsylvania in the comparison, we must anticipate her probable population fifty years hence. At this period, if we admit that the number of inhabitants is doubled once in twenty-five years, by natural increase, without the aid of foreign immigrations, the population will be equal to thirty-six for every square mile. Add to this, 400,000, for the increase by immigrants and their descendents,

---

* *Enquiry into the causes of the increase of fevers in Pennsylvania.* By Dr. Rush.

dents, which is probably not too large a number, considering the length of time—the extensive tracts of rich and vacant lands—the spirit of emmigration in the eastern states—the probable influx of inhabitants, upon the establishment and salutary operation of the new government—and the inducements which are held up to encourage settlers to fix in this state. All these things taken into view, we may venture to predict, that Pennsylvania at the end of half a century from this time, will contain two millions of souls, which is about forty-five for every square mile, equal to the present population of Connecticut.

Statement of the number of taxable inhabitants in Pennsylvania, in the year 1760, 1770, 1779, and 1786.*

	1760	1770	1779	1786
Philadelphia city and county,	8,321	10,455	{ 3,681 7,066	4,876 4,516
Bucks county,	3,148	3,177	4,067	4,237
Chester,	4,761	5,483	6,378	6,268
Lancaster,	5,631	6,608	8,433	5,839
York,	3,302	4,426	6,281	6,254
Cumberland,	1,501	3,521	5,092	3,939
Berks,	3,016	3,302	4,662	4,732
Northampton,	1,987	2,793	3,600	3,967
Bedford,	-	-	1,201	2,632
Northumberland,	-	-	2,111	2,166
Westmoreland,	-	-	2,111	2,653
Washington,	-	-	-	3,908
Fayette,	-	-	-	2,041
Franklin,	-	-	-	2,237
Montgomery,	-	-	-	3,725
Dauphin,	-	-	-	2,881
Luzerne,	-	-	-	†
Total,	31,667	39,765	54,683	66,925

The number of of militia in Pennsylvania, are reckoned at 85,000, between eighteen and fifty-three years of age.

The inhabitants of Pennsylvania consist of migrants from England, Ireland, Germany and Scotland. The Friends, and Episcopalians are chiefly of English extraction, and compose about one third of the inhabitants. They live principally in the city of Philadelphia, and in the counties

---

* So often have the counties of this state been divided and subdivided—and the boundaries altered, that a comparison in this statement can hardly be made, except between the several totals: as, for instance, it would appear from the above table that Philadelphia county had decreased in population between the years 1779 and 1786—whereas the contrary is the case—for Montgomery county was struck off from it. The same is observable of all the counties wherein a decrease appears.

† No return.

PENNSYLVANIA. 313

Counties of Chester, Philadelphia, Bucks and Montgomery. The Irish are mostly Presbyterians. Their ancestors came from the north of Ireland, which was originally settled from Scotland; hence they have sometimes been called Scotch-Irish, to denote their double descent. But they are commonly and more properly called Irish, or the descendents of people from the north of Ireland. They inhabit the western and frontier counties, and are numerous.

The Germans compose one quarter at least, if not a third of the inhabitants of Pennsylvania. They inhabit the north parts of the city of Philadelphia, and the counties of Philadelphia, Montgomery, Bucks, Dauphin, Lancaster, York and Northampton; mostly in the four last. They consist of Lutherans, (who are the most numerous sect) Calvinists, Moravians, Mennonists, Tunkers (corruptly called Dunkers) and Swingfelters, who are a species of Quakers. These are all distinguished for their temperance, industry and oeconomy.

The Germans have usually fifteen of sixty-nine members in the assembly; and some of them have arisen to the first honours in the state, and now fill a number of the higher offices. Yet the lower class are very ignorant and superstitious. It is not uncommon to see them going to market with a little bag of salt tied to their horses manes, for the purpose, they say, of keeping off the witches.

The Baptists (except the Mennonist and Tunker Baptists, who are Germans) are chiefly the descendants of emigrants from Wales, and are not numerous. A proportionate assemblage of the national prejudices, the manners, customs, religions and political sentiments of all these, will form the Pennsylvanian character. As the leading traits in this character, thus constituted, we may venture to mention industry, frugality, bordering in some instances on parsimony, enterprize, a taste and ability for improvements in mechanics, in manufactures, in agriculture, in commerce and in the liberal sciences; temperance, plainness and simplicity in dress and manners; pride and humility in their extremes; inoffensiveness and intrigue; in regard to religion, variety and harmony; liberality and its opposites, superstition and bigotry; and in politics an unhappy jargon. Such appear to be the distinguishing traits in the collective Pennsylvanian character.

In this connection, and in a work of this kind, the remarks of a citizen of Philadelphia, on 'the progress of population, agriculture, manners and government in Pennsylvania, in a letter to his friend in England,' are too valuable to be omitted.

'The first settler in the woods is generally a man who has outlived his credit or fortune in the cultivated parts of the state. His time for migrating is in the month of April. His first object is to build a small cabbin of rough logs for himself and family. The floor of this cabbin is of earth, the roof is of split logs—the light is received through the door, and, in some instances, through a small window made of greased paper. A coarser building adjoining this cabbin affords a shelter to a cow, and pair of poor horses. The labour of erecting these buildings is succeeded by killing the trees on a few acres of ground near his cabbin; this is done by cutting a circle round the trees, two or three feet from the ground. The ground around these trees is then ploughed and

Indian corn planted in it. The feafon for planting this grain is about the 20th of May—It grows generally on new ground with but little cultivation, and yields in the month of October following, from 40 to 50 bufhels per acre. After the firft of September it affords a good deal of nourifhment to his family, in its green or unripe ftate, in the form of what is called *roafting ears*. His family is fed during the fummer by a fmall quantity of grain which he carries with him, and by fifh and game. His cows and horfes feed upon wild grafs, or the fucculent twigs of the woods. For the firft year he endures a great deal of diftrefs from hunger—cold—and a variety of accidental caufes, but he feldom complains or finks under them. As he lives in the neighbourhood of Indians, he foon acquires a ftrong tincture of their manners. His exertions, while they continue, are violent; but they are fucceeded by long intervals of reft. His pleafures confift chiefly in fifhing and hunting. He loves fpirituous liquors, and he eats, drinks and fleeps in dirt and rags in his little cabbin. In his intercourfe with the world he manifefts all the art which characterize the Indians of our country. In this fituation he paffes two or three years. In proportion as population increafes around him, he becomes uneafy and diffatisfied. Formerly his cattle ranged at large, but now his neighbours call upon him to confine them within fences, to prevent their trefpaffing upon their fields of grain. Formerly he fed his family with wild animals, but thefe, which fly from the face of man, now ceafe to afford him an eafy fubfiftence, and he is compelled to raife domeftic animals for the fupport of his family. Above all, he revolts againft the operation of laws. He cannot bear to furrender up a fingle natural right for all the benefits of government; and therefore he abandons his little fettlement, and feeks a retreat in the woods, where he again fubmits to all the toils which have been mentioned. There are inftances of many men who have broken ground on bare creation, not lefs than four different times in this way, in different and more advanced parts of the ftate. It has been remarked, that the flight of this clafs of people is always increafed by the preaching of the gofpel. This will not furprife us when we confider how oppofite its precepts are to their licentious manner of living. If our firft fettler was the owner of the fpot of land which he began to cultivate, he fells it at a confiderable profit to his fucceffor; but if (as is oftener the cafe) he was a tenant to fome rich landholder, he abandons it in debt; however, the fmall improvements he leaves behind him, generally make it an object of immediate demand to a *fecond* fpecies of fettler.

This fpecies of fettler is generally a man of fome property; he pays one third or one fourth part in cafh for his plantation, which confifts of three or four hundred acres, and the reft in gales or inftalments, as it is called here; that is, a certain fum yearly, without intereft, till the whole is paid. The firft object of this fettler is to build an addition to his cabbin; this is done with hewed logs: and as faw-mills generally follow fettlements, his floors are made of boards; his roof is made of what are called clapboards, which are a kind of coarfe fhingles, fplit out of fhort oak logs. This houfe is divided by two floors, on each of which are two rooms: under the whole is a cellar walled with ftone. The cabbin ferves as a kitchen to this houfe. His next object is to clear a little meadow

dow ground, and plant an orchard of two or three hundred apple trees. His ſtable is likewiſe enlarged ; and, in the courſe of a year or two, he builds a large log barn, the roof of which is commonly thatched with rye ſtraw : he moreover encreaſes the quantity of his arable land ; and, inſtead of cultivating Indian corn alone, he raiſes a quantity of wheat and rye : the latter is cultivated chiefly for the purpoſe of being diſtilled into wiſkey. This ſpecies of ſettler by no means extracts all from the earth, which it is able and willing to give. His fields yield but a ſcanty increaſe, owing to the ground not being ſufficiently ploughed. The hopes of the year are often blaſted by his cattle breaking through his half made fences, and deſtroying his grain. His horſes perform but half the labour that might be expected from them, if they were better fed ; and his cattle often die in the ſpring from the want of proviſion, and the delay of graſs. His houſe, as well as his farm, bear many marks of a weak tone of mind. His windows are unglazed, or, if they have had glaſs in them, the ruins of it are ſupplied with old hats or pillows. This ſpecies of ſettler is ſeldom a good member of civil or religious ſociety : with a large portion of a hereditary mechanical kind of religion, he neglects to contribute ſufficiently towards building a church, or maintaining a regular adminiſtration of the ordinances of the goſpel: he is equally indiſpoſed to ſupport civil government : with high ideas of liberty, he refuſes to bear his proportion of the debt contracted by its eſtabliſhment in our country : he delights chiefly in company—ſometimes drinks ſpirituous liquors to exceſs—will ſpend a day or two in every week, in attending political meetings; and, thus, he contracts debts, which, (if he cannot diſcharge in a depreciated paper currency) compel him to ſell his plantation, generally in the courſe of a few years, to the *third* and laſt ſpecies of ſettler.

This ſpecies of ſettler is commonly a man of property and good character; ſometimes he is the ſon of a wealthy farmer in one of the interior and ancient counties of the ſtate. His firſt object is to convert every ſpot of ground, over which he is able to draw water, into meadow : where this cannot be done, he ſelects the moſt fertile ſpots on the farm, and devotes it by manure to that purpoſe. His next object is to build a barn, which he prefers of ſtone. This building is, in ſome inſtances, one hundred feet in front, and forty in depth : it is made very compact, ſo as to ſhut out the cold in winter ; for our farmers find that their horſes and cattle, when kept warm, do not require near as much food, as when they are expoſed to the cold. He uſes oeconomy, likewiſe, in the conſumption of his wood. Hence he keeps himſelf warm in winter, by means of ſtoves, which ſave an immenſe deal of labour to himſelf and his horſes, in cutting and hawling wood in cold and wet weather. His fences are every where repaired, ſo as to ſecure his grain from his own and his neighbour's cattle. But further, he increaſes the number of the articles of his cultivation, and, inſtead of raiſing corn, wheat, and rye alone, he raiſes oats, buckwheat (the fagopyrum of Linnæus) and ſpelts. Near his houſe, he allots an acre or two of ground for a garden, in which he raiſes a large quantity of cabbage and potatoes. His newly cleared fields afford him every year a large increaſe of turnips. Over the ſpring which ſupplies him with water, he builds a milk houſe : he

likewiſe

likewise adds to the number, and improves the quality of his fruit-trees: his sons work by his side all the year, and his wife and daughters forsake the dairy and the spinning-wheel, to share with him in the toils of harvest. The last object of his industry is to build a dwelling-house. This business is sometimes effected in the course of his life, but is oftener bequeathed to his son, or the inheritor of his plantation; and hence we have a common saying among our best farmers, 'that a son should always begin where his father left off;' that is, he should begin his improvements, by building a commodious dwelling-house, suited to the improvements and value of the plantation. This dwelling-house is generally built of stone; it is large, convenient, and filled with useful and substantial furniture; it sometimes adjoins the house of the second settler, but is frequently placed at a little distance from it. The horses and cattle of this species of settler, bear marks in their strength, fat, and fruitfulness—of their being plentifully fed and carefully kept. His table abounds with a variety of the best provisions; his very kitchen flows with milk and honey; beer, cyder, and wine are the usual drinks of his family; the greatest part of the clothing of his family is manufactured by his wife and daughters. In proportion as he increases in wealth, he values the protection of laws: hence he punctually pays his taxes towards the support of government. Schools and churches likewise, as the means of promoting order and happiness in society, derive a due support from him: for benevolence and public spirit, as to these objects, are the natural offspring of affluence and independence. Of this class of settlers are two-thirds of the farmers of Pennsylvania: these are the men to whom Pennsylvania owes her ancient fame and consequence. If they possess less refinement than their southern neighbours, who cultivate their lands with slaves, they possess more republican virtue. It was from the farms cultivated by these men, that the American and French armies were fed chiefly with bread during the late revolution: and it was from the produce of these farms, that those millions of dollars were obtained from the Havanna after the year 1780, which laid the foundation of the bank of North America, and which fed and clothed the American army, till the glorious peace of Paris.

This is a short account of the happiness of a Pennsylvania farmer; to this happiness our state invites men of every religion and country. We do not pretend to offer emigrants the pleasure of Arcadia; it is enough if affluence, independence, and happiness are insured to patience, industry, and labour. The moderate price of land *, the credit which

arises

---

* *The unoccupied lands are sold by the state for about six guineas, inclusive of all charges, per hundred acres. But as most of the lands that are settled, are procured from persons who had purchased them from the state, they are sold to the first settler for a much higher price. The quality of the soil; its vicinity to mills, court-houses, places of worship, and navigable water: the distance of land carriage to the sea-ports of Philadelphia or Baltimore, and the nature of the roads, all influence the price of land to the first settler. The quantity of cleared land, and the nature of the improvements, added to all the above circumstances, influence the price of farms to the second and third settlers. Hence the price*

PENNSYLVANIA. 317

arises from prudence, and the safety from our courts of law, of every species of property, render the blessings which I have described, objects within the reach of every man.

From a review of the three different species of settlers, it appears, that there are certain regular stages which mark the progress from the savage to civilized life. The first settler is nearly related to an Indian in his manners. In the second, the Indian manners are more diluted. It is in the third species of settlers only, that we behold civilization completed. It is to the third species of settlers only, that it is proper to apply the term of *farmers*.

While we record the vices of the first and second settlers, it is but just to mention their virtues likewise. Their mutual wants produce mutual dependence: hence they are kind and friendly to each other—their solitary situation makes visiters agreeable to them; hence they are hospitable to strangers: their want of money (for they raise but little more than is necessary to support their families) has made it necessary for them to associate for the purposes of building houses, cutting their grain, and the like. This they do in turns for each other, without any other pay than the pleasures which usually attend a country frolic. Perhaps, what I have called virtues, are rather *qualities* arising from necessity, and the peculiar state of society in which these people live. Virtue should, in all cases, be the offspring of principle.

I do not pretend to say, that this mode of settling farms in Pennsylvania is universal. I have known some instances where the first settler has performed the improvements of the second, and yielded to the third. I have known a few instances likewise, of men of enterprizing spirits, who have settled in the wilderness, and who, in the course of a single life, have advanced through all the intermediate stages of improvement that I have mentioned, and produced all those conveniences which have been ascribed to the third species of settlers; thereby resembling, in their exploits, not only the pioneers and light-infantry, but the main body of an army. There are instances likewise, where the first settlement has been improved by the same family, in hereditary succession, till it has reached the third stage of cultivation. There are many spacious stone houses, and highly cultivated farms in the neighbouring counties of the city of Philadelphia, which are possessed by the grandsons and great-grandsons of men who accompanied William Penn across the ocean, and who laid the foundation of the present improvements of their posterity, in such cabbins as have been described.

This price of land to the *first* settler is from a quarter of a guinea to two guineas per acre; and the price of farms is from one guinea to ten guineas per acre, to the second and third settlers, according as the land is varied by the before-mentioned circumstances. When the first settler is unable to purchase, he often takes a tract of land for seven years on a lease, and contracts, instead of paying a rent in cash, to clear fifty acres of land, to build a log cabbin, and a barn, and to plant an orchard on it. This tract, after the expiration of this lease, sells or rents for a considerable profit.

PENNSYLVANIA.

This paſſion, ſtrange and new as it may appear to an European, is wiſely calculated for the extenſion of population in America: and this it does, not only by promoting the increaſe of the human ſpecies in new ſettlements, but in the old ſettlement likewiſe. While the degrees of induſtry and knowledge in agriculture, in our country, are proportioned to farms of from 75 to 300 acres, there will be a langour in population, as ſoon as farmers multiply beyond the number of farms of the above dimenſions. To remove this langour, which is kept up alike by the increaſe of the price, and the diviſion of farms, a migration of part of the community becomes abſolutely neceſſary. And as this part of the community often conſiſts of the idle and extravagant, who eat without working, their removal, by increaſing the facility of ſubſiſtance to the frugal and induſtrious who remain behind, naturally increaſes the number of people, juſt as the cutting off the ſuckers of an apple tree increaſes the ſize of the tree, and the quantity of fruit.

I have only to add upon this ſubject, that the migrants from Pennſylvania always travel to the ſouthward. The ſoil and climate of the weſtern parts of Virginia, North and South-Carolina, and Georgia, afford a more eaſy ſupport to lazy farmers, than the ſtubborn but durable ſoil of Pennſylvania. *Here* our ground requires deep and repeated plowing to render it fruitful; *there* ſcratching the ground once or twice affords tolerable crops. In Pennſylvania, the length and coldneſs of the winter makes it neceſſary for the farmers to beſtow a large ſhare of their labour in providing for, and feeding their cattle; but in the ſouthern ſtates, cattle find paſture during the greateſt part of the winter, in the fields or woods. For theſe reaſons, the greateſt part of the weſtern counties of the ſtates, that have been mentioned, are ſettled by original inhabitants of Pennſylvania. During the late war, the militia of Orange county, in North Carolina, were enrolled, and their number amounted to 3500, *every* man of whom had migrated from Pennſylvania. From this you will ſee, that our ſtate is the great outport of the United States for Europeans; and that, after performing the office of a ſieve, by detaining all thoſe people who poſſeſs the ſtamina of induſtry and virtue, it allows a paſſage to the reſt, to thoſe ſtates which are accommodated to their habits of indolence and vice.

I ſhall conclude this letter by remarking, that in the mode of extending population and agriculture, which I have deſcribed, we behold a new ſpecies of war. The *third* ſettler may be viewed as a conqueror. The weapons with which he atchieves his conqueſts, are the implements of huſbandry: and the virtues which direct them, are induſtry and oeconomy. Idleneſs, extravagance, and ignorance fly before him. Happy would it be for mankind, if the kings of Europe would adopt this mode of extending their territories: it would ſoon put an end to the dreadful connection, which has exiſted in every age, between war and poverty, and between conqueſt and deſolation.'*

Theſe obſervations are equally applicable to the progreſs of the ſettlements in all new countries.

Religion.]

---

* See Col. Mag. Vol. I. page 117.

PENNSYLVANIA.

Religion.] We have already mentioned the prevailing religious sects in this state. A particular account of some of their peculiar customs and tenets, will here be expected.

Of the great variety of religious denominations in Pennsylvania, the FRIENDS or QUAKERS are the most numerous. George Fox is called the Father of this religious sect, because he first collected them into a society in England, about the middle of the 17th century. The true appellation of these people is FRIENDS; that of QUAKERS, was early and unjustly given them by way of contempt. They came over to America as early as 1656, but were not indulged the free exercise of their religion in New England.*

They were the first settlers of Pennsylvania in 1682, under William Penn, and have ever since flourished in the free enjoyment of their religion. They believe that God has given to all men sufficient *light* to work their salvation, unless it be resisted; that this light is as extensive as the seed of sin, and saves those who have not the outward means of salvation; that this light is a divine principle in which dwells God the Father, Son and Holy Ghost. They maintain that the scriptures are not the principal ground of all truth and knowledge; nor yet the primary rule of faith and manners; but because they give a true testimony of the first foundation, they are and may be esteemed a secondary rule, subordinate to the spirit, from whom they derive all their excellence. They believe that immediate revelation has not ceased, but that a measure of the spirit is given to every person. That as by the light or gift of God, all spiritual knowledge is received, those who have this gift, whether male or female, though without human commission of learning, ought to preach; and to preach freely, as they have freely received the gift. All true and acceptable worship of God, they maintain, is by the inward and immediate moving of his spirit; and that water baptism and the Lord's supper were commanded only for a time. They neither give titles, nor use compliments in their conversation or writings, believing that *whatsoever is more than yea, yea, and nay, nay, cometh of evil.* They conscientiously avoid, as unlawful, kneeling, bowing, or uncovering the head to any person. They discard all superfluities in dress or equipage; all games, sports, and plays, as unbecoming the christian. 'Swear not at all' is an article of their creed, literally observed in its utmost extent. They believe it unlawful, to fight in any case whatever; and think that if their enemy *smite them on the one cheek, they ought to turn to him the other also.*† They are generally honest, punctual, and even punctilious in their dealings; provident for the necessities of their poor; friends to humanity, and of course enemies to slavery; strict in their discipline; careful in the observance even of the punctilios in dress, speech and manners, which their religion enjoins; faithful in

the

---

* See Hist. of Massachusetts and Connecticut.

† During the late war, some of their number, contrary to this article of their faith, thought it their duty to take up arms in defence of their country. This laid the foundation of a secession from their brethren, and they now form a separate congregation in Philadelphia, by the name of the 'Resisting or fighting Quakers.'

PENNSYLVANIA.

the education of their children; induſtrious in their ſeveral occupations. In ſhort, whatever peculiarities and miſtakes thoſe of other denominations have ſuppoſed they have fallen into, in point of religious doctrines, they have proved themſelves to be good citizens.

Next to the Quakers, the PRESBYTERIANS are the moſt numerous; concerning whom we have nothing to add to what we have already ſaid under New York. (page 268.)

The proteſtant EPISCOPAL CHURCH of New York, New Jerſey, Pennſylvania, Delaware, Maryland, Virginia and South-Carolina, met in Convention at Philadelphia, October 1785, and reviſed the book of common prayer, and adminiſtration of the ſacraments and other rites and ceremonies, and publiſhed and propoſed the book, thus reviſed, for the uſe of the church. This reviſion was made in order to render the liturgy conſiſtent with the American revolution and the conſtitutions of the ſeveral ſtates. In this they have diſcovered their liberality and their patriotiſm. In Pennſylvania and the ſouthern ſtates this reviſed book is pretty generally uſed by the epiſcopal churches. In New York and New Jerſey it has not been adopted.

There are upwards of ſixty miniſters of the LUTHERAN and CALVINIST religion, who are of German extraction, now in this ſtate; all of whom have one or more congregations under their care; and many of them preach in ſplendid and expenſive churches: and yet the firſt Lutheran miniſter, who arrived in Pennſylvania about forty years ago, was alive in 1787, and probably is ſtill, as was alſo the ſecond Calviniſtical miniſter.

The Lutherans do not differ, in any thing eſſential, from the Epiſcopalians; nor do the Calviniſts from the Preſbyterians.

The MORAVIANS are of German extraction. Of this religion there are about 1300 ſouls in Pennſylvania; viz. between 500 and 600 in Bethlehem; 450 in Nazareth, and upwards of 300 at Litiz, in Lancaſter county. They call themſelves the 'United Brethren of the Proteſtant Epiſcopal church.' They are called Moravians, becauſe the firſt ſettlers in the Engliſh dominions were chiefly migrants from Moravia. Theſe were the remnant and genuine deſcendents of the church of the ancient United Brethren, eſtabliſhed in Bohemia and Moravia, as early as the year 1456. About the middle of the laſt century, they left their native country, to avoid perſecution, and to enjoy liberty of conſcience, and the free exerciſe of the religion of their fore-fathers. They were received in Saxony, and other Proteſtant dominions, and were encouraged to ſettle among them, and were joined by many ſerious people of other denominations. They adhere to the Auguſtan Confeſſion of Faith, which was drawn up by the Proteſtant divines at the time of the reformation in Germany, in the year 1530, and preſented at the diet of the empire at Auſburg; and which, at that time, contained the doctrinal ſyſtem of all the eſtabliſhed Proteſtant churches. They retain the diſcipline of their ancient church, and make uſe of Epiſcopal ordination, which has been handed down to them in a direct line of ſucceſſion for more than three hundred years.[*]

As

---

[*] See David Crantz Hiſt. of 'The ancient and modern United Brethren's church, tranſlated from the German, by the Rev. Benjamin La Trobe. London, 1780.

PENNSYLVANIA. 321

As to their doctrinal tenets, and the practical inferences thence deduced, they appear to be *essentially* right, and such as will not be excepted against by any candid and liberal person who has made himself acquainted with them. Those who wish to obtain a thorough and impartial knowledge of their religious sentiments and customs, may see them excellently summed up in a plain, but nervous style, in ' An exposition of Christian Doctrine, as taught in the Protestant church of the United Brethren, written in German by A. G. SPANGENBERG; and translated and published in English in 1784.' By this book nothing appears but that they are thorough in the doctrines of grace, as they are obviously exhibited in the Old and New Testament. They profess to live in strict obedience to the ordinances of Christ, such as the observation of the sabbath, infant baptism, and the Lord's Supper; and in addition to these, they practice ' The Foot-washing, the Kiss of Love, and the use of the Lot;' for which their reasons, if not conclusive, are yet plausible.

They were introduced into America by Count Zindzendorf, and settled at Bethlehem, which is their principal settlement in America, as early as 1741. The following authentic descriptions of their several settlements in this state, which was obligingly sent me by one of their own number, will afford the reader a just idea of the uncommon regularity, industry, ingenuity and œconomy which characterize these people.

Bethlehem is situated on the river Lehigh, a western branch of the Delaware, fifty-three miles north of Philadelphia, in lat. 40° 37'. The town being built partly on a high rising ground, and partly on the lower banks of the Manakes, (a fine creek, which affords trout and other fish) has a very pleasant and healthy situation, and is frequently visited in the summer-season by gentry from different parts. The prospect is not extensive, being bounded very near by a chain of the Lehigh hills. To the northward is a tract of land called the *dry lands*.

In the year 1787, the number of the inhabitants amounted to between 500 and 600, and the houses were about sixty in number, mostly good strong buildings of limestone.

Besides the church or public meeting-hall, there are three large spacious buildings, viz.

1. The single brethren's or young men's house, facing the main street or public road. Here the greatest part of the single tradesmen, journeymen and apprentices of the town are boarded at a moderate rate, under the inspection of an elder and warden, and have, besides the public meetings, their house-devotions, morning and evening prayers. Different trades are carried on in the house for the benefit of the same.

2. The single sister's, or young women's house, where they live under the care of female inspectors. Such as are not employed in private families, earn their bread mostly by spinning, sewing, fine needle work, knitting and other female occupations.

Though this house has its particular regulations to preserve order and decorum, and may perhaps bear some resemblance to a nunnery, (being sometimes improperly so called) yet the plan is very different. The ladies are at liberty to go about their business in the town, or to take a walk for recreation; and some are employed in private families, or live

S f   with

with their parents; neither are they bound to remain in the single state, for every year some of them enter into the married state.

As to their almost uniform dress, the women in general for the sake of avoiding extravagance, and the follies of fashion, have hitherto kept to a particular simple dress, introduced among them in Germany many years ago.

3. The house for the widow women; where such as have not a house of their own, or means to have their own house furnished, live nearly in the same way as do the single sisters. Such as are poor, infirm and superannuated, are assisted or maintained by the congregation, as is the case with other members of the same, that are not able to obtain subsistence for themselves.

There is, besides, an institution of a society of married men, begun since the year 1770, for the support of their widows. A considerable fund or principal has been raised by them, the interest of which, as well as the yearly contributions of the members, is regularly divided among the widows, whose husbands have been members of the institution.

In a house adjoining the church, is the school for girls; and, since the year 1787, a boarding school for young ladies from different parts, who are instructed in reading and writing, (both English and German) grammar, arithmetic, history, geography, needle-work, music, &c. The minister of the place has the special care and inspection of this as well as of the boys school, which is kept in a separate house, fitted to that purpose, and are taught reading and writing in both languages, the rudiments of the latin tongue, arithmetic, &c.

Besides the different houses for private tradesmen, mechanics and others, there is a public tavern at the north end of the town, with pretty good accommodations; also a store, with a general assortment of goods; an apothecary's shop; a large farm-yard; and on the lower part, on Manakes creek, is a large tan-yard, a curriers and dyers shop, a grist-mill, fulling-mill, oil-mill and saw-mill; and on the banks of the Lehigh, a brewery.

The town is supplied with good water from a spring, which being in the lower part of the town, is raised up the hill by a machine of a very simple construction, to the height of upwards of 100 feet, into a reservoir, whence it is conducted by pipes into the several streets and public buildings of the town.

The ferry across the river is of such particular contrivance, that a flat, large enough to carry a team of six horses, runs on a strong rope, fixed and stretched across; and, by the mere force of the stream, without any other assistance, crosses the river backwards and forwards; the flat being always put in an oblique direction, with its foremost end verging towards the line described by the rope.

The greater part of the inhabitants, as well as the people in the neighbourhood, being of German extraction, this language is more in use than the English. The latter, however, is cultivated in the schools, and divine service performed in both languages.

Nazareth is ten miles north from Bethlehem, and sixty-three north from Philadelphia. It is a tract of good land, containing about 5000 acres, purchased originally by the Rev. Mr. George Whitfield, in 1740,

and

and sold two years after to the brethren. The town was laid out almost in the center of this tract, in 1772. Two streets cross each other at right angles, and form a square, in the middle, of 340 by 200 feet. The largest building is a stone house, erected in 1755, named Nazareth-hall, 98 feet by 46 long, and 54 in height. In the lowermost story is a spacious meeting-hall, or church; the upper part of the house is chiefly fitted for a boarding school, where youth, from different parts, are under the care and inspection of the minister of the place and several tutors, and are instructed in the English, German, Latin and French languages; in history, geography, book-keeping, mathematics, music, drawing and other sciences. The front of the house faces a large square open to the south, adjoining a fine piece of meadow ground, and commands a most beautiful and extensive prospect. Another elegant building on the east side of Nazareth-hall is inhabited by single sisters, who have the same regulations and way of living as those in Bethlehem. Besides their principal manufactory for spinning and twisting cotton, they have lately begun to draw wax tapers.

At the southwest corner of the aforesaid square, in the middle of the town, is the single brethren's house, and on the east southeast corner a store. On the southermost end of the street is a good tavern. The houses are, a few excepted, built of lime stone, one or two stories high, inhabited by tradesmen and mechanics mostly of German extraction. The inhabitants are supplied with water conveyed to them by pipes from a fine spring near the town. The place is noted for having an exceedingly pleasant situation, and enjoying a very pure and salubrious air. The number of inhabitants in the town and farms belonging to it, (Schoeneck included) constituting one congregation, and meeting for divine service on Sundays and holidays at Nazareth-hall, was, in the year 1788, about 450.

Litiz is in Lancaster county, and Warwick township; eight miles from Lancaster, and seventy miles west from Philadelphia. This settlement was begun in the year 1757. There are now, besides an elegant church, and the houses of the single brethren and single sisters, which form a large square, a number of houses for private families, with a store and tavern, all in one street. There is also a good farm and several mill works belonging to the place. The number of inhabitants, including those that belong to Litiz congregation, living on their farms in the neighbourhood, amounted, in 1787, to upwards of 300.

Such is the Moravian interest in Pennsylvania. Their other settlements in America, are at Hope, in New Jersey, already described, and at Wachovia, on Yadkin river, in North Carolina, which will be described in its proper place. Besides these regular settlements, which are formed by such only as are members of the brethren's church, and live together in good order and harmony, there are, in different parts of Pennsylvania, Maryland and New Jersey, and in the cities and towns of New York, Pennsylvania, Lancaster, Yorktown, &c. congregations of the brethren, who have their own church and minister, and hold the same principles, and doctrinal tenets, and church rites and ceremonies, as the former, though their local situation does not admit of such particular regulations as are peculiar to the regular settlements.

In Pennsylvania there are sixteen congregations of English BAPTISTS. The doctrines, discipline, and worship of these, are similar to those of the New-England Baptists. In 1770, the number of this denomination of babtists was reckoned at 650 families, making, as was supposed, 3,250 souls, who were divided into ten churches, who had eighteen meeting-houses, and eleven ministers. Besides these there are a few Sabbatarian babtists, who keep the seventh day as holy time, and who are the remains of the Keithian or Quaker babtists, and a number of Tunkers and Mennonists, both of whom are professionably babtists, and are of German extraction.

The TUNKERS are so called in derision, from the word *tunken, to put a morsel in sauce.* The English word that conveys the proper meaning, of Tunkers is *Sops* or *Dippers.* They are also called Tumblers, from the manner in which they perform babtism, which is by putting the person, while kneeling, head first under water, so as to resemble the motion of the body in the action of tumbling. The Germans sound the letters *t* and *b* like *d* and *p*; hence the words Tunkers and Tumblers have been corruptly written Dunkers and Dumplers.

The first appearing of these people in America, was in the fall of the year 1719, when about twenty families landed in Philadelphia, and dispersed themselves in various parts of Pennsylvania. They are what are called General Baptists, and hold to general redemption and general salvation. They use great plainness of dress and language, and will neither swear, nor fight, nor go to law, nor take interest for the money they lend. They commonly wear their beards—keep the first day Sabbath, except one congregation—have the Lord's Supper, with its ancient attendants of love-feasts, with washing of feet, kiss of charity, and right hand of fellowship. They anoint the sick with oil for their recovery, and use the trine immersion, with laying on of hands and prayer, even while the person baptised is in the water. Their church government and discipline are the same with those of the English baptists, except that every brother is allowed to speak in the congregation; and their best speaker is usually ordained to be their minister. They have deacons, deaconesses (from among their ancient widows) and exhorters, who are all licensed to use their gifts stately. On the whole, notwithstanding their peculiarities, they appear to be humble, well-meaning Christians, and have acquired the character of the *Harmless* Tunkers.

Their principal settlement is at Ephrata, sometimes called Tunkerstown, in Lancaster county, sixty miles westward of Philadelphia. It consists of about forty buildings, of which three are places of worship: One is called Sharon, and adjoin's the sisters apartment as a chapel; another, belonging to the brother's apartment, called Bethany. To these the brethren and sisters resort, separately, to worship morning and evening, and sometimes in the night. The third is a common church, called Zion, where all in the settlement meet once a week for public worship. The brethren have adopted the White Friars' dress, with some alterations; the sisters, that of the nuns; and both, like them, have taken the vow of celibacy. All, however, do not keep the vow. When they marry, they leave their cells and go among the married people. They subsist by cultivating their lands, by attending a printing-office, a grist mill, a paper a paper mill, an oil mill, &c. and the fisters by spinning, weaving, sewing, &c. They, at first, slept on board couches, but now on beds, and have otherwise abated much of their former severity. This is the congregation who keep the seventh day Sabbath. Their singing is charming, owing to the pleasantness of their voices, the variety of parts, and the devout manner of performance. Besides this congregation at Ephrata, there were, in 1770, fourteen others in various other parts of Pennsylvania, and some in Maryland. The whole, exclusive of those in Maryland, amounted to upwards of 200 souls.

The MENNONISTS derive their name from Menno Simon, a native of Witmars in Germany, a man of learning, born in the year 1505, in the time of the reformation by Luther and Calvin. He was a famous Roman Catholic preacher till about the year 1531, when he became a Baptist. Some of his followers came into Pennsylvania from New York, and settled at Germantown, as early as 1692. This is at present their principal congregation, and the mother of the rest. Their whole number, in 1770, in Pennsylvania, was upwards of 4000, divided into thirteen churches, and forty-two congregations, under the care of fifteen ordained ministers, and fifty-three licensed preachers.

The Mennonists do not, like the Tunkers, hold the doctrine of general salvation; yet like them, they wi'l neither swear nor fight, nor bear any civil office, nor go to law, nor take interest for the money they lend, though many break this last rule. Some of them wear their beards; wash each other's feet, &c. and all use plainness of speech and dress. Some have been expelled their society for wearing buckles in their shoes, and having pocket holes in their coats. Their church government is democratical. They call themselves the Harmless Christians, Revengeless Christians, and Weaponless Christians. They are Babtists rather in name than in fact; for they do not use immersion. Their common mode of baptism is this: The person to be baptized kneels; the minister holds his hands over him, into which the deacon pours water, which runs through upon the head of the person kneeling. After this, follow imposition of hands and prayer.

Literary, Humane, and other useful Societies.] These are more numerous, and flourishing in Pennsylvania, than in any of the Thirteen States. The names of these improving institutions, the times when they were established, and a summary of the benevolent designs they were intended to accomplish, will be mentioned in their order.

1. THE AMERICAN PHILOSOPHICAL SOCIETY, HELD AT PHILADELPHIA, FOR PROMOTING USEFUL KNOWLEDGE. This society was formed January 2d, 1769, by the union of two other literary societies that had subsisted for some time in Philadelphia; and were created one body corporate and politic, with such powers, privileges, and immunities as are necessary for answering the valuable purposes which the society had originally in view, by a charter, granted by the commonwealth of Pennsylvania, on the 15th of March, 1780. This society have already published two very valuable volumes of their transactions; one in 1771, the other in 1786.

In 1771, this society consisted of nearly 300 members; and upwards of 120 have since been added; a large proportion of which are foreigners of the first distinction in Europe. This is an evidence of the increasing respectability and improvement of the society.

Their charter allows them to hold lands, gifts, &c. to the amount of the clear yearly value of ten thousand bushels of wheat. The number of members is not limited.

2. THE SOCIETY FOR PROMOTING POLITICAL ENQUIRIES; consisting of fifty members, instituted in February, 1787.

3. THE COLLEGE OF PHYSICIANS, instituted in 1787, for the promotion of medical, anatomical and chemical knowledge.

4. THE UNION LIBRARY COMPANY OF PHILADELPHIA, which was begun in 1731, incorporated by the proprietors of the province in in 1742, and united with other companies, upon a similar establishment, in 1769. The number of members in 1773 was upwards of 400. They possess (except the library of Harvard college) the most valuable collection of books in America, consisting of upwards of 7000 volumes, which are kept in Carpenters Hall. Under the same roof they have a museum, containing a collection of curious medals, manuscripts, ancient relicks, fossils, &c. and a philosophical apparatus.

5. THE PENNSYLVANIA HOSPITAL, a humane institution, which was first meditated in 1750, and carried into effect by means of a liberal subscription of about £3000, and by the assistance of the assembly who, in 1751, granted as much more for the purpose. The present building was begun in 1754, and finished in 1756. This hospital is under the direction of twelve managers, chosen annually, and is visited every year by a committee of the assembly. The accounts of the managers are submitted to the inspection of the legislature. Six physicians attend *gratis*, and generally prescribe twice or three times in a week, in their turns. This hospital is the general receptacle of lunatics and madmen, and of those affected with other disorders, and are unable to support themselves. Here they are humanely treated and well provided for.

6. THE PHILADELPHIA DISPENSARY, *for the medical relief of the poor*. This benevolent institution was established on the 12th April, 1786, and is supported by annual subscriptions of thirty-five shillings each person. No less than 1800 patients were admitted, within sixteen months after the first opening of the dispensary. It is under the direction of twelve managers, and six physicians, all of whom atttend *gratis*. This institution exhibits an application of something like the mechanical powers, to the purposes of humanity. The greatest quantity of good is produced in this way with the least money. Five hundred pounds a year defrays all the expences of the institution. The poor are taken care of in their own houses, and provide every thing for themselves, except medicines, cordial drinks, &c.

7 THE PENNSYLVANIA SOCIETY *for promoting the* ABOLITION OF SLAVERY, *and the relief of* FREE NEGROES *unlawfully held in bondage*. This society was begun in 1774, and enlarged on the 23d of April, 1787. The officers of the society consist of a president, two vice-presidents, two secretaries, a treasurer, four counsellors, an electing committee of twelve, and an acting committee of six members; all of whom except the last are to be chosen annually by ballot, on the first Monday in January. The society meet quarterly, and each member contributes ten shillings annually,

PENNSYLVANIA. 327

annually, in quarterly payments, towards defraying its contingent expences.

The legislature of this state, have favoured the humane designs of this society, by 'An Act for the gradual Abolition of Slavery;' passed on the 1st of March, 1780; wherein, among other things, it is ordained that no person born within the state, after the passing of the act, shall be considered as a servant for life; and all perpetual slavery, is by this act, forever abolished. The act provides, that those who would, in case this act had not been made, have been born servants or slaves, shall be deemed such, till they shall attain to the age of twenty-eight years; but they are to be treated in all respects as servants bound by indenture for four years.

8. THE SOCIETY OF THE UNITED BRETHREN *for propagating the gospel among the heathens*, instituted in 1787, to be held statedly at Bethlehem. An act, incorporating this society, and investing it with all necessary powers and privileges for accomplishing its pious designs, was passed by the legislature of the state, on the 27th of February, 1788. They can hold lands, houses, &c. to the annual amount of two thousand pounds.

These pious *Brethren*, commonly called Moravians, began a mission among the Mahikan, Wampano, Delaware, Shawanoe, Nantikok and other Indians, near fifty years ago, and were so successful as to add more than one thousand souls to the christian church by baptism. Six hundred of these have died in the christian faith; about 300 live with the missionaries near Lake Erie, and the rest are either dead, or apostates in the wilderness.*

9. *The* PENNSYLVANIA SOCIETY *for the encouragement of manufactures and useful arts*, instituted in 1787, open for the reception of every citizen of the United States, which will fulfil the engagements of a member of the same. The society is under the direction of a president, four vice-presidents, and twelve managers, besides subordinate officers. Each member, on his admission, pays ten shillings at least into the *general fund*; and the same sum annually, till he shall cease to be a member. Besides this, they have a *manufacturing fund*, made up of subscriptions of not less than ten pounds, for the purpose of establishing factories in suitable places, for the employment of the industrious poor. The subscribers have all the profits arising from the business. The meetings of this society are held quarterly.

Besides these, there is a SOCIETY FOR ALLEVIATING THE MISERIES OF PRISONS; and a HUMANE SOCIETY, for recovering and restoring to life the bodies of drowned persons; instituted in 1770, under the direction of thirteen managers.

Also, an *Agricultural Society*; *a Society for German emigrants*; *a Marine Society*, consisting of Captains of vessels; *a Charitable Society for the support of the widows and families of Presbyterian clergymen*; and St. George's, St. Patrick's and St. Andrew's charitable Societies; also the Society of Free and Accepted Masons.

Colleges,

---

* An affecting history of the Brethren's mission among the Indians, will shortly be published.

Colleges, Academies and Schools.] From the enterprizing and literary spirit of the Pennsylvanians, we should naturally conclude, what is fact, that these are numerous.

In Philadelphia is a UNIVERSITY, founded during the war. Its funds were partly given by the state, and partly taken from the old college of Philadelphia.

A medical school, which was founded in 1765, is attached to the university; and has professors in all the branches of medicine, who prepare the students (whose number, yearly, is 50 or 60) for degrees in that science.

DICKINSON COLLEGE, at Carlisle, 120 miles westward of Philadelphia, was founded in 1783, and has a principal—three professors—a philosophical apparatus—a library consisting of nearly 3000 volumes—four thousand pounds in funded certificates, and 10,000 acres of land; the last, the donation of the state. In 1787, there were eighty students belonging to this college. This number is annually increasing. It was named after his excellency John Dickinson, formerly president of this state.

In 1787, a college was founded at Lancaster, 66 miles from Philadelphia, and honoured with the name of FRANKLIN COLLEGE, after his excellency Dr. Franklin. This college is for the Germans; in which they may educate their youth in their own language, and in conformity to their own habits. The English language, however, is taught in it. Its endowments are nearly the same as those of Dickinson college. Its trustees consist of Lutherans, Calvinists and English; of each an equal number. The principal is a Lutheran, and the vice-principal is a Calvinist. This college, as it concentres the whole German interest, and has ample funds to support professors in every branch of science, has flattering prospects of growing importance and extensive utility.

In Philadelphia, besides the university and medical school already mentioned, there is the PROTESTANT EPISCOPAL ACADEMY, a very flourishing institution—THE ACADEMY FOR YOUNG LADIES—Another for the Friends or Quakers, and one for the Germans; besides five free schools, one for the people called Quakers, one for Presbyterians, one for Catholics, one for Germans, and one for Negroes. The Episcopalians have an academy at Yorktown, in York county. There is also an academy at Germantown, another at Pittsburgh, and another at Washington; these are endowed by donations from the legislature, and by liberal contributions of individuals.

The schools for young men and women in Bethlehem and Nazareth, under the direction of the people called Moravians, have already been mentioned, and are decidedly upon the best establishment of any schools in America. Besides these, there are private schools in different parts of the state; and to promote the education of poor children, the state have appropriated a large tract of land for the establishment of free schools. A great proportion of the labouring people among the Germans and Irish, are, however, extremely ignorant.

Chief Towns.] Philadelphia is the capital, not only of this, but of the United States. It is situated on the west bank of the river Delaware on an extensive plain, about 118 miles (some say more) from the sea. The

PENNSYLVANIA.

length of the city eaft and weft, that is from the Delaware to the Schuylkill, upon the original plan of Mr. Penn, is 10,300 feet, and the breadth, north and fouth, is 4837 feet. Not two fifths of the plot covered by the city charter is yet built. The inhabitants, however, have not confined themfelves within the original limits of the city, but have built north and fouth along the Delaware, two miles in length. The longeft ftreet is fecond ftreet, about 700 feet from Delaware river, and parallel to it. The circumference of that part of the city which is built, if we include Kenfington on the north, and Southwark on the fouth, may be about five miles.

Market-ftreet is 100 feet wide, and runs the whole length of the city from river to river. Near the middle, it is interfected at right angles by Broad-ftreet, 113 feet wide, running nearly north and fouth, quite acrofs the city.

Between Delaware river and Broad-ftreet are 14 ftreets, nearly equidiftant, running parallel with Broad-ftreet, acrofs the city; and between Broad-ftreet and the Schuylkill, there are nine ftreets, equidiftant from each other. Parallel to Market-ftreet, are eight other ftreets, running eaft and weft from river to river, and interfect the crofs ftreets at right angles; all thefe ftreets are 50 feet wide, except Arch-ftreet which is 65 feet wide. All the ftreets which run north and fouth, except Broadftreet mentioned above, are 50 feet wide. There were four fquares of eight acres each, one at each corner of the city, originally referved for public and common ufes. And in the center of the city, where Broadftreet and Market-ftreet interfect each other, is a fquare of ten acres, referved in like manner, to be planted with rows of trees for public walks.

The firft ftreet between Delaware river and the bank, is called Waterftreet. The next, on the top of the bank, is called Front-ftreet; and weft of this the ftreets are numbered, *fecond, third, fourth, &c.*

On the river Delaware, there are 16 public landings, at the diftance of 4 or 500 feet from each other; and private wharves fufficient for 200 fail of fea veffels to unload at a time; and room to build any neceffary number. There are 10 public landings on the Schuylkill, which, as the town does not yet extend fo far, are at prefent of no ufe.

Philadelphia was founded in 1682, by the celebrated William Penn, who, in October, 1701, granted a charter, incorporating the town with the privilege of choofing a mayor, recorder, eight aldermen, twelve common council men, a fheriff and clerk.

The city charter was vacated by the revolution, and has not been renewed under the new government. A bill for this purpofe is now (Nov. 1788) depending before the legiflature.

In 1749, the dwelling houfes in the feveral wards in Philadelphia, were as follows.

South suburbs,	150	High street ward,	147
Duck ward,	245	North do.	196
Walnut do.	104	Mulberry do.	488
South do.	117	Upper Delaware do.	109
Chesnut do.	110	Lower do. do.	110
Middle do.	238	North suburbs.	62
	964		1112
			964
		Total.	2076

At this time the number of inhabitants in the city were estimated at 11,000 whites, and 600 blacks. The number of churches were then, as follows,

    2 Presbyterian,   1 German Lutheran,
    2 Quaker,   1 German Calvinist,
    1 Episcopalian,   1 Moravian,
    1 Swedish,   1 Roman Catholic.
    1 Baptist,

The following will give the reader an idea of the proportional numbers of the several religious denominations in Philadelphia.

An account of births and burials in the united churches of Christ church and St. Peters's in Philadelphia, from December 25, 1781, to December 25, 1782.

Christened, {	Males	189	Buried, {	Males	110
	Females	185		Females	88
		374			198

Buried under one year,	39	From 30 to 40	16
From 1 to 3	43	—— 40 — 50	10
—— 3 — 5	8	—— 50 — 60	11
—— 5 — 10	10	—— 60 — 70	20
—— 10 — 20	9	—— 70 — 80	9
—— 20 — 30	20	—— 80 — 90	3
Swedes christenings,		34	Burials,	28
Moravians christenings,		5	do.	2
First Presbyterian burials,	40	Baptists,	18
2d. do.	28	German Lutherans,	219
3d. do.	32	German reform'd church,	68
Quakers,	102	Roman Catholics,	46
Burials this year,	820		

Philadelphia now contains about 5000 houses; in general, handsomely built of brick; and 40,000 inhabitants, composed of almost all nations and religions. Their places for religious worship are as follows.

                                                                                 The

PENNSYLVANIA.

The Friends or Quakers, have	5*	The Swedish Lutherans,	1†
The Presbyterians,	6	The Moravians,	1
The Episcopalians,	3	The Baptists,	1
The German Lutherans,	2	The Universal Baptists,	1
The German Calvinists,	1	The Methodists,	1
The Catholics,	3	The Jews.	1

The other public buildings in the city, besides the university, academies, &c. already mentioned, are the following, viz.

A state house and Offices,
A city court house,
A county court house,
A carpenters hall,
A philosophical society's hall,
A dispensary,
A hospital and offices,
An alms house,

A house of correction,
A public factory of linen, cotton and woolen,
A public observatory,
Three brick market houses,
A fish market,
A public gaol.

The state house is in Chesnut-street, between fifth and sixth streets, and was erected in 1735. The building is rather magnificent than elegant. The state house yard, is a neat, elegant and spacious public walk, ornamented with rows of trees; but a high brick wall, which encloses it, limits the prospect.

In 1787, an elegant court house was erected, on the left of the state house; and on the right a philosophical hall. These add much to the beauty of the square.

South of the state house is the public gaol, built of stone. It has a ground half story, and two stories above it. Every apartment is arched with stone against fire and force. It is a hallow square, 100 feet in front, and is the most elegant and secure building of the kind in America. To the goal is annexed a work house, with yards to each to separate the sexes, and criminals from debtors.

The hospital and poor house, in which are upwards of 300 poor people, whether we consider the buildings, or the designs for which they were erected, are unrivalled in America.

The German church, lately erected, is one of the most elegant churches in America. Mr. D. Taneberger, one of the united brethren's society at Litiz, a great mechanical genius, is erecting a large organ, of more than thirty stops, for this church.

In Market-street, between Front and Fourth Streets, is the principal market, built of brick, and is 1500 feet in length. This market, in respect to the quantity, the variety and neatness of the provisions, is not equalled in America, and perhaps not exceeded in the world.

The Philadelphians are not so social, nor perhaps so hospitable as the people in Boston, Charleston and New York. Various causes have contributed

---

* *One of these houses is for those Quakers who took up arms in defence of their country, in the late war, contrary to the established principles of the Friends. They call themselves* Free Quakers.

† *This is the oldest church, in or near the city, and has lately been annexed to the Episcopal order.*

tributed to this difference, among which the most operative has been the prevalence of party spirit, which has been, and is carried to greater lengths in this city than in any other in America: Yet no city can boast of so many useful improvements in manufactures, in the mechanical arts, in the art of healing, and particularly in the science of humanity. The tradesmen and manufacturers have become so numerous, that they are beginning to associate for mutual improvement, and to promote regularity and uniformity in their several occupations. The carpenters, the cordwainers, the taylors, the watch-makers, the joiners, and hair-dressers, have already associated, and others are forming into companies upon the same plan.

The Philadelphians have exerted their endeavours, with happy and growing success, to prevent the intemperate use of spirituous liquors. In accomplishing this benevolent purpose, on which so much of the prosperity and glory of our empire depend, every good citizen in the union will cheerfully lend his aid and influence. As one important step towards effecting their design, they are discountenancing distilleries, which are of course declining, and encouraging breweries, which are fast increasing. The increase of the consumption of beer, in the course of a few years past, in every part of America, and particularly in Pennsylvania, has been astonishing. It has become a fashionable drink, and it is not improbable but that in a few years it will come into universal use among all classes of people. In proportion as the use of beer increases, in the same proportion will the use of spirituous liquors decrease. This will be a happy exchange.

In short, whether we consider the convenient local situation, the size, the beauty, the variety and utility of the improvements in mechanics, in agriculture and manufactures, or the industry, the enterprize, the humanity and the abilities of the inhabitants of the city of Philadelphia, it merits to be viewed as the capital of the flourishing EMPIRE OF UNITED AMERICA.

LANCASTER is the largest inland town in America. It is the seat of justice in Lancaster county, and stands on Conestogo creek, 66 miles, a little to the north of the west from Philadelphia. Its trade is already large; and must increase in proportion as the surrounding country populates. It contains about 900 houses, besides a most elegant court-house, a number of handsome churches and other public buildings, and about 4,500 souls.

CARLISLE is the seat of justice in Cumberland county, and is 120 miles westward of Philadelphia. It contains upwards of 1500 inhabitants, who live in near 300 stone houses, and worship in three churches. They have also a court-house and a college. Thirty-four years ago, this spot was a wilderness, and inhabited by Indians and wild beasts. A like instance of the rapid progress of the arts of civilized life is scarcely to be found in history.

PITTSBURGH, on the western side of the Allegany mountains, is 320 miles westward of Philadelphia, is beautifully situated on a point of land between the Allegany and Monongahela rivers, and about a quarter of a mile above their confluence, in lat. 40° 26' north. It contained in 1787, 140 houses, and 700 inhabitants, who are Presbyterians and Episcopalians,

copalians. The surrounding country is very hilly, but fertile, and well stored with excellent coal. The rivers abound with fine fish, such as pike, perch, and cat-fish, which are all much larger than the same species on the eastern side of the mountains.

This town is laid out on Penn's plan, and is a thoroughfare for the incredible number of travellers from the eastern and middle states, to the settlements on the Ohio, and increases with astonishing rapidity.

Trade, manufactures and agriculture.] On the subject of exports nothing can be furnished more accurate and complete, than what is given in the American Museum for September, 1788, which follows:

Exports from Philadelphia in the years 1765, 1771, 1772, 1773, 1784, 1787.

	1765	1771	1772	1773	1784	1787
Bushels of wheat,	367,522	51,699	92,012	182,391	24,490	32,957
Barrels of flour,	148,887	252,744	284,872	265,967	201,365	193,720
Barrels of bread,	34,736	38,320	50,504	48,183	28,525	26,953
M. staves and heading,	4,270	6,188	5,867	5,141	4,083	4,333
M. shingles,	2,114	1,937	1,765	5,254		
Bushels of Indian corn	60,206	259,441	159,625	179,217	73,527	193,943
Tons of iron,	1,695	2,358	2,205	1,564	1,144	1,197
Boxes of soap,	1,644	2,936	3,231	3,743	1,733	1,544
M. hoops,	97	195	978	1,245		319
Hhds. of tobacco,	16					4,808
M. boards & scantling,	783	1,724	4,075	3,309	3,098	2,625
Barrels of beer,	1,288	1,236	1,798	1,394		604
Kegs of starch,	238	349	1,033	700		220
Bushels of flax-feed,	87,681	110,412	85,794	68,681	71,592	98,012
Packages of fur & skins	64					314
Pounds of do.		902	1,200	40		
Barrels of bees-wax,	35					161
Hogsheads of ditto,						170
Pounds of ditto,		29,261	50,140	64,540	46,585	1,347
Firkins of lard,	199	399	734	732	507	2,532
Firkins of butter,	1,501					
Barrels of beef & pork,	7,254	5,059	3,845	8,587	2,354	4,160
Barrels of hams,		778	782	1,062		1,062
Barrels of naval stores,		6,950	6,989	7,663		13,172
Walnut logs,		63	204	76		
Tons of lignum vitæ,		24	42	30		
Feet of mahogany,		108,441	142,962	63,255		
Tons of logwood,		169	425	195		
Chests of deer skins,		93	164	37		
Tons of pot-ash,		161	66	13	6	5
Tons of pearl-ash,		136	25	57		3
Cwt. brown sugar,		1,185	5,198	2,578		
Pounds of loaf sugar,		79,116	51,408	84,240		9,800
Gallons of melasses,		52,611	19,681	39,403		
Tons of wine,		24	118	68		
Gallons of oil,		5,544	10,584	4,536		1,500
Gallons of rum,		204,456	247,635	277,695		Barrels

PENNSYLVANIA.

	1765	1771	1772	1773	1784	1787
Barrels of fish,		5,128	5,776	6,430		
Boxes fperma. candles,		683	1,004	514		
Boxes tallow candles,	1,202	873	1,078	1,165	1,288	702
Boxes of chocolate,		479	385	306		629
Cwt. of coffee,		501	296	1,639		
Bufhels of falt,		64,468	42,803	39,192		
Pounds of cotton wool,		2,200	5,840	25,070		
Pounds of leather,		25,970	40,725	31,696	7,080	
Packages of ditto,						377
Sides of ditto,						970
Pounds of rice,		258,376	834,974	998,400		2,610,825

In the year 1787, befides the above articles, the following were exported:

Barrels of fhip ftuff,	1,443	Pounds of cheefe,	29,472
Barrels of rye meal,	162	Barrels of herrings,	610
Cafks of oat meal,	23	Barrels of mackerels,	174
Kegs of bread,	25,152	Quintals dry fifh,	4,718
Barrels of Indian meal,	14,710	Kegs of fturgeon,	363
Bufhels of rye,	1,140	Barrels of falmon,	17
Bufhels of barley,	306	Barrels of manhadden,	236
Bufhels of oats,	7,421	Barrels of honey,	91
Barrels of peas and beans,	919	Kegs of oyfters,	48
Barrels of apples,	2,555	Packages of cyder,	225
Barrels of dried apples,	24	Barrels of porter,	262
Bufhels of potatoes,	8,656	Hogfheads of country rum,	1,266
Bufhels of turnips,	195	Oxen,	4
Bufhels of onions,	4,373	Cows,	4
Barrels of beets,	12	Sheep,	145
Barrels of nuts,	185	Hogs,	34
Barrels of cranberries,	33	Geefe,	65
Boat boards,	740	Tons of fteel,	62
Windfor chairs,	5,731	Tons of caftings,	16
Shaken hogfheads,	4,775	Stoves,	66
Sets of wheel timbers,	1,056	Anchors,	37
Pairs of wheels,	84	Stills and worms,	48
Oars,	1,460	Bricks,	423,469
Handfpikes,	396	Bufhels of lime,	468
Mafts and fpars,	355	Barrels of glue,	15
Coaches,	8	Barrels of manufactured tobacco,	78
Chariots,	4	Cafks of fnuff,	535
Phaetons,	9	Cafks genfeng,	1,168
Carriages of different kinds,	36	Bags of farfaparilla,	8
Chaifes,	40	Cafks of indigo,	173
Kittareens,	10	Tierces of tallow,	24
Sulkeys,	7	Cafks of linfeed oil,	62
Waggons,	40	Cafks of fpirits of terpentine,	119
Wheelbarrows,	96	Boxes of hair powder,	118
Drays,	4	Barrels of ditto,	16
Ploughs,	22	Bufhels of bran,	10,306
		Harrow,	

PENNSYLVANIA.

Harrow,	1	Packages of paper,	351
Turkeys,	48	Reams of ditto,	2,481
Boxes of muftard,	42	Packages of pafteboards,	62
Barrels of fhip bread,	26,953	Box of parchment,	1
Pumps,	4	Barrels of varnifh,	5
Boats,	15	Boxes of trees and plants,	20
Flaxfeed fcreens,	14	Packages of feeds and plants,	47
Cutting boxes,	14	Pounds of faffafras,	2,000
Carts,	26	Chefts and cafks of fnake root,	34
Spinning wheels,	30	Cafks of pink root,	3
Corn mills,	4	Boxes of effence of fpruce	250
Settees,	38	Bags of hops,	30
Dutch fans,	55	Cafks of clover feed,	11
Cafks of fhip blocks,	9	Bags, of do.	7
Tons of oak bark,	45	Packages of harnefs,	10
Hogfheads of ditto,	48	Calves fkins,	72
Sifters,	286	Cafks of horn tips,	15
Logs of hickory,	13	Sheets of iron,	16
Saddle trees,	247	Share moulds,	1,233
Tons of nail rods,	133	A quantity of cedar & earthen ware.	

The following remarks of a well informed citizen of Philadelphia, are given as a proper illuftration of the foregoing accounts.

It is well known, that a confiderable part of the fouthern ftates have been in the habit of receiving their fupplies of foreign commodities thro' this city; and that, of confequence, the tranfportation of thefe articles muft have formed a confiderable part of the commerce of this port. Many of thefe articles might be afcertained with accuracy; whilft the value and quantity of others could not, from their nature, be eftimated, under our prefent export laws. But as the object here chiefly regards articles of American produce or manufacture, all others are excluded from the lift of exports for 1787. It will be fufficient to enumerate a few of the foreign articles, from which it will appear, that the obfervations on this head are ill founded. From Europe we import, among other articles, wines, brandy, geneva, falt, fruit, drugs, and dry goods of every kind; from the Weft Indies, rum, fugar, coffee, cotton, and falt; and from the Eaft Indies, teas, fpices, china ware, and dry goods; all of which articles are again exported to other ports of this continent, and the Weft Indies, to a very confiderable amount.

On a comparifon of the exports of the laft year, with thofe of the former years in the foregoing table, it will appear, that many articles, of which a confiderable value is now exported, were either not fhipped at all, or to a very fmall amount, in thofe years, whilft fome others are confiderably fhort of the quantity then exported. The firft of thefe facts may be attributed to the great improvements recently made in the agriculture and manufactures of this ftate, whilft the latter is in many inftances to be accounted for from caufes rather beneficial than injurious to the profperity of this country.

Much of the provifions which were in the period antecedent to the late conteft, fhipped to foreign markets, is now confumed by the numerous

hands

hands employed in manufacturing those articles of raw materials, which were formerly shipped to Europe, and returned to us in a manufactured state. Of these may be mentioned iron, leather, barley, tobacco, and furs, which we now manufacture into nails and steel, shoes, boots, and saddlery, porter and beer, snuff and hats, in quantities more than sufficient for our own consumption: a considerable quantity of these and other articles, formerly imported, are now manufactured by our own citizens, and form a respectable part of our exports: among these may be enumerated, as the most important, beef, pork, butter, cheese, mustard, loaf sugar, chocolate, household furniture, carriages, soap, candles, hair powder, starch, paper, and pasteboard. Upon an examination of the exports, many valuable articles will be found not enumerated: this arises from the same cause, which prevents ascertaining the amount of dry goods: namely, the impossibility of knowing either the value or contents of packages, which pay no duty or inspection; consequently are only entered in a general way, without any attention to their contents. Of goods under the last description, the exportation is very great; being articles particularly demanded by the southern states, several of which receive their principal supplies of these articles from this city; among them, the chief are, shoes, boots, hats, gloves, printed books, and other stationary, saddlery, copper, tin and brass wares, and ship chandlery.

Number of vessels entered at the custom-house, Philadelphia, in the years 1786 and 1787.

	1786.	1787.
Ships,	91	81
Brigs,	196	228
Sloops,	450	380
Schooners,	163	173
Snows,	10	6
Cutters,	-	2
Total,	910	870

From the foregoing list of articles exported from the state, it is easy to see that her manufactures and agriculture have been already advanced to a degree of improvement superior to any of her sister states. The people called Quakers and the Germans have contributed their full proportions towards this improvement.

'Since the introduction of the carding and spinning machines,' says a Philadelphian writer, ' it is found that *jeans* can be made so as to undersell those imported from England, with the unavoidable charges of importation. Every public spirited man may be supplied with this article at THE FACTORY, where the sale is very rapid, and purchases have been made by every description of the citizens of Pennsylvania, by the citizens of the adjacent states, and by some foreigners of distinction.

Another article, calls for the attention of the friends of American manufactures, and of every frugal man—thread, cotton and worsted hosiery. Several gentlemen have made a careful and impartial examination of the stockings manufactured in this city, in Germantown, in the town

PENNSYLVANIA. 337

town and county of Lancaster, Bethlehem, and Reading, and they find that the thread stockings made in Pennsylvania, and sold generally at a dollar per pair, are of the same fineness with imported stockings which are sold at 8/4 and 8/6. They also find that mixed stockings of thread and cotton, made in Pennsylvania, are sold lower in proportion compared with those of Great-Britain. Besides this difference in price, it is a well known fact that three pair of Pennsylvania made stockings will wear longer than four pair of those imported. There are now, 1788, about 250 stocking looms in the different parts of the city and state, each of which makes on a medium, one pair and a half of stockings every day. These, deducting Sundays, will amount to 117,375 pair per annum, which, at 7/6 a pair, is £.44015:12:6. The increase of wool and flax, the reduction of labor, provisions and rents, the cultivation of cotton in the southern states, and, above all, the use of machines to card spin and twist cotton thread, will greatly promote this article, of which, at two pair to each person annually, the United States require a yearly supply of near six millions of pairs—a capital domestic demand, certain, and steadily increasing with our population. The charges of importing hosiery, under the general impost of five per cent. will be twenty-three per cent. exclusive of any profit to the importer or retailer. Should the adoption of the constitution tempt any, either Americans or foreigners, to push manufactures here, this branch promises great profit, and will no doubt be among the first that will engage their attention.'

As many as two thirds of the Pennsylvanians subsist by agriculture. The articles they raise have been enumerated in the list of exports.

A gentlemen in the vicinity of Philadelphia, in the year 1788, planted one acre of carrots, which yielded him thirty tons—also an acre of pumkins, which produced the same quantity. He sows his carrots with a drill plough, and plants his pumpkins between the 1st and 10th of June. With these carrots and pumpkins only, he yearly fats a number of the best beeves that are driven to Philadelphia market.

The produce of the country east of the Susquehannah river is carried to Philadelphia in waggons drawn by horses, except what is brought down the rivers in boats. The produce of the counties of York, Cumberland and Franklin, which is principally wheat, is generally carried to Baltimore in waggons. It is probable that Pennsylvania will continue to lose the trade of these three productive counties, till good roads are made to the Susquehannah, and two free ferries established, one to Yorktown, and the other to Carlisle. These inducements would probably turn the channel of the trade of these counties from Baltimore to Philadelphia. The produce of the counties west of the Allegany mountains is principally purchased as a supply for the troops stationed in those parts, and for the numerous emigrants into the western country. Large herds of cattle are raised here with very little expence.

Curious springs.] In the neighbourhood of Reading, is a spring about fourteen feet deep, and about 100 feet square. A full mill stream issues from it. The waters are clear and full of fishes. From appearances it is probable that this spring is the opening or outlet of a very considerable river, which, a mile and an half or two miles above this place, sinks into the earth, and is conveyed to this outlet in a subterranean channel.

In the northern parts of Pennsylvania there is a creek called Oil creek which empties into the Allegany river. It issues from a spring, on the top of which floats an oil, similar to that called Barbadoes tar; and from which one man may gather several gallons in a day. The troops sent to guard the western posts, halted at this spring, collected some of the oil, and bathed their joints with it. This gave them great relief from the rheumatic complaints with which they were affected. The waters, of which the troops drank freely, operated as a gentle purge.

Remarkable caves.] There are three remarkable grottos or caves in this state; one near Carlisle, in Cumberland county; one in the township of Durham, in Bucks county, and the other at Swetara, in Lancaster county. Of the two former I have received no particular descriptions. The latter is on the east bank of Swetara river, about two miles above its confluence with the Susquehannah. Its entrance is spacious, and descends so much as that the surface of the river is rather higher than the bottom of the cave. The vault of this cave is of solid lime stone rock, perhaps 20 feet thick. It contains several appartments, some of them very high and spacious. The water is incessantly percolating through the roof, and falls in drops to the bottom of the cave. These drops petrify as they fall, and have gradually formed solid pillars which appear as supports to the roof. Thirty years ago there were ten such pillars, each six inches in diameter, and six feet high; all so ranged that the place they enclosed resembled a sanctuary in a Roman church. No royal throne ever exhibited more grandeur than this *lusus naturæ*. The resemblances of several monuments are found indented in the walls on the sides of the cave, which appear like the tombs of departed heroes. Suspended from the roof is 'the bell' (which is nothing more than a stone projected in an unusual form) so called from the sound that it occasions when struck, which is similar to that of a bell.

Some of the stalactites are of a colour like sugar-candy, and others resemble loaf sugar; but their beauty is much defaced by the country people. The water, which percolates through the roof, so much of it as is not petrified in its course, runs down the declivity, and is both pleasant and wholesome to drink. There are several holes in the bottom of the cave, descending perpendicularly, perhaps into an abyss below, which render it dangerous to walk without a light. At the end of the cave is a pretty brook, which, after a short course, loses itself among the rocks. Beyond this brook is an outlet from the cave by a very narrow aperture. Through this the vapours continually pass outwards with a strong current of air and ascend, resembling, at night, the smoak of a furnace. Part of these vapours and fogs appear, on ascending, to be condensed at the head of this great alembic, and the more volatile parts to be carried off, through the aperture communicating with the exterior air before mentioned, by the force of the air in its passage.*

Antiquities.] On a high hill, near the Tyoga river, a little to the southward of the line which divides New York from Pennsylvania, are to be seen the remains of an ancient fortification. The form of it is circular, and it is encompassed with an entrenchment. From appearances it

is

---

* *Amer. Phil. Trans. Vol. II. P. 177.*

PENNSYLVANIA. 339

is conjectured that pits were sunk in a number of places, and lightly covered over, so as to decoy the assailants in case of an attack, and defeat their attempts in storming the works. The entrenchment only remains; but it appears to have been formerly stockaded. The Indians are entirely ignorant of the origin of these works, but suppose they were erected by the Spanish Indians. The hill is an excellent station for a fort, and commands a delightful view of the country around it, which is low and fertile. There is a fortification, of a similar kind, at Unadilla, in the flat lands.

Constitution.] By the present constitution of Pennsylvania, which was established in September, 1776, all legislative powers are lodged in a single body of men, which is stiled ' The general assembly of representatives of the freemen of Pennsylvania.' The qualification required to render a person eligible to this assembly is, two years residence in the city or county for which he is chosen; no member of the house can hold any other office, except in the militia.

The qualifications of the electors, are, full age, and one years residence in the state, with payment of public taxes during that time. But the sons of freeholders are intitled to vote for representatives, without any qualification, except full age.

No man can be elected as a member of the assembly more than *four* years in *seven*.

The representatives are chosen annually on the second Tuesday in October, and they meet on the fourth Monday of the same month. A quorum of the house consists of two thirds of the whole number of members elected; and the members, before they take their seats, are obliged to take an oath or affirmation of fidelity to the state; and also subscribe a declaration or test, acknowleging their belief in one God and the inspiration of the scriptures of the Old and New Testament. The house chuse their own speaker, who, in the transaction of business, never leaves the chair. A journal of the proceedings of the assembly is published regularly, and any member may insert the reasons of his vote upon the minutes of the house. To prevent hasty determinations on matters of importance, all bills of a public nature are printed before the last reading, and, except in cases of necessity, are not passed into laws before the next session. The power of impeachment is vested in the general assembly.

The supreme executive power is lodged in a president, and a council consisting of a member from each county. The president is elected annually by the joint ballot of the assembly and council, and from the members of council. A vice president is chosen at the same time.

The counsellors are chosen by the freemen, every third year, and having served three years, they are ineligible for the four succeeding years. The appointments of one third only of the members expire every year, by which rotation no more than one third can be new members. A counsellor is, by his office, a justice of the peace for the whole state. The president and council form a court for the trial of impeachments.

The council meet at the same time and place with the general assembly.

The

PENNSYLVANIA.

The president and council appoint and commission judges of courts, naval officers, judge of the admiralty, attorney general and other officers, the appointment of whom is not expressly vested in the people or general assembly. But the freemen chuse the justices of peace, the colonels of militia, and the inferior military officers, and make a return of the persons elected, to the president and council, who are impowered to commission them. The justices of peace hold their commissions for seven years, removeable however for misconduct by the general assembly. A justice, while in office, cannot be a representative in assembly, nor take any fees but such as shall be allowed by the legislature.

The judges of the supreme court hold their office for seven years, and at the end of that term, may be re-appointed. They have a fixed salary, and are not permitted to take any fees or perquisites, or to hold any other office, civil or military.

Courts of common pleas, sessions and orphans courts are held quarterly in each city and county.

The supreme court, and courts of common pleas have the powers of chancery courts, so far as is necessary for the perpetuating of testimony, obtaining evidence from places out of the state, and the care of the persons and estates of those who are *non compotes mentis*.

Sheriffs and coroners are chosen annually by the freemen; but they can serve but three successive years, at the end of which they are ineligible during four years.

A register's office for the probate of wills, and granting letters of administration; and an office for the recording of deeds are kept in each city and county: The officers are appointed by the general assembly, removeable at their pleasure, and commissioned by the president and council.

The constitution of this state ordains, that the legislature shall regulate entails in such a manner as to prevent perpetuities.

Any foreigner of a good character may purchase and hold lands and other property, having first taken the oath of allegiance; and a years residence entitles him to the privileges of a natural born subject; except that of being eligible to a seat in the legislature.

A *Council of Censors*, composed of two members from each county, chosen by the freemen, on the second Tuesday of October every seventh year, is instituted for the purpose of enquiring whether the constitution has been preserved inviolate—whether the different branches of government have performed their duty as guardians of the people—whether the public taxes have been justly laid and collected, and in what manner the monies have been disposed of—and also whether the laws have been duly executed. For these purposes, they have power to send for persons, papers and records—to pass public censures, order impeachments, and to recommend to the legislature the repeal of laws which they deem unconstitutional. They have power also to order a convention for the purpose of amending the constitution; publishing the articles proposed to be amended six months before the election of the delegates. These powers continue in the council of censors for one year.

The people of Pennsylvania have different political sentiments according to their progress in industry and civilized life. The first class of settlers

PENNSYLVANIA.

tlers in this state, who have been described as making the first advances in the unsettled country, are attached to the present simple and visionary frame of government. The second settlers are divided in their opinions respecting it. But 99 out of an hundred of the third settlers, or real farmers, are opposed to it, and wish for a safe, stable, and compound form of government. As the first species of settlers are more idle and bold than the last, who, though the most numerous, are quiet, they have forced them to submit to it.

Among other useful laws of this state, of a public nature, are, one that declares all rivers and creeks to be high-ways—a law for the emancipation of negroes, already mentioned---a bankrupt law, nearly on the model of the bankrupt laws of England---a law commuting hard labour for a long term of years, for death, as a punishment for many crimes which are made capital by the laws of England. Murder, arson, and one or two other crimes, are yet punished with death---A bill was before the legislature last year, (1787) the purport of which was to enable foreigners, (remaining in their native allegiance) to hold lands in Pennsylvania, which is not the case in Great Britain, nor in any other of the United States.

New Inventions.] These have been numerous and useful. Among others are the following: A new model of the planetary worlds, by Mr. Rittenhouse, commonly, but improperly called an orrery---a quadrant, by Mr. Godfrey, called by the plagiary name of Hadley's quadrant---a steam-boat, so constructed, as that by the assistance of steam, operating on certain machinery within the boat, it moves with considerable rapidity against the stream, without the aid of hands. Messrs. Fitch and Rumsay, contend with each other, for the honour of this invention---a new printing-press, lately invented and constructed in Philadelphia, worked by one person alone, who performs three fourths as much work in a day, as two persons at a common press. Besides these there have been invented many manufacturing machines, for carding, spinning, winnowing, &c. which perform an immense deal of work with very little manual assistance.

History.] Pennsylvania was granted by king Charles II. to Mr. William Penn, son of the famous admiral Penn, in consideration of his father's services to the crown.* Mr. Penn's petition for the grant was presented to the king in 1680; and after considerable delays, occasioned by Lord Baltimore's agent, who apprehended it might interfere with the Maryland patent, the charter of Pennsylvania received the royal signature on the 4th of March 1681. To secure his title against all claims and prevent future altercation, Mr. Penn procured a quit-claim deed from the duke of York, of all the lands, covered by his own patent, to which the duke could have the least pretensions. This deed bears date, August 21, 1682. On the 24th of the same month, he obtained from the duke, by deed of feoffment, Newcastle, with twelve miles of the adjacent territory, and

---

* *A large debt was due from the crown to Mr. Penn, a part of which he offered to remit, on condition he obtained his grant. This, whatever benevolent motives are held out to the world, must have been a principal consideration with the king in making the grant.*

PENNSYLVANIA.

and the lands fouth to the Hoarkills. In December following, Mr. Penn effected a union of the lower counties with the province of Pennfylvania.†

The firſt frame of government for Pennfylvania, is dated in 1682. By this form, all legiſlative powers were veſted in the governor and freemen of the province, in the form of a provincial council, and a general aſſembly. The council was to conſiſt of ſeventy-two members, choſen by the freemen; of which the governor or his deputy was to be perpetual preſident, with a treble vote. One third of this council went out of office every year, and their ſeats were ſupplied by new elections.

The general aſſembly was at firſt to conſiſt of all the freemen---afterwards of two hundred, and never to exceed five hundred.

In 1683, Mr. Penn offered another frame of government, in which the number of repreſentatives was reduced, and the governor veſted with a *negative* upon all bills, paſſed in aſſembly. By ſeveral ſpecious arguments, the people were perſuaded to accept this frame of government.

Not long after, a diſpute between Mr. Penn and Lord Baltimore required the former to go to England, and he committed the adminiſtration of government to five commiſſioners, taken from the council. In 1686, Mr. Penn required the commiſſioners to diſſolve the frame of government; but not being able to effect his purpoſe, he, in 1688, appointed Capt. John Blackwell his deputy. From this period, the proprietors uſually reſided in England, and adminiſtered the government by deputies, who were devoted to their intereſt. Jealouſies aroſe between the people and their governors, which never ceaſed till the late revolution. The primary cauſe of theſe jealouſies, was an attempt of the proprietary to extend his own power, and abridge that of the aſſembly; and the conſequence was, inceſſant diſputes and diſſenſions in the legiſlature.

In 1689, governor Blackwell, finding himſelf oppoſed in his views, had recourſe to artifice, and prevailed on certain members of the council to withdraw themſelves from the houſe; thus defeating the meaſures of the legiſlature.‡ The houſe voted this to be treachery, and addreſſed the governor on the occaſion.

In 1693, the king and queen aſſumed the government into their own hands. Col. Fletcher was appointed governor of New York and Pennſylvania by one and the ſame commiſſion, with equal powers in both provinces. By this commiſſion, the number of counſellors in Pennſylvania was reduced.

Under the adminiſtration of governor Markham in 1696, a new form of government was eſtabliſhed in Pennſylvania. The election of the council and aſſembly now became annual, and the legiſlature, with their powers and forms of proceeding, was new modelled.

In 1699, the proprietary arrived from England and aſſumed the reins of government. While he remained in Pennſylvania, the laſt *charter of privileges* or frame of government, which continued till the revolution, was

---

† *See Franklin's hiſtorical review of the conſtitution and government of Pennſylvania, page* 14.

‡ *Two inſtances of a feceſſion of members from the aſſembly, with ſimilar views, have taken place ſince the revolution, and ſeem to have been copied from this example in* 1689.

PENNSYLVANIA.

was agreed upon and eſtabliſhed. This was completed and delivered to the people by the proprietary, October 28, 1701, juſt on his embarking for England. The inhabitants of the *territory,* as it was then called, or the lower counties, refuſed to accept this charter, and thus ſeparated themſelves from the province of Pennſylvania. They afterwards had their own aſſembly, in which the governor of Pennſylvania uſed to preſide.

In September 1700, the Suſquehannah Indians granted to Mr. Penn all their lands on both ſides the river. The Suſquehannah, Shawaneſe and Patomak Indians, however, entered into articles of agreement with Mr. Penn, by which, on certain conditions of peaceable and friendly behaviour, they were permitted to ſettle about the head of Patomak, in the province of Pennſylvania. The Conoſtoga chiefs alſo, in 1701, ratified the grant of the Suſquehannah Indians, made the preceeding year.

In 1708, Mr. Penn obtained from the Sachems of the country, a confirmation of the grants made by former Indians, of all the lands from Duck creek, to the mountains, and from the Delaware to the Suſquehannah. In this deed, the Sachems declared that *they had ſeen and heard read divers prior deeds which had been given to Mr. Penn, by former chiefs.*

While Mr. Penn was in America, he erected Philadelphia into a corporation. The charter was dated October 25, 1701; by which the police of the city was veſted in a mayor, recorder, aldermen and common council, with power to enquire into treaſons, murders and other felonies; and to enquire into and puniſh ſmaller crimes. The corporation had alſo extenſive civil juriſdiction; but it was diſſolved at the late revolution, and Philadelphia is governed like other counties in the ſtate.

By the favourable terms which Mr. Penn offered to ſettlers, and an unlimited toleration of all religious denominations, the population of the province was extremely rapid. Notwithſtanding the attempts of the proprietary or his governors to extend his own power, and accumulate property by procuring grants from the people, and exempting his lands from taxation, the government was generally mild, and the burdens of the people by no means oppreſſive. The ſelfiſh deſigns of the proprietaries were vigorouſly and conſtantly oppoſed by the aſſembly, whoſe firmneſs preſerved the charter rights of the province.

At the revolution, the government was aboliſhed. The proprietaries were abſent, and the people by their repreſentatives formed a new conſtitution on republican principles. The proprietaries were excluded from all ſhare in the government, and the legiſlature offered them one hundred and thirty thouſand pounds in lieu of all quit rents, which was finally accepted. The proprietaries however ſtill poſſeſs in Pennſylvania many large tracts of excellent land.

It is to be regretted that among all the able writers in this important ſtate, none has yet gratified the public with its intereſting hiſtory. As therefore hiſtory is not profeſſedly the province of a geographer, a more particular detail of hiſtorical facts, than has already been given, will not be expected. We ſhall therefore conclude the hiſtory of Pennſylvania with the following liſt of governors.

A Liſt

PENNSYLVANIA.

A List of the several PROPRIETORS, GOVERNORS, LIEUTENANT-GOVERNORS, and PRESIDENTS of the *Province*, with the times of their respective Administrations.

PROPRIETORS.

The Honorable William Penn, born 1644, died 1718.
John Penn, died 1746.
Thomas Penn,
Richard Penn, died 1771.
John Penn,

GOVERNORS, &c.

Governor,	William Penn, *Proprietor*,	from Oct. 1682, to Aug. 1684.
President,	Thomas Lloyd,	Aug. 1684, to Dec. 1688.
Lt. Governor,	John Blackwell,	Dec. 1688, to Feb. 1689-90.
President and Council governed,		Feb. 1689-90 to April 26, 1693.
Governor,	Benjamin Fletcher,	26 April 1693, to 3 June 1693.
Lt. Governor,	William Markham	3 June 1693, to Dec. 1699.
Governor,	William Penn, *Proprietor*,	3 Dec. 1699 to 1 Nov. 1701.
Lt. Governor.	Andrew Hamilton,	1 Nov. 1701, to Feb. 1702-3.
President and Council, governed		Feb. 1702-3 to Feb. 1703-4.
Lt. Governors:	John Evans,	Feb. 1703-4, to Feb. 1708-9.
	Charles Gookin,	March 1708-9, to 1717.
	Sir William Keith, *Bart.*	1717 to June 1726.
	Patrick Gordon,	June 1726 to 1736.
	George Thomas,	1738 to 1747.
President.	Anthony Palmer,	1747 to 1748.
Lt. Governors.	James Hamilton,	1748 to Oct. 1754.
	Robert Hunter Morris	Oct. 1754 to 19 Aug. 1756.
	William Denny,	19 Aug. 1756 to 17 Nov. 1759.
	James Hamilton,	17 Nov. 1759 to 31 Oct. 1763.
	John Penn,	31 Oct. 1763, to 6 May 1771.
President.	James Hamilton,	6 May 1771, to 16 Oct. 1771.
Lt. Governor,	Richard Penn,	16 Oct. 1771.
Governors.	Thomas Wharton,	March 1777, to April 1778.
	Joseph Reed,	Oct. 1778, to Oct. 1781.
	William Moore,	Nov. 1781, to Nov. 1782.
	John Dickinson,	Nov. 1782, to Oct. 1785.
	BENJAMIN FRANKLIN,	Oct. 1785, to Oct. 1788.
	Thomas Mifflin,	Oct. 1788.

DELAWARE.

DELAWARE.

SITUATION and EXTENT.

Miles.
Length 92 } Between { 38° 30' and 40° North Latitude.
Breadth 16 } { 0° and 1° 45' West Longitude.

Boundaries.] BOUNDED north, by the territorial line*, which divides it from Pennsylvania; east, by Delaware river and Bay; south, by a due east and west line, from Cape Henlopen, in lat. 38° 30' to the middle of the peninsula, which line divides the state from Worcester county in Maryland; west, by Maryland, from which it is divided by a line drawn from the western termination of the southern boundary line, northwards up the said peninsula, till it touch or form a tangent to the western part of the periphery of the above mentioned territorial circle: containing about 1400 square miles.

Climate.] In many parts unhealthy. The land is generally low and flat, which occasions the waters to stagnate, and the consequence is the inhabitants are subject to intermittents.

Civil Divisions.] The Delaware state is divided into three counties, viz.

Counties.	Chief Towns.
Newcastle,	Wilmington and Newcastle.
Kent,	DOVER.
Sussex,	Milford and Lewistown.

Rivers.] Choptank, Nanticok and Pocomoke, all have their sources in this state, and are navigable for vessels of 50 or 60 tons, 20 or 30 miles into the country. They all run a westwardly course into Chesapeek Bay. The eastern side of the state, along Delaware bay and river, is indented with a great number of small creeks, but none considerable enough to merit a description.

Soil and Productions.] The south part of the state is a low flat country, and a considerable portion of it lies in forest. What is under cultivation is chiefly barren, except in Indian corn, of which it produces fine crops. In some places rye and flax may be raised, but wheat is a foreigner in these parts. Where nature is deficient in one resource, she is generally bountiful in another. This is verified in the tall, thick forests of pines which are manufactured into boards, and exported in large quantities into every sea-port in the three adjoining states.—As you proceed north the soil is more fertile and produces wheat in large quantities, which is the staple commodity of the state. They raise all the other kinds of grain common to Pennsylvania. The state has no mountain in it, except

---

* *The* Territorial Line, *so called, is a circle described with a radius of* 12 *English miles, and whose centre is in the middle of the town of Newcastle.*

cept Thunder Hill, in the western part of Newcastle county, and is generally level, except some small parts, which are stony and uneven.

Chief Towns.] DOVER, in the county of Kent, is the seat of government. It stands on Jones' creek, a few miles from the Delaware river, and consists of about 100 houses, principally of brick. Four streets intersect each other at right angles, in the centre of the town, whose incidencies form a spacious parade, on the east side of which is an elegant state-house of brick. The town has a lively appearance, and drives on a considerable trade with Philadelphia. Wheat is the principal article of export. The landing is five or six miles from the town of Dover.

NEWCASTLE is 35 miles below Philadelphia, on the west bank of Delaware river. It was first settled by the Swedes, about the year 1627, and called Stockholm. It was afterwards taken by the Dutch, and called New Amsterdam. When it fell into the hands of the English, it was called by its present name. It contains about 60 houses, which have the aspect of decay, and was formerly the seat of government.—This is the first town that was settled on Delaware river.

WILMINGTON is situated a mile and a half west of Delaware river, on Christiana creek, 28 miles southward from Philadelphia. It is much the largest and pleasantest town in the state, containing about 400 houses, which are handsomely built upon a gentle ascent of an eminence, and show to great advantage as you sail up the Delaware.

Besides other public buildings, there is a flourishing academy of about 40 or 50 scholars, who are taught the languages, and some of the sciences, by an able instructor. This academy, in proper time, is intended to be erected into a college. There is another academy at Newark, in this county, which was incorporated in 1769, and then had 14 trustees.

MILFORD, the little emporium of Sussex county, is situated at the source of a small river, 15 miles from Delaware bay, and 150 southward of Philadelphia. This town, which contains about 80 houses, has been built, except one house, since the revolution. It is laid out with much taste, and is by no means disagreeable. The inhabitants are Episcopalians, Quakers and Methodists.

DUCK CREEK, is 12 miles north-west from Dover, and has about 60 houses, which stand on one street. It carries on a considerable trade with Philadelphia—and certainly merits a more pompous name. A mile south from this is situated Governor Collin's plantation. His house, which is large and elegant, stands a quarter of a mile from the road, and has a pleasing effect upon the eye of the traveller.

Trade.] The trade of this state, which is inconsiderable, is carried on principally with Philadelphia, in boats and shallops. The articles exported are principally wheat, corn, lumber and hay.

Religion.] There are, in this state 21 Presbyterian congregations, belonging to the Synod of Philadelphia—Seven Episcopal churches—Six congregations of Baptists, containing about 218 souls—Four congregations of the people called Quakers; besides a Swedish church at Wilmington, which is one of the oldest churches in the United States, and a number of Methodists. *All* these denominations have free toleration by the constitution, and live together in harmony.

Population

DELAWARE.

Population and Character.] In the convention held at Philadelphia, in the summer of 1787, the inhabitants of this state were reckoned at 37,000, which is about 26 for every square mile. There is no obvious characteristical difference between the inhabitants of this state and the Pennsylvanians.

Constitution.] At the revolution, the three lower counties on Delaware became independent by the name of *The Delaware State*. Under their present constitution, which was established in September, 1776, the legislature is divided into two distinct branches, which together are stiled *The General Assembly of Delaware*. One branch, called the *House of Assembly*, consists of seven representatives from each of the three counties, chosen annually by the freeholders. The other branch, called the *Council*, consists of nine members, three for a county, who must be more than twenty-five years of age, chosen likewise by the freeholders. A rotation of members is established by displacing one member for a county at the end of every year.

All money bills must originate in the house of assembly, but they may be altered, amended or rejected by the legislative council.*

A president or chief magistrate is chosen by the joint ballot of both houses, and continues in office three years; at the expiration of which period, he is ineligible the three succeeding years. If his office becomes vacant during the recess of the legislature, or he is unable to attend to business, the speaker of the legislative council is vice-president for the time; and in *his* absence, the powers of the president devolve upon the speaker of the assembly.

A privy council, consisting of four members, two from each house, chosen by ballot, is constituted to assist the chief magistrate in the administration of the government.

The three justices of the supreme court, a judge of admiralty, and four justices of the common pleas and orphans courts are appointed by the joint ballot of the president and general assembly, and commissioned by the president—to hold their offices during good behaviour. The president and privy council appoint the secretary, the attorney general, registers for the probate of wills, registers in chancery, clerks of the common

---

* *The first part of this clause is found in several of the American constitutions, and seems to have been servilely copied from the practice of originating money bills in the British house of commons. In Great-Britain this is deemed a privilege, and yet it is difficult to discover the privilege, while the house of commons have a negative upon all bills whatever. But in America, where the property of both houses is taxed alike, and the men who compose them are, at different sessions, changed from one house to the other, there seems to be not a shew of reason for giving one branch the exclusive privilege of originating money bills. To prove with how little reason this article of the constitution is introduced in America, it might be useful to read a short history of the customs in the parliament of Great-Britain—a custom introduced merely for the convenience of doing business. For this useful piece of history, the reader is referred to the American Magazine, published in New-York, 1788, by Noah Webster, Esquire, No. VII. page 456.*

mon pleas, and orphans courts, and clerks of the peace, who hold their offices during five years, unless sooner removed for mal-conduct.

The house of assembly name twenty-four persons, in each county for justices of peace, from which number the president, with the advice of his council, appoints and commissions twelve, who serve for seven years, unless sooner dismissed for mal-administration. The members of the legislative and privy councils are justices of the peace for the whole state.

The courts of common pleas and orphans courts have power to hold chancery courts in certain cases.

The clerk of the supreme court is appointed by the chief justice, and the recorders of deeds, by the justices of the common pleas, for five years, unless sooner dismissed.

All the military and marine officers are appointed by the general assembly.

The *Court of Appeals* consists of seven persons—the president, who is a member, and presides by virtue of his office, and six others, three to be chosen by the legislative council, and three by the house of assembly. To this court appeals lie from the supreme court, in all matters of law and equity. The judges hold their office during good behaviour.

The justices of the several courts, the members of the privy council, secretary, trustees of the loan office, clerks of the common pleas, and all persons concerned in army or navy contracts, are ineligible to either house of assembly. Every member, before taking his seat, must take the oath of allegiance, and subscribe a religious test, declaring his belief in God the Father, in Jesus Christ, and the Holy Ghost; and in the inspiration of the Scriptures.

The house of assembly have the privilege of impeaching delinquent officers of government, and impeachments are to be prosecuted by the attorney general, or other person appointed by the assembly, and tried before the legislative council. The punishment may extend to temporary or perpetual disability to hold offices under government, or to such other penalties as the laws shall direct.

There is, in Delaware, no establishment of one religious sect in preference to another, nor can any preacher or clergyman, while in his pastoral employment, hold any civil office in the state.

History.] The Dutch, under the pretended purchase made of Henry Hudson,* took possession of the lands on both sides the river Delaware; and as early as the year 1623, built a fort at the place which has since been called Gloucester.

In 1627, by the influence of William Useling, a respectable merchant in Sweden, a colony of Swedes and Finns came over, furnished with all the necessaries for beginning a new settlement, and landed at Cape Henlopen; at which time the Dutch had wholly quitted the country. The Dutch, however, returned in 1630, and built a fort at Lewistown, by them named Hoarkill. The year following the Swedes built a fort near Wilmington, which they called Christein or Christiana. Here also they laid out a small town, which was afterwards demolished by the Dutch. The same year they erected a fort higher up the river, upon Tenecum island, which they called New Gottenburgh; they also,

* See history of New York.

DELAWARE.

also, about the same time built forts at Chester, Elsinburgh, and other places. John Printz then governed the Swedes, who, in 1654, deputed his son-in-law, John Papgoia, and returned to Sweden. Papgoia soon followed his father-in-law to his native country, and John Ryfing succeeded to the government.

In 1655, the Dutch, under the command of Peter Stuyvesant, arrived in Delaware river, from New Amsterdam (now New York) in seven vessels, with 6 or 700 men. They dispossessed the Swedes of their forts on the river, and carried the officers and principal inhabitants prisoners to New Amsterdam, and from thence to Holland. The common people submitted to the conquerors and remained in the country.

On the first of October, 1664, Sir Robert Carr obtained the submission of the Swedes on Delaware river. Four years after, Col. Nicolls, governor of New York, with his council, on the 21st of April, appointed a *scout* and five other persons, to assist Capt. Carr in the government of the country.

In 1672, the town of Newcastle was incorporated by the government of New York, to be governed by a bailiff and six assistants; after the first year, the four oldest were to leave their office and four others to be chosen. The bailiff was president, with a double vote; the constable was chosen by the bench. They had power to try causes not exceeding £.10, without appeal. The office of *scout* was converted into that of sheriff, who had jurisdiction in the corporation and along the river, and was annually chosen. They were to have a free trade, without being obliged to make entry at New York, as had formerly been the practice.

Wampum was, at this time, the principal currency of the country. Governor Lovelace of New York, by proclamation, ordered that four white grains and three black ones, should pass for the value of a stiver or penny. This proclamation was published at Albany, Esopus, Delaware, Long Island, and the parts adjacent.

In 1674, Charles II. by a second patent, dated June 29th, granted to his brother, duke of York, all that country called by the Dutch *New Netherlands* of which the three counties of Newcastle, Kent and Suffex were a part.

In 1683, the duke of York, by deed, dated August 24th, sold to William Penn the town of Newcastle, with the district of 12 miles round the same; and by another deed, of the same date, granted to him the remainder of the territory, which, till the revolution, was called the *Three Lower Counties*, and has since been called the Delaware State. Till 1776, these three counties were considered as a part of Pennsylvania in matters of government. The same governor presided over both, but the assembly and courts of judicature were different: different as to their constituent members, but in form nearly the same.

MARYLAND.

MARYLAND.

SITUATION and EXTENT.

Miles.
Length 134 } Between { 37° 56 and 39° 44' North Latitude.
Breadth 110 }   { 0° and 4° 30' West Longitude.

Boundaries.] BOUNDED north, by Pennsylvania; east, by the Delaware State; southeast and south, by the Atlantic Ocean, and a line drawn from the ocean over the peninsula (dividing it from Accomac county in Virginia) to the mouth of Patomak river; thence up the Patomak to its first fountain; thence by a due north line till it intersects the southern boundary of Pennsylvania, in lat. 39° 43 18', so that it has Virginia on the south, southwest, and west. It contains about 14,000 square miles, of which about one-sixth is water.

Civil Divisions.] Maryland is divided into 18 counties, 10 of which are on the western, and 8 on the eastern shore of Chesapeek Bay. These, with their population in 1782, are as follows:

Counties.	Free males above 18 years of age.	Numb. of white inhabitants.	Number of Negroes in the State of Maryland, taken by the several assessors, in March. 1782.	Negroes under 8 years of age, do Males and females, from 8 to 14 years of age, do Males from 14 to 45 years of age, do Females from 14 to 36 years of age, do Males above 45 years of age, do Females above 36 years of age.	Total
St. Mary's,	1173	8,459		27,626 / 13,399 / 16,246 / 13,832 / 12,259	83,362
† Somerset,	1598	7,787			
Calvert,	894	4,012			
Montgomery,	2160	10,011			
Washington,	2579	11,488			
† Queen Ann's,	1742	7,767			
† Caroline,	1293	6,230			
† Kent,	1394	6,165			
Charles,	2115	9,804			
† Talbot,	1478	6,744			
† Dorchester,	1828	8,927			
Baltimore,	3165	17,878			
Ann Arundel,	2229	9,370			
† Worcester,	733	8,561			
Harford,	2243	9,377			
† Cœcil,	2000	7,749			
Frederick,	3785	20,495			
Prince George's,	2259	9,864			
Total	35,268	170,688			

N. B. Those counties marked (†) are on the east, the rest are on the west side of the Chesapeek Bay.

Each

MARYLAND.

Each of the counties sends four Representatives to the House of Delegates, besides which the city of Annapolis, and town of Baltimore send each two, making in the whole 76 members.

Climate.] Generally mild and agreeable, suited to agricultural productions, and a great variety of fruit trees. In the interior hilly country the inhabitants are healthy; but in the flat country, in the neighbourhood of the marshes and stagnant waters, they are, as in the other southern states, subject to intermittents.

Bays and Rivers.] Chesapeek Bay, as we have already hinted, divides this state into the eastern and western divisions. This Bay, which is the largest in the United States, was particularly described, page 47. It affords several good fisheries; and, in a commercial view, is of immense advantage to the state. It receives a number of the largest rivers in the United States. From the eastern shore in Maryland, among other smaller ones, it receives Pokomoke, Choptank, Chester and Elk rivers. From the north the rapid Susquehannah; and from the west, Patapsco, Severn, Patuxent and Patomak, half of which is in Maryland, and half in Virginia. Except the Susquehannah and Patomak, these are small rivers. Patapsco river is but about 30 or 40 yards wide at the ferry, just before it empties into the bason upon which Baltimore stands. Its source is in York county, in Pennsylvania. Its course southwardly, till it reaches Elkridge landing, about 8 miles westward of Baltimore; it then turns eastward, in a broad bay-like stream, by Baltimore, which it leaves on the north, and passes into the Chesapeek.

The entrance into Baltimore harbour, about a mile below Fell's Point, is hardly pistol-shot across, and of course may be easily defended against naval force.

Severn is a short, inconsiderable river passing by Annapolis, which it leaves to the south, emptying, by a broad mouth, into the Chesapeek Bay.

Patuxent is a larger river than the Patapsco. It rises in Ann Arundel county, and runs southeastwardly, and then east into the bay, 15 or 20 miles north of the mouth of Patomak. There are several small rivers, such as Wighcocomico, Eastern Branch, Monocasy and Conogocheague, which empty into Patomak river from the Maryland side.

Face of the Country, Soil and Productions.] East of the blue ridge of mountains, which stretches across the western part of this state, the land, like that in all the southern states, is generally level and free of stones; and appears to have been made much in the same way; of course the soil must be similar, and the natural growth not noticeably different.

The soil of the good land in Maryland, is of such a nature and quality as to produce from 12 to 16 bushels of wheat, or from 20 to 30 bushels of Indian corn per acre. Ten bushels of wheat, and 15 bushels of corn per acre, may be the annual average crops in the state at large.

Wheat and tobacco are the staple commodities of Maryland. Tobacco is generally cultivated by negroes, in setts, in the following manner: The seed is sowed in beds of fine mould, and transplanted the beginning of May. The plants are set at the distance of 3 or 4 feet from each other, and are hilled and kept continually free of weeds. When as many leaves have shot out as the soil will nourish to advantage, the top of the

plant

plant is broken of, which prevents its growing higher. It is carefully kept clear of worms, and the suckers, which put out between the leaves, are taken off at proper times, till the plant arrives at perfection, which is in August. When the leaves turn of a brownish colour, and begin to be spotted, the plant is cut down and hanged up to dry, after having sweated in heaps one night. When it can be handled without crumbling, which is always in moist weather, the leaves are stripped from the stalk, and tied in bundles, and packed for exportation in hogsheads containing 8 or 900 pounds. No suckers nor ground leaves are allowed to be merchantable. An industrious person may manage 6000 plants of tobacco, (which yield a 1000 lb.) and four acres of Indian corn.

In the interior country, on the uplands, considerable quantities of hemp and flax are raised. As long ago as 1751, in the month of October, no less than 60 waggons, loaded with flax seed, came down to Baltimore from the back country.

Among other kinds of timber is the oak of several kinds, which is of a strait grain and easily rives into staves, for exportation. The black walnut is in demand for cabinets, tables, and other furniture. The apples of this state are large, but mealy; their peaches plenty and good. From these the inhabitants distill cyder brandy and peach brandy.

The forests abound with nuts of various kinds which are collectively called *Mast*. On this Mast vast numbers of swine are fed, which run wild in the woods. These swine, when fatted, are caught, killed, barrelled and exported in great quantities. Douglass, says, that ' in the year 1733, which was a good *masting* year, one gentleman, a planter and merchant, in Virginia, salted up 3000 barrels of pork.'

Population and Character.] The population of this state is exhibited in the foregoing table. By that it appears that the number of inhabitants in the state, including the negroes, is 254,050; which is 18 for every square mile. The inhabitants, except in the populous towns, live on their plantations, often several miles distant from each other. To an inhabitant of the middle, and especially of the eastern states, which are thickly populated, they appear to live very retired and unsocial lives. The effects of this comparative solitude are visible in the countenances, as well as in the manners and dress of the country people. You observe very little of that chearful sprightliness of look and action which is the invariable and genuine offspring of social intercourse. Nor do you find that attention paid to dress, which is common, and which decency and propriety have rendered necessary, among people who are liable to receive company almost every day. Unaccustomed, in a great measure, to these frequent and friendly visits, they often suffer a negligence in their dress which borders on slovenliness. There is apparently a disconsolate wildness in their countenances, and an indolence and inactivity in their whole behaviour, which are evidently the effects of solitude and slavery. As the negroes perform all the manual labour, their masters are left to saunter away life in sloth, and too often in ignorance. These observations, however, must in justice be limited to the people in the country, and to those particularly, whose poverty or parsimony prevents their spending a part of their time in populous towns, or otherwise mingling with the world. And with these limitations they will equally apply to all the

southern

southern states. The inhabitants of the populous towns, and those from the country who have intercourse with them, are in their manners and customs like the people of the other states in like situations.

That pride which grows on slavery and is habitual to those who, from their infancy, are taught to believe and to feel their superiority, is a visible characteristic of the inhabitants of Maryland. But with this characteristic we must not fail to connect that of hospitality to strangers, which is equally universal and obvious, and is, perhaps, in part the offspring of it.

The inhabitants are made up of various nations of many different religious sentiments; few general observations, therefore, of a characteristical kind will apply.

Chief Towns.] ANNAPOLIS (city) is the capital of Maryland, and the wealthiest town of its size in America. It is situated just at the mouth of Severn river, 30 miles south of Baltimore. It is a place of little note in the commercial world. The houses, about 260 in number, are generally large and elegant, indicative of great wealth. The design of those who planned the city, was to have the whole in the form of a circle, with the streets, like radii, beginning at the center where the Stadt House stands, and thence diverging in every direction. The principal part of the buildings are arranged agreeably to this awkward plan. The Stadt House is the noblest building of the kind in America.

BALTIMORE has had the most rapid growth of any town on the continent, and is the fourth in size and the fifth in trade in the United States.* It lies in lat. 39° 21', on the north side of Patapsco river, around what is called the Bason, in which the water, at common tides, is about five or six feet deep. Baltimore is divided into the town and Fell's point, by a creek, over which are two bridges; but the houses extend, in a sparse situation, from one to the other. At Fell's point the water is deep enough for ships of burden; but small vessels, only, go up to the town. The situation of the town is low and was formerly unhealthy; but the increase of houses, and of course, of smoak, the tendency of which is to destroy or to dispel damp and unwholsome vapours, and the improvements that have been made, particularly that of paving the streets, have rendered it tolerably healthy. The houses were numbered in 1787, and found to be 1955; about 1200 of which were in the town, and the rest at Fell's point. The number of stores was 152, and of churches nine; which belong to German Calvinists and Lutherans, Episcopalians, Presbyterians, Roman Catholics, Baptists, Methodists, Quakers, Nicolites, or New Quakers. The number of inhabitants is between 10 and 11,000. Not more than one in five of these attend public worship of any kind, notwithstanding they have such a variety in their choice. Their main object (in which, indeed, they are far from being peculiar) appears to be to make their fortunes for this world; while preparation for another is either unthought of, or deferred to a *more convenient season.* There are many very respectable families in Baltimore, who live genteely—are hospitable

* *In point of size, the towns in the United States may be ranked in this order; Philadelphia, New York, Boston, Baltimore, Charleston, &c. In point of trade, New York, Philadelphia, Boston, Charleston, Baltimore, &c.*

pitable to strangers, and maintain a friendly and improving intercourse with each other; but the bulk of the inhabitants, recently collected from almost all quarters of the world—bent on the pursuit of wealth—varying in their habits, their manners and their religions, if they have any, are unsocial, unimproved and inhospitable.

Market street is the principal street in the town, and runs nearly east and west, a mile in length, parallel with the water. This is crossed by several other streets leading from the water, a number of which, particularly, Calvert, South and Gay streets, are well built. North and east of the town the land rises, and affords a fine prospect of the town and bay. Belvidera, the seat of Col. Howard, exhibits one of the finest landscapes in nature. The town—the point—the shipping both in the bason and at Fell's point—the bay as far as the eye can reach—rising ground on the right and left of the harbour—a grove of trees on the declivity at the right—a stream of water breaking over the rocks at the foot of the hill on the left, all conspire to complete the beauty and grandeur of the prospect.

FREDERICKTOWN is a fine flourishing inland town, of upwards of 300 houses, built principally of brick and stone, and mostly on one broad street. It is situated in a fertile country, about four miles south of Catokton mountain, and is a place of considerable trade. It has four places for public worship, one for Presbyterians, two for Dutch Lutherans and Calvinists and one for Baptists; besides a public goal and a brick market house.

HAGARSTOWN is but little inferior to Fredericktown, and is situated in the beautiful and well cultivated valley of Conegocheague, and carries on a considerable trade with the western country.

HEAD OF ELK is situated near the head of Chesapeek bay, on a small river which bears the name of the town. It enjoys great advantages from the carrying trade between Baltimore and Philadelphia. The tides ebb and flow to this town.

Mines and Manufactures.] Mines of iron ore, of a superior quality, are found in many parts of the state. Furnaces for running this ore into pigs and hallow ware, and forges to refine pig iron into bars, have been erected in a number of places in the neighbourhood of the mines. This is the only manufacture of importance, carried on in the state, except it be that of wheat into flour.

Trade.] On this head I can only say, that the trade of Maryland is principally carried on from Baltimore, with the other states, with the West Indies, and with some parts of Europe. To these places they send annually, about 30,000 hogsheads of tobacco, besides large quantities of wheat, flour, pig iron, lumber and corn---beans, pork and flax-feed in smaller quantities; and receive in return, clothing for themselves and negroes, and other dry goods, wines, spirits, sugars and other West India commodities. The balance is generally in their favour.

Religion.] The Roman Catholics, who were the first settlers in Maryland, are the most numerous religious sect. Besides these there are Protestant Episcopalians, English, Scotch and Irish Presbyterians, German Calvinists, German Lutherans, Friends, Baptists, of whom there are

about

MARYLAND.

about twenty congregations, Methodifts, Mennonifts, Nicolites or New Quakers.

Seminaries of Learning, &c.] Wafhington academy, in Somerfet county, was inftituted by law in 1779. It was founded and is fupported by voluntary fubfcriptions and private donations, and is authorized to receive gifts and legacies, and to hold 2000 acres of land. A fupplement to the law, paffed in 1784, increafed the number of truftees from eleven to fifteen.

In 1782, a college was inftituted at Cheftertown, in Kent county, and was honoured with the name of WASHINGTON COLLEGE, after his Excellency General Wafhington. It is under the management of 24 vifitors or governors, with power to fupply vacancies, and hold eftates whofe yearly value fhall not exceed £. 6000 current money. By a law enacted in 1787, a permanent fund was granted to this inftitution of £. 1250 a year, currency, out of the monies arifing from marriage licences, fines and forfeitures, on the Eaftern Shore.

St. John's College was inftituted in 1784, to have alfo 24 truftees, with power to keep up the fucceffion by fupplying vacancies, and to receive an annual income of £. 9000. A permanent fund is affigned this college, of £. 1750 a year, out of the monies arifing from marriage licences ordinary licences, fines and forfeitures on the Weftern Shore. This college is to be at Annapolis, where a building is now preparing for it. Very liberal fubfcriptions were obtained towards founding and carrying on thefe feminaries. The two colleges conftitute one univerfity, by the name of 'the Univerfity of Maryland,' whereof the Governor of the State, for the time being, is Chancellor, and the Principal of one of them, Vice-Chancellor, either by feniority or by election, as may hereafter be provided for by rule or by law. The Chancellor is empowered to call a meeting of the truftees, or a reprefentation of feven of each, and two of the members of the faculty of each, (the Principal being one) which meeting is ftiled 'The Convocation of the Univerfity of Maryland,' who are to frame the laws, preferve uniformity of manners and literature in the colleges, confer the higher degrees, determine appeals, &c.

The Roman Catholics have lately erected a college at George-Town, on Patomak river, for the promotion of general literature.

In 1785, the Methodifts inftituted a college at Abingdon, in Harford county, by the name of Cokefbury College, after Thomas Coke, L. L. D. and Francis Afbury, bifhops of the Methodift Epifcopal Church. The college edifice is of brick, handfomely built, on a healthy fpot, enjoying a fine air and a very extenfive profpect.

The ftudents, who are to confift of the fons of travelling preachers, the fons of annual fubfcribers, the fons of the members of the Methodift fociety and orphans, are to be inftructed in Englifh, Latin, Greek, Logic, Rhetoric, Hiftory, Geography, Natural Philofophy and Aftronomy; and when the finances of the college will admit, they are to be taught the Hebrew, French and German languages.

The college was erected and is fupported wholly by fubfcription and voluntary donations.

The ftudents have regular hours for rifing, for prayers, for their meals, for ftudy and for recreation. They are all to be in bed precifely at nine o'clock o'clock. Their recreations, (for they are to be 'indulged in nothing which the world calls *play'*) are gardening, walking, riding and bathing, without doors; and *within* doors, the carpenters, joiners, cabinet-makers or turner's business. Suitable provision is made for these several occupations, which are to be considered, not as matters of drudgery and constraint, but as pleasing and healthful recreations, both for the body and mind. Another of their rules, which though new and singular, is favourable to the health and vigour of the body and mind, is, that the students shall not sleep on feather beds, but on mattresses, and each one by himself. Particular attention is paid to the morals and religion of the students.

There are a few other literary institutions, of inferior note, in different parts of the state, and provision is made for free schools in most of the counties; though some are entirely neglected, and very few carried on with any success: so that a great proportion of the lower class of people are ignorant; and there are not a few who cannot write their names. But the revolution, among other happy effects, has roused the spirit of education, which is fast spreading its salutary influences over this, and the other southern states.

Natural Curiosities.] There are several remarkable caves in the western part of this state, but particular and accurate descriptions of them have not been received.

Expences of Government and Taxes.] The annual expences of government are estimated at about £.20,000 currency. The revenue arises from duties and imposts, on imports and exports, and taxes on real and personal property.

Constitution,] The legislature is composed of two distinct branches, a *Senate* and *House of Delegates*, and stiled *The General Assembly of Maryland*.

The senators are elected in the following manner. On the first of September, every fifth year, the freemen choose two men in each county to be electors of the senate, and one elector for the city of Annapolis, and one for the town of Baltimore. These electors must have the qualifications necessary for county delegates. These electors meet at Annapolis, or such other place as shall be appointed for convening the legislature, on the third Monday in September, every fifth year, and elect by ballot fifteen senators out of their own body or from the people at large. Nine of these must be residents on the western shore, and six on the eastern—they must be more than twenty-five years of age—must have resided in the state more than three years next preceding the election, and have real and personal property above the value of a thousand pounds. In case of the death, resignation or inability of a senator, during the five years for which he is elected, the vacancy is filled by the senate. The senate may originate any bills, except money bills, to which they can only give their assent or dissent.

The senate choose their president by ballot.

The house of delegates is composed of four members for each county, chosen annually on the first Monday in October. The city of Annapolis and town of Baltimore send, each two delegates. The qualifications of a delegate, are, full age, one year's residence in the county where he is chosen,

MARYLAND.

chosen, and real or personal property above the value of five hundred pounds.

Both houses choose their own officers and judge of the election of their members. A majority of each is a quorum.

The election of senators and delegates is *viva voce*, and sheriffs the returning officers, except in Baltimore town, where the commissioners superintend the elections and make returns. The stated session of the legislature is on the first Monday in November.

The qualifications of a freeman are full age, a freehold estate of fifty acres of land, and actual residence *in the county where he offers to vote*,— property to the value of thirty pounds *in any part of the state*, and a year's residence in the county where he offers to vote.

On the second Monday in November, annually, a governor is appointed by the joint ballot of both houses, taken in each house respectively, and deposited in a conference room; where the boxes are examined by a joint committee of both houses, and the number of votes severally reported. The governor cannot continue in office longer than three years successively, nor be elected until the expiration of four years after he has been out of office.

The qualifications for the chief magistracy, are, twenty-five years of age, five years residence in the state, next preceding the election, and real and personal estate above the value of five thousand pounds, one thousand of which must be freehold estate.

On the second Tuesday of November, annually, the senators and delegates elect by joint ballot, five able, discreet men, above twenty-five years of age, residents in the state three years next preceding the election, and possessing a freehold of lands and tenements above the value of a thousand pounds, to be a council for assisting the governor in the duties of his office.

Senators, delegates and members of council, while such, can hold no other office of profit, nor receive the profits of any office exercised by another.

Ministers of the gospel are excluded from civil offices.

The governor, with the advice of his council, appoints the chancellor, all judges and justices, the attorney general, naval and militia officers, registers of the land office, surveyors, and all other civil officers, except constables, assessors and overseers of the roads.

A court of appeals is established for the final determination of all causes, which may be brought from the general court* of admiralty or of chancery.

This constitution was established by a convention of delegates, at Annapolis, August 14, 1776.

History.] Maryland was granted by king Charles I. to Cecilius Calvert, baron of Baltimore, in Ireland, June 20, 1632. The government of the province, was, by charter, vested in the proprietary; but it appears that he either never exercised these powers alone, or but for a short time; for we find that in 1637, the freemen rejected a body of laws drawn up

in

---

* *In some of the eastern states the legislature is called* The General Court. *In some of the southern, the* General Court *is the* Supreme Judicial Court.

in England, and tranfmitted by his lordfhip, in order to be paffed for the government of the province. In the place of thefe, they propofed forty-two bills to be enacted into laws, by the confent of the proprietary. Thefe were however never enacted; at leaft they are not on record.

The hon. Leonard Calvert, efq; lord Baltimore's brother, was the firft governor, or lieutenant general. In 1638, a law was paffed, conftituting the firft regular *Houfe of Affembly*, which was to confift of fuch reprefentatives, called *Burgeffes*, as fhould be elected purfuant to writs iffued by the governor. Thefe burgeffes poffeffed *all the powers of the perfons electing them;* but any other freemen, who did not affent to the election, might take their feats in perfon. Twelve burgeffes or freemen, with the lieutenant general and fecretary, conftituted the affembly or legiflature. This affembly fat at St. Mary's, one of the fouthern counties, which was the firft fettled part of Maryland.

In 1642, it was enacted that *ten* members of the affembly, of whom the governor and fix burgeffes were to be *feven*, fhould be a houfe; and if ficknefs fhould prevent that number from attending, the members prefent fhould make a houfe.

In 1644, one Ingle excited a rebellion, forced the governor to fly to Virginia for aid and protection, and feized the records and the great feal; the laft of which, with moft of the records of the province, were loft or deftroyed. From this period, to the year 1647, when order was reftored, the proceedings of the province are involved in obfcurity.

In July, 1642, the houfe of affembly, or more properly the burgeffes, requefted they might be feparated into two branches—the burgeffes by themfelves, with a negative upon bills. This was not granted by the lieutenant general at that time; but in 1650, an act was paffed dividing the affembly into two houfes. The governor, fecretary, and any one or more of the council formed the *Upper Houfe;* the delegates from the feveral hundreds, who now reprefent the freemen, formed the *Lower Houfe*. At this time there were in the province but two counties, St. Mary's and the Ifle of Kent; but Ann Arundel was added, the fame feffion. This was during the adminiftration of governor Stone.

In 1654, during Cromwell's ufurpation in England, an act was paffed, reftraining the exercife of the Roman Catholic religion. This muft have been procured by the mere terror of Cromwell's power, for the firft and principal inhabitants were Catholics. Indeed the power of Cromwell was not eftablifhed in Maryland without force and bloodfhed. His friends and foes came to an open rupture, an engagement enfued, governor Stone was taken prifoner, and condemned to be fhot. This fentence however was not executed, but he was kept a long time in confinement.

In March, 1658, Jofiah Fendall, efq; was appointed lieutenant general of Maryland by commiffion from Oliver Cromwell. He diffolved the upper houfe, and furrendered the powers of government into the hands of the delegates.

Upon the reftoration in 1660, the hon. Philip Calvert, efq; was appointed governor; the old form of government was revived; Fendall, and one Gerrard, a counfellor, were indicted, found guilty and condemned to banifhment, with the lofs of their eftates: but upon petition they were pardoned.

MARYLAND.

In 1689, the government was taken out of the hands of lord Baltimore by the grand convention of England; and in 1692 Mr. Copley was appointed governor by commission from William and Mary.

In 1692, the *Protestant* religion was established by law.

In 1699, under the administration of governor Blackiston, it was enacted that Annapolis should be the seat of government.

In 1716, the government of this province was restored to the proprietary, and continued in his hands till the late revolution, when being an absentee, his property in the lands was confiscated, and the government assumed by the freemen of the province, who formed the constitution now existing. At the close of the war, Henry Harford, esq; the natural son and heir of lord Baltimore, petitioned the legislature of Maryland for his estate; but his petition was not granted. Mr. Harford estimated his loss of quit-rents, valued at twenty years purchase, and including arrears, at £. 259,488 : 5 : 0, dollars at 7/6—and the value of his manors and reserved lands at £. 327,441 of the same money.

LIST *of* GOVERNORS, *with the dates of their appointments.*

Hon. Leonard Calvert, esq; appointed Governor,	1637
Thomas Green, esq;	1647
William Stone, esq;	1649
The government remained in the hands of the parliament commissioners during the time of Oliver Cromwell's usurpation	1654
The commissioners by certain articles of agreement then entered into, delivered up the government into the hands of Jonah Fendale, esq; then Governor	1658
Hon. Philip Calvert made Governor	1660
Charles Calvert, esq;	1662
Upon the death of Cecilius, the government descended to Charles, lord Baltimore, who came into the province	1675
Thomas Notly, esq; Governor	1678
Who continued till his lordship returned a second time to the province in	1681
King William and queen Mary took upon them the government, and appointed Lyonel Copley, esq; Governor	1692
Francis Nicholson, esq;	1694
Upon the death of queen Mary, the government was altogether in the hands of king William the III.	1696
Nathaniel Blackiston, esq; Governor	1699
By the death of king William III. queen Ann took upon her the government—and the same governor was continued	1701-2
Thomas Finch, esq; President	1703
John Seymour, esq; Governor	1704
Edward Lloyd, esq; President	1704
John Hart, esq; Governor	1714
Upon the death of queen Ann, king George the I. took upon him the government—and the same governor was continued	1715
The government was restored to Charles, lord Baltimore, who issued a new commission to John Hart, esq;	1716
Charles Calvert, esq; Governor	1720
Benedict Leonard Calvert, esq Governor	1727

360	MARYLAND.

The Proprietor came into the province in	17 3
And returned to England	1734
Samuel Ogle, efq; Governor	1737
Thomas Bladen, efq; Governor	1742
Samuel Ogle, efq; Governor	1747
   By the death of Charles, lord Baltimore, the province defcended
ed to his fon Frederick.—Governor Ogle died the fame year	1751
Benjamin Tafker, efq; Prefident	1751
Horatio Sharp, efq; Governor	1753
Robert Eden, efq; Governor	1769
Frederick, lord baron of Baltimore, died	1771
Robert Eden, efq; Governor	1773
   The lift of the governors of this ftate, with the times of their election into office, fince the revolution, has not been received.

VIRGINIA.*

SITUATION and EXTENT.

Miles.
Length 758 } Between { 36° 30′ and 40° North Latitude.
Breadth 224 }   { The Meridian of Philadelphia, and 14 Weft Longitude.

Boundaries.] BOUNDED eaft, by the Atlantic ocean; north, by Pennfylvania and the river Ohio; weft, by the Miffifippi; fouth, by North Carolina.

Mr. Jefferfon defcribes the boundaries more particularly, as follows; ' Virginia is bounded on the eaft, by the Atlantic; on the north, by a line of latitude, croffing the eaftern fhore through Watkins's Point, being about 37° 57′ north latitude; from thence by a ftreight line to Cinquac, near the mouth of Patomak; thence by the Patomak, which is common to Virginia and Maryland, to the firft fountain of its northern branch; thence by a meridian line, paffing through that fountain till it interfects a line running eaft and weft, in latitude 39° 43′ 42.4″ which divides Maryland from Pennfylvania, and which was marked by Meffrs. Mafon and Dixon; thence by that line, and a continuation of it weftwardly to the completion of five degrees of longitude from the eaftern boundary of Pennfylvania, in the fame latitude, and thence by a meridian line to the Ohio; on the weft, by the Ohio and Miffifippi, to latitude

---

* *In the following defcription of Virginia, what is included between inverted commas, is taken from Mr. Jefferfon's notes on Virginia, except in the inftances where the reader is otherwife informed.*

VIRGINIA.   361

latitude 36° 30' north; and on the south, by the line of latitude last-mentioned. By admeasurements through nearly the whole of this last line, and supplying the unmeasured parts from good data, the Atlantic and Missisippi, are found in this latitude to be 758 miles distant, equal to 13° 38' of longitude, reckoning 55 miles and 3144 feet to the degree. This being our comprehension of longitude, that of our latitude, taken between this and Mason and Dixon's line, is 3° 13' 42.4", equal to 223.3 miles, supposing a degree of a great circle to be 69 m. 864 f. as computed by Cassini. These boundaries include an area somewhat triangular, of 121,525 miles, whereof 79,650 lie westward of the Allegany mountains, and 57,034 westward of the meridian of the mouth of the Great Kanhaway. This state is therefore one third larger than the islands of Great Britain and Ireland, which are reckoned at 88,357 square miles.

'These limits result from, 1. The antient charters from the crown of England. 2. The grant of Maryland to the Lord Baltimore, and the subsequent determinations of the British court as to the extent of that grant. 3. The grant of Pennsylvania to William Penn, and a compact between the general assemblies of the commonwealths of Virginia and Pennsylvania as to the extent of that grant. 4. The grant of Carolina, and actual location of its northern boundary, by consent of both parties. 5. The treaty of Paris of 1763. 6. The confirmation of the charters of the neighbouring states by the convention of Virginia at the time of constituting their commonwealth. 7. The cession made by Virginia to Congress of all the lands to which they had title on the north side of the Ohio.'

Rivers.] 'An inspection of a map of Virginia, will give a better idea of the geography of its rivers, than any description in writing. There navigation may be imperfectly noted.

'*Roanoke*, so far as it lies within this state, is no where navigable, but for canoes, or light batteaux; and, even for these, in such detached parcels as to have prevented the inhabitants from availing themselves of it at all.

'*James River*, and its waters, afford navigation as follows:

'The whole of *Elizabeth River*, the lowest of those which run into James River, is a harbour, and would contain upwards of 300 ships. The channel is from 150 to 200 fathoms wide, and at common flood tide, affords 18 feet water to Norfolk. The Strafford, a 60 gun ship, went there, lightening herself to cross the bar at Sowell's point. The Fier Rodrigue, pierced for 64 guns, and carrying 50, went there without lightening. Craney island, at the mouth of this river, commands its channel tolerably well.

'*Nansemond River* is navigable to Sleepy Hole, for vessels of 250 tons; to Suffolk, for those of 100 tons; and to Milner's, for those of 25.

'*Pagan Creek* affords 8 or 10 feet water to Smithfield, which admits vessels of 20 tons.

'*Chickahominy* has at its mouth a bar, on which is only 12 feet water at common flood tide. Vessels passing that, may go 8 miles up the river; those of ten feet draught may go four miles further, and those of 6 tons burthen, 20 miles further.

Z z   '*Appamattox*

'*Appamattox* may be navigated as far as Broadways, by any veſſel which has croſſed Harriſon's bar in James River; it keeps 8 or 9 feet water a mile or two higher up to Fiſher's bar, and 4 feet on that and upwards to Peterſburgh, where all navigation ceaſes.

'*James River* itſelf affords harbour for veſſels of any ſize in Hampton Road, but not in ſafety through the whole winter; and there is navigable water for them as far as Mulberry iſland. A 40 gun ſhip goes to James town, and, lightening herſelf, may paſs to Harriſon's bar, on which there is only 15 feet water. Veſſels of 250 tons may go to Warwick; thoſe of 125 go to Rocket's, a mile below Richmond; from thence is about 7 feet water to Richmond; and about the center of the town, four feet and a half, where the navigation is interrupted by falls, which in a courſe of ſix miles deſcend about 80 feet perpendicular: above theſe it is reſumed in canoes and batteaux, and is proſecuted ſafely and advantageouſly to within 10 miles of the Blue Ridge; and even through the Blue Ridge a ton weight has been brought; and the expence would not be great, when compared with its object, to open a tolerable navigation up Jackſon's river and Carpenter's creek, to within 25 miles of Howard's creek of Green Briar, both of which have then water enough to float veſſels into the Great Kanhaway. In ſome future ſtate of population, I think it poſſible, that its navigation may alſo be made to interlock with that of the Patomak, and through that to communicate by a ſhort portage with the Ohio. It is to be noted, that this river is called in the maps *James River*, only to its confluence with the Rivanna; thence to the Blue Ridge it is called the Fluvanna; and thence to its ſource, Jackſon's river. But in common ſpeech, it is called James river to its ſource.

'The *Rivanna*, a branch of James river, is navigable for canoes and batteaux to its interſection with the South Weſt mountains, which is about 22 miles; and may eaſily be opened to navigation through thoſe mountains to its fork above Charlotteſville.

'*York River*, at York town affords the beſt harbour in the ſtate for veſſels of the largeſt ſize. The river there narrows to the width of a mile, and is contained within very high banks, cloſe under which the veſſels may ride. It holds 4 fathom water at high tide for 25 miles above York to the mouth of Poropotank, where the river is a mile and a half wide, and the channel only 75 fathom, and paſſing under a high bank. At the confluence of *Pamunkey* and *Mattapony*, it is reduced to 3 fathom depth, which continues up Pamunkey to Cumberland, where the width is 100 yards, and up Mattapony to within two miles of Frazer's ferry, where it becomes $2\frac{1}{2}$ fathom deep, and holds that about five miles. Pamunkey is then capable of navigation for loaded flats to Brockman's bridge, 50 miles above Hanover town, and Mattapony to Downer's bridge, 70 miles above its mouth.

'*Piankatank*, the little rivers making out of *Mobjack Bay* and thoſe of the *Eaſtern ſhore*, receive only very ſmall veſſels, and theſe can but enter them.

'*Rappahannok* affords 4 fathom water to Hobb's Hole, and two fathom from thence to Frederickſburg.

'Patomak

Patomak is 7½ miles wide at the mouth; 4½ at Nomony Bay; 3 at Aquia; 1½ at Hallooing Point; 1¼ at Alexandria. Its foundings are, 7 fathom at the mouth; 5 at St. George's island; 4½ at Lower Matchodic; 3 at Swan's Point, and thence up to Alexandria; thence 10 feet water to the falls, which are 13 miles above Alexandria.'

The distance from the Capes of Virginia to the termination of the tide-water in this river is above 300 miles; and navigable for ships of the greatest burthen, nearly to that place. From thence this river, obstructed by four considerable falls, extends through a vast tract of inhabited country towards its source. These falls are, 1st, The *Little Falls*, three miles above tide water, in which distance there is a fall of 36 feet: 2d, The *Great Falls*, six miles higher, where is a fall of 76 feet in one mile and a quarter: 3d, The *Seneca Falls*, six miles above the former, which form short, irregular rapids, with a fall of about 10 feet; and 4th, the *Shenandoah Falls*, 60 miles from the *Seneca*, where is a fall of about 30 feet in three miles: From which last, *Fort Cumberland* is about 120 miles distant. The obstructions, which are opposed to the navigation above and between these falls, are of little consequence.

Early in the year 1785, the *Legislatures* of *Virginia* and *Maryland* passed acts to encourage opening the navigation of this river. It was estimated that the expence of the works would amount to £. 50,000 sterling, and ten years were allowed for their completion. At present the president and directors of the incorporated company suppose that £. 45,000 will be adequate to the operation, and that it will be accomplished in a shorter period than was stipulated. Their calculations are founded on the progress already made, and the summary mode lately established for enforcing the collection of the dividends, as the money may become necessary. On each share of £. 100, the payment of only £. 40 has yet been demanded.

According to the opinion of the president and directors, *locks* will be necessary at no more than two places—the *Great* and the *Little Falls*: Six at the former, and three at the latter. At the latter nothing has yet been attempted. At the *Great Falls*, where the difficulties were judged by many to be insurmountable, the work is nearly completed; except sinking the lock-seats and inserting the frames. At the *Seneca Falls* the laborious part of the business is entirely accomplished, by removing the obstacles and graduating the descent; so that nothing remains but to finish the channel for this gentle current in a workmanlike manner. At the *Shenandoah*, where the river breaks through the Blue Ridge, though a prodigious quantity of labor has been bestowed, yet much is still to be done before the passage will be perfected. Such proficiency has been made, however, that it was expected, if the summer had not proved uncommonly rainy and the river uncommonly high, an avenue for a partial navigation would have been opened by the first of January 1789, from *Fort Cumberland* to the *Great Falls*, which are within nine miles of a shipping port. As it has happened, it may require a considerable part of this year for its accomplishment.

As soon as the proprietors shall begin to receive toll, they will doubtless find an ample compensation for their pecuniary advances. By an estimate made many years ago, it was calculated that the amount, in the commencement

mencement, would be at the rate of £.11,875, Virginia currency, per annum. The toll must every year become more productive; as the quantity of articles for exportation will be augmented in a rapid ratio, with the encrease of population and the extention of settlements. In the mean time the effect will be immediately seen in the agriculture of the interior country; for the multitude of horses now employed in carrying produce to market, will then be used altogether for the purposes of tillage. But, in order to form just conceptions of the utility of this inland navigation, it would be requisite to notice the long rivers which empty into the Patomak, and even to take a survey of the geographical position of the *western waters*.

The *Shenandoah*, which disembogues just above the Blue Mountains, may, according to report, be made navigable, at a trifling expence, more than 150 miles from its confluence with the Patomak; and will receive and bear the produce of the richest part of the state. The South Branch, still higher, is navigable in its actual condition nearly or quite 100 miles, through exceedingly fertile lands. Between these, on the Virginia side, are several smaller rivers, that may with facility be improved, so as to afford a passage for boats. On the *Maryland* side are the Monocasy, Antietam, and Conegocheague, some of which pass through the state of Maryland, and have their sources in Pennsylvania.

From Fort Cumberland (or Wills' Creek) one or two good waggon roads may be had (where the distance is said by some to be 35 and by others 40 miles) to the Yohogany, a large and navigable branch of the Monongahela; which last forms a junction with the Allegany at Fort Pitt; from whence the river takes the name of the *Ohio*, until it loses its current and name in the Mississippi.

But, by passing farther up the Patomak, than Fort Cumberland, which may very easily be done, a portage by a good waggon road to the Cheat River, another large branch of the Monongahela, can be obtained through a space which some say is 20, others 22, others 25, and none more than 30 miles.

When we have arrived at either of these western waters, the navigation through that immense region is opened in a thousand directions, and to the lakes in several places by portages of less than 10 miles; and by one portage, it is asserted, of not more than a single mile.

Notwithstanding it was sneeringly said by some foreigners, at the beginning of this undertaking, that the Americans were fond of engaging in splendid projects which they could never accomplish; yet it is hoped the success of this first essay towards improving their inland navigation, will, in some degree, rescue them from the reproach intended to have been fixed upon their national character, by the unmerited imputation.

'The *Great Kanhaway* is a river of considerable note for the fertility of its lands, and still more, as leading towards the head waters of James river. Nevertheless, it is doubtful whether its great and numerous rapids will admit a navigation, but at an expence to which it will require ages to render its inhabitants equal. The great obstacles begin at what are called the Great Falls, 90 miles above the mouth, below which are only five or six rapids, and these passable, with some difficulty, even at low water

VIRGINIA. 355

From the falls to the mouth of Green Briar is 100 miles, and thence to the lead mines 120. It is 280 yards wide at its mouth.

'The *Little Kanhaway* is 150 yards wide at the mouth. It yields a navigation of 10 miles only. Perhaps its northern branch, called Junius' Creek, which interlocks with the western waters of Monongahela, may one day admit a shorter passage from the latter into the Ohio.'

Mountains.] 'For the particular geography of our mountains, I must refer to Fry and Jefferson's map of Virginia; and to Evan's analysis of his map of America for a more philosphical view of them than is to be found in any other work. It is worthy notice, that our mountains are not solitary and scattered confusedly over the face of the country; but that they commence at about 150 miles from the sea coast, are disposed in ridges one behind another, running nearly parallel with the sea coast, though rather approaching it as they advance northeastwardly. To the southwest, as the tract of country between the sea coast and the Mississippi becomes narrower, the mountains converge into a single ridge, which, as it approaches the Gulph of Mexico, subsides into plain country, and gives rise to some of the waters of that Gulph, and particularly to a river called the Apalachicola, probably from the Apalachies, an Indian nation formerly residing on it. Hence the mountains giving rise to that river, and seen from its various parts, were called the Apalachian Mountains, being in fact the end or termination only of the great ridges passing through the continent. European geographers however extended the name northwardly as far as the mountains extended; some giving it, after their separation into different ridges, to the Blue Ridge, others to the North Mountains, others to the Allegany, others to the Laurel Ridge, as may be seen in their different maps. But the fact I believe is, that none of these ridges were ever known by that name to the inhabitants, either native or emigrant, but as they saw them so called in European maps. In the same direction generally are the veins of lime-stone, coal and other minerals hitherto discovered: and so range the falls of our great rivers. But the courses of the great rivers are at right angles with these. James and Patomak penetrate through all the ridges of mountains eastward of the Allegany; that is broken by no water course. It is in fact the spine of the country between the Atlantic on one side, and the Mississippi and St. Lawrence on the other. The passage of the Patomak through the Blue Ridge is perhaps one of the most stupendous scenes in nature. You stand on a very high point of land. On your right comes up the Shenandoah, having ranged along the foot of the mountain an hundred miles to seek a vent. On your left approaches the Patomak, in quest of a passage also. In the moment of their junction they rush together against the mountain, rend it asunder, and pass of to the sea. The first glance of this scene hurries our senses into the opinion, that this earth has been created in time, that the mountains were formed first, that the rivers began to flow afterwards, that in this place particularly they have been dammed up by the Blue Ridge of mountains, and have formed an ocean which filled the whole valley; that continuing to rise they have at length broken over at this spot, and have torn the mountain down from its summit to its base. The piles of rock on each hand, but particularly on the Shenandoah, the evident marks of their disruption and avulsion from their beds by the most

powerful

powerful agents of nature, corroborate the impreffion. But the diftant finifhing which nature has given to the picture is of a very different character. It is a true contraft to the fore ground. It is as placid and delightful, as that is wild and tremendous. For the mountain being cloven afunder, fhe prefents to your eye, through the cleft, a fmall catch of fmooth blue horizon, at an infinite diftance in the plain country, inviting you, as it were, from the riot and tumult roaring around, to pafs through the breach and participate of the calm below. Here the eye ultimately compofes itfelf; and that way too the road happens actually to lead. You crofs the Patomak above the junction, pafs along its fide through the bafe of the mountain for three miles, its terrible precipices hanging in fragments over you, and within about 20 miles reach Frederick town and the fine country round that. This fcene is worth a voyage acrofs the Atlantic. Yet here, as in the neighbourhood of the natural bridge, are people who have paffed their lives within half a dozen miles, and have never been to furvey thefe monuments of a war between rivers and mountains, which muft have fhaken the earth itfelf to its center.—The height of our mountains has not yet been eftimated with any degree of exactnefs. The Alleganv being the great ridge which divides the waters of the Atlantic from thofe of the Miffifippi, its fummit is doubtlefs more elevated above the ocean than that of any other mountain. But its relative height, compared with the bafe on which it ftands, is not fo great as that of fome others, the country rifing behind the fucceffive ridges like the fteps of ftairs. The mountains of the Blue Ridge, and of thefe the Peaks of Otter, are thought to be of a greater height, meafured from their bafe, than any others in our country, and perhaps in North America. From data, which may found a tolerable conjecture, we fuppofe the higheft peak to be about 4000 feet perpendicular, which is not a fifth part of the height of the mountains of South America, nor one third of the height which would be neceffary in our latitude to preferve ice in the open air unmelted through the year. The ridge of mountains next beyond the Blue Ridge, called by us the North Mountain, is of the greateft extent; for which reafon they are named by the Indians the Endlefs Mountains.

‘ A fubftance fuppofed to be Pumice, found floating on the Miffifippi, has induced a conjecture, that there is a volcano on fome of its waters: and as thefe are moftly known to their fources, except the Miffouri, our expectations of verifying the conjecture would of courfe be led to the mountains which divide the waters of the Mexican Gulph from thofe of the South Sea; but no volcano having ever yet been known at fuch a diftance from the fea, we muft rather fuppofe that this floating fubftance has been erroneoufly deemed pumice.

Cafcades and Caverns.] ‘ The only remarkable cafcade in this country, is that of the Falling Spring, in Augufta. It is a water of James river, where it is called Jackfon's river, rifing in the warm fpring mountains about 20 miles fouthweft of the warm fpring, and flowing into that valley. About three quarters of a mile from its fource, it falls over a rock 200 feet into the valley below. The fheet of water is broken in its breadth by the rock in two or three places, but not at all in its height. Between the fheet and rock, at the bottom, you may walk acrofs dry. This cataract will bear no comparifon with that of Niagara, as to the quantity of water
compofing

composing it; the sheet being only 12 or 15 feet wide above, and somewhat more spread below; but it is half as high again, the latter being only 156 feet, according to the mensuration made by order of Mr. Vandreuil, Governor of Canada, and 130 according to a more recent account.

'In the lime-stone country, there are many caverns of very considerable extent. The most noted is called Madison's Cave, and is on the north side of the Blue Ridge, near the intersection of the Rockingham and Augusta line with the south fork of the southern river of Shenandoah. It is in a hill of about 200 feet perpendicular height, the ascent of which, on one side, is so steep, that you may pitch a biscuit from its summit into the river which washes its base. The entrance of the cave is, in this side, about two thirds of the way up. It extends into the earth about 300 feet, branching into subordinate caverns, sometimes ascending a little, but more generally descending, and at length terminates, in two different places, at basons of water of unknown extent, and which I should judge to be nearly on a level with the water of the river; however, I do not think they are formed by refluent water from that, because they are never turbid; because they do not rise and fall in correspondence with that in times of flood, or of drought; and because the water is always cool. It is probably one of the many reservoirs with which the interior parts of the earth are supposed to abound, and which yield supplies to the fountains of water, distinguished from others only by its being accessible. The vault of this cave is of solid lime-stone, from 20 to 40 or 50 feet high, through which water is continually percolating. This, trickling down the sides of the cave, has incrusted them over in the form of elegant drapery; and dripping from the top of the vault generates on that, and on the base below, stalactites of a conical form, some of which have met and formed massive columns.

'Another of these caves is near the North Mountain, in the county of Frederick, on the lands of Mr. Zane. The entrance into this is on the top of an extensive ridge. You descend 30 or 40 feet, as into a well, from whence the cave then extends, nearly horizontally, 400 feet into the earth, preserving a breadth of from 20 to 50 feet, and a height of from 5 to 12 feet. After entering this cave a few feet, the mercury, which in the open air was at 50°, rose to 57° of Farenheit's thermometer, answering to 11° of Reaumur's, and it continued at that to the remotest parts of the cave. The uniform temperature of the cellars of the observatory of Paris, which are 90 feet deep, and of all subterranean cavities of any depth, where no chymical agents may be supposed to produce a factitious heat, has been found to be 10° of Reamur, equal to 54°$\frac{1}{2}$ of Farenheit. The temperature of the cave above-mentioned so nearly corresponds with this, that the difference may be ascribed to a difference of instruments.

'At the Panther gap, in the ridge which divides the waters of the Cow and the Calf pasture, is what is called the *Blowing Cave*. It is in the side of a hill, is of about 100 feet diameter, and emits constantly a current of air of such force, as to keep the weeds prostrate to the distance of twenty yards before it. This current is strongest in dry frosty weather, and in long spells of rain weakest. Regular inspirations and expirations

expirations of air, by caverns and fissures, have been probably enough accounted for, by suppofing them combined with intermitting fountains; as they muft of courfe inhale air while their refervoirs are emptying themfelves, and again emit it while they are filling. But a conftant iffue of air, only varying in its force as the weather is drier or damper, will require a new hypothefis. There is another blowing cave in the Cumberland mountain, about a mile from where it croffes the Carolina line. All we know of this is, that it is not conftant, and that a fountain of water iffues from it.

'The *Natural Bridge*, the moft fublime of nature's works, though not comprehended under the prefent head, muft not be pretermitted. It is on the afcent of a hill, which feems to have been cloven through its length by fome great convulfion. The fiffure, juft at the bridge, is, by fome admeafurements, 270 feet deep, by others only 205. It is about 45 feet wide at the bottom, and 90 feet at the top; this of courfe determines the length of the bridge, and its height from the water. Its breadth in the middle is about 60 feet, but more at the ends, and the thicknefs of the mafs at the fummit of the arch, about 40 feet. A part of this thicknefs is conftituted by a coat of earth, which gives growth to many large trees. The refidue, with the hill on both fides, is one folid rock of lime-ftone. The arch approaches the femi-elliptical form; but the larger axis of the ellipfis, which would be the cord of the arch, is many times longer than the tranfverfe. Though the fides of this bridge are provided in fome parts with a parapet of fixed rocks, yet few men have refolution to walk to them and look over into the abyfs. You involuntarily fall on your hands and feet, creep to the parapet and peep over it. Looking down from this height about a minute, gave me a violent head ach. If the view from the top be painful and intolerable, that from below is delightful in an equal extreme. It is impoffible for the emotions arifing from the fublime, to be felt beyond what they are here: fo beautiful an arch, fo elevated, fo light, and fpringing as it were up to Heaven, the rapture of the fpectator is really indefcribable! The fiffure continuing narrow, deep, and ftreight for a confiderable diftance above and below the bridge, opens a fhort but very pleafing view of the North mountain on one fide, and Blue Ridge on the other, at the diftance each of them of about five miles. This bridge is in the county of Rock bridge, to which it has given name, and affords a public and commodious paffage over a valley, which cannot be croffed elfewhere for a confiderable diftance. The ftream paffing under it is called Cedar creek. It is a water of James river, and fufficient in the drieft feafons to turn a grift-mill, though its fountain is not more than two miles above.'* There is a natural bridge, fimilar to the one above defcribed, over Stock creek, a branch of Pelefon river, in Wafhington county.

Mines

---

* Don Ulloa mentions a break, fimilar to this, in the province of Angaraez, in South America. It is from 16 to 22 feet wide, 111 deep and of 1¾ miles continuance, Englifh meafure. Its breadth at top is not fenfibly greater than at bottom.

VIRGINIA. 369

Mines and Minerals.] ' I knew a single instance of gold found in this state. It was interspersed in small specks through a lump of ore, of about four pounds weight, which yielded seventeen penny-weight of gold, of extraordinary ductility. This ore was found on the north side of Rappahannock, about four miles below the falls. I never heard of any other indication of gold in its neighbourhood.

' On the Great Kanhaway, opposite to the mouth of Cripple creek, and about 25 miles from our southern boundary, in the county of Montgomery, are mines of lead. The metal is mixed, sometimes with earth, and sometimes with rock, which requires the force of gunpowder to open it; and is accompanied with a portion of silver, too small to be worth separation under any process hitherto attempted there. The proportion yielded is from 50 to 80 lb. of pure metal from 100 lb. of washed ore. The most common is that of 60 to the 100 lb. The veins are at sometimes most flattering; at others they disappear suddenly and totally. They enter the side of the hill, and proceed horizontally. Two of them are wrought at present by the public, the best of which is 100 yards under the hill. These would employ about 50 labourers to advantage. We have not, however, more than 30 generally, and these cultivate their own corn. They have produced 60 tons of lead in the year; but the general quantity is from 20 to 25 tons. The present furnace is a mile from the ore bank, and on the opposite side of the river. The ore is first waggoned to the river, a quarter of a mile, then laden on board of canoes and carried across the river, which is there about 200 yards wide, and then again taken into waggons and carried to the furnace. This mode was originally adopted, that they might avail themselves of a good situation on a creek, for a pounding mill: but it would be easy to have the furnace and pounding mill on the same side of the river, which would yield water, without any dam, by a canal of about half a mile in length. From the furnace the lead is transported 130 miles along a good road, leading through the peaks of Otter to Lynch's ferry, or Winston's, on James river, from whence it is carried by water about the same distance to Westham. This land carriage may be greatly shortened, by delivering the lead on James river, above the Blue Ridge, from whence a ton weight has been brought in two canoes. The Great Kanhaway has considerable falls in the neighbourhood of the mines. About seven miles below are three falls, of three or four feet perpendicular each; and three miles above is a rapid of three miles continuance, which has been compared in its descent to the great fall of James river. Yet it is the opinion, that they may be laid open for useful navigation, so as to reduce very much the portage between the Kanhaway and James river.

' A valuable lead mine is said to have been lately discovered in Cumberland, below the mouth of Red river. The greatest, however, known in the western country, are on the Mississippi, extending from the mouth of Rock river 150 miles upwards. These are not wrought, the lead used in that country being from the banks on the Spanish side of the Mississippi, opposite to Kaskaskia.

' A mine of copper was once opened in the county of Amherst, on the north side of James River, and another in the opposite county, on the south side. However, either from bad management or the poverty of the

A a a veins

veins, they were discontinued. We are told of a rich mine of native copper on the Ouabache, below the upper Wiaw.

'The mines of iron worked at present are Callaway's, Ross', and Ballendine's, on the south side of James river; Old's on the north side, in Albemarle: Miller's in Augusta, and Zane's in Frederick. These two last are in the valley between the Blue Ridge and North Mountain. Callaway's, Ross', Miller's, and Zane's make about 150 tons of bar iron each, in the year. Ross' makes also about 1600 tons of pig iron annually; Ballendine's 1000; Callaway's, Miller's, and Zane's, about 600 each. Besides these, a forge of Mr. Hunter's, at Frederickburgh, makes about 300 tons a year of bar iron, from pigs imported from Maryland; and Taylor's forge on Neapsco of Patomak, works in the same way, but to what extent I am not informed. The indications of iron in other places are numerous, and dispersed through all the middle country. The toughness of the cast iron of Ross' and Zane's furnaces is very remarkable. Pots and other utensils, cast thinner than usual, of this iron, may be safely thrown into, or out of the waggons in which they are transported. Salt-pans made of the same, and no longer wanted for that purpose, cannot be broken up, in order to be melted again, unless previously drilled in many parts

'In the western country, we are told of iron mines between the Muskingum and Ohio; of others on Kentucky, between the Cumberland and Barren rivers, between Cumberland and Tennissee, on Reedy creek, near the Long Island, and on Chesnut creek, a branch of the Great Kanhaway, near where it crosses the Carolina line. What are called the Iron Banks, on the Missisippi, are believed, by a good judge, to have no iron in them. In general from what is hitherto known of that country, it seems to want iron.

'Considerable quantities of black lead are taken occasionally for use from Winterham, in the county of Amelia. I am not able, however, to give a particular state of the mine. There is no work established at it, those who want, going and procuring it for themselves.

'The country on James river, from 15 to 20 miles above Richmond, and for several miles northward and southward, is replete with mineral coal of a very excellent quality. Being in the hands of many proprietors, pits have been opened, and, before the interruption of our commerce, were worked to an extent equal to the demand.

'In the western country coal is known to be in so many places, as to have induced an opinion, that the whole tract between the Laurel Mountain, Missisippi, and Ohio, yields coal. It is also known in many places on the north side of the Ohio. The coal at Pittsburg is of a very superior quality. A bed of it at that place has been a-fire since the year 1765. Another coal-hill on the Pike Run of Monongahela has been a-fire ten years; yet it has burnt away about 20 yards only.

'I have known one instance of an emerald found in this country. Amethysts have been frequent, and chrystals common; yet not in such numbers any of them as to be worth seeking.

'There is very good marble, and in very great abundance, on James river, at the mouth of Rockfish. The samples I have seen, were some of them of a white as pure as one might expect to find on the surface of the earth

earth: but most of them are variegated with red, blue, and purple. None of it has been ever worked. It forms a very large precipice, which hangs over a navigable part of the river. It is said there is marble at Kentucky.

'But one vein of lime-stone is known below the Blue Ridge. Its first appearance, in our country, is in Prince William, two miles below the Pignut Ridge of mountains; thence it passes on nearly parallel with that, and crosses the Rivanna about five miles below it, where it is called the Southwest Ridge. It then crosses Hardware, above the mouth of Hudson's creek, James river at the mouth of Rockfish, at the marble quarry before spoken of, probably runs up that river to where it appears again at Rofs' iron-works, and so passes off southwestwardly by Flat creek of Otter river. It is never more than 100 yards wide. From the Blue Ridge westwardly the whole country seems to be founded on a rock of lime-stone, besides infinite quantities on the surface, both loose and fixed. This is cut into beds, which range, as the mountains and sea coast do, from southwest to northeast, the lamina of each bed declining from the horizon towards a parallelism with the axis of the earth. Being struck with this observation, I made, with a quadrant, a great number of trials on the angles of their declination, and found them to vary from $22°$ to $60°$, but averaging all my trials, the result was within one-third of a degree of the elevation, of the pole or latitude of the place, and much the greatest part of them taken separately were little different from that: by which it appears, that these lamina are, in the main, parallel with the axis of the earth. In some instances, indeed, I found them perpendicular, and even reclining the other way: but these were extremely rare, and always attended with signs of convulsion, or other circumstances of singularity, which admitted a a possibility of removal from their original position. These trials were made between Madison's cave and the Patomak. We hear of lime-stone on the Mississippi and Ohio, and in all the mountainous country between the eastern and western waters, not on the mountains themselves, but occupying the valleys between them.

'Near the western foot of the North Mountain are immense bodies of *Schist*, containing impressions of shells in a variety of forms. I have received petrified shells of very different kinds from the first sources of the Kentucky, which bear no resemblance to any I have ever seen on the tide-waters. It is said that shells are found in the Andes, in South America, 15,000 feet above the level of the ocean.'

Medicinal springs.] 'There are several medicinal springs, some of which are indubitably efficacious, while others seem to owe their reputation as much to fancy, and change of air and regimen, as to their real virtues. None of them having undergone a chymical analysis in skilful hands, nor been so far the subject of observations as to have produced a reduction into classes of the disorders which they relieve, it is in my power to give little more than an enumeration of them.

'The most efficacious of these are two springs in Augusta, near the first sources of James river, where it is called Jackson's river. They rise near the foot of the ridge of mountains, generally called the Warm spring mountain, but in the maps Jackson's mountains. The one is distinguished by the name of the Warm Spring, and the other of the Hot

Spring. The Warm Spring issues with a very bold stream, sufficient to work a grist-mill, and to keep the waters of its bason, which is 30 feet in diameter, at the vital warmth, viz. 96° of Farenheit's thermometer. The matter with which these waters is allied is very volatile; its smell indicates it to be sulphureous, as also does the circumstance of turning silver black. They relieve rheumatisms. Other complaints also of very different natures have been removed or lessened by them. It rains here four or five days in every week.

'The *Hot Spring* is about six miles from the Warm, is much smaller, and has been so hot as to have boiled an egg. Some believe its degree of heat to be lessened. It raises the mercury in Farenheit's thermometer to 112 degrees, which is fever heat. It sometimes relieves where the Warm Spring fails. A fountain of common water, issuing within a few inches of its margin, gives it a singular appearance. Comparing the temperature of these with that of the hot springs of Kamschatka, of which Krachininnikow gives an account, the difference is very great, the latter raising the mercury to 200°, which is within 12° of boiling water. These springs are very much resorted to in spite of a total want of accommodation for the sick. Their waters are strongest in the hottest months, which occasions their being visited in July and August principally.

'The sweet springs are in the county of Botetourt, at the eastern foot of the Allegany, about 42 miles from the warm springs. They are still less known. Having been found to relieve cases in which the others had been ineffectually tried, it is probable their composition is different. They are different also in their temperature, being as cold as common water: which is not mentioned, however, as a proof of a distinct impregnation. This is among the first sources of James river.

'On Patomak river, in Berkeley county, above the North Mountain, are medicinal springs, much more frequented than those of Augusta. Their powers, however are less, the waters weakly mineralized, and scarcely warm. They are more visited, because situated in a fertile, plentiful, and populous country, better provided with accommodations, always safe from the Indians and nearest to the more populous states.

'In Louisa county, on the head waters of the South Anna branch of York river, are springs of some medicinal virtue. They are not much used however. There is a weak chalybeate at Richmond; and many others in various parts of the country, which are of too little worth, or too little note to be enumerated after those before mentioned.

'We are told of a Sulphur Spring on Howard's creek of Green Briar and another at Boonsborough on Kentucky.

'In the low grounds of the Great Kanhaway, 7 miles above the mouth of Elk River, and 67 above that of the Kanhaway itself, is a hole in the earth of the capacity of 30 or 40 gallons, from which issues constantly a bituminous vapour in so strong a current, as to give to the sand about its orifice the motion which it has in a boiling spring. On presenting a lighted candle or torch within 18 inches of the hole, it flames up in a column of 18 inches diameter, and four or five feet in height, which sometimes burns out within 20 minutes, and at other times has been known to continue three days, and then has been left still burning. The flame is unsteady, of the density of that of burning spirits, and smells

like

VIRGINIA. 373

like burning pit coal. Water sometimes collects in the bason, which is remarkably cold, and is kept in ebullition by the vapour issuing through it. If the vapour be fired in that state, the water soon becomes so warm that the hand cannot bear it, and evaporates wholly in a short time. This, with the circumjacent lands, is the property of his Excellency General Washington and of General Lewis.

' There is a similar one on Sandy river, the flame of which is a column of about 12 inches diameter, and 3 feet high. General Clarke, who informs me of it, kindled the vapour, staid about an hour, and left it burning.

' The mention of uncommon springs leads me to that of Syphon fountains. There is one of these near the intersection of the lord Fairfax's boundary with the North mountain, not far from Brock's gap, on the stream of which is a grift-mill, which grinds two bushels of grain at every flood of the spring. Another near the Cow-pasture river, a mile and a half below its confluence with the Bull-pasture river, and 16 or 17 miles from the Hot Springs, which intermits once in every twelve hours. One also near the mouth of the North Holston.

After these may be mentioned the Natural Well, on the lands of a Mr. Lewis in Frederick county. It is somewhat larger than a common well: the water rises in it as near the surface of the earth as in the neighbouring artificial wells, and is of a depth as yet unknown. It is said there is a current in it tending sensibly downwards. If this be true, it probably feeds some fountain, of which it is the natural reservoir, distinguished from others, like that of Madison's cave, by being accessible. It is used with a bucket and windlass as an ordinary well.'

Population.]

VIRGINIA.

Population.] 'The following table shews the number of persons imported for the establishment of our colony in its infant state, and the census of inhabitants at different periods, extracted from our historians and public records, as particularly as I have had opportunities and leisure to examine them. Successive lines in the same year shew successive periods of time in that year. I have stated the census in two different columns, the whole inhabitants having been sometimes numbered, and sometimes the tythes only. This term, with us, includes the free males above 16 years of age, and slaves above that age of both sexes.

TABLE.

Years	Settlers imported.	Census of Inhabitants.	Years	Settlers imported.	Census of Inhabitants.	Census of Tythes.
1607	100		1618		600	
		40	1619	1216		
		120	1621	1300		
1608		130	1622		3800	
		70			2500	
1609		490	1628		3000	
		16	1632			2,000
		60	1644			4,822
1610	150		1645			5,000
		200	1652			7,000
1611	3 shiploads		1654			7,209
		300	1700			22,000
1612	80		1748			82,100
1617		400	1759			105,000
1618	200		1772			153,000
		40	1782		567,614	

* A further examination of our records would render this history of our population much more satisfactory and perfect, by furnishing a greater number

number of intermediate terms. Those however which are here stated will enable us to calculate, with a considerable degree of precision, the rate at which we have increased. During the infancy of the colony, while numbers were small, wars, importations, and other accidental circumstances render the progression fluctuating and irregular. By the year 1654, however, it becomes tolerably uniform, importations having in a great measure ceased from the dissolution of the company, and the inhabitants become too numerous to be sensibly affected by Indian wars. Beginning at that period, therefore, we find that from thence to the year 1772, our tythes had increased from 7209 to 153,000. The whole term being of 118 years, yields a duplication once in every $27\frac{1}{4}$ years. The intermediate enumerations taken in 1700, 1748, and 1759, furnish proofs of the uniformity of this progression. Should this rate of increase continue, we shall have between six and seven millions of inhabitants within 95 years. If we suppose our country to be bounded, at some future day, by the meridian of the mouth of the Great Kanhaway, (within which it has been before conjectured, are 64,491 square miles) there will then be 100 inhabitants for every square mile, which is nearly the state of population in the British islands.

' Here I will beg leave to propose a doubt. The present desire of America is to produce rapid population by as great importations of foreigners as possible. But is this founded in good policy ? The advantage proposed is the multiplication of numbers. Now let us suppose (for example only) that, in this state, we could double our numbers in one year by the importation of foreigners; and this is a greater accession than the most sanguine advocate for emigration has a right to expect. Then I say, beginning with a double stock, we shall attain any given degree of population only 27 years and 3 months sooner than if we proceed on our single stock. If we propose 4,500,000 as a competent population for this state, we should be $54\frac{1}{2}$ years attaining it, could we at once double our numbers; and $81\frac{3}{4}$ years, if we rely on natural propagation, as may be seen by the following table.

T A B L E.

	Proceeding on our present stock.	Proceeding on a double stock.
1781	567,614	1,135,228
$1808\frac{1}{4}$	1,135,228	2,270,456
$1835\frac{1}{2}$	2,270,456	4,540,912
$1862\frac{3}{4}$	4,540,912	

' In the first column are stated periods of $27\frac{1}{4}$ years; in the second are our numbers, at each period, as they will be if we proceed on our actual stock; and in the third are what they would be, at the same periods, were we to set out from the double of our present stock. I have taken the term of 4,500,000 inhabitants for example's sake only. Yet I am persuaded it is a greater number than the country spoken of, considering how much inarable land it contains, can clothe and feed, without a material

rial change in the quality of their diet. But are there no inconveniences to be thrown into the scale against the advantage expected from a multiplication of numbers by the importation of foreigners? It is for the happiness of those united in society to harmonize as much as possible in matters which they must of necessity transact together. Civil government being the sole object of forming societies, its administration must be conducted by common consent. Every species of government has its specific principles. Ours perhaps are more peculiar than those of any other in the universe. It is a composition of the freest principles of the English constitution, with others derived from natural right and natural reason. To these nothing can be more opposed than the maxims of absolute monarchies. Yet, from such, we are to expect the greatest number of emigrants. They will bring with them the principles of the governments they leave, imbibed in their early youth; or, if able to throw them off, it will be in exchange for an unbounded licentiousness, passing, as is usual, from one extreme to another. It would be a miracle were they to stop precisely at the point of temperate liberty. These principles, with their language, they will transmit to their children. In proportion to their numbers, they will share with us the legislation. They will infuse into it their spirit, warp and bias its direction, and render it a heterogeneous, incoherent, distracted mass.

'I may appeal to experience, during the present contest, for a verification of those conjectures. But, if they be not certain in event, are they not possible, are they not probable? Is it not safer to wait with patience 27 years and three months longer, for the attainment of any degree of population desired, or expected? May not our government be more homogeneous, more peaceable, more durable? Suppose 20 millions of republican Americans thrown all of a sudden into France, what would be the condition of that kingdom? If it would be more turbulent, less happy, less strong, we may believe that the addition of half a million of foreigners to our present numbers would produce a similar effect here. If they come of themselves, they are entitled to all the rights of citizenship: But I doubt the expediency of inviting them by extraordinary encouragements. I mean not that these doubts should be extended to the importation of useful artificers. The policy of that measure depends on very different considerations. Spare no expence in obtaining them. They will after a while go to the plough and the hoe; but, in the mean time, they will teach us something we do not know. It is not so in agriculture. The indifferent state of that among us does not proceed from a want of knowledge merely; it is from our having such quantities of land to waste as we please. In Europe the object is to make the most of their land, labour being abundant: here it is to make the most of our labour, land being abundant.

'It will be proper to explain how the numbers for the years 1782 have been obtained; and it was not from a perfect census of the inhabitants. It will at the same time develope the proportion between the free inhabitants and slaves. The following return of taxable articles for that year was given in.

Free

VIRGINIA. 377

Free males above 21 years of age	53,289
Slaves of all ages and sexes	211,698
Not distinguished in the returns but, said to be titheable slaves.	23,766
Horses	195,439
Cattle	609,734
Wheels of riding carriages	5,126
Taverns	191

'There were no returns from the 8 counties of Lincoln, Jefferson, Fayette, Monongalia, Yohogania, Ohio, Northampton, and York. To find the number of slaves which should have been returned instead of the 23,766 titheables, we must mention that some observations on a former census had given reason to believe that the numbers above and below 16 years of age were equal. The double of this number, therefore, to wit, 47,532 must be added to 211,698, which will give us 259,230 slaves of all ages and sexes. To find the number of free inhabitants, we must repeat the observation, that those above and below 16 are nearly equal. But as the number 53,289 omits the males between 16 and 21, we must supply them from conjecture. On a former experiment it had appeared that about one-third of our militia, that is, of the males between 16 and 50, were unmarried. Knowing how early marriage takes place here, we shall not be far wrong in supposing that the unmarried part of our militia are those between 16 and 21. If there be young men who do not marry till after 21, there are as many who marry before that age. But as the men above 50 were not included in the militia, we will suppose the unmarried, or those between 16 and 21, to be one-fourth of the whole number above 16, then we have the following calculation:

Free males above 21 years of age	53,289
Free males between 16 and 21	17,763
Free males under 16	71,052
Free females of all ages	142,104
Free inhabitants of all ages	284,208
Slaves of all ages	259,230
Inhabitants, exclusive of the 8 counties from which were no returns	543,438

In these 8 counties in the years 1779 and 1780 were 3,161 militia. Say then,

Free males above the age of 16	3,161
Ditto under 16	3,161
Free females	6,322
Free inhabitants in these 8 counties	12,644

To find the number of slaves, say, as 284,208 to 259,230, so is 12,644 to 11,532. Adding the third of these numbers to the first, and the fourth to the second, we have,

B b b   Free

Free inhabitants - - 296,852
Slaves - - - - 270,762

Inhabitants of every age, sex, and condition   567,614

'But 296,852, the number of free inhabitants, are to 270,762, the number of slaves, nearly as 11 to 10. Under the mild treatment our slaves experience, and their wholesome, though coarse, food, this blot in our country increases as fast, or faster, than the whites. During the regal government, we had at one time obtained a law, which imposed such a duty on the importation of slaves, as amounted nearly to a prohibition, when one inconsiderate assembly, placed under a peculiarity of circumstance, repealed the law. This repeal met a joyful sanction from the then sovereign, and no devices, no expedients, which could ever after be attempted by subsequent assemblies, and they seldom met without attempting them, could succeed in getting the royal assent to a renewal of the duty. In the very first session held under the republican government, the assembly passed a law for the perpetual prohibition of the importation of slaves. This will in some measure stop the increase of this great political and moral evil, while the minds of our citizens may be ripening for a complete emancipation of human nature.'

Climate.] In an extensive country, it will be expected that the climate is not the same in all its parts. It is remarkable that, proceeding on the same parallel of latitude westwardly, the climate becomes colder in like manner as when you proceed northwardly. This continues to be the case till you attain the summit of the Allegany, which is the highest land between the ocean and the Mississippi. From thence, descending in the same latitude to the Mississippi, the change reverses; and, if we may believe travellers, it becomes warmer there than it is in the same latitude on the sea side. Their testimony is strengthened by the vegetables and animals which subsist and multiply there naturally, and do not on our sea coast. Thus catalpas grow spontaneously on the Mississippi, as far as the latitude of 37°, and reeds as far as 38°. Perroquets even winter on the Sioto, in the 39th degree of latitude. In the summer of 1779, when the thermometer was at 90°, at Monticello, and 96° at Williamsburg, it was 110° at Kaskaskia. Perhaps the mountain, which overhangs this village on the north side, may, by its reflection, have contributed somewhat to produce this heat.'

Militia.

VIRGINIA.   379

Militia.] 'The following is a state of the militia, taken from returns of 1780 and 1781, except in those counties marked with an asterisk, the returns from which are somewhat older.

TABLE.

Situation	Counties	Militia	Situation	Counties	Militia
Westward of the Allegany. 4458.	Lincoln	600	Between James river and Carolina. 6950.	Greenesville	500
	Jefferson	300		Dinwiddie	*750
	Fayette	156		Chesterfield	655
	Ohio			Prince George	382
	Monongalia	*1000		Surry	380
	Washington	*829		Sussex	*700
	Montgomery	1071		Southampton	874
	Green-briar	502		Isle of Wight	*600
				Nansemond	*644
Between the Allegany & Blue Ridge. 7673.	Hampshire	930		Norfolk	*880
	Berkley	*1100		Princess Anne	*594
	Frederick	1142	Between James and York rivers. 3009.	Henrico	619
	Shenando	*925		Hanover	796
	Rockingham	875		New Kent	*418
	Augusta	1375		Charles City	286
	Rockbridge	*625		James City	235
	Botetourt	*700		Williamsburg	129
Between the Blue Ridge and Tide waters. 18,828.	Loudoun	1746		York	*244
	Fauquier	1078		Warwick	*100
	Culpeper	1513		Elizabeth City	182
	Spotsylvania	480	Between York and Rappahanoc. 3269.	Caroline	805
	Orange	*600		King William	436
	Louisa	603		King and Queen	500
	Goochland	*550		Essex	468
	Fluvanna	*296		Middlesex	*210
	Albemarle	873		Gloucester	850
	Amherst	896	Between Rappahanoc and Patowmak. 4137.	Fairfax	652
	Buckingham	*625		Prince William	614
	Bedford	1300		Stafford	*500
	Henry	1004		King George	483
	Pittsylvania	*725		Richmond	412
	Halifax	*1139		Westmoreland	544
	Charlotte	612		Northumberland	630
	Prin. Edward	589		Lancaster	302
	Cumberland	408	East Shore 1638	Accomac	*1208
	Powhatan	330		Northampton	*430
	Amelia	*1125	Whole Militia of the State		49,971
	Lunenburg	677			
	Mecklenburg	1100			
	Brunswic	559			

Every

'Every able-bodied freeman, between the ages of 16 and 50, is enrolled in the militia. Those of every county are formed into companies, and these again into one or more battalions, according to the numbers in the county. They are commanded by colonels, and other subordinate officers, as in the regular service. In every county is a county lieutenant, who commands the whole militia in his county, but ranks only as a colonel in the field. We have no general officers always existing. These are appointed occasionally, when an invasion or insurrection happens, and their commission determines with the occasion. The governor is head of the military, as well as civil power. The law requires every militia-man to provide himself with the arms usual in the regular service. But this injunction was always indifferently complied with, and the arms they had have been so frequently called for to arm the regulars, that in the lower parts of the country they are entirely disarmed. In the middle country a fourth or fifth part of them may have such firelocks as they had provided to destroy the noxious animals which infest their farms; and on the western side of the Blue Ridge they are generally armed with rifles.'

Civil Divisions.] 'The counties have already been enumerated. They are 74 in number, of very unequal size and population. Of these 35 are on the tide waters, or in that parallel; 23 are in the midlands, between the tide waters and Blue Ridge of mountains; 8 between the Blue Ridge and Allegany; and 8 westward of the Allegany.

'The state, by another division, is formed into parishes, many of which are commensurate with the counties: but sometimes a county comprehends more than one parish, and sometimes a parish more than one county. This division had relation to the religion of the state, a parson of the Angilcan church, with a fixed salary, having been heretofore established in each parish. The care of the poor was another object of the parochial division.

'We have no townships. Our country being much intersected with navigable waters, and trade brought generally to our doors, instead of our being obliged to go in quest of it, has probably been one of the causes why we have no towns of any consequence. Williamsburg, which, till the year 1780, was the seat of our government, never contained above 1800 inhabitants; and Norfolk, the most populous town we ever had, contained but 6000. Our towns, but more properly our villages or hamlets, are as follows.

'On *James River* and its waters, Norfolk, Portsmouth, Hampton, Suffolk, Smithfield, Williamsburg, Petersburg, Richmond the seat of our government, Manchester, Charlottesville, New London.

'On *York River* and its waters, York, Newcastle, Hanover.

'On *Rappahannock*, Urbanna, Port Royal, Fredericksburg, Falmouth.

'On *Patomak* and its waters, Dumfries, Colchester, Alexandria, Winchester, Staunton.

'There are other places at which, like some of the foregoing, the *laws* have said there shall be towns; but *nature* has said there shall not, and they remain unworthy of enumeration. Norfolk will probably be the emporium for all the trade of the Chesapeek Bay and its waters; and a canal of 8 or 10 miles will bring it to all that of Albemarle sound and its waters. Secondary to this place, are the towns at the head of the tide-

waters

VIRGINIA.

waters, to wit, Petersburg on Appamattox, Richmond on James River, Newcastle on York River, Alexandria on Patomak, and Baltimore on the Patapsco. From these the distribution will be to subordinate situations of the country. Accidental circumstances however may controul the indications of nature, and in no instances do they do it more frequently than in the rise and fall of towns.'

To the foregoing general account, we add the following more particular descriptions.

ALEXANDRIA stands on the south bank of Patomak river. Its situation is elevated and pleasant. The soil is clay; and the water so bad, that the inhabitants are obliged to send nearly a mile for that which is drinkable. The original settlers, anticipating its future growth and importance, laid out the streets upon the plan of Philadelphia. It contains upwards of 300 houses, many of which are handsomely built. This town, upon the opening of the navigation of Patomak river, will probably be one of the most thriving commercial places on the continent.

MOUNT VERNON, the celebrated seat of GENERAL WASHINGTON, is pleasantly situated on the Virginia bank of the river Patomak, where it is nearly two miles wide, and is about 280 miles from the sea. It is 9 miles below Alexandria, and 4 above the beautiful seat of the late Col. Fairfax, called Bellevoir. The area of the mount is 200 feet above the surface of the river, and, after furnishing a lawn of five acres in front, and about the same in rear of the buildings, falls off rather abruptly on those two quarters. On the north end it subsides gradually into extensive pasture-grounds; while on the south it slopes more steeply, in a shorter distance, and terminates with the coach-house, stables, vineyard and nurseries. On either wing is a thick grove of different, flowering forest trees. Parallel with them, on the land side, are two spacious gardens, into which one is led by two serpentine gravel-walks, planted with weeping willows and shady shrubs. The *Mansion-House* itself (though much embellished by, yet not perfectly satisfactory to the chaste taste of the present possessor) appears venerable and convenient. The superb banquetting room has been finished since he returned home from the army. A lofty portico, 96 feet in length, supported by eight pillars, has a pleasing effect when viewed from the water; and the *tout ensemble* the whole assemblage, of the green-house, school-house, offices and servants halls, when seen from the land side, bears a resemblance to a rural village—especially as the lands in that side are laid out somewhat in the form of English gardens, in meadows and grass grounds, ornamented with little copses, circular clumps and single trees. A small park on the margin of the river, where the English fallow-deer, and the American wild-deer are seen through the thickets, alternately with the vessels as they are sailing along, add a romantic and picturesque appearance to the whole scenery. On the opposite side of a small creek to the northward, an extensive plain, exhibiting cornfields and cattle grazing, affords in summer a luxuriant landscape to the eye: while the blended verdure of woodlands and cultivated declivities on the Maryland shore variegates the prospect in a charming manner. Such are the philosophic shades to which the late Commander in Chief of the American Armies has retired from the tumultuous scenes of a busy world.

FREDERICKSBURGH

VIRGINIA.

Fredericksburg is situated on the south side of Rappahannok river, 110 miles from its mouth; and contains about 200 houses, principally on one street, which runs nearly parallel with the river.

Richmond, the present seat of government, stands on the north side of James river, just at the foot of the falls, and contains about 300 houses; part of which are built upon the margin of the river, convenient for business; the rest are upon a hill which overlooks the lower part of the town, and commands an extensive prospect of the river and adjacent country. The new houses are well built. A large and elegant statehouse or capitol, has lately been erected on the hill. The lower part of the town is divided by a creek, over which is a bridge, that, for Virginia, is elegant. A handsome and expensive bridge, between 3 and 400 yards in length, constructed on boats, has lately been thrown across James river at the foot of the falls, by Col. John Mayo, a wealthy and respectable planter, whose seat is about a mile from Richmond. This bridge connects Richmond with Manchester; and as the passengers pay toll, it produces a handsome revenue to Col. Mayo, who is the sole proprietor.

The falls, above the bridge, are 7 miles in length. A canal is cutting on the north side of the river, which is to terminate in a bason of about two acres, in the town of Richmond. From this bason to the wharves in the river, will be a land carriage of about 400 yards. This canal is to be cut by a company, who have calculated the expence at 30,000 pounds, Virginia money. This they have divided into 500 shares of 60 pounds each. The opening of this canal promises the addition of much wealth to Richmond.

Petersburg, 25 miles southward of Richmond, stands on the south side of Appamatox river, and contains nearly 300 houses, in two divisions; one is upon a clay, cold soil and is very dirty—the other upon a plain of sand or loam. There is no regularity, and very little elegance in Petersburg. It is merely a place of business. The Free Masons have a hall tolerably elegant; and the seat of the Bowling family, is pleasant and well built. It is very unhealthy. About 2200 hogsheads of tobacco are inspected here annually. Like Richmond, Williamsburg, Alexandria and Norfolk, it is a corporation; and what is singular, Petersburg city comprehends a part of three counties. The celebrated Indian queen, Pocahonta, from whom descended the Randolph and Bowling families, formerly resided at this place.

Williamsburg is 60 miles eastward of Richmond, situated between two creeks; one falling into James, the other into York river. The distance of each landing place is about a mile from the town, which, with the disadvantage of not being able to bring up large vessels, and want of enterprize in the inhabitants, are the reasons why it never flourished. It consists of about 200 houses, going fast to decay, and not more than 900 or 1000 souls. It is regularly laid out in parallel streets, with a square in the center, through which runs the principal street, E. and W. about a mile in length, and more than 100 feet wide. At the ends of this street are two public buildings, the college and capitol. Besides these there is an Episcopal church, a prison, a hospital for lunatics, and the palace; all of them extremely indifferent. In the capitol is a large marble statue, in the likeness of Narbone Berkley, lord Botetourt, a man

distinguished

VIRGINIA.

distinguished for his love of piety, literature and good government, and formerly governor of Virginia. It was erected at the expence of the state, since the year 1771. The capitol is little better than in ruins, and this elegant statue is exposed to the rudeness of negroes and boys, and is shamefully defaced.

Every thing in Williamsburg appears dull, forsaken and melancholy—no trade—no amusements, but the infamous one of gaming—no industry, and very little appearance of religion. The unprosperous state of the college, but principally the removal of the seat of government, have contributed much to the decline of this city.

YORKTOWN, 13 miles eastward from Williamsburg, is a place of about 100 houses, situated on the south side of York river. It was rendered famous by the capture of lord Cornwallis and his army, on the 19th of October, 1781, by the united forces of France and America.

Colleges, Academies, &c.] 'The college of William and Mary is the only public seminary of learning in this state. It was founded in the time of king William and queen Mary, who granted to it 20,000 acres of land, and a penny a pound duty on certain tobaccoes exported from Virginia and Maryland, which had been levied by the statute of 25 Car. 2. The assembly also gave it, by temporary laws, a duty on liquors imported, and skins and furs exported. From these resources it received upwards of £. 3000 *communibus annis*. The buildings are of brick, sufficient for an indifferent accommodation of perhaps 100 students. By its charter it was to be under the government of 20 visitors, who were to be its legislators, and to have a president and six professors, who were incorporated. It was allowed a representative in the general assembly. Under this charter, a professorship of the Greek and Latin languages, a professorship of mathematics, one of moral philosophy, and two of divinity, were established. To these were annexed, for a sixth professorship, a considerable donation by a Mr. Boyle of England, for the instruction of the Indians, and their conversion to christianity. This was called the professorship of Brafferton, from an estate of that name in England, purchased with the monies given. The admission of the learners of Latin and Greek filled the college with children. This rendering it disagreeable and degrading to young gnntlemen already prepared for entering on the sciences, they were discouraged from resorting to it, and thus the schools for mathematics and moral philosophy, which might have been of some service, became of very little. The revenues too were exhausted in accommodating those who came only to acquire the rudiments of science. After the present revolution, the visitors, having no power to change those circumstances in the constitution of the college which were fixed by the charter, and being therefore confined in the number of professorships, undertook to change the objects of the professorships. They excluded the two schools for divinity, and that for the Greek and Latin languages, and substituted others; so that at present they stand thus:—A Professorship for Law and Police—Anatomy and Medicine—Natural Philosophy and Mathematics—Moral Philosophy, the Law of Nature and Nations, the Fine Arts—Modern Languages—For the Brafferton.

'And it is proposed, so soon as the legislature shall have leisure to take up this subject, to desire authority from them to increase the number of professorships,

professorships, as well for the purpose of subdividing those already instituted, as of adding others for other branches of science. To the professorships usually established in the universities of Europe, it would seem proper to add one for the antient languages and literature of the North, on account of their connection with our own language, laws, customs, and history. The purposes of the Brafferton institution would be better answered by maintaining a perpetual mission among the Indian tribes, the object of which, besides instructing them in the principles of christianity, as the founder requires, should be to collect their traditions, laws, customs, languages, and other circumstances which might lead to a discovery of their relation with one another, or descent from other nations. When these objects are accomplished with one tribe, the missionary might pass on to another.'

The college edifice is a huge, misshapen pile. ' which, but that it has a roof, would be taken for a brick-kiln.' In 1787, there were about 30 young gentlemen members of this college, a large proportion of which were law-students.

There are a number of flourishing academies in Virginia---one in Prince Edward county---one at Alexandria---one at Norfolk---one at Hanover; and others in other places.

Since the declaration of independence, the laws of Virginia have been revised by a committee appointed for the purpose, who have reported their work to the assembly. One object of this revisal was to diffuse knowledge more generally through the mass of the people. The bill for this purpose ' proposes to lay off every county into small districts of five or six miles square, called hundreds, and in each of them to establish a school for teaching reading, writing, and arithmetic. The tutor to be supported by the hundred, and every person in it entitled to send their children 3 years gratis, and as much longer as they please, paying for it. These schools to be under a visitor, who is annually to chuse the boy, of best genius in the school, of those whose parents are too poor to give them further education, and to send him forward to one of the grammar schools, of which twenty are proposed to be erected in different parts of the country, for teaching Greek, Latin, geography, and the higher branches of numerical arithmetic. Of the boys thus sent in any one year, trial is to be made at the grammar schools one or two years, and the best genius of the whole selected, and continued six years, and the residue dismissed. By this means twenty of the best geniusses will be raked from the rubbish annually, and be instructed, at the public expence, so far as the grammar schools go. At the end of six years instruction, one half are to be discontinued (from among whom the grammar schools will probably be supplied with future masters); and the other half, who are to be chosen for the superiority of their parts and disposition, are to be sent and continued three years in the study of such sciences as they shall chuse, at William and Mary college, the plan of which is proposed to be enlarged, as will be hereafter explained, and extended to all the useful sciences. The ultimate result of the whole scheme of education would be the teaching all the children of the state reading, writing, and common arithmetic: turning out ten annually of superior genius, well taught in Greek, Latin, geography, and the higher branches of arithmetic,

rithmetic: turning out ten others annually, of still superior parts, who, to those branches of learning, shall have added such of the sciences as their genius shall have led them to: the furnishing to the wealthier part of the people convenient schools, at which their children may be educated, at their own expence.—The general objects of this law are to provide an education adapted to the years, to the capacity, and the condition of every one, and directed to their freedom and happiness. Specific details were not proper for the law. These must be the business of the visitors entrusted with its execution. The first stage of this education being the schools of the hundreds, wherein the great mass of the people will receive their instruction, the principal foundations of future order will be laid here. Instead therefore of putting the Bible and Testament into the hands of the children, at an age when their judgments are not sufficiently matured for religious enquiries, their memories may here be stored with the most useful facts from Grecian, Roman, European and American history. The first elements of morality too may be instilled into their minds; such as, when further developed as their judgments advance in strength, may teach them how to work out their own greatest happiness, by shewing them that it does not depend on the condition of life in which chance has placed them, but is always the result of a good conscience, good health, occupation, and freedom in all just pursuits.—Those whom either the wealth of their parents or the adoption of the state shall destine to higher degrees of learning, will go on to the grammar schools, which constitute the next stage, there to be instructed in the languages. The learning Greek and Latin, I am told, is going into disuse in Europe. I know not what their manners and occupations may call for: but it would be very ill-judged in us to follow their example in this instance. There is a certain period of life, say from eight to fifteen or sixteen years of age, when the mind, like the body, is not yet firm enough for laborious and close operations. If applied to such, it falls an early victim to premature exertion; exhibiting indeed at first, in these young and tender subjects, the flattering appearance of their being men while they are yet children, but ending in reducing them to be children when they should be men. The memory is then most susceptible and tenacious of impressions; and the learning of languages being chiefly a work of memory, it seems precisely fitted to the powers of this period, which is long enough too for acquiring the most useful languages antient and modern. I do not pretend that language is science. It is only an instrument for the attainment of science. But that time is not lost which is employed in providing tools for future operation: more especially as in this case the books put into the hands of the youth for this purpose may be such as will at the same time impress their minds with useful facts and good principles. If this period be suffered to pass in idleness, the mind becomes lethargic and impotent, as would the body it inhabits if unexercised during the same time. The sympathy between body and mind during their rise, progress and decline, is too strict and obvious to endanger our being misled while we reason from the one to the other.—As soon as they are of sufficient age, it is supposed they will be sent on from the grammar schools to the university, which constitutes our third and last stage, there to study those sciences which may be adapted to their views.—By that part of our plan which prescribes

scribes the selection of the youths of genius from among the classes of the poor, we hope to avail the state of those talents which nature has sown as liberally among the poor as the rich, but which perish without use, if not sought for and cultivated.—But of all the views of this law none is more important, none more legitimate, than that of rendering the people the safe, as they are the ultimate, guardians of their own liberty. For this purpose the reading in the first stage, where *they* will receive their whole education, is proposed, as has been said, to be chiefly historical. History by apprising them of the past will enable them to judge of the future; it will avail them of the experience of other times and other nations; it will qualify them as judges of the actions and designs of men; it will enable them to know ambition under every disguise it may assume; and knowing it, to defeat its views. In every government on earth is some trace of human weakness, some germ of corruption and degeneracy, which cunning will discover, and wickedness insensibly open, cultivate, and improve. Every government degenerates when trusted to the rulers of the people alone. The people themselves therefore are its only safe depositories. And to render even them safe their minds must be improved to a certain degree. This indeed is not all that is necessary, though it be essentially necessary. An amendment of our constitution must here come in aid of the public education. The influence over government must be shared among all the people. If every individual which composes their mass participates of the ultimate authority, the government will be safe; because the corrupting the whole mass will exceed any private resources of wealth: and public ones cannot be provided but by levies on the people. In this case every man would have to pay his own price. The government of Great Britain has been corrupted, because but one man in ten has a right to vote for members of parliament. The sellers of the government therefore get nine-tenths of their price clear. It has been thought that corruption is restrained by confining the right of suffrage to a few of the wealthier of the people: but it would be more effectually restained by an extension of that right to such numbers as would bid defiance to the means of corruption.'

The excellent measures for the diffusion of useful knowledge, which the fore-mentioned bill proposes, have not yet been carried into effect. And it will be happy if the great inequality in the circumstances of the citizens —the pride, the independence, and the indolence of one class—and the poverty and depression of the other, do not prove insuperable difficulties in the way of their universal operation.

Religion.] ' The first settlers in this country were emigrants from England, of the English church, just at a point of time when it was flushed with complete victory over the religions of all other persuasions. Possessed, as they became, of the powers of making, administering, and executing the laws, they shewed equal intolerance in this country with their Presbyterian brethren, who had emigrated to the northern government. The poor Quakers were flying from persecution in England. They cast their eyes on these new countries as asylums of civil and religious freedom; but they found them free only for the reigning sect. Several acts of the Virginia assembly of 1659, 1662, and 1693, had made it penal in parents to refuse to have their children baptized; had prohibited the unlawful assembling of Quakers; had made it penal for any master of a vessel

VIRGINIA. 387

fel to bring a Quaker into the state; had ordered those already here, and such as should come thereafter, to be imprisoned till they should abjure the country; provided a milder punishment for their first and second return, but death for their third; had inhibited all persons from suffering their meetings in or near their houses, entertaining them individually, or disposing of books which supported their tenets. If no capital execution took place here, as did in New England, it was not owing to the moderation of the church, or spirit of the legislature, as may be inferred from the law itself; but to historical circumstances which have not been handed down to us. The Anglicans retained full possession of the country about a century. Other opinions began then to creep in, and the great care of the government to support their own church, having begotten an equal degree of indolence in its clergy, two-thirds of the people had become dissenters at the commencement of the present revolution. The laws indeed were still oppressive on them, but the spirit of the one party had subsided into moderation, and of the other had risen to a degree of determination which commanded respect.'

The present denominations of christians in Virginia are, Presbyterians, who are the most numerous, and inhabit the western parts of the state; Episcopalians, who are the most ancient settlers, and occupy the eastern and first settled parts of the state. Intermingled with these are great numbers of Baptists and Methodists. The proportional numbers of these several denominations have not been ascertained. The Episcopalians, or as Mr. Jefferson calls them, the 'Anglicans,' have, comparatively, but few ministers among them; and these few, when they preach, which is seldom more than once a week, preach to very thin congregations.——The Presbyterians, in proportion to their numbers, have more ministers, who preach oftener, and to larger audiences. The Baptists and Methodists are generally supplied by itinerant preachers, who have large and promiscuous audiences, and preach almost every day, and often several times in a day.

The bulk of these religious sects are of the poorer sort of people, and many of them are very ignorant, (as is indeed the case with the other denominations) but they are generally a moral, well-meaning set of people. They exhibit much zeal in their worship, which appears to be composed of the mingled effusions of piety, enthusiasm, and superstition.

Character, Manners and Customs.] Virginia has produced some of the most distinguished and influential men that have been active in effecting the two late grand and important revolutions in America. Her political and military character will rank among the first in the page of history. But it is to be observed that this character has been obtained for the Virginians by a few eminent men, who have taken the lead in all their public transactions, and who, in short, govern Virginia; for the great body of the people do not concern themselves with politics—so that their government, though nominally republican, is, in fact, oligarchal or aristocratical.

The Virginians pride themselves in inheriting the *ancient dominion*, and think that this does, or ought to, entitle them to the first rank in the union. Age is indeed honorable, and ought to be respected, in proportion to the wisdom which it discovers; but it is often proud and petulent; and, in view of what it has *once* been, claims a rank and respect which are

not

VIRGINIA.

not its due; and this is never more likely to be the case, than when there is a lack of that wisdom which long experience ought to produce. Whether this is the case with Virginia, I will not pretend to determine. It is certain, however, that her northern sisters, though willing to yield to her in point of age, believe, not only that she is not superior, but that she is far from being equal to some of them, in point of literary, mechanical, nautical, agricultural, and manufactural improvements. A few singular instances excepted, the Virginians have made very little progress in the arts and sciences. Of their skill in architecture, Mr. Jefferson gives the following account: 'The private buildings are very rarely constructed of stone or brick; much the greatest proportion being of scantling and boards, plaistered with lime. It is impossible to devise things more ugly, uncomfortable, and happily more perishable. There are two or three plans, on one of which, according to its size, most of the houses in the state are built. The poorest people build huts of logs, laid horizontally in pens, stopping the interstices with mud. These are warmer in winter, and cooler in summer, than the more expensive constructions of scantling and plank.—The only public buildings worthy mention are the Capitol, the Palace, the College, and the Hospital for Lunatics, all of them in Williamsburg. There are no other public buildings but churches and courthouses, in which no attempts are made at elegance. Indeed it would not be easy to execute such an attempt, as a workman could scarcely be found here capable of drawing an order. The genius of architecture seems to have shed its maledictions over this land. Buildings are often erected, by individuals, of considerable expence. To give these symmetry and taste would not increase their cost. It would only change the arrangement of the materials, the form and combination of the members. This would often cost less than the burthen of barbarous ornaments with which these buildings are sometimes charged. But the first principles of the art are unknown, and there exists scarcely a model among us sufficiently chaste to give an idea of them. Architecture being one of the fine arts, and as such within the department of a professor of the college, according to the new arrangement, perhaps a spark may fall on some young subjects of natural taste, kindle up their genius, and produce a reformation in this elegant and useful art.'

A sensible gentleman* who travelled through the middle settlements in America, about 30 years ago, has given the Virginians the following character.

'The climate and external appearance of the country conspire to make them indolent, easy and good-natured: extremely fond of society, and much given to convivial pleasures. In consequence of this, they seldom show any spirit of enterprize, or expose themselves willingly to fatigue. Their authority over their slaves renders them vain and imperious, and intire strangers to that elegance of sentiment, which is so peculiarly characteristic of refined and polished nations. Their ignorance of mankind and of learning, exposes them to many errors and prejudices, especially in regard to Indians and Negroes, whom they scarcely consider as of the human species; so that it is almost impossible, in cases of violence,

---

* *The Rev. Andrew Burnaby, Vicar of Greenwich.*

lence, or even murder, committed upon thofe unhappy people by any of the planters, to have the delinquents brought to juftice: for either the grand jury refufe to find the bill, or the petit jury bring in their verdict, not guilty.

'The difplay of a character thus conftituted, will naturally be in acts of extravagance, oftentation, and a difregard of oeconomy; it is not extraordinary, therefore, that the Virginians out-run their incomes; and that having involved themfelves in difficulties, they are frequently tempted to raife money by bills of exchange, which they know will be returned protefted, with 10 per cent. intereft.

'The public or political character of the Virginians, correfponds with their private one: They are haughty and jealous of their liberties, impatient of reftraint, and can fcarcely bear the thought of being controuled by any fuperior power. There are but few of them that have a turn for bufinefs, and even thofe are by no means adroit at it. I have known them, upon a very urgent occafion, vote the relief of a garrifon, without once confidering whether the thing was practicable, when it was moft evidently and demonftrably otherwife.* In matters of commerce they are ignorant of the neceffary principles that muft prevail between a colony and the mother country; they think it a hardfhip not to have an unlimited trade to every part of the world. They confider the duties upon their ftaple as injurious only to themfelves; and it is utterly impoffible to perfuade them that they affect the confumer alfo. Upon the whole, however, to do them juftice, the fame fpirit of generofity prevails here which does in their private character; they never refufe any neceffary fupplies for the fupport of government when called upon, and are a generous and loyal people.

'The women are, upon the whole, rather handfome, though not to be compared with our fair country-women in England. They have but few advantages, and confequently are feldom accomplifhed; this makes them referved, and unequal to any interefting or refined converfation. They are immoderately fond of dancing, and indeed it is almoft the only amufement they partake of: But even in this they difcover great want

of

* *The garrifon here alluded to, was that of Fort Loudoun, in the Cherokee country, confifting of a lieutenant, and about fifty men. This unfortunate party being befieged by the Cherokee Indians, and reduced to the laft extremity, fent off runners to the governors of Virginia and Carolina, imploring immediate fuccour; adding that it was impoffible for them to hold out above twenty days longer. The affembly of Virginia, commiferating their unhappy fituation, very readily voted a confiderable fum for their relief. With this, troops were to be levied; were to rendezvous upon the frontiers 200 miles diftant from Williamfburg; were afterward to proceed to the fort 200 miles farther through a wildernefs, where there was no road, no magazines, no pofts, either to fhelter the fick, or cover a retreat in cafe of any difafter; fo that the unfortunate garrifon might as effectually have been fuccoured from the moon. The author taking notice of thefe difficulties to one of the members, he frankly replied, "Faith, it is true: But we have had an opportunity at leaft of fhowing our loyalty." In a few days after arrived the melancholy news, that this unfortunate party was intirely cut off.*

of taste and elegance, and seldom appear with that gracefulness and ease which these movements are so calculated to display. Towards the close of an evening, when the company are pretty well tired with country-dances, it is usual to dance jiggs; a practice originally borrowed, I am informed, from the Negroes. These dances are without any method or regularity: A gentlemen and lady stand up, and dance about the room, one of them retiring, the other pursuing, then perhaps meeting, in an irregular fantastical manner. After some time, another lady gets up, and then the first lady must sit down, she being, as they term it, cut out: The second lady acts the same part which the first did, till somebody cuts her out. The gentlemen perform in the same manner. The Virginian ladies, excepting their amusements, and now and then a party of pleasure into the woods to partake of a barbacue, chiefly spend their time in sewing and taking care of their families: They seldom read, or endeavour to improve their minds; however, they are in general good housewives; and though they have not, I think, quite so much tenderness and sensibility as the English ladies, yet they make as good wives, and as good mothers, as any in the world.' This character was drawn from personal observation, and, in general, appears to be just.

'The Virginians,' says another discerning traveller, 'who are rich, are in general sensible, polite and hospitable, and of an independent spirit. The poor are ignorant and abject—and all are of an inquisitive turn, and in many other respects, very much resemble the people in the eastern states. They differ from them, however, in their morals; the former being much addicted to gaming, drinking, swearing, horse-racing, cock-fighting, and most kinds of dissipation. There is a much greater disparity between the rich and the poor, in Virginia, than in any of the northern states.'

'The young men' another traveller observes, generally speaking, 'are gamblers, cock-fighters, and horse-jockies. To hear them converse, you would imagine that the grand point of all science was properly to fix a gaff, and touch, with dexterity, the tail of a cock while in combat. He who won the last match, the last game or the last horse-race, assumes the airs of a hero or German Potentate. The ingenuity of a Locke, or the discoveries of a Newton, are considered as infinitely inferior to the accomplishments of him, who knows when to shoulder a blind cock, or start a fleet horse.' A spirit for literary enquiries, if not altogether confined to a few, is, among the body of the people, evidently subordinate to a spirit of gaming and barbarous sports. At almost every tavern or ordinary, on the public road, there is a billiard-table, a back-gammon table, cards and other implements for various games. To these public houses, the gambling gentry in the neighbourhood resort to *kill time*, which hangs heavily upon them; and at this business they are extremely expert, having been accustomed to it from their earliest youth. The passion for cock-fighting, a diversion not only inhumanly barbarous, but infinitely beneath the dignity of a man of sense, is so predominant that they even advertise their matches in the public news papers.* This dissipation

* *A traveller through Virginia observes,* 'Three or four matches were advertized in the public prints at Williamsburg; and I was witness of five in the course of my travels from that to Port Royal.'

dissipation of manners is the fruit of indolence and luxury, which are the fruit of the African slavery.

Constitution, Courts and Laws.] ' The executive powers are lodged in the hands of a governor, chosen annually, and incapable of acting more than three years in seven. He is assisted by a council of eight members. The judiciary powers are divided among several courts, as will be hereafter explained. Legislation is exercised by two houses of assembly, the one called the House of Delegates, composed of two members from each county, chosen annually by the citizens possessing an estate for life in 100 acres of uninhabited land, or 25 acres with a house on it, or in a house or lot in some town: the other called the Senate, consisting of 24 members, chosen quadrennially by the same electors, who for this purpose are distributed into 24 districts. The concurrence of both houses is necessary to the passage of a law. They have the appointment of the governor and council, the judges of the superior courts, auditors, attorney general, treasurer, register of the land office, and delegates to Congress. As the dismemberment of the state had never had its confirmation, but, on the contrary, had always been the subject of protestation and complaint, that it might never be in our own power to raise scruples on that subject, or to disturb the harmony of our new confederacy, the grants to Maryland, Pennsylvania, and the two Carolinas, were ratified.

' This constitution was formed when we were new and unexperienced in the science of government. It was the first too which was formed in the whole United States. No wonder then that time and trial have discovered very capital defects in it.

1. ' The majority of the men in the state, who pay and fight for its support, are unrepresented in the legislature, the roll of freeholders intitled to vote, not including generally the half of those on the roll of the militia, or of the tax-gatherers.

2. ' Among those who share the representation, the shares are very unequal. Thus the county of Warwick, with only 100 fighting men, has an equal representation with the county of Loudon, which has 1746. So that every man in Warwick has as much influence in the government as 17 men in Loudon. But lest it should be thought that an equal interspersion of small among large counties, through the whole state, may prevent any danger of injury to particular parts of it, we will divide it into districts, and shew the proportions of land, of fighting men, and of representation in each.

	Square miles.	Fighting men.	Delegates	Senators.
Between the sea coast and falls of the rivers	11,205	19,012	71	12
Between the falls of the rivers and the Blue Ridge of mountains	18,759	18,828	46	8
Between the Blue Ridge and the Allegany	11,911	7,673	16	2
Between the Allegany and Ohio	79,650	4,458	16	2
Total	121,525	49,971	149	24

'An inspection of this table will supply the place of commentaries on it. It will appear at once that nineteen thousand men, living below the falls of the rivers, possess half the senate, and want four members only of possessing a majority of the house of delegates; a want more than supplied by the vicinity of their situation to the seat of government, and of course the greater degree of convenience and punctuality with which their members may and will attend in the legislature. These nineteen thousand, therefore, living in one part of the country, give law to upwards of thirty thousand, living in another, and appoint all their chief officers executive and judiciary. From the difference of their situation and circumstances, their interests will often be very different.

'There are three superior courts,' to which appeals lie from the courts below, 'to wit, the high court of chancery, the general court, and court of admiralty. The first and second of these receive appeals from the county courts, and also have original jurisdiction where the subject of controversy is of the value of ten pounds sterling, or where it concerns the title or bounds of land. The jurisdiction of the admiralty is original altogether. The high court of chancery is composed of three judges, the general court of five, and the court of admiralty of three. The two first hold their sessions at Richmond at stated times, the chancery twice in the year, and the general court twice for business civil and criminal, and twice more for criminal only. The court of admiralty sits at Williamsburg whenever a controversy arises.

'There is one supreme court, called the Court of Appeals, composed of the judges of the three superior courts, assembling twice a year at stated times at Richmond. This court receives appeals in all civil cases from each of the superior courts, and determines them finally. But it has no original jurisdiction.

'If a controversy arise between two foreigners of a nation in alliance with the United States, it is decided by the consul for their state, or, if both parties chuse it, by the ordinary courts of justice. If one of the parties only be such a foreigner, it is triable before the courts of justice of the country. But if it shall have been instituted in a county court, the foreigner may remove it into the general court, or court of chancery, who are to determine it at their first sessions, as they must also do if it be originally commenced before them. In cases of life and death, such foreigners have a right to be tried by a jury, the one half foreigners, the other natives.

'All public accounts are settled with a board of auditors, consisting of three members, appointed by the general assembly, any two of whom may act. But an individual, dissatisfied with the determination of that board, may carry his case into the proper superior court.'

In 1661, the laws of England were expressly adopted by an act of the assembly of Virginia, except so far as 'a difference of condition' rendered them inapplicable. To these were added a number of acts of assembly, passed during the monarchy, and ordinances of convention, and acts of assembly since the establishment of the republic. The following variations from the British model are worthy of notice.

'Debtors unable to pay their debts, and making faithful delivery of their whole effects, are released from their confinement, and their persons

VIRGINIA.   393

for ever disharged from restraint for such previous debts: But any property they may afterwards acquire will be subject to their creditors.

' The poor, unable to support themselves, are maintained by an assessment on the titheable persons in their parish.

' A foreigner of any nation, not in open war with us, becomes naturalized by removing to the state to reside, and taking an oath of fidelity; and thereupon acquires every right of a native citizen.

' Slaves pass by descent and dower as lands do.

' Slaves, as well as lands, were entailable during the monarchy: But, by an act of the first republican assembly, all donees in tail, present and future, were vested with the absolute dominion of the entailed subject.

' Gaming debts are made void, and monies actually paid to discharge such debts (if they exceeded 40 shillings) may be recovered by the payer within three months, or by any other person afterwards.

' Tobacco, flour, beef, pork, tar, pitch and turpentine, must be inspected by persons publicly appointed, before they can be exported.'

In 1785, the assembly enacted that no man should be compelled to support any religious worship, place or minister whatsoever, nor be enforced, restrained, molested or burdened in his body or goods, nor otherwise suffer on account of his religious opinions or belief; but that all men should be free to profess, and by argument, to maintain their opinions in matters of religion; and that the same should in no wise diminish, enlarge or affect their civil capacities.

In October 1786, an act was passed by the assembly prohibiting the importation of slaves into the commonwealth, upon penalty of the forfeiture of the sum of £1000 for every slave. And every slave imported contrary to the true intent and meaning of this act, becomes free.

Manufactures and commerce.] ' We never had an interior trade of any importance. Our exterior commerce has suffered very much from the beginning of the present contest. During this time we have manufactured within our families the most necessary articles of cloathing. Those of cotton will bear some comparison with the same kinds of manufacture in Europe; but those of wool, flax and hemp are very coarse, unsightly and unpleasant: And such is our attachment to agriculture, and such our preference for foreign manufactures, that be it wise or unwise, our people will certainly return as soon as they can, to the raising raw materials, and exchanging them for finer manufactures than they are able to execute themselves.

VIRGINIA.

'Before the present war we exported, *communibus annis*, according to the best information I can get, nearly as follows:

TABLE.

ARTICLES.	Quantity.	Price in dollars.	Am. in dollars.
Tobacco	55,000 hhds. of 1000 lb.	at 30 d. per hhd.	1,650,000
Wheat	800,000 bushels	at $\frac{5}{6}$ d. per bush.	666,666$\frac{2}{3}$
Indian corn	600,000 bushels	at $\frac{1}{3}$ d. per bush.	200,000
Shipping	—	—	100,000
Masts, planks, scantling, shingles, staves	—	—	66,666$\frac{2}{3}$
Tar, pitch, turpentine	30,000 barrels	at 1$\frac{1}{3}$ d. per bar.	40,000
Peltry, viz. skins of deer, beavers, otters, muskrats, racoons, foxes	180 hhds. of 600 lb.	at 1$\frac{5}{12}$ d, per lb.	42,000
Pork	4,000 barrels	at 10 per barrel	40,000
Flax-feed, hemp, cotton	—	—	8,000
Pit-coal, pig-iron	—	—	6,666$\frac{2}{3}$
Peas	5,000 bushels	at $\frac{2}{3}$ d. per bush.	3,333$\frac{1}{3}$
Beef	1,000 barrels	at 3$\frac{1}{3}$ d. per bar.	3,333$\frac{1}{3}$
Sturgeon, white shad, herring	—	—	1,666$\frac{2}{3}$
Brandy from peaches and apples, and whisky	—	—	1,666$\frac{2}{3}$
Horses	—	—	
			2,833,333$\frac{1}{3}$ d.

This sum is equal to £.850,000 Virginia money, 607,142 guineas.

VIRGINIA. 395

‘ In the year 1758, we exported seventy thousand hogsheads of tobacco, which was the greatest quantity ever produced in this country in one year. But its culture was fast declining at the commencement of this war and that of wheat taking its place: And it must continue to decline on the return of peace. I suspect that the change in the temperature of our climate has become sensible to that plant, which, to be good, requires an extraordinary degree of heat. But it requires still more indispensably an uncommon fertility of soil: And the price which it commands at market will not enable the planter to produce this by manure. Was the supply still to depend on Virginia and Maryland alone, as its culture becomes more difficult, the price would rise, so as to enable the planter to surmount those difficulties and to live. But the western country on the Mississippi, and the midlands of Georgia, having fresh and fertile lands in abundance, and a hotter sun, will be able to undersell these two states, and will oblige them to abandon the raising tobacco altogether. And a happy obligation for them it will be. It is a culture productive of infinite wretchedness. Those employed in it are in a continued state of exertion beyond the powers of nature to support. Little food of any kind is raised by them; so that the men and animals on these farms are badly fed, and the earth is rapidly impoverished. The cultivation of wheat is the reverse in every circumstance. Besides cloathing the earth with herbage, and preserving its fertility, it feeds the labourers plentifully, requires from them only a moderate toil, except in the season of harvest, raises great numbers of animals for food and service, and diffuses plenty and happiness among the whole. We find it easier to make an hundred bushels of wheat than a thousand weight of tobacco, and they are worth more when made. The weavil indeed is a formidable obstacle to the cultivation of this grain with us. But principles are already known which must lead to a remedy. Thus a certain degree of heat, to wit, that of the common air in summer, is necessary to hatch the egg. If subteranean granaries, or others, therefore, can be contrived below that temperature, the evil will be cured by cold. A degree of heat beyond that which hatches the egg, we know will kill it. But in aiming at this we easily run into that which produces putrefaction. To produce putrefaction, however, three agents are requisite, heat, moisture, and the external air, If the absence of any one of these be secured, the other two may safely be admitted. Heat is the one we want. Moisture then, or external air, must be excluded. The former has been done by exposing the grain in kilns to the action of fire, which produces heat, and extracts moisture at the same time: The latter, by putting the grain into hogsheads, covering it with a coat of lime, and heading it up. In this situation its bulk produces a heat sufficient to kill the egg; the moisture is suffered to remain indeed, but the external air is excluded. A nicer operation yet has been attempted; that is, to produce an intermediate temperature of heat between that which kills the egg, and that which produces putrefaction. The threshing the grain as soon it is cut, and laying it in its chaff in large heaps, has been found very nearly to hit this temperature, though not perfectly, nor always. The heap generates heat sufficient to kill most of the eggs, whilst the chaff commonly restrains it from rising into putrefaction. But all these methods abridge too much the quantity

which

which the farmer can manage, and enable other countries to underfell him which are not infested with this insect. There is still a desideratum than to give with us decisive triumph to this branch of agriculture over that of tobacco. The culture of wheat, by enlarging our pasture, will render the Arabian horse an article of very considerable profit. Experience has shewn that ours is the particular climate of America where he may be raised without degeneracy. Southwardly the heat of the sun occasions a deficiency of pasture, and northwardly the winters are too cold for the short and fine hair, the particular sensibility and constitution of that race. Animals transplanted into unfriendly climates, either change their nature and acquire new fences against the new difficulties in which they are placed, or they multiply poorly and become extinct. A good foundation is laid for their propagation here by our possessing already great numbers of horses of that blood, and by a decided taste and preference for them established among the people. Their patience of heat without injury, their superior wind, fit them better in this and the more southern climates even for the drudgeries of the plough and waggon. Northwardly they will become an object only to persons of taste and fortune, for the saddle and light carriages. To these and for these uses, their fleetness and beauty will recommend them.—Besides these there will be other valuable substitutes when the cultivation of tobacco shall be discontinued, such as cotton in the eastern parts of the state, and hemp and flax in the western.

'It is not easy to say what are the articles either of necessity, comfort, or luxury, which we cannot raise, and which we therefore shall be under a necessity of importing from abroad, as every thing hardier than the olive, and as hardy as the fig, may be raised here in the open air. Sugar, coffee, and tea, indeed, are not between these limits; and habit having placed them among the necessaries of life with the wealthy part of our citizens, as long as these habits remain, we must go for them to those countries which are able to furnish them.'

Public Revenue and Expences.] 'The nominal amount of these varying constantly and rapidly, with the constant and rapid depreciation of our paper money, it becomes impracticable to say what they are. We find ourselves cheated in every essay by the depreciation intervening between the declaration of the tax and its actual receipt. It will therefore be more satisfactory to consider what our income may be when we shall find means of collecting what the people may spare. I shall estimate the whole taxable property of this state at an hundred million of dollars, or thirty millions of pounds our money. One per cent on this, compared with any thing we ever yet paid, would be deemed a very heavy tax. Yet I think that those who manage well, and use reasonable œconomy, could pay one and a half per cent, and maintain their houshold comfortably in the mean time, without aliening any part of their principal, and that the people would submit to this willingly for the purpose of supporting their present contest. We may say then, that we could raise, and ought to raise, from one million to one million and a half of dollars annually, and that is from three hundred to four hundred and fifty thousand pounds, Virginia money.

'Of

VIRGINIA. 397

Of our expences it is equally difficult to give an exact state, and for the same reason. They are mostly stated in paper money, which varying continually, the legislature endeavours at every session, by new corrections, to adapt the nominal sums to the value it is wished they should bear. I will state them therefore in real coin, at the point at which they endeavour to keep them.

	Dollars.
The annual expences of the general assembly are about	20,000
The governor - - - -	$3,333\frac{1}{3}$
The council of state - - -	$10,666\frac{2}{3}$
Their clerks - - -	$1,166\frac{2}{3}$
Eleven judges - - - - -	11,000
The clerk of the chancery - -	$666\frac{2}{3}$
The attorney general - - - -	1,000
Three auditors and a a solicitor - -	$5,333\frac{1}{3}$
Their clerks - -	2,000
The treasurer - - - - -	2,000
His clerks - - -	2,000
The keeper of the public jail - - -	1,000
The public printer - - - -	$1,666\frac{2}{3}$
Clerks of the inferior courts - - -	$43,333\frac{1}{3}$
Public levy: this is chiefly for the expences of criminal justice	40,000
County levy, for bridges, court houses, prisons, &c. -	40,000
Members of Congress - - - -	7,000
Quota of the Federal civil list, supposed $\frac{1}{6}$ of about 78,000 dollars - - - -	13,000
Expences of collection, 6 per cent. on the above -	12,310
The clergy receive only voluntary contributions: suppose them on an average $\frac{1}{8}$ of a dollar a tythe on 200,000 tythes - - - -	25,000
Contingencies, to make round numbers not far from truth	$7,523\frac{1}{3}$
	250,000

Dollars, or 53,571 guineas. This estimate is exclusive of the military expence. That varies with the force actually employed, and in time of peace will probably be little or nothing. It is exclusive also of the public debts, which are growing while I am writing, and cannot therefore be now fixed. So it is of the maintenance of the poor, which being merely a matter of charity, cannot be deemed expended in the administration of government. And if we strike out the 25,000 dollars for the services of the clergy, which neither makes part of that administration, more than what is paid to physicians or lawyers, and being voluntary, is either much or nothing as every one pleases, it leaves 225,000 dollars, equal to 48,208 guineas, the real cost of the apparatus of government with us. This, divided among the actual inhabitants of our country, comes to about two-fifths of a dollar, 21d. sterling, or 42 sols, the price which each pays annually for the protection of the residue of his property, that of his person, and the other advantages of a free government. The public revenues of Great Britain divided in like manner on its inhabitants would

be

be sixteen times greater. Deducting even the double of the expences of government, as before estimated, from the million and a half of dollars which we before supposed might be annually paid without distress, we may conclude that this state can contribute one million of dollars annually towards supporting the federal army, paying the federal debt, building a federal navy, or opening roads, clearing rivers, forming safe ports, and other useful works.'

History.] We have already given a brief historical account of the first settlement of Virginia, till the arrival of lord Delaware in 1610. His arrival with a fresh supply of settlers and provisions revived the drooping spirits of the former company, and gave permanency and respectability to the settlement.

In April 1613, Mr. John Rolfe, a worthy young gentleman, was married to *Pocahontas*, the daughter of *Powhatan*, the famous Indian chief. This connexion, which was very agreeable both to the English and Indians, was the foundation of a friendly and advantageous commerce between them.

In 1616, Mr. Rolfe, with his wife Pocahontas, visited England, where she was treated with that attention and respect which she had merited by her important services to the colony in Virginia. She died the year following at Gravesend, in the 22d year of her age, just as she was about to embark for America. She had embraced the Christian religion; and in her life and death evidenced the sincerity of her profession. She left a little son, who, having received his education in England, came over to Virginia, where he lived and died in affluence and honor, leaving behind him an only daughter. Her descendents are among the most respectable families in Virginia.

Tomocomo, a sensible Indian, brother-in-law to Pocahontas, accompanied her to England; and was directed by Powhatan to bring him an exact account of the numbers and strength of the English. For this purpose, when he arrived at Plymouth, he took a long stick, intending to cut a notch in it for every person he should see. This he soon found impracticable and threw away his stick. On his return, being asked by Powhatan, how many people there were, he is said to have replied, 'Count the stars in the sky, the leaves on the trees, and the sands on the sea shore; for such is the number of the people in England.'

' In pursuance of the authorities given to the company by their several charters, and more especially of that part in the charter of 1609, which authorised them to establish a form of government, they, on the 24th of July, 1621, by charter under their common seal, declared, That from thence forward there should be two supreme councils in Virginia, the one to be called the council of state, to be placed and displaced by the treasurer, council in England, and company, from time to time, whose office was to be that of assisting and advising the governor; the other to be called the general assembly, to be convened by the governor once yearly or oftener, which was to consist of the council of state, and two burgesses out of every town, hundred, or plantation, to be respectively chosen by the inhabitants. In this all matters were to be decided by the greater part of the votes present; reserving to the governor a negative voice; and they were to have power to treat, consult and conclude all

emergent

VIRGINIA.

emergent occasions concerning the public weal, and to make laws for the behoof and government of the colony, imitating and following the laws and policy of England as nearly as might be: Providing that these laws should have no force till ratified in a general quarter court of the company in England, and returned under their common seal, and declaring that, after the government of the colony should be well framed and settled, no orders of the council in England should bind the colony unless ratified in the said general assembly. The king and company quarrelled, and, by a mixture of law and force, the latter were ousted of all their rights, without retribution, after having expended 100,000l. in establishing the colony, without the smallest aid from government. King James suspended their powers by proclamation of July 15, 1624, and Charles I. took the government into his own hands. Both sides had their partisans in the colony: But in truth the people of the colony in general thought themselves little concerned in the dispute. There being three parties interested in these several charters, what passed between the first and second it was thought could not affect the third. If the king seized on the powers of the company, they only passed into other hands, without increase or diminution, while the rights of the people remained as they were. But they did not remain so long. The northern parts of their country were granted away to the Lords Baltimore and Fairfax, the first of these obtaining also the rights of separate jurisdiction and government. And in 1650 the parliament, considering itself as standing in the place of their deposed king, and as having succeeded to all his powers, without as well as within the realm, began to assume a right over the colonies, passing an act for inhibiting their trade with foreign nations. This succession to the exercise of the kingly authority gave the first colour for parliamentary interference with the colonies, and produced that fatal precedent which they continued to follow after they had retired, in other respects, within their proper functions. When this colony, therefore, which still maintained its opposition to Cromwell and the parliament, was induced in 1651 to lay down their arms, they previously secured their most essential rights, by a solemn convention.

' This convention entered into with arms in their hands, they supposed had secured the antient limits of their country—its free trade—its exemption from taxation, but by their own assembly, and exclusion of military force from among them. Yet in every of these points was this convention violated by subsequent kings and parliaments, and other infractions of their constitution, equally dangerous, committed. Their general assembly, which was composed of the council of state and burgesses, sitting together and deciding by plurality of voices, was split into two houses, by which the council obtained a separate negative on their laws. Appeals from their supreme court, which had been fixed by law in their general assembly, were arbitrarily revoked to England, to be there heard before the king and council. Instead of 400 miles on the sea coast, they were reduced, in the space of 30 years, to about 100 miles. Their trade with foreigners was totally suppressed, and, when carried to Great Britain, was there loaded with imposts. It is unnecessary, however, to glean up the several instances of injury, as scattered through American and British history, and the more especially as, by passing on to the accession of the present king,

we

we shall find specimens of them all, aggravated, multiplied and crouded within a small compass of time, so as to evince a fixed design of considering our rights natural, conventional and chartered as mere nullities. The following is an epitome of the first fifteen years of his reign. The colonies were taxed internally and externally; their essential interests sacrificed to individuals in Great Britain; their legislatures suspended; charters annulled; trials by juries taken away; their persons subjected to transportation across the Atlantic, and to trial before foreign judicatories; their supplications for redress thought beneath answer; themselves published as cowards in the councils of their mother country and courts of Europe; armed troops sent among them to enforce submission to these violences; and actual hostilities commenced against them. No alternative was presented but resistance, or unconditional submission. Between these could be no hesitation. They closed in the appeal to arms. They declared themselves independent states. They confederated together into one great republic; thus securing to every state the benefit of an union of their whole force.'

The state of Virginia has taken a leading, active and influential part in bringing about the late grand revolution in our Federal Government.* This event, however, has unhappily divided the citizens into two parties of nearly equal strength. Though they were united in the opinion that an alteration in our government, they have not agreed in the plan. While one party warmly espouses the present system of government, the other as violently opposes its going into operation without amendments. Their debates run high. What will be their issue cannot be predicted.

LIST of PRESIDENTS and GOVERNORS of *Virginia, from its first settlement to the year* 1624.†

Edward Maria Wingfield, from May,	1607,	to Sept.	1607.
John Ratcliffe,	Sept. 1607,	to July,	1608.
Mat. Scrivener, *Vice President*,	July, 1608,	to Sept.	1608.
John Smith,	Sept. 1608,	to Sept.	1609.
George Percy, *Governor*,	Sept. 1609,	to May,	1610.
Sir Thomas Gates,	May, 1610,	to June,	1610.
Lord Delaware,	June, 1610,	to March	1611.
George Percy,	March, 1611,	to May,	1611.
Sir Thomas Dale,	May, 1611,	to Aug.	1611.
Sir Thomas Gates,	August, 1611,	to	1614.
Sir Thomas Dale,	1614,	to	1616.
George Yeardley,	1616,	to	1617.
Samuel Argall,	1617,	to	1619.
George Yeardley,	1619,	to Nov.	1621.
Sir Francis Wyat,	Nov. 1621,	to	1624.

INDIANA.

* See *History of the United States*, page 122.

† Stith brings down the *History of Virginia* no farther than this period. A list of the Governors since has not been received.

INDIANA.

INDIANA, so called, is a tract of land lying on the Ohio river, in the state of Virginia, ceded to William Trent and twenty two others, Indian traders, by the Shawwanese, Delaware and Huron tribes, as a compensation for the losses the former had sustained by the depredations of the latter, in the year 1763. This cession was made in a congress of the representatives of the Six nations, at Fort Stanwix, by an indenture, signed the 3d of November, 1768, witnessing, 'That for and in consideration of £85,916:10:8, York currency, (the same being the amount of the goods seized and taken by said Indians from said Trent, &c.) they did grant, bargain, sell, &c. to his majesty, his heirs and successors, for the only use of said William Trent, &c. All that tract or parcel of land, beginning at the southerly side of the little Kanhaway creek, where it empties itself into the river Ohio; and running thence southeast to the Laurel Hill; thence along the Laurel Hill until it strikes the river Monongahela; thence down the stream of the said river according to the several courses thereof, to the southern boundary line of the province of Pennsylvania; thence westwardly along the course of the said province boundary line as far as the same shall extend; thence by the same course to the river Ohio, and then down the river Ohio to the place of beginning, inclusively.' This indenture was signed by six Indian chiefs, in presence of twelve witnesses.

Since the Indians had an undisputed title to the above limited territory, either from pre-occupancy or conquest; and their right was expressly acknowledged by the above deed of cession to the crown, it is very evident that Mr. Trent, in his own right, and as attorney for the traders, hath a good, lawful and sufficient title to the land granted by the said deed of conveyance.

This matter was laid before congress in the year 1782, and a committee appointed to consider it, who, in May, reported as follows: ' On the whole, your committee are of opinion that the purchases of Colonel Croghan and the Indian company, were made *bona fide* for a valuable consideration, according to the then usage and customs of purchasing Indian lands from the Indians, with the knowledge, consent and approbation of the crown of Great Britain, the then government of New York and Virginia, and therefore do recommend that it be

Resolved, That if the said lands are finally ceded or adjudged to the United States in point of jurisdiction, that congress will confirm to such of the said purchasers who are, and shall be, citizens of the United States, or either of them, their respective shares and proportions of said lands, making a reasonable deduction for the value of the quit-rents reserved by the crown of England.'

KENTUCKY.

[Belonging, at prefent, to the State of Virginia.]

SITUATION and EXTENT.

Miles.		
Length 250	Between	36° 30.' and 39° 30' North Latitude.
Breadth 200		8° and 15° Weft Longitude.

Boundaries.] BOUNDED northweft, by the river Ohio; weft, by Cumberland river; fouth, by North Carolina; eaft, by Sandy river, and a line drawn due fouth from its fource, till it ftrikes the northern boundary of North Carolina.

Civil divifion.] Kentucky was originally divided into two counties, Lincoln and Jefferson. It has fince been fubdivided into feven, which follow:

Counties.	Chief towns.	Counties.	Chief towns.
Jefferfon,	LOUISVILLE,	Nelfon,	Bardftown,
Fayettee,	LEXINGTON,	Maddifon,	
Bourbon,		Lincoln,	
Mercer,	Harrodftown,		

As moft of thefe counties are very large, it is probable that fubdivifions will continue to be made, as population increafes.

Rivers.] The river Ohio wafhes the northweftern fide of Kentucky, in its whole extent. Its principal branches, which water this fertile tract of country, are Sandy, Licking, Kentucky, Salt, Green and Cumberland rivers. Thefe again branch in various directions, into rivulets of different magnitudes, fertilizing the country in all its parts. At the bottoms of thefe water-courfes the lime-ftone rock, which is common to this country, appears of a greyifh colour; and where it lies expofed to the air, in its natural ftate, it looks like brown free-ftone. On the banks of thefe rivers and rivulets, this ftone has the appearance of fine marble, being of the fame texture, and is found in the greateft plenty.

Sandy, Licking and *Kentucky* rivers ride near each other, in the Cumberland Mountains. Of thefe, *Sandy* river only breaks through the mountain. This river conftitutes a part of the eaftern boundary of Kentucky.

Licking river runs in a northweft direction, upwards of 100 miles, and is about 100 yards broad at its mouth.

Kentucky is a very crooked river, and after running a courfe of more than 200 miles, empties into the Ohio by a mouth 150 yards broad.

Salt river rifes at four different places near each other. The windings of this river are curious. The four branches, after a circuitous courfe around a fine tract of land, unite; and after running about 15 miles, empty into the Ohio, 20 miles below the falls. Its general courfe is weftward—its length about 90 miles—and at its mouth is 80 yards wide.

Green river purfues a weftern courfe upwards of 150 miles, and by a mouth 80 yards wide, falls into the Ohio, 120 miles below the *Rapids*.

Cumberland

KENTUCKY.

Cumberland river interlocks with the northern branch of Kentucky, and rolling round the other arms of Kentucky, among the mountains, in a southern course, 100 miles—then in a southwestern course for above 200 more—then in a southern and southwestern course for about 250 more, finds the Ohio, 413 miles below the Falls. At Nashville, this river is 200 yards broad, and at its mouth 300. The river in about half its course, passes through North Carolina.

These rivers are navigable for boats almost to their sources, without rapids, for the greatest part of the year. The little rivulets which checker the country, begin to lessen in June, and quite disappear in the months of August, September and October. The autumnal rains, however, in November, replenish them again. The method of getting a supply of water in the dry season is by sinking wells, which are easily dug, and afford excellent water. The want of water in autumn, is the great complaint. Mills that may be supplied with water, eight months in a year, may be erected in a thousand different places. Wind mills and horse mills may supply the other four months.

The banks of the rivers are generally high and composed of lime-stone. After heavy rains the water in the rivers, rises from 10 to 30 feet.

Springs.] There are five noted salt springs or licks in this country ; viz. The higher and lower Blue Springs, on Licking river, from some of which, it is said, issue streams of brinish water—the Big Bone lick, Drennon's licks ; and Bullet's lick, at Saltsburg. The last of these licks, though in low order, has supplied this country and Cumberland with salt at 20 shillings the bushel, Virginia currency ; and some is exported to the Illinois country. The method of procuring water from these licks, is by sinking wells from 30 to 40 feet deep. The water drawn from these wells is more strongly impregnated with salt than the water from the sea. A streight road, 40 feet wide, has been cut from Saltsburg to Louisville, 24 miles.

Face of the country, soil and produce.] This whole country, as far as has yet been discovered, lies upon a bed of lime-stone, which in general lies about six feet below the surface, except in the vallies, where the soil is much thinner. A tract of about 20 miles wide, along the banks of the Ohio, is hilly, broken land, interspersed with many fertile spots. The rest of the country is agreeably uneven, gently ascending and descending at no great distances. The angles of ascent are from 8 to 24 degrees, and sometimes more. The vallies in common, are very narrow, and the soil in them is very thin, and of an inferior quality ; and that along the ascending ground is frequently not much better ; for where you see a tree blown up, you find the roots clinging to the upper parts of the rock. The soil, on these agreeable ascents, (for they cannot be called hills) is sufficiently deep, as is evident from the size of the trees. The soil is either black or tinged with a lighter or deeper vermillion, or is of the colour of dark ashes. In many places there are appearances of potters clay, and coal in abundance. The country promises to be well supplied with wholesome, well-tasted water. In Nelson county, northwest of Rolling fork, a branch of Salt river, is a tract of about 40 miles square, mostly barren, interspersed with plains and strips of good land, which are advantageous situations for raising cattle, as the neighbouring barrens

are

are covered with grafs and afford good pafturage. The lands eaft of No-
lin creek, a branch of Green river, are in general of an inferior quality;
but the banks of Green river afford many defirable fituations.

Towards the head waters of Kentucky river, which interlock with the
waters of Cumberland and Sandy rivers, and the whole country eaftward
and foutheaftward as far as the Holftein river, is broken, mountainous
and almoft impenetrable; and from the defcription given by hunters, it
is much doubted whether it will ever be practicable to make a paffable
road from Kentucky acrofs to Winchefter, in Virginia, on the eaft fide
of the mountains, which, on a ftraght line, is not perhaps more than
400 miles, and the way now travelled is 600.

No country will admit of being thicker fettled with farmers, who confine themfelves to agriculture, than this. But large ftocks of cattle, except in the neighbourhood of barrens, cannot be raifed.

Elkhorn river, a branch of the Kentucky, from the foutheaft, waters
a country fine beyond defcription. Indeed, the country eaft and fouth
of this, including the head waters of Licking river, Hickman's and Jef-
famine creeks, and the remarkable bend in Kentucky river, may be called
an extenfive garden. The foil is deep and black, and the natural growth,
large walnuts, honey and black locuft, poplar, elm, oak, hickory, fugar tree, &c. Grape vines, running to the tops of the trees; and the
furface covered with clover, blue grafs and wild rye. On this fertile
tract, and on the Licking river, and the head waters of Salt river, are the
bulk of the fettlements in this country. The foil within a mile or two
of Kentucky river is generally of the third and fourth rates; and as you
advance towards the Ohio, the land is poor and hilly.

Dick's river runs through a great body of firft rate land, abounding
with cane, and affords many excellent mill feats. Salt river has good
lands on its head waters, except that they are low and unhealthy, but for
25 miles before it empties into the Ohio, the land on each fide is level
and poor, and abounds with ponds.

Cumberland river, fo much of it as paffes through Kentucky, traverfes,
fome few parts excepted, a hilly poor country.

Green river overflows its banks a confiderable way up, at the feafon
when the Ohio fwells, which is in April. This fwell in Green river,
occafions feveral of its large branches to overflow, and cover the low
grounds with water, leaves and vegetable fubftances, which in fummer
become noxious and unhealthy. Its banks are fine and fertile. There
is a great body of good land near the falls or rapids in the Ohio, called
Bare grafs; but the climate is rendered unhealthy by ponds of ftagnant
water, which may be eafily drained.

This country in general is well timbered. Of the natural growth which
is peculiar to this country, we may reckon the fugar, the coffee, the pa-
paw and the cucumber tree. The two laft are a foft wood, and bear a
fruit of the fhape and fize of a cucumber. The coffee tree refembles the
black oak, and bears a pod, which enclofes good coffee. Befides thefe
there is the honey locuft, black mulberry, wild cherry, of a large fize,
buckeye, an exceedingly foft wood—the magnolia, which bears a beautiful bloffom of a rich and exquifite fragrance. Such is the variety and
beauty of the flowering fhrubs and plants which grow fpontaneoufly in

this

KENTUCKY.

this country, that in the proper season the wilderness appears in blossom.

The accounts of the fertility of the soil in this country have, in some instances, exceeded belief; and probably have been exaggerated.—That some parts of Kentucky, particularly the high grounds, are remarkably good, all accounts agree. The lands of the first rate are too rich for wheat, and will produce 50 and 60, and in some instances, it is affirmed, 100 bushels of good corn, an acre. In common, the land will produce 30 bushels of wheat or rye an acre. Barley, oats, cotton, flax, hemp, and vegetables of all kinds common in this climate, yield abundantly. The old Virginia planters say, that if the climate does not prove too moist, few soils known, will yield more and better tobacco.

In the rivers are plenty of buffalo and catfish of uncommon size, salmon, mullet, rock, perch, garfish, eel, suckers, sunfish, &c.—Trout, shad and herrings have not been caught in the western waters.

Swamps are rare in Kentucky; and of course the reptiles which they produce, such as snakes, frogs, &c. are not numerous. The honey-bee may be called a domestic insect, as it is not found but in civilized countries. This is confirmed by a saying which is said to be common among the Indians, when they see a swarm of bees in the woods, ' Well brothers, it is time for us to decamp, for the white people are coming.'

The quadrupeds, except the buffalo, are the same as in Virginia and Carolinas.

Climate.] Healthy and delightful, some few places in the neighbourhood of ponds and low grounds excepted. The inhabitants do not experience the extremes of heat and cold. Snow seldom falls deep, or lies long.—The winter, which begins about Christmas, is never longer than three months, and is commonly but two, and is so mild as that cattle can subsist without fodder.

Chief Towns.] LEXINGTON, which stands on the head waters of Elkhorn river, is reckoned the capital of Kentucky. Here the courts are held, and business regularly conducted. In 1786, it contained about 100 houses, and several stores, with a good assortment of dry goods. It must have greatly increased since.

LEESTOWN is west of Lexington on the eastern bank of Kentucky river. It is regularly laid out and is flourishing. The banks of Kentucky river are remarkably high, in some places 3 and 400 feet, composed generally of stupendous perpendicular rock; the consequence is, there are few crossing places. The best is at Leestown, which is a circumstance that must contribute much to its increase.

Louisville stands on the Kentucky side of the Ohio, opposite Clarksville, at the falls, in a fertile country, and promises to be a place of great trade. Its unhealthiness, owing to stagnated waters back of the town, has considerably retarded its growth. Besides these there is Bardstown, in Nelson county, and Harrodsburg, in Mercer county, both on the head waters of Salt river ; Danville, Boonsborough and Granville are also increasing towns.

Population and Character.] It is impossible to ascertain, with any degree of accuracy, the present number of inhabitants ; owing to the numerous

rous acceffions which are made almoft every month. In 1783, in the county of Lincoln* only, there were, on the militia rolls, 3570 men, chiefly emigrants from the lower parts of Virginia. In 1784, the number of inhabitants were reckoned at upwards of 30,000. From the accounts of their aftonifhing increafe fince, we may now fafely eftimate them at 100,000. It is afferted that at leaft 20,000 migrated here in the year 1787. Thefe people, collected from different ftates, of different manners, cuftoms, religions, and political fentiments, have not been long enough together to form a uniform and diftinguifhing character. Among the fettlers there are many gentlemen of abilities, and many genteel families, from feveral of the ftates, who give dignity and refpectability to the fettlement. They are, in general, more orderly, perhaps, than any people who have fettled a new country.

Religion.] The Baptifts are the moft numerous religious fect in Kentucky. In 1787 they had 16 churches eftablifhed, befides feveral congregations where churches were not conftituted. Thefe were fupplied with upwards of 30 minifters or teachers. There are feveral large congregations of Prefbyterians, and fome few of other denominations.

Government.] The fame as Virginia. But they expect to be admitted into the union as an independent ftate, in a convenient time after the new government is put in operation. The inconveniencies to which they are neceffarily fubjected, from their connexion with Virginia, are great. Thefe inconveniencies the legiflature of Virginia have confidered; and, in their feffion of 1786, paffed an act, providing, on their part, for the erection of the diftrict of Kentucky into an independent ftate. In no part of the United States is juftice adminiftered with more propriety and difpatch.

Literature and Improvements.] The legiflature of Virginia have made provifion for a college in Kentucky, and have endowed it with very confiderable landed funds. The Rev. John Todd has given a very handfome library for its ufe. Schools are eftablifhed in the feveral towns, and, in general, regularly and handfomely fupported. They have a printing office, and publifh a weekly Gazette. They have erected a paper mill, an oil mill, fulling mills, faw mills, and a great number of valuable grift mills. Their falt works are more than fufficient to fupply all the inhabitants, at a low price. They make confiderable quantities of fugar from the fugar trees. Labourers, particularly tradefmen, are exceedingly wanted here. No tradefman will work for lefs than fifty per cent. advance upon the Philadelphia price.

Curiofities.] The banks, or rather precipices, of Kentucky and Dick's rivers, are to be reckoned among the natural curiofities of this country. Here the aftonifhed eye beholds 3 or 400 feet of folid perpendicular rock, in fome parts of the lime-ftone kind, and in others of fine white marble, curioufly checkered with ftrata of aftonifhing regularity. Thefe rivers have the appearance of deep, artificial canals. Their banks are level and covered with red-cedar groves.

Caves have been difcovered in this country, of feveral miles in length, under a fine lime-ftone rock, fupported by curious arches and pillars.

Springs

---

* *This county, it is to be remembered, has fince been divided.*

KENTUCKY.

Springs that emit sulphurous matter have been found in several parts of the country. One is near a salt spring, in the neighbourhood of Boonsborough. There are three springs or ponds of bitumen near Green river, which do not form a stream, but empty themselves into a common reservoir, and when used in lamps, answer all the purposes of the best oil. Copperas and allum are among the minerals of Kentucky.——Near Lexington are found curious sepulchres full of human skeletons. I have been told that a man, in or near Lexington, having dug 5 or 6 feet below the surface of the ground, came to a large flat stone, under which was a well of common depth, regularly and artificially stoned.

History.] *The first white man we have certain accounts of, who discovered this province, was one James M'Bride, who in company with some others, in the year 1754, passing down the Ohio in canoes, landed at the mouth of Kentucky river, and there marked a tree, with the first letters of his name, and the date, which remains to this day. These men reconnoitred the country, and returned home with the pleasing news of their discovery of the best tract of land in North America, and probably in the world. From this period it remained concealed till about the year 1767, when one John Finley and some others, trading with the Indians, fortunately travelled over the fertile region, now called Kentucky, then but known to the Indians, by the name of the Dark and Bloody Grounds, and sometimes the Middle Ground. This country greatly engaged Mr. Finley's attention. Some time after disputes arising between the Indians and traders, he was obliged to decamp; and returned to his place of residence in North Carolina, where he communicated his discovery to Col. Daniel Boon, and a few more, who conceived it to be an interesting object, agreed in the year 1769 to undertake a journey in order to explore it. After a long fatiguing march, over a mountainous wilderness, in a westward direction, they at length arrived upon its borders; and from the top of an eminence, with joy and wonder, descried the beautiful landscape of Kentucky. Here they encamped, and some went to hunt provisions, which were readily procured, there being plenty of game, while Col. Boon and John Finley made a tour through the country, which they found far exceeding their expectations, and returning to camp, informed their companions of their discoveries: But in spite of this promising beginning, this company, meeting with nothing but hardships and adversity, grew exceedingly disheartened, and was plundered, dispersed and killed by the Indians, except Col. Boon, who continued an inhabitant of the wilderness until the year 1771, when he returned home.

About this time Kentucky had drawn the attention of several gentlemen. Doctor Walker of Virginia, with a number more, made a tour westward for discoveries, endeavouring to find the Ohio river; and afterwards he and General Lewis, at Fort Stanwix, purchased from the Five Nations of Indians the lands lying on the north side of Kentucky. Col. Donaldson, of Virginia, being employed by the state to run a line from six miles above the Long Island, on Holstein, to the mouth of the Great Kanhaway,

---

* *The following history is mostly taken from Mr. John Filson's account of the discovery and settlement of Kentucky. To this gentleman I am indebted for much of the information contained in the foregoing description.*

Kanhaway, and finding thereby that an extensive tract of excellent country would be cut off to the Indians, was solicited, by the inhabitants of Clench and Holstein, to purchase the lands lying on the north side of Kentucky river from the Five Nations. This purchase he compleated for five hundred pounds, specie. It was then agreed, to fix a boundary line, running from the Long Island on Holstein to the head of Kentucky river; thence down the same to the mouth; thence up the Ohio, to the mouth of Great Kanhaway; but this valuable purchase the state refused to confirm.

Col. Henderson, of North Carolina, being informed of this country by Col. Boon, he, and some other gentlemen, held a treaty with the Cherokee Indians at Wataga, in March 1775, and then purchased from them the lands lying on the south side of Kentucky river for goods, at valuable rates, to the amount of £. 6000 specie.

Soon after this purchase, the state of Virginia took the alarm, agreed to pay the money Col. Donaldson had contracted for, and then disputed Col. Henderson's right of purchase, as a private gentleman of another state, in behalf of himself: However, for his eminent services to this country, and for having been instrumental in making so valuable an acquisition to Virginia, that state was pleased to reward him with a tract of land, at the mouth of Green river, to the amount of 200,000 acres; and the state of North Carolina gave him the like quantity in Powel's Valley. This region was formerly claimed by various tribes of Indians; whose title, if they had any, originated in such a manner, as to render it doubtful which ought to possess it: Hence this fertile spot became an object of contention, a theatre of war, from which it was properly denominated the Bloody Grounds. Their contentions not being likely to decide the right to any particular tribe, as soon as Mr. Henderson and his friends proposed to purchase, the Indians agreed to sell; and notwithstanding the valuable consideration they received, have continued ever since troublesome neighbours to the new settlers.'

The progress in improvements and cultivation which have been made in this country, almost exceeds belief.—Eleven years ago Kentucky lay in forest, almost uninhabited, but by wild beasts. Now, notwithstanding the united opposition of all the western Indians, she exhibits an extensive settlement, divided into seven large and populous counties, in which are a number of flourishing little towns—containing more inhabitants than are in Georgia, Delaware or Rhode Island states—and nearly or quite as many as in New Hampshire. An instance of the like kind, where a settlement has had so large and so rapid a growth, can scarcely be produced from the page of history.

NORTH

NORTH CAROLINA.

SITUATION and EXTENT.

Miles.
Length 758 } Between { 34° and 36° 30' North Latitude.
Breadth 110 } { 1° and 16° West Longitude.

Boundaries.] BOUNDED north, by Virginia; east, by the Atlantic Ocean; south, by South Carolina and Georgia; west, by the Mississippi.*

Rivers.] *Chowan* river is formed by the confluence of three rivers, viz. the Meherrin, Nottaway and Black rivers; all of which rise in Virginia. It falls into the northwest corner of Albemarle sound, and is three miles wide at its mouth, but narrows fast as you ascend it.

Roanoke is a long rapid river, formed by two principal branches, Staunton river, which rises in Virginia, and Dan river which rises in North Carolina. This river is subject to inundations, and is navigable but for shallops, nor for these, but about 60 or 70 miles, on account of falls, which in a great measure obstruct the water communication with the back country. It empties, by several mouths, into the southwest end of Albemarle sound. The planters on the banks of this river are supposed to be the wealthiest in North Carolina. One of them, it is said, raises about 3000 barrels of corn, and 4000 bushels of peas annually.

Cushai is a small river, which empties into Albemarle sound between Chowan and the Roanoke.

Pamlico or *Tar* river opens into Pamlico sound. Its course is from northwest to southeast. It is navigable for vessels drawing nine feet water to the town of Washington, about 40 miles from its mouth; and for

F f f   scows

---

* *The charter limits of North Carolina are a line beginning on the sea side, at a cedar stake, at or near the mouth of a little river, (being the southern extremity of Brunswick county) and running thence a northwest course through the boundary house, in lat. 33° 56' to lat. 35°, and on that parallel west as far as is mentioned in the charter of king Charles II. to the original proprietors of Carolina, viz. to the South Sea. Their northern line begins on the sea coast in lat. 36° 30', and runs due west to the termination of the southern line. This line strikes the Mississippi 15 miles below the mouth of the Ohio. These limits were ascertained and confirmed agreeably to an order of George II. in council in the year ———. Great Britain, by the treaty of 1763, gave up her claim to all territory to the westward of the Mississippi, and the courts of France and Spain, at the same time, gave her the free navigation of the Mississippi. By the treaty of 1783, Great Britain yielded her interest in that river to the United States. But since Spain now claims the exclusive right of navigating the Mississippi, which right she had given up by the treaty of 1763 as abovementioned, North Carolina resumes her claim to the lands beyond the Mississippi, included within the limits of her original charter.*

NORTH CAROLINA.

scows or flats, carrying 30 or 40 hogsheads, 50 miles further, to the town of Tarborough. Beyond this place the river is inconsiderable and is not navigable.

Neus river empties into Pamlico sound below Newbern. It is navigable for sea vessels about 12 miles above the town of Newbern; for scows 50 miles, and for small boats 200 miles.

Trent river, from the southwest, falls into the Neus at Newbern. It is navigable for sea vessels about 12 miles above the town, and for boats thirty.

There are several other rivers of less note, among which are the *Pasquetank*, *Perquimins*, *Little River*, *Alligator*, &c. which discharge themselves into Albemarle sound. All the rivers in North Carolina, and, it may be added, in South Carolina, Georgia, and the Floridas, which empty into the Atlantic Ocean, are navigable by any vessel that can pass the bar at their mouths. While the water courses continue broad enough for vessels to turn round, there is generally a sufficient depth of water for them to proceed.

Cape Fear river opens into the sea at Cape Fear, in about lat. 33° 45'. As you ascend it, you pass Brunswick on the left, and Wilmington on the right. The river then divides into northeast and northwest branches, as they are called. It is navigable for large vessels to Wilmington, and for boats to Fayetteville, near 90 miles farther. This river affords the best navigation in North Carolina. Yadkin river rises in this state, and running southeastwardly, crosses into South Carolina, where it takes the name of Pedee, and passes to sea at George-town.

Pelison, *Holstein*, *Noley Chuckey*, and *Frank* rivers are all branches of the Broad Tennesee, falling into it from the northeast. This noble river crosses the parallel of 35° north latitude into the state of Georgia, just before it passes through Cumberland or Laurel Mountains. The passage of the river through these mountains, occasions a remarkable *whirl*. The river, which a few miles above is half a mile wide, is here compressed to the width of about 100 yards. Just as it enters the mountain, a large rock projects from the northern shore in an oblique direction, which renders the bed of the river still narrower, and causes a sudden bend; the water of the river is of course thrown with great rapidity against the southern shore, whence it rebounds around the point of the rock and produces the whirl, which is about 80 yards in circumference. Canoes have often been carried into this whirl, and escaped without damage.—In less than a mile below the whirl, the river spreads into its common width, and, except Muscle shoals, flows beautiful and placid, till it mingles with the Ohio.

Sounds, Capes, Inlets, Swamps, &c.] Pamlico sound is a kind of lake or inland sea, from 10 to 20 miles broad, and nearly 100 miles in length. It is separated from the sea, in its whole length, by a beach of sand hardly a mile wide, generally covered with small trees or bushes. Through this bank are several small inlets, by which boats may pass. But Ocrecok inlet is the only one that will admit vessels of burden into the districts of Edenton and Newbern. This inlet is in lat, 35° 10', and opens into Pamlico sound, between Ocrecok island and Core bank; the land on the north is called *Ocrecok*; and on the south *Portsmouth*. A bar of hard sand crosses this inlet, on which, at low tide, there are 14 feet water. Six miles

miles within this bar, is a hard sand shoal, called the *Swash*, lying across the channel. On each side of the channel are dangerous shoals, sometimes dry. There is from 8 to 9 feet water at full tide, according to the winds, on the Swash. Common tides rise 18 inches on the bar, and 10 on the Swash. Between the bar and the Swash is good anchoring ground, called the Upper and Lower Anchorages. Ships drawing 10 feet water do not come far her than the first anchorage, till lightened. Few mariners, though acquainted with the inlets, choose to bring in their own vessels, as the bar often shifts during their absence on a voyage. North of Pamlico sound, and communicating with it, is Albemarle sound, 60 miles in length, and from 8 to 12 in breadth.

Core sound lies south of Pamlico, and communicates with it. These sounds are so large when compared with their inlets from the sea, that no tide can be perceived in any of the rivers which empty into them; nor is the water salt even in the mouths of these rivers.

Cape Hatteras is in lat. 35° 15'. In old charts the shoals of this cape are marked as having in some places only 3, 4 and 5 feet water upon them. Experienced pilots and mariners, however, now say that there is in no place, after you get two miles from the land, less than nine feet water. The best channel for vessels is about a league and a half from the land at the cape, having in no place, at this distance, less than two and a half fathoms of water. Vessels from the northward, by displaying a jack from the fore-top-mast, are usually boarded by a pilot from the land. Some of the pilots carry branches, and some good ones, carry none. This cape has been dreaded by mariners sailing southward when they have been in large vessels; for if they come within 20 miles of the land at the cape, it is in some places too shoal for them; if they stand further off they are in danger of falling into the Gulph Stream, which would set them 3 or 4 miles an hour northward. It is observeable that violent storms of rain and gusts of wind, are uncommonly frequent around this cape.

Cape Lookout is south of Cape Hatteras, opposite Core sound, and has already been mentioned as having had an excellent harbour entirely filled up with land since the year 1777.

Cape Fear is remarkable for a dangerous shoal called, from its form, the *Frying-pan*. This shoal lies at the entrance of Cape Fear river.

Dismal Swamp spreads over the whole tract of country which lies between Pamlico and Albemarle sounds, and needs no other description than is conveyed by its name. There is another large swamp north of Edenton, which lies partly in this state and partly in Virginia.

This swamp is owned by two companies; the Virginia company, of which General Washington is a member, hold 100,000 acres; and the North Carolina company, who hold about 40,000 acres. It is in contemplation to cut a canal through this swamp, from the head of Pasquetank, to the head of Elizabeth river, in Virginia, 12 or 14 miles in length.

Civil Divisions.] This state is divided into 8 districts, which are subdivided into 58 counties, as follows:

Districts.

NORTH CAROLINA.

Districts.	Counties.	Districts.	Counties.
Edenton, 9 counties	Chowan, Currituck, Cambden, Pasquetank, Perquimins, Gates, Hertford, Bertie, Tyrrel.	Halifax, 7 counties.	Halifax, Northampton, Martin, Edgecomb, Warren, Franklin, Nash.
Wilmington, 8 counties.	New Hanover, Brunswick, Cumberland, Robinson, Duplin, Beaden, Wayne, Moore.	Hillsborough, 9 counties.	Orange, Chatan, Granville, Johnston, Caswell, Sampson, Wake, Guilford, Randolph.
Newbern, 8 counties.	Craven, Beaufort, Carteret, Pitt, Dobbs, Hyde, Jones, Onslow.	Salisbury, 8 counties.	Rowan, Mecklenburg, Rockingham, Surry, Montgomery, Anson, Wilkes, Richmond.

The above three districts are on the sea coast, extending from the Virginia line southwestward to South Carolina.

		Morgan, 7 counties.	Burk, Green, Rutherford, Washington, Sullivan, Lincoln, Hawkins.

Davidson, 2 counties.	Davidson, Sumner.		

These five districts, beginning on the Virginia line, cover the whole state west of the three maritime districts before mentioned; and the greater part of them extend quite across the state from north to south.

Principal Towns.] Newbern, Edenton, Wilmington, Halifax, Hillsborough and Fayetteville, each in their turns have been considered as the capital of the state. At present they have no capital. The convention which met to consider the new constitution, fixed on a place in Wake county to be the seat of government, but the town is not yet built.

NEWBERN is the largest town in the state. It stands on a flat, sandy point of land, formed by the confluence of the rivers Neus on the north, and Trent on the south. Opposite the town, the Neus is about a mile and a half, and the Trent three quarters of a mile wide. The town contains about 400 houses, all built of wood, excepting the palace, the church, the goal and two dwelling houses, which are of brick. The palace is a building erected by the province before the revolution, and was formerly the residence of the governors. It is large and elegant, two stories high, with

two

two wings for offices, a little advanced in front towards the town; these wings are connected with the principal building by a circular arcade. This once handsome and well furnished building is now much out of repair. One of the halls is used for a dancing, and another for a school room —which are the only present uses of this palace. The arms of the king of Great Britain still appear in a pediment in front of the building. The Episcopal church is a small brick building, with a bell. It is the only house for public worship in the place. A rum distillery has been lately erected in this town. It is the county town of Craven county, and has a courthouse and goal. The court-house is raised on brick arches, so as to render the lower part a convenient market-place; but the principal marketing is done with the people in their canoes and boats at the river side.

EDENTON is situated on the north side of Albemarle Sound; and has about 150 indifferent wood houses, and a few handsome buildings. It has a brick church for Episcopalians, which for many years has been much neglected, and serves only to shew that the people once had a regard, at least, for the *externals* of religion. Its local situation is advantageous for trade, but not for health. It is the county town of Chowan county, and has a court house and gaol. In or near this town lived the proprietory, and the first of the royal governors.

WILMINGTON is a town of about 180 houses, situated on the east side of the eastern branch of Cape Fear river, 34 miles from the sea. The course of the river, as it passes by the town, is from north to south, and is about 150 yards wide.

In 1786, a fire broke out, supposed to have been kindled by negroes, and consumed about 25 or 30 houses. The town is rebuilding slowly. A printing office was established here in 1788.

WASHINGTON and TARBOROUGH are two flourishing, trading towns on Tar river. About 130 small vessels enter annually at the customhouse for this river.

HILLSBOROUGH is an inland town, situated in a high, healthy and fertile country, 180 miles north of the west from Newbern. It is settled by about 60 or 70 families, and has an academy of 60 or 80 students, under the care of suitable instructors, and patronized by the principal gentlemen in the state, who have been liberal in their donations.

Face of the country, Soil and Productions.] North Carolina, in its whole width, for 60 miles from the sea, is a dead level. A great proportion of this tract lies in forest, and is barren. On the banks of some of the rivers, particularly of the Roanoke, the land is fertile and good. Interspersed through the other parts, are glades of rich swamp, and ridges of oak land, of a black, fertile soil. In all this champagne country, marine productions are found by digging 18 or 20 feet below the surface of the ground. The sea coast, the sounds, inlets and lower parts of the rivers, have uniformly a muddy, soft bottom. Sixty and 80 miles from the sea, the country rises into hills and mountains, as described under this head in South Carolina and Georgia.

That part of North Carolina which lies west of the mountains, a tract about 500 miles in length, east and west, and upwards of 100 in breadth, (except the Cumberland barrens, and some broken lands) is a fine fertile country, watered by the broad Tennessee, and abounds with

oaks,

oaks, locust trees of several kinds, walnut, elm, linn and cherry trees some of which are three feet in diameter.

Wheat, rye, barley, oats and flax grow well in the back hilly country. Indian corn and pulse of all kinds in all parts. Ground peas run on the surface of the earth, and are covered by hand with a light mould, and the pods grow under ground. They are eaten raw or roasted, and taste much like a hazlenut. Cotton is also considerably cultivated here, and might be raised in much greater plenty. It is planted yearly : The stalk dies with the frost.

Trade.] A great proportion of the produce of the back country, consisting of tobacco, wheat, Indian corn, &c. is carried to market in South Carolina and Virginia. The southern interior counties, carry their produce to Charleston ; and the northern to Petersburg in Virginia. The exports from the lower parts of the state, are tar, pitch, turpentine, rosin, Indian corn, boards, scantling, staves, shingles, furs, tobacco, pork, lard, tallow, bees-wax, myrtle-wax, and a few other articles. Their trade is chiefly with the West Indies, and the northern states. From the latter they receive flour, cheese, cyder, apples, potatoes, iron wares, cabinet wares, hats, and dry goods of all kinds imported from Great Britain, France and Holland, teas, &c. From the West Indies, rum, sugar, and coffee.

Climate, diseases, &c.] In the flat country near the sea coast, the inhabitants, during the summer and autumn, are subject to intermitting fevers which often prove fatal, as bilious or nervous symptoms prevail. These fevers are seldom immediately dangerous to the natives who are temperate, or to strangers who are prudent. They, however, if suffered to continue for any length of time, bring on other disorders, which greatly impair the natural vigor of the mind, debilitate the constitution, and terminate in death. The countenances of the inhabitants during these seasons, have generally a pale yellowish cast, occasioned by the prevalence of bilious symptoms. They have very little of the bloom and freshness of the people in the northern states.

It has been observed that more of the inhabitants, of the men especially, die during the winter, by pleurisies and peripneumonies, than during the warm months by bilious complaints. These pleurisies are brought on by intemperance, and by an imprudent exposure to the weather. Were the inhabitants cautious and prudent in these respects, it is alledged by their physicians, that they might in general, escape the danger of these fatal diseases. The use of flannel next to the skin is reckoned an excellent preventative, during the winter, of the diseases incident to this climate. The western hilly parts of the state are as healthy as any of the United States. That country is fertile, full of springs and rivulets of pure water. The air there is serene a great part of the year, and the inhabitants live to old age, which cannot so generally be said of the inhabitants of the flat country. Though the days in summer are extremely hot, the nights are cool and refreshing. Autumn is very pleasant, both in regard to the temperature and serenity of the weather, and the richness and variety of the vegetable productions which the season affords. The winters are so mild in some years, that autumn may be said to continue till spring. Wheat harvest is the beginning of June, and that of Indian corn early in September. *Natural*

NORTH CAROLINA. 415

Natural history.] The large natural growth of the plains in the low country, is almost universally pitch pine; which is a tall, handsome tree, far superior to the pitch pine of the northern states. This tree may be called the staple commodity of North Carolina. It affords pitch, tar, turpentine and various kinds of lumber, which together constitute at least one half of the exports of this state. This pine is of two kinds, the common and the long leaved. The latter has a leaf shaped like other pines, but is nearly half a yard in length, hanging in large clusters. No country produces finer white and red oak for staves. The swamps abound with cypress and bay trees. The latter is an ever-green, and is food for cattle in the winter. The leaves are shaped like those of the peach tree, but larger. The most common kinds of timber in the back country, are, oak, walnut and pine. A species of oak grows in the moist, gravelly soil, called Black Jack. It seldom grows larger than 8 or 9 inches diameter. It is worthy of remark, that the trees in the low country, near the sea coast, are loaded with vast quantities of a long, spongy kind of moss, which, by absorbing the noxious vapour that is exhaled from stagnated waters, contributes much, it is supposed, to the healthiness of the climate. This hypothesis is confirmed by experience, since it is commonly observed, that the country is much less healthy after having been cleared, than while in a state of nature.

The Missletoe is common in the back country. This is a shrub which differs in kind, perhaps, from all others. It never grows out of the earth, but on the tops of trees. The roots, (if they may be so called) run under the bark of the tree, and incorporate with the wood. It is an ever-green, resembling the garden box-wood.

The principal wild fruits are plums, grapes, strawberries and blackberries.

The country is generally covered with herbage of various kinds, and a species of wild grass. It abounds with medicinal plants and roots. Among others are the ginseng, Virginia snake root, Seneca snake root, an herb of the emetic kind, like the epicacuana. Lyons hart, which is a sovereign remedy for the bite of a serpent. A species of the sensitive plant is also found here; it is a sort of brier, the stalk of which dies with the frost, but the root lives through the winter, and shoots again in the spring. The lightest touch of a leaf causes it to turn and cling close to the stalk. Although it so easily takes the alarm, and apparently shrinks from danger, in the space of two minutes after it is touched, it perfectly recovers its former situation. The mucipula veneris is also found here. The rich bottoms are overgrown with canes. Their leaves are green all the winter, and afford an excellent food for cattle. They are of a sweetish taste, like the stalks of green corn, which they in many respects resemble.

Religion.] The western parts of this state, which have been settled within the last 35 years, are chiefly inhabited by Presbyterians from Pennsylvania, the descendents of people from the North of Ireland, and are exceedingly attached to the doctrines, discipline and usages of the church of Scotland. They are a regular industrious people. Almost all the inhabitants between the Catawba and Yadkin rivers, are of this denomination, and they are in general well supplied with a sensible and learned ministry.

ministry. There are interspersed some settlements of Germans, both Lutherans and Calvinists, but they have very few ministers.

The Moravians have several flourishing settlements in this state. In 1751, they purchased of Lord Granville one hundred thousand acres of land, between Dan and Yadkin rivers, about 10 miles south of Pilot mountain, in Surry county, and called it Wachovia, after an estate of Count Zinzendorf, in Austria. In 1755, this tract, by an act of assembly, was made a separate parish by the name of Dobb's parish. The first settlement, called Bethabara, was begun in 1753, by a number of the brethren from Pennsylvania, in a very wild, uninhabited country, which, from that time, began to to be rapidly settled by farmers from the middle states.

In 1759, Bethany, a regular village, was laid out and settled. In 1766, Salem, which is now the principal settlement, and nearly in the center of Wachovia, was settled by a collection of tradesmen. The same constitution and regulations are established here, as in other regular settlements of the united brethren. Besides, there are in Wachovia three churches, one in Friedland, one in Friedberg and another at Hope, each of which has a minister of the Brethren's church. These people, by their industry and attention to various branches of manufacture, are very useful to the country around them.

The Friends or Quakers, have a settlement in New Garden, in Guilford county, and several congregations at Perquimins and Pasquetank. The Methodists and Baptists are numerous and increasing. Besides the denominations already mentioned, there is a very numerous body of people, in this, and in all the southern states, who cannot properly be classed with any sect of christians, having never made any profession of christianity, and are literally, as to religion, NOTHINGARIANS.

The inhabitants of Wilmington, Newbern, Edenton and Halifax districts, making about three-fifths of the state, once professed themselves of the Episcopal church. The clergy, in these districts, were chiefly missionaries; and in forming their political attachments, at the commencement of the late war, personal safety, or real interest, or perhaps a thorough conviction of the injustice and impolicy of opposing Great Britain from whence they received their salaries, induced them almost universally to declare themselves in favour of the British government, and to emigrate. There may be one or two of the original clergy remaining, but at present they have no particular pastoral charge. Indeed the inhabitants in the districts abovementioned, seem now to be making the experiment, whether christianity can exist long in a country where there is no visible christian church. Thirteen years experience has proved that it probably cannot, for there is very little *external* appearance of religion among the people in general. The Baptists and Methodists have sent a number of missionary preachers into these districts; and some of them have pretty large congregations. It is not improbable that one or the other of the denominations, and perhaps both, may acquire consistency and establish permanent churches.

Colleges and Academies.] There is no university or college in the state. In the original constitution it is declared that ' There shall be one or more seminaries of learning maintained at the public expence.' But the legis-
ture

NORTH CAROLINA.

ture, hitherto, have not confidered that claufe as binding. Probably they do not like it. Academies are eftablifhed at Newbern, Salifbury and Hillfborough. The latter has been already mentioned and defcribed. The one at Salifbury had, in 1786, about fifty fcholars, under the tuition of a worthy clergyman. It is fituated in a rich, healthy country, and is flourifhing.

Population, character, manners and cuftoms.] The inhabitants of this ftate are reckoned at 270,000, of which 60,000 are negroes. The North Carolinians are moftly planters, and live from half a mile to 3 and 4 miles from each other, on their plantations. They have a plentiful country—no ready market for their produce—little intercourfe with ftrangers, and a natural fondnefs for fociety, which induce them to be hofpitable to travellers. In the lower diftricts the inhabitants have very few places for public and weekly worfhip of any kind; and thefe few, being deftitute of minifters, are fuffered to ftand neglected. The fabbath of courfe, which, in moft civilized countries, is profeffionally and externally, at leaft, regarded as holy time, and which, confidered merely in a civil view, is an excellent eftablifhment for the promotion of cleanlinefs, friendfhip, harmony and all the focial virtues, is here generally difregarded, or diftinguifhed by the convivial vifitings of the white inhabitants, and the noify diverfions of the negroes. The women, except in fome of the populous towns, have very little intercourfe with each other, and are almoft entirely deftitute of the bloom and vivacity of the north: Yet they poffefs a great deal of kindnefs, and, except that they fuffer their infant babes to fuck the breafts of their black nurfes, are good mothers, and *obedient* wives.

The general topics of converfation among the men, when cards, the bottle, and occurrences of the day do not intervene, are negroes, the prices of indigo, rice, tobacco, &c. They appear to have as little tafte for the fciences as for religion. Political enquiries, and philofophical difquifitions are attended to but by a few men of genius and induftry, and are too laborious for the indolent minds of the people at large. Lefs attention and refpect are paid to the women here, than in thofe parts of the United States where the inhabitants have made greater progrefs in the arts of civilized life. Indeed, it is a truth, confirmed by obfervation, that in proportion to the advancement of civilization, in the fame proportion will refpect for the women be increafed; fo that the progrefs of civilization in countries, in ftates, in towns and in families, may be marked by the degree of attention which is paid by hufbands to their wives, and by the young men to the young women.

Temperance and induftry, are not to be reckoned among the virtues of the North Carolinians. The time which they wafte in drinking, idling and gambling, leaves them very little opportunity to improve their plantations or their minds. The improvement of the former is left to their overfeers and negroes; the improvement of the latter is too often neglected. Were the time, which is thus wafted, fpent in cultivating the foil, and in treafuring up knowledge, they might be both wealthy and learned; for they have a productive country, and are by no means deftitute of genius.

NORTH CAROLINA.

Time that is not employed in study or useful labour, in every country, is generally spent in hurtful or innocent exercises, according to the custom of the place or the taste of the parties. The citizens of North Carolina, who are not better employed, spend their time in drinking, or gaming at cards or dice, in cock-fighting or horse-racing. Many of the interludes are filled up with a boxing match; and these matches frequently become memorable by feats of *gouging**

In a country that pretends to any degree of civilization, one would hardly expect to find a prevailing custom of putting out the eyes of each other. Yet this more than barbarous custom is prevalent in both the Carolinas, and in Georgia, among the lower class of people. Of the origin of this custom we are not informed. We presume there are few competitors for the honor of having originated it; and equally as few who are envious of the *pleasure* of those who have the *honor* to continue it.

North Carolina has had a rapid growth. In the year 1710, it contained but about 1200 fencible men. It is now, in point of numbers, the fourth state in the union. During this amazing progress in population, which has been greatly aided by immigrations from Pennsylvania, Virginia and other states, while each has been endeavoring to increase his fortune, the human mind, like an unweeded garden, has been suffered to shoot up in wild disorder. But when we consider that, during the late revolution, this state produced many distinguished patriots and politicians, that she sent her thousands to the defence of Georgia and South Carolina, and gave occasional succours to Virginia—when we consider too the difficulties she has had to encounter from a mixture of inhabitants, collected from different parts, strangers to each other, and intent upon gain, we shall find many things worthy of praise in her general character.

Constitution.] By the constitution of this state, which was ratified in December, 1776, all legislative authority is vested in two distinct branches, both dependent on the people, viz. A *Senate* and *House* of *Commons*, which, when convened for business, are styled the *General Assembly*.

The Senate is composed of representatives, one for each county, chosen annually by ballot.

The House of Commons consists of representatives chosen in the same way, two for each county, and one for each of the towns of Edenton, Newbern, Wilmington, Salisbury, Hillsborough and Halifax.

The qualifications for a senator, are one years residence, immediately preceding his election, in the county in which he is chosen, and 300 acres of land in fee.

A

---

* *The delicate and entertaining diversion, with propriety called gouging, is thus performed. When two boxers are worried with fighting and bruising each other, they come, as it is called, to close quarters, and each endeavours to twist his forefingers in the ear-locks of his antagonist. When these are fast clinched, the thumbs are extended each way to the nose, and the eyes gently turned out of their sockets. The victor for his expertness, receives shouts of applause from the sportive throng, while his poor, eyeless antagonist is laughed at for his misfortune.*

A member of the House of Commons must have usually resided in the county in which he is elected, one year immediately preceding his election, and for six months shall have possessed, and continue to possess, in the county which he represents, not less than 100 acres of land in fee, or for the term of his own life.

A freeman of 21 years of age, who has been an inhabitant in the state twelve months immediately preceding the day of any election, and who had possessed a freehold of fifty acres of land within the county for six months next before, and at the day of election, is entitled to vote for a member of the senate.

All freemen of 21 years of age, who have been inhabitants of the state the year next before the election, and have paid public taxes, may vote for members of the House of Commons.

The Senate and House of Commons, when convened, choose, each their own speaker, and are judges of the qualifications and elections of their members. They jointly, by ballot at their first meeting after each annual election, choose a governor for one year, who is not eligible to that office longer than three years in six succeffive years; and who must possess a freehold of more than £1000, and have been an inhabitant of the state above five years. They, in the same manner and at the same time, elect seven persons to be a council of state for one year, to advise the governor in the execution of his office. They appoint a treasurer or treasurers for the state. They triennially choose a state secretary. They jointly appoint judges of the supreme courts of law and equity—judges of admiralty, and the attorney general, who are commissioned by the governor and hold their offices during good behaviour. They prepare bills—which must be read three times in each house, and be signed by the speaker of both houses, before they pass into laws.

Judges of the supreme court—members of council—judges of admiralty —treasurers—secretaries—attorney generals for the state—clerks of record—clergymen—persons denying the Being of a God—the truth of the protestant religion, or the divine authority of the Old or New Testament —receivers of public monies, whose accounts are unsettled—military officers in actual service, are all ineligible to a seat either in the Senate or House of Commons—justices of the peace, being recommended by the representatives, are commissioned by the governor, and hold their offices during good behaviour. The constitution allows of no religious establishment. The legislature are authorized to regulate entails so as to prevent perpetuities—a majority of both houses is necessary to do business.

New Settlements, Roads, &c.] Davidson county, in this state, is one of the most western settlements in the United States. This county was established by the name of Davidson, in honor of brigadier general William Davidson, who fell opposing the army under lord Cornwallis, across the Yadkin river, in the year 1781, and begins where the river Tenneffee or Cherokee intersects the north boundary of the state; thence due east with the said boundary to the second intersection of the said boundary, by the Cumberland or Shawanee river, being 140 miles; thence south 55 geographical miles; thence west to the Tenneffee; thence down the meanders thereof to the beginning. The Tenneffee crosses the north boundary of the state 58 miles, and the south boundary thereof about 80 miles east of of the Miffifippi.—In the year 1782, the legiflature of North Carolina appointed commiffioners to explore the weftern part of the ftate, (by which is meant as well the lands at prefent included in Davidfon county as thofe between the fouth boundary of the ftate and the fouth boundary of this county, and thofe between the rivers Miffifippi and Tenneffee) and report to the fucceeding legiflature, which part was beft for the payment of the bounty promifed to the officers and foldiers of the Continental Line of that ftate; and they accordingly did explore the before defcribed tract of country and reported to the legiflature in the fpring of the year 1783.— Although this county was not eftablifhed by law before the laft mentioned period, yet a few families had fettled in the year 1780, principally under the guidance and direction of James Robertfon (at prefent colonel of that county) on Cumberland river, and called the place Nafhville, in honor of brigadier general Francis Nafh, who fell at Germantown in the year 1777; but he had but few followers until the year 1783, after the peace had taken place, and after an act had paffed directing the military or bounty warrants of the officers and foldiers to be located in this county. Thefe circumftances induced many officers and foldiers to repair immediately thither, to fecure and fettle their lands; and fuch as did not choofe to go, fold their warrants to citizens who did go. Many people from almoft every ftate in the Union became purchafers of thefe military warrants, and are fince become refidents of this county; and many valuable and opulent families have removed to it from the Natches.—Colonel Robertfon, when he fettled at Nafhville, was upwards of 200 miles diftant (to the weftward) from any other fettlement in his own ftate, and was equally diftant from the then fettled parts of Kentucky. Hence it will readily be fuppofed that himfelf and party were in danger every hour of being cut off by the Indians, againft whom his principal fecurity was, that he was nearly as diftant from them as from the white people; and flender as this fecurity may appear, his party never fuftained any damage from the Indians, but what was done by parties of hunters who happened to find out his fettlements.—The face of this country is in general level, and the foil very rich, equal to any other part of America, and produces in abundance every thing that can be expected from fo temperate a climate and fo rich a foil. It is common for the planter to gather from his fields, upon an average, 60 bufhels of Indian corn per acre. This county is well watered by the rivers Tenneffee and Cumberland, and their branches. Both of thefe rivers empty into the Ohio fhortly after they pafs the north boundary of the ftate. As the waters of the Cumberland from Nafhville, and of the Tenneffee from the Mufcle Shoals to the Ohio, are equally deep as the waters of the Ohio and Miffifippi, the people, of courfe, who live in this county, or the adjacent country, have the fame advantages of water conveyance for trade, as thofe who live on the Ohio or Miffifippi, to New Orleans or elfewhere.

Befides, there is another probable avenue through which trade will be carried on with this county and the adjacent country, which is from Mobille, up the waters of the Mobille river as far as navigable, thence by a land carriage of about 50 miles (at moft) to Ocochappo creek, which empties into the Tenneffee at the lower end of the Mufcle Shoals.—The

mouth

mouth of this creek is the center of a piece of ground, the diameter of which is 5 miles, ceded by the southern Indians at the treaty at Hopwell, on Keeowee, to the United States for the establishment of trading posts.

At Nashville, the inferior and superior courts of the county are held, in which good order is observed, and justice speedily and satisfactorily administered. Two houses in this town are set apart for divine worship, in which divine service is regularly performed on the sabbath.

The legislature of North Carolina, at their session in the year 1786, passed a law for the establishment of an academy in this town, with liberal endowments.

It is to be observed that this county, though it lies upwards of 200 miles west of what is commonly called the state of Franklin, never departed from her allegiance to the state of North Carolina, but continued to send her members to the legislature, although they had to pass through the state of Franklin.

The following are the distances on the new road from Nashville, in Davidson county, to Fort Campbell, near the junction of Holstein river with the Tennessee.

	miles.		miles.
From Nashville to Stony river	9	From Grovet's creek -	7
Big Spring -	6	The foot of Cumberland	
Cedar Lick -	4	Mountain -	2
Little Spring -	6	Through the mountain	
Barton's creek -	4	to Emmeries river, a	
Spring creek -	5	branch of the Pelison	11
Martin's Spring -	5	To the Pappa Ford of	
Blair's Spring -	5	the Pelison or Clinch	
Buck Spring -	12	river -	12
Fountaines -	8	To Campbell's station	
Smith's creek -	6	near Holstein -	10
Coney river -	11	To the Great Island	100
Mine Lick -	9	To Abingdon in Wash-	
Falling creek -	9	ington county	35
War Path -	7	To Richmond in Virgi-	
Bear creek - -	18	nia -	280
Camp creek -	8		
King's Spring -	16	Total	605

By this new road, a pleasant passage may be had to the western country with carriages, as there will be only the Cumberland mountain to pass; and that is easy of ascent—and beyond it, the road is generally level and firm; abounding with fine springs of water.

History.] The history of North Carolina is less known than that of any of the other states. From the best accounts that history affords, the first permanent settlement in North Carolina was made about the year 1710, by a number of Palatines from Germany, who had been reduced to circumstances of great indigence, by a calamitous war. The proprietors of Carolina, knowing that the value of their lands depended on the strength

of

of their settlements, determined to give every possible encouragement to such emigrants. Ships were accordingly provided for their transportation—and instructions were given to governor Tynte to allow an hundred acres of land for every man, woman and child, free of quit-rents for the first ten years; but at the expiration of that term, to pay one penny per acre, annual rent forever, according to the usages and customs of the province. Upon their arrival, governor Tynte granted them a tract of land in North Carolina, since called Albemarle and Bath precincts, where they settled, and flattered themselves with having found, in the hideous wilderness, a happy retreat from the desolations of a war which then raged in Europe.

In the year 1712, a dangerous conspiracy was formed by the Coree and Tuscorora tribes of Indians, to murder and expel this infant colony. The foundation for this conspiracy is not known. Probably they were offended at the encroachments upon their hunting ground. They managed their conspiracy with great cunning and profound secrecy. They surrounded their principal town with a breast-work to secure their families. Here the warriors convened to the number of 1200. From this place of rendezvous they sent out small parties, by different roads, who entered the settlement under the mask of friendship. At the change of the full moon, all of them had agreed to begin their murderous operations the same night. When the night came, they entered the houses of the planters, demanding provisions, and pretending to be offended, fell to murdering men, women and children without mercy or distinction. One hundred and thirty-seven settlers, among whom were a Swiss baron, and almost all the poor Palatines that had lately come into the country, were slaughtered the first night. Such was the secrecy and dispatch of the Indians in this expedition, that none knew what had befallen his neighbour, until the barbarians had reached his own door. Some few, however, escaped and gave the alarm.—The militia assembled in arms, and kept watch day and night, until the news of the sad disaster had reached the province of South Carolina. Governor Craven lost no time in sending a force to their relief.—The assembly voted £. 4000 for the service of the war. A body of 600 militia, under the command of colonel Barnwell, and 366 Indians of different tribes, with different commanders, marched with great expedition, through a hideous wilderness, to their assistance. In their first encounter with the Indians, they killed 300 and took 100 prisoners. After this defeat, the Tuscororas retreated to their fortified town—which was shortly after surrendered to colonel Barnwell. In this whole expedition it was computed that near a thousand Tuscororas were killed, wounded and taken. The remainder of the tribe soon after abandoned their country, and joined the Five Nations, with whom they have ever since remained. After this the infant colony remained in peace, and continued to flourish under the general government of South Carolina, till about the year 1729, when seven of the proprietors, for a valuable consideration,* vested their property and jurisdiction in the crown, and the colony was erected into a separate province, by the name of North Carolina, and its present limits
established

* See Page 31.

NORTH CAROLINA.

established by an order of George II. From this period to the revolution in 1776, the history of North Carolina is unpublished, and of course unknown, except to those who have had access to the records of the province. Some of the most important events that have since taken place, have been already mentioned in the general history of the United States.

In the year 1785, the inhabitants of the counties of Sullivan, Washington and Green, which lie directly west of the mountains in this state, convened in committees—appointed and held a convention—framed a constitution—elected their governor—and in short erected themselves into a separate, independent state, by the name of the *New State of Franklin*. This premature state, was to comprehend all that tract of country which lies between the mountains and the *Suck* or *Whirl*, in the Tennessee river. These proceedings occasioned great confusion and warm disputes in North Carolina, which continued to rage till the year 1788, when all pretensions to independency were relinquished, and tranquillity was restored to the state.

The western and frontier settlements, for some time past, have been, and still are harrassed by the Creek and Cherokee Indians, who have done considerable damage and killed many of the inhabitants. The latest accounts from this state are, that the assembly have voted to raise an army of 1500 men, not only to prevent the incursions of the enemy, but to carry war into their own country, and to compel them to sue for peace.

SOUTH CAROLINA.

SITUATION and EXTENT.

Miles.
Length 200 } Between { 32° and 35° North Latitude.
Breadth 125 }   { 4° and 9° West Longitude.

Boundaries.] BOUNDED east, by the Atlantic ocean; north, by North Carolina; southwest and south, by Savannah river, which divides it from Georgia. The western boundary has not yet, with accuracy, been ascertained.*

Climate.] The climate is different in different parts of the state. Along the sea coast, bilious diseases and fevers of all kinds are prevalent between July and October. The probability of dying is much greater between the 20th of June and the 20th of October, than in the other eight months in the year.

One

SOUTH CAROLINA.

One cause of these diseases is, a low marshy country, which is overflowed for the sake of cultivating rice. The exhalations from these stagnated waters—from the rivers—and from the neighbouring ocean—and the profuse perspiration of vegetables of all kinds, which cover the ground, fill the air with moisture. This moisture falls in frequent rains and copious dews. From actual observation it was found that the average annual fall of rain for ten years was 42 inches; without regarding the moisture that fell in fogs and dews. The great heat of the day relaxes the body, and the agreeable coolness of the evening invites to an exposure to these heavy dews. But a second, and probably a more operative cause in producing diseases, is the indolence of the inhabitants. On this, physicians say, more than on any unavoidably injurious qualities in the air, are chargeable the diseases so common in this country. The upper country, situated in the medium, between heat and cold, is as healthful as any part of the United States.

Rivers.] This state is watered by four large, navigable rivers, besides a great number of smaller ones, which are passable in boats. The river *Savannah* washes it in its whole length from northwest to southeast. The *Edisto* rises in two branches from a remarkable ridge in the interior part of the state. These branches unite a little below Orangeburgh, which stands on the North Fork, and form Edisto river, which, having passed Jacksonsburgh, branches and embraces Edisto island.

Santee is the largest, and longest river in this state. It empties into the ocean by two mouths, a little south of Georgetown. About 120 miles, in a direct line from its mouth, it branches into the *Congaree* and *Wateree*; the latter or northern branch passes the Catabaw nation of Indians, and bears the name of the *Catabaw* river from this settlement to its source. The *Congaree* branches into *Saluda* and *Broad* rivers. Broad river again branches into *Enoree, Tyger* and *Pacolet* rivers; on the latter of which are the celebrated Pacolet Springs. Just below the junction of Saluda and Broad Rivers, on the Congaree, stands the town of COLUMBIA, which is intended to be the future seat of government in this state.

Pedee river rises in North Carolina, where it is called *Yadkin* river. In this state, however, it takes the name of Pedee, and receiving Lynche's creek and Wakkamaw river, passes by George-town, which it leaves on the east, and 12 miles below, it empties into the ocean. All the forementioned rivers, except Edisto, rise from various sources in that ridge of mountains which divides the waters which flow into the Atlantic Ocean from those which fall into the Mississippi.

The rivers of a secondary size, many of which are no more than arms of the sea; the others rising from swamps or savannahs, are Caafaw, Combahee, Wakkamaw, Ashley, Cooper and Black rivers.

The tide, in no part of the state, flows more than 25 miles from the sea shore.

Mountains.] The Tryon and Hogback mountains, are 220 miles northwest from Charleston, in latitude 35° and longitude 6° 30' from Philadelphia. The elevation of these mountains above their base is 3840 feet; and above the sea coast 4640.—The ascent from the sea shore being eight

* See History.

SOUTH CAROLINA.

eight times as great as the difference between the sphere of the horizon and that of an even plane, there is exhibited from the top of these mountains an extensive view of this state, North Carolina and Georgia. And as no object intervenes to obstruct the view, a man with *telescopic* eyes, might discern vessels at sea. The mountains west and northwest rise much higher than these and form a ridge, which divides the waters of Tennessee and Santee rivers.

Harbours.] The only harbours of note are those of Charleston, Port Royal and George-town. Charleston harbour is spacious, convenient and safe. It is formed by the junction of Ashley and Cooper rivers. Its entrance is guarded by Fort Johnson. Twelve miles from the city is a bar, over which are four channels: One by the name of Ship Channel, has 18 feet water; another $16\frac{1}{2}$, the other two are for smaller vessels. The tide rises about 9 feet. Port Royal has an excellent harbour, of sufficient extent to contain the largest fleet in the world.

The entrance into George-town harbour is impassable to large ships, which is a great obstruction to the growth of that place.

Islands.] The sea coast is bordered with a chain of fine sea islands, around which the sea flows, opening an excellent inland navigation for the conveyance of produce to market.

The principal of these are James Island, opposite Charleston, on which are about 50 families.——Further southwest is John's Island, larger than James. Next is Edisto. Each of these islands has a Presbyterian church.

On the other side of St. Helena sound, from Edisto, lies a cluster of islands, one of the largest of which is Port Royal. Adjacent to Port Royal lie St. Helena, Ladies Island, Paris Island, and the Hunting Islands, 5 or 6 in number, bordering on the ocean, so called from the number of deer and other wild game found upon them; and over across Broad river, is Hilton Head Island. All these islands, except the three first mentioned, belong to St. Helena parish.

The soil and natural growth of these islands are not noticeably different from the adjacent main land. They are in general favorable for the culture of indigo.

Civil Divisions.] The proprietors who first sent settlers to Carolina, divided it into counties and parishes. The counties were generally named after the proprietors. No county courts, however, were established, and this division, though for a long time kept up in the province, became in a great measure obsolete, previous to the revolution. Since the revolution, county courts have been established, and the state is now divided into districts and counties—and the counties are subdivided; in the lower country, into parishes—and in the upper country, into smaller or voting districts.

There are seven districts, in which are 35 counties, as follows:

Counties.

District	Counties	District	Counties
BEAUFORT DISTRICT, on the sea coast, between Combahee and Savannah rivers. Chief town BEAUFORT.	Hilton, Lincoln, Granville, Shrewsbury	ORANGE DISTRICT, west of Beaufort district. Chief town ORANGEBURG.	Lewisburg, Orange, Lexington, Winton.
CHARLESTON DISTRICT between Santee and Combahee rivers. Chief town CHARLESTON.	Charleston, Washington, Marion, Berkeley, Colleton, Bartholomew.	CAMDEN DISTRICT, west of George-town district. Chief town CAMDEN.	Clarendon, Richland, Fairfield, Cleremont, Lancaster, York, Chester.
GEORGE-TOWN DISTRICT, between Santee river and North Carolina. Chief town GEORGE-TOWN.	Winyah, Williamsburg, Kingston, Liberty.	NINETY SIX DISTRICT, comprehends all other parts of the state, not included in the other district. Ch. t. CAMBRIDGE.	Abbeville, Edgefield, Newbury, Union, Laurens, Spartanburgh, Greenville.
CHERAWS DISTRICT west of George town district. Chief town ———.	Marlborough, Chesterfield, Darlington.		

The committee appointed by act of assembly to divide the districts into counties, were directed to lay them as nearly 40 miles square as was practicable, due regard being paid to situations, natural boundaries, &c.

As the lower country was originally settled by people from Europe under the proprietary government and influence, all the then counties were divided into parishes. And even now, although the old counties are done away, the boundaries altered, and new ones established, the division of parishes subsists in the three lower districts, the people choose their senators and representatives by parishes, as formerly. But in the middle and upper districts, which were settled by people of various nations from Europe, but principally by northern emigrants, parishes are hardly known, except perhaps in Orangeburgh district. In these districts the people vote in small divisions as convenience dictates.

Chief Towns.] CHARLESTON is the only considerable town in South Carolina. It is situated on the tongue of land which is formed by the confluence of Ashley and Cooper rivers, which are large and navigable. These rivers mingle their waters immediately below the town, and form a spacious and convenient harbour, which communicates with the ocean at Sullivan's island, seven miles south east of the town. In these rivers the tide rises, in common, about five feet. The continued agitation which this occasions in the waters which almost surround Charleston, and the refreshing sea breezes which are regularly felt, render Charleston more healthy than any part of the low country in the southern states. On this account it is the resort of great numbers of gentlemen, invalids from the West India islands, and of the rich planters from the country, who come here to spend the *sickly months*, as they are called, in quest of health and of the social enjoyments which the city affords. And in no part of America are the social blessings enjoyed more rationally and liberally than in Charleston. Unaffected hospitality—affability—ease in manners and address—and a disposition to make their guests welcome, easy and pleased with themselves, are characteristics of the respectable people in Charleston.

The land on which the town is built is flat and low, and the water brackish and unwholsome. The inhabitants are obliged to raise banks of earth as barriers to defend themselves against the higher floods of the sea. The streets from east to west extend from river to river, and running in a straight line, not only open beautiful prospects each way, but afford excellent opportunities, by means of subterranean drains, for removing all nuisances and keeping the city clean and healthy. These streets are intersected by others, nearly at right angles, and throw the town into a number of squares, with dwelling houses in front, and office houses and little gardens behind. Some of the streets are conveniently wide, but most of them are much too narrow, especially for so populous a city, in so warm a climate. Besides their being a nursery for various diseases from their confined situation, they have been found extremely inconvenient in case of fires, the destructive effects of which have been frequently felt in this city. The houses, which have been lately built, are brick, with tiled roofs. Some of the buildings in Charleston are elegant, and most of them are neat, airy and well furnished. The public buildings are an exchange, state house, armoury, poor house, two large churches for Episcopalians, two for Congregationalists or Independents, one for Scotch Presbyterians,

two

two for the Baptists, one for the German Lutherans, one for the Methodists, one for French Protestants—besides a meeting house for Quakers, and two Jewish synagogues, one for the Portuguese, the other for the German Jews. There are upwards of a thousand Roman Catholics in Charleston, but they have no public building for worship.

In 1787, there were 1600 houses in this city, and 9600 white inhabitants, and 5400 negroes; and what evinces the healthiness of the place, upwards of 200 of the white inhabitants were above 60 years of age.

Charleston was incorporated in 1783, and divided into 13 wards, who choose as many wardens, who, from among themselves, elect an intendant of the city. The intendant and wardens form the city council, who have power to make and enforce bye laws for the regulation of the city.

BEAUFORT, on Port Royal island, is the seat of justice in Beaufort district. It is a pleasant, thriving little town, of about 50 or 60 houses, and 200 inhabitants, who are distinguished for their hospitality and politeness.

GEORGE-TOWN, the seat of justice in George-town district, stands on a spot of land near the junction of a number of rivers, which, when united in one broad stream, by the name of Pedee, fall into the ocean 12 miles below the town. Besides these, are Purysburgh, Jacksonsborough, Orangeburg, Wynnsborough, Cambridge, Camden and Columbia, the intended capital of the state, which are all inconsiderable villages of from 30 to 60 dwelling houses.

General face of the country.] The whole state, to the distance of 80 miles from the sea, is level, and almost without a stone. In this distance, by a gradual ascent from the sea coast, the land rises about 190 feet. Here commences a curiously uneven country. The traveller is constantly ascending or descending little sand hills, which nature seems to have disunited in a frolic. If a pretty high sea were suddenly arrested, and transformed into sand hills, in the very form the waves existed at the moment of transformation, it would present the eye with just such a view as is here to be seen. Some little herbage, and a few small pines grow even on this soil. The inhabitants are few, and have but a scanty subsistence on corn and sweet potatoes, which grow here tolerably well. This curious country continues for 60 miles, till you arrive at a place called *The Ridge*, 140 miles from Charleston. This ridge is a remarkable tract of high ground, as you approach it from the sea, but level as you advance northwest from its summit. It is a fine high, healthy belt of land, well watered and of a good soil, and extends from the Savannah to Broad river, in about 6° 30′ west longitude from Philadelphia. Beyond this ridge, commences a country exactly resembling the northern states. Here hills and dales, with all their verdure and variegated beauty, present themselves to the eye. Wheat fields, which are rare in the low country, begin to grow common. Here Heaven has bestowed its blessings with a most bounteous hand. The air is much more temperate, and healthful than nearer to the sea. The hills are covered with valuable woods—the vallies watered with beautiful rivers, and the fertility of the soil is equal to every vegetable production. This, by way of distinction, is called the upper country, where are different modes and different articles of cultivation

where

SOUTH CAROLINA.

where the manners of the people, and even their language, have a different tone. The land still rises by a gradual ascent; each succeeding hill overlooks that which immediately preceeds it, till, having advanced 220 miles in a northwest direction from Charleston, the elevation of the land above the sea coast is found by mensuration, to be about 800 feet. Here commences a mountainous country, which continues rising to the western terminating point of this state.

Soil and productions.] The soil may be divided into four kinds, first, the *Pine-barren*, which is valuable only for its timber. Interspersed among the pine-barren, are tracts of land free of timber, and of every kind of growth but that of grass. These tracts are called *Savannas*, constituting a second kind of soil, good for grazing. The third kind is that of the *swamps* and *low grounds* on the rivers, which is a mixture of black loam and fat clay, producing naturally canes in great plenty, cypress, bays, &c. In these swamps rice is cultivated, which constitutes the staple commodity of the state. The *high-lands*, commonly known by the name of oak and hiccory lands, constitute the fourth kind of soil. The natural growth is oak, hiccory, walnut, pine and locust. On these lands, in the low country, are cultivated, Indian corn, principally; and in the back country, besides these, they raise tobacco in large quantities, wheat, rye, barley, oats, hemp, flax, cotten and silk.*

At the distance of about 110 miles from the sea, the river swamps for the culture of rice, terminate, and the high lands extend quite to the rivers, and form banks, in some places, several hundred feet high from the surface of the water, and afford many extensive and delightful views. These high banks are interwoven with layers of leaves and different colored earth, and abound with quarries of free stone, pebbles, flint, chrystals, iron ore in abundance, silver, lead, sulphur and coarse diamonds.

It is curious to observe the gradations from the sea coast to the upper country, with respect to the produce—the mode of cultivation, and the cultivators. On the islands upon the sea coast, and for 40 or 50 miles back (and on the rivers much farther) the cultivators are all slaves. No white man, to speak generally, ever thinks of settling a farm, and improving it for himself without negroes. If he has no negroes, he hires himself as overseer, to some rich planter, who has more than he can or will attend to, till he can purchase for himself. The articles cultivated, are corn and potatoes, which are food for the negroes; rice and indigo, for exportation. The soil is cultivated almost wholly by manual labor. The plough, till since the peace, was scarcely used, and prejudices still exist against it.—In the middle settlements negroes are not so numerous. The master attends personally to his own business, and is glad to use the plough to assist his negroes, or himself, when he has no negroes. The soil is not rich enough for rice. It produces moderately good indigo weed; no tobacco is raised for exportation. The farmer is contented to raise corn potatoes, oats, poultry and a little wheat.—In the upper country, many men have a few negroes, and a few have many; but generally speaking, the farmers have none, and depend, like the inhabitants of the northern

---

* See the nature of the soil more particularly described under this head in the description of Georgia.

SOUTH CAROLINA.

northern states, upon the labor of themselves and families for subsistance. The plough is used almost wholly. Indian corn, wheat, rye, potatoes, &c. are raised for food, and large quantities of tobacco and some wheat and indigo for exportation.

Manufactures.] In the middle, and especially in the upper country, the people are obliged to manufacture their own cotton and woolen clothes, and most of their husbandry tools; but in the lower country the inhabitants for these articles, depend almost entirely, on their merchants. It is a fact to be lamented, that manufactures and agriculture, in this and the two adjoining states, are yet in the first stages of improvement.

Constitution.] In 1776, a temporary form of government was agreed to by the freemen of South Carolina, assembled in congress; and on the 19th of March 1778, it was established by an act of the legislature. By this constitution, the legislative authority is vested in a general assembly, to consist of two distinct bodies, a senate and house of representatives. These two bodies, jointly by ballot, at their every first meeting, choose a governor and lieutenant governor, both to continue for two years, and a privy council, (to consist of the lieutenant governor and eight other persons) all of the protestant religion.

The governor and lieutenant governor must have been residents in the state, for 10 years, and the members of the privy council 5 years, preceeding their election, and possess a freehold in the state of the value of at least ten thousand pounds currency, clear of debt.

The governor is eligible but two years in six years, and is vested with the executive authority of the state.

The senate are chosen by ballot, biennially, on the last Monday in November—thirteen make a quorum. A senator must be of the protestant religion—must have attained the age of 30 years—must have been a resident in the state at least 5 years; and must possess a freehold in the parish or district for which he is elected, of at least £2000 currency, clear of debt.

The last Monday in November, biennially, two hundred and two persons are to be chosen in different parts of the state, (equally proportioned) to represent the freemen of the state in the general assembly, who are to meet with the senate, annually, at the seat of government, on the first Monday in January.

All free whitemen of 21 years of age, of one years residence in the state, and possessing freeholds of 50 acres of land each, or what shall be deemed equal thereto, are qualified to elect representatives.

Every fourteen years the representation of the whole state is to be proportioned in the most equal and just manner, according to the particular and comparative strength and taxable property of the different parts of the same.

All money bills, for the support of government, must originate in the house of representatives, and shall not be altered or amended by the senate, but may be rejected by them.*

Ministers of the gospel are ineligible to any of the civil offices of the state.

The

---

* *This is in imitation of the British constitution, while the reasons for this imitation do not exist.*

SOUTH CAROLINA. 431

The power of impeaching officers of the state is vested in the house of representatives.

The lieutenant governor, and a majority of the privy council, exercise the powers of a court of chancery.

Justices of the peace are nominated by the senate and representatives, jointly, and commissioned by the governor during pleasure.

All other judicial officers are chosen by the senate and representatives, jointly (and except the judges of the court of chancery) commissioned by the governor during good behaviour.

All religious societies, who acknowledge that there is one God---a future state of rewards and punishments, and that God is to be publickly worshipped, are freely tolerated.

The liberty of the press is to be preserved inviolate.

No part of this constitution is to be altered, without a notice of ninety days being previously given, nor then, without the consent of a majority of the members of the senate and house of representatives.

Laws.] The laws of this state have nothing in them of a particular nature, excepting what arises from the permission of slavery. The evidence of a slave cannot be taken against a white man, and the master who kills his slave is not punishable, otherwise than by a pecuniary mulct, and 12 months imprisonment.

In an act of this state for regulating and fixing the salaries of several officers, passed in March 1787, it was ordered that the governor should receive a salary of £ 900 sterling,

Four associate judges, £500 each,	2000
Attorney general, - - -	200
Three delegates to congress, £600 each. -	1800
Auditor of public accounts, - -	373 : 6 : 8
Commissioners of the treasury, - -	571 : 8 : 8
Other salaries of public officers mentioned in said act to the amount of	2,114 : 0 : 0
Total,	£7,958 : 15 : 4

State of Literature.] Gentlemen of fortune, before the late war, sent their sons to Europe for education. During the war and since, they have generally sent them to the middle and northern states. Those who have been at this expence in educating their sons, have been but comparatively few in number, so that the literature of the state is at a low ebb. Since the peace, however, it has begun to flourish. There are several flourishing academies in Charleston—one at Beaufort, on Port Royal island—and several others in different parts of the state. Three colleges have lately been incorporated by law—one at Charleston, which is merely nominal—one at Winnsborough, in the district of Camden—the other at Cambridge, in the district of ninety six. The public and private donations for the support of these three colleges, were originally intended to have been appropriated jointly, for the erecting and supporting of one respectable college. The division of these donations has frustrated this design. The Mount Sion college, at Winnsborough, is supported by a respectable society

SOUTH CAROLINA.

ciety of gentlemen, who have long been incorporated. This institution flourishes and bids fair for usefulness. The college at Cambridge, is no more than a grammar school. That the literature of this state might be put upon a respectable footing, nothing is wanting but a spirit of enterprize among its wealthy inhabitants.

Indians.] The Catabaws are the only nation of Indians in this state. They have but one town, called Catabaw, situated on Catabaw river, in latitude $34^\circ\ 49'$ on the boundary line between North and South Carolina, and contains about 450 inhabitants, of which about 150 are fighting men.

Religion.] The people of this state, by the constitution, are to enjoy the right of electing their own pastors or clergy; and what is peculiar to this state, the minister, when chosen, is required by the constitution, to subscribe to the following declaration (viz.) ' That he is determined, by God's grace, out of the holy scriptures, to instruct the people committed to his charge, and to teach nothing (as required of necessity to eternal salvation) but that which he shall be persuaded may be concluded and proved from the scripture; that he will use both public and private admonitions, as well to the sick as to the whole, within his cure, as need shall require, and occasion shall be given, and that he will be diligent in prayers, and in reading of the holy scriptures, and in such studies as help to the knowledge of the same—that he will be diligent to frame his own self and family according to the doctrine of Christ, and to make both himself and them, as much as in him lieth, wholesome examples and paterns to the flock of Christ; that he will maintain and set forward as much as he can, quietness, peace and love among all people, and especially among those that are or shall be committed to his charge.'

Since the revolution, by which all denominations were put on an equal footing—there have been no disputes between different religious societies. They all agree to differ.

The upper parts of this state are settled chiefly by Presbyterians, Baptists and Methodists. From the most probable calculations, it is supposed that the religious denominations of this state, as to numbers, may be ranked as follows: Presbyterians, including the Congregational and Independant churches—Episcopalians, Baptists, Methodists, &c.

Population and Character.] The best estimate of the inhabitants in this state which has been made, fixes their number at 80,000 white people, and as many negroes—some say there is 120,000 negroes in this state; but no actual census has lately been made. On the sea coast there are many more slaves than freemen. The bulk of the white population is in the western parts of the state. There is no peculiarity in the manners of the inhabitants of this state, except what arises from the mischievous influence of slavery; and in this, indeed, they do not differ from the inhabitants of the other southern states. Slavery, by exempting great numbers from the necessities of labour, leads to luxury, dissipation and extravagance. The absolute authority which is exercised over their slaves, too much favors a haughty supercilious behaviour. A disposition to obey the christian precept, ' To do to others as we would that others should do unto us,' is not cherished by a daily exhibition of many made for one. The Carolinians sooner arrive at maturity, both in their bodies and minds, than the natives of colder climates. They possess a natural quickness and vivacity of

genius

genius superior to the inhabitants of the north; but too generally want that enterprize and perseverance, which are necessary for the highest attainments in the arts and sciences. They have, indeed, few motives to enterprize. Inhabiting a fertile country, which by the labor of the slaves, produces plentifully, and creates affluence—in a climate which favors indulgence, ease, and a disposition for convivial pleasures, they too generally rest contented with barely knowledge enough to transact the common affairs of life. There are not a few instances, however, in this state, in which genius has been united with application, and the effects of their union have been happily experienced, not only by this state, but by the United States.

The wealth produced by the labor of the slaves, furnishes their proprietors with the means of hospitality; and no people in the world use these means with more liberality. Many of the inhabitants spare no pains nor expence in giving the highest polish of education to their children, by enabling them to travel, and by other means unattainable by those who have but moderate fortunes.

The Carolinians are generally affable and easy in their manners, and polite and attentive to strangers. The ladies want the bloom of the north, but have an engaging softness and delicacy in their appearance and manners, and many of them possess the polite and elegant accomplishments.

Hunting is the most fashionable amusement in this state. At this the country gentlemen are extremely expert, and with surprizing dexterity pursue their game through the woods. Theatrical exhibitions have been prohibited in Charleston. Gaming of all kinds is more discountenanced among fashionable people in this, than in any of the southern states. Twice a year, statedly, a class of sportive gentlemen, in this and the neighbouring states, have their horse-races. Bets of ten and fifteen hundred guineas are sometimes laid on these occasions.

There is no instance, perhaps, in which the richer class of people trespass more on propriety than in the mode of conducting their funerals. That a decent respect be paid to the dead, is the natural dictate of refined humanity; but this is not done by sumptuous and expensive entertainments, splendid decorations, and pompous ceremonies, which a misguided fashion has here introduced and rendered necessary. In Charleston and other parts of the state, no persons attend a funeral any more than a wedding, unless they are particularly invited. Wine, punch and all kinds of liquors, tea, coffee, cake, &c. in profusion, are handed round on these solemn occasions. In short, one would suppose that the religious proverb of the wise man, ' It is better to go to the house of mourning than to the house of feasting,' would be unintelligible and wholly inapplicable here, as it would be difficult to distinguish the house of mourning from the house of feasting.

The Jews in Charleston, among other peculiarities in burying their dead, have this: After the funeral dirge is sung, and just before the corpse is deposited in the grave, the coffin is opened, and a small bag of earth, taken from the grave, is carefully put under the head of the deceased; then some powder, said to be earth brought from Jerusalem, and carefully kept for this purpose, is taken and put upon the eyes of the corpse, in token of their remembrance of the holy land, and of their expectations of returning thither in God's appointed time. *Military*

Military Strength.] There are about 20,000 fighting men in this state. About 10 men are kept to guard Fort Johnson, on James Island, at the entrance of Charleston harbour, by which no vessel can pass, unless the master or mate make oath that there is no malignant distemper on board. These 10 men are the only standing force of this state. The militia laws, enacting that every freeman between 16 and 50 years of age, shall be prepared for war, have been but indifferently obeyed since the peace.

Public Revenue and Expences.] The public revenue of this state is, nominally, about £. 90,000 sterling. But a great part of this is either not collected, or paid in public securities, which are much depreciated. The expences of government are about £. 16,000 sterling.

Mode of Levying Taxes.] There is a general impost of 3 per cent. and other imposts varying from 3 to 10 per cent. payable on the importation of merchandize from foreign countries. The great bulk of the revenue of the state, is raised by a tax on lands and negroes. The lands, for the purpose of being taxed according to their value, are divided into three grand divisions; the first reaches from the sea coast to the extent of the flowing of the tides; the second from these points to the falls of the rivers; and thence to the utmost verge of the western settlement makes the third. These grand divisions, for the sake of more exactly ascertaining the value of the lands, are subdivided into 21 different species. The most valuable of which is estimated at six pounds, and the least valuable at one shilling per acre. One per cent. on the value thus estimated, is levied from all granted lands in the state. The collection of taxes is not annexed to the office of sheriff, but is committed to particular gentlemen appointed for that purpose.

Estimate of Damages sustained in the late War.] The damages which this state sustained in the late war are thus estimated. The two entire crops of 1780 and 1781, both of which were used by the British——The crop of 1782 taken by the Americans——About 25,000 negroes——Many thousands of pounds worth of plate, and houshold furniture in abundance.——The villages of George-town and Camden burnt——The loss to the citizens directly by the plunderings and devastations of the British army——and indirectly by American impressments, and by the depreciation of the paper currency, together with the heavy debt of £. 1,200,000 sterling, incurred for the support of the war, in one aggregate view, make the price of independence to South Carolina, exclusive of the blood of its citizens, upwards of £. 3,000,000 sterling.

State of the Practice of Physic.] The practice of physic throughout the state, is reputable, particularly in Charleston, which contains more regular bred physicians, in proportion to its numbers, than any city in the United States. It is to be lamented, however, that, in common with the other parts of America, extraordinary merit is unrewarded, and persons of real skill rarely fare better, and sometimes worse, than those of moderate talents and contracted education.

SOUTH CAROLINA. 435

Commerce.] The little attention that is paid to manufactures, occasions a vast consumption of foreign imported articles; but the quantities and value of their exports, generally leave a balance in favor of the state, except when there are large importations of negroes. The following list of exports, which was copied from the custom-house books in Charleston, will give an accurate and satisfactory idea of the variety and quantity of articles exported from the port of Charleston.

General EXPORTS from Charleston, South Carolina, from November, 1786, to November 1787.

Barrels rice,	61,754	Logs cedar,	2,726
Half bls. ditto,	6,882	Plank,	514
Hogsheads tobacco,	5,493	Feet cedar,	8,800
Casks indigo,	2,783	Bushels corn,	29,088
Hhds. deer skins,	205	Firkins Butter,	1,111
Bales ditto,	256	Barrels beef,	362
Racoon skins,	767	Barrels pork,	176
Otter skins,	12	Boxes soap,	259
Hhd. Beaver skins,	1	Boxes candles,	119
Bale, do.	1	Casks bees wax,	42
Box, do.	1	Casks ground nuts,	51
Pounds, do.	875	Hogsheads Pink root,	4
Bag wool,	1	Casks snake ditto,	28
Bags cotton,	33	Boxes genseng ditto,	3
Pounds ditto,	131	Bales sarsaparilla,	10
Bags feathers,	31	Casks ditto,	15
Pounds ditto,	600	Bundles ditto,	57
Barrels pitch,	1,904	Hides leather,	3,308
Barrels tar,	2,230	Sides ditto,	4,212
Barrels rozin,	739	Casks bacon hams,	13
Barrels turpentine,	3,707	Pounds ditto,	3,455
Blls. spirits of terpentine,	32	Casks oranges,	21
Feet lumber,	1,057,600	Bricks,	97,000
Feet shingles,	3,689,600	Reeds,	121,800
Feet staves,	1,023,700	Horns,	6,900

AMERICAN produce imported into, and exported from Charleston.

Barrels flour,	8,783	Bushels ditto,	1,238
Barrels bread,	735	Barrels onions,	36
Kegs ditto,	835	Bunches ditto,	14,624
Barrels fish,	965	Bushels oats,	360
Quintals, do	110	Barrels apples,	72
Pounds ditto,	900	Barrels cyder,	56
Barrels potatoes,	360		

FOREIGN produce imported into, and exported from Charleston.

Hhds. and puncheons Rum, W. I. & N. E.	354	Casks and barrels ditto.	121
		Pipes wine,	31
		Hogsheads ditto,	41

Casks

SOUTH CAROLINA.

Casks ditto,	569	Pieces cane wood, — 79
Cases ditto.	358	Pieces elephants teeth, — 15
Pipes brandy, —	91	Tons iron, — $22\frac{1}{4}$
Casks ditto.	88	Bars ditto. — 229
Cases gin, —	1,561	Tons coal, — 220
Hhds. and casks porter,	324	Tons Russia hemp, — 7
Bushels salt, —	16,332	Pounds ditto. — 11,200
Hhdds. molasses, —	560	Cables, — 6
Hhdds. sugar, —	32	Coils cordage, — 8
Chests ditto. —	375	Pounds ditto — 10,000
Casks ditto. —	276	Anchors, — 6
Hhdds. coffee, —	3	Hhdds. goods of different
Casks ditto. —	182	kinds exported, — 58
Bags ditto. —	71	
Pounds ditto.	5,500	Casks ditto. — 552
Hhdds. cocoa, —	30	Bales ditto. — 150
Casks ditto.	94	Trunks ditto. 148
Bags ditto. —	106	Cases and boxes ditto. — 490
Bags pimento, —	143	Crates ditto. — 102
Tons logwood, —	$220\frac{3}{4}$	Bundles ditto. — 51
Quintals ditto. —	300	Jugs & jars ditto. — 209
Pieces ditto. —	598	Kegs ditto. — 477
Tons fustick, —	$41\frac{1}{2}$	Loose pieces duck & osnaburg, 185
Pieces ditto. —	2,078	Iron pots, — 512
Tons lignum vitæ, —	$50\frac{1}{4}$	Grind & queen stones, 45
Pieces ditto.	300	Logs mahogany, — 2,967
Pieces yellow sanders, —	249	Feet ditto. — 18,638
Pounds ditto. —	6,450	

VESSELS cleared out at the custom house, Charleston, from November 1786, to November 1787, belonging to the following nations.

AMERICA.

40	Ships measuring	7,372	Tons.
3	Snows ditto.	252	ditto.
95	Brigs ditto.	9,824	ditto.
285	Sloops ditto.	11,650	ditto.
312	Schooners ditto.	12,433	ditto.
735	Vessels.	41,531	Tons.

GREAT BRITAIN.

35	Ships, measuring	7,152	Tons.
4	Snows ditto.	535	ditto.
46	Brigs ditto.	5,652	ditto.
35	Sloops ditto.	2,160	ditto.
28	Schooners ditto.	1,288	ditto.
148	Vessels.	16,787	Tons.

SPAIN.

SOUTH CAROLINA.

SPAIN.

2	Brigs, measuring, - -	273	Tons,
3	Sloops ditto. - - -	150	ditto,
39	Schooners ditto, - - -	650	ditto.
44	Vessels. - - -	1,073	Tons,

FRANCE,

1	Snow, measuring - -	180	Tons,
3	Brigs ditto. -	235	ditto,
2	Sloops ditto, - - -	138	ditto.
2	Schooners ditto. - -	162	ditto.
8	Vessels. - - -	715	Tons,

UNITED NETHERLANDS.

1	Ship, measuring - -	290	Tons,
4	Brigs ditto. - -	509	ditto.
5	Vessels. - - -	799	Tons,

IRELAND.

1	Ship measuring - -	218	Tons,
1	Brig ditto. - -	101	ditto,
2	Vessels, - - -	319	Tons,

1	Ship, Altona, - - -	280	ditto.
1	Brig, Bremen, - • -	193	ditto.
1	Brig, Denmark, - -	164	ditto.
1	Brig, Hamburg, - -	130	ditto.
1	Brig, Austria, - -	127	ditto.

Tot. 947	Vessels, measuring - - -	62,118	Tons.

The amount of the above exports in sterling money, has been estimated at £.505,279:19:5. In the most successful seasons there have been as many as 140,000 barrels of rice, and 1,300,000 pounds of indigo, exported in one year. The average price of rice, since the peace, has been from 12 to 14 shillings sterling the hundred; and of indigo, of the different sorts, 3 shillings and 9 pence. Since the peace of 1783, in consequence of the depopulation of labourers, the bad state of the fields, and from a succession of bad seasons, the planters have made yearly but little more than half a common crop.

The following 'abstract' from a gentleman accurately informed on the subject, contains much useful information, and demands a place under this head.

GENERAL

SOUTH CAROLINA.

General Abstract of the Debt of the State of South Carolina,

Last Balances.	Supposed value of imports of West India and European goods, as per entries, made at the treasury office.	Amount of imports, with charges on dry goods, which are included in the European invoices, though not in the entries at the treasury, the average of which is from 10 to 15 per cent.	Number of Negroes imported.	Supposed neat proceeds of negroes, for which the vender here is held accountable to the merchant in Europe.	One year's interest on the last balances.
500,000	280,000	315,000	1003	40,471 1	25,000
745,775 1	700,000	787,500	4434	178,911 18	37,288 15
1,376,224 10	390,000	438,750	2768	111,688 16	68,811 4
1,624,613 14	280,000	315,000	532	21,466 4	81,230 14
4,246,613 5	1,650,000	1,856,250	8737	352,537 19	212,330 13

N. B. Vast quantities of goods imported in the above years, were on account of foreigners, and sold at vendue and otherwise, greatly under their first cost, in Europe, and many bad debts were contracted, both which ought to be deducted from the above balance of £. 1,626,761 : 16, which deducted, it is computed, will reduce the balance to about £. 1,400,000.—It is computed that the goods now left in stores, will amount to at least £. 500,000; but as there was likewise a considerable value at the evacuation, as well as debts contracted during the time the British held the city as a garrison, no deduction can, with propriety, be made on that account.

Statement of the supposed future trade of the State (allowing an annual importation private debts of the State,

Supposed last balances, deducting bad debts, on account of foreigners and specie.	Supposed value of imports of West India and European goods as per entries at the treasury.	Charges on goods included in the invoices, and payable by the importer, though not taken notice of in the entries made in the treasury.	Number of negroes imported.	Neat proceeds of negroes payable in Europe.	Total amount of imports of negroes and goods including charges.
1,250,000	200,000	25,000	1000	40,000	265,000
1,077,500	200,000	25,000	1000	40,000	265,000
896,375	200,000	25,000	1000	40,000	265,000
706,193 15	200,000	25,000	1000	40,000	265,000
506,503 8 9	200,000	25,000	1000	40,000	265,000
296,129 12	200,000	25,000	1000	40,000	265,000

SOUTH CAROLINA.

from 1st of January, 1783, to 1st January, 1787, both inclusive.

Total amount of the import of negroes, European and West India goods, including charges.	Totals, including Interest on last balance.	Periods.	Supposed value of exports here.	Supposed neat proceeds of Exports from hence.	Balances.
355,471 1	880,471 1	1783 to 1784	178,370	134,696	745,775 1
966,411 18	1,749,475 14	1784 to 1785	466,564	373,251 4	1,376,224 10
550,438 16	1,995,474 10	1785 to 1786	463,576	370,860 16	1,624,613 14
336,466 4	2,042,310 12	1786 to 1787	519,436	415,548 16	1,626,761 16
2,208,787 19	6,667,731 13		1,617,946	1,294,356 16	5,373,375 1

N. B. The above exports are the produce of South Carolina, and are exclusive of dry goods, rum, sugar, salt, coffee, &c. shipped to North Carolina, Georgia, East Florida, Bahamas and Savannah, neither are the exports from George-town, and Beaufort included therein, though at a moderate calculation all those articles for the above years may be estimated at

In the exports, specie is not included, though it is thought that the sum annually sent from hence is from £. 150,000 to £. 200,000 at least.

of 1000 negroes) to shew the period of time necessary for the extinguishment of the on the foregoing principles.

One years interest on the last balance.	Totals, including interest on last balance.	Periods.	Supposed val. of exports here	Supposed neat proceeds of exports.	Balances.
62,500	1,577,500	1 Jan. 87 to 1 Jan. 88	500,000		1,077,500
53,875	1,396,375	1 Jan. 88 to 1 Jan. 89	500,000		896,375
44,818 15	1,206,193 15	1 Jan. 89 to 1 Jan. 90	500,000		706,193 15
35,309 13 9	1,006,503 8 0	1 Jan. 90 to 1 Jan. 91	500,000		506,503 8 9
25,325 3 3	796,828 12	1 Jan. 91 to 1 Jan. 92	500,000		296,828 12
14,841 8	576,670	1 Jan. 92 to 1 Jan. 93	500,000		76,670

The

SOUTH CAROLINA.

The balance of £. 500,000 sterling is the supposed amount of the foreign private debt of this state at the commencement of the late war.

The foregoing calculations were made during the period the instalment act was in progress in the legislature, and is more unfavorable to the state of the debt, than any other that was produced at that time, except some that were calculated with a view to extend the instalments as far as possible; but as the importation of negroes is prohibited for three years, the balance of debt at the end of that time, say March 1790, will be reduced to £. 580,093.

It is to be observed that the value of exports in this calculation, are not rated higher than the nominal value here in the late bad seasons; so that a few successful crops would decrease the debt in a much greater degree.

Practice of the Law, Courts, &c.] From the first settlement of this country in 1669, to the year 1769, a single court, called the Court of *Common Pleas*, was thought sufficient to transact the judicial business of the state. This court was invariably held at Charleston, where all the records were kept, and all civil business transacted. As the province increased, inconveniences arose, and created uneasiness among the people.

To remedy these inconveniences an act was passed in 1769, by which the province was divided into seven districts, which have been mentioned. The Court of Common Pleas (invested with the powers of the same court in England) sat four times a year in Charleston. By the abovementioned act, the Judges of the Court of Common Pleas were empowered to sit as Judges of the Court of Sessions, invested with the powers of the Court of King's Bench, in England, in the criminal jurisdiction. The act likewise directed the Judges of the Courts of Common Pleas and Sessions in Charleston district, to divide, and two of the Judges to proceed on what is called the Northern Circuit, and the other two on the Southern Circuit, distributing justice in their progress. This was to be done twice in the year. This mode of administering justice continued till 1785, when, by the unanimous exertions of the two upper districts, an act was passed, establishing county courts in all the counties of the four districts of Camden, Ninety Six, Cheraws and Orangeburg; in the two last, however, the law has not taken effect. The County Courts are empowered to sit four times in a year. Before the establishment of county courts, the lawyers all resided at Charleston, under the immediate eye of government; and the Carolina bar was as pure and genteel as any in the United States. Since this establishment, lawyers have flocked in from all quarters, and settled in different parts of the country, and law-suits have been multiplied beyond all former knowledge.

History.] The reformation in France occasioned a civil war between the Protestant and Catholic parties in that kingdom. During these domestic troubles Jasper de Coligni, a principal commander of the Protestant army, fitted out two ships, and sent them with a colony to America, under the command of Jean Ribaud, for the purpose of securing a retreat from persecution. Ribaud landed at the mouth of what is now called Albemarle river, in North Carolina. This colony, after enduring incredible hardships, were extirpated by the Spaniards. No further attempts were made to plant a colony int his quarter, till the reign of Charles II, of England. Mention is, however, made of Sir Robert Heath's having obtained

SOUTH CAROLINA.

tained a grant of Carolina, from Charles I. in 1630; but no settlements were made in consequence of this grant.

In 1662, after the restoration of Charles II. Edward, earl of Clarendon, and seven others, obtained a grant of all lands lying between the 31st and 36th degrees of north latitude.

A second charter, given two years after, enlarged their boundaries, and comprehended all that province, territory, &c. extending eastward as far as the north end of Currotuck inlet, upon a streight line westerly to Wyonoke creek, which lies within, or about latitude 36° 30'; and so west, in a direct line as far as the South sea; and south and westward as far as 29° north latitude, inclusive, and so west in direct lines to the South sea.* Of this large territory, the king constituted these eight persons absolute lords Proprietors—investing them with all necessary powers to settle and govern the same.

Nothing was successfully done towards the settlement of this country till 1669. At this time, the proprietors, in virtue of their powers, engaged the famous Mr. Locke to frame, for them, a constitution and body of laws. This constitution, consisting of 120 articles, was aristocratical and though ingenious in theory, could never be successfully reduced to practice.

K k k Three

---

* *Various causes have rendered it expedient to divide this extensive territory. In 1728 North Carolina was erected into a separate province. In 1732, George II. granted to certain trustees therein mentioned, and to their successors, a charter of all that part of Carolina, lying between the most northern stream of Savannah river; along the sea coast, to the most southern stream of Alatamaha river; westward, from the heads of these rivers, respectively in direct lines to the South sea, inclusively, with all islands within 20 leagues of the same.*

In 1762, the governor of South Carolina, conceiving that the lands lying south of Alatamaha river, belonged to South Carolina, granted several tracts of said land. Upon complaint being made by the government of Georgia, of this supposed encroachment on their territory, his majesty issued a proclamation in 1763, annexing to Georgia all the lands lying between the rivers Alatamaha and St. Mary's. The boundary line, dividing the two provinces (now states) of South Carolina and Georgia, has long been the subject of controversy; the former claiming the lands lying between the North Carolina line, and a line to run due west from the mouth of Tugulo and Keowee rivers; consequently that that spot was the head of Savannah river; the latter contended that the source of Keowee river, was to be considered as the head of Savannah river.

For the purpose of settling this controversy, commissioners were appointed in April 1787, by the contending states—vested with full powers to determine the controverted boundary, which they fixed as follows:

' The most northern branch or stream of the river Savannah, from the sea or mouth of such stream, to the fork or confluence of the rivers now called Tugulo and Keowee, and from thence the most northern branch or stream of the said river Tugulo till it intersects the northern boundary line of South Carolina, if the said branch of Tugulo extends so far north, reserving all the islands in

Three claffes of nobility were to be eftablifhed, (viz.) barons, caffiques and landgraves. The firft to poffefs twelve—the fecond twenty-four—the third forty-eight thoufand acres of land, which was to be unalienable.

In 1669, William Sayle, being appointed firft governor of this country, embarked with a colony, and fettled on the neck of land where Charlefton now ftands.

During the continuance of the proprietary government, a period of 50 years (reckoning from 1669 to 1719) the colony was involved in perpetual quarrels. Oftentimes they were harraffed by the Indians—fometimes infefted with pirates—frequently invaded by the French and Spanifh fleets—conftantly uneafy under their injudicious government—and quarrelling with their governors.—But their moft bitter diffentions, were refpecting religion. The epifcopalians, being more numerous than the diffenters, attempted to exclude the latter from a feat in the legiflature. Thefe attempts were fo far fucceeded, as that the church of England, by a majority of votes, was eftablifhed by law. This illiberal act threw the colony into the utmoft confufion, and was followed by a train of evil confequences, which proved to be the principal caufe of the revolution. Notwithftanding the act eftablifhing the church of England was repealed, tranquility was not reftored to the colony. A change of government was generally defired by the colonifts. They found that they were not fufficiently protected by their proprietory conftitution, and effected a revolution about the year 1719, and the government became regal.

In 1728, the proprietors accepted £22,500 fterling from the crown, for the property and jurifdiction, except Lord Granville, who referved his 8th of the property, which has never yet been formally given up. At this time the conftitution was new modelled, and the territory, limited by the original charter, was divided into North and South Carolinas.

From this period the colony began to flourifh. It was protected by a government, formed on the plan of the Englifh conftitution. Under the foftering care of the mother country, its growth was aftonifhingly rapid. Between the years 1763 and 1775, the number of inhabitants, was more than doubled. No one indulged a wifh for a change in their political conftitution, till the memorable ftamp act, paffed in 1765.

From this period till 1775, various attempts were made by Great Britain to tax her colonies without her confent. Thefe attempts were invariably oppofed. The Congrefs, who met at Philadelphia this year, unanimoufly

the faid rivers Savannah and Tugulo to Georgia—but if the faid branch or ftream of Tugulo does not extend to the north boundary line of South Carolina, then a weft line to the Miffifippi to be drawn from the head fpring or fource of the faid branch of Tugulo river, which extends to the higheft northern latitude, fhall forever hereafter form the feparation limit and boundary between the ftates of South Carolina and Georgia.'

It is fuppofed, in the map of this ftate, that the moft northern branch of Tugulo river, interfects the northern boundary of South Carolina, which, if it be fact, brings the ftate to a point in latitude 35°, and about 8° 35' weft longitude from Philadelphia.

unanimously approved the opposition, and on the 19th of April, war commenced.

During the vigorous contest for independence, this state was a great sufferer. For three years it was the seat of the war. It feels and laments the loss of many of its noble citizens. Since the peace, it has been emerging from that melancholy confusion and poverty, in which it was generally involved by the devastations of a relentless enemy. The inhabitants are fast multiplying by immigrations from other states—the agricultural interests of the state are reviving—commerce is flourishing—oeconomy is becoming more fashionable—and science begins to spread her salutary influences among the citizens.—And should the political difficulties, which have for several years past, unhappily divided the inhabitants, subside, as is hoped, upon the operation of the new government, this state, from her natural commercial and agricultural advantages, and the abilities of her leading characters, promises to become one of the richest in the union.

GEORGIA.

SITUATION and EXTENT.

Miles.
Length 600 } Between { 31° and 35° North Latitude.
Breadth 250 }   { 5° and 16° West Longitude.

Boundaries.] BOUNDED east, by the Atlantic Ocean; south, by East and West Floridas; west, by the river Mississippi; north and northeast, by South Carolina, and by lands ceded to the United States by South Carolina.

Civil divisions.] That part of the state which has been laid out in counties, is divided as follows:

Counties.	Principal Towns.
Chatham,	SAVANNAH, lat. 32° 5.
Effingham,	Ebenezer.
Burke,	Waynesburgh and Louisville.
Richmond,	AUGUSTA.
Wilkes,	Washington.
Liberty,	Sunbury.
Glynn,	Brunswick.
Camden,	St. Patrick's.
Washington,	Golphinton.
Greene,	Greensburg.
Franklin,	

Before

GEORGIA.

Before the revolution, Georgia, like all the southern states, was divided into parishes; but this mode of division is now abolished, and that of counties has succeeded in its room.

Chief Towns.] The present seat of government in this state is AUGUSTA. It is situated on the southwest bank of Savannah river, about 134 miles from the sea, and 117 northwest of Savannah. The town, which contains not far from 200 houses, is on a fine large plain; and as it enjoys the best soil, and the advantage of a central situation between the upper and lower counties, is rising fast into importance.

SAVANNAH, the former capital of Georgia, stands on a high sandy bluff, on the south side of the river of the same name, and 17 miles from its mouth. The town is regularly built in the form of a parallellogram, and, including its suburbs, contains 227 dwelling houses, one Episcopal church, a German Lutheran church, a Presbyterian church, a Synagogue and Court-house. The number of its inhabitants, exclusive of the blacks, amount to about 830, seventy of whom are Jews.

In Savannah, and within a circumference of about 10 miles from it, there were, in the summer of 1787, about 2300 inhabitants. Of these 192 were above 50 years of age, and all in good health. The ages of a lady and her six children, then living in the town, amounted to 385 years. This computation, which was actually made, serves to shew that Savannah is not really so unhealthy as has been commonly represented.

SUNBURY is a sea port town, favored with a safe and very convenient harbour. Several small islands intervene, and partly obstruct a direct view of the ocean; and, interlocking with each other, render the passage out to sea winding, but not difficult. It is a very pleasant, healthy town, and is the resort of the planters from the adjacent places of Midway and Newport, during the sickly months. It was burnt by the British in the late war, but is now recovering its former populousness and importance.

BRUNSWICK, in Glynn county, lat. 31° 10', is situated at the mouth of Turtle river, at which place this river empties itself into St. Simon's sound. Brunswick has a safe harbour, and sufficiently large to contain the whole of his Most Christian Majesty's fleet; and the bar, at the entrance into it, has water deep enough for the largest vessel that swims. The town is regularly laid out, but not yet built. From its advantageous situation, and from the fertility of the back country, it promises to be hereafter one of the first trading towns in Georgia.

FREDERICA, on the island of St. Simon, is nearly in lat. 31° 15' north. It stands on an eminence, if considered with regard to the marshes before it, upon a branch of Alatamaha river, which washes the west side of this agreeable island, and after several windings, disembogues itself into the sea at Jekyl sound: It forms a kind of bay before the town, and is navigable for vessels of the largest burthen, which may lie along the wharf in a secure and safe harbour.

The town of LOUISVILLE, which is designed as the future seat of government in this state, has lately been laid out on the bank of Ogeechee river, about 70 miles from its mouth, but is not yet built.

Rivers.] Savannah river forms a part of the divisional line, which separates this state, from South Carolina. Its course is nearly from northwest to south east. It is formed principally of two branches, by the names
of

of Tugulo and Keowee, which spring from the mountains. It is navigable for large vessels up to Savannah, and for boats, of 100 feet keel, as far as Augusta. After rising a fall just above this place, it is passable for boats to the mouth of Tugulo river. Tybee bar, at its entrance in lat. 31° 57', has 16 feet water at half tide.

Ogeechee river, about 18 miles south of the Savannah, is a smaller river, and nearly parallel with it in its course.

Alatamaha,* about 60 miles south of Savannah river, is formed by the junction of the Okonee and Okemulgee branches. It is a noble river, but of difficult entrance. Like the Nile it discharges itself by several mouths into the sea.

Besides these there is *Turtle river*, *Little Sitilla*, *Great Sitilla*, *Crooked river*, and *St. Mary's*, which forms a part of the southern boundary of the United States. St. Mary's river empties into Amelia sound, lat 30° 44, and is navigable for vessels of considerable burden for 90 miles. Its banks afford immense quantities of fine timber, suited to the West India market. Along this river, every four or five miles, are bluffs convenient for vessels to haul too and load.

The rivers in the middle and western parts of this state are, Apalachicola, which is formed by the Chatahouchee and Flint rivers, Mobile, Pascagoula and Pearl rivers. All these running southwardly, empty into the Gulph of Mexico. The fore mentioned rivers abound with a great variety of fish, among which are the mullet, whiting, cat, rock, trout, brim, white, shad and sturgeon.

Climate, Diseases, &c.] In some parts of this state, at particular seasons of the year, the climate cannot be esteemed salubrious. In the low country near the rice swamps, bilious complaints and fevers of various kinds are pretty universal during the months of July, August and September, which, for this reason, are called the sickly months.

The disorders peculiar to this climate, originate chiefly from the badness of the water, which is generally brackish, and from the noxious putrid vapours which are exhaled from the stagnant waters in the rice swamps. Besides, the long continuance of warm weather produces a general relaxation of the nervous system, and as they have no necessary labor to call them to exercise, a large share of indolence is the natural consequence; and indolence, especially amongst a luxurious people, is ever the parent of disease. The immense quantities of spiritous liquors, which are used to correct the brackishness of the water, form a species of intemperance which too often proves ruinous to the constitution. Parents of infirm, sickly habits, often, in more senses than one, have children of their own likeness. A considerable part of the diseases of the present inhabitants may therefore be viewed as hereditary. I must add as a general observation, that to the three last mentioned causes, may be ascribed no inconsiderable part of those disorders which prevail in southern climates.

Before the sickly season commences, many of the rich planters of this state, remove with their families to the sea islands, or some elevated healthy situation, where they reside three or four months, for the benefit of fresh air. In the winter and spring, pleurisies, peripneumonies and other inflammatory

---

* *Pronounced Ollamawhaw.*

inflammatory diforders, occafioned by fudden and violent colds, are confiderably common and frequently fatal. Confumptions, epilepfies, cancers, palfies and apoplexies, are not fo incident to the inhabitants of the fouthern as northern climates.

The winters in Georgia are very mild and pleafant. Snow is feldom or never feen. Vegetation is not frequently prevented by fevere frofts. Cattle fubfift tolerably well through the winter, without any other food than what they obtain in the woods and favannahs,* and are fatter in that feafon than in any other. In the hilly country, which begins about 80 or 100 miles from the fea, the air is pure and falubrious, and the water plenty and good. In the flat country there is here and there a fpring only, which is clear and pretty good. Neither is the air here fo pure as in the hilly country, being more confined and lefs fubject to agitations from the winds, and withal impregnated with putrid vapour from the rice fwamps.

In the foutheaft parts of this ftate, which lie within a few degrees of the torrid zone, the atmofphere is kept in motion by impreffions from the trade winds. This ferves to purify the air, and render it fit for refpiration; fo that it is found to have a very advantageous effect on perfons of confumptive habits.

Face of the Country.] The eaftern part of the ftate, between the mountains and the ocean, and the rivers Savannah and St. Mary's, a tract of country more than 120 miles from north to fouth, and 40 or 50 eaft and weft, is entirely level, without a hill or a ftone. At the diftance of about 40 or 50 miles from the fea board, or falt marfh, the lands begin to be more or lefs uneven. The ridges gradually rife one above another into hills, and the hills fucceffively increafing in height, till they finally terminate in mountains. That vaft chain of mountains which commences with Katts Kill, near Hudfon's river, in the ftate of New York, known by the names of the Allegany and Apalachian Mountains, terminate in this ftate, about 60 miles fouth of its northern boundary.—From the foot of this mountain, fpreads a wide extended plain, of the richeft foil, and in a latitude and climate favorably adapted to the cultivation of moft of the Eaft India productions.

Soil and Productions.] The foil and its fertility are various, according to fituation and different improvement. The iflands on the fea board, in their natural ftate, are covered with a plentiful growth of pine, oak, and hiccory, live oak and fome red cedar. The foil is a mixture of fand and black mould, making what is commonly called a grey foil. A confiderable part of it, particularly that whereon grow the oak, hiccory and live oak, is very fertile, and yields on cultivation good crops of indigo, cotton, corn and potatoes. Thefe iflands are furrounded by navigable creeks, between which and the main land is a large extent of falt marfh, fronting the whole ftate, not lefs, on an average, than 4 or 5 miles in breadth, interfected with creeks in various directions, admitting, through the whole, an inland navigation, between the iflands and mainland, from the northeaftward to the foutheaftward corners of the ftate. The foil of the main land, adjoining the marfhes and creeks, is nearly of the fame quality with
that

---

* *A* favannah *is a tract of ground covered with grafs, but without any trees or fhrubs. They are often to be found in pine lands in the fouthern ftates.*

GEORGIA.

that of the islands; except that which borders on those rivers and creeks which stretch far back into the country. On these, immediately after you leave the salts, begin the valuable rice swamps, which, on cultivation, afford the present principal staple of commerce. The most of the rice lands lie on rivers, which, as far as the tide flows, are called Tide-lands, or on creeks and particular branches of water flowing in some deeper or lower parts of the lands, which are called inland-swamps, and extend back in the country from 15 to 25 miles, beyond which very little rice is planted, though it will grow exceedingly well, as experiment has proved, 120 miles back from the sea. The intermediate lands, between these creeks and rivers, are of an inferior quality, being of a grey soil, covered chiefly with pine, and a sort of wild grass and small reeds, which afford a large range of feeding ground for stock both summer and winter. Here and there, are interspersed oak and hiccory ridges, which are of a better soil, and produce good crops of corn and indigo, but these are very little elevated above the circumjacent lands. The lands adjoining the rivers are nearly level, and, for an hundred miles in a direct line from the sea, continue a breadth from 2 to 3 or 4 miles, and wherever, in that distance, you find a piece of high land that extends to the bank of the river on one side, you may expect to find the low or swamp ground proportionably wide on the opposite side of the river. This seems to be an invariable rule till you come to that part where the river cuts the mountains.

The soil between the rivers, after you leave the sea board and the edge of the swamps, at the distance of 20 or 30 miles, changes from a grey to a red colour, on which grows plenty of oak and hiccory, with a considerable intermixture of pine. In some places it is gravelly, but fertile, and so continues for a number of miles, gradually deepening the redish colour of the earth, till it changes into what is called the Mulatto soil, consisting of a black mould and red earth. The composition is darker or lighter according as there is a larger or smaller portion of the black or red earth in it. The mulatto lands are generally strong, and yield large crops of wheat, tobacco, corn, &c. To this kind of land succeeds by turns a soil nearly black and very rich, on which grow large quantities of black walnut, mulberry, &c. This succession of different soils continues uniform and regular, though there are some large veins of all the different soils intermixed, and what is more remarkable, this succession, in the order mentioned, stretches across this state nearly parallel with the sea coast, and extends through the several states, nearly in the same direction, to the banks of Hudson's river. In this state are produced by culture, rice, indigo, cotton, silk, (though not in large quantities) Indian corn, potatoes, oranges, figs, pomegranates, &c. Rice, at present, is the staple commodity; and as a small proportion only of the rice ground is under cultivation, the quantity raised in future must be much greater than at present. But the rapid increase of the inhabitants, chiefly by immigrations, whose attention is turned to the raising of tobacco, and the vast extent of land, with a richness of soil suited to the culture of that plant, renders it probable, that tobacco will shortly become the staple of this state.

The tobacco lands are equally well adapted to wheat, which may hereafter make an important article of commerce.

On

On the dry plains, grow large crops of sweet patatoes, which are found to afford a wholsome nourishment, and from which is made, by distillation, a kind of whisky, tolerably good, but inferior to that made from rye. It is by properly macerating and washing this root, that a sediment or starch is made, which has obtained the name of Sago, and answers all the purposes of the India sago.

Most of the tropical fruits would flourish in this state with proper attention. The rice plant has been, and the tea plant, of which such immense quantities are consumed in the United States, may undoubtedly be, transplanted with equal advantage. The latitude, the soil, and the temperature of climate, all invite to make the experiment.

From many considerations, we may perhaps venture to predict, that the southwestern part of this state, and the parts of East and West Florida, which lie adjoining, will, in a few years, become the vineyard of America.

Remarkable Springs.] In the county of Wilkes, within a mile and an half of the town of Washington, is a medicinal spring, which rises from a hallow tree, four or five feet in length.—The inside of the tree is covered with a coat of nitre, an inch thick, and the leaves around the spring are incrusted with a substance as white as snow.—It is said to be a sovereign remedy for the scurvy, scrofulous disorders, consumptions, gouts, and every other disease arising from humours in the blood.—A person, who had a severe rheumatism in his right arm, having, in the space of ten minutes, drank two quarts of the water, experienced a momentary chill, and was then thrown into a perspiration, which, in a few hours, left him entirely free from pain, and in perfect health.

This spring, situated in a fine, healthy part of the state, in the neighbourhood of Washington, where are excellent accommodations, will no doubt prove a pleasant and salutary place of resort for invalids from the maritime and unhealthy parts of this and the neighbouring states.

Curiosities.] About 90 miles from the sea, as you advance towards the mountains, is a very remarkable bank of oyster shells, of an uncommon size. They run in a direction nearly parallel with the sea coast, in three distinct ridges near each other, which together occupy a space of seven miles in breadth. The ridges commence at Savannah river, and have been traced to the northern branches of the Alatamaha. This remarkable phenomenon has already been accounted for (page 49.) But by whatever means these shells were placed there, they are an inexhaustible source of wealth and convenience to the neighbouring inhabitants, as from them they make their lime for building, and for the making of indigo, in which it is indispensibly necessary.

Commerce, manufactures and agriculture.] The chief articles of export from this state are rice, tobacco, indigo, sago, lumber of various kinds, naval stores, leather, deer skins, snake root, myrtle, bees wax, corn, live stock, &c. The value of the exports from this state in 1772, was £121,677 sterling. The number of vessels employed this year, was 217, whose tonnage was 11,246, as will be seen in the following statement.

Exports

GEORGIA. 449

Exports of Georgia, of the crops of 1755, 1760, 1765, 1770, *and* 1772.

	1755.	1760.	1765.	1770.	1772.
Barrels of rice,	2,399	3,283	12,224	22,129	23,540
Pounds of indigo,	4,508	11,746	16,019	22,336	11,882
Lbs. deer skins,	49,995	65,765	200,695	284,840	213,475
Lbs. beaver skins,	120	2,29	1,800	1,469	632
Lbs. raw silk,	438	558	711	290	485
Lbs. tanned leather,	3,250	34,725	34,575	44,539	52,126
M. Feet of timber.	387	283	1,879	1,806	2,163
Lbs. of tobacco,				13,447	176,732
M. staves,	203	80	661	466	988
M. shingles,	240	581	3,722	2,897	3,525
Oars & handspikes,		1,112	528	96	
Lbs. of hemp.				1,860	259
Bbls. turpentine,				103	40
Barrels of pitch,				80	364
Barrels of tar,	45	425	486	105	298
Barrels of pork,	20	8	394	521	628
Barrels of beef,	40	14	141	639	555
Hogs and shoats,	76		1,360	605	574
Bushels of corn,	600		7,805	13,598	11,444
Lbs. of flour,					1,000
Bushels rough rice,	237	208	3,113	7,064	2,627
Bushels of peas,	400		300	601	140
Lbs. sago powder,				18,405	14,435
Gals. orange juice,				605	284
Lbs. of tallow,			100	1,079	
Lbs. of bees and myrtle wax,		960	3,910	2,170	4,058	1,954
Horses,	48		200	345	257
Mules,				30	10
Steers and cows,	16		69	25	136

Value, in sterling money, of the exports of Georgia, for eighteen years.

	£.		£.		£.
1755,	15,744	1761,	15,870	1767,	67,092
1756,	16,776	1762,	27,021	1768,	92,284
1757,	15,649	1763,	47,551	1769,	86,480
1758,	8,613	1764,	55,025	1770,	99,383
1759,	12,694	1765,	73,426	1771,	106,387
1760,	20,852	1766,	81,228	1772,	121,677

Statement of the number of vessels cleared out of Georgia, from 1755 *to* 1772.

	Square rigged	Sloops	tons.		Square rigged	Sloops	tons.
1755,	9	43	1,899	1759,	13	35	1,981
1756,	7	35	1,799	1760,	7	30	1,457
1757,	11	33	1,559	1761,	9	36	1,604
1758,	4	17	665	1762,	22	35	2,784

Lll

1759,

450   G E O R G I A,

1763,	34	58	4,761	1768,	77	109	10,406
1764,	36	79	5,586	1769,	87	94	9,276
1765,	54	94	7,685	1770,	73	113	10,514
1766,	68	86	9,974	1771,	64	121	9,553
1767,	62	92	8,465	1772,	84	133	11,246

It is impossible to tell, with accuracy, what has been the amount of exports in any one year since the peace, owing to the confusion into which affairs of this kind were thrown by the late war. In return for the numerated exports are imported, West India goods, teas, wines, various articles of clothing, and dry goods of all kinds—From the northern states, cheese, fish, potatoes, apples, cyder and shoes. The imports and exports of this state are to and from Savannah, which has a fine harbour, and is a place where the principal commercial business of the state is transacted. The manufactures of this state have hitherto been very inconsiderable, if we except indigo, silk and sago. In 1766, 1084 lbs. of raw silk were exported. So large a quantity, however, has not been exported in any one year before or since. The culture of silk and the manufacture of sago, are at present but little attended to. The people in the lower part of this state manufacture none of their own clothing for themselves or their negroes. For almost every article of their wearing apparel, as well as for their husbandry tools, they depend on their merchants, who import them from Great Britain and the northern states. In the upper part of the country, however, the inhabitants manufacture the chief part of their clothing from cotton and from flax.

Military strength.] In Georgia there are supposed to be about 8000 fighting men, between 16 and 50 years of age. Of these 2340 are in Wilkes county, 600 in Chatham, and 424 in Liberty county.

Population, Character, Manners, &c.] No actual census of the inhabitants of this state has been taken since the war. Population, since the peace of 1783, has increased with a surprising rapidity. It is conjectured that emigrations from Europe, the northern states, but principally from the back parts of Virginia, and North and South Carolinas, have more than tripled the number of inhabitants in the last six years. From the most probable calculations there are, exclusive of Indians, upwards of 40,000 inhabitants in Georgia, of whom one third part at least are slaves.

In the grand convention at Philadelphia, in 1787, the inhabitants of this state were reckoned at 90,000, including three-fifths of 20,000 negroes. But from the number of the militia, which has been ascertained with a considerable degree of accuracy, there cannot be at most, more than half that number.

No general character will apply to the inhabitants at large. Collected from different parts of the world, as interest, necessity or inclination led them, their character and manners must of course partake of all the varieties which distinguish the several states and kingdoms from whence they came. There is so little uniformity, that it is difficult to trace any governing principles among them. An aversion to labour is too predominant, owing in part to the relaxing heat of the climate, and partly to the want of necessity to excite industry. An open and friendly hospitality, particu-
                                                                      larly

larly to ftrangers, is an ornamental characteriftic of a great part of this people.

Their diverfions are various. With fome, dancing is a favorite amufement. Others take a fancied pleafure at the gaming table, which, however, frequently terminates in the ruin of their happinefs, fortunes, and conftitutions. In the upper counties, horfe racing and cock fighting prevail, two cruel diverfions imported from Virginia, and the Carolinas, from whence thofe who practice them principally emigrated. But the moft rational and univerfal amufement is hunting, and for this Georgia is particularly well calculated, as the woods abound with plenty of deer, raccoons, rabits, wild turkies, and other game; at the fame time the woods are fo thin and free from obftructions, that you may generally ride half fpeed in the chace, without danger. In this amufement pleafure and profit are blended. The exercife, more than any other, contributes to health, and fits for activity in bufinefs, and expertnefs in war; the game alfo affords them a palatable food, and the fkins a profitable article of commerce.

Religion.] In regard to religion, politics and literature, this ftate is yet in its infancy. In Savannah is an Epifcopal church, a Prefbyterian church, a Synagogue, where the Jews pay their weekly worfhip, and a German Lutheran church, fupplied occafionally by a German minifter from Ebenezer, where there is a large convenient ftone church, and a fettlement of fober induftrious Germans of the Lutheran religion. In Augufta they have an Epifcopal church. In Midway is a fociety of Chriftians, eftablifhed on the congregational plan. Their meeting houfe was burnt by the Britifh, 1778; fince which they have erected a temporary one in its room. Their anceftors emigrated in a colony from Dorchefter, near Bofton, about the year 1700, and fettled at a place named Dorchefter, about 20 miles fouthweft of Charlefton, South Carolina. In 1752, for the fake of a better climate, and more land, almoft the whole fociety removed and fettled at Midway. With few interruptions, occafioned by the deaths of their minifters, and the late war, in which they greatly fuffered, they have had a preached gofpel conftantly among them. They, as a people, retain, in a great meafure, that fimplicity of manners, that unaffected piety and brotherly love, which characterized their anceftors, the firft fettlers of New England. The upper counties are fupplied, pretty generally, by Baptift and Methodift minifters. But the greater part of the ftate, is not fupplied by minifters of any denomination.

Conftitution.] The numerous defects in the prefent conftitution of this ftate, induced the citizens, pretty univerfally, to petition for a revifion of it. It was according revifed, or rather a new one was formed, in the courfe of the laft year, nearly upon the plan of the conftitution of the United States—but has not yet been adopted by the ftate.

The ftate of literature.] The literature of this ftate, which is yet in its infancy, is commencing on a plan which affords the moft flattering profpects. It feems to have been the defign of the legiflature of this ftate, as far as poffible, to unite their literary concerns, and provide for them in common, that the whole might feel the benefit, and no part be neglected or left a prey to party rage, private prejudices and contentions, and confequent ignorance, their infeparable attendant. For this purpofe, the literature of this ftate, like its policy, appears to be confidered as one object,

ject, and in the same manner subject to common and general regulations for the good of the whole. The charter containing their present system of education, was passed in the year 1785. A college, with ample and liberal endowments, is instituted in Louisville, a high and healthy part of the country, near the center of the state. There is also provision made for the institution of an academy, in each county in the state, to be supported from the same funds, and considered as parts and members of the same institution, under the general superintendence and direction of a president and board of trustees, appointed, for their literary accomplishments, from the different parts of the state, invested with the customary powers of corporations. The institution thus composed, is denominated 'The University of Georgia.'

That this body of literati, to whom is intrusted the direction of the general literature of the state, may not be so detached and independent, as not to possess the confidence of the state, and in order to secure the attention and patronage of the principal officers of government, the governor and council, the speaker of the house of assembly, and the chief justice of the state, are associated with the board of trustees, in some of the great and more solemn duties of their office, such as making the laws, appointing the president, settling the property, and instituting academies. Thus associated, they are denominated 'The Senate of the University,' and are to hold a stated, annual meeting, at which the governor of the state presides.

The senate appoint a board of commissioners in each county, for the particular management and direction of the academy, and the other schools in each county, who are to receive their instructions from, and are accountable to the senate. The rector of each academy is an officer of the university, to be appointed by the president, with the advice of the trustees, and commissioned under the public seal, and is to attend with the other officers at the annual meeting of the senate, to deliberate on the general interests of literature, and to determine on the course of instruction for the year, throughout the university. The president has the general charge and oversight of the whole, and is from time to time to visit them, to examine into their order and performances.

The funds for the support of their institution, are principally in lands, amounting in the whole to about fifty thousand acres, a great part of which is of the best quality, and at present very valuable. There are also nearly six thousand pounds sterling in bonds, houses and town lots in the town of Augusta. Other public property to the amount of £1000, in each county, has been set apart for the purposes of building and furnishing their respective academies. The funds originally designed for the support of the orphan house, are chiefly in rice plantations and negroes. As the countess of Huntingdon has not, since the revolution, expressed her intention concerning them, they lie at present in a very unproductive situation.

Islands.] The whole coast is bordered with islands, affording, with few interruptions, an inland navigation from the river Savannah to St. Mary's. The principal islands are Skidaway, Wassaw, Ossabaw, St. Catharines, Sapelo, Frederica, Jekyl, Cumberland and Amelia.

Indians.] The MUSKOGEE or CREEK Indians inhabit the middle parts of this state, and are the most numerous tribe of Indians of any within the

GEORGIA.   453

limits of the United States. Their whole number is 17,280, of which 5,860, are fighting men. Their principal towns lie in latitude 32° and longitude 11° 20' from Philadelphia. They are settled in a hilly but not mountainous country. The soil is fruitful in a high degree, and well watered, abounding in creeks and rivulets, from whence they are called the *Creek Indians.*

The SEMINOLAS, a division of the creek nation, inhabit a level, flat country on the Appalachicola and Flint rivers, fertile and well watered.

The CHACTAWS, or flat heads, inhabit a very fine and extensive tract of hilly country, with large and fertile plains intervening, between the Alabama and Mississippi rivers, in the western part of this state. This nation have 43 towns and villages, in three divisions, containing 12,123 souls, of which 4,041 are fighting men.

The CHICASAWS are settled on the head branches of the Tombeckbe, Mobile and Yazoo rivers, in the northwest corner of the state. Their country is an extensive plain, tolerably well watered from springs, and of a pretty good soil. They have 7 towns, the central one of which is in latitude 34° 23', and longitude 14° 30' west. The number of souls in this nation have been reckoned at 1725, of which 575 are fighting men.

History.] The settlement of a colony between the rivers Savannah and Alatamaha, was meditated in England in 1732, for the accommodation of poor people in Great Britain and Ireland, and for the further security of Carolina. Private compassion and public spirit conspired to promote the benevolent design.—Humane and opulent men suggested a plan of transporting a number of indigent families, to this part of America, free of expence. For this purpose they applied to the King, George the II. and obtained from him letters patent, bearing date June 9th, 1732, for legally carrying into execution what they had generously projected. They called the new province GEORGIA, in honor of the King, who encouraged the plan. A corporation, consisting of 21 persons, was constituted by the name of the Trustees, for settling and establishing the colony of Georgia; which was separated from Carolina by the river Savannah.—The Trustees having first set an example themselves, by largely contributing to the scheme, undertook also to solicit benefactions from others, and to apply the money towards clothing, arming, purchasing utensils for cultivation, and transporting such poor people as should consent to go over and begin a settlement. They did not confine their charitable views to the subjects of Britain alone, but wisely opened a door, for the indigent and oppressed protestants of other nations. To prevent a misapplication of the money, it was deposited in the bank of England.

About the middle of July 1732, the Trustees for Georgia, held their first meeting, and chose Lord Percival president of the corporation—and ordered a common seal to be made.——In November following, 116 settlers embarked for Georgia, to be conveyed thither free of expence, furnished with every thing requisite for building and for cultivating the soil. James Oglethorpe, one of the trustees, and an active promoter of the settlement, embarked as the head and director of these settlers. They arrived at Charlestown early in the next year, where they met a friendly reception from the governor and council. Mr. Oglethorpe, accompanied by William Bull, shortly after his arrival, visited Georgia, and after
reconnoitering

reconnoitring the country, marked the spot on which Savannah now stands, as the fittest to begin their settlement. Here they accordingly began and built a small fort; a number of small huts for their defence and accommodation.——Such of the settlers as were able to bear arms, were embodied, and well appointed with officers, arms and amunition.—— A treaty of friendship was concluded between the settlers and their neighbours and the Creek Indians, and every thing wore the aspect of peace and future prosperity.

In the mean time the trustees for Georgia had been employed in framing a plan of settlement, and establishing such public regulations as they judged most proper for answering the great end of the corporation. In this general plan they considered each inhabitant both as a planter and a soldier, who must be provided with arms and amunition for defence, as well as with tools and utensils for cultivation. As the strength of the province was their chief object in view, they agreed to establish such tenures for holding lands in it as they judged most favorable for a military establishment. Each tract of land granted was considered as a military fief, for which the possessor was to appear in arms, and take the field, when called upon for the public defence. To prevent large tracts from falling in process of time into one hand, they agreed to grant their lands in tail male in preference to tail general. On the termination of the estate in tail male, the lands were to revert to the trust; and such lands thus reverting were to be granted again to such persons, as the common council of the trust should judge most advantageous for the colony; only the trustees in such a case were to pay special regard to the daughters of such persons as had made improvements on their lots, especially when not already provided for by marriage. The wives of such persons as should survive them, were to be during their lives, entitled to the mansion-house, and one half of the lands improved by their husbands. No man was to be permitted to depart the province without licence. If any of the lands granted by the trustees, shall not be cultivated, cleared, and fenced round about with a worm fence, or pales, six feet high, within eighteen years from the date of the grant, such part was to revert to the trust, and the grant with respect to it to be void. All forfeitures for non-residence, high-treason, felonies, &c. were to the trustees for the use and benefit of the colony. The use of negroes was to be absolutely prohibited, and also the importation of rum. None of the colonists were to be permitted to trade with Indians, but such as should obtain a special licence for that purpose.

These were some of the fundamental regulations established by the trustees of Georgia, and perhaps the imagination of man could scarcely have framed a system of rules worse adapted to the circumstances and situation of the poor settlers, and of more pernicious consequence to the prosperity of the province. Yet, although the trustees were greatly mistaken, with respect to their plan of settlement, it must be acknowledged their views were generous. As the people sent out by them were the poor and unfortunate, who were to be provided with necessaries at their public store, they received their lands upon condition of cultivation, and by their personal residence, of defence. Silk and wine being the chief articles intended to be raised, they judged negroes were not requisite to these purposes.

poses. As the colony was designed to be a barrier to South Carolina, against the Spanish settlement at Augustine, they imagined that negroes would rather weaken than strengthen it, and that such poor colonists would run in debt, and ruin themselves by purchasing them. Rum was judged pernicious to health, and ruinous to the infant settlement. A free trade with Indians was considered as a thing that might have a tendency to involve the people in quarrels and troubles with the powerful savages, and expose them to danger and destruction. Such were probably the motives which induced those humane and generous persons to impose such foolish and ridiculous restrictions on their colony. For by granting their small estates in tail male, they drove the settlers from Georgia, who soon found that abundance of lands could be obtained in America upon a larger scale, and on much better terms. By the prohibition of negroes, they rendered it impracticable in such a climate to make any impression on the thick forests, Europeans being utterly unqualified for the heavy task. By their discharging a trade with the West Indies, they not only deprived the colonists of an excellent and convenient market for their lumber, of which they had abundance on their lands, but also of rum, which, when mixed with a sufficient quantity of water, has been found in experience the cheapest, the most refreshing, and nourishing drink for workmen in such a foggy and burning climate. The trustees, like other distant legislators, who framed their regulations upon principles of speculation, were liable to many errors and mistakes, and however good their design, their rules were found improper and impracticable. The Carolinians plainly perceived that they would prove insurmountable obstacles to the progress and prosperity of the colony, and therefore from motives of pity began to invite the poor Georgians to come over Savannah river, and settle in Carolina, being convinced that they could never succeed under such impolitic and oppressive restrictions.

Besides the large sums of money which the trustees had expended for the settlement of Georgia, the parliament had also granted during the two last years £. 36,000 towards carrying into execution the humane purpose of the corporation. But after the representation and memorial from the legislature of Carolina reached Britain, the nation considered Georgia to be of the utmost importance to the British settlements in America, and began to make still more vigorous efforts for its speedy population. The first embarkations of poor people from England, being collected from towns and cities, were found equally idle and useless members of society abroad, as they had been at home. An hardy and bold race of men, inured to rural labour and fatigue, they were persuaded would be much better adapted both for cultivation and defence. To find men possessed of these qualifications, they turned their eyes to Germany and the Highlands of Scotland, and resolved to send over a number of Scotch and German labourers to their infant province. When they published their terms at Inverness, an hundred and thirty Highlanders immediately accepted them, and were transported to Georgia. A township on the river Alatamaha, which was considered as the boundary between the British and Spanish territories, was allotted for the Highlanders, on which dangerous situation they settled, and built a town, which they called New Inverness. About the same time an hundred and seventy Germans embarked with James Oglethorpe,

and

and were fixed in another quarter; fo that, in the fpace of three years, Georgia received above four hundred Britifh fubjects, and about an hundred and feventy foreigners. Afterwards feveral adventurers, both from Scotland and Germany, followed their countrymen, and added further ftrength to the province, and the truftees flattered themfelves with the hopes of foon feeing it in a promifing condition.

Their hopes, however, were vain. Their injudicious regulations and reftrictions——the wars in which they were involved with the Spaniards and Indians—and the frequent infurrections among themfelves, threw the colony into a ftate of confufion and wretchednefs too great for human nature long to endure. Their oppreffed fituation was reprefented to the truftees by repeated complaints; till at length, finding that the province languifhed under their care, and weary with the complaints of the people, they, in the year 1752, furrendered their charter to the king, and it was made a royal government. In confequence of which, his majefty appointed John Reynolds, an officer of the navy, governor of the province, and a legiflature, fimilar to that of the other royal governments in America, was eftablifhed in it. Great had been the expence which the mother country had already incurred, befides private benefactions, for fupporting this colony; and fmall had been the returns yet made by it. The veftiges of cultivation were fcarcely perceptible in the forefts, and in England all commerce with it was neglected and defpifed. At this time the whole annual exports of Georgia did not amount to £. 10.000 fterling. Though the people were now favored with the fame liberties and privileges enjoyed by their neighbours under the royal care, yet feveral years more elapfed before the value of the lands in Georgia was known, and that fpirit of induftry broke out in it, which afterwards diffufed its happy influence over the country.

In the year 1740, the rev. George Whitefield founded an orphan houfe academy in Georgia, about 12 miles from Savannah.—For the fupport of this, in his itenerations, he collected large fums of money of all denominations of chriftians, both in England and America. A part of this money was expended in erecting proper buildings to accommodate the ftudents, and a part in fupporting them. In 1768, it was propofed that the orphan houfe fhould be erected into a college. Whereupon Mr. Whitefield applied to the crown for a charter, which would have been readily granted, on condition that the prefident fhould, in all fucceffions, be an Epifcopalian, of the Church of England. Several letters paffed between the archbifhop of Canterbury and Mr. Whitefield on the fubject, in which the archbifhop infifted on this condition. But Mr. Whitefield, though himfelf an Epifcopalian, declined it, alledging to his grace, that it would be unjuft to limit that office to any particular fect, when the donations for the foundation of the inftitution had been made and intrufted to him by the various religious denominations, both in England and America. In confequence of this difpute, the affair of a charter was given up, and Mr. Whitefield made his affignment of the orphan houfe in truft to the countefs of Huntington. Mr. Whitefield died at Newbury Port, in New England, in October, 1770, in the 56th year of his age, and was buried under the Prefbyterian church in that place.

Soon

Soon after his death a charter was granted to his institution in Georgia, and the rev. Mr. Percy was appointed president of the college. Mr. Percy accordingly came over to execute his office, but unfortunately, on the 30th of May, 1775, the orphan house building caught fire, and was entirely consumed, except the two wings, which are still remaining. The American war soon after came on, and put every thing into confusion, and the funds have ever since lain in an unproductive state. It is probable that the college estate, by the consent of the countess of Huntington, may hereafter be so incorporated with the university of Georgia, as to subserve the original and pious purposes of its founder.

From the time Georgia became a royal government, in 1752, till the peace of Paris, in 1763, she struggled under many difficulties, arising from the want of credit, from friends, and the frequent molestations of enemies. The good effects of the peace were sensibly felt in the province of Georgia. From this time it began to flourish, under the fatherly care of governor Wright. To form a judgment of the rapid growth of the colony, we need only attend to its exports.

In the year 1763, the exports of Georgia consisted of 7,500 barrels of rice, 9,633 pounds of indigo, 1,250 bushels of Indian corn, which, together with deer and beaver skins, naval stores, provisions, timber, &c. amounted to no more than £27,021 sterling. Ten years afterwards, in 1773, it exported commodities to the value of £121,677 sterling.

During the late war, Georgia was over-run by the British troops, and the inhabitants were obliged to flee into the neighbouring states for safety. The sufferings and losses of her citizens, were as great, in proportion to their numbers and wealth, as in any of the states. Since the peace, the progress of the population of this state has been astonishingly rapid. Its growth in improvement and population, has been checked by the hostile irruptions of the Creek Indians, which have been frequent, and very distressing to the frontier inhabitants for these two years past. This formidable nation of Indians, headed by one Mac Gilvery, an inhabitant of Georgia, who sided with the British in the late war, still continue to harrass the frontiers of this state. Treaties have been held, and a cessation of hostilities agreed to between the parties; but all have hitherto proved ineffectual to the accomplishment of a peace. It is expected that, under the new government, conciliatory measures will be adopted, and tranquillity restored to the state.

The WESTERN TERRITORY.

UNDER this name is comprehended all that part of the United States which lies northwest of the Ohio. Bounded west, by the Mississippi river; north, by the Lakes; east, by Pennsylvania; southeast and south, by the Ohio river. Containing, according to Mr. Hutchins, 411,000 square miles, equal to 263,040,000 acres—from which, if we deduct

deduct 43,040,000 acres for water, there will remain 220,600,000 of acres, belonging to the federal government, to be sold for the discharge of the national debt; except a narrow strip of land, bordering on the south of Lake Erie, and stretching 120 miles west of the western limit of Pennsylvania, which belongs to Connecticut.

But a small proportion of these lands is yet purchased of the natives, and to be disposed of by congress. Beginning on the meridian line, which forms the western boundary of Pennsylvania, seven ranges of townships have been surveyed and laid off by order of congress. As a north and south line strikes the Ohio in an oblique direction, the termination of the 7th range falls upon that river, 9 miles above the Muskingum, which is the first large river that falls into the Ohio. It forms this junction 172 miles below Fort Pitt, including the windings of the Ohio, though in a direct line it is but 90 miles.

The lands in which the Indian title is extinguished, and which are now purchasing under the United States, are bounded by Pennsylvania on the east, by the Great Miami on the west, by the Ohio on the south, and extend nearly to the head waters of the Muskingum and Sioto on the north. On these lands two settlements are commencing, one at Marietta,* at the mouth of Muskingum, under the direction of the Ohio company. This settlement consists at present, of about 220 souls, and is almost daily increasing. The other between the Miami rivers, under the direction of Colonel Symmes, which, though very small at present, is in prospect of a rapid enlargement. There are several other tracts, delineated on the map, which have been granted by congress to particular companies, and other tracts for particular uses, which remain without any English settlements.

Rivers.] The *Muskingum* is a gentle river, confined by banks so high as to prevent its overflowing. It is 250 yards wide at its confluence with the Ohio, and navigable by large batteaux and barges to the Three Legs; and, by small ones, to the lake at its head. From thence, by a portage of about one mile, a communication is opened to Lake Erie, through the Cayahoga, which is a stream of great utility, navigable the whole length, without any obstruction from falls. From Lake Erie, the avenue is well known to the Hudson in the state of New York.

The *Hockhocking* resembles the Muskingum, though somewhat inferior in size. It is navigable for large boats about 70 miles, and for small ones much farther. On the banks of this very useful stream are found inexhaustible quarries of free-stone, large beds of iron ore, and some rich mines of lead. Coal mines and salt springs are frequent in the neighbourhood of this stream, as they are in every part of the western territory. The salt that may be obtained from those springs will afford an inexhaustible store of that necessary article. Beds of white and blue clay, of an excellent quality, are likewise found here, suitable for the manufacture of glass, crockery and other earthen wares. Red bole and many other useful fossils have been observed on the branches of this river.

The *Sioto* is a larger river than either of the preceding, and opens a more extensive navigation. It is passable for large barges for 200 miles,

with

* *This place was first called* Adelphi, *and is so called in the map.*

The WESTERN TERRITORY.

with a portage of only 4 miles to the Sandusky, a good navigable stream that falls into the Lake Erie. Through the Sandusky and Sioto lies the most common pass from Canada to the Ohio and Missisippi; one of the most extensive and useful communications that are to be found in any country. Prodigious extensions of territory are here connected; and, from the rapidity with which the western parts of Canada, Lake Erie and the Kentucky countries are settling, we may anticipate an immense intercourse between them. The lands on the borders of these middle streams, from this circumstance alone, aside from their natural fertility, must be rendered vastly valuable. There is no doubt, but flour, corn, flax, hemp, &c. raised for exportation in that great country between the Lakes Huron and Ontario, will find an easier outlet through Lake Erie and these rivers, than in any other direction. The Ohio merchant can give a higher price than those of Quebec, for these commodities; as they may be transported from the former to Florida and the West India islands, with less expence, risk and insurance, than from the latter; while the expence from the place of growth to the Ohio will not be one fourth of what it would be to Quebec, and much less than even to the Oneyda lake. The stream of Sioto is gentle, no where broken by falls: At some places, in the spring of the year, it overflows its banks, providing for large natural rice plantations. Salt springs, coal mines, white and blue clay, and free-stone, abound in the country adjoining this river.

The *Little Miami* is too small for batteaux navigation. Its bank are good land, and so high as to prevent, in common, the overflowing of the water.

The *Great Miami* has a very stoney channel, and a swift stream, but no falls. It is formed of several large branches, which are passable for boats a great distance. One branch comes from the west, and rises in the Wabash country: Another rises near the head waters of Miami river, which runs into Lake Erie; and a short portage divides another branch, from the west branch of Sandusky river.

The *Wabash* is a beautiful river, with high and fertile banks. It empties into the Ohio, by a mouth 270 yards wide, 1020 miles below Fort Pitt. In the spring, summer and autumn, it is passable with batteaux, drawing three feet water, 412 miles, to Ouitanon, a small French settlement, on the west side of the river; and for large canoes 197 miles further, to the Miami carrying place, 9 miles from Miami village. This village stands on Miami river, which empties into the southwest part of Lake Erie. The communication between Detroit, and the Illinois, and Ohio countries is, down Miami river to Miami village, thence, by land, 9 miles when the rivers are high—and from 18 to 30 when they are low, through a level country, to the Wabash, and through the various branches of the Wabash to the places of destination.

A silver mine has been discovered about 28 miles above Ouiatanon, on the northern side of the Wabash. Salt springs, lime, free-stone, blue, yellow and white clay are found in plenty upon this river.

The rivers *A Vase* and *Kaskaskias* empty into the Missisippi from the northeast; the former is navigable for boats 60, and the latter about 130 miles. They both run through a rich country, which has extensive meadows.

Between

Between the Kaskaskias and Illinois rivers, which are 84 miles apart, is an extensive tract of level, rich land, which terminates in a high ridge, about 15 miles before you reach the Illinois river. In this delightful vale are a number of French villages, which, together with those of St. Genevieve and St. Louis, on the western side of the Missisippi, contained in 1771, 1,273 fencible men.

One hundred and seventy-six miles above the Ohio, and 18 miles above the Missouri, the Illinois empties into the Missisippi from the northeast by a mouth about 400 yards wide. This river is bordered with fine meadows, which in some places extend as far as the eye can reach: This river furnishes a communication with Lake Michigan, by the Chicago river, between which and the Illinois, are two portages, the longest of which does not exceed 4 miles. It receives a number of rivers which are from 20 to 100 yards wide and navigable for boats from 15 to 180 miles. On the northwestern side of this river is a coal mine, which extends for half a mile along the middle of the bank of the river. On the eastern side, about half a mile from the river, and about the same distance below the coal mine, are two salt ponds, 100 yards in circumference, and several feet in depth. The water is stagnant, and of a yellowish colour; but the French and natives make good salt from it. The soil of the Illinois country is, in general, of a superior quality—its natural growth are oak, hiccory, cedar, mulberry, &c. hops, dying drugs, medicinal plants of several kinds, and excellent wild grapes. In the year 1769, the French settlers made 110 hogsheads of strong wine from these grapes.

There are many other rivers of equal size and importance with those we have been describing, which are not sufficiently known for accurate descriptions.

Population.] It is impossible to tell the exact population of this country. Mr. Hutchins, the geographer of the United States, who is the best acquainted with the country, estimates them at about 6000 souls, exclusive of Indians. This number is made up of French, English emigrants from the original states, and negroes.

Face of the country, soil and productions.] To the remarks on these heads, interspersed in the description of the rivers, we will add some observations from an anonymous pamphlet, lately published, which we presume are the most authentic, respecting that part of the country which has been purchased of the Indians, of any that have been given.

' The undistinguished terms of admiration, that are commonly used in speaking of the natural fertility of the country on the western waters of the United States, would render it difficult, without accurate attention in the surveys, to ascribe a preference to any particular part; or to give a just description of the territory under consideration, without the hazard of being suspected of exaggeration: But in *this* we have the united opinion of the geographer, the surveyors, and every traveller that has been intimately acquainted with the country, and marked every natural object with the most scrupulous exactness—That no part of the federal territory unites so many advantages, in point of health, fertility, variety of production, and foreign intercourse, as that tract which stretches from the Muskingum to the Sioto and the Great Miami rivers.

Colonel Gordon, in his journal, speaking of a much larger range of country, in which this is included, and makes unquestionably the finest

part,

part, has the following obfervation:—" The country on the Ohio is every where pleafant, with large level fpots of rich land; and remarkably healthy. One general remark of this nature will ferve for the whole tract of the globe comprehended between the weftern fkirts of the Allegany mountains; thence running fouthweftwardly to the diftance of 500 miles to the Ohio falls; then croffing them northerly to the heads of the rivers that empty themfelves into the Ohio; thence eaft along the ridge that feparates the lakes and Ohio's ftreams, to French creek—This country may, from a proper knowledge, be affirmed to be the moft healthy, the moft pleafant, the moft commodious and moft fertile fpot of earth, known to the European people."

' The lands that feed the various ftreams abovementioned, which fall into the Ohio, are now more accurately known, and may be defcribed with confidence and precifion. They are interfperfed with all the variety of foil which conduces to pleafantnefs of fituation, and lays the foundation for the wealth of an agricultural and manufacturing people. Large level bottoms, or natural meadows, from 20 to 50 miles in circuit, are every where found bordering the rivers, and variegating the country in the interior parts. Thefe afford as rich a foil as can be imagined, and may be reduced to proper cultivation with very little labour. It is faid, that in many of thefe bottoms a man may clear an acre a day, fit for planting with Indian corn; there being no under wood; and the trees, growing very high and large, but not thick together, need nothing but girdling.

' The prevailing growth of timber and the more ufeful trees are, maple or fugar tree, fycamore, black and white mulberry, black and white walnut, butternut, chefnut, white, black, Spanifh and chefnut oaks, hickory, cherry, buckwood, honey locuft, elm, horfe chefnut, cucumber tree, lynn tree, gum tree, iron wood, afh, afpin, faffafras, crab apple tree, pawpaw or cuftard apple, a variety of plumb trees, nine bark fpice, and leather wood bufhes. General Parfons meafured a black walnut tree near the Mufkingum, whofe circumference, at 5 feet from the ground, was 22 feet. A fycamore, near the fame place, meafures 44 feet in circumference, at fome diftance from the ground. White and black oak, and chefnut, with moft of the abovementioned timbers, grow large and plenty upon the high grounds. Both the high and low lands produce vaft quantities of natural grapes of various kinds, of which the fettlers univerfally make a fufficiency for their own confumption of rich red wine. It is afferted in the old fettlement of St. Vincent's, where they have had opportunity to try it, that age will render this wine preferable to moft of the European wines. Cotton is the natural production of this country, and grows in great perfection.

' The fugar maple is a moft valuable tree for an inland country. Any number of inhabitants may be forever fupplied with a fufficiency of fugar, by preferving a few trees for the ufe of each family. A tree will yield about ten pounds of fugar a year, and the labour is very trifling: The fap is extracted in the months of February and March, and granulated, by the fimple operation of boiling, to a fugar equal in flavour and whitenefs to the beft Mufcovado.

' Springs of excellent water abound in every part of this territory; and fmall and large ftreams, for mills and other purpofes, are actually interfperfed terspersed, as if by art, that there be no deficiency in any of the conveniencies of life.

'Very little waste land is to be found in any part of this tract of country. There are no swamps; and though the hills are frequent, they are gentle and swelling, no where high nor incapable of tillage. They are of a deep, rich soil, covered with a heavy growth of timber, and well adapted to the production of wheat, rye, indigo, tobacco, &c.

'The communications between this country and the sea will be principally in the four following directions.

'1. The rout through the Sioto and Muskingum to Lake Erie, and so to the river Hudson; which has been already described.

'2. The passage up the Ohio and Monongahela to the portage abovementioned, which leads to the navigable waters of the Powtomac. This portage is 30 miles, and will probably be rendered much less by the execution of the plans now on foot for opening the navigation of those waters.

'3. The Great Kanhaway, which falls into the Ohio from the Virginia shore, between the Hockhocking and the Sioto, opens an extensive navigation from the south east, and leaves but 18 miles portage from the navigable waters of James river, in Virginia. This communication, for the country between Muskingum and Sioto, will probably be more used than any other, for the exportation of manufactures, and other light and valuable articles; and, especially, for the importation of foreign commodities, which may be brought from the Chesapeek to the Ohio much cheaper than they are now carried from Philadelphia to Carlisle and the other thick settled back counties of Pennsylvania.

'4. But the current down the Ohio and the Mississippi, for heavy articles that suit the Florida, and West India markets, such as corn, flour, beef, lumber, &c. will be more frequently loaded than any streams on earth. The distance from the Sioto to the Mississippi is 800 miles; from thence to the sea is 900. This whole course is easily run in 15 days; and the passage up those rivers is not so difficult as has usually been represented. It is found, by late experiments, that sails are used to great advantage against the current of the Ohio: And it is worthy of observation, that in all probability steam boats will be found to do infinite service in all our extensive river navigation.

'As far as observations in passing the rivers, and the transitory remarks of travellers, will justify an opinion, the lands farther down, and in other parts of the unappropriated country, are not equal, in point of soil and other local advantages, to the tract which is here described. This, however, cannot be accurately determined, as the present situation of these countries will not admit of that minute inspection which has been bestowed on the one under consideration.

'It is a happy circumstance, that the *Ohio Company* are about to commence the settlement of this country in so regular and judicious a manner. It will serve as a wise model for the future settlement of all the federal lands; at the same time that, by beginning so near the western limit of Pennsylvania, it will be a continuation of the old settlements, leaving vacant no lands exposed to be seized by such lawless banditti as usually infest the frontiers of countries distant from the seat of government.

'The

The design of Congress and of the settlers is, that the settlements shall proceed regularly down the Ohio; and northward to Lake Erie. And it is probable that not many years will elapse, before the whole country above Miami will be brought to that degree of cultivation, which will exhibit all its latent beauties, and justify those descriptions of travellers which have so often made it the garden of the world, the seat of wealth, and the centre of a great empire.'

Animals, &c.] ' No country is better stocked with wild game of every kind: Innumerable herds of deer, elk, buffalo, and bear, are sheltered in the groves, and fed in the extensive bottoms that every where abound; an unquestionable proof of the great fertility of the soil: Turkies, geese, ducks, swans, teal, pheasants, patridges, &c. are, from observation, believed to be in greater plenty here, than the tame poultry are in any part of the old settlements in America.

' The rivers are well stored with fish of various kinds, and many of them of an excellent quality. They are generally large, though of different sizes: The cat fish, which is the largest, and of a delicious flavour, weighs from 30 to 80 pounds.'

Antiquities and Curiosities.] The number of old forts found in the Kentucky country are the admiration of the curious, and a matter of much speculation. They are mostly of a circular form, situated on strong, well chosen ground, and contiguous to water. When, by whom, and for what purpose, these were thrown up, is uncertain. They are certainly very ancient, as there is not the least visible difference in the age or size of the timber growing on or within these forts, and that which grows without; and the oldest natives have lost all tradition respecting them. They must have been the efforts of a people much more devoted to labour than our present race of Indians; and it is difficult to conceive how they could be constructed without the use of iron tools. At a convenient distance from these always stands a small mount of earth, thrown up in the form of a pyramid, and seems in some measure proportioned to the size of its adjacent fortification. On examination, they have been found to contain a chalky substance, supposed to be bones, and of the human kind.

On an extensive plain, or, as the French term it *parara*,* between Post St. Vincent and Cuscusco river, is what is called the *Battle Ground*, where the Siack and Cuscusco Indians fought a desperate battle, in which about 800 were killed on each side. On this spot, the ground for two miles, is covered with skulls and other human bones.

Forts.] The stations occupied by the troops of the United States on the frontiers, are the following.

FORT FRANKLIN—On French creek, near to the post formerly called Venango, is a small strong fort with one cannon, was erected in 1787, and garrisoned

---

* *A* parara, *which answers to what in the southern states is called a savannah, is an extensive, rich plain without trees, and covered with grass. Some of these pararas, between Post St. Vincent and the Mississippi are 30 or 40 miles broad, and several hundred miles in length. In passing them, as far as the eye can reach there is not a tree to be seen; but there is plenty of buffaloes, deer, elks, bears, and wolves, and innumerable flocks of turkies; these, with the green grass, form a rich and beautiful prospect.*

garrisoned with one company. The excellent construction and execution of this work reflects honor on the abilities and industry of Captain Hart, who garrisons it with his company, and who was his own engineer.

This post was established for the purpose of defending the frontiers of Pennsylvania, which are much exposed by the facility with which the Indians can cross from Lake Erie, either to French creek or the Jadagghue Lake and the Conneawango branch, and thence descend the rapid river Allegany.

FORT PITT—Has only an officer, and a few men to receive the supplies and dispatches forwarded to the troops by the Secretary at War.

FORT M'INTOSH—Is ordered to be demolished and a block-house to be erected in lieu thereof, a few miles up the Big Beaver creek to protect the communication up the same, and also to cover the country.

FORT HARMAR—At the mouth of Muskingum, is a well constructed fort, with five bastions, and three cannons mounted.

It is at present garrisoned with four companies and is considered as head quarters, being conveniently situated to reinforce any of the posts either up or down the river Ohio.

FORT STEUBEN—At the rapids of the Ohio, on the west side is a well constructed small fort, with one cannon, and is garrisoned with a major and two companies. This post is established to cover the country from the incursions of the Indians, and it also serves as a post of communication to Post Vincennes on the Wabash.

POST VINCENNES—On the Wabash, is a work erected during the year 1787, and has four small brass cannon. It is garrisoned by a major and two companies.

It is established to curb the incursions of the Wabash Indians into Kentucky country, and to prevent the usurpation of the federal lands, the fertility of which have been too strong a temptation to the lawless people of the frontiers, who posted themselves there in force in the year 1786. Brigadier-General Harmar, by orders of Congress, formed an expedition in August, 1787, for the purpose of dispossessing them; but previous to his arrival, most of the intruders had abandoned their settlement.

Government, &c.] By an ordinance of congress, passed on the 13th of July 1787, this country, for the purposes of temporary government, was erected into one district, subject, however, to a division, when circumstances shall make it expedient.

In the same ordinance it is provided, that congress shall appoint a governor, whose commission shall continue in force three years, unless sooner revoked.

The governor must reside in the district, and have a freehold estate therein, in 1000 acres of land, while in the exercise of his office.

Congress, from time to time, are to appoint a secretary, to continue in office four years, unless sooner removed, who must reside in the district, and have an estate of 500 acres of land, while in office.

The business of the secretary is, to keep and preserve the acts and laws of the legislature, and the public records of the district, and the proceedings of the governor, in his executive department; and to transmit authentic copies of such acts and proceedings, every six months, to the secretary of Congress.

The

The ordinance provides that Congress shall appoint three judges, possessed each of 500 acres of land in the district in which they are to reside, and to hold their commissions during good behaviour, any two of whom, shall form a court, who shall have a common law jurisdiction. The governor and judges are authorized to adopt and publish in the district, such laws of the original states, criminal and civil, as may be necessary and best suited to the circumstances of the district, and report them to Congress, and if approved they shall continue in force, till the organization of the general assembly of the district, who shall have authority to alter them. The governor is to command the militia, and appoint and commission their officers, except general officers, who are to be appointed and commissioned by Congress.

Previous to the organization of the assembly, the governor is to appoint such magistrates and civil officers, as shall be deemed necessary for the preservation of peace and order.

So soon as there shall be 5000 free male inhabitants of full age, in the district, they shall receive authority to elect representatives, one for every 500 free male inhabitants, to represent them in the general assembly ; the representation to encrease progressively with the number of free male inhabitants, till there be 25 representatives; after which the number and proportion of the representatives shall be regulated by the legislature. A representative must possess, in fee simple, 200 acres of land, and be a resident in the district—and must have been a citizen of the United States, or a resident in the district, three years preceding his election. An elector must have 50 acres of land in the district—must have been a citizen of one of the states—and must be a resident in the district—or must possess the same freehold—and have been two years a resident in the district. The representatives, when duly elected, are to continue in office two years.

The general assembly, or legislature, shall consist of the governor, legislative council, and house of representatives. The legislative council shall consist of five members, to continue in office five years, unless sooner removed by Congress. Three make a quorum.—The council are to be thus appointed : The governor and representatives, when met, shall nominate ten persons, residents in the district, and each possessed of a freehold in 500 acres of land, and return their names to Congress, who shall appoint and commission five of them to serve as aforesaid.

All bills passed by a majority in the house, and in the council, shall be referred to the governor for his assent; but no bill or legislative act whatever, shall be of force without his assent. The governor shall have power to convene, prorogue, and dissolve the general assembly, when, in his opinion, it shall be expedient.

The legislature, when organized, shall have authority, by joint ballot, to elect a delegate to Congress, who shall have a seat in Congress, with a right of debating, but not of voting, during this temporary government.

' And for extending the fundamental principles of civil and religious liberty, which form the basis whereon these republics, their laws and constitutions, are erected ; to fix and establish those principles as the basis of all laws, constitutions and governments, which forever hereafter shall be formed

formed in the said territory; to provide also for the establishment of states, and permanent government therein, and for their admission to share in the federal councils on an equal footing with the original states, at as early periods as may be consistent with the general interest:

'It is hereby ordained and declared by the authority aforesaid, That the following articles shall be considered as articles of compact, between the original states and the people, and states in the said territory, and forever remain unalterable, unless by common consent, to wit:

'Article 1st. No person demeaning himself in a peaceable and orderly manner shall ever be molested on account of his mode of worship or religious sentiments in the said territory.

'Article 2d. The inhabitants of the said territory shall always be entitled to the benefits of the writ of habeas corpus, and of the trial by jury, of a proportionate representation of the people in the legislature, and of judicial proceedings according to the course of the common law: all persons shall be bailable unless for capital offences, where the proof shall be evident, or the presumption great: all fines shall be moderate, and no cruel or unusual punishment shall be inflicted; no man shall be deprived of his liberty or property but by the judgment of his peers, or of the law of the land; and should the public exigencies make it necessary for the common preservation to take any person's property, or to demand his particular services, full compensation shall be made for the same; and in the just preservation of the rights and property it is understood and declared, that no law ought ever to be made, or have force in the said territory, that shall in any manner whatever interfere with, or affect private contracts or engagements *bona fide* and without fraud previously formed.

'Article 3d. Religion, morality and knowledge, being necessary to good government and the happiness of mankind, schools and the means of education shall forever be encouraged, the utmost good faith shall always be observed towards the Indians; their lands and property shall never be taken from them without their consent; and in their property, rights and liberty, they shall never be invaded or disturbed, unless in just and lawful wars authorised by Congress; but laws founded in justice and humanity shall from time to time be made, for preventing wrongs being done to them, and for preserving peace and friendship with them.

Article 4th. The said territory, and the states which may be formed therein, shall forever remain a part of this confederacy of the United States of America, subject to the articles of confederation, and to such alterations therein as shall be constitutionally made; and to all the acts and ordinances of the United States, in Congress assembled, conformable thereto. The inhabitants and settlers in the said territory, shall be subject to pay a part of the federal debts contracted, or to be contracted, and a proportionable part of the expences of government to be apportioned on them by Congress, according to the same common rule and measure, by which apportionments thereof shall be made on the other states, and the taxes for paying their proportion, shall be laid and levied by the authority and direction of the legislatures of the district or districts, or new states, as in the original states, within the time agreed upon by the United Sates, in Congress assembled. The legislatures of those districts, or new states, shall never interfere with the primary disposal of the soil, by the United States,

States in Congress assembled, nor with any regulations Congress may find necessary for securing the title in such soil to the *bona fide* purchasers. No tax shall be imposed on lands the property of the United States; and in no case shall non-resident proprietors be taxed higher than residents. The navigable waters leading into the Mississippi and St. Lawrence, and the carrying places between the same shall be common highways, and forever free, as well to the inhabitants of the said territory, as to the citizens of the United States, and those of any other states that may be admitted into the confederacy, without any tax, impost, or duty therefor.

' Article 5th. There shall be formed in the said territory, not less than three, nor more than five states; and the boundaries of the states, as soon as Virginia shall alter her act of cession and consent to the same, shall become fixed and established as follows, to wit: The western state in the said territory, shall be bounded on the Mississippi, the Ohio, and Wabash rivers; a direct line drawn from the Wabash and Post Vincent's due north to the territorial line, between the United States and Canada, and by the said territorial line to the Lake of the Woods and Mississippi. The middle state shall be bounded by the said direct line, the Wabash from Post Vincent's to the Ohio; by the Ohio, by a direct line drawn due north from the mouth of the Great Miami to the said territorial line, and by the said territorial line. The eastern state shall be bounded by the last mentioned direct line, the Ohio, Pennsylvania, and the said territorial line: Provided however, and it is further understood and declared, that the boundaries of these three states, shall be subject so far to be altered, that if Congress hereafter shall find it expedient, they shall have authority to form one, or two states in that part of the said territory which lies north of an east and west line drawn through the southerly bend or extreme of Lake Michigan: and when any of the said states shall have 60,000 free inhabitants therein, such state shall be admitted by its delegates into the Congress of the United States, on an equal footing with the original states in all respects whatever; and shall be at liberty to form a permanent constitution and state government: Provided the constitution and government so to be formed, shall be republican, and in conformity to the principles contained in these articles, and so far as it can be consistent with the general interest of the confederacy, such admission shall be allowed at an earlier period, and when there may be a less number of free inhabitants in the state than 60,000.

Article 6th. There shall be neither slavery nor involuntary servitude in the said territory, otherwise than in the punishment of crimes, whereof the party shall have been duly convicted: Provided always, that any person escaping into the same, from whom labour or service is lawfully claimed in any one of the original states, such fugitive may be lawfully reclaimed and conveyed to the person claiming his or her labour or service as aforesaid.'

Such is the present government of the Western Territory, and such the political obligations of the adventurers into this fertile and delightful part of the United States.

' * In the ordinance of Congress, for the government of this territory, it is provided, that, after the said territory acquires a certain degree of population

---

* *From the anonymous pamphlet before quoted.*

population, it shall be divided into states. The eastern state, that is thus provided to be made, is bounded on the Great Miami on the west, and by the Pennsylvania line on the east. The centre of this state will fall between the Sioto and the Hockhocking. At the mouth of one of these rivers will probably be the seat of government for this state: And, if we may indulge the sublime contemplation of beholding the whole territory of the United States settled by an enlightened people, and continued under one extended government—on the river Ohio, and not far from this spot, will be the seat of empire for the whole dominion. This is central to the whole; it will best accommodate every part; it is the most pleasant, and probably the most healthful.'

In this connection we must not omit to add, that a settlement is commencing, with advantageous prospects, on the western side of the Missisippi, opposite the mouth of the Ohio. The spot on which the city is to be built, is called New Madrid, after the capital of Spain. This settlement, which is without the limits of the United States, in the Spanish dominions, is conducting by Colonel Morgan, under the patronage of the Spanish king.

The settlers are to form their own constitution, make their own laws, (provided they do not counteract the laws of Spain) choose their own magistrates and civil officers, and are to enjoy free toleration in religion. They are, however, to be subjects of the king of Spain. As an encouragement to settlers, they are to be indulged with some peculiar commercial privileges.

New Madrid, from its local situation and adventitious privileges, is in prospect of being the great emporium of the western country, unless the free navigation of the Missisippi should be opened to the United States. And even should this desired event take place, which probably will not without a rupture with Spain, this must be a place of great trade. For here will naturally center, the immense quantities of produce that will be borne down the Illinois, the Missisippi, the Ohio, and their various branches; and if the carriers can find as good a market for their cargoes here, as at New Orleans or the West Indies, and can procure the articles they desire, they will gladly save themselves the difficulties and dangers of navigating the long Missisippi.

It has been supposed by some that all settlers who go beyond the Missisippi, will be forever lost to the United States. There is, I believe little danger of this, provided they are not provoked to withdraw their friendship. The emigrants will be made up of citizens of the United States. They will carry along with them their manners and customs, their habits of government, religion and education; and as they are to be indulged with religious freedom, and with the privilege of making their own laws, and of conducting education upon their own plans, these *American* habits will undoubtedly be cherished. If so, they will be Americans in fact, though nominally the subjects of Spain.

It is true Spain will draw a revenue from them, but in return they will enjoy peculiar commercial advantages, the benefit of which will be experienced by the United States, and perhaps be an ample compensation for the loss of so many citizens as may migrate thither. In short, this settlement, if conducted with judgment and prudence, may be mutually serviceable

both

VERMONT.

both to Spain and the United States. It may prevent jealousies—lessen national prejudices—promote religious toleration, preserve harmony, and be a medium of trade reciprocally advantageous.

Besides, it is well known that empire has been travelling from east to west. Probably her last and broadest seat will be America. Here the sciences and the arts of civilized life are to receive their highest improvement. Here civil and religious liberty are to flourish, unchecked by the cruel hand of civil or ecclesiastical tyranny. Here Genius, aided by all the improvements of former ages, is to be exerted in humanizing mankind—in expanding and inriching their minds with religious and philosophical knowledge, and in planning and executing a form of government, which shall involve all the excellencies of former governments, with as few of their defects as is consistent with the imperfection of human affairs, and which shall be calculated to protect and unite, in a manner consistent with the natural rights of mankind, the largest empire that ever existed. Elevated with these prospects, which are not merely the visions of fancy, we cannot but anticipate the period, as not far distant, when the AMERICAN EMPIRE will comprehend millions of souls, west of the Mississippi. Judging upon probable grounds, the Mississippi was never designed as the western boundary of the American empire. The God of nature never intended that some of the best part of his earth should be inhabited by the subjects of a monarch, 4000 miles from them. And may we not venture to predict, that, when the rights of mankind shall be more fully known, and the knowledge of them is fast increasing both in Europe and America, the power of European potentates will be confined to Europe, and their present American dominions, become, like the United States, free, sovereign and independent empires.

VERMONT.

SITUATION and EXTENT.

Miles.
Length 155 } Between { 42° 50' and 45° North Latitude.
Breadth 60 }   { 1° 30' and 3° East Longitude.

Boundaries. BOUNDED north, by Canada; east, by Connecticut river, which divides it from New Hampshire; south, by Massachusetts; west, by New York.

Civil divisions.] Vermont is divided into the seven following counties:

Counties.	Chief Towns.	Counties.	Chief Towns.
Bennington,	BENNINGTON.	Chittendon.	
Rutland.		Orange.	
Addison.		Windsor.	
Windham.			

These

These counties are divided into townships, which are generally six miles square. In every township is a reserve of two rights of land, of 350 acres each, one to be appropriated for the support of public schools; the other to be given in fee to the first minister who settles in the township. A part of the townships were granted by the governor of New Hampshire, and the other part by that of Vermont. In those townships granted by the former, a right of land is reserved for the support of the gospel in foreign parts; in those granted by the latter, a college right, and a right for the support of county grammar schools, are reserved. In these reservations, liberal provision is made for the support of the gospel, and for the promotion of common and collegiate education.

Rivers.] This state, on the east side of the mountain, is watered by Paupanhoosak, Quechey, Welds, White, Black and West rivers, which run from west to east into Connecticut river; and west of the mountains, by the river Lamoil, over which is a natural stone bridge, 7 or 8 rods in length, by Onion river and Otter Creek, which empty by one mouth into Lake Champlain, 20 or 30 miles south of St. John's. Otter Creek is navigable for boats 50 miles. The lands adjacent are of an excellent quality, and are annually enriched by the overflowing of the water, occasioned by the melting of the snow on the Green Mountains.

Mountains.] A chain of high mountains, running north and south, divides this state nearly in the center between Connecticut river and Lake Champlain. The height of land is generally from 20 to 30 miles from the river, and about the same distance from the New York line. The natural growth upon this mountain, is hemlock, pine, spruce, and other evergreens; hence it has always a green appearance, and on this account has obtained the descriptive name of *Ver Mont, Green Mountain.* On some high parts of this mountain, snow lies till May, and sometimes till June.

Face of the country, soil and productions.] The country is generally hilly, but not rocky. It is finely watered and affords the best of pasturage for cattle. On the banks of the lakes, rivers and rivulets, are many fine tracts of rich interval land. The heavy growth of timber, which is common throughout the state, evince the strength and fertility of the soil. Elm, black birch, maple, ash and bass wood, grow in the moist low ground; and the banks of the rivers are timbered principally with white pine, intermingled with vales of beech, elm and white oak. The inhabitants cultivate wheat, 25 and 30 bushels of which grow on an acre, rye, barley, oats, Indian corn, &c. The corn, however, is frequently cut off by the early frosts, especially on the mountains and hills. That which grows on the banks of the rivers, is not so frequently injured. Flax is raised in considerable quantities, and the soil is good for hemp. Potatoes, pumpkins, and garden roots and vegetables, grow here in great plenty. Large quantities of sugar, of a good quality and flavour, are made from the sugar maple.

Climate.] None in the world more healthy. Snow begins to fall, commonly in the beginning of November, and is generally gone by the middle of April. During this season, the inhabitants generally enjoy a serene sky, and a keen cold air. The ground is seldom frozen to any great depth, being covered with a great body of snow, before the severe frosts begin. In the spring, the snow, in common, is gradually dissolved by the warm influences of the sun. In this way the earth is enriched and moistened, and spring advances with surprizing quickness.

Militia, population and character.] There are upwards of 17,000 men upon the militia rolls of this state. These consist of two divisions, one on the west, the other on the east side of the mountain. In these two divisions are 7 brigades, which are made up of 21 regiments. From the number of militia, reckoning 5 for one, we may estimate the number of inhabitants in the state at 85,000. Others, who reckon 6 for one, estimate them at 100,000. The bulk of the inhabitants are emigrants from Connecticut and Massachusetts, and their descendents. There is one settlement of Scotch people, which are almost the only foreigners in the state. As to the character, the manners, the customs, the laws, the policy and the religion of the people in Vermont, it is sufficient to say they are New Englandmen.

Curiosities.] In the township of Tinmouth, on the side of a small hill, is a very curious cave. The chasm, at its entrance, is about four feet in circumference. Entering this you descend 104 feet, and then opens a spacious room 20 feet in breadth and 100 feet in length. The angle of descent it about 45 degrees. The roof of this cavern is of rock, through which the water is continually percolating. The stalactites which hang from the roof appear like icicles on the eves of houses, and are continually increasing in number and magnitude. The bottom and sides are daily incrusting with spar and other mineral substances. On the sides of this subterraneous hall, are tables, chairs, benches, &c. which appear to have been artificially carved. This richly ornamented room, when illuminated with the candles of the guides, has an enchanting effect upon the eye of the spectator. If we might be indulged in assigning the general cause of these astonishing appearances, we should conclude from the various circumstances accompanying them, that they arise from water filtrating slowly through the incumbent *strata*; and taking up in its passage a variety of mineral substances, and becoming thus saturated with metallic particles, gradually exsuding on the surface of the caverns and fissures, in a quiescent state, the aqueous particles evaporate, and leave the mineral substances to unite according to their affinities.

At the end of this cave is a circular hole, 15 feet deep, apparently hewn out, in a conical form, enlarging gradually as you descend, in the form of a sugar loaf. At the bottom is a spring of fresh water, in continual motion, like the boiling of a pot. Its depth has never been founded.

Constitution.] The inhabitants of Vermont, by their representatives in convention, at Windsor, on the 25th of December, 1777, declared that the territory called Vermont, was, and of right ought to be a free and independent state; and for the purpose of maintaining regular government in the same, they made a solemn declaration of their rights, and ratified a constitution, of which the following is an abstract.

Their declaration, which makes a part of their constitution, asserts that all men are born equally free—with equal rights, and ought to enjoy liberty of conscience—freedom of the press—trial by jury—power to form new states in vacant countries, and to regulate their own internal police

police—that all elections ought to be free—that all power is originally in the people—that government ought to be instituted for the common benefit of the community—and that the community have a right to reform or abolish government—that every member of society hath a right to protection of life, liberty and property—and in return is bound to contribute his proportion of the expence of that protection, and yield his personal service when necessary—that he shall not be obliged to give evidence against himself—that the people have a right to bear arms—but no standing armies shall be maintained in time of peace—that the people have a right to hold themselves, their houses, papers, and possessions free from search or seizure—and therefore warrants without oaths first made, affording sufficient foundation for them, are contrary to that right and ought not to be granted—that no person shall be liable to be transported out of this state for trial for any offence committed within this state, &c.

By the frame of government, the supreme legislative power is vested in a house of representatives of the freemen of the state of Vermont, to be chosen annually by the freemen on the first Tuesday in September, and to meet the second Thursday of the succeeding October—this body is vested with all the powers necessary for the legislature of a free state—two thirds of the whole number of representatives elected, make a quorum.

Each inhabited town throughout the state, has a right to send one representative to the assembly.

The supreme executive power is vested in a governor, lieutenant governor, and twelve counsellors to be chosen annually in the same manner, and vested with the same powers as in Connecticut.

Every person of the age of 21 years, who has resided in the state one whole year next before the election of representatives, and is of a quiet, peaceable behaviour, and will bind himself by his oath, to do what he shall in conscience judge to be most conducive to the best good of the state, shall be entitled to all the privileges of a freeman of this state.

Each member of the house of representatives before he takes his seat, must declare his belief in one God—in future rewards and punishments, and in the divinity of the scriptures of the Old and New Testament, and must profess the protestant religion.

Courts of justice are to be established in every county throughout the state.

The supreme court, and the several courts of common pleas of this state, besides the powers usually exercised by such courts, have the powers of a court of chancery, so far as relates to perpetuating testimony, obtaining evidence from places not within the state, and the care of the persons and estates of those who are *non compotes, mentis* &c. All prosecutions are to be commenced in the name, and by the authority of the freemen of the state of Vermont. The legislature are to regulate entails so as to prevent perpetuities.

All field and staff officers, and commissioned officers of the army, and all general officers of the militia shall be chosen by the general assembly, and be commissioned by the governor.

Every

BRITISH AMERICAN DOMINIONS.

Every seventh year, beginning with the year 1785, thirteen persons (none of whom are to be of the council or assembly) shall be chosen by the freemen, and be called 'the council of censors,' whose duty it shall be to enquire whether the constitution has been preserved inviolate in every part—whether the legislative and executive powers have been properly exercised—taxes justly laid and collected—the public monies rightly disposed of—and the laws duly executed.—For these purposes, they shall have power to send for persons, papers, &c.—to pass public censures—to order impeachments, and to recommend the repeal of all laws enacted contrary to the principles of the constitution. They are to be vested with these powers for one year only, after the day of their election.

The council of censors, when necessary, may call a convention, to meet within two years after their sitting—to alter the constitution—the proposed alterations to be published at least six months before the election of delegates to such convention.

Chief town.] BENNINGTON is the principal town in Vermont. It is situated in the southwest corner of the state, near the foot of the Green Mountain. Its public buildings are a church for congregationalists, a court house and gaol. It has a number of elegant houses, and is a flourishing town. Near the center of the town is *Mount Anthony*, which rises very high in the form of a sugar loaf. The assembly commonly hold their sessions at Windsor.

✢✢✢✢✢✢✢✢✢✢✢✢✢✢✢✢✢✢✢✢✢✢✢✢✢✢✢✢✢✢✢✢✢✢✢✢✢✢

British American dominions.

NEW BRITAIN.

UNDER this name is comprehended all the tract of country, which lies north of Canada, commonly called the Eskimaux country, including Labrador, now North and South Wales; said to be 850 miles long, and 750 broad.

To speak generally, this is a mountainous, frozen, barren country, abounding with lakes, rivers and bays, that furnish a plenty of fish. The fur of the various animals is close, soft and warm. The fishery and the fur trade are the only things which render this country valuable. This trade is in the hands of a company of nine or ten persons, who received a charter in 1670, and whose profits are not inconsiderable. One year they carried from Great Britain articles, to the amount of £16,060; and in return, carried furs and fish to the amount of £29,380.

The country is very thinly inhabited, by a people resembling the Laplanders, and the other nations in the northwestern parts of Europe, from whence their ancestors probably migrated.

BRITISH AMERICAN DOMINIONS.

CANADA.

SITUATION and EXTENT.

Length 600 Miles, Breadth 200 } Between { 61° and 81° West Long. from London. 45° and 52° North Latitude.

Boundaries.] BOUNDED north, by New Britain; east, by the Bay of St. Lawrence; south, by Nova Scotia and the United States; west, by unknown lands.

Rivers.] The principal are, the Outtauais, St. John's Seguina, Desprairies and Trois rivieres, which are large, bold and deep, and are all swallowed up by the river St. Lawrence, which falls into the ocean at Cape Rosieres, by a mouth 90 miles broad.

Chief Towns.] QUEBEC is the capital of Canada. It is built on the bank of St. Lawrence river, on a rock, in two divisions, 320 miles from the sea, and contained in 1784, 6,472 inhabitants. One hundred and seventy miles from Quebec, as you ascend the St. Lawrence, stands MONTREAL, on a beautiful island in the river. It is nearly as large as Quebec.

Population.] In 1784, a census of the inhabitants of the Province of Quebec was taken, by order of General Haldimand, when they amounted to 113,012 English and French, exclusive of the Loyalists, who have lately settled in the upper parts of the province, to the number, it is said, of 10,000.

Constitution.] The constitution of the province is founded on the 14th of George the III. called the Quebec bill. By this bill the legislative power is vested in the governor and legislative council. The council is composed of the lieutenant governor, chief justice and secretary for the time being, and twenty other members, nearly one half of whom are French. They are appointed by the crown, and receive £100 a year as a salary. Their power extends to almost all the necessary purposes of government, except the levying of taxes, wherein the said statute inhibits, whereby Great Britain pays the salaries to the counsellors, and all the expences of the civil list of the province, which amount to £25,000 per annum exclusive of the governor general's salary.

Trade.] The amount of the exports from the province of Quebec in the year 1786, was £343,262 : 19 : 6. The amount of imports in the same year was £325,116. The exports consisted of wheat, flour, biscuit, flaxseed, lumber of various kinds, fish, potash, oil, ginseng and other medicinal roots, but principal of furs and peltries, to the amount of £285,977. The imports consisted of rum, brandy, molasses, coffee, sugar, wines, tobacco, salt, chocolate, provisions for the troops and dry goods.

History.] This country was discovered by the English, as early as about 1497, and settled by the French in 1608, who kept possession of it till 1763, when, after a long and bloody war, it fell into the hands of the British, to whom it has ever since belonged.

BRITISH AMERICAN DOMINIONS.

NOVA SCOTIA.

Miles.
Length 350 } Between { 43° and 49° North Latitude.
Breadth 250 } { 60° and 67° West Longitude from London.

Boundaries.] BOUNDED weft, by the eaftern boundary of the United States; north, by the river St. Lawrence; eaft and fouth, by the Gulph of St. Lawrence and the Atlantic Ocean. It has about 90 leagues of fea coaft, on the Atlantic Ocean. In 1784, this province was divided into two governments. One of the governments is called *New Brunfwick*, and lies bordering on the United States.

Rivers and Bays.] The rivers Rifgouche and Nipifiguit run from weft to eaft, and fall into the Bay of St. Lawrence. St. John's, Paffamagnadi, and St. Croix, run from north to fouth into the Bay of Fundy, or the fea. Nova Scotia is indented with numerous bays, which afford many commodious, bold harbours. The Bay of Fundy is the largeft of the bays, and extends 50 leagues into the country. Here the ebb and flow of the tide is from 45 to 60 feet.

Climate, Soil, Productions and Trade.] During a great part of the year the atmofphere is clouded with thick fog, which renders it unhealthy for the inhabitants; and four or five months it is intenfely cold. A great part of this country lies in foreft, and the foil, in moft parts, is thin and barren. On the banks of the rivers, and fome other parts the foil is good; many of the bays, and falt water rivers, and fome parts of the fea coaft, are bordered with tracts of falt marfh. The inhabitants do not raife provifion enough for home confumption. They fubfift principally by the lumber trade, which is fupplied by their forefts; and by the fifhery, which is very profitable. The fifhery on the fea coaft of the ifland of Cape Breton, in the year 1743, while in poffeffion of the French, yielded 1,149,000 quintals of dried fifh, and 3,900,000 quintals of mud fifh; the value of both, including $3116\frac{1}{4}$ tons of train oil, was eftimated at £.926,577 : 10 fterling. Five hundred and fixty-four fhips, befides fhallops, and 27,000 feamen, were employed in this trade.

Chief Towns.] HALIFAX is the capital of Nova Scotia, and ftands on Chebucto Bay. It has a good harbour, fufficiently large and fafe to fhelter a fquadron of fhips through the winter. The town has an entrenchment, and is ftrengthened with forts of timber. It is commodioufly fituated for the fifhery. ANNAPOLIS ftands on the eaft fide of the Bay of Fundy, and has one of the fineft harbours in the world. ST. JOHN'S is a new fettlement at the mouth of the river of the fame name. Since the conclufion of the war, there have been large emigrations of the refugees from the United States to this province. They have built feveral new towns, the largeft of which is SHELBURNE, which is faid to contain 9000 inhabitants.

Hiftory and Government.] Notwithftanding the forbidding afpect of this country, it was here that fome of the firft European fettlements were made. The firft grant of land in it, was made by James I. to his fecretary

tary William Alexander, who named it Nova Scotia, or New Scotland.—Since that time it has frequently changed from one private proprietor to another, and repeatedly from the French to the English. At the peace of Utrecht is was confirmed to the English, under whose government it has ever since continued.

✦✦✦✦✦✦✦✦✦✦✦✦✦✦✦✦✦✦✦✦✦✦✦✦✦✦✦✦✦✦✦✦✦✦✦

Spanish dominions.

EAST AND WEST FLORIDA.

Miles.
Length 600 } Between { 25° and 31° North Latitude.
Breadth 130 }   { 5° and 17° West Longitude from Philadelphia.

Boundaries.] BOUNDED north, by Georgia; east, by the Atlantic Ocean; South by the Gulph of Mexico; west by the Mississippi; lying in the form of an *L*.

Rivers.] St. John's and Indian rivers, which empty into the Atlantic Ocean; Seguana, Apalachicola, Chatahatchi, Escambia, Mobile, Pascagoula and Pearl rivers, all of which rise in Georgia, and run southerly into the Gulph of Mexico.

Climate.] Very little different from that of Georgia.

Soil and Productions.] There are, in this country, a great variety of soils.—The eastern part of it, near and about St. Augustine, is far the most unfruitful; yet even here two crops of Indian corn a year are produced. The banks of the rivers which water the Floridas, and the parts contiguous, are of a superior quality, and well adapted to the culture of rice and corn, while the more interior country, which is high and pleasant, abounds with wood of almost every kind; particularly white and red oak, pine, hiccory, cypress, red and white cedar. The intervals between the hilly part of this country are extremely rich, and produce spontaneously the fruits and vegetables that are common to Georgia and the the Carolinas. But this country is rendered valuable in a peculiar manner, by the extensive ranges for cattle.

Chief Towns.] ST. AUGUSTINE, the capital of E. Florida, is situated on the sea coast—is of an oblong figure, and intersected by four streets, which cut each other at right angles. The town is fortified with bastions, and enclosed with a ditch. It is likewise defended by a castle, called Fort St. John, which is well appointed as to ordnance. The north and south breakers, at the entrance of the harbour, form two channels, whose bars have eight feet water.

The principal town in West Florida is PENSACOLA. It lies along the beach, and, like St. Augustine, is of an oblong form.—The water approach to the town, except for small vessels, is obstructed by a low and sandy shore. The bay, however, on which the town stands, forms a very commodious harbour, and vessels may ride here secure from every wind.

History.

SPANISH DOMINIONS.

History.] The Floridas have experienced the vicissitudes of war, and frequently changed masters, belonging alternately to the Frecnh and Spaniards. It was ceded by the latter to the English at the peace of 1763. During the last war it was again reduced by the arms of his Catholic Majesty, and was guaranteed to the crown of Spain by the late definitive treaty. Its first discoverer was Sebastian Cabot, in 1497.

LOUISIANA.

Boundaries.] BOUNDED by the Missisippi east; by the Gulph of Mexico south; by New Mexico west; and runs indefinitely north.

Rivers.] It is intersected by a number of fine rivers, among which are the Natchitoches, which empties into the Missisippi at Point Coupee, and the Adayes or Mexicano river, emptying into the Gulph of Mexico.

Capital.] NEW ORLEANS. It stands on the east side of the Missisippi, 105 miles from its mouth, in latitude 30° 2' north. In the beginning of the last year it contained about 1100 houses, seven-eights of which were consumed by fire, in the space of five hours, on the 19th of March 1788. It is now fast rebuilding. Its advantages for trade are very great. Situated on a noble river, in a fertile and healthy country, within two weeks sail of Mexico by sea, and still nearer to the British, French and Spanish West India islands, with a moral certainty of its becoming the general receptacle for the produce of that extensive and valuable country on the Missisippi and Ohio, are sufficient to ensure its future growth and commercial importance.

Religion, &c.] The greater part of the white inhabitants are Roman Catholics. They are governed by a viceroy from Spain, and their number is unknown.

Climate, Soil and Produce.] Louisiana is agreeably situated between the extremes of heat and cold. Its climate varies as it extends towards the north. The southern parts, lying within the reach of the refreshing breezes from the sea, are not scorched like those under the same latitudes in Africa; and its northern regions are colder than those of Europe under the same parallels, with a wholesome serene air. To judge of the produce to be expected from the soil of Louisiana, let us turn our eyes to Egypt, Arabia Felix, Persia, India, China and Japan, all lying in corresponding latitudes. Of these China alone has a tolerable government; and yet it must be acknowledged they all are, or have been, famous for their riches and fertility. From the favourableness of the climate, two annual crops of Indian corn, as well as rice, may be produced; and the soil, with little cultivation, would furnish grain of every kind in the greatest abundance. Their timber is as fine as any in the world, and the quantities of live oak, ash, mulberry, walnut, cherry, cypress and cedar, are astonishing. The neighbourhood of the Missisippi, besides, furnishes the richest fruits in great variety; the soil is particularly adapted for hemp, flax and tobacco; and indigo is at this time a staple commodity, which commonly yields the planter three or four cuttings a year. In

a word

a word, whatever is rich and rare in the moſt deſirable climates in Europe, ſeems to be the ſpontaneous production of this delightful country. The Miſſiſippi furniſhes in great plenty ſeveral ſorts of fiſh, particularly perch, pike, ſturgeon and eels.

Hiſtory.] The Miſſiſippi, on which the fine country of Louiſiana is ſituated, was firſt diſcovered by Ferdinand de Soto, in 1541. Monſieur de la Salle was the firſt who traverſed it. He, in the year 1682, having paſſed down to the mouth of the Miſſiſippi, and ſurveyed the adjacent country, returned to Canada, from whence he took paſſage to France.

From the flattering accounts which he gave of the country, and the conſequential advantages that would accrue from ſettling a colony in thoſe parts, Louis XIV. was induced to eſtabliſh a company for the purpoſe. Accordingly a ſquadron of four veſſels, amply provided with men and proviſions, under the command of Monſieur de la Salle, embarked, with an intention to ſettle near the mouths of the Miſſiſippi. But he unintentionally ſailed 100 leagues to the weſtward of it, where he attempted to eſtabliſh a colony; but through the unfavourableneſs of the climate, moſt of his men miſerably periſhed, and he himſelf was villainouſly murdered, not long after, by two of his own men. Monſieur Ibberville ſucceeded him in his laudable attempts. He, after two ſucceſsful voyages, died while preparing for a third. Crozat ſucceeded him; and in 1712. the king gave him Louiſiana. This grant continued but a ſhort time after the death of Louis XIV. In 1763 Louiſiana was ceded to the king of Spain, to whom it now belongs.

NEW MEXICO AND CALAFORNIA.

Miles.
Length 2000 } Between { 94° and 126° Weſt Long. from London.
Breadth 1600 } { 23° and 43° North Latitude.

Boundaries.] BOUNDED north, by unknown lands; eaſt, by Louiſiana; ſouth by Old Mexico and the Pacific Ocean; weſt, by the ſame ocean.

Diviſions,	Subdiviſions.	Chief Towns.
Northeaſt diviſion	New Mexico Proper,	Santa Fe, W. Longitude 104°. North Latitude 36°.
Southeaſt diviſion	Apacheira,	St. Antonio.
South diviſion	Sonora,	Tuape.
Weſt diviſion	Calafornia, a peninſula,	St. Juan.

Climate, ſoil and productions.] The climate of this country, if we may judge from its ſituation, muſt be very agreeable. Towards the cloſe of the laſt century, the Jeſuits, who had great merit in exploring the neglected province of California, and in civilizing its rude inhabitants, ſeem
ſtudiouſly

studiously to have depreciated this country, for political reasons, by representing the climate as so disagreeable and unwholesome, and the soil as so barren, that nothing but their zealous endeavours to convert the natives, could have induced them to settle there. The falsehood of this representation, however, has since been detected, and a very favourable account has been given of the climate and soil. A valuable pearl fishery has been found on its coasts, and mines of gold have been discovered of a very promising appearance. In California, there falls in the morning a great quantity of dew, which, settling on the rose leaves, candies, and becomes hard like manna, having all the sweetness of refined sugar, without its whiteness. There is also another very singular natural production. In the heart of the country there are plains of salt, quite firm and clear as crystal, which, considering the vast quantities of fish found on its coasts, might render it an invaluable acquisition to an industrious nation.

Inhabitants and character.] The number of inhabitants, as far as can be known, do not exceed 300,000. The characteristics of the Californians, are stupidity and insensibility; want of knowledge and reflection; inconstancy, impetuosity, and blindness of appetite; an excessive sloth, and abhorrence of all labour and fatigue; an excessive love of pleasure and amusement of every kind, however trifling or brutal; pusillanimity; and, in fine, a most wretched want of every thing which constitutes the real man, and renders him rational, inventive, tractable, and useful to himself and society.

History.] Cortes, the great conqueror of Mexico, discovered the extensive peninsula of California in the year 1536, after enduring incredible hardships, and encountering dangers of almost every species. During a long period it continued to be so little frequented, that even its form was unknown, and in most maps it was represented as an island. Sir Francis Drake was the first who took possession of it in 1578, and his right was confirmed by the principal king or chief in the whole country.

✛✛✛✛✛✛✛✛✛✛✛✛✛✛✛✛✛✛✛✛✛✛✛✛✛✛✛✛✛✛✛✛✛

OLD MEXICO, or NEW SPAIN.

Miles.
Length 2000 } Between { 83° and 110° West Long. from London,
Breadth 600 } { 8° and 30° North Latitude.

Boundaries, BOUNDED north, by New Mexico; northeast, by the Gulph of Mexico; southeast, by Terra Firma; southwest, by the Pacific Ocean; divided into the three following audiences, viz.

Audiences.	Chief Towns.
Galicia or Guadalajarra,	Gaudalajarra,
Mexico Proper,	Mexico N. Lat. 19° 54'. Acapulco, Vera Cruz,
Guatimala,	Guatimala. *Climate,*

SPANISH DOMINIONS.

Climate, soil and productions.] Mexico, lying principally in the torrid zone, is excessively hot. This country is mountainous in the interior parts, but along the eastern shore, it is flat and marshy, and is overflowed in the rainy seasons, which renders it very unhealthy. The trees are cloathed with perpetual verdure, and blossom and bear almost the whole year round. The cotton and cedar trees, and those which bear the cocoa, of which chocolate is made, abound here. Mexico, like all the tropical countries, is rather more abundant in fruits than in grain. Pine apples, pomegranates, oranges, lemons, citrons, figs, &c. are here in great plenty and perfection. Mexico produces also a great quantity of sugar, especially towards the Gulf of Mexico.

The chief mines of gold are in Veragua and New Grenada, bordering upon Darien and Terra Firma. Those of silver, which are much more rich, as well as numerous, are found in several parts, particularly in the province of Mexico.

The mines of both kinds are always found in the most barren and mountainous parts of the country; nature making amends in one respect for defects in another.

Of the gold and silver which the mines of Mexico afford, great things have been said. Those who have enquired most into this subject compute the revenues at twenty-four millions of money; and this account is probably just, since it is well known that this, with the other Spanish provinces in South America, supply the whole world with silver.

The Spanish commerce in the article of cocoa is immense. It grows on a tree of a middling size, which bears a pod about the size of a cucumber, containing the cocoa. It is said that a small garden of cocoas, produces to the owner twenty thousand crowns a year.

Inhabitants, character and government.] The present inhabitants of Mexico, may be divided into whites, Indians and negroes. The whites are born in Old Spain, or they are creoles, that is, natives of Spanish America. The former are chiefly employed in government and trade, and have nearly the same character with the Spaniards in Europe; only a larger share of pride; for they consider themselves as intitled to every high distinction as natives of Europe, and look on the other inhabitants as many degrees beneath them. The creoles have all the bad qualities of the Spaniards, from whom they are descended, without that courage, firmness and patience, which make the praiseworthy part of the Spanish character. Naturally weak and effeminate, they dedicate the greatest part of their lives to loitering and inactive pleasures. Luxurious without variety or elegance, and expensive with great parade, and little convenience, their character is nothing more than a grave, specious insignificance. From idleness and constitution, their whole business is amour and intrigue; their ladies, of consequence, are not distinguished for their chastity or domestic virtues.

The Indians, who, notwithstanding the devastations of the first invaders, remain in great numbers, are become, by continual oppression and indignity, a dejected, timorous and miserable race of mortals.

The blacks here, like those in other parts of the world, are stubborn, robust and hardy, and as well adapted for the gross and inhuman slavery they endure, as any human beings. This may serve for the general

character,

character, not only of the Mexicans, but for the greater part of the Spanish colonies in South America.

The civil government of Mexico is administered by tribunals, called audiences. In these courts the viceroy of the king of Spain presides. His employment is the greatest trust and power his catholic majesty has at his disposal, and is perhaps the richest government entrusted to any subject in the world. The viceroy continues in office but three years.

The clergy are extremely numerous in Mexico. The priests, monks and nuns of all orders, make a fifth part of the white inhabitants, both here and in other parts of Spanish America.

Chief towns.] MEXICO, the capital of this place, is situated on a large plain, environed by mountains of such height, that, though within the torrid zone, the temperature of its climate is mild and healthful.

All the buildings are convenient; and the public edifices, especially the churches, are magnificent. The revenue of the grand cathedral amounts to near £80,000 sterling a year, of which the archbishop has £15,000, besides vast sums arising from perquisites. The inhabitants are reckoned at 150,000, who draw annually from the mines above ten millions of money, exclusive of the vast sums secreted, and applied to private uses; yet with these almost incredible treasures, the people may be reckoned poor, as most of them live beyond their fortunes, and commonly terminate a life of profusion, in extreme indigence.

ACAPULCO stands on a bay of the South Sea, about 210 miles south-east of Mexico. In this harbour, which is very commodious, the Manilla galleon takes in at least ten millions of dollars, in return for the goods she brings thither, and for the payment of the Spanish garrisons in the Phillippine isles.

History] The empire of Mexico was subdued by Cortes in the year 1521. Montezuma was at that time emperor of Mexico. In the course of the war, he was treacherously taken by Cortes, and held as a prisoner. During the imprisonment of Montezuma, Cortes and his army had made repeated attacks on his subjects, but without success. Cortes was now determined, as his last resource, to try what effect the interposition of Montezuma might have to sooth, or overawe his subjects. This unfortunate prince, at the mercy of the treacherous Spaniards, and reduced to the sad necessity of becoming the instrument of his own disgrace, and of the slavery of his subjects, advanced to the battlements in his royal robes, with all the pomp in which he used to appear on solemn occasions. At sight of their sovereign, whom they had long been accustomed to honour, and almost to revere as a God, the weapons dropped from their hands, every tongue was silent, all bowed their heads, and many prostrated themselves on the ground. Montezuma addressed them with every argument that could mitigate their rage, or persuade them to cease from hostilities. When he ended his discourse, a sullen murmur of disapprobation ran through the crowd; to this succeeded reproaches and threats; and their fury rising in a moment, they violently poured in whole flights of arrows, and vollies of stones, upon their unhappy monarch; two of the arrows struck him in the body, which, with the blow of a stone on his temple, put an end to his life. Guatimozin succeeded Montezuma, and maintained a vigorous opposition against the assaults of Cortes. But he like his predecessor, after a noble defence, was forced to submit. Previous to this, being aware of his impending fate, he had ordered that all his treasures should be thrown into the lake. While a prisoner, on suspicion of his having concealed his treasure, he was put to the torture, which was done by laying him on burning coals; but he bore whatever the refined cruelty of his tormentors could inflict, with the invincible fortitude of an American warrior. One of his chief favourites, his fellow sufferer, being overcome by the violence of the anguish, turned a dejected eye towards his master, which seemed to implore his permission to reveal all that he knew. But the high spirited prince, darted on him a look of authority, mingled with scorn, and checked his weakness by asking, ' Am I now reposing on a bed of flowers ?' Overawed by the reproach, he persevered in dutiful silence and expired. Cortes, ashamed of a scene so horrid, rescued the royal victim from the hands of his torturers, and prolonged a life for new indignities and sufferings. Cortes died in Spain, in the year 1547, in the 62d year of his age. Envied by his contemporaries, and ill requited by the court which he served, he has been admired and celebrated by succeeding ages. By his own desire he was carried to Mexico, and buried there.

SOUTH AMERICA.

IS a peninsula, joined to North America by the Isthmus of Darien, and divided as follows:

Countries.	Chief Towns.	Belonging to
Terra Firma,	Panama,	Spain,
Peru,	Lima,	Spain,
Amazonia,	St. Pedro,	Spain,
Guiana,	Surinam,	Dutch,
Brazil,	St. Sebastian,	Portugal,
Paragua, or La Plata,	Buennos Ayres,	Spain,
Chili,	St. Jago,	Spain,
Patagonia,		The natives.

TERRA FIRMA or CASTILE DEL ORO.

Miles.
Length 1400 } Between { 60° and 82° West Longitude.
Breadth 700 } { The Equator, and 12° North Latitude.

Boundaries. BOUNDED north, by the Atlantic ocean; east, by the same ocean and Surinam; south, by Amazonia and Peru; west, by the Pacific ocean.

Climate,

SPANISH DOMINIONS. 483

Climate, soil and productions.] The climate here, especially in the northern parts, is extremely hot and sultry during the whole year. From the month of May to the end of November, the season called winter by the inhabitants, is almost a continual succession of thunder, rain and tempests; the clouds precipitating the rains with such impetuosity, that the low lands exhibit the appearance of an ocean. Great part of the country is of consequence almost continually flooded; and this, together with the excessive heat, so impregnates the air with vapours, that in many provinces, particularly about Popayan and Porto Bello, it is extremely unwholesome. The soil of this country is very different, the inland parts being exceedingly rich and fertile, and the coasts sandy and barren. It is impossible to view without admiration, the perpetual verdure of the woods, the luxuriancy of the plains, and the towering height of the mountains. This country produces corn, sugar, tobacco and fruits of all kinds; the most remarkable is that of the manzanillo tree. It bears a fruit resembling an apple, but which, under this specious appearance, contains the most subtile poison. The bean of Carthagena is the fruit of a species of willow about the bigness of a bean, and is an excellent and never failing remedy for the bite of the most venomous serpents, which are very frequent all over this country. Among the natural merchandize of Terra Firma, the pearls found on the coast, particularly in the bay of Panama, are not the least considerable. An immense number of Negroe slaves are employed in fishing for these, and have arrived at a wonderful dexterity in this occupation. They are sometimes, however, devoured by sharks, while they dive to the bottom, or are crushed against the shelves of the rocks.

Chief Towns.] PANAMA is the capital of Terra Firma Proper, and is situated upon a capacious bay to which it gives its name. It is the great receptacle of the vast quantities of gold and silver, with other rich merchandize, from all parts of Peru and Chili: here they are lodged in storehouses, till the proper season arrives to transport them to Europe.

PORTO BELLO is situated close to the sea, on the declivity of a mountain which surrounds the whole harbour. The convenience and safety of this harbour is such, that Columbus, who first discovered it, gave it the name of Porto Bello, or the Fine Harbour.

History.] This part of South America was discovered by Columbus, in his third voyage to this continent. It was subdued and settled by the Spaniards about the year 1514, after destroying, with great inhumanity, several millions of the natives. This country was called Terra Firma, on account of its being the first part of the continent which was discovered, all the lands discovered previous to this being islands.

PERU.

PERU.

Miles.
Length 1800 } Between { 60° and 81° West Longitude,
Breadth 500 }   { The Equator and 25° South Latitude.

Boundaries.] BOUNDED north, by Terra Firma; east, by the Andes; south, by Chili; west, by the Pacific ocean.

Rivers.] A prodigious number of rivers rise in the Andes, and run through this country, among which are the Granada or Cagdalena, Orinoco and Amazon. The last has its source in Peru, and after running eastward upwards of three thousand miles, falls into the Atlantic ocean. This river, like all other tropical rivers, annually overflows its banks.

Climate, soil and productions.] Though Peru lies within the torrid zone, yet, having the Pacific ocean on the west, and the Andes on the east, the air is not so sultry, as is usual in tropical countries. The sky is generally cloudy, so that the inhabitants are shielded from the direct rays of the sun; but what is extremely singular, it never rains in Peru. This defect, however, is sufficiently supplied by a soft and gentle dew, which falls every night on the ground, and so refreshes the plants and grass, as to produce in many places the greatest fertility. In the inland parts of Peru, and by the banks of the rivers, the soil is generally very fertile, but along the sea coast it is a barren sand. The productions of this country are, Indian corn, wheat, balsam, sugar, wine, cotton,—cattle, deer, poultry, parrots, wild fowls, lions, bears, monkeys, &c. Their sheep are large, and work as beasts of burden. Another extraordinary animal here is the vicunna, or Indian goat, in which is found the bezoar stone, celebrated for expelling poisons. The province of Quito abounds with cedar, cocoa, palm trees, and the kinguenna, which affords the Peruvian or Jesuits bark; also the storax, guiacum, and several other gums and drugs. Gold and silver mines are found in every province, but those of Potosi are the richest. The mountain of Potosi alone, is said to have yielded to the Spaniards the first forty years they were in possession of it, two thousand millions of pieces of eight.

Government.] Peru is governed by a viceroy, who is absolute; but it being impossible for him to superintend the whole extent of his government, he delegates a part of his authority to the several audiences and courts, established at different places throughout his dominions.

Chief Towns.] Lima, the capital of Peru, and residence of the viceroy, is large, magnificent and populous; and for the splendor of its inhabitants, the grandeur of its public festivals, the extent of its commerce, and the delightfulness of its climate, is superior to all cities in South America. These eminent advantages are, however, considerably overbalanced by the dreadful earthquakes which frequently happen here. In the year 1747 a most tremendous earthquake laid three fourths of this city level with the ground, and entirely demolished Callao, the port town belonging to it. Never was any destruction more complete or terrible: but one, of 3,000 inhabitants, being left to record this dreadful calamity, and he by a providence the most singular and extraordinary imaginable.

Lima

Lima contains 60,000 inhabitants, of whom the whites amount to a sixth part.

All travellers speak with amazement of the decoration of the churches with gold, silver and precious stones, which load and ornament even the walls. Quito is next to Lima in populousness.

History.] The Spaniards first visited Peru in 1526. Pizarro, with an army of about 160 men, after a series of treacherous and cruel acts, made a conquest of the whole country, for the king of Spain, in 1533, to whom it has ever since been subject. The natives have frequently attempted to regain their liberty, but have hitherto been unsuccessful. Some late insurrections have happened, but the consequences are not yet particularly known.

✣✣✣✣✣✣✣✣✣✣✣✣✣✣✣✣✣✣✣✣✣✣✣✣✣✣✣✣✣✣✣✣✣✣✣✣

C H I L I.

Miles.
Length 1200 } Between { 25° and 45° South Latitude.
Breadth 500 }   { 65° and 85° West Longitude.

Boundaries.] BOUNDED north, by Peru; East, by La Plata; south, by Patagonia; west, by the Pacific ocean.

Climate, soil and productions.] The air of Chili, though in a hot climate, is remarkably temperate, occasioned by the refreshing breezes from the sea, and the cool winds from the top of the Andes, which are covered with eternal snows. This country is free from lightning, and although thunder is frequently heard, it is far up in the mountain. Spring begins here about the middle of August, and continues till November. It is summer from November till February. Autumn continues till May; and winter till August. It rarely snows in the vallies, though the mountains are always covered. This country is entirely free from all kinds of ravenous beasts, poisonous animals and vermin; not even so much as a fly is to be found here. The soil is extremely fertile, being watered with numberless little rivulets from the mountains. It produces, in the greatest abundance, apples, pears, plums, peaches, quinces, apricots, almonds, olives, grapes, cocoa-nuts, figs, and straw berries as large as pears,—wheat, oats, corn, garden flowers and fruits of almost every kind. It abounds in gold, silver and lead mines, and the rivers themselves roll on golden sands. But their staple commodity is cattle; they have them in such abundance, as frequently to cast the flesh into the rivers, reserving the hides, tallow and tongues for exportation.

History, inhabitants, &c.] The Spaniards made several attempts to reduce this country, but with no great success till the year 1541, when they built the capital St. Jago, now the residence of the Spanish governor, and a bishop's see; and afterwards Coquimbo, Conception, and Baldivia. The natives are remarkable for wit, fortitude and patience; and the Spaniards to this day have never been able to subdue them; they

continue

continue still masters of part of the inland country. There have lately been some formidable insurrections against the Spaniards by the natives, which have greatly alarmed the Spanish court.

✣✣✣✣✣✣✣✣✣✣✣✣✣✣✣✣✣✣✣✣✣✣✣✣✣✣✣✣✣✣✣✣✣✣✣✣✣

PARAGUA or LA PLATA.

Length 1500 } Between { 12° and 37° South Latitude.
Breadth 1000 } { 50° and 75° West Longitude.

Boundaries.] BOUNDED north, by Amazonia; east, by Brazil; south, by Patagonia; west by Peru and Chili.

Rivers and Mountains.] This country, besides an infinite number of small rivers, is watered by three principal ones, which united near the sea, form the famous Rio de la Plata, or Plate river, and which annually overflow their banks, and, on their recess, leave them enriched with a slime, that produces great plenty of whatever is committed to it. This river, where it unites with the ocean, is 150 miles broad. At 100 miles from its mouth, a ship in the middle of the channel, cannot be seen from either shore; and at Buenos Ayres, 100 miles still further back, one cannot discern the opposite shore. There are no mountains of consequence here, excepting that remarkable chain which divides South America, called the Andes. The height of Chimborazo, the most elevated point in these mountains, is 20,280 feet; which is above 5000 feet higher than any other mountains in the known world.

Climate, Soil and Produce.] This country consists of extensive plains, 300 leagues over, except on the east, where it is separated by high mountains from Brazil. La Plata is a most desirable climate, and one of the most fruitful countries in the world. The cotton and tobacco produced here, with the herb called Paragua, which is peculiar to this country, would alone be sufficient to form a flourishing commerce. There are here also several gold and silver mines.

Chief Towns.] BUENOS AYRES, the capital of La Plata, is the most considerable sea port town in South America. It is situated on the south side of the river La Plata, 200 miles from the mouth of it. The river is upwards of 20 miles broad at this place. From this town a great part of the treasure of Chili and Peru is exported to Old Spain. The natives of Tacuman are said to have wooden houses built on wheels, which they draw from place to place as occasion requires.

History and Religion.] The Spaniards first discovered this country in the year 1515, and founded the town of Buenos Ayres in 1535. Most of the country is still inhabited by the native Americans. The Jesuits have been indefatigable in their endeavours to convert the Indians to the belief of their religion, and to introduce among them the arts of civilized life, and have met with surprizing success. It is said that above 340,000 families

PORTUGUESE DOMINIONS. 487

milies, several years ago, were subject to the Jesuits, living in obedience and an awe, bordering on adoration, yet procured without any violence or constraint. In 1767, the Jesuits were sent out of America, by royal authority, and their subjects were put upon the same footing with the rest of the country.

✤✤✤✤✤✤✤✤✤✤✤✤✤✤✤✤✤✤✤✤✤✤✤✤✤✤✤✤✤✤✤✤✤✤

BRAZIL, belonging to Portugal.

Miles.
Length 2500 } Between { 35° and 60° West Longitude.
Breadth 700 } { The Equator and 35° South Latitude.

Boundaries.] BOUNDED north, by the mouth of the river Amazon and the Atlantic Ocean; east, by the same ocean; south, by the mouth of the river La Plata; west, by a chain of mountains, which divides it from Paragua, and the country of the Amazons.

Air, Soil and Produce.] The air of this country is hot, but healthy, and the soil exceedingly fertile in maize, millet, rice, fruits, saffron, balsam of capivi, ginger, indigo, amber, rosin, train oil, cotton, the best of tobacco, fine sugar, brazil-wood, &c. Here also are mines of gold, silver and diamonds, and a great quantity of excellent crystal and jasper. This country also abounds in cattle, apes, parrots, and beautiful birds. The rivers and lakes are stored with fish, and there is a whale fishery on the coast.

Inhabitants, Religion, &c.] The coast of this large country is only known; the natives still possess the inland parts; whereof those towards the north are called Tapayers, and those in the south Tupinamboys. These natives seem to have little religion, and no temple or place for public worship; but yet are said to believe a future state, and have some notion of rewards and punishments after this life.

History, &c.] The Portuguese discovered this country in the year 1500, but did not plant it till the year 1549, when they took possession of All Saints Bay, and built the city of St. Salvador, which is now the residence of the viceroy and archbishop. The Dutch invaded Brazil in 1623, and subdued the northern provinces; but the Portuguese agreed, in 1661, to pay the Dutch eight tons of gold, to relinquish their interest in this country, which was accepted, and the Portuguese remained in peaceable possession of all Brazil till about the end of 1762, when the Spanish governor of Buenos Ayres, hearing of a war between Portugal and Spain, took, after a month's siege, the Portuguese frontier fortress, called St. Sacrament; but by the treaty of peace it was restored.

GUIANA.

GUIANA, belonging to the French and Dutch.

IS divided into Cayenne, which belongs to the French, and into Surinam, which is a Dutch province.

Cayenne extends 240 miles along the coast of Guiana, and near 300 within land. It is bounded north, by Surinam; east, by the Atlantic; south, by Amazonia; west by Guiana. All the coast is very low, but within land there are fine hills, very proper for settlements. The commodities are similar to those of the West India Islands.

Surinam is one of the richest and most valuable colonies belonging to the United Provinces. The chief trade of Surinam consists in sugar cotton, coffee of an excellent kind, tobacco, flax, skins, and some valuable dying drugs. They trade with the United States, of whom they receive horses, live cattle, and provisions, and give in exchange large quantities of molasses. The Torporific eel is found in the rivers of Guiana, which, when touched either by the hand, or by a rod of iron, gold, copper, or by a stick of some particular kinds of heavy wood, communicates a shock perfectly like that of electricity. There is an immense number and variety of snakes in this country, and which form one of its principal inconveniencies.

✤✤✤✤✤✤✤✤✤✤✤✤✤✤✤✤✤✤✤✤✤✤✤✤✤✤✤✤✤✤✤✤✤✤✤✤✤✤

AMAZONIA.

Length 1200——Breadth 960 miles.

Boundaries.] BOUNDED north, by Terra Firma and Guiana; east, by the Atlantic Ocean and Brazil; south, by La Plata; and west, by Peru.

Rivers.] From the discoveries of Orellana, and others made since his time, it appears that the Amazon is one of the largest rivers in the world. It runs a course from west to east of about 3000 miles, and receives near 200 other rivers, many of which have a course of 5 or 600 leagues, and some of them not inferior to the Danube or the Nile. The breadth of this river at its mouth, where it discharges itself by several channels into the ocean, almost under the equator, is 150 miles; and 1500 miles from its mouth it is 30 or 40 fathoms deep. In the rainy season it overflows its banks, and waters and fertilizes the adjacent country.

Climate, Soil and Produce.] The fair season here is about the time of the solstices, and the wet or rainy season, at the time of the equinoxes. The trees, fields and plants, are verdant all the year round. The soil is extremely rich, producing corn, grain, and fruits of all kinds, cedar trees, brazil wood, oak, ebony, logwood, iron wood, dying woods, cocoa, tobacco, sugar canes, cotton, cassavi root, potatoes, yams, sarsaparilla, gums, raisins, balsams of various kinds, pine apples, guavas, bonanas, &c. The forests are stored with wild honey, deer, wild fowls and parrots.

rots. The rivers and lakes abound with fish of all sorts; but are much infested with crocodiles, alligators and water serpents.

Inhabitants.] The Indian nations inhabiting this wide country are very numerous; the banks of almost every river are inhabited by a different people, who are governed by petty sovereigns, called Caciques, who are distinguished from their subjects by coronets of beautiful feathers. They are idolators, and worship the images of their ancient heroes. In their expeditions they carry their gods along with them.

History.] The first discovery of this country was made by Francisco Orellana, about the year 1580, who coming from Peru, sailed down the river Amazon to the Atlantic Ocean. He observed on the banks of the river, companies of women in arms, and from thence called the country Amazonia, or the land of the Amazons; and gave the name of Amazon to the river, which formerly had been called Maragon. The Spaniards made several attempts to plant this country, but always met with so many difficulties and disasters as rendered all their designs abortive. The Portuguese have some small settlements on that part of the coast which lies betwixt Cape North and the mouth of the river Amazon; but this excepted, the natives are in the sole possession of all the country.

✢✢✢✢✢✢✢✢✢✢✢✢✢✢✢✢✢✢✢✢✢✢✢✢✢✢✢✢✢✢✢✢✢✢✢✢

PATAGONIA.

IS a tract of country, 7 or 800 miles long, and 2 or 300 broad, at the southern extremity of the American continent.

Climate, Soil and Productions.] This country is full of high mountains, which are covered with snow most of the year. The storms of wind, rain and snow here are terrible. The soil is very barren and has never been cultivated.

Inhabitants, Character, &c.] The natives live in thatched huts, and wear no cloaths, notwithstanding the rigour of the climate. They live chiefly on fish and game, and what the earth spontaneously produces. They are of a tawny complexion, have black hair, and are a gigantic, brave, hardy, active race. Their arms are bows and arrows headed with flints. We know nothing of their government or religion.

History.] Ferdinand Magellan, a Portuguese in the service of Spain, first discovered this country; at least he was the first that sailed through the straits called by his name. Magellan passed these straits in the year 1519. The continent is often called Terra Magellanica; and the largest of the neighbouring isles, from a volcano in it. is called Terra del Fuego, the most southerly point of which is called Cape Horn.

Upon the first discovery of the Straits of Magellan, the Spaniards built forts and sent some colonies thither; but most of the people perished with cold and hunger; since which time no settlements have been attempted here by any Europeans.

West India Islands.

These belong to Great Britain, Spain, France, Holland and Denmark.

TO GREAT BRITAIN belong, Bermudas, the Bahama islands, Jamaica, Barbadoes, Antigua, St. Christopher's, Grenada, and the Grenadines, Nevis, Montserrat, Barbuda, Dominica, St. Vincent, Anguilla,—to which we may add their northern islands, Newfoundland, Cape Breton, and St. John's. Jamaica, the largest of the West India islands, is computed to produce annually 70,000 tons of sugar, upwards of 4,000,000 gallons of rum, besides coffee, cocoa, indigo and pepper.

To SPAIN belong, the island of Cuba, one half of St. Domingo, Porto Rico, Trinidad, Margaretta, Tortuga, Virgin Islands, to which we may add the island of Juan Fernandes, which lies 300 miles west of Chili, in the Pacific Ocean, famous for having given rise to the celebrated romance of Robinson Crusoe. The story is this: One Alexander Selkirk, a Scotchman, was left ashore in this solitary place, where he lived a number of years, till he was taken up by Capt. Rogers 1709; he had almost forgotten his native language, seeming to speak his words by halves. During his residence on the island, he had killed 500 goats by running them down, and he had marked as many more on the ear which he had let go. Upon his return to England he was advised to publish an account of his life and adventures, in his little kingdom. For this purpose he gave his papers into the hands of one Defoe, to prepare them for publication. But the writer, by the help of these papers, transformed Alexander Selkirk into Robinson Crusoe.

To the FRENCH belong, the largest part of the island of St. Domingo, the islands of Martinique, Guadaloupe, St. Lucia, Maria Galante, Tobago, St. Bartholomew, and Deseada, and the North American islands St. Pierre and Miquelon.—These, with their African and Asiatic possessions, and their settlements at Guiana and Cayenne, contain, according to Mr. Necker, 600,000 inhabitants.

To HOLLAND belong the islands of St. Eustatia, Saba and Curracoa.
To DENMARK belong the islands of St. Croix, St. Thomas, and St. John. In these islands the Moravians have useful establishments.

EUROPE.

Miles.
Length 3000 } Between { 10° West and 65° East Longitude from London.
Breadth 2500 } { 36° and 72° North Latitude.

Boundaries.] BOUNDED north, by the Frozen Ocean; east, by Asia; south, by the Mediterranean Sea, which divides it from Africa; west, by the Atlantic Ocean, which separates it from America. Containing 2,627,574 square miles.

Divisions,

EUROPE.

Divisions, Population, &c.] The following table,* exhibits the latest and most accurate account of the grand divisions of Europe—of their extent, and real and comparative population, of any extant.

Grand divisions of Europe.	Area of these states in square miles.	Population.	Number of inhabitants in each square mile.	Public Revenue in sterling money.
Russia, (in Europe)	1,104,976	20,000,000	20	£5,800,000
Sweden,	209,392	3,000,000	14	1,300,000
Denmark,	182,400	2,200,000	12	1,000,000
Poland & Lithuania	160,800	8,500,000	53	
Germany,	192,000	26,000,000	135	
The kingdom of Prussia alone,	22,144	1,500,000	67	3,600,000
France,	163,200	24,800,000	152	18,000,000
Holland,	10,000	2,360,000	236	4,000,000
Great Britain and Ireland,	100,928	11,000,000	109	14,500,000
Switzerland,	15,296	1,500,000	117	
Gallizia and Lodomiria,	20,480	2,800,000	136	
Italy,	90,000	16,000,000	180	
Portugal,	27,376	2,000,000	65	1,800,000
Hungary & Transylvania,	92,112	5,170,000	56	
Spain,	148,448	10,000,000	68	5,000,000‡
Turkey,	182,562	7,000,000	38	5,000,000
Total	2,712,114	144,130,000	140	

Military

* From Zimmermann's ' Political Survey and Present State of Europe,' published in London, 1787.
§ Exclusive of Ireland.   ‡ Of Old Spain alone.

EUROPE.

Military and Marine Strength.] The land forces of the European states, in the year 1783, were as follows:

France	300,000	Holland	37,000
Austria	282,000	Naples and Sicily	30,000
Russia, (450,000 in all) in Europe	290,000	Electorate of Saxony	26,000
Prussia	224,000	Portugal	20,000
Turkey, (210,000 in all) in Europe, only	170,000	Electorate of Bavaria and the Palatinate	24,000
Spain (including militia)	60,000	Hesse Cassel	15,000
Denmark	72,000	Hanover	20,000
Great Britain (including militia)	58,000	Poland	15,000
		Venice	8,000
Sweden	50,000	Wurtemburg	6,000
Sardinia	40,000	The Ecclesiastical state	5,000
		Tuscany	3,000

Including the parts o[f] [E]urope omitted in this calculation, the armies of all the countries of Eu[rop]e, amount to two millions of men; so that supposing one hundre[d and] forty millions of inhabitants in Europe, no more than $\frac{1}{7^\circ}$ [of th]e population are soldiers.

Number of Ships of the Line, Frigates, Cutters, Sloops, &c.

England	465	Russia	63
France	266	Sardinia	32
Spain	130	Venice	30
Holland	95	Sicily	25
Sweden	85	Portugal	24
Denmark	60		
Turkey	50	Total	1325

Religion.] The religions of Europe are the Christian, the Jewish and the Mahometan. The two first are spread all over Europe; the first and last are the only established ones, the Jewish being merely tolerated. The chief divisions of the Christian, are the Greek, the Roman Catholic, and the Protestant. The Greek religion is established only in Russia, and tolerated in some parts of the Austrian dominions, in Poland, and chiefly in Turkey: subdivisions of the Greek church, are the Armenian and Nestorian church. Of the Roman Catholic church, Jansenism is a subdivision. The protestant religion is subdivided into the Lutheran and Calvinist, or reformed religion: Of the former the Episcopal church of England and Ireland is a branch: Of the latter the Presbyterian church of Scotland. There are, besides, many sects adapted to the different degrees of theological knowledge, or to the different warmth of imagination of those that adhere to them: The principal of these sects are Arminians, Mennonists, Socinians, Unitarians, Moravian Brethern, Quakers and Methodists. The portion of the surface of the countries, in which the Protestant religion is established, to those in which the Roman Catholic religion prevails, is nearly as 3 to 4: The number of Roman Catholics, according to the best

best calculations, is about 90,000,000; the number of Protestants only 24,000,000, which is a proportion of nearly 4 to 1.

A concise view of the several countries of Europe, proceeding from south to north, follows. My authorities are Zimmermann and Guthrie.

✛✛✛✛✛✛✛✛✛✛✛✛✛✛✛✛✛✛✛✛✛✛✛✛✛✛✛✛✛✛✛✛✛✛✛✛

PORTUGAL.

Miles.
Length 300 } Between { 37° and 42° North Latitude.
Breadth 100 } { 7° and 10° West Longitude.

Boundaries.] BOUNDED north and east, by Spain; south and west, by the Atlantic Ocean. Containing 19 towns, 527 villages, 3343 parishes.

Rivers.] Every brook in Portugal is called a river. Its rivers rise in Spain and run west through Portugal, into the Atlantic. The most noted is the Tagus.

Capital.] LISBON, at the mouth of the Tagus, containing about 150,000 inhabitants. In 1755, it was laid level with the ground by a tremendous earthquake, which was succeeded by a general conflagration, in which catastrophe upwards of 10,000 people lost their lives.

Climate, Productions and Commerce.] Portugal, situated in a genial climate, abounds in excellent natural productions, and is well watered. It possesses very rich provinces in, and upon the coast of, Asia, Africa and America. It is, however, not proportionably powerful; its inhabitants are indigent, and the balance of trade is against it. It is even obliged to import the necessaries of life, chiefly corn, from other countries. Portugal produces wine, wool, oil, silk, honey, aniseed, sumac, a variety of fine fruits, some corn, flax and cork. In 1785, the goods imported from Great Britain and Ireland into Portugal, consisting of woolens, corn, fish, wood and hard ware, amounted to upwards of 960,000 sterling. The English took in return, of the produce of Portugal and Brasil, to the amount of £728,000 sterling. Only 15 millions of livres are supposed to circulate in a country which draws annually upwards of £1,500,000 sterling, or 36 millions of livres, from the mines of Peru. Since the discovery of these mines, that is, within 60 years, Portugal has brought from Brasil about 2400 millions of livres, or £100,000,000 sterling.

Government and religion.] Since the *council* of the three estates, viz. the clergy, the nobility, and the cities, the members of which are nominated by the king, was substituted in the room of diets or meetings of the states (which event took place the latter end of the last century) the government of the kingdom of Portugal has been absolutely monarchical. The proceedings of the courts of justice are slow and arbitrary, and the number of lawyers and law officers is exceedingly great.

The

PORTUGAL.

The state of religion in Portugal is the same as in Spain. The Portugese clergy consist of one patriarch, a dignity granted to the church of Portugal in the year 1716, of 3 archbishops and 15 bishops. The whole number of ecclesiastics is 200,000: 30,000 of which, and some say 60,000 are monks and nuns. The number of convents is 745. The number of clerical persons to that of the laymen is as 1 to 11.

History.] Portugal was anciently called Lusitania, and inhabited by tribes of wandering people, till it became subject to the Carthaginians and Phœnicians, who were dispossessed by the Romans 250 years before Christ. In the fifth century it fell under the yoke of the Suevi and Vandals, who were driven out by the Goths of Spain, in the year 589; but when the Moors of Africa made themselves masters of the greatest part of Spain, in the beginning of the eighth century, they penetrated into Lusitania: there they established governors, who made themselves kings. After many fruitless attempts made by the kings of Leon on this part of Spain, Alonzo V. king of Castile and Leon, carried here his victorious arms, and to insure his conquest, he gave it, in the year 1088, with the title of count, or earl, to Henry, grandson of Robert king of France, who had married Theresa, Alonzo's natural daughter. Henry was succeeded in his earldom by his son Alonzo, who, encouraged by his conquests over the Moors, in the year 1139 assumed the title of king of Portugal. His successors continued till 1580, when, upon the death of Henry, surnamed the Cardinal, it was seized upon by Philip II. king of Spain, after a war of two or three years; but in 1640, the people rebelled, shook off the Spanish yoke, and elected for their king the duke of Braganza, who took the name of John IV. in whose family it has ever since remained independent of Spain. Her present Majesty's name is Mary Frances Isabella, who acceded to the throne in the year 1777.

✤✤

SPAIN.

Miles.
Length 700 } Between { 36° and 44° North Latitude.
Breadth 500 }   { 3° and 10° East Longitude.

Boundaries.] BOUNDED west, by Portugal and the Atlantic; north, by the Bay of Biscay and the Pyrenean mountains, which divide it from France; east and south, by the Mediterranean sea, and the Straits of Gibraltar.

Spain is divided into 14 districts, in which are 139 towns, and 21,083 villages and boroughs.

Rivers.] The Deuro, the Tagus, the Guadiana, the Guadalquiver, all which fall into the Atlantic ocean, and the Ebro, the ancient Iberus, which falls into the Mediterranean.

Capital.] MADRID, situated on a branch of the river Tagus, containing 140,000 inhabitants. CADIZ, situated on the Atlantic, a little to the northward of the Straits of Gibraltar, is the great emporium of Spain, and contains 80,000 inhabitants.

Wealth and commerce.] The advantages of Spain, as to climate, foil, natural productions, rivers, navigation and foreign poffeffions, which are immenfely rich, ought to raife this monarchy high above all other powers of Europe. Yet the reverfe is the cafe: Spain is but thinly peopled—has but little commerce—few manufactures—and what commerce it has, is almoft entirely in the hands of ftrangers, notwithftanding the impediments thrown in their way by the government.

Spain produces excellent oranges, lemons, almonds, figs, grapes, pomegranates, dates, piftachios, capers, chefnuts,—tobacco, foda, faffron, honey, falt, faltpetre, wines, of a rich and delicious flavour; cotton, rice, corn, oil, wool, filk, hemp, flax, &c. which, with proper induftry, might be exported to an amazing amount. And yet all the exports of Spain, moft articles of which no other country can fupply, are eftimated at only £3,333,333 fterling. Spain does not produce corn enough for its own confumption, and is under the neceffity of importing large quantities.

Government.] Spain is an abfolute monarchy. The provinces of Navarre, Bifcay and Arragon, have preferved fome of their ancient privileges. The kings edicts muft be regiftered in the court of Carlifle, before they acquire the force of laws. The crown is hereditary both in the male and female line. By a law made in 1715, female heirs cannot fucceed till after the whole male line is extinct.

Religion.] The Roman Catholic religion, to the exclufion of all others, is the religion of the Spanifh monarchy; and it is, in thefe countries, of the moft bigotted, fuperftitious and tyrannical character. All other denominations of Chriftians, as well as Jews, are expofed to all the feverities of perfecution. The power of the court of Inquifition, eftablifhed in Spain in 1578, has been diminifhed, in fome refpects, by the interference of the civil power. It is fuppofed that the clergy of this kingdom amount to 200,000, half of whom are monks and nuns, diftributed in 3000 convents. The revenue of the archbifhop of Toledo is 300,000 ducats. There are in the kingdom of Spain 8 archbifhops, 46 bifhops; in America fix archbifhops and 28 bifhops; in the Phillippine ifles, one archbifhop and 3 bifhops. All thefe dignities are in the gift of the king. Fifty two inferior ecclefiaftical dignities and offices are in the gift of the pope.

Hiftory.] The firft inhabitants of Spain were the Celtæ, a people of Gaul; after them the Phœnicians poffeffed themfelves of the moft fouthern parts of the country, and may well be fuppofed to have been the firft civilizers of this kingdom, and the founders of the moft ancient cities. After thefe followed the Grecians; then the Carthaginians, on whofe departure, fixteen years before Chrift, it became fubject to the Romans, till the year 400, when the Goths, Vandals, Suevi, Alans and Sillingi, on Conftantine's withdrawing his forces from that kingdom to the eaft, invaded it, and divided it amongft themfelves; but the Goths in a little time were fole mafters of it under their king ALARICK I. who founded the Spanifh monarchy. After a regular fucceffion of monarchs, we come to the prefent king CHARLES III. who afcended the throne upon the death of his half brother FERDINAND VI. in the year 1759.

FRANCE.

FRANCE.

Miles.
Length 600 } Between { 45° and 51° North Latitude.
Breadth 500 }   { 5° and 8° East Longitude.

Boundaries.] BOUNDED north, by the English channel and the Netherlands; east, by Germany, Switzerland and Italy; south, by the Mediterranean and Spain; west, by the Bay of Biscay. Containing 400 cities, 1500 smaller towns, 43,000 parishes, 100,000 villages.

Climate, soil, rivers, commerce, &c.] France is situated in a very mild climate. Its soil in most parts is very fertile; it is bounded by high ridges of mountains, the lower branches of which cross the greater part of the kingdom; it consequently abounds with large rivers, such as the Rhone, the Loire, the Garonne, the Seine, &c. to the amount of 200 which are navigable; and it is contiguous to two oceans. These united advantages render this kingdom one of the richest countries of Europe, both with respect to natural productions and commerce. Wine is the staple commodity of France. One million six hundred thousand acres of ground are laid out in vineyards; and the net profit from each acre is estimated at from 4 to 7 pounds sterling. France annually exports wines to the amount of 24 millions of livres. The fruits and other productions of France, do not much differ from those of Spain, but are raised in much greater plenty. France has very important fisheries, both on her own, and on the American coast.

In 1773, there were in France 1500 silk mills, 21,000 looms for silk stuffs, 12,000 for ribbands and lace, 20,000 for silk stockings, and the different silk manufactures employed 2,000,000 of people.

In point of commerce, France may be ranked next to England and Holland. The French have the greatest share of the Levant trade—they enjoy some valuable commercial privileges in Turkey—but their West India possessions, which are admirably cultivated and governed, are the richest. Before the late American war, the balance of commerce in favour of France was estimated at 70,000,000 livres, and has not since been diminished.

Government.] France is at present one of the most absolute monarchies in Europe. The king is exclusively possessed of the supreme power of the state, and according to the doctrine of the French law, he is to be considered as the vicegerent of God, from whom alone he derives his authority. There are now in France twelve parliaments or assemblies of provincial states, which are properly supreme courts of justice and appeal, with some few political rights—one is to remonstrate against the edicts of the king that appear unjust.

Religion.] The established religion of this kingdom is the Roman Catholic; and since the year 1685, in which the edict of Nantes was repealed, greatly to the prejudice of the kingdom, no other christian sect is

legally

legally tolerated. Even in the present enlightened age, the penal laws against the protestants are not abolished; a pressure that continues to be severely felt by the latter, although it has been found expedient not to put the laws against them in execution. Alsatia is the only province where they enjoy the free exercise of their religion. This province is said to contain 3,000,000 of souls.

In France there are 18 archbishops, 111 bishops, 166,000 clergymen, 5400 convents, containing 200,000 persons devoted to monastic life.

Learning.] The sciences have arisen to a very great height in this kingdom, and this nation can boast of having produced great master pieces in almost every branch of scientific knowledge and elegant literature. There are 20 universities in France. The royal academies of sciences, of the French language, and of inscriptions and antiquities at Paris, are justly celebrated.

History.] France was originally the country of the ancient Gauls, and was conquered by the Romans twenty-five years before Christ. The Goths, Vandals, Alans and Suevi, and afterwards the Burgundi, divided it amongst them from A. D. 400 to 476, when the Franks, another set of German emigrants, who had settled between the Rhine and the Maine, completed the foundation of the present kingdom under Clovis. It was conquered, except Paris, by Edward III. of England, between 1341 and 1359. In 1420 an entire conquest was made by Henry V. who was appointed regent, during the life of Charles VI. acknowledged heir to the crown of France, and homage paid to him accordingly. The English crown lost all its possessions in France during the reign of Henry VI. between 1434 and 1450.

The present king of this potent empire, is Lewis XVI. who was born Aug. 23, 1754; married Maria Antonietta of Austria, May 16, 1770; acceded to the throne upon the death of his grand-father Lewis XV. May 10, 1774, and was crowned at Rheims, June 12, 1775.

✤✤✤✤✤✤✤✤✤✤✤✤✤✤✤✤✤✤✤✤✤✤✤✤✤✤✤✤✤✤✤✤✤✤✤✤

ITALY.

Miles.

Length 600 } Between { 38° and 47° North Latitude.
Breadth 400 } { 7° and 19° East Longitude.

ITALY is a large peninsula, shaped like a boot and spur; and is bounded north, by the Alps, which divide it from France and Switzerland; east, by the gulf of Venice, or Adriatic Sea; south and west, by the Mediterranean sea.

The whole of the Italian dominions comprehending Corsica and Sardinia, are divided as follows:

To the kingdom of Sardinia, belong
{ Piedmont,
  Savoy,
  Montferrat.
  Alessandrine,
  Oneglia,
  Sardinia island,

To their respective Princes.
{ Tuscany,
  Massa,
  Parma,
  Modena,
  Piombino,
  Monaco.

The

To the kingdom of Naples,	Naples, Scicily island,	Republics,	Lucca, St. Marino, Genoa,
To the Emperor,	Milan, Mantua, Mirandola.	To France,	Corsica Island.
Popes dominions.		To the republic of Venice.	Venice, Istria, Dalmatia, Isles of Dalmatia

Islands in the Venetian dominions.

Air, soil and productions.] Italy is the most celebrated country in Europe, having been formerly the seat of the Roman empire, and is at present of the Pope. The country is so fine and fruitful, that it is commonly called the garden of Europe. The air is temperate and wholesome, excepting the territory of the church, where it is very indifferent. The soil is fertile and produces wheat, rice, wine, oil, oranges and all sorts of fruits, flowers, honey, silk; and in the kingdom of Naples are cotton and sugar. The forests are full of all kinds of game. On the mountains are fine pastures, which feed great numbers of cattle.

Inhabitants and character.] Italy contains between 12 and 13 millions of inhabitants. The Italians excel in complaisant, obliging behaviour to each other, and affability to foreigners; observing a medium between the levity of the French, and the starch'd gravity of the Spaniards, and are by far the soberest people that are to be found in the christian world, though they abound in the choicest of wines. Nothing of luxury is to be seen at the tables of the great. They are generally men of wit, and have a genius for the arts and sciences; nor do they want application. Music, poetry, painting, sculpture and architecture are their favourite studies, and there are no people on the face of the earth who have brought them to greater perfection. But they are amorous and addicted to criminal indulgences, revengeful, and masters of the art of dissimulation. The women say they only desire good features, they can make their complexion what they please.

Religion.] The Italians are zealous professors of the doctrine of the church of Rome. The Jews are here tolerated in the public exercise of their religion. The natives, either in reverence to the Pope, or by being industriously kept in ignorance of the protestant doctrines, entertain monstrous notions of all the dissenters from the church of Rome. The inquisition here is little more than a sound. In Naples there are 20 archbishops, 107 bishops: in Sicily 3 archbishops, and 8 bishops. In the year 1782 there were in Naples alone, 45,525 priests, 24,694 monks, 20,793 nuns. In 1783, government resolved to dissolve 466 convents of nuns.

Chief city.] Rome, once the capital of the world, is now the chief city in Italy. It contained, in the year 1714, 143,000 inhabitants, and is situated upon the river Tyber. It was founded by Romulus 750 years before Christ, and was formerly three times as large as at present; and is now one of the largest and handsomest cities in Europe.

Mountains.] Mount Vesuvius, in the kingdom of Naples, and Ætna, in Sicily, are remarkable for their fiery eruptions, which frequently bury whole cities in ruins.

Government.]

SWITZERLAND. 499

Government.] The government of Venice is aristocratical, under a chief magistrate called a *Doge*, who is said to be a king as to robes, a senator in the council-house, a prisoner within the city, and a private man out of it.

There are many different sovereignties in Italy. It is divided into little republics, principalities, and dukedoms, which, in spiritual matters, are subject to the Pope, who, like the ghost of the deceased Roman empire, sits crowned upon its grave.

History.] The æra of the foundation of Rome begins April 20, 753 years before the birth of Christ. Authors generally assign the honour to Romulus its first king, who was but eighteen years old. He was a wise, courageous and politic prince.

St. Peter is placed at the head of the popes or bishops of Rome, in the 33d year of the common æra. The present pope is Pius VI. elected February 15, 1775.

✦✦

SWITZERLAND.

Miles.
Length 260 } Between { 6° and 11° East Longitude.
Breadth 100 } { 45° and 48° North Latitude.

Boundaries.] BOUNDED north, by Germany; east, by Tirol, Trent and Lake Constance; south, by Italy; west, by France.

Cities.] BERN, on the river Aar, is the most considerable city in Switzerland. BASIL, on the banks of the Rhine, contains 220 streets, and by some is reckoned the capital of all Switzerland.

Rivers.] The principal rivers are the Rhine and Rhone, both of which rise in the Alps.

Air, soil and productions.] This country is full of mountains; on the tops of some of them the snow remains the year round; the air of consequence is keen, and the frosts severe. In the summer the inequality of the soil renders the same province very unequal in its seasons. On one side of the mountains, called the Alps, the inhabitants are often reaping, while they are sowing on the other. The vallies however, are warm, fruitful and well cultivated. The water of Switzerland is excellent, descending from the mountains in beautiful cataracts, which have a most pleasing and delightful effect. Its productions are, sheep, cattle, wine, flax, wheat, barley, apples, peaches, cherries, chesnuts and plums.

Population and character.] For the number of inhabitants, see table of Europe.

The Swifs are a brave, hardy, industrious people, remarkable for their fidelity and their zealous attachment to the liberties of their country. A general simplicity of manners, an open, unaffected frankness, together with

SWITZERLAND.

with an invincible spirit of freedom, are the most distinguishing characteristics of the inhabitants of Switzerland. On the first entrance into this country, travellers cannot but observe the air of content and satisfaction, which appears in the countenances of the inhabitants. A taste for literature is prevalent among them, from the highest to the lowest rank. These are the happy consequences of a mild republican government.

Religion.] The established religions are calvinism and popery; though, in some doctrinal points, they differ much from Calvin. Their sentiments on religious toleration are much less liberal, than upon civil government.

Government.] Switzerland comprehends thirteen cantons, that is, so many different republics, all united in one confederacy, for their mutual preservation. The government is partly aristocratical, and partly democratical. Every canton is absolute in its own jurisdiction. But whether the government be aristocratical, democratical or mixed, a general spirit of liberty pervades and actuates the several constitutions. The real interests of the people appear to be attended to, and they enjoy a degree of happiness, not to be expected in despotic governments.

History.] The old inhabitants of this country were called Helvetii; they were defeated by Julius Cæsar, 57 years before Christ, and the territory remained subject to the Romans, till it was conquered by the Alemans, German emigrants, A. D. 395; who were expelled by Clovis, king of France, in 496. It underwent another revolution in 888, being made part of the kingdom of Burgundy. In 1032, it was given, by the last king of Burgundy, to Conrad II. emperor of Germany; from which time it was held as part of the empire, till the year 1307, when a very singular revolt delivered the Swiss cantons from the German yoke. Grisler, governor of these provinces for the emperor Albert, having ordered one William Tell, an illustrious Swiss patriot, under pain of death, to shoot at an apple, placed on the head of one of his children, he had the dexterity, though the distance was very considerable, to strike it off without hitting the child. The tyrant perceiving that he had another arrow under his cloak, asked him for what purpose? to which he boldly replied, "To have shot you to the heart, if I'd had the misfortune to kill my son." The enraged governor ordered him to be hanged, but his fellow citizens, animated by his fortitude, and patriotism, flew to arms, attacked and vanquished Grisler, who was shot dead by Tell, and the independency of the several states of this country, now called the Thirteen Cantons, under a republican form of government, took place immediately; which was made perpetual by a league among themselves, in the year 1315; and confirmed by treaty with the other powers of Europe 1649. Seven of these cantons are Roman catholics, and six protestants.

TURKEY,

TURKEY.

TURKEY, in Europe.

Miles.

Length 1000 } Between { 17° and 40° East Longitude.
Breadth 900 } { 36° and 49° North Latitude.

Boundaries.] BOUNDED north, by Russia, Poland and Sclavonia; east, by Circassia, the Black Sea, the Propontis, Hellespont and Archipelago; south by the Mediterranean Sea; west, by the same sea, and the Venetian and Austrian territories.

Soil, air and productions.] Nature has been lavish of her blessings upon the inhabitants of Turkey in these particulars. The soil, though unimproved, through the indolence of the Turks, is luxuriant beyond description. The air is salubrious and friendly to the imagination, unless corrupted by the neighbouring countries, or through the uncleanliness of its inhabitants. The seasons here are regular and pleasant, and have been celebrated from the remotest times of antiquity. The Turks are invited to frequent bathings, by the purity and wholsomeness of the water, in every part of their dominions. Raw silk, cotton, oil, leather, tobacco, cake-soap, honey, wax, manna, and various fruits and drugs, are here produced in plenty.

Chief Cities.] CONSTANTINOPLE, the capital of this empire, stands on the west side of the Bosphorus, in the province of Romania, was rebuilt by the emperor Constantine in the fourth century, who transferred hither the seat of the Roman government; upon his death it obtained the name of Constantinople.

It is of a triangular shape, washed by the sea on two sides, and rising gradually from the shore, in the form of an amphitheatre. The view of it from the harbour is confessedly the finest in the world, exhibiting a multitude of magnificent mosques, or temples, with their domes and minarets, and the seraglio intermixed with gardens and groves of evergreens. The expectations excited by this prospect, however, are disappointed on entering the city, where we find the streets narrow, the houses of the common people low and built of boards, and the palaces of the great men concealed by high walls before them. The city is surrounded by a wall about twelve miles in circumference, and the suburbs are very extensive. It contains 1,000,000 souls, of which 200,000 are Greeks, 40,000 Armenians, and 60,000 Jews.

Mountains,] In Thessaly, besides mount Olympus, which the ancients esteemed one of the highest mountains in the world, are those of Pelion and Ossa, mentioned so often by the poets; between these mountains, lie the celebrated plains of Tempe, represented by the ancients as equal to the Elysian Fields.

Religion.] The established religion in this empire is the Mahometan, of the sect the Sunnites. All other religions are tolerated on paying a certain capitation. Among the Christians residing in Turkey, those of the orthodox Greeks are the most numerous, and they enjoy, among other privileges, that of being advanced to dignities and posts of trust and profit.

fit. The Turkish clergy are numerous, being composed of all the learned in the empire, and are the only teachers of the law, and must be consulted in all important cases.

Government.] The Turkish emperor, who is usually called the Grand Seignior, has an unlimited power over the lives and fortunes of his subjects. But this he exercises chiefly towards his ministers and officers of state. Their laws in general are equitable, if duly executed, but justice is frequently bought and sold.

Character.] A Turk, or Persian, contemplates his emperor with fear and reverence, as a superior being to whose pleasure it is his duty to submit, as much as unto the laws of nature and the will of Providence.

History.] The *Ottoman* empire, or sovereignty of the Turkish empire, was founded at Constantinople by Othman I. upon the total destruction of the empire of the eastern Greeks in the year 1300, who was succeeded by a race of the most warlike princes that are recorded in history. The Turkish throne is hereditary in the family of Osman. The present Ottoman, or Turkish emperor, is ABDELHAMET or ACHMET III. who had been in confinement forty-four years. He succeeded his brother Mustapha III. January 21, 1774.

✧✧✧✧✧✧✧✧✧✧✧✧✧✧✧✧✧✧✧✧✧✧✧✧✧✧✧✧✧✧✧✧✧✧✧✧

HUNGARY, belonging to the house of Austria.

Miles. Sq. M.
Length 300 } Between { 17° and 23° East Longitude. } 36,060.
Breadth 200 }   { 45° and 49° North Latitude. }

Boundaries.] BOUNDED north, by Poland; east, by Transylvania and Walachia; south, by Sclavonia; west, by Austria and Moravia. Divided into *Upper Hungary*, north of the Danube; and *Lower Hungary*, south of the Danube.

Population.] See table of Europe.

Air, soil and produce.] The air in the southern parts of Hungary is very unhealthy, owing to stagnated waters in lakes and marshes. The air in the northern parts is more serene and healthy. The soil in some parts is very fertile, and produces almost every kind of fruits. They have a fine breed of mouse coloured horses, much esteemed by military officers.

Religion.] The established religion in Hungary is the Roman Catholic, though the greater part of the inhabitants are Protestants or Greeks; and they now enjoy the full exercise of their religious liberties.

Government.] By the constitution of Hungary, the crown is still held to be elective. This point is not disputed. All that is insisted on is, that the heir of the house of Austria shall be elected as often as a vacancy happens.

The regalia of Hungary, consisting of the crown and sceptre of St. Stephen, the first king, are deposited in Presburg. These are carefully secured

secured by seven locks, the keys of which are kept by the same number of Hungarian noblemen. No prince is held by the populace as legally their sovereign, till he be crowned with the diadem of king Stephen; and they have a notion that the fate of their nation depends upon this crown's remaining in their possession; it has therefore been always removed in times of danger, to places of the greatest safety.

Chief Towns.] Presburg, in Upper Hungary, is the capital of the whole kingdom. It is well built on the Danube, and, like Vienna, has suburbs more magnificent than itself. In this city the states of Hungary hold their assemblies, and in the cathedral church the sovereign is crowned.

History.] This kingdom is the ancient Pannonia. Julius Cæsar was the first Roman that attacked Hungary, and Tiberius subdued it. The Goths afterwards took it; and in the year 376, it became a prey to the Huns and Lombards. It was annexed to the empire of Germany under Charlemange, but became an independent kingdom in 920. It was the seat of bloody wars between the Turks and Germans, from 1540 to 1739, when, by the treaty of Belgrade, it was ceded to the latter, and is now annexed to the German empire. Formerly it was an assemblage of different states, and Stephen was the first who assumed the title of king, in the year 997. He was distinguished with the appellation of SAINT, because he first introduced christianity into this country. The present sovereign is, MARIA THERESA, who succeeded her father CHARLES VI. February 12, 1736. She married Francis Stephen grand duke of Lorain, chosen emperor September, 1745; who died in August, 1765, by whom she had the present emperor Joseph II.

✠✠✠✠✠✠✠✠✠✠✠✠✠✠✠✠✠✠✠✠✠✠✠✠✠✠✠✠✠✠✠✠✠✠✠✠✠✠✠

GERMANY

Miles.
Length 600 } Between { 45° 4' and 54° 40' North Latitude.
Breadth 520   5° and 19° East Longitude.

Boundaries.] BOUNDED north, by the German Ocean, Denmark, and the Baltic; east, by Poland and Hungary; south, by Switzerland and the Alps, which divide it from Italy; west, by the dominions of France and the Low Countries, from which it is separated by the Rhine, Moselle, and the Mease.

Divisions.] The German empire is divided into ten circles, viz.

Circles.	Population.	Circles.	Population.
Upper Saxony	3,700,000	Burgundy	1,880,000
Lower Saxony	2,100,000	Franconia	1,000,000
Westphalia	2,300,000	Swabia	1,800,000
Upper Rhine	1,000,000	Bavaria	1,600,000
Lower Rhine	1,100,000	Austria,	4,182.000

Besides

Besides these ten circles there belong also to the German empire,

	Population.
The kingdom of Bohemia, divided into 16 circles	2,266,000
The Marquisate of Moravia, in 5 circles,	1,137,000
The Marquisate of Lusatia, (belonging to the elector of Saxony)	400,000
Silesia, (belonging to the Roman empire)	1,800,000

Productions and Commerce.] From the advantageous situation and the great extent of Germany, from the various appearance of the soil, the number of its mountains, forests and large rivers, we should be led to expect, what we actually find, a great variety and plenty of useful productions. The northern, and chiefly the northeastern parts, furnish many sorts of peltry, as skins of foxes, bears, wolves, squirrels, lynxes, wild-cats, boars, &c.—The southern parts produce excellent wines and fruits; and the middle provinces great plenty of corn, cattle and minerals. Salt is found in Germany in greater abundance and purity than in most other countries.

If the Germans are inferior to the English in the manufactures of cloth, hardware, and in the articles of luxury, it must be accounted for from the political situation of their country: The great number of princes, the variety of the forms of government, the different interests and mutual jealousies of the petty states, operate as checks on the commerce and prosperity of the whole; and the difficulty of obtaining their concurrence in measures of general utility, is frequently the cause, why there are so few canals and good roads, to facilitate travelling and inland trade.

Government.] The German empire, which till the year 843, was connected with France, now forms a state by itself, or may be considered as a combination of upwards of 300 sovereignties, independent of each other, but composing one political body under an elective head, called the Emperor of Germany, or the Roman Emperor. All other sovereigns allow him the first rank among the European monarchs. Eight princes of the empire, called Electors, have the right of electing the emperor. The electors are divided into ecclesiastical and temporal.

Ecclesiastical.
- The Archbishop of Mentz,
- The Archbishop of Treves,
- The Archbishop of Cologne.

Temporal.
- The King or Elector of Bohemia,
- The Elector of the Palatine of Bavaria,
- The Elector of Saxony,
- The Elector of Brandenburg,
- The Elector of Brunswick, (Hanover) Temporal.

The emperor, upon his election, engages to protect the Roman Catholic religion and the Holy See. He is lord Paramount of the Roman empire, of whom the princes are supposed to hold their dominions in fee—He has power to assemble the Diet, over which he presides in person or by his commissary, and of ratifying their resolutions by his confirmation—He is supreme judge—has power to confer titles of nobility—to establish post offices throughout the empire—to give charters to the universities, and to confer

confer academical degrees. The Diet, which is composed of the emperor and of the immediate states of the empire, have power to levy taxes, give laws, make war, and conclude treaties of peace, by which the whole empire is bound. The states of the empire, which are differently constituted and governed, considered in their separate capacity, enjoy sovereign power in their respective dominions, limited only by the above mentioned laws.

Religion.] Since the year 1555, the Roman Catholic, the Lutheran, and the Calvinist, generally called the Reformed Religion, have been the established religions of Germany. The first prevails in the south of Germany, the Lutheran in the north, and the Reformed near the Rhine.

Capital.] VIENNA, on the Danube is the capital of Austria, and of the whole German empire; and is the residence of the Emperor.

Improvements.] The Germans can boast of a greater number of useful discoveries and inventions in arts and sciences than any other European nation. They have the honour of inventing the art of printing, about the year 1450.

History, &c.] Charlemange, or Charles the Great, king of France was the founder of the German empire, in 800. Joseph II. the present emperor, was born March 13, 1741, and crowned king of the Romans, 1764. In 1765, he was elected emperor, upon the death of his father Francis I.

The German empire, when considered as one single power or state, with the emperor at its head, is of no great political consequence in Europe; because, from the inequality and weak connection of its parts, and the different nature of their government, from the insignificancy of its ill composed army, and above all from the different views and interests of its masters, it is next to impossible its force should be united, compact and uniform.

✧✧✧✧✧✧✧✧✧✧✧✧✧✧✧✧✧✧✧✧✧✧✧✧✧✧✧✧✧✧✧✧✧✧✧✧✧

THE NETHERLANDS, OR FLANDERS.

Miles.
Length 220 } Between { 49° and 52° North Latitude.
Breadth 200 } { 2° and 7° East Longitude.

Boundaries.] BOUNDED north, by Holland; east, by Germany; south and west, by France and the English Sea.

Divisions.] This country is divided into ten provinces, named,

Provinces	Chief Towns.
Brabant, belonging to the Dutch and Austrians,	{ Breda, Brussels.
Antwerp, Malines. } subject to the house of Austria,	Antwerp.
	Limburg,

HOLLAND, OR THE UNITED PROVINCES.

Provinces.	Chief Towns.
Limburg, belonging to the Dutch and Auſtrians,	Limburg.
Luxemburg, Auſtrian and French,	Luxemburg.
Namur, middle parts belonging to Auſtria,	Namur.
Hainault, Auſtrian and French,	Mons.
Cambreſis, ſubject to France,	Cambray.
Artois, ſubject to France,	Arras.
Flanders, belonging to the Dutch, Auſtrians and French	Ghent, Oſtend.

Inhabitants and religion.] The Netherlands are inhabited by about 1,500,000 ſouls. The Roman Catholic is the eſtabliſhed religion, but Proteſtants and Jews are not moleſted.

Manufactures.] Their principal manufactures are, fine lawns, cambrics, lace and tapeſtry, with which they carry on a very advantageous traffic, eſpecially with England, from whence, it is computed, they receive a balance of half a million annually in time of peace.

Chief towns.] BRUSSELS is the chief town of Brabant and the capital of Flanders. Here the beſt camblets are made, and moſt of the fine laces, which are worn in every part of the world.

Antwerp, once the emporium of the European continent, is now reduced to be a tapeſtry and thread-lace ſhop. One of the firſt exploits of the Dutch, ſoon fter they ſhook off the Spaniſh yoke, was to ruin at once the commerce of Antwerp, by ſinking veſſels loaded with ſtone in the mouth of the river Scheldt; thus ſhutting up the entrance of that river to ſhips of burden. This was the more cruel, as the people of Antwerp had been their friends and fellow ſufferers in the cauſe of liberty.

Hiſtory.] Flanders, originally the country of the ancient Belgæ, was conquered by Julius Cæſar forty-ſeven years before Chriſt; paſſed into the hands of France A. D. 412; and was governed by its earls, ſubject to that crown, from 864 to 1369. By marriage it then came into the houſe of Auſtria; but was yielded to Spain in 1556. Shook off the Spaniſh yoke 1572, and in the year 1725, by the treaty of Vienna, was annexed to the German empire.

✣✣✣✣✣✣✣✣✣✣✣✣✣✣✣✣✣✣✣✣✣✣✣✣✣✣✣✣✣✣✣✣✣✣✣✣✣✣

HOLLAND, OR THE UNITED PROVINCES.

	Miles.			Sq. Mil.
Length	180	Between	$51°\ 20'$ and $53°\ 30'$ N. Lat.	10,000
Breadth	145		$2°$ and $7°$ Eaſt Longitude.	

Boundaries.] BOUNDED eaſt, by Germany; ſouth, by the Auſtrian and French Netherlands; weſt and north by the German Ocean. Containing 113 towns, 1400 villages.

Divided

HOLLAND, or the UNITED PROVINCES.

Divided into seven provinces.

Provinces.	Chief Towns.	Inhab.	Provinces.	Chief Towns.
Gelder,	Nimweguen,	12,000.	Friesland,	Leuwarden.
Holland,	Amsterdam,	212,000.	Overyssel,	Deventer.
Utrecht,	Utrecht,	30,000.	Groenigen,	Groenigen.
Zeeland,	Middleburg,	24,000.		

Country of Drenthe, under the protection of the United Provinces. Lands of the Generality, commonly called Dutch Brabant.

Wealth and commerce.] The seven United Provinces afford a striking proof, that unwearied and persevering industry is capable of conquering every disadvantage of climate and situation. The air and water are bad; the soil naturally produces scarcely any thing but turf; and the possession of this soil, poor as it is, is disputed by the ocean, which, rising considerably above the level of the land, can only be prevented by strong and expensive dykes, from overflowing a spot which seems to be stolen from its natural domains. Notwithstanding these difficulties, which might seem insurmountable to a less industrious people, the persevering labours of the patient Dutchmen have rendered this small, and seemingly insignificant territory, one of the richest spots in Europe, both with respect to population and property. In other countries, which are possessed of a variety of natural productions, we are not surprized to find manufactures employed in multiplying the riches which the bounty of the soil bestows. But to see, in a country like Holland, large woolen manufactures, where there are scarcely any flocks; numberless artists employed in metals, where there is no mine; thousands of saw-mills, where there is scarcely any forest; an immense quantity of corn exported from a country where there is not agriculture enough to support one half of its inhabitants, must strike every observer with admiration. Among the most valuable productions of this country may be reckoned their excellent cattle. They export large quantities of madder, a vegetable much used in dying. Their fisheries yield a clear profit of many millions of florins. The trade of Holland extends to almost every part of the world, to the exclusion, in some branches, of all their European competitors.

Capital.] AMSTERDAM, which is built on piles of wood, and is one of the most commercial cities in the world. It has more than one half the trade of Holland; and, in this celebrated centre of an immense commerce, a bank is established of that species, called a Giro Bank, of very great wealth and greater credit.

Government.] Since the great confederation of Utrecht, made in the year 1579, th Seven United Provinces must be looked upon as one political body, united for the preservation of the whole, of which each single province is governed by its own laws, and exercises most of the rights of a sovereign state. In consequence of the union, the seven Provinces guarantee each other's rights, they make war and peace, they levy taxes, &c. in their joint capacity; but as to internal government, each province is independent of the other provinces, and of the supreme power of the republic. The provinces rank in the order they are mentioned. They send deputies, chosen out of the provincial states, to the general assembly, called

called the *States General*, which is invested with the supreme legislative power of the confederation. Each province may send as many members as it pleases, but it has only one voice in the assembly of the states. According to the latest regulations, that assembly is composed of 58 deputies. At the head of this republican government, is the Prince Stadtholder or Governor, who exercises a very considerable part of the executive power of the state.

Religion.] The Calvinist or Reformed Religion is established in Holland; but others are tolerated.

None but Calvinists can hold any employment of trust or profit. The church is governed by presbyteries and synods. Of the latter there are nine for single provinces, and one national synod, subject, however, to the controul of the States General. The French and Walloon Calvinists have synods of their own. In the seven provinces are 1579 ministers of the established church, 90 of the Walloon church, 800 Roman Catholic, 53 Lutheran, 43 Arminian, and 312 Baptist ministers. In the East Indies there are 46, and in the West Indies 9 ministers of the established church.

History.] These provinces were originally an assemblage of several lordships, dependent upon the kings of Spain; from whose yoke they withdrew themselves during the reign of Philip II. in the year 1579, under the conduct of the Prince of Orange, and formed the republic now called the Seven United provinces, or Holland, that being the most remarkable province. The office of stadtholder, or captain-general of the United Provinces, was made hereditary in the Prince of Orange's family, not excepting females, 1747.

✳✤✤✤✤✤✤✤✤✤✤✤✤✤✤✤✤✤✤✤✤✤✤✤✤✤✤✤✤✤✤✤✤✤✤✤✤✤✤

POLAND AND LITHUANIA.

Miles.
Length 700 } Between { 16° and 34° East Longitude.
Breadth 680 }   { 46° and 57° North Latitude.

Boundaries.] BEFORE the extraordinary partition of this country by the king of Prussia, aided by the emperor and empress queen, and the empress of Russia, which event happened since the year 1771, the kingdom of Poland, with the dutchy of Lithuania annexed, was bounded north, by Livonia, Muscovy, and the Baltic; east, by Muscovy; south, by Hungary, Turkey and Little Tartary; west, by Germany. Containing 230 towns.

In Poland, are villages 2,377, convents of nuns 86, noblemen's estates 22,032, abbeys 37, convents of monks 579, houses in general 1,674,328, pesants 1,243,000, Jews 500,000.

Divisions.] The kingdom of Poland contains 155 towns, and is divided into, 1. Great Poland, which is subdivided into 12 districts, called Woidwodships. 2. Little Poland, three woidwodships. 3. Polachia, three

three counties, 4. Chelm, remaining part of Red Ruffia. 5. Podolia and Bratzaw. 6. Kow. 7. Volhynia. 8. The great dutchy of Lithuania, which includes White Ruffia, Black Ruffia, Polefia and the dutchy of Szamaite.

Wealth and commerce.] Poland is one of the weakeft ftates in Europe, owing to the oppreffion of the trades-people in the towns, and the flavery of the peafantry. If the fkill of the natives in agriculture, bore any proportion to the fertility of the foil, Poland might be one of the richeft countries in the world; for though a large part of it lies uncultivated, it exports no inconfiderable quantity of corn. Want of induftry and of freedom, are the chief reafons that the balance of trade is fo much againft Poland. The exports are corn, hemp, flax, horfes, cattle, (about 100,000 oxen every year) peltry, timber, metals, manna, wax, honey, &c. the value of them in the year 1777, amounted to nearly 30 millions of dollars. The imports, confifting chiefly in wine, cloth, filk, hardware, gold, filver, Eaft and Weft India goods, were fuppofed to amount to no lefs the 47 millions of dollars.

Government.] Since the late revolution, the government of Poland is ariftocratical. Its nominal head is an elective king, fo limited, that in public acts he is often called only the firft order of the republic. On being elected he is obliged immediately to fign the *Pacta Conventa* of Poland. The fovereign power is vefted in the hands of the three orders of the ftate, the king, the fenate and the nobility.

Religion.] The eftablifhed religion is the Roman Catholic. Proteftants, to whom the name of diffidents is now confined, are tolerated. The power of the pope and of the priefts is very great.

Capital.] WARSAW, fituated on the river Viftula, in the center of Poland, containing 50,000 inhabitants.

Hiftory.] Poland was anciently the country of the Vandals, who emigrated from it to invade the Roman empire. It was erected into a duchy, of which Lechus was the firft duke, A. D. 694. In his time the ufe of gold and filver was unknown to his fubjects, their commerce being carried on only by exchange of goods. It became a kingdom in the year 1000; Otho III. emperor of Germany, conferring the title of king on Boleflaus I. Red Ruffia was added to this kingdom by Boleflaus II. who married the heirefs of that country, A. D. 1059. Difmembered by the emperor of Germany, the emprefs of Ruffia, and the king of Pruffia, who, by a partition treaty, feized the moft valuable territories, 1772.

PRUSSIA.

THE countries belonging to this monarchy, are fcattered, and without any natural connection. The kingdom of Pruffia is bounded north, by part of Samogitia; fouth, by Poland Proper and Mafovia; eaft, by part of Lithuania; weft, by Polifh Pruffia and the Baltic; 160 miles

510 P R U S S I A.

miles in length, and 112 in breadth. Its capital is KONINGSBERG, containing 54,000 inhabitants. Prussia extends to 55° north latitude, and is divided into

	Population.	Capital.	Towns.
The countries which are independent of the German Empire.	6,000,000	BERLIN. 145,136 inhabitants.	570
The countries which are dependent.	6,400,000		

Wealth and commerce.] The different provinces of the Prussian monarchy are by no means equal to one another, with respect to fertility and the articles of their produce. The kingdom of Prussia, being the most northern part of the monarchy, is rich in corn, timber, manna grass, flax and peltry of all sorts, and exports these articles. Amber is exported annually, to the value of 20,000 dollars. Prussia wants salt, and has no metals but iron. The profits of its fisheries are considerable. Other parts of the monarchy produce various metalic ores, minerals and precious stones. The sum accruing to the king from the mines, amounts to 800,000 dollars, and the profits of private proprietors, to 500,000 dollars. Five thousand hands are employed in the silk manufactures. Prussia annually exports linen to the value of 6 millions of dollars. Their manufactures of iron, cloth, silk, linen, leather, cotton, porcelaine, hard ware, glass, paper and their other principal manufactures, employ upwards of 165,000 hands, and the produce of their industry is estimated at upwards of 30 millions of dollars.

Government and religion.] The Prussian monarchy resembles a very complicated machine, which, by its ingenious and admirable construction, produces the greatest effects with the greatest ease, but in which the yielding of a wheel, or the relaxation of a spring, will stop the motion of the whole. The united effects of flourishing finances, of prudent œconomy, of accuracy and dispatch in every branch of administration, and of a formidable military strength, have given such consequence to the Prussian monarchy, that the tranquillity and security, not only of Germany, but of all Europe, depend in a great measure on the politics of its cabinet. The administration of justice is likewise admirably simplified, and executed with unparalleled quickness.

Under the reign of the late king, Frederick the great, all professions of faith lived peaceably together, because the established religion, which is the reformed, had no power to oppress those of a different persuasion. Roman Catholics and Jews are very numerous in the Prussian dominions; they enjoy the most perfect freedom in the exercise of their religion.

History.] Prussia was anciently inhabited by an idolatrous and cruel people. The barbarity and ravages they were continually making upon their neighbours, obliged Conrad, duke of Masovia, about the middle of the thirteenth century, to call to his assistance the knights of the Teutonic order, who were just returned from the holy land. These knights chose a grand master, attacked those people with success, and after a bloody war of fifty years, reduced them to obedience, and obliged them to embrace christianity. They maintained their conquest till 1525, when Albert, Margrave of Blandenburg, their last grand master, having made

himself

himself master of all Prussia, ceded the western part to the king of Poland, and was acknowledged duke of the eastern part, but to be held as a fief of that kingdom. The elector, Frederick-William, surnamed the Great, by a treaty with Poland in 1656, obtained a confirmation of this part of Prussia to him and his heirs, free from vassalage, and in 1663 he was declared independent and sovereign duke. With these titles, and as grand master of the Teutonics, they continued till 1701, when Frederick, son of Frederick-William the great, and grandfather of the late king, raised the duchy of Prussia to a kingdom, and on January 18, 1701, in a solemn assembly of the states of the empire, placed the crown with his own hands upon his head; soon after which he was acknowledged as king of Prussia by all the other European powers. Frederick III. died August 17, 1786, and was succeeded by his nephew, Frederick-William, who was born 1744.

✧✧✧✧✧✧✧✧✧✧✧✧✧✧✧✧✧✧✧✧✧✧✧✧✧✧✧✧✧✧✧✧✧✧✧✧✧✧✧

RUSSIA.

Length } Between { 44° 40' and 72° North Lat. } 4,880,000 Sq. Mil.
Breadth   23° and 62° East Longitude.

THIS is the largest empire in the world, extending from the Baltic and Sweden on the west; to Kamtschatka, and the eastern ocean; and on the north, from the frozen ocean to the 44th degree of latitude.

Divisions.] Russia is at present divided into 42 governments, which are comprehended again under 19 general governments, viz.

	Government.	Inhab.	Capital.
European part of Russia,	30	20 millions.	Petersburg.
Asiatic Russia,	12	4 do.	Casan.

The superiority of the European part over the vast but uncultivated provinces of Asia is striking. The provinces acquired by the division of Poland, are highly valuable to Russia, to which the acquisition of Crimea is by no means comparable in value.

This immense empire comprehends upwards of 50 different nations, and the number of languages is supposed not to be less than the number of nations.

Wealth and commerce.] In so vast a tract of country, as the empire of Russia, spreading under many degrees of latitude, watered by more than 8 rivers, which run through the space of 2000 miles, and crossed by an extensive chain of mountains, we may expect to find an infinite number of natural productions, though we must make some allowances for the great deserts of Siberia, and the many parts, not yet thoroughly investigated by natural historians. The species of plants peculiar to this part of the globe, which have already been discovered, amount to many thousands. The soil contains almost all minerals, tin, platina and some semi-metals

metals excepted. Ruffia abounds with animals of almoft all the various kinds, and has many that have never been defcribed. It has the greateft variety of the fineft furs. In 1781, there were exported from Peterfburg alone, 428,877 fkins of hares, 36,904 of grey fquirrels, 1,354 of bears, 2,018 of ermine, 5,639 of foxes, 300 of wild cats, befides thofe of wolves and of the *fuflic* (a beautiful animal of the rat kind) exclufive of the exportation of the fame articles from Archangel, Riga and the Cafpian fea. In one year there were exported from Archangel 783,000 pud of tallow (a pud is equal to 40 lb.) 8,602 pud of candles, and 102 pud of butter. In 1781 from Peterfburg, 148,099 pud of red leather, 10,885 pud of leather for foles, 530,646 pud of candles, 50,000 pud of foap, 27,416 pud of ox bones, 990 calve fkins. The fifheries belonging to Ruffia are very productive. The forefts of fir trees are immenfely valuable. Oaks and beeches do not grow to a ufeful fize beyond the 60th degree of north latitude. They export timber, pitch, tar and potafh to a vaft amount. Rye, wheat, tobacco, hemp, flax fail-cloth, linfeed-oil, flax-feed, iron, filver, copper, falt, jafper, marble, granit, &c. are among the productions of Ruffia. The whole of the exports of Ruffia amounted in 1783 to near 13 millions of rubles; the imports did not much exceed the fum of 12 millions. The imports confift chiefly of wine, fpices, fruits, fine cloth and other manufactured commodities and articles of luxury. There are at prefent no more than 484 manufacturers in the whole empire.

Government.] The emperor or autocrator of Ruffia, (the prefent emprefs ftyles herfelf autocratrix,) is abfolute. He muft be of the Greek church by the ancient cuftom of the empire. The only written fundamental law exifting is that of Peter the firft, by which the right of fucceffion to the throne depends entirely on the choice of the reigning monarch, who has unlimited authority over the lives and property of all his fubjects. The management of public affairs is entrufted to feveral departments. At the head of all thofe concerned in the regulation of internal affairs (the ecclefiaftical fynod excepted) is the fenate, under the prefidency of a chancellor and vice chancellor. The fovereign nominates the members of this fupreme court which is divided into 6 chambers, 4 at Peterfburg and 2 at Mofcow. The provinces are ruled by governors appointed by the fovereign.

Religion.] The religion eftablifhed in the Ruffian empire is the Greek. The moft effential point in which their profeffion of faith differs from that of the latin church, is the doctrine, that the Holy Ghoft proceeds from the Father only. Their worfhip is as much overloaded with ceremonies as the Roman Catholic. Saints are held in veneration, and painted images of them, but no ftatues are fuffered in the churches. The church has been governed fince the time of Peter the great by a national council called the Holy Synod. Marriage is forbid, to the archbifhops and bifhops, but is allowed to the inferior clergy. There are 479 convents for men, 74 for women, in which are about 70,000 perfons. Above 900,000 peafants belong to the eftates in poffeffion of the clergy.

Hiftory.] The earlieft authentic account we have of Ruffia is A. D. 862, when Rurick was grand duke of Novogorod in this country. In the year 981, Wolidimer was the firft chriftian king. The Poles conquered it about 1058, but it is uncertain how long they kept it. Andrey I. began his reign 1158, and laid the foundation of Moscow. About 1200 of the Mungls Tartars conquered it, and held it subject to them till 1540, when John Bafilowitz reftored it to independency. About the middle of the fixteenth century, the Ruffians difcovered and conquered Siberia. It became an empire 1721, when Peter I. affumed the title of emperor of all the Ruffias, which was admitted by the powers of Europe to be obferved in future negociations with the court of Peterfburg.

The reign of Elizabeth, in the courfe of the prefent century, is remarkable, on account of her abolifhing the ufe of torture, and governing her fubjects for twenty years without inflicting a fingle capital punifhment.

The prefent emprefs is actually employed in founding a number of fchools, for the education of the lower claffes of her fubjects, throughout the beft inhabited parts of the empire; an inftitution of the mo beneficial tendency, which, if rightly executed, will entitle the great Catharine, more than any of her predeceffors, to the gratitude of the Ruffian nation.

✠✠✠✠✠✠✠✠✠✠✠✠✠✠✠✠✠✠✠✠✠✠✠✠✠✠✠✠✠✠✠✠✠✠✠✠✠✠✠

SWEDEN.

Miles.

Length 1300 } Between { 50° and 70° North Latitude.
Breadth 600 } { 10° and 30° Eaft Longitude.

Boundaries.] BOUNDED north, by the Frozen Ocean; eaft, by Ruffia; fouth, by Denmark and the Baltic; weft, by Norway. The whole kingdom of Sweden contains 104 towns, 80,250 villages, and 1,200 eftates of the nobility.

Divifions.	Square miles.	Population.	Cap. Towns.
1 Sweden Proper,	} 64,000	2,100,00	Stockholm.
2 Gothland,			80,000 inhabitants.
3 Nordland,	95,472	150,00	Lund.
4 Lapland,			
5 Finland,	48,780	624,000	Abo.
6 Swedifh Pomerania,	1,440	100,560	Bergen.

7 In the Weft Indies, Sweden obtained from France, in the year 1785 the ifland of Barthelemi.

Climate, exports and imports.] Sweden has an inhofpitable climate, and the greater part of the foil is barren, upwards of 110,000 fquare miles lie uncultivated. Yet the induftry of the inhabitants in arts and agriculture, has raifed it to the rank of a fecondary European power. Sweden imports 300,000 tons of corn, and 4,535 hogfheads of fpirituous liquors, befides hemp, flax, falt, wine, beef, filk, paper, leather and Eaft and Weft India goods. The exports of Sweden confift chiefly of wood, pitch, tar, fifh, furs, copper, iron, fome gold and filver, and other minerals, to the amount, in the year 1768, of upwards of 13 millions of dollars; and their

imports,

imports, in the same year amounted to little more than 10 millions of dollars. The Swedes trade to all parts of Europe, to the Levante, the East and West Indies, to Africa and China.

Government.] Since the memorable revolution in 1772, Sweden may be called a monarchy. The senate still claim some share in the administration, but its members are chosen by the king. The king has the absolute disposal of the army, and has the power of calling and of dissolving the assembly of the states; but he cannot impose any new tax, without consulting the diet. The senate is the highest court or council in the kingdom, and is composed of 17 senators, or supreme counsellors. The provinces are under governors, called provincial captains.

Religion.] The religion established in Sweden is the Lutheran, which the sovereign must profess, and is engaged to maintain in the kingdom. Calvinists, Roman Catholics and Jews are tolerated. The superior clergy of Sweden have preserved the dignities of the Roman Catholic church; it is composed of the archbishop of Upsal, of 14 bishops, and of 192 presidents. The jurisdiction in ecclesiastical matters is in the hands of 19 consistories. The number of the inferior clergy, comprehending the ministers of parishes, &c. amounts only to 1387.

History.] We have no account of this country till the reign of Bornio III. A. D. 714. Margaret, queen of Denmark and Norway, was called to the throne of Sweden, on the forced resignation of Albert, their king, A. D. 1387. It remained united to the Danish crown till 1523, when the famous Gustavus Vasa expelled the Danes, and ever since it has remained independent; but was made an absolute monarchy by the present king in 1772.

Possessions of DENMARK in Europe.

ALL the Danish provinces contain 182,400 square miles, and, including the colonies 2,500,000 inhabitants.

Divisions.	Square miles.	Population.	Chief Towns.	Inhab.
1 Denmark Proper, on the Baltic sea.	13,000	1,125,000	COPENHAGEN,	87,000
2 Dutchy of Holstein in Germany.	2,800	310,000	Glukstadt,	2483
3 Norway, which has the Atlantic west.	112,000	723,141	Bergen,	18,000
4 Faroe islands,	—	5,000	—	—
5 Iceland,	46,400	46,201	Skalholt.	—

The whole of Denmark contains 68 towns, 22 boroughs, 15 earldoms, 16 baronies, 932 estates of the inferior nobility, 7000 villages.

Norway, contains only 18 towns, two earldoms, and 27 estates of the other nobility.

GREAT BRITAIN AND IRELAND.

The Danes have settlements at Coromandel in Asia. On the coast of Guinea and other places in Africa, and in Greenland, in America. Greenland is divided into East and West Greenland, a very extensive country, but thinly inhabited. *Crantz* reckons only 957 stated, and 7,000 wandering inhabitants in West Greenland. The Danes are the only nation who have settlements in West Greenland; where, under their protection, the Moravian brethren have missionaries, and very useful establishments.

Wealth and commerce.] If the cold and barren kingdom of Norway did not require large supplies of corn from Denmark, the latter could export a considerable quantity of it. Slefwic, Jutland, Seeland and Leland, are very rich corn countries, and abound in black cattle. The chief produce of Norway is wood, timber, and a great variety of peltry. The mines of Norway are very valuable, as well as its fisheries. Only one fourteenth part of it is fit for agriculture. The balance of trade is in favour of Norway, and against Denmark. The whole of the exports of Denmark and Holstein, amounted, in 1768, to 1,382,681 rix dollars; the imports to 1,976,800. The exports of Norway, to 1,711,369, and the imports to 1,238,284 dollars. Manufactures do not thrive in Denmark.

Religion.] The same as in Sweden.

Government.] Denmark is an hereditary kingdom, and governed in an absolute manner; but the Danish kings are legal sovereigns, and perhaps the only legal sovereigns in the world; for the senators, nobility, clergy, and commons divested themselves of their right, as well as power in the year 1661, and made a formal surrender of their liberties to the then king Frederick III.

History.] Denmark, the ancient kingdom of the Goths, was little known till the year 714, when Gormo was king. Christian VII. is the present sovereign; he visited England in 1768. His queen, the youngest sister of George III. king of Great Britain, was suddenly seized, confined in a castle as a state prisoner, and afterwards banished the kingdom. The counts Struensee and Brandt (the first prime minister, and the queen's physician) were seized at the same time, January 1772, and beheaded the same year.

Bartholinus, celebrated for his knowledge of anatomy and Tico-Brache, the famous astronomer, were natives of this country.

✣✣✣✣✣✣✣✣✣✣✣✣✣✣✣✣✣✣✣✣✣✣✣✣✣✣✣✣✣✣✣✣✣✣✣

GREAT BRITAIN AND IRELAND.

Lie between 49° and 58° 50' North Latitude, and 2° East and 6° 20' West Longitude.

Divisions.	Sq. Mil.	Population.	Capital.	Inhab.
ENGLAND and Wales,	54,112	7,000,000	London,	800,000
Scotland,	25,600	1,300,000	Edinburgh,	80,000
Ireland,	21,216	2,161,514	Dublin,	160,000

Counties.

GREAT BRITAIN AND IRELAND.

	Counties.		Counties.
England is divided into	40	Scotland	31 and 2 stewardships.
Wales	12	Ireland	32 in 4 provinces.

The English possess the fortress of Gibraltar, and valuable settlements in Asia, Africa and America.

Wealth and commerce.] The two divisions of Great Britain, England, and Scotland, differ widely with respect to their natural fertility, and to the wealth of their inhabitants. South Britain, or England, abounds with all the useful productions of those countries of Europe, which are in parallel latitudes, wine, silk, and some wild animals excepted. Agriculture, gardening, the cultivation of all those plants which, are most useful for feeding cattle, and breeding horses and sheep, are carried on in England to an astonishing height. Of about 42,000,000 acres, which England contains, only 9,500,000 produce corn; the rest is either covered with wood, or laid out in meadows, gardens, parks, &c. and a considerable part is still waste land. Yet out of the crops obtained from the fifth part of the lands, there have been exported, during the space of five years, from 1745 to 1750, quantities of corn to the value of £. 7,600,000 sterling. The net produce of the English corn-land is estimated at £. 9,000,000 sterling. The rents of pasture ground, meadows, &c. at £. 7,000,000. The number of people engaged in, and maintained by farming, is supposed to be 2,800,000. England abounds in excellent cattle and sheep. In the beginning of the present century, there were supposed to be 12 millions of sheep, and their number has since been increasing. In the years 1769, 1770 and 1771, the value of the woollens, exported from England, including those of Yorkshire, amounted to upwards of £. 13,500,000 sterling.

Copper, tin, lead and iron are found in great abundance in Great Britain, where there is made every year 50—60,000 tons of pig-iron, and 20—30,000 tons of bar-iron.

England possesses a great treasure in its inexhaustible coal mines, which are worked chiefly in the northern counties, whence the coal is conveyed by sea, and by the inland canals to every part of the kingdom. The mines of Northumberland alone, send every year upwards of 600,000 chaldrons of coals to London, and 1500 vessels are employed in carrying them along the eastern coast of England.

SCOTLAND's natural productions are greatly inferior to those of England, both with respect to plenty and variety. It produces chiefly, flax, hemp, coal, some iron and much lead. The trade of this country consists chiefly in linen, thread and coals; they have lately begun to manufacture, cloth carpets, sugar, &c.

IRELAND is, in most of its provinces, not inferior in fertility to England, but very far behind it in point of civilization and industry. This inferiority must be partly attributed to the idleness, ignorance and oppression of its inhabitants; and partly to the commercial jealousy of the British legislation, from which Ireland has at length been emancipated. The chief articles of its produce are cattle, sheep, hogs and flax; large quantities of excellent salted pork, beef and butter, are annually exported.

The

GREAT BRITAIN AND IRELAND.

The Irish wool is very fine. The principal manufacture of Ireland is that of linen, which at prefent, is a very valuable article of exportation. Fifteen hundred perfons are employed in the filk manufactures at Dublin.

With the increafe of liberty and induftry, this kingdom will foon rife to the commercial confequence to which it is intitled by its fertility and fituation.

The total value of the exports from Ireland to Great Britain, in 1779 and 1780, at an average, was £. 2,300,000. The balance is greatly in favour of Ireland.

The manufactures in England are confeffedly, with very few exceptions, fuperior to thofe of other countries. For this fuperiority they are nearly equally indebted to national character, to the fituation of their country, and to their excellent conftitution.

The Englifh government, favourable to liberty and to every exertion of genius, has provided, by wife and equitable laws, for the fecure enjoyment of property acquired by ingenuity and labour, and has removed obftacles to induftry, by prohibiting the importation of fuch articles from abroad which could be manufactured at home.

The Britifh iflands, among other advantages for navigation, have coafts, the fea line of which, including both Great Britain and Ireland, extends nearly 3800 miles, whereas the fea coaft of France has but 1000 miles. The commerce of Great Britain is immenfe, and increafing. In the years 1783 and 1784, the fhips cleared outwards, amounting to 950,000 tons, exceeded the number of tons of the fhips employed in 1760, (24 years before) by upwards of 400,000 tons. The value of the cargoes exported in 1784, amounted to upwards of £. 15,000,000 fterling; and the net cuftoms paid for them into the exchequer were upwards of £. 3,000,000 fterling; and even this fum was exceeded the following year, 1785, by upwards of £. 1,000,000 fterling.—The balance of trade in favour of England is eftimated at £. 3,000,000. The inland trade is valued at £. 42,000,000 fterling.—The fifheries of Great Britain are numerous and very productive. The privileged trading companies, of which the Eaft India Company, chartered in the reign of queen Elizabeth, is the principal, carry on the moft important foreign commerce.

The bank of England was incorporated in 1694: This company, by the fanction of parliament, deals in bills of exchange—it buys and fells bullion, and manages government annuities paid at its office. Its credit is the moft extenfive of any in Europe. It is one of the principal creditors of the nation, and the value of the fhares in its ftock runs very high.

Government.] The government of Great Britain may be called a limited monarchy. It is a happy combination of a monarchial and popular government. The king has only the executive power; the legiflative is fhared by him and the parliament, or more properly by the people. The crown is hereditary; both male and female defcendents are capable of fucceffion. The king muft profef the Proteftant religion.

Religion.] The eftablifhed religion in that part of Great Britain, called England, is the Epifcopal Church of England, of which the king, without any fpiritual power, is the head. The revenues of the Church of England are fuppofed to be about £. 3,000,000 fterling. All other denominations of chriftians, called Diffenters, and Jews are tolerated.—

Four-

Four-fifths of the people of Ireland are Roman Catholics, and are consequently excluded from all places of trust and profit. Their clergy are numerous.—The Scotch are Presbyterians, and are strictly Calvinists in doctrine and form of ecclesiastical government. The other most considerable religious sects in England are Unitarians, Baptists, Quakers (60,000), Methodists, Roman Catholics (60,000), 12,000 families of Jews—and French and German Lutherans and Calvinists.

History.] Britain was first inhabited by a tribe of Gauls. Fifty-two years before the birth of Christ, Julius Cæsar subjected them to the Roman empire. The Romans remained masters of Britain 500 years, till they were called home in defence of their native country against the invasions of the Goths and Vandals. The Picts, Scots and Saxons then took possession of the island. In 1066, William duke of Normandy, obtained a complete victory over Harold king of England, which is called the Norman Conquest. *Magna Charta* was signed by John 1216. This is called the bulwark of English liberty. In 1485, the houses of York and Lancaster were united in Henry VII. after a long and bloody contest. The usurpation of Cromwell took place in 1647. The revolution (so called on account of James the second's abdicating the throne, to whom William and Mary succeeded) happened 1688. Queen Anne succeeded William and Mary in 1702, in whom ended the Protestant line of Charles I. and George the I. of the house of Hanover, ascended the throne in 1714, and the succession has since been regular in this line. George the III. who is reported to be in a state of insanity, is the present king.

✢✢

ISLANDS, SEAS, MOUNTAINS, &c.

OF EUROPE.

THE principal islands of Europe, are, Great Britain and Ireland in the north. In the Mediterranean sea, are, Yvica, Majorca, and Minorca, subject to Spain. Corsica, subject to the French. Sardinia is subject to its own king; and Sicily is governed by a viceroy under the king of Naples, to whom the island belongs. The islands of the Baltic, the Adriatic and Ionian seas are not worthy of notice.

The principal seas, gulphs, and bays in Europe, are the Adriatic Sea, between Italy and Turkey; the Baltic Sea, between Denmark, Poland and Sweden; the Bay of Biscay, between France and Spain; the English Channel, between England and France; the Euxine or Black Sea, between Europe and Asia; the German Ocean, between Germany and Britain; and the Mediterranean Sea, between Europe and Africa.

The chief Mountains in Europe, are the Alps, between France and Italy; the Apennine Hills in Italy; the Pyrenean Hills, that divide France from Spain; the Carpathian Mountains, in the south of Poland; the Peak in Derbyshire; the Plinlimmon in Wales: besides the terrible Volcanos,

A S I A. 519

canos, or Burning Mountains, of Vesuvius and Stromboli, in Naples; Etna, in Sicily, and Ecla, in the cold island of Iceland.

✣✣✣✣✣✣✣✣✣✣✣✣✣✣✣✣✣✣✣✣✣✣✣✣✣✣✣✣✣✣✣✣✣✣✣✣✣✣✣

A S I A.

THIS immense tract of country, stretches into all climates, from the frozen wilds of Siberia, where the hardy inhabitants, clothed in fur, are drawn in sledges over the snow; to the sultry regions of India and Siam, where, seated on the huge elephants, the people shelter themselves from the scorching sun by the spreading umbrella.

This is the principal quarter of the globe; for in Asia the All Wise Creator planted the garden of Eden, in which Adam and Eve were formed, from whom the whole human race have derived their existence. Asia became again the nursery of the world after the deluge, whence the descendents of Noah dispersed their various colonies into all the other parts of the globe. It was here our Saviour was born, and accomplished the great and merciful work of our redemption, and it was hence, that the light of his glorious gospel was carried, with amazing rapidity, into all the surrounding nations by his disciples and followers. This was, in short, the theatre of almost every action recorded in the Holy Scriptures.

This vast tract of land was, in the earliest ages, governed by the Assyrians, Medes, Persians and Greeks. Upon the extinction of these empires, the Romans carried their arms even beyond the Ganges, till at length the Mahometans, or as they are usually called Saracens, spread their devastations over this continent, destroying all its ancient splendor, and rendering the most populous and fertile spots of Asia, wild and uncultivated deserts.

Among the highest mountains of Asia are Arrarat, near the Caspian Sea, on which the ark of Noak rested, when the waters of the deluge subsided; and Horeb and Sinai in Arabia.

Asia is bounded north, by the Frozen Ocean; west, by Europe and the Mediterranean and Red Seas; south, by the Indian Ocean; east, by the Pacific Ocean; and is reckoned to be 4800 miles in length, and 4300 in breadth; comprehending, besides islands,

	Chief Towns	Sq. Miles.
The Empire of China,	Pekin,	1,105,000.
The several nations of Tartary,	Tobolski, Tibet,	4,479,000.
Persia,	Ispahan,	800,000.
India, or the Mogul Empire,	Delhi,	1,867,500.
Turkey, in Asia,	Jerusalem,	1,112,500.
Arabia,	Mecca.	

TARTARY.

TARTARY.

Boundaries.] BOUNDED north, by the Frozen ocean; east, by the Pacific; south, by China, India, Persia and the Caspian sea; west, by Russia; 3000 miles long, 2250 broad.

Air, soil and productions.] The northern parts are excessively cold and barren, but the southern more temperate and fertile. The country abounds with unwholesome lakes and marshes, mountains and sandy deserts. Their commodities are chiefly skins of foxes, sables, ermine, lynxes and other furrs, also, flax, musk, rhubarb, and cinnamon.

Religion.] The Tartars are chiefly pagans, mahometans or christians; the first are most numerous.

Government.] Muscovite Tartary is subject to the empress of Russia; Chinese Tartary to the emperor of China; other parts of Tartary have their own princes, or *Chams*, and some are subject to Persia and the great Mogul.

Character.] The Tartars are in general strong made, stout men; some are honest and hospitable, others barbarous and live by plundering. The beauty of the Circassian women is a kind of staple commodity in that country; for parents there make no scruple of selling their daughters, to recruit the seraglio's of the great men of Turkey and Persia. They avoid all labour as the greatest slavery. Their only employment is tending their flocks, hunting and managing their horses. If they are angry with a person, the worst they wish him is, that he may live in one fixed place and work like a Russian.

History.] The first acknowledged sovereign of these dismal territories, was the famous Jenghis Khan, A. D. 1206. His descendants possessed it till 1582, when Mungls revolted to the Manchew Tartars, who reign in China. The Eluths became an independent state about 1400, and so remain.

✢✢✢✢✢✢✢✢✢✢✢✢✢✢✢✢✢✢✢✢✢✢✢✢✢✢✢✢✢✢✢✢✢✢✢✢✢

CHINA.

CHINA is bounded on the north, by part of Tartary; east, by the Pacific ocean; south, by part of the Indian ocean; west, by India without the Ganges; 1450 miles long, 1260 broad.

Rivers.] The principal rivers are, the Yamour, Argun, Yellow River and the Tay; besides a prodigious number of navigable canals, which are very convenient. Great numbers of the Chinese live constantly on the waters in these canals.

Chief cities.] This empire is said to contain 4400 walled cities; the chief of which are, Pekin, the capital, Nankin and Canton. Pekin is reckoned to contain 2,000,000 inhabitants. The city is entered by seven iron gates, within side of each is a guard-house.

Government.]

CHINA.

Government.] The emperor of China is absolute. He is, however, obliged, by a maxim of state, to consider his subjects as children, and they regard him no longer, than while he behaves like a parent. The emperor is styled, *Holy Son of Heaven, Sole Governor of the Earth, Great Father of his People.* The present emperor is descended from a Tartarian family; for about 150 years ago the Tartars over-ran and conquered this fine country. However, Tartary may now rather be said to be subject to China, than China to Tartary, since all the wealth of the United Empire centers in China, and Tartary is no small addition to its strength.

Religion.] Natural religion, as explained by their celebrated philosopher Confucius, is the established religion of China. But the greater part of the people are gross idolators, and the most numerous sect are those who worship the idol Fohi, which was brought from Tibet soon after the death of our Saviour. The Mahometans have been tolerated in China for 6 or 700 years, and the Jews much longer. Christianity had gained considerable footing in this empire, by the labours of the Jesuits; but in the year 1726, those missionaries, being suspected of designs against the government, and teaching doctrines destructive of it, were quite expelled, and the christian churches demolished.

Character and inhabitants.] It is said that China contains 158 millions of inhabitants, between 20 and 60 years of age, who pay an annual tax. The Chinese in their persons are middle sized, their faces broad, their eyes black and small, and their noses rather short. It is thought good policy to forbid women from all trade and commerce, which they can only benefit by letting them alone. The women have little eyes, plump, rosy lips, black hair, regular features and a delicate though florid complexion: the smallness of their feet is reckoned a principal part of their beauty, and no swathing is omitted when they are young, to give them that accomplishment; so that when they grow up, they may be said to totter rather than to walk.

Air, soil and productions.] The air of China is generally temperate and good, though sometimes very hot in the southern provinces, and very cold in the northern. It is one of the most fruitful countries in the world; the mountains themselves being cultivated to the top. The principal productions of China are silks, cotton, precious stones, porcelain or china ware, quicksilver, tea, which is peculiar to this country, ginger, camphire, japan'd works, gold, silver, copper, &c.

Curiosities.] One of the greatest curiosities of China, and perhaps in the world, is that stupendous wall, separating China from Tartary, to prevent the incursions of the Tartars. It is supposed to extend 1500 miles, and is carried over mountains and vallies, from 20 to 25 feet high, and broad enough at the top for six horsemen to travel abreast with ease. The Chinese have upwards of 20,000 letters or characters in their language.

History.] This empire is reported to have been founded by Fohi, who is said to have been the Noah mentioned in the bible, about 2240 years before Christ. It is now governed by the emperors of the Dynasty of the Manchew Tartars, who conquered it, A. D. 1645.

INDIA AND PERSIA.

INDIA IN GENERAL.

BOUNDED north, by Tartary; east, by China and the Chinese Sea; south, by the Indian Ocean; west, by the same ocean and Persia; length 4000 miles, breadth 2500.

Chief Towns.] The capital cities of the Mogul's empire, are Agra and Delhi.

Air, soil and productions.] In the northern parts of India the air is temperate; but very hot in the southern. The heats, however, are moderated by refreshing breezes from the sea, and from the rains that fall continually from the end of June to the end of October. Some part of India, especially the northern provinces of the Mogul's empire, are sandy, mountainous and barren; but in general the soil is fertile, producing plenty of corn, and the finest fruits. It is well watered with rivers, the chief are the Ganges and the Indus. Their commodities are silks, cottons, callicoes, muslins, fattins, taffeties, carpets, gold, silver, diamonds, pearls, porcelain, rice, ginger, amber, pepper, cinnamon and a great variety of medicinal drugs.

Government.] The Great Mogul is an absolute monarch; but there are some princes in his dominions, called Rajahs, who maintain their independency. The other kings and princes of India are likewise absolute, but some of them tributary, the weaker to the more powerful.

Religion.] The Moors or Moguls, who are a mixture of Tartars, Persians, Arabs, &c. are Mahometans; but the natives of India, who are by far the most numerous, are chiefly Pagans, worshipping idols of various shapes; many christians are settled on the coast.

Character.] In general the Indians are ingenious in arts, civil to strangers, and pretty just in their dealings; some are of a swarthy complexion, others are black as jet. They marry very young, the males before 14, females at 10 or 11. A man is in the decline of life at 30, and the beauty of the women is on the decay at 18; at 25 they have all the marks of old age.

History.] The first conqueror of the whole of this country was Jenghis Khan, a Tartarian prince, who died A. D. 1226. In 1399, Timur Bek, by conquest, became Great Mogul. The Dynasty continued in his family till the conquest of Tamerlane in the 15th century, whose descendents have possessed the throne from that time; but Kouli Khan, the famous Sophi of Persia, considerably diminished the power of the Moguls, carried away immense treasures from Delhi; and since that event many of the Rajahs and Nabobs, have made themselves independent.

✣✣✣✣✣✣✣✣✣✣✣✣✣✣✣✣✣✣✣✣✣✣✣✣✣✣✣✣✣✣✣✣

PERSIA.

BOUNDED north, by the Caspian Sea; east, by India; south, by the Persian Gulf and Indian Ocean; west, by Asiatic Turkey. Its length 1450 miles; its breadth 1250.

Capital.

ARABIA

Capital.] The chief city and residence of the sovereign is Ispahan, a fine spacious town.

Air, soil and productions.] The north and east parts of Persia are mountainous and cold; the provinces to the south-east are sandy and desart; those on the south and west are very fertile. The air in the south, is extremely hot in summer, and very unwholsome. There is scarcely any country that has more mountains and fewer rivers. The productions of Persia are similar to those of India.

Character of the inhabitants.[The Persians are a brave, polite and ingenious people; honest in their dealings and civil to strangers. Their great foible seems to be ostentation in their equipages.

Religion.] The Persians in general, are strict followers of Mahomet's doctrine, but differ considerably from the Turks. There are many Christians in Persia, and a sect who worship fire, the followers of Zoroaster.

Government.] Persia is governed by an absolute monarch, called Shah or King, and frequently Sophi. The crown is hereditary, but females are excluded.

History.] The Persian empire was founded by Cyrus, after his conquest of Media, 536 years before Christ. It continued till it was overthrown by Alexander the Great, 331 years before Christ. A new empire, styled the Parthian, was formed by the Persians under Arbaces, 250 years before Christ; but in A. D. 229, Artaxerxes restored it to its ancient title; and in 651, the Seracens put an end to that empire. From this time Persia was a prey to the Tartars, and a province of Indostan, till Thomas Kouli Khan, once more raised it to a powerful kingdom. He was assassinated in 1747.

ARABIA

BOUNDED north, by Turkey; east, by the Gulphs of Persia and Ormus; south, by the Straits of Babel-mandel and the Indian Ocean; west, by the Red Sea; length 1300, breadth 1200.

In that part of Arabia called the Holy Land, the inhabitants enjoy a pure and healthful air, and a fertile soil. The middle, called Arabia Deserta, is overspread with barren mountains, rocks and sandy deserts. But the southern parts, deservedly called the Happy, although the air is hot and unwholsome, is blessed with an excellent, and very fertile soil, producing balm of Gilead, manna, myrrh, cassia, aloes, frankincense, spikenard and other valuable gums;—cinnamon, pepper, oranges, lemons, &c. — The Arabians, like most of the Asiatics, are of a middling stature, thin and of a swarthy complexion, with black hair and black eyes. They are much addicted to thieving. In 1750, a body of 50,000 Arabians, attacked a caravan of merchants and pilgrims, returning from Mecca, killed 60,000 persons, and plundered them of every thing valuable, though escorted by a Turkish army.—The Arabians in general are Mahometans though there are some Pagans.—They have many princes, some tributary to the

the Turks, others independent.—The Arabs are descended from Ishmael, of whose posterity it was foretold, that they should be invincible, and have their hands against every man, and every man's hands against them. The famous imposter Mahomet was born at Mecca in the 6th century. He fled to Medina, A. D. 622. This is called the Hegira or Flight, from whence the Mahometans compute their time. He died 629, having propogated his doctrines through Arabia, Syria, Egypt and Persia, leaving two branches of his race, both esteemed divine by their subjects.

✢✢✢✢✢✢✢✢✢✢✢✢✢✢✢✢✢✢✢✢✢✢✢✢✢✢✢✢✢✢✢✢

TURKEY IN ASIA

BOUNDED north, by the Black Sea and Circassia; east, by Persia; south, by Arabia and the Levant Sea; west, by the Archipelago, the Hellespont and Propontis; length 1000 miles, breadth 800.

The air is naturally delightful, serene and salubrious, yet the inhabitants are frequently visited with the plague. The soil is calculated to produce all the necessaries, agreeables, and even luxuries of life.—The Grand Seignior is absolute sovereign of the Turkish empire, who appoints Bashaws or Beglerbegs to govern the several provinces,—Mahometanism is the established religion of the Turkish dominions.—The Turks, when young, are well made and robust, Their eyes and hair are black. The women look old at 30.——Turkey in Asia contains many large provinces, particularly Syria, Judea, or Palestine, Phœnicia, &c. which are subject to the Turks. In Palestine, or the Holy Land, and the countries adjacent, were Babylon, Damascus, Nineveh, Tyre, Sidon, Samaria, Bethlehem, Nazareth, and Jerusalem the capital, which was taken, pillaged, burnt, and entirely razed to the ground by Titus the Roman general, under Domitian, in the year 70, and is now a very inconsiderable place, and only famous for what it has been; for there Jesus Christ preached the christian religion, and was crucified by the Jews upon mount Calvary. Ephesus is in the lesser Asia, famous for the temple of Diana, which Eroftratus burnt, in order to immortalize his memory. Near Jerusalem is the lake *Asphaltites* or the *Dead Sea*, being the place where Sodom and Gomorrah stood. In Mesopotamia, between the Euphrates and the Tigris, is supposed to have been the Garden of Eden. There are now no remains of the tower of Babel, or the city of Babylon, nor is the place where they stood exactly known. Owls now dwell there, and wild beasts and dragons in their pleasant places *(Isaiah* xiii. 20, &c.) Nineveh too, once the capital of the Assyrian empire, is now known only by its ruins,

ASIATIC ISLES.

THE Japan Iflands, forming an empire governed by a moft defpotic king, lie about 150 miles eaft of China. The foil and productions of thefe iflands are much the fame as thofe of China. The Japanefe are the groffeft idolaters, and irreconcileable to Chriftianity. They are of a yellow complexion, narrow eyes, fhort nofes, black hair. A famenefs of drefs prevails through the whole empire, from the emperor to the peafant. The firft compliment offered to a ftranger in their houfes, is a difh of tea, and a pipe of tobacco. Obedience to parents, and refpect to fuperiors characterize the nation. Their penal laws are very fevere, but punifhment is feldom inflicted. The inhabitants have made great progrefs in commerce and agriculture.

Formofa, is a fine ifland eaft of China, abounding in all the neceffaries of life.

The Philippines, 1100 in number, lying 200 miles foutheaft of China, belonging to Spain, are fruitful in all the neceffaries of life, and beautiful to the eye. They are however fubject to earthquakes, thunder and lightning, venomous beafts and noxious herbs, whofe poifon kills inftantaneoufly. They are fubject to the Spanifh government. The Sultan of Mindanao is a Mahometan.

Borneo, 800 miles long, and 700 broad, is thought to be the largeft ifland in the world. It lies on the equator, and is famous for being the native country of the Ouran Outang, which, of all irrational animals, refembles a man the moft.

Sumatra, weft of Borneo, produces fo much gold that it is thought to be the Ophir mentioned in the Scriptures.

Ceylon belongs to the Dutch, and is faid to be by nature the richeft and fineft ifland in the world. The natives call it, with fome fhew of reafon, the terreftial paradife. They are a fober inoffenfive people; but idolaters. This ifland is noted for the cinnamon tree.

✣✣✣✣✣✣✣✣✣✣✣✣✣✣✣✣✣✣✣✣✣✣✣✣✣✣✣✣✣✣✣✣✣✣✣✣✣

AFRICA.

AFRICA is fituated fouth of Europe, and furrounded on all fides by the fea, except a narrow neck of land about 60 miles over, called the Ifthmus of Suez, which joins it to Afia at the north end of the Red Sea. Africa is about 4300 miles in length, and 3500 in breadth; and lies chiefly in the torrid zone, the equator running through the middle of it. Here once dwelt the queen of Sheba, who, on paying a vifit to the magnificent king Solomon, ftood amazed at his wifdom and the glory of his court. Here we find a race of people quite black, fuppofed to be defcendants of *Ham*.

EGYPT AND BARBARY

Africa will be considered under the 7 following divisions:
1. Egypt,
2. Barbary,
3. Zaara or the Desert,
4. Negroland,
5. Guinea,
6. Ethopia,
7. The African Islands.

EGYPT.

Boundaries.] BOUNDED east, by the Red sea and the Isthmus of Suez; west, by Barca; north, by the Mediterranean; south, by Nubia and Abyssinia; 600 miles in length, and 350 in breadth, including the Deserts.

Capital.] Grand Cairo, one of the most populous cities in the world, and a place of great trade and riches.

Air, soil and productions.] The air of Egypt is for the most part very hot and unwholsome; but the soil is exceedingly fruitful, occasioned by the annual overflowing of the Nile, which leaves a fattening slime behind it. Those parts not overflowed by the Nile are uncultivated, sandy and barren. Egypt produces corn, rice, sugar, flax, linen, salt, sal ammoniac, balsam and various sorts of fruits and drugs.

Religion and government.] Egypt is governed by a Bashaw sent from Constantinople, being a province of the Turkish empire. The Turks and Arabs are Mahometans. Mahometanism is the established religion of Egypt; but there are many Christians called Copts, and the Jews are very numerous.

Egypt is famous for its pyramids, those stupendous works of folly. The Egyptians were the only people who were acquainted with the art of embalming or preserving dead bodies from putrefaction. Here is the river Nile celebrated for its fertilizing inundations, and for the subtle, voracious crocodiles which inhabit its shores. This was the theatre of those remarkable transactions, which make up the beautiful and affecting history of Joseph. Here Pharaoh exhibited scenes of cruelty, tyranny and oppression towards the Israelites in the course of their 400 years bondage to the Egyptians. Here too Moses was born, and was preserved in the little ark, among the flags on the banks of the Nile. Here, through the instrumentality of this great man, the Egyptians were afflicted with many grievous plagues, which induced them at last to *let Israel go.* Here Moses, with his rod, divided the Red sea, and Israel passed it on dry land; which the Egyptians attempting to do, were overwhelmed by the returning of the waters. To this scene, succeeded the Israelites memorable 40 years march through the deserts of Arabia, before they reached the land of Canaan.

BARBARY.

BARBARY (including Bildulgerid) is bounded south, by Zaara; east, by Egypt; north, by the Mediterranean; west, by the Atlantic ocean; length 2300 miles, breadth 700. *Air,*

Air, soil and productions.] Thefe ftates, under the Roman empire, were juftly denominated the garden of the world. The air is temperate and generally healthful. The foil is rich, producing plenty of corn, fruits and pafture. But fome parts are fandy and barren, and others are overrun with woods and mountains.

Character.] The Moors, who are the original inhabitants of Barbary, dwell chiefly in Morocco, and are faid to be a covetous, inhofpitable, treacherous people. The Arabs, who are difperfed all over this country, follow their common trade of robbing travellers.

The women of Tunis are exceffively handfome and very delicate. They improve the beauty of their eyes, by the ufe of the powder of lead-ore, fuppofed to be the fame pigment that Jezebel made ufe of II. Kings ix. 30.) to paint her face ; the words in the original fignifying, that fhe fet off her eyes with the powder of lead-ore.

Religion and government.] Mahometanifm, in its worft form, prevails throughout the ftates of Barbary. The emperor of Morocco is an arbitrary prince. Algiers is governed by a Prince, called the Dey, elected by the army. The fovereigns of Tunis and Tripoli, called Beys, are not fo independent as the former. Thefe three ftates may be looked upon as republics of foldiers under the protection of the Grand Seignior. Algiers belongs to the Spaniards, and is a neft of pirates. On this coaft ftood the famous city of Carthage, which was deftroyed by the Romans. Among the great men Africa has produced, are Tertullian, Cyprian, Julius Africanus, Arnobius, Lactantius and St. Auftin, all bifhops of the church. The warriors of note are Hamilcar, Hannibal and Afdrubal. Among the poets, are Terence and Apuleius.

ZAARA or the DESERT.

IT has Barbary north ; Egypt and Nubia eaft ; Negroland and Guinea fouth ; and the Atlantic weft ; 2500 miles long, and 500 broad.

The air of this country is very hot, but wholefome to the natives. The foil is generally fandy and barren; infomuch that the Caravans crofling this country, to and from Negroland, are often reduced to great extremities. The inhabitants of this country are wild and ignorant. They have a number of petty princes, but for the moft part, have few figns of any government at all. The Mahometan religion is profeffed throughout the country.

NEGROLAND.

THIS country lies fouth of Zaara ; 2300 mile long and 700 broad. The air is very hot, but wholefome. The foil is fertile, efpecially near the river Niger, which runs through the country from eaft to weft,

and

528   ETHIOPIA AND AFRICAN ISLANDS.

and overflows at a certain time of the year like the Nile. The commodities of this country are gold, flaves, elephants-teeth, bees-wax and fome drugs. There is a well here, whofe water is as fweet as ordinary fugar. The Negroes are an uncivilized, ignorant, crafty, robuft people. Their colour is deep black, their hair fhort, like wool, flat nofes, thick lips, and white, even teeth. The Negroes are governed by a number of abfolute princes. The inhabitants are moftly pagans and idolaters.

GUINEA lies fouth of Negroland, 1890 miles long, 600 broad. The foil is preferable to that of Negroland. The inhabitants are more courteous and fenfible; in other refpects the difference is immaterial. The greater part of the poor Negroes in the Weft Indies and the fouthern ftates, were brought from thefe two countries.

✠✠✠✠✠✠✠✠✠✠✠✠✠✠✠✠✠✠✠✠✠✠✠✠✠✠✠✠✠✠✠✠✠✠

ETHIOPIA.

UNDER the general name of Ethiopia is included all the remaining part of Africa; containing an extent of 3600 miles from north to fouth, and 2000 from eaft to weft. The air of this country is generally exceffively hot, and the foil barren, though on the banks of the rivers it is fertile, and produces rice, citrons, lemons, fugar canes, &c. The Ethiopians are an ignorant, uncivilized, fuperftitious people. Their government is abfolute, lodged in the hands of a great number of princes, the fmall ones are tributary to the greater. The Mahometan and Pagan religions prevail in Ethiopia.

✠✠✠✠✠✠✠✠✠✠✠✠✠✠✠✠✠✠✠✠✠✠✠✠✠✠✠✠✠✠✠✠✠✠

AFRICAN ISLANDS.

AT the mouth of the Red Sea, is the ifland that failors now call Socatra, famous for its aloes, which are efteemed the beft in the world. Sailing down, fouthward, we come to the ifland Madagafcar, or Lawrence, abounding in cattle and corn, and moft of the neceffaries of life, but no fufficient merchandize to induce Europeans to fettle colonies; it has feveral petty favage kings of its own, both Arabs and Negroes, who making war on each other, fell their prifoners for flaves to the fhipping which call here, taking cloaths, utenfils and other neceffaries in return.

Near it are the four Comorra ifles, whofe petty kings are tributary to the Portuguefe; and near thefe lies the French ifland Bourbon; and a little higher Maurice, fo called by the Dutch, who firft touched here in 1598. It is now in poffeffion of the French.

Quitting the eaftern world and the Indies, and paffing round the Cape of Good Hope, into the wide Atlantic ocean, the firft ifland is the fmall, but pleafant St. Helena, at which place all the Englifh Eaft India fhips ftop to get water and frefh provifions in their way home. Near this are

the

GENERAL REMARKS.

the Guinea islands, St. Matthew, St. Thomas and others, not far from the coast under the Equinoctial line, belonging to the Portuguese. These were so named by the sailors, who first found them on St. Helen's, St. Thomas's and St. Matthew's festivals.

Thence northward, are the Cape Verd islands, so called from their verdure. They now belong to the Portuguese, who are furnished from thence with salt and goats skins.

Farther north are the pleasant Canaries, belonging to the Spaniards, from whence first came Canary wine, and the beautiful singing birds, called Canary Birds. The ancients called them the Fortunate Isles, and placed there the Elysian fields. They are ten or twelve in number, the chief are Teneriffe, Gomera, Ferro and Great Canary. The fertile islands of Madeira lie still higher north, and are famous for the best stomachic wine. They belong to the Portuguese.

GENERAL REMARKS.

'THE varieties among the human race, says Dr. Percival, enumerated by Linnæus and Buffon, are six. The first is found under the polar regions, and comprehends the Laplanders, the Esquimaux Indians, the Samoeid Tartars, the inhabitants of Nova Zembla, the Borandians, the Greenlanders, and the people of Kamschatka. The visage of men, in these countries, is large and broad; the nose flat and short; the eyes of a yellowish brown, inclining to blackness; the cheek bones extremely high; the mouth large; the lips thick, and turning outwards; the voice thin and squeaking; and the skin a dark grey colour. The people are short in stature, the generality being about four feet high, and the tallest not more than five. Ignorance, stupidity, and superstition are the mental characteristics of the inhabitants of these rigorous climates. For here

> Doze the gross race. Nor sprightly jest nor song,
> Nor tenderness they know, nor aught of life,
> Beyond the kindred bears that stalk without.

The Tartar race, comprehending the Chinese, and the Japanese, forms the second variety in the human species. Their countenances are broad and wrinkled, even in youth; their noses short and flat; their eyes little, sunk in the sockets, and several inches asunder; their cheek bones are high; their teeth of a large size and separate from each other; their complexions are olive, and their hair black. These nations, in general, have no religion, no settled notions of morality, and no decency of behaviour. They are chiefly robbers; their wealth consists in horses, and their skill in the management of them.

The third variety of mankind is that of the southern Asiatics, or the inhabitants

inhabitants of India. These are of a slender shape, have long straight black hair, and generally Roman noses. These people are slothful, luxurious, submissive, cowardly and effeminate.

———The parent Sun himself
Seems o'er this world of slaves to tyrannize;
And, with oppressive ray, the roseate bloom
Of beauty blasting, gives the gloomy hue,
And features gross: or worse, to ruthless deeds,
Mad jealousy, blind rage, and fell revenge,
Their fervid spirit fires. Love dwells not there.
The soft regards, the tenderness of life,
The heart-shed tear, th' ineffable delight
Of sweet humanity: these court the beam
Of milder climes; in selfish fierce desire,
And the wild fury of voluptuous sense,
There lost. The very brute creation there
This rage partakes, and burns with horrid fire.

The negroes of Africa constitute the fourth striking variety in the human species: But they differ widely from each other; those of Guinea, for instance, are extremely ugly, and have an insupportably offensive scent; while those of Mosambique are reckoned beautiful, and are untainted with any disagreeable smell. The negroes are, in general, of a black colour; and the downy softness of hair, which grows upon the skin, gives a smoothness to it, resembling that of velvet. The hair of their heads is woolly, short and black; but their beards often turn grey, and sometimes white. Their noses are flat and short, their lips thick and tumid, and their teeth of an ivory whiteness.

The intellectual and moral powers of these wretched people are uncultivated; and they are subject to the most barbarous despotism. The savage tyrants, who rule over them, make war upon each other for *human plunder!* and the wretched victims, bartered for spirituous liquors, are torn from their families, their friends, and their native land, and consigned for life to misery, toil and bondage. But how am I shocked to inform you, that this infernal commerce is carried on by the humane, the polished, the christian inhabitants of Europe; nay even by Englishmen, whose ancestors have bled in the cause of liberty, and whose breasts still glow with the same generous flame! I cannot give you a more striking proof of the ideas of horror, which the captive negroes entertain of the state of servitude they are to undergo, than by relating the following incident from Dr. Goldsmith.

' A Guinea captain was, by distress of weather, driven into a certain harbour, with a lading of sickly slaves, who took every opportunity to throw themselves over-board, when brought upon deck for the benefit of fresh air. The captain perceiving, among others, a female slave attempting to drown herself, pitched upon her as a proper example for the rest. As he supposed that they did not know the terrors attending death, he ordered the woman to be tied with a rope under the arm-pits, and let down into the water. When the poor creature was thus plunged in, and about half way down, she was heard to give a terrible shriek, which at first was

ascribed

GENERAL REMARKS. 531

afcribed to her fears of drowning; but foon after, the water appeared red around her, fhe was drawn up, and it was found that a fhark, which had followed the fhip, had bitten her off from the middle.'

The native inhabitants of America make a fifth race of men. They are of a copper colour, have black, thick, ftraight hair, flat nofes, high cheek bones, and fmall eyes. They paint the body and face of various colours, and eradicate the hair of their beards and other parts, as a deformity. Their limbs are not fo large and robuft, as thofe of the Europeans. They endure hunger, thirft, and pain with aftonifhing firmnefs and patience; and, though cruel to their enemies, they are kind and juft to each other.

The Europeans may be confidered as the laft variety of the human kind. They enjoy fingular advantages from the fairnefs of their complexions. The face of the African Black, or of the olive-coloured Afiatic, is a very imperfect index of the mind, and preferves the fame fettled fhade in joy and forrow, confidence and fhame, anger and defpair, ficknefs and health. The Englifh are faid to be of the faireft of the Europeans; and we may therefore prefume, that their countenances beft exprefs the variations of the paffions and viciffitudes of difeafe. But the intellectual and moral characteriftics of the different nations, which compofe this quarter of the globe, are of more importance to be known. Thefe, however, become gradually lefs difcernable, as fafhion, learning, and commerce prevail more univerfally.

APPENDIX.

APPENDIX.

NOTE I.

THE following note will correct what was said, page 87, in respect to the state of our commerce with France.

'A distinction must be made between the arret of 1785 and that of 1787. The first grants privileges in certain cases to all neutrals, the second is entirely in favour of the Americans. But both are for their advantage. Whenever they shall enjoy a permanent and solid government, on whose measures some reliance may be given, then it may be expected that the king of France will give effect to the disposition which his majesty has constantly harboured towards the United States. But no regulation can be solid which is not founded on reciprocal advantage. To obtain, a nation should be able to grant. That has not been the case with the United States towards France. They have not ever been able to make good the treaty of commerce on which their first connection with France is grounded. Many grievances exist against the United States, where the few French navigators have been liable to many inconveniences from the fickleness and imperfection of the laws of individual states. Justice must be the first basis on which industry may repose. France will always grant more than she may receive, but her subjects must find in the United States protecting and solid laws. That will certainly be the effect of a wise and a general government. It may then be pronounced that the æra of the new constitution will also be the æra of a renewal of a lasting and useful connection between two nations, who have no motive for rivalship, and who have many natural reasons to be strongly connected besides what sentiment may inspire.

No. II.

The following Extract from the Journals of Mr. ELKANAH WATSON, a gentleman who has travelled extensively both in Europe and America, merits a place in a book of this kind, and would have been inserted in the body of the work, had the journals been timely received.

'When the extent of America is considered, boldly fronting the old world—blessed with every climate—capable of every production—abounding with the best harbours and rivers on the globe, and already overspread with three millions of souls, mostly descendents of Englishmen—inheriting all their ancient enthusiasm for liberty, and enterprizing almost to a fault—what may be expected from such a people in such a country?——The partial hand of nature has laid off America upon a much larger scale than any other part of the world. Hills in America are mountains in Europe—brooks are rivers, and ponds are swelled into lakes. In short the map of the world cannot exhibit a country uniting so many natural advantages, so pleasingly diversified, and that offers such abundant and easy resources to agriculture and commerce.

In contemplating *future America*, the mind is lost in the din of cities—in harbours and rivers clouded with sails—and in the immensity of her population. Admitting her present population to be three millions, and

calculating

calculating her progressive increase to continue doubling once in twenty years, as has hitherto been the case, at the end of one hundred years there will be ninety-six millions of souls in United America; which is two-thirds as many as there are at present in all Europe. And when we consider the probable acquisition of people, by foreign immigrations, and that the interior and unsettled parts of America are amply sufficient to provide for this number, the presumption is strong, that this estimation will not differ materially from the event.

Europe is already aware of the rising importance of America, and begins to look forward with anxiety to her West India Islands, which are the natural legacy of this continent, and will doubtless be claimed as such when America shall have arrived at an age which will enable her to maintain her right.

The northern and southern states differ widely in their customs, climate, produce, and in the general face of the country. The middle states preserve a medium in all these respects; they are neither so level and hot as the states south; nor so hilly and cold as those north and east. The inhabitants of the north are hardy, industrious, frugal, and in general well informed; those of the south are more effeminate, indolent and imperious. The fisheries and commerce are the sinews of the north; tobacco, rice and indigo, of the south. The northern states are commodiously situated for trade and manufactures; the southern, to furnish provisions and raw materials; and the probability is, that the southern states will one day be supplied with northern manufactures instead of European, and make their remittances in provisions and raw materials.'

No. III.

The following observations on the subject of the probable revenue that would result to the United States from the impost and excise, were communicated by a gentleman who, from his situation in public life, from the attention he has paid to the sources of public revenue in this country, and from the pains he has taken to collect the facts on which the following estimate is founded, is capable of giving as accurate information on the subject as the nature of the case will admit

From the want of accurate documents of former collections under the state regulations, it is not possible to determine with precision, the amount of the revenue which may be relied on from these sources, under the new form of government.—I am, however, clearly of opinion, from several returns I have seen of the former impost and excise duties, in some principal importing states, that after the regulations adopted by Congress, have had their complete operation, the produce of these duties, without encouraging contraband, or other frauds on the revenue, may be estimated at 2,000,000 dollars.—This sum, it is true, will at present fall short of what is necessary to defray the expences of the civil government, and to discharge the interest of the foreign and domestic debt.—But by the aids of a national bank properly organized, it will be easy and perfectly safe to borrow in anticipation, such sums as may be deficient, annually for those purposes, pledging the above revenue (which will constantly encrease rapidly with the population of the country) as a fund of reimbursement.—This is practised in other countries, under similar circumstances, in support of public credit, and may undoubtedly be done in this,—more especially

especially, as the Capital of the domestic debt will be constantly decreasing by a judicious disposal of lands in the Western Territory, and means may be devised of inducing the domestic creditors to agree to a reduction of the present rate of interest.

With respect to direct taxes, I am of opinion, that in times of peace, little, if any, recourse need be had to them;—It is, however, absolutely necessary that the general government should be invested with the power of levying them, because in times of war, or the calamities, to which all nations are subjected, the sources of impost and excise may be so diminished as not to be adequate to the means of national defence—and every government ought undoubtedly to have the means of preserving itself.

I know it has been said, that on such great occasions, requisitions may be relied on; but past experience proves the fallacy of this observation; for if during a war, whose object was to rescue the whole body of the people, from the most ignominious slavery, the earnest and repeated recommendations of Congress, could not draw forth from the states any contributions of money in the least degree proportionate to the public exigencies, what could be expected on future occasions? Nothing else than subjecting the citizens of the states most contiguous to the scene of action to a ruinous depredation of property; whilst those in the distant states would not only be perfectly free of any burthen, but dispute, when the danger was over, the justice of reimbursement.—To such acts of violation of private rights it is well known that the citizens of New York, Jersey, and Pennsylvania, were peculiarly subjected, during the late war; and if they are wise, they will never again expose themselves to the same hazard.'

F I N I S.

THE Reader is defired to notice and correct the following errors, fome of which are errors of the Prefs, and others have been difcovered in confequence of information received after it was too late to correct them in the Manufcript.

Page 3, two lines from the bottom, for 335 read 355.
Page 31, line 25, for 1654, read 1754.
Page 47, line 19, for Wahant, read Nahant.
Page 117, line 8, for offenfive, read defenfive.
Page 156, line 4, for Andrew, read Sir Edmund Andross.
Page 157, line 30, for Boyntow, read Boynton.
Page 162, line 9 from bottom, for Nywichwannot, read Nywichwannok.
Page 178, line 5 from bottom, for Pychon, read Pynchon.
Page 218, line 5, for Middlefex, read Middleton.
Page 227, line 3 from bottom, for the 20th of Auguft, read 10th of September.
Page 253 line 16, dele few.
Page 257, line 6, for pond, read fpring.
Page 283, line 33, for beems, read beam.
Page 320, line 13, after the words *was made*, add *in part*.

DIRECTIONS for the BINDER.

LET the MAP of the Southern ftates front the INTRODUCTION—And the MAP of the Northern ftates page 33.

CORRECTIONS RESPECTING FRANCE.

SINCE the Abridgement of Zimmermann's Political Survey was made and printed, a better acquaintance with facts has given room for the following obfervations on the paragraphs concerning the Religion and Government of France.

A folemn law, which does much honor to Louis XVI. the prefent king of France, who has been ftyled by the United States, ' the Protector of the Rights of Mankind,' has granted to his *non-Roman Catholic* fubjects, as they are called, all the civil advantages and privileges of their Roman Catholic brethren.

His Moft Chriftian Majefty is far from being, or ftyling himfelf, an Abfolute Monarch. In the ceremony of his coronation, he takes the oath of never infringing the rights and privileges of the nation, or altering the conftitutional laws without their confent. Like his Britannic majefty, he ftyles himfelf *King by the Grace of God;* but it is no more underftood in France than in England that the king is the vicegerent of God, and holds his power by divine right.

There are 13 parliaments in France. They are fupreme courts of juftice and appeal—they have the right of remonftrating againft the legiflative acts, and of regiftering them before they are deemed binding laws. Their other powers are an ufurpation upon the States General of the kingdom, who have not been convened during the laft 150 years. They are not reprefentatives of the people, and are very different bodies from the Provincial States. Thefe have been re-eftablifhed in all the provinces by Louis XVI. upon the moft perfect fyftem of reprefentation yet known. The States General are to meet in May 1789, and the king has announced his intention of eftablifhing with them, the conftitution of the nation upon the enlightened principles of the eighteenth century. The Americans view with great pleafure, that the fame fovereign, who has generoufly fupported their independence, is no lefs liberal in reftoring to his fubjects their unalienable, but long neglected rights. He is, however, oppofed, in the laft undertaking, by the parliaments, the clergy, and part of the nobility, as he was in the former by the arms of Great Britain.